THEY CALLED IT PEARSON

The History of Mata Ortiz
and the Casas Grandes Valley

RICHARD D. O'CONNOR WALTER P. PARKS

Parks O'Connor Publishing
San Diego and Riverside, California

Parks O'Connor Publishing
San Diego and Riverside, California
parksoconnorpublishing@gmail.com

Includes bibliographical references and index

ISBN 979-8-9879499-0-0 (paperback)
ISBN 979-8-9879499-1-7 (ebook)

Library of Congress Control Number: 2023904934

Printed in the United States of America

Book design: Clarity Designworks

Table of Contents

Introduction

We discovered the pottery first, then the people, and then the land and its stories. The more we delved into the past, the more we discovered. Finally, we decided to compile into one place the scattered history of Mata Ortiz and the Casas Grandes Valley. We were first lured to Mata Ortiz in Mexico's remote northern Chihuahua almost 40 years ago by the extraordinary pottery that had begun to appear in exhibitions and galleries in the United States. Gradually as we became more involved with the village, we began to pay attention to the local stories. The more we heard, the more intrigued we became. A closer look showed the Casas Grandes Valley and the dusty town of Mata Ortiz to be in the eye of a swirling storm of history that included the extensive remnants of a lost civilization; centuries of brutal Apache warfare; *hacendados* with multi-million acre ranches; Latter-day Saint colonists fleeing U.S. anti-polygamy laws; and Yankee entrepreneurs with grandiose but mostly failed schemes. We also heard about larger-than-life characters such as Pancho Villa, Geronimo, and Dr. Fred Stark Pearson who built the world's largest lumber mill in Mata Ortiz in the middle of the Mexican Revolution.

In the available books, dissertations, and articles, we found only passing references to the Casas Grandes Valley. None told the whole story. We began searching through old archives and obscure journals and following leads through personal communication to find everything we could, particularly about Mata Ortiz and Dr. Fred Stark Pearson, the town founder.

It did not take us long to discover that certain pieces of misinformation had persisted as fact in academic publications as well as regional lore.

The local version of Mata Ortiz's origin story tells of a Dr. Pearson, an English lord, who built the railway through the Casas Grandes Valley to serve his new lumber mill, the largest sawmill in the world, in the town he founded called Pearson. Before the mill was in full operation, Dr. Pearson died in the sinking of the Titanic.

With a few embellishments, this was the conventional story even among academics, when we began our research. With a little work, we found a great deal about Weetman Pearson, the English Lord Cowdrey, who developed oil fields and railroads in Mexico. However, his biography and other references gave no indication he had ever been in Chihuahua, let alone invest there. Also, he died in bed in his castle, years after the Titanic hit the iceberg.

More work revealed another Pearson, Dr. Fred Stark Pearson (most sources erroneously called him Frederick). This Pearson, a pioneering electrical engineer and inventor, a contemporary of Edison and Westinghouse, built major hydroelectric and streetcar systems throughout the world. His brilliantly-conceived project in the Casas Grandes Valley suffered from

Juan Mata Ortiz. Photo: 1984

terrible timing. A year after he arrived the Mexican Revolution erupted, followed by World War I. Dr. Pearson and his wife Mabel perished when the British ship Lusitania was torpedoed off the Irish coast in 1915—a different marine disaster.

Time and the machinations of Dr. Pearson's enemies have obscured and even sullied his memory. Soon after his tragic death, he was forgotten. Even the name of the town he founded was changed from Pearson to Juan Mata Ortiz in 1925, when Anglo names became politically unacceptable. Part of our purpose here is to tell the story of this unique, brilliant man whose accomplishments still affect people around the world.

Much has been written about certain topics that relate to our work, Pancho Villa, the Apache Wars and the Revolution. We make no attempt to be completely comprehensive on these or other well-covered subjects. The Apaches had a huge impact on the Casas Grandes Valley, but their overall story is very complex and can be found in detail elsewhere. We did not differentiate among the numerous Apache groups, using only the term "Apache" or sometimes "Chiricahua," the dominant group in northern Chihuahua.

Even more has been written about the Mexican Revolution and its most famous rebel, Pancho Villa. No attempt has been made to present that complete story, only those parts that relate to the Casas Grandes Valley.

Sometimes we did need to stray from the Valley into other regions as the complexities of Mexican history evolved. These diversions were intended to provide background for understanding what happened (or did not happen) in the Valley.

Members of the Church of Jesus Christ of Latter-day Saints played an important role in Casas Grandes Valley history. The Church declared in August 2018 that the word "Mormon" should no longer be used to describe the Church or its members. Out of respect, we have used "LDS colonists," Saints, or similar terms to identify the Church settlers.

We first saw the village as the rutted road we followed topped a gentle rise. We had no idea the original name was Pearson nor that the full correct name was Juan Mata Ortiz. For most of this book, we chose to drop the "Juan" and use the more common abbreviated version of the village name.

We were not the first North Americans to discover the village, but we have remained continuously involved and watched as high-quality pottery became the main livelihood for the once poor village. We made lifelong friends there and helped them organize the first public library, rebuild the kindergarten complex, and add rooms and computers to the middle and high schools.

It is our hope that our narrative will bring additional attention to the creative people of this unique corner of the earth.

Walter Parks and Richard O'Connor

The Terrain

The Casas Grandes Valley lies in the remote northwest corner of the state of Chihuahua. To the west stands the massive dark wall of the Sierra Madre Occidental. The Continental Divide follows an invisible line through the Sierra's jagged peaks, ridges, and canyons, that separate Chihuahua from Sonora. Along its edges, subsidiary ranges with different names have fractured away from the main massif.

On the east side of the valley, a jumble of "basin and range" hills and mountains run roughly north and south. These unique geologic formations are often completely separate "sky islands" with different flora and fauna. Others lock together in a continuous line. Many appear to be benign rolling hills, which often hide steep, rough terrain, forcing the traveler to seek distant passes.

Just south of the old Spanish town of Casas Grandes and the ruins of the prehistoric city of Paquimé, the San Diego Valley branches from the main Casas Grandes Valley. Mata Ortiz is located in this branch valley. At the southern end, the Sierra Madre bulges to the east and joins a series of small ranges enclosing the San Diego Valley. The small basin and range mountains above Mata Ortiz on the east side of the branch valley are the Sierra de Anchón, capped by the notched crag called *El Indio*. At 8,200 feet above sea level and 3,200 feet above the high plains surrounding Mata Ortiz, this much-photographed peak creates a dramatic backdrop for the village. Its rarely used official name, *Cerro Rajado,* translates "Split Hill."

The Casas Grandes and Santa María Rivers flow north through parallel valleys to Laguna Guzmán and Laguna Santa María near the New Mexico Border.

The small ranges continue on the east side of the valley, past Mata Ortiz to the north, separating San Diego from the main Casas Grandes Valley. In the other direction, fifty miles south of the old Mata Ortiz railroad station, the mountains rise to 7,000 feet at La Cumbre summit.

From the mountains at the south end of the San Diego Valley, creeks and small rivers flow down and join to form the Palanganas River (on old maps, the San Miguel). The Palanganas flows north past Mata Ortiz to a junction with the Piedras Verdes River to form the Casas Grandes River, just east of the old Hacienda San Diego.

West of Mata Ortiz, the Piedras Verdes originates in the Sierra Madre Mountains and flows through Cave Valley, site of the famous Cave of the Olla, before descending to the plains. Tributary streams Tinaja and Tapiecitas join the Piedras Verdes about three miles west of its junction with the Palanganas to form the Casas Grandes River. This important stream flows north through the main Casas Grandes Valley, past the old pueblo of Casas Grandes and the much larger Nuevo Casas Grandes, past the Corralitos ranch and the Mennonite community of Capulín, until it makes a fishhook turn to the east and south and empties into *Laguna Guzmán*. This rather strange body of water has no outlet and can be twenty-five miles across or an almost dry swamp, depending on precipitation and irrigation demand. The river and its tributaries are the lifeblood of the region's productive farmland. Beyond the rivers and related irrigation systems, millions of acres of rangeland extend to the mountain foothills and north and northeast to the Chihuahuan Desert.

In the north corner of the Casas Grandes Valley, another river, the San Pedro, labeled the Janos River on some maps, flows east from the Sierra Carcay section of the Sierra Madre across open plains, the *Llano de Carretas*, toward Janos, the northernmost outpost of the valley. The usually dry river arroyo passes under a bridge on Highway 10 at the south end of the town. It joins the Río Casas Grandes north of Janos, east of Highway 2.

Over the mountains to the east, the Santa Maria Valley parallels the Casas Grandes Valley. The Santa Maria River runs north to *Laguna Santa Maria,* another lake with no outlet. Historic events and old trails and roads have linked the two valleys for centuries.

These valleys are located in the northwest corner of Chihuahua, Mexico's largest state by area. Two thirds of its 3.8 million people reside in either Ciudad Juárez, the city across the border from El Paso, or due south in the capital, Ciudad Chihuahua in the center of the state. Nuevo Casas Grandes, with a population of nearly 70,000, has evolved into the agricultural, financial, commercial, and educational center of the Casas Grandes Valley. For the most part, northern Chihuahua is a land of small towns and wide-open spaces with a mountain range on every horizon, near or far.

The Sierra Madre dominates the view west from Mata Ortiz. The mountain terrain is considered some of the roughest in the world and provided impenetrable hideouts for Apaches, outlaws, and rebels. In other places, the gorges widen into lovely, fertile valleys. Prehistoric mankind and later people such as the Ópata Indians, Spanish missionaries, Mexican pioneers,

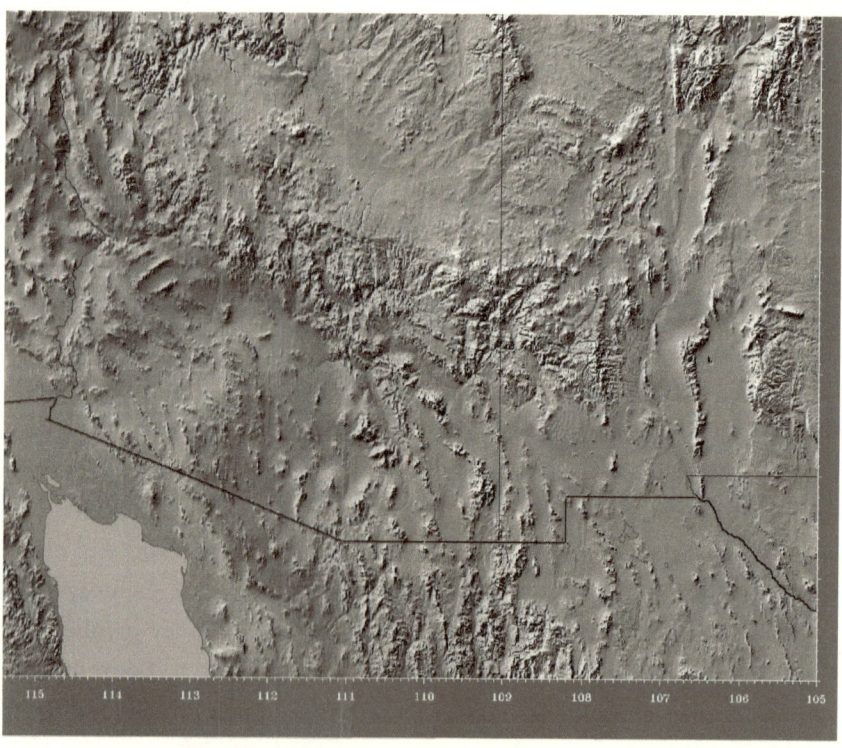

Basin and Range country of northern Mexico made east-west travel difficult. The line represents the U.S. border with Sonora and Chihuahua.

and LDS colonists, miners, and logging entrepreneurs all discovered and settled these valleys.

Access was and remains difficult. Ancient traders found three rugged but accessible passes, which enabled them to penetrate into the valleys and through the mountains to the coast. The best known, almost due west of Janos, is *Púlpito* Pass, named for a distinctive rock formation near the entrance. Today, the rough pass is rarely used, but Janos remains a crossroads for travelers between Ciudad Juárez/El Paso, Casas Grandes, and Agua Prieta on the Arizona border.

The second of the three passes, *Carretas* Pass, twenty miles to the south of Púlpito, is even more rugged with dangerous drop offs. The name is a contradiction because *carretas* or wagons could not negotiate these trails, only horses or mules. The wagons had to be left at the bottom at a place that became known as *Las Carretas*. A mission was established there in the 17th century. In reading the accounts of early explorers, it is often unclear which of these two passes was used as they both descend to the Llano de Carretas not far from Janos.

About 50 miles farther south and due west of Mata Ortiz, the Sierra Madre skyline slopes away from a highpoint, the pyramid-shaped Pico Picacho. The low point south of the peak marks *Puerto San Diego,* the third major entrance into the mountainous interior, sometimes called locally *El Caracol* or snail. This twisting route leads to high valleys, including the famous Cave of the Olla, and to dirt-road routes through mountain communities in both Chihuahua and Sonora.

The Puerto San Diego arroyo system drains the mountain canyons around the Caracol. One of these arroyos, *Arroyo Los Poños,* goes due east across the plains and joins the Palanganas River just south of Mata Ortiz. A branch arroyo, *La Sección*, separates the southern part of the town, *Barrio Porvenir* from *Barrio Centro*.

For all time, nomadic hunter/gatherers, *conquistadores*, explorers, settlers, army generals, and railroad engineers had to contend with the rugged terrain surrounding the Casas Grandes Valley. North-south travel was relatively easy but movement east or west required finding a way through miles of mountains and across rivers. This formidable geography slowed the otherwise relentless Spanish incursion, even halting it altogether for long periods of time. After initial efforts, most conquistadores, colonists, and missionaries found easier routes, traveling east along the Rio Grande Valley up to Santa Fe or to the west in the valleys of Sonora and Sinaloa. Eventually, explorers and settlers discovered the Casas Grandes Valley and its rich farm and ranch lands. Development gradually occurred but always within the framework of the terrain.

1

A Look Back

In 1884, pioneer anthropologist Adolph F.A. Bandelier rode up a steep escarpment into the Sierra Madre Occidental Mountains. Pausing, he looked back to the east across the broad plain of the San Diego Valley to a thin line of green that marked a branch of the Casas Grandes River. He called the branch by its new name, *Río Palanganas*, which old maps show as *Río San Miguel*. Beyond the river a small range, capped by a notched crag, ran parallel to the river north and south as far as he could see. Bandelier wrote in his journal that the plain was alive with antelope grazing in the tall grass. Looking east to the notched crag, later call El Indio, as far north and south as he could see, there was no sign of human occupation, that is, of contemporary inhabitants. An ancient people, however, had left their mark everywhere.

Bandelier had scrambled all over *Paquimé*, the great ruined central city of the Casas Grandes Pueblo culture. That massive ruin with its high thick walls lay to the northeast of Bandelier's mountain-side position beyond hills that extended north from the *El Indio* crag. What he had found in recent days fascinated him. Evidence of this great culture was everywhere. He had followed the Casas Grandes River and its two main branches, the Palanganas and the Piedras Verdes, for miles in all directions and found hundreds of ruins and mounds. Along the base of the hills, he could clearly see remnants of rock erosion-control structures called *trincheras* put in place hundreds of years before. He wrote that the region must have supported a population much larger than any in the Southwest. However, within his vast view over the plains, there was nothing of modern man with one exception—the ruins of a rancho called San Diego. Bandelier had camped there near the junction of the Palanganas and the Piedras Verde Rivers, the two branches that form the Casas Grandes River. He noted that it had been abandoned twenty-five years before.[1]

The plains were empty of settlement because raiding Apaches had intermittently controlled vast regions of northern Chihuahua for two hundred years. Spanish and later Mexican settlements like San Diego would succeed for a while until decimated by sudden attack. In desperation, the Spanish viceroys developed a chain of military-towns, *presidios*, and provided incentives of land and tax breaks to settlers to form militias and other defenses. These measures continued after Mexican independence. No presidio towns existed along the Palanganas within Bandelier's view. As he rode, he was very aware of the Apache and his vulnerability, but the centuries-old Apache Wars were almost over.

Just four years before, in 1880, the great warrior Victorio had been killed at the Battle of Tres Castillos in the Chihuahua desert. Historians

Bandelier's view east to the San Diego Valley from the Caracol in the Sierra Madre.

say this was the beginning of the end of the Apache menace. Just months before Bandelier entered the Sierra Madre, Gerónimo had surrendered for the first time. Some Apaches had disappeared into the Sierra Madre, creating a multitude of stories of attacks and depredations, a few even true, that continued well into the 20th century. Bandelier and his companions were wary, and they did see Apaches. However, those were quietly moving north to reservations in Arizona.

That year, 1884, was a turning point for northern Chihuahua. Entrepreneurs like Luis Terrazas, a hero of the war against the French, already claimed huge tracts of land that for centuries had been too dangerous to settle. The next year, Latter-day Saints from now-monogamous Utah would begin their Diaspora to the Casas Grandes Valley. Encouraged by President Porfirio Díaz, foreign and domestic mining, lumbering, and railroad operators expanded fledgling works and sought out new resources. Luis Terrazas would own all that Bandelier could see from north to south. A railroad would run parallel to the green line of cottonwood trees. This is the land pertinent to the Pearson/Mata Ortiz part of the story.

2

La Entrada

Los Conquistadores

When Bandelier crossed into Sonora, Mexico, he followed in the opposite direction the routes conquistadores had opened in the 16th century.

Spanish exploration of Mexico began with Hernán Cortez's trek from Veracruz on the coast to the center of the Aztec Empire in 1519. Spanish conquerors gradually widened their exploration in all directions in the land they called New Spain. They had several objectives, ranging from greed—the incessant search for gold—through settlement and development of the land, to the most noble—saving souls and bringing civilization to the "primitive" peoples. By 1531, a coastal outpost had been established on the northern frontier at San Miguel de Culiacán in what is now the state of Sinaloa. Five years later, Cabeza de Vaca passed through, nearing the end one of the most incredible journeys and survival stories in the history of man. Shipwrecked on the Texas coast, he and three companions walked to Mexico City. It took them eight years. He told many fabulous tales including seeing cities made of pure gold—the Seven Cities of Cíbola. These stories captivated the imagination of the Spanish authorities, including the Viceroy of New Spain. His fascination stimulated one of the earliest and most ambitious of the Spanish expeditions. The commander, Francisco Vázquez de Coronado y Lujan, was a man of high standing, no less than the governor of the province of Nuevo Galicia, centered in Guadalajara.

14

In order to administer the vast area of New Spain, which encompassed much of North America, King Carlos I had established a vice king or "viceroy" in Mexico City. New Spain was subdivided into provinces, such as Nuevo Galicia, ruled by powerful governors, who served as military commanders as well as chief administrators.

Appointed by the viceroy to command the largest exploration ever into the northern frontier, Coronado organized an expeditionary force consisting of at least, as sources vary, 400-500 Spaniards, 1,200 Indian auxiliaries, and thousands of horses, mules, cows, and sheep. In the spring of 1540, they assembled at Culiacán and followed their dream of golden cities up the west coast and valleys of Sinaloa and Sonora of the western Sierra Madre, continuing toward Arizona and as far as Kansas. To be more efficient on the trail, Coronado divided his large force into smaller, more flexible units. These could forage independently as well as be assigned to scout ahead or make side explorations. He left some as garrison troops in native towns deemed promising for future settlement.

Four Franciscan padres accompanied Coronado, but this was not a missionary expedition. Gold was the driving force behind this enormous effort.

Trekking north, they followed roughly the route Cabeza de Vaca blazed four years before going in the opposite direction. Coronado entered the Sonora River Valley following trails along the river and its tributaries that today constitute the 200-mile stretch of highway from Hermosillo to Cananea. This was the heart of Ópata country, a fierce indigenous people at the height of their power. Prior to contact with the Spanish, the Ópata had expanded control over most of Sonora. Their economy could support a warrior class strong enough to dominate the region and at least initially confront the Spanish.

At first the Ópata were hospitable toward Coronado and his soldiers, possibly because of an amicable relationship with the recent wayfarer Cabeza de Vaca. After Coronado continued north, however, a weakness showed in his divided-command concept. The garrison left behind in a town the Spaniards called San Gerónimo, near present day Ures, so antagonized the local Ópata that they attacked. Using deadly poison arrows, they annihilated the garrison soldiers, their horses, and their Indian auxiliaries.[2] On the return trail home, two years later, Coronado carefully avoided

Ópata country, where his subordinates had turned the hospitable natives into a fierce enemy.

The Coronado expedition explored vast areas of northern Mexico, Arizona, and New Mexico. Elements of Coronado's troop traveled as far as Kansas. The way was opened for future exploration and settlement. However, the closest Coronado came to gold was the sun reflecting off of the adobe walls of Zuni Pueblo. He did not meet his golden objective, nor as it happens, did he see or enter the Casas Grandes Valley or the ruined city of Paquimé to the east of his route. What he did was to set the stage for another explorer, who did visit the Casas Grandes Valley.

Francisco de Ibarra, Teen-Age Conquistador

Baltasar de Obregón, the chronicler of the Francisco de Ibarra expedition, filed the first report ever about the Casas Grandes region in 1565. The exhausted troop stumbled out of the mountain wilderness into the ruins of Paquimé, the great central city of the Casas Grandes culture that had been abandoned only about 125 years before their arrival.

Francisco de Ibarra, the commander at age 25, was no longer a teenager, but he had been commanding, governing, and leading expeditions since he was seventeen. At fifteen, he had come to New Spain from his home in Durango in the Vizcaya (Biscayne) province of old Spain. He went to Zacatecas, then on the edge of New Spain's northwest frontier, to live with an uncle who had made a fortune in the great silver mine nearby and who was a founder of Zacatecas. Gold in large quantities having eluded the conquistadores in the northwest, they settled for silver. They discovered large deposits and silver mining became a major economic activity of this frontier land, one reason the viceroy urged his provincial governors to push north in search of more.

In two years, young Ibarra finished his education, married the viceroy's daughter, and accepted the command of an expedition to explore beyond Zacatecas. Just seventeen, he led the hardened men of his command for three months, discovering several sites that developed into successful mining communities. Having proven his abilities, the viceroy gave him more exploratory assignments that he successfully executed. By 1562 when the viceroy decided to create a new province north of New Galicia, the young, capable Ibarra was the obvious choice for governor and captain general. It did not hurt that he was married to the viceroy's daughter and that his rich uncle could afford to finance his expeditions. At first, the new province had no name, but Ibarra, remembering his home in Spain, chose *Nueva Vizcaya.* He made Durango the capital, a town he founded near a newly discovered mine.[3]

Under the young governor, more profitable mines were discovered, developed, and more settlements established. In May 1565, Ibarra launched the last major expedition that he personally led. The objective this time was to explore Coronado's route into northern Nueva Vizcaya and to put to rest the legend of Cíbola that still tantalized the Spaniards. Ibarra had 60 soldiers, less than 15 percent of Coronado's large force. Most of these men were *arcabuceros,* armed with the arquebus that had such a traumatic effect (both the noise and deadly bullets), against Indian attackers.[4] Like Coronado, Ibarra divided his men into smaller, more mobile units. They blazed a new trail to Culiacán, still a frontier outpost, and then followed Coronado's trail north straight into that conquistador's brutal legacy. The Ópatas had not forgotten the mistreatment of their people nor their victory and complete annihilation of the garrison left behind at San Gerónimo. The Ópatas organized all of their own people as well as other Indian groups to repel these new foreigners. Accounts vary as to the details, but it is clear that the Ópatas and their confederates harassed Ibarra's troop and in one engagement killed 14 invaluable horses with their lethal poison arrows. This occurred near the Ópata town of Saguaripa, later to become a Jesuit mission town in 1627. Under Ibarra's skilled leadership, the soldiers fought back, using their horses, armor, and arquebuses effectively against greater numerical odds. However, their position was untenable, and Ibarra's only option was to order a retreat deeper into the mountains. Survival now became the expedition's sole objective. Moving northeast along the Bavispe River, they encountered an east-west trail, a so called "shell trail," used by native traders. They followed this and found a narrow, rocky pass, through which they descended carefully out on to the broad plain of the Llano de Carretas. The pass that enabled them to escape the Ópatas and the mountains could have been either Púlpito or Carretas.

Out on the plains, groups of Indians approached and greeted Ibarra's weary and wary troop. The Indians turned out to be not only hospitable but more than friendly. They danced and sang, treating the arrival of the tattered Spaniards as a grand occasion. Most sources refer to these natives as the Sumas. Charles Di Peso, the archeologist famed for his excavation and study of Paquimé, quoted chronicler Obregón's description of the descent from the mountains to "tablelands occupied by Querechos."[5]

Querechos or Suma? The names of the numerous nations, tribes, and language groups that the Spaniards encountered, fought, married, enslaved, baptized, and employed over three and a quarter centuries are confusing. Often the names the Spanish used simply were born of a communication misunderstanding. What the native groups called themselves turned out to be something entirely different. Tribal name changes in the latter part of the 20th century, such as Papago to Tohono O'odham reflect those early misunderstandings. Cabeza de Vaca, after his long trek, came to Mexico City with a long list of names he had applied for one reason or another to the groups he encountered. Subsequent explorers followed suit, applying their own versions, sometimes giving one name to a large group with many internal differences, while giving different names to closely related subgroups. Also, the Indians themselves changed. The romantic concept of native peoples living a quiet, bucolic existence in one place for centuries prior to being ravaged by Western Civilization does not apply. Various groups merged with each other, sometimes forcefully, subjugating, displacing, or assimilating other, weaker groups. Some were sedentary and others nomadic raiders. The Ópatas, who controlled much of Sonora at the time of the Spanish *entrada,* were relative latecomers to the area.

Whatever their name, these native people that Ibarra's troop encountered were nomadic not sedentary agriculturalists. They made it clear when they showed the Spaniards the ruins of Paquimé that their people had not constructed the great houses. They indicated vaguely that the original builders had gone off somewhere to the north.

Whoever the Paquimé builders were, what they left behind impressed the Spaniards as they wandered among four-story buildings organized around large, paved plazas with well-made canals bringing water from a spring over a mile away. Obregón wrote that "this large city ... contains buildings that seemed to have been constructed by the ancient Romans. It is marvelous to look upon."[6]

Marvelous or not, Ibarra's men were exhausted. The Suma talked of golden cities to the north, but for most of the troopers that dream was over. They camped among the ruins, arguing among themselves. Ibarra, the young leader, wanted to push on to the north. This was his land, Nueva Vizcaya, and he wanted to explore and push the frontiers northward. Obregón and other officers agreed. However, for the soldiers seeking their own fortunes, the incentive was to find promising lands that would be awarded to them by Ibarra, their governor and captain general. Settlements in Sonora and Sinaloa looked far better to them than this hostile land. Ibarra wisely placed the issue before his men, and the "return" contingent won by single vote.[7] Reluctantly, Ibarra gave the order to start south, to Obregón's everlasting disgust. He later wrote how disappointed he was that "...because of fear and cowardice ... they lost the honor and profit of discovering New Mexico." That honor belonged to Cabeza de Vaca. As it was, Ibarra's expedition barely made it back.

From Paquimé, they went south, probably along the Casas Grandes and Palanganas Rivers; the route later followed by Bandelier in 1884. The scanty information available suggests they might have turned from the river at the Arroyo Poños near the future Mata Ortiz site, just as Bandelier did, and followed the San Diego Canyon route into the mountains. Obregón's chronicle and other reports are not clear. Whatever the route, Ibarra and his men wanted to go far enough south to avoid the Ópata before entering the Sierra Madre and crossing into Sonora. Unfortunately, they turned too soon and not only encountered hostile Ópata but became lost among the ridges and canyons probably in the region of the confluence of the Aros, Bavispe, and Yaqui Rivers. The story again becomes a saga of survival. After days of wandering and fighting off Indians, and killing their mules for food, they found themselves in a deep river canyon. The situation was beyond desperate. Baltasar de Obregón, weak as he was, had enough spirit to volunteer to find a way out. He somehow climbed up the canyon wall. From the top could see the way to the Río Sonora Valley and the coast. Energized, Ibarra and the remaining troopers made it out of the canyon and eventually to the coast, probably somewhere near Guaymas.

While this expedition cannot be considered a great success, Ibarra did expand the known limits of Nueva Vizcaya, and he forever remains the first European to enter Paquimé, now a World Heritage Site. He may have been the first European to pass by the future site of Mata Ortiz. That trip ended his trekking. He never personally led another major expedition. Young as he was, the grueling trips took a physical toll. He governed capably for ten more years until his death in 1575 at age 36. Ibarra is rightly called the "Father of Nueva Vizcaya," which in turn makes him the Father of Chihuahua. Many governors succeeded him, but most references comment on their activities in relation to what Ibarra accomplished. His light hand with the various indigenous groups he encountered helped promote development and spread of European culture. The relationships with these groups, always somewhat rocky, deteriorated dramatically in Nueva Vizcaya in the succeeding three centuries, particularly in the north.

Over those centuries, province boundaries changed. In Ibarra's day, the Nueva Vizcaya province extended vaguely north to include the modern states of Durango, Sinaloa, and Sonora to the east, Coahuila to the west, and Texas, New Mexico, and whatever lands lay beyond. Chihuahua remained in the center. After the House of Bourbon replaced the Hapsburgs as the rulers of Spain in the early 1700s, the new king made numerous administrative changes, gradually establishing separate provinces for those surrounding locations, leaving Chihuahua as the remainder of Nueva Vizcaya, still a vast region.

3

The Prehistoric Beginning
Casas Grandes, Mimbres,
and the Ancient Inspiration

What They Saw

Starting almost four and a half centuries ago, conquistadors, explorers, travelers, traders, and scientists have filed reports on the dramatic remnants of what became known as the Casas Grandes culture. Francisco de Ibarra's chronicler Baltasar de Obregón was the first. Others followed, culminating in Dr. Charles Di Peso's eight-volume *Casas Grandes, a Fallen Trading Center of the Gran Chichimeca*. This massive report covered the first major excavation of Paquimé, the accompanying research, and an analysis of the surrounding area. Many anthropologists and archaeologists followed Di Peso, challenging, refining, and adding to his basic theories about this distinct culture that took form about 1000 AD and disappeared in the mid-1400s.

Left behind were the ruins of a multi-storied city with its outlying suburbs. They stretched dozens of miles along the Casas Grandes River and its tributaries into the Sierra Madre west and along the basin and range terrain north into New Mexico and south over the Sierra Madre. Some experts, including Di Peso, argued that the founders of Paquimé came from the central Mexico portion of Mesoamerica. Others acknowledge the Mesoamerican connection but theorize that the people migrated to the

21

Casas Grandes Valley from the north after the expansion or dissolution of prehistoric pueblos in the U.S. Southwest.

For close to 600 years, Paquimé sat abandoned, its thick walls and towers crumbling in the wind and rain. Some passersby wondered at its size and complexity. Others gave it only a few cursory lines in their reports. In later centuries, individuals and government officials became curious and began to examine the ruins more carefully.

Nicolás de Lafora and Marqués de Rubí

Representatives sent out by the Spanish Crown in the 18th century to inspect the conditions in the vast northern province called Nueva Vizcaya did not concern themselves with prehistoric sites. Their reports filed with the viceroy in Mexico City only briefly mentioned their impressions of the wonders of Paquimé. One of these early reports was written by Nicolás de Lafora, the chronicler for the inspection expedition led by Marqués de Rubí in 1766-1768.

The Spanish nobleman from Barcelona, Cayetano María Pignatelli Rubí Corbera y San Climent, Marqués de Rubí, held the rank of field marshal in the Spanish army. He came to Mexico in the fall of 1764 as part of a team selected by King Carlos III to organize a regular Mexican army. The king knew the situation in his vast northern Mexican realm was chaotic, and in an attempt to do something about it, sent new orders to Rubí. The king appointed Rubí inspector of the presidios and frontier settlements of all the northern provinces. He was to report on deficiencies, corruption, mismanagement, and make specific recommendations.

Nicolás de Lafora, a captain in the Spanish army engineers, had arrived in Mexico a year before the Marqués. The viceroy responsible for organizing Rubí's expedition appointed Lafora as engineer, cartographer, and chronicler. In addition to his formal report, Lafora wrote a detailed narrative of what he saw. For decades, scholars have found his descriptions of the regions north and south of the modern border to be invaluable.

What was not known to the academic world was that the Marqués himself kept a private journal. Found in an obscure collection in 1989, this added another view of the 18[8] century frontier.[8] Rubí did not mention Paquimé, and Lafora's description is brief. He wrote:

After fording it (the Casas Grandes River) one sees on a small elevation the remains of a very old town, called Las Casas Grandes de Moctezuma. Its ruins show it to have been of several levels. On one side of the rectangle which is formed by two plazas is a number of small rooms in two rows. According to their dimensions and measurements, they seem to me to have been intended for wild animal cages. On the other side are fragments of walls several *varas* (about 2.74 feet per vara) high and constructed of blocks of earth three to five feet in thickness, plastered in parts and whitewashed with a white earth which the Spaniards in this country still use.

José Agustín de Escudero

José Agustín de Escudero is considered to be Chihuahua's first historian. Born in Parral in 1801, he grew up in Ciudad Chihuahua when the state was still Spanish Nueva Vizcaya. He received the formal education offered in that day and became a lawyer and politician. His life spanned revolution, Apache depredation, war, and foreign occupation. He visited Paquimé in 1819 but did not publish his observations until 1834.[9]

Lieutenant R.W.H. Hardy, R.N.

The first publication describing Paquimé since Nicolás de Lafora is credited to the English Navy officer, Lieutenant R.W.H. Hardy, R.N. He rode through Mexico in 1825-28 and published in 1829, five years before Escudero.

As a boy of 12, he went to sea on a warship as a midshipman. He found himself "on the beach" during the era of world peace after the Napoleonic Wars. He spent time in Argentina, and in 1825 was in Mexico City negotiating with the newly independent Mexican government for a concession in the Gulf of California for the General Pearl and Coral Association, a British joint-stock company. With the concession granted, he explored the Gulf in a company sailing ship and returned by land through Sonora, Chihuahua, Mexico City to Veracruz and by sea back to England. After diving for pearls in the Gulf bays around Loreto with meager results, he apparently decided investigating mines in the Sierra Madre would be more lucrative.

From Hermosillo, he traveled up the valleys to the Bavispe River, then north to the presidio town of Bavispe that had a population of about 300. He described the town layout as a walled square with a church built for defense against the Apaches, similar to other towns in Sonora.

He followed the Carretas Pass trail down into the Casas Grandes Valley and to Casas Grandes. He spent a day at Paquimé. He described how the great walls of the city were intact but the roofs had collapsed filling the rooms with rubble. He said he could see where "Apaches" dug into the rooms looking for shell ornaments and pottery. Why he referred to Apaches as the diggers, he does not explain. He bought or was given a polychrome pot which appears to have pleased him. A drawing of this pot appears in his book. As far as is known, this is the first illustration to appear anywhere of Casas Grandes pottery.[10] After Hardy returned to England, he published his experiences, including what he saw at Paquimé, in a travel book, a popular format in that era.

R.W.H. Hardy's drawing, 1829. Believed to be the first illustration of a Casas Grandes pot.

John Russell Bartlett and the Boundary Survey

The Mexican American War ended with the Treaty of Guadalupe in 1848, but the boundary between the two countries remained in dispute. In 1850, President Millard Fillmore appointed John Russell Bartlett as U.S. Boundary Commissioner, charged with finding a solution. This was a political appointment. Bartlett was an expert on the English language and had other talents, but he knew little about surveying and nothing about the southwest. What he had was a curious mind and a desire to travel. He negotiated an agreement with his Mexican counterpart, but Congress rejected it because of an error that put the boundary forty-two miles north of El Paso. The boundary issues were not finally resolved until the Gadsden Purchase in 1854.

As Commissioner, Bartlett had a fine time traveling extensively along the border of the new U.S. territories and into northern Mexico. Bartlett became famous or infamous for constantly making side trips that had little to do with the task at hand. While in Chihuahua, he left the survey route and travelled to Hacienda Corralitos, the mining and ranching center southeast of Janos, along the Casas Grandes River. He and an assistant continued to Casas Grandes and spent a day there tramping over the ruins and picking up artifacts. He noted that an active relic market existed and locals at this very early date were already looting the sites for specimens to sell in Ciudad Chihuahua.

Bartlett wrote a personal narrative in order he said to "keep before the reader a correct idea of the character of the country throughout which he was to follow me without lists and descriptions, scientific or otherwise of every plant, quadruped, bird, and reptile that came my way." Included in the narrative are his drawings and sketches that have survived as the earliest known pictures of Paquimé. The resulting book, *Narrative of Explorations and Incidents in Texas, New Mexico, California, Sonora and Chihuahua, 1850-1853*, is Bartlett's legacy.

Edmond Guillemin-Tarayre

During the French occupation (1862-66), Napoleon III authorized the establishment of the Commission Scientifique du Mexique. The Commission assigned mineralogist Edmond Guillemin-Tarayre to explore a number of sites. He visited Paquimé and in his writings referred to the meteorite that apparently had been discovered recently by Enrico Müller.[11]

The Mysterious Meteorite, the Great Slice

Astral bodies streaking across the sky and crashing into earth have always fascinated mankind. Archaeologists have found sites in both the old and new worlds where man-made structures around these chunks of iron or stone clearly identified them as objects of veneration. When researchers attempted to decipher and document these findings, they often heard old, conflicting stories. That happened with the Casas Grandes Meteorite.

In one story dating to the 1860s, Enrique Müller, the director of the Chihuahua mint, hired workers to tunnel into the Paquimé ruins. In a buried room, they discovered several mummies wrapped in rough cotton cloth surrounding a large turtle-shaped object wrapped in the same cloth.[12] Enrique (sometimes Enrico, or Henry) Müller's name appears in various references as a German immigrant and entrepreneur in Chihuahua during the economic boom of the late 1880s. He and Luis Terrazas, the most powerful man in Chihuahua, did business together and were operating partners for one large hacienda. It is not known why Müller had men burrow into the ruins. Perhaps he had heard stories of buried treasure. What is known is the meteorite ended up in the Smithsonian in the Janet Annenberg Hooker Hall of Geology in 1876, where it is still displayed. No one is sure how this 4,400-pound piece of almost solid iron got there.

In another story, William M. Pierson, the U.S. vice consul in El Paso, gives himself the credit. In a wonderfully flamboyant letter written to the State Department in 1873, he said:

A party of Mexican mountaineers as a matter of curious speculation, commenced excavating in the old ruins of the Montezuma Casas Grandes ... One, Teodoro Alvarado, more fortunate than the others, drifted into a large room, in the middle of which, there appeared a kind of tomb made of brick. Curiosity led this bold Knight of the Crowbar to renew his excavations, and when he had reached the middle of this tomb, he there found this curious mass of meteoric iron, carefully and curiously wrapped in a kind of coarse linen …[13]

Alvarado, the "Knight of the Crowbar" found a way to move the heavy mass to his yard in Casas Grandes. Pierson does not say where he saw the meteorite. He said only that, along with partners, he intended to buy and haul it by freight wagon to the consulate in El Paso. This apparently never happened. The mysterious mass, at least most of it, was still in Casas Grandes in 1875.

According to O.C. Farrington, the leading expert on meteorites at the turn of the 19th century, the Smithsonian received only a "piece" along with Pierson's report in 1873. Farrington went on to say that in 1876, the Smithsonian received as a gift the "uncut" mass along with other Mexican minerals that had been exhibited at the Centennial Exposition.[14] The obvious contradiction by the leading expert adds to the confusion. The brief interpretive material in Hooker Hall describes the display as "… once part of a single gigantic crystal found in an ancient Mexican Temple."[15] Also, it was recorded that at some unknown time, a slab was cut from the meteorite's rough outer surface to reveal the crystalline structure.[16]

Another version of the story is found in an obscure journal that led to an equally obscure autobiography by a Texas freight hauler. These accounts, despite obvious inaccuracies in the autobiography, pull together the other stories into a plausible scenario.

In 1939, Oscar E. Monnig from Fort Worth, Texas submitted an article to the Society for Research on Meteorites.[17] As president of a department store chain, Monnig was a successful businessman, but his passion was astronomy. He became a recognized meteorite expert and a leader in a group of like-mined amateurs called the Texas Observers. Monnig was aware of the Casas Grandes Meteorite and the gaps and contradictions in its story. A friend gave him a book written by August Santleben and published in 1910. Santleben started the first stage line between Texas and Mexico and was a major freight hauler. He told of hauling bullion, of confrontations with Indians, and of life on the prairies in both countries. In one story, he recounted how he heard about the meteorite, "said to be one of the most massive in the scientific world." He decided to find out if he could take it to the Centennial International Exhibition in Philadelphia, America's first official world's fair.[18]

Monnig carefully reviewed Santleben's story and combined it with research from Farrington and others to prepare his article. He recognized that Santleben made many factual errors, but the overall story was still very important. Santleben said that the meteorite fell on Enrique Müller's hacienda at San Lorenzo. Monnig dismisses this but accepts that Müller had the meteorite (likely in Alverado's yard in Casas Grandes). Santleben, also a German immigrant, knew Enrique Müller because he hauled loads of silver coin in his large wagons from Müller's Chihuahua mint. According to Santleben, Müller willingly gave up the meteorite as it had no value for him. However, the Mexican government heard about it and insisted that because the object came from outer space, it could not be owned by an individual. Santleben disagreed. He always maintained he owned the meteorite, but he went along to get the Mexican permit at the border allowing him to transport the object to the U.S. for display. Both Santleben and Müller posted a bond guaranteeing its return by a certain date at no cost to the government. Santleben was very concerned about the cost of shipping the meteorite to Philadelphia. He felt it would be a big attraction and admission fees would cover his expenses.

He had a fleet of about ten very large wagons. The beds were 24 feet long compared to the classic Conestoga wagon that measured 18 feet. The back wheels were almost six feet in diameter and six inches wide. The front wheels were five feet in diameter. Ten mules pulled each ponderous vehicle. At the mint, the teamsters loaded silver coin worth $200,000 for delivery to the trailhead at Luling, Texas, for transshipment to Galveston. Why such a fortune in Mexican coin was to be delivered through hostile Indian and outlaw border country to a port in the U.S. is unclear. Santleben made several such trips and, to his own amazement after many scrapes, never lost a coin.

The teamsters left one wagon empty and piled cow hides high on the boxes of coins in the others. Led by Santleben they diverted to Casas Grandes from the direct Chihuahua/El Paso road to load the meteorite. Santleben said hauling the object gave them trouble because it was "dead weight."

The road passed through a series of Texas forts—Davis, Stockton, and Conchos—before reaching San Antonio. One night as they camped with Texas Rangers, hunters came in with the news that a Comanche war party was nearby. Most in the Ranger command had left in pursuit of other raiders. A small detachment from the remaining soldiers and campers rode out, found the Comanche and killed three in a battle. None of the pursuers were hurt. Santleben continued on to San Antonio without further incident. His teamsters parked the meteorite wagon behind a house, while they rested two days. Hundreds of people came to the back yard and peered into the wagon to see the "stone" from the sky.

The railhead at Luling was 47 miles west of San Antonio. They arrived there two days before the train to Galveston. Luling, founded just the year before, was a wide-open frontier town. Santleben stayed up both nights with his guns guarding the wagons.

He had gone this far but could not continue to Philadelphia. His wagons stood empty, and there were contracts to fulfill in Mexico. He put the meteorite on the train and paid to have it shipped by boat from Galveston to Philadelphia. That happened and apparently, the exhibit was a great success. However, Santleben never saw the meteorite again, nor did he receive any of the exhibition receipts. The object gained enough publicity that the Mexican government claimed ownership under the Antiquities Laws and decided it would be advantageous to give it to the Smithsonian in Washington DC. This really annoyed Santleben, who considered himself the legal owner. He made claims but was ignored. He was a long distance away and had no clear idea as to what had happened. He even thought the meteorite had gone to the British Museum. As a practical businessman, he cut his losses and moved on. At least the Mexican government did not hold him to the meteorite bond.

Oscar Monnig considers this a plausible explanation of how the Casas Grandes meteorite got to the Smithsonian. The dates quoted from the stories fit together. The discoverer of the meteorite in the Paquimé, Teodora Alvarado, could have been employed by Enrique Müller. Until another old story surfaces, it is assumed that the Mexican government made a gift to the Smithsonian at August Santleben's expense.

The meteorite sat in the Smithsonian's Hooker Gallery undisturbed until the 21st century. By that time Paquimé had been professionally excavated, declared a World Heritage Site, and designated the Casas Grandes Archaeological Site managed by the Chihuahua office of the Instituto Nacional de Antropología e Historia (INAH). Researchers and others connected to the Mexican museum world began to discuss the meteorite. Should not at least a part of this unusual object that was venerated by the prehistoric people be on display in the museum? This led to inquiries to the Smithsonian. The persistence of several people paid off, including Eduardo Gamboa Carrera, the director of the Museo de las Culturas del Norte; Jorge Carrera, the director of the Chihuahua's INAH office; Javier Pedraza, the President of Pueblo Mágico de Casas Grandes; and Spencer MacCallum. Smithsonian officials liked the concept, but they wanted to make sure whatever they sent was secure; specifically, they specified video camera surveillance. A local businessman, José Luis Rodriquez of Central Alarmas y Comunicación, graciously provided the required security system.

The Smithsonian technicians cut a large slice, *La Gran Rebanada,* showing the crystalline structure and shipped it to the museum. It arrived on March 6, 2018. A small ceremony was held the following week to honor the return of a piece of the Casas Grandes Meteorite that crashed nearby in prehistoric times and left under somewhat mysterious circumstances 143 years before.

Adolph Bandelier, the First Real Scientist

In 1884, Adolph Bandelier, one of the most important and influential Southwest anthropologists of the late 19th century, reconnoitered northern Mexico during the months of January through June. He followed Coronado's approximate route along the western slope of the Sierra Madre through the Río Sonora Valley before turning northeast to the Bavispe Valley. Descending the rugged Carretas Pass to Chihuahua, he crossed the Llano de Carretas. At Janos he turned south to visit Paquimé and the surrounding area before making another trip back into the mountains, perhaps riding near the future site of Pearson/Mata Ortiz. He returned to the plains, followed the Casas Grandes River northward, and crossed back into the U.S. in June. He described this trip in detailed hand-written journals with illustrations, which have been edited and published.[19]

Bandelier was a prolific writer, including even one novel. In his later years, he spent much time studying archival material and writing. On his first trip to Mexico, he met and became friends with Mexico's most noted 19th century historian/archivist, Joaquín García Icazbalceta. The Spanish had left behind detailed records of the entrada and their interactions with the native peoples. Icazbalceta was an expert with these colonial records. Both tireless researchers, they worked together side-by-side for six months comparing and trying to find links between Indians of Mexico and the tribal groups of New Mexico. After Bandelier returned to the U.S., they continued to correspond regularly, exchanging research until Icazbalceta's death in 1894.[20] In 1887 Bandelier also prepared a bulky manuscript with full-color illustrations for Archbishop Salpointe of Santa Fe. The manuscript, now in the Vatican Library, contains more than 90 illustrations of pottery, stone tools, and site plans.

Adolph Bandelier's willingness to go deep into the rugged terrain of northern Mexico to find and research prehistoric sites stemmed from his many attributes. A quintessential late 19th century man, he combined a brilliant mind, a facility with languages, and an insatiable curiosity with a sense of romance. Adding courage and stamina to the mix, he became a sort of an early-day Indiana Jones. In 1880, the fledgling American Institute of Archaeology (AIA), later chartered by the U.S. Congress, and today one of the largest and most important archaeological institutions in the world, chose Bandelier as its first field researcher in the Southwest. With this initial support, he began a quarter century of ethnographic, anthropological, and archaeological research in the American Southwest, Mexico, and South America, performing the first truly scientific exploration of many sites. His reports to the AIA dispelled myths—myths that had in some cases had been perpetuated since Spanish times, such as the Seven Cities of Cíbola and supposed Aztec involvement with cultures of the Southwest. In remote areas, he often lived with the local people, eating their food, hearing their stories and absorbing their culture. Bandelier died in 1914. Two years later, President Wilson signed a law designating a magnificent 33,600-acre ruin site on the Pajarito Plateau in north-central New Mexico as the Bandelier National Monument.[21]

In 1883, Bandelier began his expedition into Mexico from the Gila Cliffs area in New Mexico, now a National Monument. He rode and sometimes walked southwest into Arizona, past Tucson and Tombstone, along the Huachuca Mountains to the Mexican border. At Fort Huachuca, he met Lt. Frank West, who described landmarks and ruins he had seen in the rugged region of the Bavispe River headwaters while pursuing Gerónimo's band. Bandelier crossed into the state of Sonora on January 19, 1884. He worked his way south through the Sierra Madre until he was in the Bavispe Valley almost directly west of the Casas Grandes Valley in Chihuahua. Local guides showed him numerous prehistoric sites with buildings substantially intact and others not much more than melted adobe mounds. He measured and carefully recorded everything he saw, describing and sketching the various artifacts—pottery, stone mortars, metates, axes—that lay scattered about, relatively untouched.

In March during Holy Week, he witnessed dances and ceremonies of the Ópata, descendants of the warriors that so harassed Coronado and Francisco de Ibarra. It is remarkable that these people had survived in their ancient homeland with something of their identity intact. After the cultural disruption of the Spanish *entrada* and the Apache intrusion, many Ópata had moved away, some to the Janos area where they joined the Spanish in the fight against the raiding Apaches. There in Janos over the centuries, they were absorbed into the mestizo culture.

In the mountains, around campfires, Bandelier listened to their old stories, such as the origin of the sun and moon, and details of ancient battles with the people of Casas Grandes to the east. Elders said these enemies to the east were also Ópata. Others said they were a different people altogether.[22] Whoever lived there, the Casas Grandes Valley and the ruins of Paquimé would be Bandelier's next destination.

By the end of April, he was in Bavispe, Sonora, 78 miles from Janos in the valley west of the Sierra Madre crest. On May 1, he started up the stony trail. His entourage consisted of 24 men and a mix of 78 horses, mules, and burros. They climbed the Carretas Pass trail, possibly the same route taken by the desperate Francisco de Ibarra over three hundred years before. The trail featured dangerous precipices plus lurid stories of Apache ambushes. Bandelier seemed wary but not overly concerned about the Apaches since an old Ópata Apache fighter had assured him that none were in the pass. Whatever the potential dangers, after three days of hard travel, Bandelier arrived safely in Janos on May 3, where he rested at the home of a local resident.

The Janos area had suffered. The Mexican government closed the presidio and removed the protective garrison 27 years before. Ongoing Apache raids had forced many people to leave, reducing the population from 4,590 in 1831 to 600 by 1884. Ranchos in the immediate area were abandoned.[23]

Bandelier was undeterred. His main concern was the ruins, and he found many. He noted in his journal that there were some along the San Pedro River and many more along the Casas Grandes River all the way to San Diego. He stayed one night at Hacienda Corralitos and on May 8 rode south alone to Casas Grandes. He described the valley as very fertile. The town of Casas Grandes itself probably had about 1,600 to 1,700 "souls." The local leaders received him cordially and provided guides. On a hill about two miles north of town, stood a ruined structure with high adobe walls, *El Convento*. Bandelier, at first, was not sure what it was, and he probably never learned the full story of the failed attempt to start the Mission San Antonio de Padua 200 years before.

He spent most of May 1884, investigating Paquimé, making measurements, maps, drawings, and extensive notes. He concluded that the region must have supported a population much larger than any of the Pueblo cultures in the North American Southwest.

Late in the month, he and two Mexican companions rode south from San Diego along the Palanganas River before heading west across the plains into the Sierra Madre. He noted at least three substantial ruins in the general area of what is now Mata Ortiz. From his journal description, he must have seen *Los Cables*, a large Mimbres/Casas Grandes site on a bluff just north of the village, well known to local pot hunters.

South of Los Cables, he turned toward the dip in the wall of mountains across the plains. Following the descriptions in his journal, he likely turned at Arroyo de los Poños, an arroyo near the site of present-day Mata Ortiz that crosses the plains to the Sierra Madre.[24] Again, this may have been the same route taken by Francisco de Ibarra and his trail-weary troop three centuries before. Bandelier followed this arroyo west to where it joined the Puerto San Diego arroyo system draining the canyons at the base of the mountains. Antelope were all around, and the two Mexican guides blazed away with their guns and according to Bandelier "did some very bad shooting indeed, missing every shot."

Prehistoric *trincheras* or dikes of rock lined the plains around the arroyos creating farm plots. Bandelier had seen similar elaborate rock structures designed to control the flow of water, on the slopes and arroyos higher in the mountains. Near the farm plots were ruins of ancient Casas Grandes-style houses with metates and pottery shards scattered about. Farmers from Mata Ortiz today work these same plots, called *labores*. They find shards and occasionally a complete pot.

Past the farms, the trail left the valley floor and continued into the steep *Cañón de San Diego*, climbing the north side into forests of pine—forests whose exploitation for lumber would lead to the creation of Pearson/Mata Ortiz 25 years later. Bandelier's objective for this short trip was to familiarize himself with this part of the mountain range, which was east of the areas he had explored earlier. He recognized landmarks that Lt. Frank West had described when they met at Fort Huachuca.

Before returning, Bandelier explored caves along the Piedras Verdes River region. He made no mention of the now-famous Cave of the Olla with its twelve-foot-high granary. It sat then as it does now at the edge of a large cave high on a canyon wall above the river in what is now called Cave Valley.

He did note an arch in a rock formation rising about 60 feet above another little valley. Above and behind the arch on the cliff, he found a cave with plastered interior walls. This little valley with the arch, *El Arco*, was named *Cuesta Blanca*. Ron Bridgemon of Tucson, Arizona and his wife Sue have spent over 20 years exploring northern Chihuahua. Ron has been in *Cuesta Blanca* many times and has located the cave, which still shows traces of plaster on the interior walls.

Bandelier's notation about El Arco places him not far from the future LDS community of Pacheco established three years later.

On May 27, Bandelier left the mountains and returned to a campsite not far from San Diego. After resting a day, Bandelier and a guide climbed Cerro Moctezuma, the prominent little mountain west of Paquimé between the Casas Grandes and San Diego Valleys. This mountain dominates the view today when looking east from the Mata Ortiz highway.

Bandelier and his guide followed clearly defined trails from the north and west leading to a plateau north of the main peak. There they found rock houses and walls, which could have been dwellings or fortifications. Some were well built, and others appeared to be no more than temporary shelters. Shards and metates suggested people had lived there for a long time. Yet, Bandelier could find no water source anywhere. A well-defined trail led around the west slope to the top. There he found a round tower or fort of stone, eight feet tall with walls five feet thick and forty feet in diameter. Inside the wide interior were other walls and structures but no evidence of prolonged habitation. Bandelier thought it might have been a place of refuge or fortification. The view in all directions was magnificent. He claimed in his notes that he could see clear to the Sierra de Hacha in New Mexico.

After so long on the trail, Bandelier was ready to go home, After resting a few days at Corralitos, while vaqueros rounded up his lost horse, he started out. It was early June. He rode northeast, crossed the border, and reached Deming, New Mexico one week later. This ended the explorations of the first scientist to study the Casas Grandes culture.

After Bandelier

Bandelier's expedition and research in northern Mexico were extraordinary for the time. However, after Bandelier, and partly because of his work in New Mexico and what became the Bandelier National Monument, exploration of the prehistoric North American Southwest dominated the attention of U.S. scientists and the popular news. In Mexico City, academics were preoccupied with the rich archeological challenges all around them in central and southern Mexico. Casas Grandes was in the distant north. Ralph L. Beals noted in 1932, during the heyday of Southwest exploration, that "Perhaps no region of North America is so little known to the anthropologist as northern Mexico ..."[25]

Beals exaggerated somewhat. Casas Grandes remained in the shadow of scientific study but was not unknown. Carl S. Lumholtz certainly was aware of it when he began his expedition six years after Bandelier. He referred to the "famous ruins of the Casas Grandes." In 1890, this meticulous Norwegian ethnographer with an entourage of scientists began an eight-year in-depth study of the human cultures, geology, flora and fauna of Mexico that included almost three years in the northern Sierra Madre area. One result was Lumholtz's well-known book *Unknown Mexico, Exploration in the Sierra Madre and Other Regions, 1890-1898."* First published in 1902 and still in print, it reads well and introduced the general public to the mysteries of the Sierra Madre and the Casas Grandes region.[26]

Carl Lumholtz, the Next Scientist

Lumholtz's work among the aborigines in Australia earned him a reputation sufficient to gain the backing of the American Museum of Natural History for an extensive expedition into Mexico. His particular interest was finding native peoples that still practiced their old ways. The concept of modern-day "cavemen" fascinated him. However, as a man of science, he wanted his research to be as broad as possible. The personnel of this first Mexican expedition covered most of the physical sciences including two geographers, two archaeologists, two botanists, a mineralogist, and a zoologist. One of the botanists was Carl V. Hartman from Sweden. As one of his tasks, Hartman studied the wild plants still used by the Indians. He became so intrigued dealing directly with these people, and influenced by Lumholtz, he later changed professions from botany to anthropology. When Lumholtz was away, he took over camp management and supervised the archeological excavations.

The first expedition lasted three years. Lumholtz started with 35 men—scientists, guides, cooks, and *arrieros,* the muleteers. The arrieros had charge of almost a hundred animals—horses, mules, and burros—needed to transport men, gear, food, scientific and photographic equipment. Lumholtz recruited men and obtained most of the non-scientific items including, supplies, and animals, in the mining boom town of Bisbee, Arizona. Like Bandelier, Lumholtz was the quintessential 19th century man—tough, fearless, with an insatiable intellectual curiosity coupled with the same sense of romance. He needed all his skills dealing with Bisbee's horse traders and the rough border crowd from which he tried to select recruits. He eventually replaced most of the North American non-scientists with Mexicans hired along the way, whom he found to be more reliable. He learned the trick of going first to the village elders before hiring.

The results of his first expedition were dramatic. The scientists collected hundreds of species of plants including 27 that were previously unknown to the academic world. They collected 1,000 bird and 55 mammal specimens. They also excavated prehistoric mounds and ruins, gathering artifacts including outstanding examples of Casas Grandes pottery. One interesting sidelight is that in preparing for the expedition, Lumholtz made the long trip to Mexico City to seek permission to explore. High government officials welcomed him warmly, and he even met with President Porfirio Díaz for over an hour to discuss his expedition plans. He received documents that permitted him to do almost anything he wanted, including excavation and exportation of artifacts, normally prohibited by Mexican law. Much of what Lumholtz and the other scientists collected on this first expedition was exhibited in the World Columbian Exposition in Chicago that began in 1893. Carl Hartman, the botanist turned anthropologist, helped prepare the displays and interpretive material. Afterwards, everything went to the American Museum of Natural History in New York City. The collection remains uniquely important because in contrast to many of the collections in the U.S. and Mexico, the provenance of each piece was recorded.

One advantage Lumholtz had over Bandelier was photography. The earlier explorer had a camera, but the plates did not survive. Lumholtz had four cameras. In his book, he uses many pictures including the first published photographs of Casas Grandes pottery.[27] A drawing in the book shows the animal assigned to carry the photo equipment, known as the "Photographic Mule."[28] Two of the four cameras were large-format, glass-plate devices that were bulky and took time to set up. He also had two Kodaks. Eastman had just introduced the box camera, and Lumholtz had Eastman's second version, a Kodak 2, that shot round pictures. He also had a more sophisticated model with an adjustable lens, the Kodak 4. Each camera took three or four steps to shoot a picture, but it could be done from the saddle.

Like Bandelier, Lumholtz's expedition crossed the border into Sonora and followed the river system on the east side of the crest of the Sierra

Madre. Also like Bandelier, he investigated the many mounds and ruins along the route. It is not known how much detailed information Lumholtz had of Bandelier's work. He was certainly aware of his predecessor, and he refers to one of Bandelier's comments about the elaborate stone *trincheras* in the mountain valleys.[29]

Another advantage Lumholtz had over Bandelier was the presence of the Church of Jesus Christ of Latter-day Saints colonists. In 1885, one year after Bandelier left northern Chihuahua, they began arriving. These intrepid settlers left Utah and Arizona with their families, stock, farm equipment, and everything else they owned to move to this foreign place to escape U.S. anti-polygamy laws. They settled in the Casas Grandes Valley and on arable land in the mountains. The first community in the valley was Colonia Juárez and in the mountains Pacheco, established in 1886 among the pines near the Piedras Verdes River.

Lumholtz's expedition continued south to Nácori in Sonora, then turned northeast, cresting the Sierra at 8,000 feet into Chihuahua. They

Cave of the Olla — Photo PHO25-1-1-112 Courtesy of the University of Texas at El Paso Library, Special Collections Department

38

descended about 1,000 feet to reach Pacheco. The scattered wooden cabins there housed 16 families with 80 children. The LDS Settlers greeted them warmly, provided food, guides, and local information.

While camped at Pacheco, Lumholtz heard of a beautiful little valley along the river just five miles away called Cave Valley. The steep cliffs surrounding this valley contained caves with evidence of early people. The next morning, he found the valley and a nearby settlement of eight houses, where he was greeted warmly again and shown a good campsite. The Piedras Verdes River over time has cut through the volcanic rock, leaving a relatively level area surrounded by cliffs. These cliffs in turn have been eroded into fantastic shapes featuring towers, minarets, crenellations, and deep caves.

The focal point, then and now, is a twelve-foot-high granary standing majestically like a giant pot on the lip of a wide, deep cave on the canyon wall. Known as the Cave of the Olla, it can be seen clearly from the campsites below. Lumholtz described the "olla" in detail in his book. According to his analysis, the ancient people constructed it of large coils of grass laid on top of each other and covered with plaster inside and out. Adobe walls along the side and back of the cave formed six to eight rooms. The cave opening was broad and extended back at least 60 feet.

The LDS colonists cultivated fields on the level areas near the river where prehistoric people long ago had grown corn. They practiced a branch of the LDS religion; a collectivist style of living called the United Order of Enoch.[30] The settlers claimed the valley was also a hideout for the Apaches.

The land was owned by Moses Thatcher, an Apostle of the Church, who had helped establish the first LDS colonies.[31] Lumholtz met Apostle Thatcher, who had just returned from Utah for an inspection tour. He gave Lumholtz permission to make excavations in Cave Valley and "take away anything of interest to science." His only restriction concerned the burials. He did not want any mummies removed.

The little valley enchanted Lumholtz, and he decided to make it his base camp, despite his concern about the Apaches. He was far more nervous about the Apaches than Bandelier. Gerónimo and the other famous leaders had surrendered or were dead. Still, attacks in the remote mountains occurred or were rumored to have occurred.

He sent Hartman on to begin work at San Diego, where they had permission from a Mr. Gavin, then leasing the property, to excavate mound sites.

Lumholtz systematically examined the caves, taking measurements, making floor plans and sketches, as well as excavating. The expedition broke camp in early spring and pushed on to Colonia Juárez. At the top of the pass, Lumholtz paused to look at the "charming" view across the San Diego Valley to the future site of Mata Ortiz, framed by the Sierra de Anchón. He noted that antelope could only be found in isolated herds. Bandelier enjoyed the same view with the plains covered with antelope, suggesting that hunting had reduced their numbers in just a few years. In modern times, Bishop John Hatch of Casas Grandes has seen antelope, but sightings are rare.[32]

They reached Colonia Juárez in one day. Lumholtz was impressed with the new town. Only four years old, it had well-laid out streets lined with cottonwood trees and houses surrounded by gardens. He was also impressed with the richness of the archaeological sites. He counted over 50 mounds in the San Diego area. One of his teams found caves and structures along the Palanganas River, well past the Pearson/Mata Ortiz site, similar to Cave Valley. All interesting, but the main attraction was Paquimé.

The crew camped right in the ruins on the highest mound. They unearthed many artifacts, particularly pottery. Lumholtz described the Casas Grandes ware as "far superior in quality and in decoration to anything made in Mexico," and "is superior in quality as well as decoration to that produced by the Pueblos of the Southwest of the United States."[33] He also described local pot hunters digging up the site looking for pieces to sell.

From the mounds at Paquimé, he could see the tower or fort on Cerro Moctezuma west about five miles. His observations of the huge fort and the other structures matched those of Bandelier as did his total enjoyment of the magnificent view in all directions.

After making the arrangements for shipping the collected artifacts back to New York, he shut down the camp, and rode south through the mountains into Tarahumara country to continue his expedition looking for people who lived in caves.

Cave of the Olla

The little valley with its spectacular Cave of the Olla, that so appealed to Lumholtz, soon became an attraction. Families from below started making the trip just to see it. The old circuitous route from Colonia Juárez covered 35 miles. A new road built sometime after 1894 cut off six miles, but it remained a rough all-day trip. Over the decades, additional switchbacks enabled wagons and later diesel trucks to haul lumber and logs down the steep grade. By the end of the 20th century, the drive up still took four hours, assuming no problems. Once there, families would explore, scramble in and out of the caves, and enjoy a picnic.

Drivers on the slow narrow dirt switchbacks always faced the possibility of meeting a semi-truck with worn brakes and a precarious load of logs around the next curve.

At the summit, the road led across a concrete bridge over the Piedras Verdes River to the village of Ignacio Zaragoza. The concrete bridge made the crossing easier, but a huge flood in the 1980s tipped the bridge to one side. A modern steel span called the Stevens Bridge replaced it in 2007.

The nickname for Ignacio Zaragoza is El Willy. Locals say the name came from a character named Willy, who operated a still during Prohibition. A more mundane and probably more factual version gives credit to an LDS settler named George Williams, who owned a ranch nearby.

In 1988, a small sawmill still operated close to El Willy. Beyond the village, the road entered the private *Rancho de Casa Blanca*. The road in fact went through a pasture gate right in front of the ranch house, *Casa Blanca*, a large, very old, but still functioning, adobe home. Cave Valley lay about one half mile from the gate at the back end of the pasture. It was necessary to get permission to cross the property from the owner, Señor Cuauhtémoc López. He always granted it. Next to the pasture, he and his brothers had a sugar cane field. When the cane was ready, family members and workers cut the cane and stacked it near an old-fashioned sugar mill, a *rastra*, at the edge of the field. A mule, harnessed to a wooden beam, walked around and around a mill connected to the other end of the beam. Workers fed cane stalks into the top of the mill, and the juice flowed out the bottom into a metal can. The resulting molasses sugar was formed into cone-shaped *piloncillos* that were sold in the store in El Willy.

The little valley has been used by Apaches, Ópatas, and their prede-cessors back through prehistoric time. Tiny corn cobs found in the nearby caves appeared to be a variety used in ancient times. They probably came from the still-active corn field that stretches along the river.

The large olla-shaped granary survived a century of visitors, but many of the adobe walls within the caves around it were damaged. INAH, the federal agency responsible for historic sites, assumed control in the early 2000s and installed an on-site supervisor. It remains an attraction, easily accessible on the paved highway with road signs directing the way.

Other Scientists

While scientific interest in Casas Grandes remained in the shadow of the northern pueblos (U.S. Southwest) and the numerous and often spectacular sites of Mesoamerica, some study continued after Bandelier and Lumholtz. At least five notable anthropologists/archaeologists spent time in the Casas Grandes cultural region in the decades following the turn of the century.

Jesse Walter Fewkes

Jesse Walter Fewkes was an expert on northern pueblo cultures and one of the most important early anthropologists. He lived among pueblo peoples in Arizona, and New Mexico and was unique in that he was accepted into their societies. He was the first to record ceremonial songs, made on wax cylinders. In 1901, he traveled through west Texas into Chihuahua to Casas Grandes. He worked at Paquimé, making what some called the most exten-sive study of the ruins ever up until that time.[34]

Edgar Lee Hewett

Edgar Lee Hewett, fifteen years younger than Fewkes, had an enormous impact on early anthropology and archaeology. He is particularly remem-bered as the driving force behind the federal Antiquities Act of 1906, which helped save and conserve prehistoric Southwest sites, such as the Bandelier National Monument.

In 1898, the New Mexican territorial government appointed him president of the newly formed New Mexico Normal University at Las Vegas, New Mexico (today New Mexico Highlands University) where he founded the first college classes devoted to anthropology in the United States.[35] In 1901, he left the university and committed himself to archaeology and anthropology. He must have been a dynamic character because soon he held several offices in archaeological institutions in Washington D.C. and New Mexico and was deeply involved in conservation causes. In 1909, he founded and was the first director of the Museum of New Mexico and the School of American Research in Santa Fe.

His efforts were not all administrative and political. In 1906, he spent a year exploring sites from Mesa Verde, Colorado to Mexico City. Traveling south, often on horseback, he entered the Casas Grandes Valley and visited several sites. He was welcomed at the haciendas, and he stayed at Hacienda Ramos and the Hearst Ranch at San José de Babícora. At Hacienda Ramos, he met Mrs. E. C. Houghton, the wife of the Corralitos Company manager. Ramos was then part of Corralitos. Mrs. Houghton was an amateur archaeologist. She had explored the prehistoric sites nearby and dug up over 200 pots. Perhaps some or all were for sale because Hewett lamented he did not have money to make a purchase. He corrected that deficiency years later.

He made other trips to Chihuahua between 1906 and 1926, and his writings are considered a major contribution to the understanding of the U.S. Southwest and northwest Mexico and of "Oasisamerica," the concept of agricultural settlements near water in these arid regions.

During his frenetic career, he made many investigative trips not only to the Southwest and Mexico but to sites around the world. He wrote over 250 books, monographs, and articles, many published by the University of New Mexico Press, which he helped found.

Alfred V. Kidder

Alfred V. Kidder had a boyhood fascination for anthropology and archaeology. As a Harvard student, he spent the summer of 1907 assisting the great Walter Fewkes at Mesa Verde in Colorado.

After receiving his PhD in 1914, Kidder established his own reputation at the Pecos Pueblo in New Mexico, which, largely to his efforts, became the Pecos National Historic Park. The huge region contained an enormous amount of prehistoric pottery, and he became an expert in classifying shards and whole pots. For Pecos and for his expeditions elsewhere, he usually was sponsored by either Harvard's Peabody Museum of Archaeology and Ethnology or the Robert S. Peabody Museum of Archaeology at Phillips Academy in Andover, Massachusetts.

In 1927, he used the Pecos Pueblo name and founded the Pecos Conference, an annual three-day professional meeting of southwestern U.S. and northwestern Mexican archaeologists. The conference was held in or near prehistoric sites including Paquimé in 1961, 1991 (hosted by Dr. R.B. "Ben" Brown), and 2003.

Between 1922 and 1924, Kidder made trips to study the Casas Grandes culture region as far south as the Babícora plain over the mountains from the San Diego Valley. In 1916 prior to his first visit, he made a detailed study of the Philips collection of Casas Grandes pottery at the Peabody Museum and other major collections. His descriptions, written over a hundred years ago, in the monograph, *The Pottery of the Casas Grandes District, Chihuahua* remain useful to students today.[36]

Edwin Booth Sayles

Edwin Booth (Ted) Sayles was a kind of Renaissance man in that he dabbled successfully in completely different activities. He had a real estate career, became a famous anthropologist, an *Arizona Highways* photographer, and writer of children's books. While he always had an interest in anthropology and archaeology, he was 38 years old before he made this avocation his profession.

He began working for Harold S. Gladwin and his wife Winifred in 1931 at the Gila Pueblo Archaeological Foundation in Globe, Arizona. Harold Gladwin was a successful New York stockbroker. After he and Winifred were introduced to A.V. Kidder, they became fascinated with Southwestern archaeology. They came west and established the foundation dedicated to archaeological research. It operated until 1950, when it closed and its collections and archives were transferred to the Arizona State Museum on the University of Arizona campus in Tucson.

Sayles worked at Gila Pueblo for over ten years. He participated in several expeditions including a survey of the Casas Grandes region in 1933. He wrote several articles for the Gila Pueblo publication, *Medallion Papers,* including two on the survey. He left in 1943 to become curator of the Arizona State Museum, where he served in various capacities until retirement in 1961. His papers in the museum archives are a major resource for researchers, particularly those interested in his description and classification of Casas Grandes pottery.

Donald Brand

Donald Brand's writings about pottery are also studied and widely quoted. His expertise included geography as well as anthropology. One of his university appointments was called "Anthrogeography." He had a long academic career that started at the University of California and included several years at each of the Universities of New Mexico, Michigan, and Texas.

In addition to his academic work, he was a tireless field researcher, which included many trips to Mexico. In 1931, he made an extensive tour of Casas Grandes ruins and mounds or *moctezumas* as he called them, using the local Mexican term. He covered almost all the Casas Grandes region in Mexico from the U.S. border with New Mexico south to the Babícora plains.

While at the University of New Mexico between 1934 and 1947, he took a two-year leave to work in Mexico, sponsored by the Smithsonian Institution. During the summer of 1936, he took a group of New Mexico students to northern Chihuahua to record cave sites. He continued his field work for the next two decades, seeking among other objectives to establish the connection between the Casas Grandes culture and Mesoamerica. During his trips, he recorded hundreds of sites, and studied thousands of pots and shards. Brand's articles in 1935 and 1936 helped establish nomenclature for various pottery types.

A few other professionals visited the Casas Grandes region, but those listed here did the most significant work. Even they faced obstacles. Not only was the focus of expedition sponsors on the northern pueblos and Mesoamerica, but the Mexican government placed restrictions on excavations.[37] Also, sponsor financing and access to the sites were handicapped by revolution, two wars, and the Depression. Nevertheless, the work of this handful of scientists remains significant and laid the groundwork for the largest study ever in the Casas Grandes Valley.

Charles Di Peso and Joint Expedition

It was not until 1958, well after most of the major U.S. Southwest sites had been thoroughly studied, placed into national monument or park status, and turned into tourist attractions, that archaeologist Charles Di Peso put together a team to systematically excavate Paquimé and study the surrounding area. The Joint Casas Grandes Expedition was sponsored by the Amerind Foundation of Dragoon, Arizona in conjunction with the *Instituto Nacional de Antropología e Historia* (INAH). Di Peso and Dr. Eduardo Contreras of INAH and their team worked on site for three years, 1959-61. Afterwards, they spent the next decade producing an eight-volume illustrated report, one of the most comprehensive archaeological reports ever. Entitled *Casas Grandes, A Fallen Trading Center of the Gran Chichimeca,* the first two volumes, *Viejo and Medio,* tell the story of the Casas Grandes people, their predecessors and antecedents, based on excavation findings. The third volume, *Tardio,* covers the Spanish period, based on excavations and archival study.[38] The remaining five volumes contain the detailed data. Illustrating the text with photos and elaborate caricature-style drawings, Di Peso and Contreras captured the sweep of the grand story of a lost culture that had been so long ignored. Dr. Contreras became the first INAH official in charge of conservation of the Paquimé site, a position he held until 1985.[39] The Nuevo Casas Grandes library is named after him.

Details within each part of this prehistoric and historic sequence are complex. Simply put, the Viejo Period represented the early transition of nomadic people into a settled society and the beginnings of agriculture. The classic corn, bean, and squash culture came late to the Casas Grandes Valley. Hunter-gatherers had wandered the land for eons, long after the people of central Mexico or Mesoamerica, south of the Tropic of Cancer, had organized into agriculture-based city-state "civilizations." From approximately 700 to 1000 A.D., some of the wandering people transitioned to sedentary living based on primitive agriculture. Pit houses are characteristic of this period. They consisted of a shallow pit covered with an above-ground wicker-like framework plastered with mud. These evolved into more substantial above-ground structures, along with improved tools and pottery making.

According to Di Peso and Contreras, the arrival among the Viejo people of more sophisticated outsiders marked the beginning of the Medio Period, which saw a very rapid flowering of accomplishment, followed by stagnation, decline, and sudden oblivion. The currently accepted dates for the Medio Period are approximately 1200 to 1450 A.D.

Di Peso proposed that sophisticated traders from Mesoamerica came north to the Casas Grandes Valley and founded an urban trading center among the pit-house residents. According to Di Peso, these traveling entrepreneurs, referred to as *pochtecas*, organized the locals into a stratified society capable of building a large multi-storied city, Paquimé, supported by hundreds of outlying settlements spreading for miles in every direction along rivers and streams, including both sides of the Palanganas River near Mata Ortiz. Farming techniques included elaborate irrigation systems and hillside erosion-control terraces called *trincheras*.

The entrepreneurs of the Medio Period developed an economy based on trade with routes that extended west across the mountains to the Pacific Ocean, east across desert and mountains to the Gulf of Mexico, south to the cultures of Mesoamerica, and north to the pueblo cultures across today's modern borders as far as Colorado and Kansas.

Beyond the practical matters of farming and trade was the evidence of an elaborate and powerful metaphysical system of which Paquimé appears to be the core. Part of this evidence was the large number of ball courts and stone platforms suggesting religious-oriented activities. Similar structures have been found within twenty miles of the Paquimé core area, including four at Arroyo de Tinaja, Casas Grandes' second largest site and two at El Alamito. Fewer are found beyond, suggesting that Paquimé's religious influence diminished as distance away increased.[40] Designs and images on Casas Grandes pottery can be interpreted as religious motifs.

Architecture and pottery are two of the most distinct features that mark the Casas Grandes culture, allowing researchers to identify sites and trace trade routes. The architecture has characteristics similar to the northern pueblos, but the basic construction was different. The walls were not made of adobe bricks or rock masonry. The Casas Grandes builders poured adobe and conglomerate into forms creating large blocks for the walls, a procedure called "rammed earth." They covered the interiors and exteriors of the thick walls with layers of plaster to prevent melting and as a base for decoration.

The most distinctive marker of the culture is the pottery. Archaeologists are experts at using pottery and pottery shards to track and identify cultural patterns. Casas Grandes provided abundance with which to work. The polychrome and monochrome pottery is so distinctive and so prevalent that even an informed amateur usually can make a positive identification.

The final report of the joint expedition contains detailed descriptions of the regional category types of Casas Grandes pottery. The descriptions are accompanied by pages of designs illustrating each type. The report references Kidder's work but is far more extensive and establishes the basic nomenclature categories commonly used to differentiate the pottery types.

One thing that Di Peso and the other writers did not cover was firing, the final step in the pottery-making process. It is not clear how the Casas Grandes potters fired the thousands of pots they made. What sort of kiln and fuel did they use? A discovery by Juan Quezada in the 1970s provides a clue. He found a prehistoric polychrome pot on the ground in a pile of ashes, surrounded by a wall of volcanic rock. The inside of the wall was about four inches from the pot surface. For some unknown reason the pot had been abandoned. Juan determined that fragments in the rocks were pine bark. He experimented with using the bark in a firing and it worked as well as cow chips.[41] In modern times, Mata Ortiz potters have used cottonwood bark to provide the desired steady even combustion similar to cow chips. Pine bark worked just as well.

While this does not completely solve the mystery of how thousands of prehistoric pots were fired, Juan's discovery and careful observations show that at least some ancient potters used the readily available volcanic rock and pine bark.

In the later phase of the Casas Grandes era, the culture began to stagnate. The excavations revealed that Paquimé's later structures were less well built. Older structures had not been maintained and even collapsed before the city was abandoned. These signs suggested that the vitality of this once vigorous culture had decayed. According to Di Peso and Contreras, the demise of Casas Grandes occurred when a nomadic people attacked and destroyed Paquimé in one cataclysmic event. The survivors abandoned the city and the outlying settlements. No one knows where they went. Anthropologists and archaeologists have theories but no compelling evidence.

The study by the Di Peso/Contreras team continued after the Medio Period into the Tardio Period, the Spanish *entrada* era, covering the 16th through the early 18th centuries. Excavations included El Convento, the original San Antonio de Padua de Casas Grandes mission site. They found a rich trove of artifacts that enabled them to reconstruct the Spanish era history. The data was added to the information found in thousands of documents their researchers copied from old Spanish archives, particularly from Parral in Durango.

The mass of data, collected and organized into the eight thick volumes, has been studied, rehashed, extolled and criticized by anthropologists and archaeologists for almost 50 years. Subsequent research shows Di Peso's dating to be off by about 100 years. The final cataclysmic event appears to have occurred in the mid-1400s rather than the 1300s as Di Peso thought.[42] The challenges to his theories have generated numerous articles, theses, and dissertations. What is definite is that Charles Di Peso and Eduardo Contreras brought the magnificent Paquimé site to the attention of the academic world and put Casas Grandes in its rightful place among the great prehistoric cultures of the Americas. Many contradict and even criticize their conclusions. No one ignores them.

Casas Grandes, A Three-Dimensional Puzzle

The excavation at Paquimé revealed a grand city that exceeded all expectations. Impressive walls, rooms, and towers always had been visible above ground, but beneath the accumulated rubble, researchers found an untold number of artifacts of an advanced culture.

Di Peso's and Contreras' team carefully cleared approximately 37 of Paquimé's estimated 88 acres. They found thick-walled buildings of one to four stories with hundreds of rooms designed for every purpose—domestic to ceremonial. The excavation team found several Mesoamerican features in addition to the stone ceremonial platforms and ball courts, such as evidence of macaw aviculture and plumed serpent motifs. One long undulating serpent-like wall ended in a head with a large horn or plume. These features reinforced Di Peso's *pochteca* thesis while others argue that the actual founders of Paquimé could have come from the north.

Anthropologist Steven Lekson of the University of Colorado in his book, *The Chaco Meridian,* postulates that Casas Grandes lay on the north-south meridian line that included the Anasazi or Ancestral Pueblo Aztec ruins, Chaco National Historic Park, and lesser sites in New Mexico. Lekson theorized that the Chaco Pueblo culture followed that meridian line south to the Casas Grandes Valley and Paquimé. While Lekson was challenged harshly ("provocative, and wrong"), the hypothesis was made.[43]

Whatever its origins, the culture flourished for about 300 years, declined, and disappeared. Anthropologists ponder what happened to the survivors. Di Peso believed they became the Tarahumara, an indigenous people now living in the deep recesses of the Sierra Madre. Others theorize that the Ópata, who gave Francisco de Coronado and Francisco de Ibarra so much grief, may be the descendants.[44] Nomadic groups, like the Suma, were living in the area when Francisco de Ibarra arrived, but none seemed to have a direct connection to the Casas Grandes people. The mystery remains. Who were they and where did they go? Dr. R. B. Brown, the INAH representative in charge of Paquimé in the 1980s, described Casas Grandes as a "three-dimensional jigsaw puzzle missing 90 percent of the pieces."[45]

Museo de las Culturas del Norte

For more than thirty years after Charles Di Peso and Eduardo Contreras completed their excavation, Paquimé lay open to the public with minimal protection or interpretation. Visitors roamed the site, climbing on walls and enjoying family picnics. A small building served as the office and "interpretive center" with a few pots displayed on shelves and some written handouts. Site directors, starting with Eduardo Contreras in the early 60s and continuing to R. B. Brown in the 80s and early 90s, had few resources to deal with the enormous conservation and interpretation challenges of the site with its massive crumbling walls. Most of the Casas Grandes pottery and other artifacts unearthed were dispersed to other museums. After an initial flurry of interest, the archeology world largely ignored Paquimé until Carlos Salinas de Gortari became president in 1988. After taking office, he established several agencies to develop, conserve, and promote Mexico's art, historic and prehistoric sites. While his motives have been questioned (some considered it a payoff to silence criticism of his regime by the intelligentsia), his action brought long-needed attention and resources to Paquimé.

The award-winning architect Mario Schjetnan was hired to design a state-of-the-art museum. Schjetnan had received many awards and was known for creating modern buildings that blended with the surrounding landscape. His *Museo de las Culturas del Norte* at Paquimé fits these criteria with earthen exterior colors and a low-lying almost subterranean appearance. Inside, exhibition space, meeting rooms, offices, and a gift shop surround an interior patio.

Construction began in 1993, the next-to-last year of Salinas de Gortari's term. The following year, the project looked like an anthill as workers from all trades climbed over the emerging building. According to a local rumor, a huge effort was underway to complete the museum before the president's term ended in 1994. The deadline passed, but a fine facility did emerge and was formally inaugurated February 2, 1996. Interpretive kiosks were installed and access restricted to paths through the site.

Pottery and artifacts were returned to fill out the displays. The New Mexico State University Museum in Las Cruces, New Mexico had 386 Casas Grandes pots donated by a private couple. Laurena and Andres Babey had discovered Casas Grandes pottery at a time when many pieces were taken across the border and sold around the country. Their crusade was to keep as much as possible in the Southwest. Most of the pieces went to New Mexico State. When the collection manager and other officials heard of the museum construction at Paquimé, they decided that most of the Babey collection should be repatriated. The university entered into a mutually beneficial agreement with INAH to permanently loan the Babey collection to the Museo de las Culturas del Norte in turn for access to the museum and site by university researchers. The pots were delivered and a celebration reception held on July 2, 1994 in the uncompleted museum.

UNESCO designated Paquimé a World Heritage site in 1998.

First the Mimbres

Mimbres was one of the influences from the north. This branch of the Mogollon culture extended from New Mexico along the basin and range country into northern Chihuahua and the Casas Grandes Valley. The Mogollon represented one of the three major cultures (Mogollon, Hohokam, and Anasazi or Ancestral Pueblo) that existed in the Southwest in the millennium before the arrival of the Spanish.

Centered in southwestern New Mexico, the Mimbres gained modern fame when archeologists and pot hunters discovered their unique bowls in burial sites. The bowls usually were found placed over the faces of the mummified dead. Ancient artists painted the inside bottom of each bowl with single human, animal, or anthropomorphic figure. These images so intrigued artists, anthropologists, and collectors that not only did the individual pots become valuable, but the images became universal in modern Native American art. The problem was finding "good" pots. Those long-ago burial teams indiscriminately punched a hole in the bottom of each pot, the so called "spirit hole," before placing it over the face of the deceased. More often than not this damaged the design, much to the consternation of collectors.

The Mimbres region extended well into northern Chihuahua. Researchers suggest that a some of these early pottery makers were absorbed into the emerging Casas Grandes culture in the 1100s, and their unique clay bowls influenced the later Casas Grandes potters.[46] Interestingly, Juan Quezada agrees. From his lifelong observation of the country surrounding his home, he is very clear that the earlier people, prior to *Paquimé* (the local term for the Casa Grandes culture) were *Mimbreños.*

The prehistoric site called Los Cables covers several acres on a little mesa about a mile north of Mata Ortiz, just to the east of the river and the old railroad right of way. In May 1986, Juan guided a small group, including Dr. R.B. Brown, then in charge of the Paquimé site, to walk north down the track to Los Cables. Francisco de Ibarra must have passed this way in 1565 in the opposite direction as did Adolph Bandelier in 1884.

On the mesas, Juan's group saw an ancient site full of holes made by pot hunters and littered with shards and fragments of metates. Dr. Brown was shocked. For an archeologist this was about as bad as it could get. Nevertheless, Juan was able to show Dr. Brown that the underlying portion of Los Cables was *Mimbreño* with later Casas Grandes structures on top of about half of the site. Juan knew that local pot hunters had dug up several Mimbres-style pots there as well as numerous Casas Grandes pieces. He showed the group charred wood fragments that were the remnants of the four corner posts of a pit house, a Mimbres dwelling.

The well-known potter, Héctor Gallegos confirmed that there were Mimbres habitation sites overlaid by Casas Grandes right in Mata Ortiz. His father owned property along the road above the river that now features a row of houses. The house at the north end of the row now belongs to

The fine bowls of the Mimbres culture influenced the early Casas Grandes potters. Courtesy of ROM (Royal Ontario Museum), Toronto, Canada. ©ROM

the Cota family. Héctor grew up there, and as a boy in the 1950s, watched Casas Grandes pots being dug up from the top layer of the earth near his house and Mimbres pots retrieved from the layer below. After becoming a potter, Héctor worked versions of the images he saw on these ancient pieces into his modern pot designs.

The Mimbres culture and pottery became part of Casas Grandes and in turn an inspirational root of the modern Mata Ortiz ceramic art movement.

Casas Grandes Pottery

Pottery making on a small scale may go back as far as 2,000 years in northern Chihuahua. It grew slowly because as a practical matter nomadic people did not have large pack animals and could not carry many relatively heavy, breakable pots. By the Viejo Period, approximately 1,000 years ago, different pottery types appeared and became commonplace. The nomenclature varied over time among archaeologists but followed a general pattern.

Alfred V. Kidder in his monograph organized the pottery into broad categories such as Rough Dark Ware, Polished Blackware, Redware, and Chihuahua Painted Ware. One Painted Ware variation, referred to as Red-on-Brown Ware, was also called "Mata Ware," an interesting nomenclature coincidence.[47] Another variation, Textured Ware, had a series of indentations on all or part of the pot surface.

Charles Di Peso, Eduardo Contreras and their Joint Expedition colleagues devoted Volume Six of eight volumes to an incredible array of data and detailed descriptions, accompanied by dozens of pictures of Viejo and Medio Period pottery shapes, designs, and classifications.[48] While Volume Six includes far more illustrations and subsidiary detail, the basic classifications are similar to those in Kidder's monograph.

Although many details of the Viejo Period remain vague, it is clear that people in the Casas Grandes Valley gradually became agriculturalists and relatively settled. They used local clay to make pottery for cooking, storage, and perhaps ceremonial purposes. In the later phases of the Viejo Period, some of the ancient potters began to decorate pieces, such as the Mata Ware.

The most common clay in the area is a naturally gray color and fires to various shades of beige, brown, or yellow, called *baya*. Much of the clay contained a natural volcanic ash "temper," the inert material potters often add to clay to give it strength. Commonly used tempers such as sand result in a rough surface that must be covered with a liquid clay or "slip" as a smooth base for painting designs. Volcanic ash leaves a smooth surface and most Casas Grandes Valley potters, from the Viejo and Medio Periods to the modern Mata Ortiz ceramic art era, painted directly on the clay body.

Potters used pinch pot and coil-and-smooth techniques to form the pieces. The red pigment for the early designs was made from hematite, a readily available iron oxide present in local rocks. There were at least two possible sources for the black pigment. One was magnesium oxide, a relatively uncommon mineral. One source exists today in the valley. The other is a technique used by the northern pueblos, which is boiling Rocky Mountain Bee Weed into thick syrup and mixing it with hematite.

Painted pots along with textured and plain ware were found at Viejo sites in and around the Casas Grandes Valley, sometimes mixed with Mimbres pieces.

The Medio Period began around 1200-1250 when Di Peso's pochtecas or other outsiders entered the Casas Grandes Valley and integrated with the indigenous Viejo Period settlers. Very soon they constructed the great city at Paquimé and developed the advanced features that characterize Casas Grandes culture. Artisans began making a thin-walled finely painted polychrome ware that incorporated a great variety of forms from the Viejo Period, Mesoamerica, and Mimbres. The Casas Grandes pieces, particularly those that became known as Ramos Ware, arguably surpassed in quality and variety any produced by other prehistoric pueblos. The handful of researchers that began to seriously study these pieces were lavish in their praise. Cornelia G. Harcum, an expert on Greek art at the Royal Ontario Museum, saw the pottery for the first time when the museum received a large collection in 1923. She wrote, "Casas Grandes is a rare achievement of early ceramic art. It is distinguished by beauty both of form and decoration and by perfection of technical skill."[49]

Donald Brand on his many trips did not have permits to excavate. His objective was to locate as many sites as he could and describe the surface artifacts—shards, metates, stone tools—exposed by weather and pot hunters. Many of the hundreds of sites he and his teams examined contained shards from other Chihuahua sites, from Sonora, and from as far away as Arizona, New Mexico, and Texas. These trade wares, mixed with remnants of the local ware, were more common in sites closer to main trails. The amount found demonstrates the significant trade in the Medio Period. The presence of foreign wares also suggests that the later Casas Grandes pottery would be influenced by the numerous styles of the U.S. Southwest.

The amount produced in those ancient times is staggering. Thousands of pieces were found in the rubble of Paquimé and in the numerous surrounding satellite sites throughout northern Chihuahua, northeast Sonora, and southern Arizona and New Mexico.

These included pots, jars, and bowls of every shape, double pots, (cuates), and effigies representing humans, birds, and animals. Most clay bodies fired various shades of beige or baya, depending on the clay source. Some were white. Baya clays are plentiful in the region, but white kaolin clays are hard to find. It took Juan Quezada and his brothers years to find a source.

For the most part, little is known of the Casas Grandes religion. The pots, especially the effigies provide clues, suggesting a complex pantheon of gods and elaborate rituals. The effigies, which have no other practical function, often were found in burials or near what appeared to be altars. The iconography on these vessels has been interpreted as depicting images of Mesoamerican gods, the most famous being Quetzalcóatl, the plumed serpent. Early archaeologists were typically less interested in the meaning of the iconography than they were in the sources and physical descriptions of the shapes and designs.

Generalizations for Casas Grandes pottery are difficult because of the wide variety of decoration. However, many basic designs on bowls and jars, followed the Viejo Period Mata Ware pattern with the design applied only to the sides between a line around the neck of the pot below the lip and an "equator" line around the pot above the bottom. The lip and bottom were left unpainted. On the "canvas" between the two lines, the artists painted a variety of repetitive, usually geometric designs in red, black, or the bare "negative" clay color outlined with one or more thin lines. The artists sometimes painted the lips of jars and the interiors of open bowls. They often added animal, bird, and human figures within the triangles and rectangles. Macaw images were common, and like the other figures, varied from realistic to abstract. Most of the overall decoration on each pot was divided in half with each design element duplicated in form and placement on both sides. Another design variation was a snake-like band around the pot with the head of a plumed serpent or macaw. The design elements illustrated in Kidder's monograph and Di Peso's Volume Six, constituted an inventory that could be mixed and matched on the pot as the artist chose.

Regional differences in the designs and clay color caused archaeologists to create style classifications for identification. Some of these differences are subtle. Not all researchers agree or use them, but certain names have come into common use. In the U.S. Southwest, there are multiple classifications, sub-classifications, and variants. Chihuahua pottery is typically grouped into two general types, Ramos and Babícora.

Babícora Ware

Babícora may be earlier, descending directly from Viejo Period Painted Ware, while Ramos may be later reflecting outsider influence.[50] There are differences in clay and form, but the primary difference is painting style. On Babícora Ware, red and black paint do not touch. On Ramos Ware, adjacent paint colors sometimes touch and the red designs or panels are outlined with one or more fine black lines. These differences were recognized early by Casas Grandes researchers. Donald Brand, writing in 1935, noted the two general styles that he called Babícora Polychrome and Chihuahua Black-on-Red.[51]

Babícora Ware received its name from the broad plains over the Sierra Madre south of the San Diego Valley. The Hearst Ranch occupied much of this large basin. This was also the southern margin of the Casas Grandes cultural area. Babícora Ware tended to be produced in the cultural-area peripheries. On the eastern periphery, the production area extended northeast through Buenaventura, Galeana, and the Santa María Valley through Villa Ahumada. Lack of design detail and thicker less precise lines indicate

*Babícora Polychrome found for the most part on the periphery of the
Casas Grandes culture area. Courtesy of ROM (Royal Ontario Museum),
Toronto, Canada. ©ROM*

that Babícora may have a direct extension of the Viejo Period with less
influence from the Paquimé core of Medio Period growth.

Beyond the Casas Grandes Valley to the east, the town of Villa Ahumada sits on north-south highway 45 that links Ciudad Juárez and Ciudad
Chihuahua. The surrounding broad region, once part of one of Luis Terrazas's haciendas, was an outlying extension of the Casas Grandes culture.
Artists there produced a great deal of pottery, classified as Villa Ahumada
Ware, a form of Babícora-style ware. Pots were made from a variety of
clays. An identifying feature is white slip on the pot sides above the equator line as a base for the black and red design. Other versions of the ware
had no slip. Overall, Villa Ahumada, like most Babícora, was not as finely
done as Ramos.

The sites are clustered around the numerous springs in the area. Brand
discovered a large amount of the white-slipped ware at site about two miles
north of the town at a place called *Loma de Moctezumas.*

Other Classifications

Di Peso's Joint-Expedition study report identified, and classified by location, other pottery in the Casas Grandes Valley. These were early versions of Ramos Ware. The sites include Huérigos, Carretas, Corralitos, and Dublán.[52]

The most northerly site in Chihuahua, Huérigos, is located in the foothills in the extreme northwest corner of the state about 25 miles west of the Antelope Wells/El Berrendo border crossing into New Mexico. Many streams flow out of the Sierra Madre and disappear into the vast plain of the Llano de Carretas. Prehistoric people lived along the few larger rivers that flowed all year and in the arroyo valleys of the foothills, where streams ran. The Huérigos Arroyo, a northern tributary of the Carretas River, apparently was a major production area as it yielded a large quantity of shards and pottery. Huérigos clay tended to fire to a light shade of orange. Huérigos potters often used an off-white slip to cover part of the piece.

South of Huérigos near the road from the plains into the mountains via Carretas Pass is the Carretas Ware area. Donald Brand found many moctezumas in the arroyos and along the drainage of the Carretas River. Carretas Ware is virtually identical to Huérigos except for the lack of slip.

The Dublán Ware production area was a narrow band along the west side of Casas Grandes River through much of the valley. As an early Ramos type, it faded when the more sophisticated ware began to dominate. Jars typically had textured necks with relatively simple black and red designs on the sides.

The name Corralitos appeared in the archaeological literature as early as 1934. Harold S. Gladwin and his wife Winifred, founders of the Gila Pueblo Archaeological Foundation, published a monograph in *Medallion Papers* on the classification of pottery in the southern areas of Arizona, New Mexico, and Chihuahua.[53] The pottery classification was established when Brand's survey located several moctezumas south of the Corralitos ranch compound. Textured designs, bordered by black and red lines, are characteristics. It is similar to Dublán Ware and like Dublán, faded in the Ramos era.

Ramos Ware

For most, Ramos Polychrome is the pottery of Casas Grandes. It is one the most distinguishing features of the culture during the zenith of the Medio Period. Widely produced in the core Casas Grandes Valley cultural area, it only gave way to the Babícora in the outlying regions.

The artists' skill and the large variety of design elements utilized distinguish Ramos Ware. Parallel lines are typically thin, uniform, and perfectly spaced whether straight or curved. The iconography ranges from realistic to abstract with elements associated with Mesoamerica and others clearly inspired by Mimbres.

Ramos Ware was the primary inspiration of the Mata Ortiz ceramic art movement.

The Origin of the Ramos Name

Because so much Ramos Polychrome was found around Ojo de Ramos, later Hacienda Ramos, it is logical for this to be the source of the name, but when and how did it begin to be used? Other names were used well into the middle of the 20th century such as Painted Polychrome, Chihuahua Painted Ware, and Casas Grandes Polychrome.

Located midway between Janos and Casas Grandes, Ojo de Ramos featured a natural spring from which water flowed east through the Arroyo Ramos, eventually disappearing in a grove of mesquite a few miles southwest of the Corralitos Hacienda ranch compound. Prehistoric people settled there as did the Spanish Captain Francisco Ramírez because of the reliability of abundant water. Bandelier, Lumholtz, Brand, and Sayles, all worked the Ramos site. Shards and broken stone tools still can be easily found on two *moctezumas* on small hills a short walk just east of the ranch buildings. A channel, lined with stone slabs, brought water to the site. Señor Victor "Cacho" Barrio, the current owner, inherited the rancho from his father. After a lifetime observing the land and weather, he thinks the ancient people lived on the higher knolls to keep watch in all directions and to avoid the periodic floods that still occur. Corn and other crops were grown in the rich soil around the knolls. Señor Barrio grows pecan trees on one of these ancient plots. He said the previous owner of the rancho had filled his house with pots dug from the moctezumas.

The first time "Ramos" or "Ramos Polychrome" appears in print was in the Gladwin's seminal 1934 monograph in the *Medallion Papers*. The Gladwins organized prehistoric pottery into categories and established nomenclature. Most of their classifications related to sites in southern Arizona, New Mexico, and Texas. However, in two tables showing cultural groupings, the term Ramos is used along with Corralitos and Babícora. Footnotes for each table cite a monograph by E.B "Ted" Sayles, not published until two years later. Sayles' name does not appear in the Gladwin's bibliography.[54]

Ted Sayles surveyed Chihuahua for the Gila Pueblo Archaeological Foundation in 1933 and wrote two monographs in the *Medallion Papers*, published in 1936, two years after the Gladwin article. In the foreword of first volume, *Medallion XXI*, he wrote that Brand had seen a draft and approved the use of synonyms for the nomenclature previously used by

Ramos Polychrome, one of the distinguishing features of the Casas Grandes culture. Courtesy of ROM (Royal Ontario Museum), Toronto, Canada. ©ROM

Brand.[55] A section in Sayles' monograph was devoted to "Ramos Polychrome." He noted this was a synonym for what Brand called Casas Grandes Polychrome and Kidder called Chihuahua Painted Ware. Sayles' publication established the use of the name Ramos Polychrome. In a footnote on the very first page, he made it clear that the terms the Gladwins had used in the tables of their earlier monograph had come originally from his manuscript, just now published.

Since Sayles was the first to formally use the term, what motivated him to make the change?

A prominent El Paso citizen with a somewhat dubious past, at least by today's standards, now enters the picture. Edward Ledwidge was the tax and claims agent for the Mexico North Western Railway in Ciudad Juárez, the rail system Dr. Fred Stark Pearson created.[56] During his career, Ledwidge was responsible for most of the major Casas Grandes pottery collections owned privately as well as those found in museums. Some of the most important North American archaeologists were his friends. Basically, Ledwidge was a pottery smuggler. He acquired Casas Grandes pots, probably from a network of suppliers, and transported them across the border in the railroad shipments he controlled. He then sold them to an apparently ready market in the U.S. In the 1920s, Ledwidge obtained a collection of exceptionally high-quality pots that appear to have been the ones collected years before by Mrs. E.C. Houghton at Hacienda Ramos. This was the collection Edgar Hewett saw in 1906 when he visited Mrs. Houghton at the Hacienda, augmented by what she found over the intervening years. Aided by Hewett, the Gladwins obtained parts of the collection in 1926 and again in 1931 and took the pottery to the Gila Pueblo in Globe, Arizona. Gladwin later said that some of the pots in the Gila Pueblo collection came from Ledwidge and others interestingly enough, directly from Mrs. Houghton, then a widow living in Amarillo.

Sayles became very familiar with the pots and wrote that Ledwidge told him the pots came from Ramos. All of this happened before Sayles' 1933 expedition and before his and the Gladwin's monographs were written. When they did begin to write, they were all aware as they organized their classifications and prepared their monographs that the finest polychrome ware in the Gila Pueblo collection came from Hacienda Ramos.

The name remained on the highest-quality pottery of the Casas Grandes Valley, described as a "rare achievement of early ceramic art."

Collectors and Collecting

Casas Grandes potters produced thousands of pieces. At least seventy percent were elaborately painted wares that have attracted collectors for well over 100 years. Great collections were amassed privately and by institutions from the San Diego Museum on Man in California (Museum of Us since 2020) to the Smithsonian in Washington D.C. and from the Royal Ontario Museum in Canada to the Museo de las Culturas del Norte in Casas Grandes and the Museo Nacional de Antropología in Mexico City. This stimulated looting for pots, particularly in the early decades of the 20th century, which continues today on a reduced scale. The early archaeology professionals like Edger Lee Hewett believed amassing collections was part of their duties as protectors of past heritages. This belief reflects the late 19th century's awakening interest in ancient civilizations that filled the British Museum with Egyptian mummies and Greek marbles. In 1907, a year after Hewett had seen Mrs. Houghton's accumulation of pots, Dr. John C. Phillips traveled to Corralitos and Ramos with his friend and Corralitos board member Thomas Wentworth Peirce, Jr. Dr. Phillips graduated from Harvard in 1899 and from Medical School in 1904. Both men came from elite New England families and likely became friends at Harvard. This was a working trip for Peirce and apparently Phillips was invited along. In Chihuahua, he purchased a collection of pots, metates, stone implements, stone effigies, and a few crania. He donated all of this to the Peabody Museum at Harvard in 1907. The only paperwork is an invoice on Corralitos Company letterhead with E.C Houghton listed as one of the officers. The invoice indicated 149 pots had been sold.[57] All indications are that these were Mrs. Houghton's pots and her first sale. They formed the basis for the Peabody collection that A.V. Kidder analyzed in his 1916 article.

Another sale of pots involved Ted Sayles, working for the Gladwins, and Gustavo E. McGinnis, William Randolph Hearst's lawyer in Mexico. McGinnis moved to Casas Grandes in 1903, where he married a local Mexican woman. He commuted to Hearst's San José Babícora ranch and in his travels began acquiring pots in the 1920s. After meeting Sayles and making the sale, 203 pots were shipped to El Paso and stored. When Sayles retrieved the pots to take to the Gila Pueblo in Globe, he found only 198. Well aware of this transaction was pot-trader Edward Ledwidge. When the inventory proved to be short, he immediately produced five pots to make up the difference. All parties were satisfied.

Sources describe Edward Ledwidge in different ways. He worked for Pearson's Mexico Northwestern Railway and was responsible for collecting fees from shippers. His obituary described him as a prominent and generous El Paso philanthropist. He died in 1934 not long after the McGinnis sale. As he was directly involved with the railroad's shipping, he undoubtedly transported the pots across the border in company railway cars.

What surfaces after some study is the fact that Ledwidge supplied a significant percentage of the pottery acquired by U.S. museums and private collections between 1914 and 1934, during the collection heyday. It is estimated that a minimum of 2,000 pots passed through his hands.[58] Early archaeologists did not condemn Ledwidge. Rather, they respected him as a savior of antiquities. When Ledwidge got in trouble with Mexican authorities and had to dispose of his inventory, Hewett, with all of his contacts, was the link.

Dr. Eduardo Noguera became one of Mexico's most distinguished archaeologists and one of the first to officially represent the Mexican government. In 1921, he was put in charge of a large northern region that included Chihuahua. He took his duties very seriously and confronted Ledwidge in El Paso. He had no direct power over Ledwidge, but he had enough influence, through diplomatic connections, to embarrass the prominent citizen, who was smuggling pottery. Ledwidge agreed to cease pot trading and divest himself of all of his Chihuahua pottery.

Hewett stepped up, well aware of what was going on. His own institution, the Museum of New Mexico, did not have sufficient funds to purchase the entire inventory. Ledwidge was not embarrassed enough by Dr. Noguera not to want cash for the pots. His price was $6,000. Hewett arranged for two other institutions to participate. He was closely associated and an officer with the Archaeological Society in Washington D.C. That institution bought 497 pots, most of which were turned over to the Smithsonian's

National History Museum. Charles Trick Currelly, the legendary first director of the Royal Ontario Museum in Toronto, Canada, took 400 pieces.[59] In 2019, two hundred pieces from that collection were exhibited in the museum for only the second time in 100 years. The curator commented that virtually all the pots were whole and unbroken, very unusual for prehistoric work.

If attempts were made today to dig and transport pots from Mexico to the U.S. and then to Canada, laws of three countries plus international law would be violated. Attitudes towards antiquities collection have changed. Still, in a different era, Hewett, Ledwidge, and the others saved work that for all time will be preserved, studied, and enjoyed in museum settings under professional guidance.

Within a few years of selling his collection at Dr. Noguera's insistence in 1922, Ledwidge reverted to smuggling again. After his death in 1935, his estate gave a large collection to the Wilderness Museum, now the El Paso Museum of Archaeology.

Casas Grandes Influence on Mata Ortiz Ceramics

The Mata Ortiz ceramic art movement can be likened to a great multi-colored flowering tree with flowers representing the endless variety of pottery. The multiple limbs and twigs represent family, group and sub-group styles. These branch from large, heavy limbs representing significant early potters that in turn branch from the trunk that is Juan Quezada. Some may argue that Juan was not the very first potter in the area, and there is no question that major limbs of the movement, representing such early potters as Félix Ortiz, branch off very low from the main trunk. The point here is that this flowering tree has two deep prehistoric roots. The largest is Casas Grandes pottery, particularly Ramos Ware while the other is Mimbres most notably the images on its famous bowls.

4

The Spanish Keep Trying

Eye of the Storm

After the fall of Paquimé, and for most of the three centuries following Francisco de Ibarra's expedition, there is little evidence of human activity on the site of the future Pearson/Mata Ortiz community. Vaqueros chased cows and Apaches passed through but neither lingered. It lay like the eye of a storm in the Casas Grandes Valley, with a dramatic, often violent history surrounding it, century after century.

The Spanish continued to try to colonize all of Nueva Vizcaya using their established three-pronged method of military exploration and dominance, religious conversion, and civil settlement: the Sword, the Cross and the Plow. Cattle ranching, farming, and mining sustained the growth of settlements, moving north from the Durango area—especially silver mining. The searchers never found the gold bonanza they sought, but they found an abundance of silver and lesser metals such as copper and lead.

Franciscan padres had always accompanied military expeditions, and Francisco de Ibarra, while governor, encouraged these mendicant missionaries to expand their efforts. Members of the Society of Jesus, the well-trained, energetic missionary and teaching order commonly called Jesuits, arrived in Durango in 1574. They directed their efforts to the west, following the trails of the conquistadores to establish missions in Sinaloa and Sonora. As noted by Charles Di Peso, the Cross and Plow were beginning to replace the Sword on the frontier.[60] However, religion and settlement

66

were not the only motives for braving the hardships of the forbidding frontier wilderness. Images of golden cities still lingered in the dreams of the young Spanish *hidalgos* seeking their fortunes. Coronado, de Ibarra, and others had searched for Cíbola by going north through Sinaloa and Sonora. They blazed trails for Jesuit padres and other settlers but found no treasure. Later, at the end of the century and well into the 17th century, other explorers tried another route on the east side of Chihuahua searching for the *Gran Quivira*, where it was said cups of gold hung from trees. This route followed the Río Conchos to the Rio Grande and beyond through *El Paso del Norte*. Eventually this became a major road, called a *camino real* or royal road, opening New Mexico to missions, settlement, and trade. Spanish explorers established Santa Fe in 1607 and San Fernando de Taos in 1615.

The First Attempt

Stated simply, the early expeditions went north up the left side of the map of Nueva Vizcaya, through the coastal plains and mountains of Sinaloa and Sonora. The later expeditions went up the right side on the eastern border to Texas and New Mexico. In the map's center, the valleys of the Casas Grandes and Santa María rivers remained almost untouched for decades after Ibarra's hurried passage in 1565.

Three Franciscan monks, alone and without soldiers, did venture out onto the *Llano de Carretas* plains in 1580.[61] They found a place they deemed appropriate for a mission, where trails intersected along the Janos/San Pedro River, a tributary of the Casas Grandes. The three named their new *misión* Santa María de Carretas and went to work. While the land was not as good as that of the valley 40 miles south near Paquimé, the rolling hills and broad valleys were far better than the narrow valleys and canyons of the Sierra Madre. The river flowed and even overflowed when it rained in the mountains and became a dry sandy wash when the rains stopped. Beneath the sand, aquifers held enough water to support farming and ranching, a characteristic common to southwestern rivers.

For some indigenous peoples, the Cross had not quite replaced the Sword. A group described only as *rebeldes* sacked and pillaged the fledgling mission and murdered the three padres. These padres, Agustín Rodríguez, Francisco López, and Juan Santamaría, became a footnote in history—the first Europeans to settle in the Casas Grandes River region and the first to be massacred.[62] Many more would follow to experience both.

A Lonely Outpost

No one knows who killed the three padres. Several indigenous groups occupied or passed through the region. Some accepted the padres' teaching and their God, while others remembered the heavy-handed conquistadores. Still others made a habit of preying on their neighbors, regardless of who they were. Unrest and marauding became a fact of life to be dealt with by any settled group, indigenous or European.

The Indian populations were in a great state of flux in Nueva Vizcaya. Details are poorly understood, but tribal groups split apart or were absorbed by others. Sedentary groups became nomadic. Some abandoned traditional homelands for other locations, fleeing either the padres or other more powerful tribes. The Suma and their close relations the Janos emerged as significant groups in the valley at the time of Spanish contact. The Concho were to the southeast and the Tarahumara in the mountains to the southwest.

The history of the Casas Grandes River region is vague for the 100 years between 1580 and 1680. About 1640, the Franciscans returned to the site on the Janos River and re-established the mission, calling it Nuestra Señora de la Soledad de Janos. Solitude was an apt name for Nueva Vizcaya's isolated, most northern outpost. Remote and lonely as it was and still seems today, Janos held a strategic position at a three-way intersection. Travelers reaching Janos from the south could go northeast to the Rio Grande and Santa Fe, Taos, or El Paso, or they could take the left fork west over the mountain passes to Sonora and Arizona. Traders from ancient times had followed the trail linking the Rio Grande Valley to the Pacific Ocean, the "Shell Trail," that had helped Francisco de Ibarra escape the Sierra Madre. Rocky trails became cart tracks, roads, and eventually major highways. The intersection at Janos today appears to be nothing more than a truck stop. However, sharp-eyed travelers can spot the old mission church above the tops of brake shops and convenience stores to the southwest of the main intersection, a remnant of an earlier, often violent time. Travel on these trails could be perilous; much of Janos' history features a violent bloody struggle between and among various ethnic groups vying for survival.

The Cross

The northern reaches of Nueva Vizcaya were too far removed and resources too thin for effective control by the Spanish from the center of Mexico. Civil authorities and soldiers sent by the viceroy often had limited administrative skills and little understanding or sympathy with the complex indigenous cultures. Some brutalized the people in their charge with cruel punishments and abused women despite specific Crown policies to the contrary in the Laws of the Indies.

The padres did better. Many worked hard to protect their charges from the abuses of soldiers and settlers. The Jesuits in particular made an effort to learn native languages and understand local customs. While the padres' single-minded agenda to convert pagan souls ran roughshod over the cultures they encountered, they did have a certain degree of success. It is not fashionable to discuss the work of the missionary padres in a positive way, but they at least sometimes, succeeded in transforming their charges into *gente de razón*, "people of reason." The Spanish used this term to describe the Crown's basic policy to convert "primitive" or "savage" peoples, into European-style Christian mold; whereby they would learn farming, animal husbandry, blacksmithing, carpentry, and other trades to become productive, tax-paying citizens of the Spanish Empire.

If the tide of Western Civilization was inevitable, then it can be said the missionary padres helped with the transition.

San Antonio de Padua de Casas Grandes

Another important development occurred in 1663. The Suma, the indigenous people that Francisco de Ibarra met on the plains after escaping from the Ópata in the mountains, requested a mission. This is curious because the Suma were nomadic and not inclined to the sedentary farming culture of the missions. The Nueva Vizcaya governor agreed to found a mission on the Casas Grandes site. He sent Padre Andrés Páez from San Buenaventura de Atotonilco, an almost-defunct mission far to the southeast, to establish the new mission. The governor also authorized the Franciscans to establish a mission near the Carretas Pass and gave it the old name of the Janos mission that had been destroyed some 80 years before, Santa María de Carretas. Another, Misión Santa Ana del Torreón, was established near present-day San Buenaventura in the Santa María River Valley.

To complete the other segments of the Spanish colonization policy of Sword, Cross, and Plow, the governor sent Captain Andrés López de Gracia from El Paso to Casas Grandes. His orders were to promote the settlement of Casas Grandes and to bring to the mission as many Indians as possible. After the long trip, he rode into the Paquimé area leading a train of soldiers, family members, and settlers.[63] De Gracia and his family have the distinction of being the first European settlers in the southern Casas Grandes Valley.[64] Family members included de Gracia's son-in-law, the soldier Francisco Ramírez de Salazar. Captain Ramírez would play a major role over the next thirty years as a large landowner and as a commander leading soldiers in the field against Apaches.

Few personal descriptions exist of these early historical figures. The surviving reports retrieved from archives typically reveal just names, status, requests, orders, and cryptic descriptions of events. Rarely does a personality or an image emerge from these dry, handwritten pages. One exception adds at least a hazy picture to de Gracia's name by describing him as a tall, slim, swarthy man with a scar on the left side of his forehead just at the hairline. Born in Puebla de Los Angeles in 1616, he was 47 when he rode to Paquimé. We can imagine a tall, dark bearded man, in a heavy leather jerkin and steel helmet, riding at the head of a column of settlers, pack mules, and wagons.[65]

At age 30, seventeen years before, he joined a fourteen-man wagon-train escort traveling 1,200 miles from Mexico City to New Mexico. He stayed and by 1661 had risen through the ranks and was appointed the first *alcalde* (a magistrate, which is essentially a combination of mayor and judge) of El Paso. When the governor sent him to Casas Grandes, he received the same title and office for the new settlement, apparently as an incentive for making the move. He also was the local military commander. Di Peso suggests he and his small band of followers initially may have sought shelter in Paquimé, roofing the abandoned rooms and concentrating on their fields and stock, before making the adobe bricks necessary for constructing their own homes, barns, and corrals.[66]

Captain de Gracia and Padre Páez located the mission buildings on a hill north of the ruins of Paquimé. They named their new mission San Antonio de Padua de Casas Grandes after one of the most important Franciscan saints. San Antonio is the patron saint of bountiful harvests, which unfortunately were to be few for this mission during the brief years it existed. Páez directed the construction of the main buildings on a site that had been used for farming in ancient times and was still suitable for corn, the new-world crop, and wheat, the old-world crop.[67] They built a multipurpose structure to serve as a church and as a fortress with two guard towers. How effective church services were is unknown, but the thick walls and towers served the settlers well during the upcoming violence.

Today the local people call this place *El Convento.* A large, high-walled adobe ruin located on a barren hill north of town, is all that remains of this ill-fated venture.

In August 1991, archaeologists, attending the Pecos Conference in Casas Grandes, led a field trip to *El Convento.* Walking the site, they noted shallow depressions in the otherwise flat earth surface that they identified as the remnants of pit houses.

For water, the new settlers used a lateral that ran east from the main *acequia* or canal. The same source brought water to ancient Paquimé from a hot spring now called *Ojo de Vareleño*, after the Varela family, prominent in Casas Grandes history. The spring exists today as a small resort catering to weddings, fiestas and bird watching. The lateral is still used and is called *La Turbina.*[68]

Captain de Gracia and Padre Páez worked out a plan with the Suma in which the settler's land, including the mission church, workshops, living quarters, fields, and grazing lands would be located south of the water canal. Land to the north of the canal was allocated to the Suma. These lands extended north for miles along the Casas Grandes River, past today's Nuevo Casas Grandes, almost to what became Hacienda Corralitos, southeast of

Janos. The plan was specific, designating the Suma land just north of the lateral with direct access to water as farm land. The next parcel was pasture for sheep and goats, the next range land for cattle, and the next hunting grounds. All of this was written into a formal treaty, recorded with Spanish authorities.[69]

Hacienda Ojo de Ramos

Presumably de Gracia, son-in-law Ramírez and others were assigned *mercedes de reales*, the prevailing Spanish system for allocating land and mining claims. Technically, the Crown owned all land, including mineral and water rights.

Development was strictly regulated by a body of law that evolved over the centuries called the Laws of the Indies. The Laws provided for grants or *mercedes*, and specific rules for their use including the layout of towns. The fact that most Mexican towns are a grid of streets surrounding a central plaza traces directly back to the Laws. Awarding mercedes was not a casual thing. Abandonment of the granted property without official permission could be punishable by death. Later, this would become an issue for the Casas Grandes settlers. Captain Ramírez established himself at a place of natural springs called *Ojo de Ramos* about 25 miles southwest of Janos, 20 miles north of Casa Grandes, and west of the designated Suma hunting grounds.[70] It is clear that Captain Ramírez picked this place because of the water. The water table was high, and water flowed east through the rancho in the Arroyo Ramos, eventually disappearing in a grove of mesquite a few miles southwest of Corralitos. Prehistoric ruins along the arroyo meant ancient people also liked the site.[71] He located his headquarters just south of a long flat mountain called Cerro Ramos, a landmark visible for miles in all directions.

In addition to the ranch buildings, Captain Ramírez built three silver smelters. Indian raiders destroyed them in 1684, but while they lasted, they represented the first effort at mining in the Casas Grandes Valley. The source of the ore is not known. According to the current Ramos owner, Señor Victor "Cacho" Barrio, there used to be silver mines in the Sierra Pajarito, a small range visible to the south. He said the section of the old road that linked Casas Grandes, Ramos, Corralitos, and Janos ran along the east side of Sierra Pajarito past Ramos. A branch road led to the ranch compound.[72] Ore might have come from the mountains as the Spanish already had several mines on the Sonora side of the Sierra Madre. A few years later, nearby Corralitos became the mining center of the Valley.

However he acquired the property, Ramírez retained it until his death in 1693. Most of those intervening years, he spent leading armed expeditions against the Apaches in Chihuahua and Sonora. Apparently, he and his wife Josefa had little time for a family because they left no surviving heirs. In 1704, eleven years after Ramírez died, his nephew, Gerónimo Varela de Losada, testified in a hearing concerning Ramírez's estate. Two others, presumably brothers also were involved in the proceedings—Joseph Varela de Losada and Juan Varela de Losada. This suggests that the hacienda passed into the Varela branch of Ramírez's family.

There is little recorded about Ojo de Ramos for the entire 18th century. The Varela family probably continued the ranching operation despite the Apache threat. Eighteenth-century Puebla majolica ceramic pieces found by archeologists indicate workers and their families lived on the property. A chapel was built during Spanish times. Charles Di Peso noted the building still stood in use as a barn in 1960. A moldering wall of adobe bricks

All that remains of the Ojo de Ramos chapel. The original chapel dates to the 17th century. Photo: 2018

near the ranch house marks the location today. Señor Barrio said a previous owner tore down the old building some years before Barrio's father bought the property.

Casas Grandes Struggles

Charles Di Peso and his team of archaeologists working at Paquimé, 1959-62, also excavated the Convento area. They devoted much of Volume 3 of their eight-volume report to their findings supplemented by research into historic records. An outline emerges of the early Europeans (Di Peso calls them Iberians) in the Casas Grandes Valley. Even after the extensive research, Di Peso noted how much of the story's detail either still was missing or appeared contradictory.

Di Peso stated that the Spanish settler land may have extended south to the junction where the Piedras Verdes River, flowing east out of the Sierra Madre, joins the Palanganas flowing north, to form the Casas Grandes River. This area, later part of Hacienda San Diego, is only about seven miles north of Mata Ortiz. It is intriguing to think that Captain de Gracia's grazing lands might have extended these few more miles, and that he and his vaqueros chased cows over the Pearson/Mata Ortiz site.

The Casas Grandes settlement was not successful in the early years, despite the richness of the valley. Padres Pedro Aparicio and Nicolás Hidalgo replaced Padre Páez in 1665. Padre Aparicio seems to have related well with the Suma, but he died after just two years. This gave the Suma an excuse to leave the mission. For unexplained reasons Captain de Gracia also left and relocated his family near Galeana in the Santa María Valley. He remained an important figure in the region until he died in 1706 with the honorific of being the first settler in the Casas Grandes Valley and possibly the first owner of Mata Ortiz land.[73]

The Suma returned for a short while, but it is a mystery why they ever asked for a mission and agreed to settle in one place. After twenty years, few ever became *gente de razón*. Hard times contributed. Both the settlers and Suma suffered years of epidemics and poor crops. By 1680, the region was ripe for revolt. Then came the Apache.

The Apache, Trading and Raiding

Most sources say that the people who became the Apaches migrated relatively late to the Southwest. They may have come from as far away as northwest Canada and Alaska as they share the Athabascan language with indigenous groups there. Other experts have different theories.[74] Regardless, by the 18th century, various Apache subgroups had spread across a vast area that extended more than 200 miles north of the border into Arizona, New Mexico, and Texas and south of the border into Sonora and Chihuahua. A subgroup, based along the Gila River, which became known as the Chiricahua Apache, began to interact with the various sedentary agricultural pueblos strung through the Rio Grande Valley from northern New Mexico down into Texas.

While the Apaches did some farming, they were basically nomadic hunter/gatherers and raiders. The cultural collision between these nomads and the pueblo agriculturalists evolved into a strange interdependent relationship labeled "trading and raiding."[75] Each had products from the soil or from the hunt not readily available to the other. European animals entered the product mix as well as human beings—slaves. When trade became inconvenient or inadequate, the Apaches raided pueblo fields and towns taking what they needed. In spite of this trait, they were not considered a real threat until they began to use horses. Wild horse herds, descended from conquistador strays, had been around for most of the seventeenth century. The Apaches initially killed them for food. They soon learned to capture and ride them and eventually to fight on horseback. These large fleet animals supplanted dogs as beasts of burden. Most Southwest indigenous people used the horse but none like the Apaches. Their skilled hands created a mounted force so formidable that just the word "Apache" struck terror into generations of Puebloans, Spanish, Mexicans, and North Americans. Adolph Bandelier was wary as late as 1884 as he worked in the Sierra Madre Mountains near the old hideouts, even though the Apache Wars were supposedly over. Stories of Apache raiding and even murder persisted into the 20th century. Some say they might still exist in the hidden canyons of the Sierra Madre. Grenville Goodwin in *Apache Diaries* sums up the Apaches in one sentence. "As a people, the Apaches were never Christianized, never urbanized, never colonized, never enslaved, never broken."[76]

After the Spanish blazed trails north to the New Mexican pueblos, trade intensified. All three cultural groups, the nomadic Apache, the sedentary Pueblos, and the European Spanish, had something the others wanted. The Apaches initially traded horses for buffalo hides with Plains Indians, who were located farther north from the wild horse herds. Later, horses became an important trade item with the Spanish and Mexican settlers. This set up a trading and raiding pattern for the next two centuries—the Apaches stealing horses and mules from one area and driving them to another to sell before being caught by the pursuing victims.

Human trafficking became an important item as each needed slaves, women, and children for different reasons. All profited, but the cultural clash, mixed with raiding, retaliation, and resentment against the Spanish, led finally to rebellion.

The Great Pueblo Revolt, 1680

It was the Indian pueblos that revolted in 1680 in a beautifully coordinated effort. The pueblos scattered along the Rio Grande in New Mexico Province coordinated with the Hopi and Zuni in what is today's Arizona to rise up and literally drive out all Spanish and their Indian converts. No single event so affected the American Southwest or the Mexican Northwest, as the Great Pueblo Revolt. All Spanish and those identified with the Spanish were killed or driven out of Santa Fe and the pueblos. The rebels burned every Spanish building—dwellings, churches, stables—everything. They tried to eliminate all traces of the Spanish in New Mexico. Almost 2,000 refugees retreated to El Paso. The governor of New Mexico (now a separate province from Nueva Vizcaya) ordered the people to remain there pending re-conquest of the pueblos. However, about 500 continued south some stopping at Janos and some continuing to Casas Grandes—becoming the second wave of immigration to the Casas Grandes Valley. The New Mexicans found the potential of the rich valley to their liking, so much so, that they refused to return to New Mexico when ordered by New Mexico's governor.

Their arrival and settlement had positive and negative effects. All evidence suggests they became productive citizens, always ready to pick up a sword to defend themselves and their neighbors against Indian attack. On the negative side, they arrived at a very delicate time in the relationship of the two cultures. The scent of rebellion was in the air, and when the New Mexicans moved onto Indian lands, they tipped the balance.

When the uprising started, the Apaches were on the sidelines, probably as surprised as the Spanish at the thoroughness and intensity of the pueblo revolt. They occasionally harassed the refugee columns fleeing to El Paso, but for the most part avoided the conflict. It soon became apparent they had a problem. Trading with the Spanish for needed goods and raiding their herds for stock had become the economic base for their way of life. Groups of Chiricahua Apaches did the logical thing, drifting to El Paso and the valleys to the south in the wake of the Spanish refugees. They reestablished their pattern of trading and raiding in northern Nueva Vizcaya with a stepped-up level of intermittent violence. In the Casas Grandes and Santa María Valleys, it did not take long for either the Spanish or the Apaches, to kill or absorb most of the indigenous peoples. By the early 1700s, groups such as the Suma, Janos, and Conchos were effectively gone. The Tarahumara, after their own uprising in 1690, retreated into the deep canyons of the Sierra Madre as did some Ópata. The two interloper cultures, Spanish and Apache, remained in a combustible faceoff that lasted another 200 years.[77]

The Apaches move south into Mexico coincided with their development as warrior horsemen. They had refined hit and run tactics, and rapid deployment methods that enabled them to move quickly, keeping ahead of their enemies, even while encumbered with their families.[78]

The Chiricahua first penetrated into the Casas Grandes Valley in March 1682.[79] An unknown number rode south and attacked Captain Ramírez's rancho, Ojo de Ramos. What actually happened is not reported. They probably intended to run off stock to eat or trade. Whatever they did enraged Captain Ramírez. This tough, local leader, now *alcalde* after his father-in-law, Captain de Gracia, moved to Galeana, assembled his men and rode after the raiders, the first of innumerable pursuits over the next two centuries.

While anyone can understand Ramírez's reaction to the violation of this property, his hot pursuit had the unintended consequence of further destabilizing an already fragile situation. His troop, including a few Indian scouts, trailed the Apache to Janos to find them long gone into the Sierra Madre. While at Janos, one of his Concho Indians, acting on an old grudge, murdered a Janos Indian. This act infuriated the Janos people and drove them into the arms of the Apaches. These fierce newcomers had arrived, more would follow, and they now had allies.

The incursion of the Apaches destabilized the region and set the stage for the expansion of the Great Pueblo Revolt into the Great Southwest Revolt.

The Great Southwest Revolt

After the initial uprising in New Mexico, the revolt expanded south. Messengers and passionate spokesmen from the pueblos slowly but effectively spread the word. In 1684, indigenous groups from the El Paso area through Janos, Casas Grandes, and over the mountains to the Santa María Valley rose up almost at once. The Great Pueblo Revolt morphed into the Great Southwest Revolt. Like the Pueblo Revolt, these uprisings seemed to be coordinated. At two in the morning on May 6, 1684, the Janos and Suma Indians at Nuestra Señora de la Soledad at Janos burst out of their huts and began ransacking the mission. In three days of terror, they burned the buildings, killed the two resident priests, the captain of the guard, and a servant. They then left for the mountains, carrying off six women and three boys.

Captain Ramírez at Hacienda Ojo de Ramos heard nothing until May 11, when a wounded mission servant staggered in from Janos with a tale of death and destruction.[80] The exhausted man, who had somehow covered the 25 miles from Janos, told Ramírez that a band of the rebel Suma and Janos were on their way south to attack San Antonio de Padua de Casas Grandes. The Captain knew he needed more fighting men, and he sent messengers to El Paso and Parral for help. Two days later, another messenger came in with the news that Casas Grandes was burning. Ramírez saddled and with his few men rode through the night over the 20 miles to Casas Grandes. All Indians were gone, both attackers and "Christianized" residents. The thick walls of El Convento were intact but the surrounding Indian village was burned. Ramírez found the resident padre, Juan de Porras, inside, alone but unhurt. The old reports of this attack mention nothing of the nearby settlers. Apparently, the Suma focused their rage only on the church area and their own dwellings. After their rampage at Janos and Casas Grandes, they joined other rebel groups in the Sierra Madre, which probably now included Apaches.

Simultaneous uprisings occurred in the Santa María Valley as far south as Namiquipa. Captain Ramírez desperately needed more men. He sent messengers in all directions asking for help, including the governors of Nueva Vizcaya and New Mexico. Ramírez himself rode up the Carretas Pass into Sonora to the Ópata mission town of Santa María Bacerac (close to the area Francisco de Ibarra passed through while escaping the Ópata in 1595) looking for help. The commander there sent 30 troopers, a generous act at a time when other besieged commanders would not spare a man.

The Carretas Pass and access to Sonora was soon cut off as the Indians destroyed the mission at Santa María de las Carretas. The padre there barely escaped to Casas Grandes. He reported that everything in the mission sanctuary had been smashed. The raiders tore the cloth from the *retablo* and made bags to haul away loot, a shocking desecration to a man who had spent a lifetime revering the objects of his church.

Captain Juan Fernández de la Fuente led the relief troops from Sonora. He would play an important role in the upcoming Apache wars. Other troopers arrived from El Paso within a few days, an amazingly quick response considering the vast distances to cover on horseback. These mounted reinforcements were well-armed with arquebuses, a smoothbore early musket, swords, and lances. Loyal Indians accompanied them, eager to take on old tribal enemies. They waited impatiently for more help that never came. Captain Ramírez and Captain Fernández now had a force totaling 62 Spaniards and about an equal number of loyal Indians. From scouting reports they knew that at least 2,000 Suma and their allies, men, women, and children, had fortified a position in the mountains called Peñón del Diablo.[81] More Indian warriors came into the stronghold every day, and the Spaniards knew they could not wait any longer. On June 2, they rode into the mountains, found the entrenched rebel Indians, and prepared to attack.

The meager descriptions available suggest the Indians had built redoubts of stacked rocks on the sides of a rough canyon. The terrain forced the attackers to dismount and leave behind their lances, which meant losing part of their advantage in battle. Boys took the horses back down the trail and held them out of range of the fighting. The Spanish advanced on foot. They all carried arquebuses that provided deadly fire whenever the Indians exposed themselves.[82] Some probably wore bits and pieces of armor—helmets, breast plates, and chain mail vests—whatever they had available and whatever they could stand to wear on their long rides in the heat. Most wore a version of the *escuapil,* a multi-layered deerskin cape or long jacket that had evolved on the frontier from the layered-cloth armor worn by the Aztec warriors that met Hernán Cortés. All carried swords, most of fine Toledo steel, lethal at close range. Some carried bull-hide shields, tough enough to block an arrow. The Indian auxiliaries may have had steel weapons. It is unlikely any had arquebuses. Indians possessing firearms was a sensitive issue.

It is not known how skilled the Suma and Janos rebel Indians were with bows in combat or whether they were backed by Apache warriors in the redoubts. If they used powerful four-to-five foot Apache bows, they would have shot volleys of three-foot arrows that could pierce an unprotected enemy at 200 yards. For close combat, the rebels might have had a few steel weapons but likely were dependent on stone axes and clubs.

The battle lasted all day. No one knows the rebel Indian casualties, but they held. Even with superior weapons, the Spanish were too few and the Indians too many and too well protected in the rocks. By four in the afternoon, a Spanish captain from El Paso was dead along with six loyal Indians. Thirty more of the combined forces were wounded. Ramírez could see they were getting nowhere. He ordered his bugler to sound retreat. His exhausted fighters fell back to their horses, mounted, and returned to Casas Grandes and the thick walls of El Convento.

The rebel Suma and Janos continued random attacks in the following days. Ramírez and his small force would sortie in response, sometimes locating and engaging in indecisive battles. In September, a band lured his troop north toward El Paso, and then doubled back and this time laid waste to the Casas Grandes settlements south of El Convento. The raiders ran off all stock—horses, mules, cattle, and sheep—everything. There is no proof, but the clever ruse, luring the experienced captain north, suggests the hand of the Apache. The now defenseless settlers, about 15 families, fled to *El Convento*. They stayed there for the rest of 1684 and most of the following year. In October 1685, Ramírez and his troopers did find and defeat a large rebel force and recover some stock and more importantly, rescued captured women and children. However, the genie was out of the bottle. What started as the Great Southwest Revolt would ebb and flow for the next twelve years.

The initial phase of colonization was over in northern Nueva Vizcaya. Most of the destroyed missions would never be rebuilt. Many Spanish settlements as far south as Encinillas on the Sacramento River just north of Ciudad Chihuahua were depopulated.[83] In Casas Grandes, the settlers, huddled in *El Convento* overlooking their devastated fields, wanted out. Their contract with the Crown stated they must stay with the land granted to them under penalty of death. That was the deal and they understood it. They saw their other options as either dying of starvation or being clubbed to death. They convinced Captain Ramírez, their *alcalde*, to make the long ride south to Parral with a written petition asking the Nueva Vizcaya governor for relief from their contract. The captain did not take that much convincing. Ojo de Ramos had been raided again, and the buildings burned. In Parral, the governor not only refused the petition, but he ordered Ramirez to enforce all agreed-upon terms. Somehow the desperate settlers held on for another year, living inside El Convento. They even managed to round up a few hundred head of stock.

The governor received word from a colonist who had escaped capture that the Indian renegades were planning an elaborate ruse to kill all the Casas Grandes settlers. The alarmed governor sent orders to Captain Francisco de Archuleta in El Paso to accompany troops to Casas Grandes to head off the attack and to find out once and for all who was responsible for the uprisings and devastation in the Casas Grandes Valley. With the appearance of the troops, the plot collapsed. Captain Archuleta formed a group, presumably of El Paso soldiers, to begin a series of interrogations. Given the few facts available, it does not appear they did a very good job. They tortured uncooperative witnesses, and finally concluded that the instigators of the Southwest Revolt in the Casas Grandes Valley were the Suma acolytes, who had been converted by the San Antonio de Padua padres and had been quietly working and serving the mission. When determined guilty, Captain

Archuleta ordered 43 men to be executed by clubbing. Captain Ramírez and Padre Porras protested and wrote the governor requesting clemency. The request was denied and the sentence carried out. The smashed bodies were stacked in a room attached to the mission church building adjacent to the grave yard. In 1959, two hundred and seventy-four years later, Charles Di Peso's team found the bones under dirt and debris when they excavated El Convento. After examination, the remains were left in place at the request of the Catholic Church and citizens of Casas Grandes.

In December 1685, Ramírez presented a revised petition stating that the settlers would move only as far as Janos. The governor agreed, and some Casas Grandes settlers moved north to new lands. It is not known how many left. Clear title to the new lands was uncertain, and the governor of New Mexico continued to bicker with the governor of Nueva Vizcaya over territorial jurisdiction and the Great Pueblo Revolt refugees settling in the Casas Grandes Valley rather than returning to New Mexico as he ordered.

Subsequent references to Indian attacks and other events at Casas Grandes suggest that at least some stayed or returned later. Captain Ramírez remained at Hacienda Ojo de Ramos with enough men to pursue raiders. However, the mission itself did not survive. By 1786, the Misión San Antonio de Padua de Casa Grandes was abandoned forever—the thick walls standing for over three centuries to become an archeological curiosity. The last Franciscan padre moved to the Santa María Valley.

Another change involved Captain Ramírez. He was given command of the military forces in Sonora, a thankless task.[84] He led an expedition deep into the heart of country dominated by rebellious tribes. As with many frontiersmen, the rugged life in the saddle caught up with him. In 1693, he rode to Mexico City to seek more men. The viceroy granted his request, but Ramírez died on the return trip.

By the time the Casas Grandes settlers moved to Janos, the viceroy already was exasperated by the reports describing the chaos in his far northern domain. As the Crown's representative, he had begun to change the policies for occupying and colonizing the north. Depending on missionaries had not worked. Resources had to be found and allocated toward building and manning additional forts, *presidios*, in a series of defensive positions to block marauders. In early 1686, the viceroy ordered a presidio built at Casa Grandes, which was relocated almost immediately to the more strategic Janos crossroads. On the specific orders of the Viceroy, the military assigned 50 soldiers armed with a newer-style musket. Captain Juan Fernández de la Fuente from Sonora, who had responded to Captain Ramírez's call for help two years before, became the first commander.[85] They named the completed fort San Felipe de Santiago de Janos. The *presidio* with its well-armed garrison swung the regional balance-of-power pendulum back to the center, but just to the center. Roving Apaches and their indigenous allies could not dominate the region as they had for the past two years. Neither could the Spanish leave their defensive walls and completely conquer the roaming people that stood in their way.[86]

This balance of power introduced the next era to Nueva Vizcaya, an era with some curious aspects. Two separate peoples, representing two very different cultures, coexisted in the same space in a sort of symbiotic relationship. The familiar pattern of trading and raiding continued, centered on Janos, and areas to the west in Sonora and to the east and south through the Santa María Valley. The southern part of the Casas Grandes Valley definitely played a part in the presidio era of trading and raiding. However, Casas Grandes, San Diego, and the future site of Pearson/Mata Ortiz remained on the periphery of the main drama. References mention people going and coming to Casas Grandes, attacks were recorded, but only a few clues suggest who the people were or how they lived.

During the 1690s and early 1700s, it appears that a small, mixed-group of Indians, Suma, Ópatas, and Conchos remained near El Convento, administered by a padre. A census in 1716 reported eleven Indian families. The number had decreased to 23 Indians by 1728. These statistics suggest that a few old Indians eked out an existence near El Convento. No doubt each had an interesting story as to how they ended in this place. As they died, their stories died with them. By 1767, both the Indian sites above the acequia and the Spanish site below were reported vacant.[87]

The Revolts died away by the end of the 17th century. In New Mexico, the Spanish worked hard to reclaim Santa Fe and the pueblos along the Rio Grande Rivers. By 1695, they were back in control, and by 1698, Spanish officials presided, and padres were restoring the churches. The Hopi to the west never submitted nor did any of the Apache groups, some of whom eventually aligned with the pueblos in the fight. Other Pueblo people seeking freedom actually fled and became part of the Apaches. A sidelight for pottery *aficionados* was the flight of Tewa Pueblo people west to Hopi. They brought skills that evolved into the now-famous pottery tradition of First Mesa.

In Spanish Nueva Vizcaya, the presidio era had begun, an era that would last well beyond Mexican Independence.

Corralitos, the Early Days

The ranch buildings of Hacienda Corralitos are southeast of Janos and northeast of Nuevo Casas Grandes, about a one-and one-half hour's drive from Mata Ortiz. The Spanish established a settlement there along the Casas Grandes River about 1740. The land was part of a huge Spanish land grant given to Juan Azcárate's father sometime before 1775. The grant included land from El Paso to Corralitos and the Casas Grandes Valley. The grant with its mines and ranches plus the extensive land holdings around El Paso of his mother's family, Ponce de León, made Azcárate a prominent citizen.

Ruins of the Corralitos smelter. Photo: 2018

About 1800, he and his wife Eugenia moved their headquarters to Corralitos, where they built their *Casa de Amo*. William Wallace II, the late patriarch of the family that has owned the modern-day version of the ranch (much reduced in size but still significant), stated in an interview that he believed the surviving ranch house at Corralitos was built around 1800 and is the original Casa de Amo. He did extensive research as had his interviewer C.E. Campbell, the author of *Mines, Cattle, and Rebellion, the History of the Corralitos Ranch*. Both failed to find definitive information regarding dates, the origins of the house, or other details.[88] What is known is that Corralitos became a ranching and mining center. Long caravans of mules, traveling about 20 miles a day, brought ore to the Corralitos smelter to be processed into silver ingots.

Sometime about 1840, Azcárate sold Hacienda Corralitos to Carlos Zuloaga, the patriarch of another powerful family. The sale covered 688,260 hectares (1.7 million acres).

The family and their hacienda would play a significant role in Chihuahua's presidio era.

Two Hundred Years to Geronimo

Elements of History

It was just over 200 years from the Great Pueblo Revolt of 1680 to the final surrender of Gerónimo in 1886. Over those centuries, two elements defined settlement and development in the Casas Grandes Valley: the local Apache, and the politics in faraway Mexico City and even farther away Spain. Both the Apache and the Spanish settlers were interlopers in the valley. The two cultures either displaced or absorbed the previous inhabitants and entered into the strange interdependent relationship described as "trading and raiding." Periods of peace alternated with raiding, killing and vicious retaliation. At the same time, the backlash of national and world events washed over the northern valleys with intended and unintended consequences affecting organization, administration, and resources.

Survival of the Species

To persist as a people, births, augmented by an infusion of outsiders, must exceed deaths. The Apaches presumably had a high death rate—combat, disease, infant mortality—but they readily absorbed other tribes peacefully or forcefully. By the middle of the 18th century, the word "Apache" stood for nearly all the nomads interfacing with the Casas Grandes and Santa Maria Valleys. They periodically added to their population by raiding Indian and European settlements. Captured native women and the occasional

European woman became wives. The Apache particularly wanted young boys who could be incorporated into families and raised as warriors. Humans had always been traded among the Indians, but with the arrival of the Spanish, they became an even more desirable commodity.

In the non-mechanized European world, human labor got the work done. Fields, workshops, mines, ranches, and private homes needed hands from whatever available source—family member, employee, indentured servant, or slave. Expanding a field, adding capacity to a workshop, or raising more cattle—all required more labor. Human trafficking had picked up considerably in the 17th century to meet the need for slaves to work in Nueva Vizcaya's booming silver-mine industry. Janos, located at a crossroads, emerged as the trading hub of Nueva Vizcaya's far north. The Janos traders bartered with Apache for this human commodity, often captives from other tribes. The Apaches themselves sometimes became slaves after capture by punitive expeditions. Whether conceived willingly or forcefully, mixed children became a significant factor as decade followed decade. A few former African slaves entered the mix and gradually the *mestizo*, the quintessential Mexican, became the dominant settler at Janos. This classic mixture stretches back through time and myth to the union of conquistador Hernán Cortés and his interpreter/mistress Malinche.

The evolution of mixed bloodlines throughout New Spain created a complicated class system, *sistema de castas,* particularly in the central, more settled regions. The proud Spaniard born in Spain remained very much at the top of the class hierarchy, while his brother, born in Mexico of the same Spanish parents, was a step inferior. Social stratification under the *casta* system proceeded down through the various *mestizo* mixes to the mulattos, Indians, with slaves at the bottom. The Crown always appointed Spanish-born viceroys and most of the high officials were also *peninsulares* or *españoles* as they were known. *Gachupines* was a more derisive term. The intent was to keep decision-makers, those in power, close and loyal to the mother country. Those born in New Spain (and anywhere in New World for that matter) of Spanish parents were called *criollos.* Those in this societal level usually had lower job assignments at least in the government. Class distinctions solidified over the centuries in colonial Spain. The resulting animosities imparted a class warfare aspect to the future struggles for independence in Mexico as well as throughout the New World.

In the remote frontier of Nueva Vizcaya, these distinctions existed but meant far less to those just trying to survive. Florence and Robert Lister in their aptly titled book, *Chihuahua, Storehouse of Storms*, made the point that a man of mixed blood is just as capable of shooting an Apache as pure-blooded *hidalgo* born in Spain.[89] The mestizos of the northern regions became fiercely independent, developing and protecting their property, families, and community with minimal assistance or interference from the central government. At the same time, at least in the earlier days, the Chihuahuenses were politically conservative, remaining loyal to a remote European king, of whom they knew little and who had done little for them. Later, as conservatives and liberals battled for control of the central government, Chihuahua politics became a unique mixture of left and right, always retaining an element of fierce independence. This explains, at least in part, why so much of the Revolution in 1910 against the oppression of the Porfirio Díaz dictatorship centered on Chihuahua and nearby northern states.

Chihuahua Booms

As the 17th century gave way to the 18th in northwestern Nueva Vizcaya, life continued the pattern of trading and raiding. The Apache had extended their reach deep into the province. Violence slowed and sometimes reversed the flow of colonization as settlers were killed and ranchos abandoned. The center of what became the state of Chihuahua was no less violent than the north around Janos and the Casas Grandes Valley, but the stakes would soon become much higher. Miners with their passion to find the big bonanza have always taken personal risks. Just before the turn of the 18th century, some of these single-minded prospectors braved a particularly inhospitable, waterless, treeless group of hills, where the Apache had already driven off previous explorers. One story says a Christianized Indian showed the miners the location.[90] However it happened, they found silver, a great deal of silver, in what became one of the richest mining strikes ever. Mexico soon would produce one half of the silver mined in the world.

Miners established legal claims and the rush was on. In 1708, the governor of Nueva Vizcaya province declared the area, now called Santa Eulalia, a *real de minas*, the term for an official mining district. Despite the designation, the problems of location remained. Santa Eulalia had nothing to offer except the silver. Water had to be hauled in on mules from miles away. Even for the first half of the 20th century, water had to be transported to the mining district by railroad tank cars.[91] Many miners favored locating the main town fifteen miles west at the junction of the Sacramento and Chuvíscar Rivers. Others felt the main town should be right at the mines, not a half day's ride away. The governor intervened and conducted a democratic vote (in itself an indication of the changing times) and those willing to commute from a more pleasant location prevailed. The relocated town soon became the focal point for commerce, transportation, farming, ranching, and culture for the northern half of Nueva Vizcaya (the half that became the state of Chihuahua). The governor insisted that the town be laid out in conformance with the detailed instructions in the 1573 version of the Laws of the Indies. These called for the classic plaza with the main church at one end facing the town hall, *casa de ayuntamiento* on the other. The plaza and buildings remain the center of today's city. The original name San Francisco de Cuellar honored the viceroy of the time. This was changed in 1718 when the next viceroy granted the status of *villa* to the rapidly expanding community and gave it the official name San Felipe Real de Chihuahua—today's *Ciudad* Chihuahua. A *villa* is a chartered frontier town with its own coat of arms, council, and special privileges.[92]

By 1716, fifteen mines produced ore for eighteen processing mills.[93] The newly rich built homes of adobe, adding second stories, porches, balconies, and wrought-iron grills. They ordered furnishings from Mexico City, some of which came from as far away as China. These luxury items had to be hauled in mule trains over dangerous trails to the salons of the *nouveau riche*.

The Changing World

Chihuahua's growth was not the only change in 18th century Nueva Vizcaya. Political change was in the wind. Politics had always been a bit messy in the north with jurisdictional disputes among the viceroys, province governors, Church leaders, local military captains, and *alcaldes*. Even European geopolitics affected the remote province. Real or perceived threats of French expansion beyond Louisiana (the huge region of the later Louisiana Purchase) and Texas alarmed the Spanish military. They reasoned that a trained, European-style army could be landed in Texas and march right through the few hundred garrison troops stationed in the widely scattered *presidios* of the northern frontier.

In Europe the century started with the death of the last Hapsburg king in 1700. After a bloody war involving the French, Netherlands, and England, the War of the Spanish Succession, 1701-1714, the Bourbon monarchy secured the throne.

The Bourbons brought new energy and an "enlightened" philosophy to the administration of their colonies. Seeds of these new 18th century European ideas, when carried across the Atlantic, eventually had unintended consequences, blossoming into struggles for independence throughout the New World. Rebellions would come later. The new monarchy had immediate problems across the entire empire, including the northern frontiers of New Spain.

The flow of the *quinto real*, the Crown's one fifth of all mining proceeds, was critical to a royal treasury depleted by constant war. However, the interruption of this flow by Apache attacks on the mule trains carrying the treasure and the constant reports of other Apache depredations vexed the Spanish authorities at all levels. The viceroy, far to the south in Mexico City, also received reports of corruption and abuse within the presidio garrisons charged with protecting the frontier. To compound the problem, the Spanish continued to worry about French incursions into Texas and Nueva Vizcaya from Louisiana. The French already had attacked Pensacola in Spanish Florida.

To address the situation, like governments for all time, they decided to hire consultants to do a study. This approach to the problem already had been used in the late 17th century and earlier inspection expeditions had led to the establishment of the Janos presidio, San Felipe y Santiago de Janos, as well as other presidios stretching into east Texas.

The first consultant brought in after the start of the 18th century was Brigadier Pedro de Rivera de Villalón, one of several Spanish officials sent by the crown to resolve Mexico's problems. He was first assigned to command the military installations at Veracruz, the main east coast port of New Spain. In 1723, the viceroy instructed Rivera to organize and lead an inspection expedition in the north. For more than three years, Rivera and his crew of soldiers, engineers, cartographers, and chroniclers traveled across 7,000 miles of uncharted northern frontier, inspecting presidios and missions. They ranged from Texas on the Louisiana border through Nueva Vizcaya into Sonora, an incredible feat of logistics. The expedition stopped at Janos twice. After the first inspection, the Brigadier declared the men of the fifty-man Janos garrison to be "ideal" and their captain able. They maintained a condition of readiness not often found at other presidios. His only criticism was that the cost of supplies deducted from soldiers' pay was excessive.[94] During his second trip to Janos, where his expedition waited out winter snow, 70 Suma Indians came in and requested that they be allowed to settle with the Janos Indians already living near the presidio. Rivera, as representative of the viceroy, had the power to grant this request. The Suma did not stay long, but their appearance was part of a pattern of Indians living peacefully for varying lengths of time in camps, called *rancherias*, close to the Spanish and later Mexican settlements. At times, this included even the Apaches.

From Janos, Rivera traveled south to the settlement of San Buenaventura in the Santa Maria River Valley, just over the mountains southeast of Casas Grandes. The mestizos there had done well developing their farms and marketing their harvests to the miners at San Felipe el Real de Chihuahua. In route, he passed through Casas Grandes and saw the ruins at Paquimé. He noted five Indian families living in the small village with Franciscan padres.[95] This is an important observation, documenting that in 1727 there was a presence, however small at Casas Grandes. Most of the reported activities of that time centered on Janos and Ciudad Chihuahua and said little about Casas Grandes.

Rivera wrote an extensive report for the viceroy. His recommendations on the reorganization and administration of the presidios came out as the *Reglamento de 1729*. Some of these regulations helped. The military organized a convoy system of armed escorts to protect the silver-laden mule trains. Also, the cartographers produced excellent maps and detailed descriptions of the terrain, flora, and fauna.[96]

Like so many consultants, Rivera was so concerned with reorganization and "efficiencies" that he missed the fundamental point. The Apaches remained a very dangerous enemy and continued to cause a huge loss of life, resources, and the Crown's quinto real. The solution, one that politicians did not want to hear, was to spend more, significantly more, on troops, arms, horses, and fortifications.

The Reglamento was barely published when the criticism began to flow, particularly from Church officials angered by the closure of the east Texas missions. Most notable was the writing of the Franciscan padre Juan Agustín Morfi. He published a history in 1783 that excoriated Rivera for his recommendations to pull back across Texas Province from the Louisiana border. Rivera had argued that the missions were failing and the presidios were too weak to control the region. Others also criticized the Regulations, primarily because they weakened the presidios.[97]

As it turned out, the critics were right. After Rivera's *Reglamento* reorganization, things got worse, at least in northern Nueva Vizcaya. The future state of Durango south of Chihuahua stabilized and by midcentury could be considered relatively safe with only an occasional Apache raid disturbing the peace. The opposite occurred in the Chihuahua portion of Nueva Vizcaya. Over the next two decades, raiding escalated. The situation worsened, partly because of the reduced resources caused by the "efficiencies" called for in the *Reglamento* and partly because more Apache groups moved in after being squeezed out of the Texas plains by the expansion of the powerful Comanche. The stepped-up Apache activity fell heavily on Janos but was felt throughout Chihuahua.

An experienced frontiersman, Captain José de Berroterán, commander of the presidio San Francisco de los Conchos south near Parral, filed another report in 1748, stating in detail just how bad the situation had become. He described the thousands of Apaches and their allies that continued to threaten the region. He criticized the *Reglamento* and made his own recommendations. His report was filed away, but later in the century, authorities at both the province governor and viceroy level reexamined it and incorporated Berroterán's recommendations into new presidio regulations.

In the meantime, in 1742, the viceroy commissioned another study. The job was given to a man with the elaborate name José Antonio Villaseñor y Sánchez. His published findings had an even more elaborate title, *Teatro Americano: Descripción General de los Reinos y Provincias de la Nueva España y sus Jurisdicciones.*[98] Summary information from this report in Oakah L. Jones' detailed book, *Nueva Vizcaya,* provides a picture of conditions in the Casas Grandes Valley. Janos had two plazas, four military towers, and 51 soldiers, essentially the same complement established almost 50 years before. In Casas Grandes, Villaseñor saw just a few families living in misery, unable to farm because of Apache raids, conditions no better and perhaps worse than when Rivera passed through 15 years before. Over in the Santa Maria Valley, San Buenaventura managed to remain productive even bountiful in spite of Apache harassment.

Though trading and raiding continued as a way of life in Nueva Vizcaya through the first half of the century, change did occur. As noted, the south, centered in Durango, calmed considerably. On the political side, Sinaloa and Sonora became separate provinces in 1733, and the southeastern portion of Nueva Vizcaya became part of Coahuila Province. These changes helped centralize government responsibility and simplify the task of the governor. Economically, the early 1700s featured rapid growth stimulated by the Santa Eulalia mining, a boom that had setbacks but never busted. Growth carried on into the second half of the century, but the predominant feature of the time was political reorganization—reorganization at all levels, civil, military, and religious, primarily to deal with the never-ending Apache issue. Different leaders tried a variety of approaches—diplomacy, eradication by any means, more studies. Nothing really worked. Throughout the century, the balance of power between the Apache and Spanish swung back and forth. Over the decades, the Apaches killed thousands of settlers, ran off tens of thousands of animals, and burned hundreds of homesteads and ranchos.[99] Still, settlers brought more stock or traded back for stolen animals. Miners struck new bonanzas, and more presidios were built.

Captain Berroterán and others had made several very practical recommendations on the military situation. The Spanish government needed to finance additional presidios manned by more soldiers with better officers, better training and with modern weapons. In 1757, ten years after Berroterán's report, the viceroy in Mexico City held a council of war. Among other things, he authorized two new presidios, one near present day Ojinaga on the Texas border. Today a branch of the *Chihuahua al Pacífico* railroad line begins in Ojinaga crosses Chihuahua, becoming the famed Copper Canyon line.

The other presidio was built on the hacienda El Carrizal on the north-south trail (now Highway 45) between Ciudad Chihuahua and El Paso.[100] The site was referred to as a hacienda, but probably was established to collect the salt created by evaporation in the local desert lakes. Today, the tiny town's claim to fame is that the Battle of El Carrizal was fought there in June 1916, between General John Pershing's Punitive Expedition cavalry and troops of Venustiano Carranza's government. It also played a role in the Apache Victorio's last raiding campaign in 1880.

While it lay many miles over the mountains to the east, El Carrizal relieved the pressure on Janos. This time the viceroy allocated sufficient resources. The Nueva Vizcaya governor himself rode north from Durango to El Carrizal to supervise, inspect and inventory the new garrison. Jones, in *Nueva Vizcaya*, summarizes the governor's findings that provide another look into the lifestyle on the Apache frontier. One hundred and ninety-four people were listed: 97 adults, with an almost equal number of men and women, and 97 children. Each head of household typically had a shotgun, sword, lance, cartridge case, thick leather jacket or *escuapil*, bull-hide shield, saddle, three horses, three head of cattle, two yokes of oxen, farm tools, hatchet, and digging stick. The government also provided 10-15 bushels of wheat as start-up subsistence. Officers were assigned to train the settlers and lead them into combat when necessary. The Bishop of the Diocese, based in Durango, assigned a parish priest. No mission was established.

The arms assigned to each man were standard for the time and place and were not that different than those used by Captain Ramírez's troopers at the Battle of Peñón del Diablo in 1684. The shotgun, or *escopeta* (probably many were muskets rather than shotguns), had replaced the arquebus, but the other arms had changed little. While working cattle, the settlers used their long lances to prod and drive their half-wild range animals. When called upon to fight, the lance in their practiced hands became a powerful weapon, able to hold off charging Apaches. Their long leather jackets that protected them from wind and cold often had four to six layers of thick hide and acted as lightweight armor.[101]

While these defenses made sense, they seemed only to stimulate the Apache to more activity. The frustrated Spanish called for more inspections and more reports. Between 1759 and 1763, Bishop Pedro Tamarón y Romeral conducted one of the most thorough ever. Based in Durango, his diocese included most of the provinces of Nueva Vizcaya, Sonora, Sinaloa, New Mexico, and Nueva Galicia. The bishop obviously took his responsibilities very seriously as he traveled an estimated 7,000 miles over rugged and dangerous trails to visit every community under his jurisdiction. His assistants performed a census and recorded a description of all aspects of the administration and economy of each community. He personally "confirmed" over 90,000 people, a religious rite only a bishop can perform. His report, finished in 1765, stated that Nueva Vizcaya had a population of 94,727, much larger than the other provinces. Most were in or around the large towns such as Durango (8,937) and Parral (2,693) in the south and San Felipe el Real de Chihuahua (4,652) and Santa Eulalia (4,755) in the center. In spite of its miserable site, Santa Eulalia was slightly larger than its more attractive neighbor because of the need for many hands to work the rich mines.[102] The Bishop's population figures appear to include the Indians in settlements but not those who remained nomads. It is doubtful any of the Bishop's assistants, no matter how dedicated, went out to count the Apaches. At the time of the Bishop's visit, Janos still had 50 soldiers, but the surrounding ranches were devastated. All of these reports make the poignant observation of the rich potential for agriculture, ranching, and mining if only the Apache could be controlled. As far as is known, no one was counted in the valley around Casas Grandes.

Hard on the heels of the Bishop was the Marqués de Rubí with another inspection tour, this one ordered directly by the Crown. Once again, the snarled complexities of European politics had reached across the Atlantic to affect events in Mexico's remote north. England had defeated France and its ally Spain in the Seven Years War (known as the French and Indian

War in the North American colonies in which young George Washington learned military skills). The resulting treaty in 1763 passed around huge pieces of the New World like a giant game of Monopoly. Great Britain got Canada, Florida, and everything else east of the Mississippi and gave Cuba back to Spain. Spain also got the vast area west of the Mississippi known as Louisiana that stretched north from the Gulf of Mexico into Alberta, Canada. New problems on the frontiers were substituted for old. The French in Louisiana had met the trading and raiding dilemma by trading guns to the Indians, a policy strictly forbidden by the Spanish. Spanish sovereignty over Louisiana could not stop this trade, and Apache raiders armed with pistols and muskets began to appear in Nueva Vizcaya.

The French were gone, but the powerful British in Florida were now just across the Mississippi from the thin Spanish presidio line. British corsairs had always roamed the Spanish Main preying on shipping. Now they had ports close by on the Gulf of Mexico from which to easily interdict galleons loaded with the king's treasure. To make matters worse, Spanish authorities in Madrid and Mexico received continuous reports of Russian incursions far to the northwest. No living Spaniard had ever seen the northern reaches of lands they claimed, but they were paranoid that forces of the British or Russian Empires somehow would sweep down across mountains and desert to attack Nueva Vizcaya and conquer the rich silver region.

The progressive Bourbon Carlos III assumed the Spanish throne in 1759 and reigned until 1788. He supported George Washington during the Revolution against England, apparently not considering the success of the colonists would sow seeds for later rebellion in Latin America.

The king had enough problems of his own. He inherited an expensive war, an over-powerful and zealot Jesuit order that operated virtually independent theocracies in the colonies, and the excesses of the Spanish Inquisition. The Mexican government's finances and military were not in good order, and the government could not control Apache depredations in the north. This directly affected the monarchy's quinto real. Reports of corruption and abuses by presidio captains reached Madrid. Frustrated, Carlos took direct action. He sent a message to the viceroy stating that three high-ranking officials would be sent to Mexico with extraordinary powers to reorganize the army, reorganize the government finances, and find a solution to the ever-increasing Apache problem. The officials were accompanied by Spanish-army generals, engineers, and other specialists. Sweeping changes were made in the government and military. Other draconian measures included the virtual overnight expulsion of all Jesuits from Mexico and the colonization of California by Franciscan missionaries.

The official selected to inspect the northern presidios and develop a plan to solve the real and perceived problems was Cayetano María Pignatelli Rubí Corbera y San Climent, Marqués de Rubí, who also was a Knight of the Order of Alcántara and Baron of Llinás and most importantly, a field marshall in the Spanish Army.[103]

Marqués de Rubí

The Marqués de Rubí was an excellent choice. For two years, 1766-68, the Marqués and his chronicler/engineer, Captain Nicolás de Lafora, led an officially sanctioned expedition to inspect the presidios. With engineers, cartographers, and escorting soldiers, they, like Bishop Pedro de Rivera, travelled an estimated 7,600 miles, inspecting the 27 presidios in Baja California, Sonora, Chihuahua, Coahuila, Nuevo León, New Mexico, and Texas as far as the modern Louisiana border. The extent of their travel attests to the vastness of the region the Spanish were trying to control and colonize. They found that in just the short time since the Bishop's tour the situation in the northern provinces had deteriorated even further. Hostilities had virtually shut down the mines at Santa Eulalia, which devastated the economy of Ciudad Chihuahua. Families there now lived in fear of direct attack by the "enemies," to use Lafora's words. After inspecting the defenses, Rubí's expedition moved north to San Buenaventura. Lafora reported the location of the presidio there to be too far in the mountains to be effective, and Rubí recommended it be moved north near Laguna de Ascensión. The trail continued north through low hills by a pass called Chocolate Pass. Lafora identified the hill bordering the pass as Chocolate Hill. He said the pass was open and not dangerous.[104] One hundred and fifteen years later, Juan Mata Ortiz would find it a very dangerous when ambushed there by descendants of Lafora's "enemies." The next objective was the presidio at Janos.

Several miles beyond Chocolate Pass, the troop turned northwest, forded the Casas Grandes River, and rode into what they called Las Casas Grandes Moctezuma. It was empty. No one was there. The Apaches had killed or driven away all the settlers, Indian or Spanish.[105] Lafora wrote a brief description of the Paquimé ruins and noted the wrecked, empty houses nearby and the many crosses along the trail, marking the graves of those killed in ambush. They did not linger in Paquimé but rode north through a pass near Ojo de Ramos, where Lafora noted more crosses. He made no mention of the hacienda.

The garrison at Janos hung on with 51 soldiers guarding a total population of 455. The surrounding settlements were mostly abandoned. The balance of power in the region had swung to the Apaches.

Marqués de Rubí's recommendations in his formal report called, the *dictamen,* together with previous reports, resulted in the promulgation of new royal regulations, the *Reglamento de 1772,* which called for the complete reorganization of the presidio system. All were closed in east Texas. Designed to solve the same problem as Rivera's *Reglamento de 1729,* this later model took a much tougher approach. Rubí's theory, based on his own observations as well as Berroterán's earlier report, was to create a line of seventeen presidios. The line started at the crossroads settlement of La Bahía, present-day Goliad, Texas and extended to San Antonio de Bexar, present-day San Antonio. It then crossed west Texas to El Paso, proceeding along the Rio Grande to northern Chihuahua. It ran past Carrizal then west to Janos and through northern Sonora to the Pacific. Rubí considered this a practical defensive line, protecting lands Spain actually occupied, rather than just claimed. The *Reglamento* called for bringing the poorly equipped, poorly trained, and poorly paid presidio garrison troops up to regular Spanish Army standards. Articles 21 and 27 of the Dictamen recommended for each presidio a compliment of 50 men including three officers, a sergeant, and 20 mounted "riflemen." Additional soldiers at Santa Fe and elsewhere raised the total to 940, which seems paltry in view of the vast territory they must defend. Rubí argued that properly led by competent officers, these upgraded forces would not only man the defensive positions but would engage in coordinated offensive expeditions.[106] Reorganization and combat operations would be carried out by an independent military commander for all of Nueva Vizcaya and Sonora, reporting directly to the viceroy. After a council of war, the viceroy accepted the plan and published it as the *Reglamento of 1772.*

The Marqués concluded as did Pedro de Rivera that Spain could not control all of Spain's lands. The difference was that Rivera's plan cut resources while Rubí's plan would commit more of the Crown's resources and add well-equipped and well-led presidios. In contrast to Rivera, Rubí's plan initially was well received. Even Padre Morfi, who had been so critical of Rivera, approved in spite of the closure of more missions. Some presidio officers, charged with implementing the plan, objected to the presidio placement and the distance between them. Later historians would disagree on the presidio concept as the best policy for the defense of the northern provinces. Best policy or not, the Reglamento of 1772 guided the defenses of Nueva Vizcaya for decades into Mexican times.[107]

The Red Captain

An unlikely character now enters the story as the enforcer of the new *Reglamento.* In October 1771, Hugo O'Conor of the Royal Armies, Knight of Calatrava, and newly appointed Commandant Inspector of the Interior Provinces left Mexico City and rode 1,100 miles to Ciudad Chihuahua to take up his new assignment. What made Colonel O'Conor unique, other than his long military experience, was the fact that he was born and raised in Ireland and had long, flaming red hair and fierce determination. His high rank in the Spanish army was another byproduct of Europe's convoluted politics. O'Conor was one of the "Wild Geese," those thousands of frustrated young Irishmen who crossed the Channel to join foreign armies on the continent after Protestant England dominated Catholic Ireland in the late 17th century. Spain supported the restoration of the Catholic Stuarts to the English throne, and the Wild Geese saw Spain as their savior and the vehicle for independence from England. In Spain, young men by the thousands filled all-Irish regiments that gained fame and respect in the innumerable Spanish wars. The first Spanish Bourbon king, Philip V, even tried twice, in 1719 and 1745, to invade the British Isles and restore the Stuart monarchy. Storms wrecked both attempts.

The Irish saw these failures as acts of good faith, and even more joined the Spanish king's ranks.

Hugh O'Conor (most sources use the Spanish "Hugo") left for Spain as a teenager about 1750. He had been born in 1734 into a family that claimed descent from the last Irish king, Roderic O'Conor. As there are several O'Conor lineages and most descendants (including the co-author of this book) claim the royal line, Hugo's family claim may be suspect. Questionable or not, the prestige of the name brought him to the attention of high-ranking Irish officers serving in Spain and helped his career.[108]

As a young officer, O'Conor fought in campaigns in Portugal during the Seven Years War. After that war, he was promoted and assigned to Cuba to help oversee the transition from British back to Spanish control. This included complete reorganization of the island's defenses, a task at which O'Conor proved to be especially competent. While in Cuba, the king approved his application for knighthood in the Order of Calatrava, one of three ancient military orders in Spain dating back to the Crusades. Admission to these prestigious ranks was difficult for any officer, particularly a foreigner. This honor provides a clue to as to how highly regarded he was by his superiors. When authorities in New Spain requested competent officers to help reorganize the military, O'Conor was one of those selected. He received orders to proceed to Mexico City and report directly to the viceroy. These orders sealed his destiny.

His assignment was supposed to be to help organize a "Mexican" army made up of local people to alleviate the need for sending regular-army soldiers from Spain. However, the viceroy had another problem. In Texas Province, bad blood between the governor and the military commander plus blatant corruption (O'Conor later refused large bribes from both sides) caused the disgusted viceroy to send O'Conor to Texas to clean up the mess, which he did, eventually arresting the culprits and traveling all over the province to square away the garrisons. As a result, he was appointed acting governor for almost five years. In his first year, he led 30 troopers into a successful battle against 300 Apaches—the first of many such battles for Hugo O'Conor. Riding into the enemy that first time with red hair streaming over a red uniform, the Apache called him *el capitán colorado,* a title that stuck and became known throughout the northern provinces.[109]

O'Conor not only impressed the Apaches, but he impressed an important visitor, the Marqués de Rubí. While on his inspection tour, the Marqués met O'Conor and liked what he saw of the man and his work in Texas. This led to his recommendation to the viceroy that the Red Captain be appointed as the new commandant to carry out the *Reglamento*. The viceroy, Antonio María de Bucareli, also appears in history as a major supporter of Padre Junípero Serra and his work establishing missions in Alta California.

For five years the indefatigable captain (now promoted to colonel) rode the high plains, mountains, and deserts of the northern provinces. In four major reconnaissance expeditions, he visited all of the existing presidios, closing some, relocating others, and founding new ones, to create the fortress-line alignment called for in the *Reglamento*. He inspected, reorganized, and drilled the garrisons following strict regular-army discipline. When he found poor arms and equipment, which was often, he badgered the vice-royal bureaucracy to send replacements. Strict discipline did not go over well with those along the distant frontier provinces used to a more egalitarian style. It is hard to guess how far the liberal 17th century European ideas had penetrated, but revolution was not that far into the future. Such ideas had nothing to do with the Red Captain or his single-minded approach to his task at hand.

On a raw January day in 1774, O'Conor rode into Janos escorted by a troop of worn-out dragoons. The presidio captain mustered his company: a lieutenant, ensign, chaplain, two corporals, and 40 men, roughly the same compliment as previous decades. Colonel O'Conor looked critically over the ragged ranks and recognized tough men of the frontier. He found them to be skilled shooting muskets and wielding their lances. They could ride for days in all kinds of weather subsisting on pinole and using a *sarape* for shelter.[110] However, their equipment—saddles, bridles, muskets, shields, leather body armor—all were worn out. O'Conor could see that Janos occupied a key strategic position. He had made many changes in other presidios, even moving some to different locations. Here he re-designed some of the defensive walls, but otherwise left it and the complement much as it was. He and his dragoons, after their brief rest, saddled up once more and rode southeast to San Buenaventura. Presumably, he sent an order to

Mexico City for new equipment because Janos received 92 firearms, 204 pistols, 86 swords, and 112 lances that year.[111]

In the process of carrying out this exhausting assignment, Colonel O'Conor played both sides of the trading and raiding game, negotiating truces and alliances with some hostile bands and leading troopers on desperate campaigns of annihilation against others.

By 1776, (a year of turmoil in the British colonies) Colonel, soon to be Brigadier General, O'Conor felt he had completed the job. A cordon of evenly spaced, well-equipped presidios lined the frontier. He had accomplished this despite opposition from quarreling civil governors and constant physical hardship. The trading and raiding pendulum swung back toward to a position favorable to the colonists. It was a huge effort, and that effort had taken its toll on the Red Captain. After ten years of harsh traveling and brutal fighting, he petitioned Viceroy Bucareli for relief and a transfer. Bucareli, a sound administrator, felt he could not spare him and denied the petition. European politics had intervened again.

The Bourbon monarchy from its distant viewpoint had never been happy with events in Nueva Vizcaya and its other northern provinces. Court intrigue changed the power structure, eliminating those who supported the existing organization. Representatives of the Spanish Crown stepped in directly over the head of the viceroy and created a new independent province, *Provincias Internas* (Internal Provinces), out of all the Northern provinces: Nueva Vizcaya, Sonora, Sinaloa, New Mexico, Coahuila, and Texas, plus Nuevo Santander (essentially the present-day state of Tamaulipas on the Gulf of Mexico coast), and Nuevo Reino de León (present day Nuevo León). All affairs, civil, military, and fiscal of this vast region would under the authority of one man, the *comandante general.* The center of this authority would be in the north not in faraway Mexico City. The first comandante located his headquarters in Arizpe, Sonora, a Jesuit mission community and today a small town whose claim to fame is an 18th century church, the burial site of the trailblazer, Juan Bautista De Anza.

Everyone agreed, even opponents of this radical reorganization including Viceroy Bucareli, that it would not work to make Colonel O'Conor a subordinate to the new *comandante*, after he had exercised total military control over significant portions of the new internal province for years.

Politicians solved their problem in a political way. O'Conor was promoted and sent to Yucatán Province as governor and captain general. After a difficult 16-day sail from Veracruz, he arrived in Campeche in August 1779. He started immediately to work inspecting the port fortifications, but he had little left to give. One of the most prominent of Ireland's Wild Geese, a Knight of Calatrava, died seven months later at age forty-four He is buried in Veracruz.

Provincias Internas

The Provincias Internas idea was not a bad concept. All of the governors, military commanders, and other officials would be under the authority of one commander whether they liked it or not, and many in their fiefdoms did not like it. The new system did work for a time, essentially building on O'Conor's legacy. The first commandant general was an elegant Frenchman, Chevalier Teodoro de Croix, who had for some reason joined the Spanish army also as a teenager and had risen through the ranks to high command, even higher than the Red Captain.

Chevalier de Croix arrived in Durango in September 1777, accompanied by Padre Juan Agustín Morfi, his personal chaplain.[112] Padre Morfi authored the 1783 publication that so criticized the Regulations resulting from Pedro de Rivera's earlier expedition, and approved of those of the Marqués de Rubí. The outspoken padre served as chronicler for de Croix, keeping a detailed diary of their travels. In 1779, they rode through the little valley near where the Casas Grandes River is formed by the junction of the San Miguel (Palanganas) and Piedras Verdes Rivers. Morfi wrote in his diary that this was the San Diego Valley, the first recorded mention of this name.

Before establishing his headquarters at Arizpe in Sonora, de Croix spent two years in San Felipe el Real de Chihuahua (shortened to Chihuahua in 1823), where he created a social sensation. Parisian style became the fad for the gentry made rich by the silver flowing again from the Santa Eulalia mines. Fine gowns and fancy uniforms graced lavish events. Not far away, men and women of another world, dressed in animal skins, rode, camped, and waited.

On the military side, Commandant General de Croix was initially impressed by the Reglamento de 1772. Upon further reading, he changed his mind. He still believed in a strong presidio system but felt Rubí and O'Conor had located them in the wrong places.[113] He made changes in the line and poured in more resources with more or less the same results. They pushed the Apaches back, secured some areas, and even "pacified" some bands that moved into semi-permanent settlements near the presidios. These efforts never could eliminate the pervasive threat.

On the civil side, de Croix encouraged settlers to remain in northern Nueva Vizcaya. He granted land to be owned in common (*ejidos*) by the communities in the Casas Grandes and Santa Maria Valleys. His edict established the Casas Grandes *ejido* on November 15, 1778. It was 12 miles wide and 60 miles long, stretching between the mountains and the Palanganas River.[114] Communal land was an inducement, but wary settlers were slow to take advantage of the opportunity. Four families came in 1778. One, the Miranda family, had descendants that continued to reside in Casas Grandes and were active in land dealings as late as 1907.[115] Another probably was the Quevedo family, later one of the most prominent local families in the 20th and 21st centuries.

Commandant General de Croix's 18th century establishment of communal lands had long-range ramifications. Casas Grandes residents used the old documents as the basis for their claim for ejido land 150 years later in the post-Revolution era.

Casas Grandes in the 18th Century

Except for a few Indians, the Casas Grandes settlement had been essentially abandoned for much of the 18th century. Violent action swirled around Janos to the north and beyond to New Mexico and Texas and to towns in Sonora to the west. The fields around *El Convento* and Paquimé lay fallow. The archived reports available say little. In January 1757, a thirty-two-man Janos patrol, riding south along the Casas Grandes River in pursuit of Apaches, passed through the "abandoned settlement at Casas Grandes."[116] Twenty years later Casas Grandes became an ejido, suggesting that settlers were present. Commandant General de Croix's inducements apparently made Casas Grandes more attractive.

However it happened, by the 1790s settlers were plowing the previously abandoned fields and running cattle around Paquimé. It is not known exactly when the first family or families arrived. An unknown number were reported there in 1792. Sixty, including men, women, children, and nine servants were recorded in April 1795. By the end of that year, the number had increased to 100 plus 51 soldiers detached from the Janos presidio. Four new houses had been constructed. This was almost a mini-land rush. The original settlers, Spanish and Indian, were gone. This second group provided the base for the modern population.[117] They were able to build homes, plow fields, and tend their sheep and cattle in relative safety. The concentration of violence remained in that northwest to southeast arc, centered at Janos. Casas Grandes began to prosper.

Hacienda Ojo de Ramos

One of the original Casas Grandes Valley settlements that appears sporadically in the old records is Ramos. It dates back to Captain Ramírez's Hacienda Ojo de Ramos and the time the valley was first settled in 1663. The property is located north of present-day Nuevo Casas Grandes and west of the highway to Janos. The main ranch buildings lined the old road that connected Casas Grandes with Corralitos. Hacienda Ramos remained with a branch of the Ramírez family, named Varela, at least into the 1830s. Mariano Varela, the owner in 1831, apparently had good relations with at least some of the Apache groups.[118] The relationship ended violently in December 1837. Apaches sacked Ramos and killed the owner, Juan María Varela, and seven others returning from a cattle roundup at Corralitos.[119] The hacienda was abandoned.[120] It is not known exactly when the family returned, but José Varela had a herd of mules stolen near Casas Grandes in 1842, which indicates the Varela family was still in the area.[121]

In 1855, a report from the Janos military commander mentions the abandoned Ramos rancho. Other than this passing reference, Ramos disappears from the records for years. In 1880, the Zuloaga heirs of Hacienda

Corralitos sold that huge property to two North Americans. That same year, they resold it along with a mining operation to E.D. Morgan, a Wall Street banker. He and his investors formed the Corralitos Cattle Company. The company acquired other ranchos including Ramos. In a short time Corralitos expanded to 607,000 hectares (1.5 million acres) with over 3,000 employees—vaqueros, miners, craftsmen, and farmers.

The Last Years of Spanish Empire

Commandant General Teodoro de Croix left in 1783 to become viceroy of Peru. He was succeeded by Felipe de Neve a former governor of Alta California and founder of Los Angeles. He died after one year and was replaced by a series of successors as a potentially effective system, based on absolute control by the commander, began to unravel. Dissatisfied Spanish authorities thousands of miles away began to meddle, rearrange the organization, and divide and recombine the commands repeatedly for the next 30 years.

In 1804, the viceroy regained some authority and by 1811was in overall charge of the *Provincias Internas* for the remainder of the Spanish period, not long as it turned out.

The erratic administration can be attributed partially to slow communication over great distances. Messages traveled in mule trains to Mexico City and then to Veracruz to reach a ship that may or may not be departing for the port of Sevilla on Spain's Guadalquivir River.

It also seems likely that this administrative thrashing about for so many years was an indication the Spanish monarchy was losing its grip on its New World empire. Enlightenment philosophies, such as popular sovereignty and the inalienable rights of man, had shaken the absolute monarchies of Europe. The American Revolution followed by the French Revolution helped spread these concepts to the New World, spawning more unrest. In France, the revolution disintegrated into chaos. In 1790, ten years after Louis XV was beheaded, General Napoleon Bonaparte emerged as the absolute leader of France. He went on to dominate much of Europe. In 1808, he forced out the Spanish Bourbon king, Ferdinand VII, and put his brother Joseph Bonaparte on the Spanish throne. While Joseph undoubtedly was more capable than his predecessor, the move enraged the Spanish people and many in New Spain. This led to war between France and Spanish forces loyal to Ferdinand, referred to as the Peninsular War.

The Apache, of course, took advantage of any lapses in the Spanish defenses. After decades of confrontation, their numbers seemed never to diminish with young warriors replacing the old and those lost in battle. Yet the balance of power continued to swing in favor of the Spanish. This is curious considering the Spanish leadership was so erratic. It seems Western Civilization's inexorable march through the New World had reached the *Provincias Internas* in spite of being hobbled by the Apaches. In 1790, Nueva Vizcaya's population had reached 124,151. Fifty thousand more were added over the next 20 years.[122] It remained the largest of the northern provinces and the economic center for mining, ranching, and agriculture. Durango, still peaceful, was becoming quite urban. Ciudad Chihuahua was not far behind even though its residents still faced Apache threats. Farther north around Janos, the area remained an on-and-off battlefield.

In spite of the chaotic organizational structure, some leaders had effective strategies that accounted for change and progress in the late 18th century. One was Viceroy Bernardo de Gálvez, who came into office in 1785. He had been governor of Spanish Louisiana, and incidentally had significantly aided the American Revolution by smuggling in large quantities of munitions and supplies to George Washington's beleaguered army and later opening a second front against the British in the south. The city of Galveston is named after him. From Mexico City, Gálvez issued a new order, the *Instrucción* of 1786. This was a compilation of the many orders and reports that had been filed with the Viceroy's office over the past 20 years. It was long and detailed but made two basic points: continue to bear down hard on the Apaches, but if they ask for peace, grant it immediately. Give gifts, followed by a stipend of regular rations. Gálvez had too much experience on the frontier to have any illusions about his policy. For him a bad peace was better than a good war. He said, "a bad peace with all the tribes which ask for it would be more fruitful than the gains of a successful war."[123] He reasoned that if the Apache had enough to survive, this would be a strong incentive, especially knowing the Spanish would retaliate severely if the peace was broken. Retaliation included exiling captured Apache leaders, to

Cuba, a very undesirable fate. In contrast, any leader who came in peacefully would be exempted.

This worked to some extent. When raiding continued, the Janos troops did their job, including capturing family members of the warriors. Freeing family added to the incentive to come in peacefully. Several hundred did, taking up residence in *rancherias* around Janos. This ushered in a period of relative peace that lasted until after Mexican independence. The term "relative" must be emphasized because raiding and retaliation continued. A few Apache groups never came in. Others settled around Janos but continued to raid elsewhere. Still others settled quietly. Some of these actually became scouts, joining the Spanish soldiers in the retaliation campaigns, Apache fighting Apache. It was Gálvez's bad peace, but as he said, it was better than all-out war. It lasted approximately 40 years from 1790 to 1830.[124] This period of relative peace was the primary reason new settlers felt comfortable taking over the abandoned lands of Casas Grandes.

El Grito

On September 16, 1810, Padre Miguel Hidalgo y Costilla stood on the steps of the parish church in the small town of Dolores and delivered his famous *Grito de Dolores,* his Cry or Shout of Dolores, a speech that ignited the Mexican War of Independence. Already in South America in 1808, Simón Bolivar and José de San Martín had led successful revolts against the Spanish *gachupines.* It took thirteen years, but by 1821, the Spanish were gone from the southern continent, leaving behind their language, culture, and nine new countries.

The struggle in South America had been basically the *criollos* against the *gachupines* backed by armies from Spain. The situation was different in Mexico. The mestizos, Indians, and others of the lower classes tended to despise their criollo betters as much as the gachupines. Hidalgo's cry set off a volatile mix. Indians and mestizos flocked to him. Without much planning, he quickly assembled a peasant army of no less than 50,000 that also included many idealistic criollos. A young army officer named Ignacio Allende raised a regiment and joined him. They marched through central Mexico, looting and pillaging. They sacked Guanajuato, murdering a number of *gachupines* hiding in the *Alhóndiga de Granaditas*, the large granary exchange building. They even had some military success until the mob army began to disintegrate in the face of stiff resistance by units of Spain's professional army. After a number of unsuccessful forays, Hidalgo and Allende decided to go north to Texas, where they had convinced themselves there would be support from the Spanish-hating Texans. In route, a *criollo* officer betrayed them and both were captured and taken to Ciudad Chihuahua for trial and execution. This brings Nueva Vizcaya briefly into the main stream of this phase of Mexican revolutionary history. The military commandant in Chihuahua set up a civil tribunal to try all rebels. The bishop in Durango convened an ecclesiastical tribunal for Hidalgo. That body "degraded" him, an official punishment that stripped him of all ecclesiastic authority and benefits but did allow him the Holy Sacrament as part of the last rites. The bishop himself administered these rites to Hidalgo following the verdict of death by the civil tribunal. A twelve-man firing squad executed the defrocked priest along with twenty-other rebels over the following month. Seven rebels were sentenced to hard labor at the Janos presidio.[125] Faraway Janos at the head of the Casas Grandes Valley was considered a place of exile at that time.

The Spanish authorities were not done. They ordered the bodies of Hidalgo, Allende, and two others decapitated, and the heads hung on the high corners of the Alhóndiga de Granaditas, the grain exchange building, in the recently sacked city of Guanajuato. This sent a very graphic, grisly message to all who might consider challenging the Spanish Crown, at that time worn by Joseph Bonaparte of France.

The Spanish had crushed Hidalgo's rebellion, but the proverbial genie was out of the bottle. He had given the Mexican people—Indians, mestizos, intellectuals—a glimpse of a life of freedom and equality, a glimpse that led to a dream and to a struggle that would continue in one form or other for the next one hundred years. Hidalgo himself would become the symbol of that struggle, *El Padre de la Patria*. Every year on September 16, the anniversary of his grito, Mexicans from the southern tropics to the northern deserts gather to hear a local dignitary voice his version of the grito, often including an enthusiastic "Viva Mexico."

The heads of the four freedom fighters remained displayed on the Alhóndiga de Granaditas for over a decade before being reunited with their bodies. All parts are now interred alongside other martyrs in the *Ángel de la Independencia* monument and mausoleum in downtown Mexico City. Designed by Antonio Rivas Mercado, construction of this elaborate edifice began ironically in 1910 during the regime of President/Dictator Porfirio Díaz, who himself soon would fall victim to a new revolution inspired by the dreams and ideals of those honored by the monument.

Nueva Vizcaya was a long way from central Mexico. The first reaction of the leaders in Ciudad Chihuahua after hearing news of rebellion was to support the Crown, the legitimate Crown as they saw it, belonging to King Ferdinand VII. The *comandante general* started a subscription drive to raise 50,000 pesos to send to Spain to help Ferdinand drive out the Bonaparte usurper. This was a large sum. To put it in perspective, the governor's annual salary was 1,830 pesos.[126] Many throughout Mexico felt this way. This is one of several curious aspects regarding the War of Independence. For them, the war began as a struggle of Ferdinand against the French Bonapartes. As the viceroy and the highest Spanish authorities were official appointees of King Joseph Bonaparte, the initial insurrection was against them. Gradually the revolt evolved into an all-out war throughout Mexico against all Spanish and all of Spain, regardless of who wore the Crown—except in Nueva Vizcaya. The governor, commandant, bishop, and other local officials ruthlessly repressed any revolutionary activity. As Mexican politics split into conservative and liberal wings in the years following independence, Chihuahua officials remained conservative.

North of Ciudad Chihuahua, in the Casas Grandes and San Buenaventura Valleys, the need to survive had long since leveled the social and racial *casta* system, even on the feudal-like haciendas. Most thought rule by the Spanish Crown was just fine if they thought about it at all. The seven rebel prisoners arriving at the Janos presidio to perform hard labor would have been a curiosity. Any that survived likely were absorbed into the thick mix of the local Janos culture and their past forgotten.

José María Morelos

It was a different story in the various regions of central and southern Mexico. After Hidalgo's fall, the movement simmered as a harassing guerilla action under local chieftains. Then it boiled over again when a strong, competent leader emerged to consolidate most, if not, all of the fractionalized units into a unified rebel force. The leader, who so successfully picked up Hidalgo's fallen banner of independence, was José María Morelos, a short, taciturn mestizo priest. Henry Bamford Parkes in his *History of Mexico* calls Morelos "a military genius and one of the most clear-sighted political thinkers in Mexican history."[127] Heavy praise certainly, but this quiet small-town priest deserves it. With no military training, he raised and trained a citizen army that he led into battle against the best the Spanish could muster. He knew when to fight and when to retreat. By the end of 1811, he and his able lieutenants had conquered most of southern Mexico and established a three-branch—executive, legislative, and judicial—civil government for the lands they controlled. One of his ablest lieutenants was Hermenegildo Galeana. The central plaza in Casas Grandes bears his name.

For Morelos, this was definitely a social revolution. The façade of supporting King Ferdinand fell away. He believed Mexico should be a republic, subject to the will of all people of all races and all classes. The great haciendas should be broken up and the lands distributed. While he remained devout, he advocated for Church reform, eliminating privileges that oppressed the people such as mandatory tithing and the accumulation of large, tax-free land holdings. Unfortunately for the future of Mexico, other leaders of the movement, both civil and military, had their own agendas and could not rise to his level of competence and unselfishness. Meddling and lack of cooperation began to cause battlefield losses. This interference plus a clever political maneuver by the Spanish finally doomed Morelos' social revolution.

Simply put, the Spanish were able to turn a significant portion of the war-weary middle class, the *criollos,* the people of property with everything to lose, against the peons of Hidalgo and Morelos, who had nothing and nothing to lose. The Spanish armed the *criollos* and the tide turned.

It took time, but by the middle of 1817, the social revolution essentially was over, as was the fighting. A few disciples of Morelos survived with guerilla bands, such as Guadalupe Victoria, Vicente Guerrero, and Juan Álvarez, names that would resurface in later phase of Mexico's convoluted political scene. Morelos was captured when he put himself in harm's way fighting a rearguard action to cover the escape of the surviving members of his rebel government. The Spanish quietly executed him to avoid creating a martyr. It didn't work. He is considered one of the great heroes of Mexican history. His body lies alongside Hidalgo and the other martyrs of the War of Independence in the Ángel de la Independencia monument in Mexico City.

An Emperor Succeeds the King

Strengthening the *criollos* backfired on the Spanish. This class within the Mexican *casta* system ranged from an elite group with ties to Spanish nobility to a middle class owning or managing the mines, haciendas, and commercial operations. They were barred from the coveted high offices because they lacked a Spanish birth certificate. Others wanted to expand their haciendas into Indian lands. Spanish law as spelled out in Laws of the Indies specifically protected the Indians and their rights to certain lands. If the Spanish were gone, so would their laws. Still other *criollos* had more altruistic motives, believing in the principles of the Enlightenment including self-determination. Regardless of motive, all saw that the time to act was now and agreed the *gachupines* should be deported. The question was how to proceed.

The great irony of the War of Independence, a time of many ironies, was that the inheritor of the movement, who emerged to lead the war to its conclusion, was an elite *criollo* officer with family connections to ancient Spanish nobility, who had spent the previous several years fighting against independence. Agustín de Iturbide was everything a military leader of the era should be, and he was at the right time for rapid military advancement. Handsome, even dashing, and a fine horseman, he competently led his dragoons into battle as a young lieutenant against Morelos' insurgents. For early exploits, he was promoted to captain, then quickly to colonel and finally to general through the decade of the war. He broke Morelos' siege of the city of Valladolid with a well-timed and well-executed cavalry charge. This battle finished Morelos' army as an effective force while creating another bit of irony. Both Iturbide and Morelos were born in Valladolid and the city's name was later changed to Morelia to honor the vanquished Morelos. No cities were named after Iturbide.

By 1820, Iturbide had risen to command the Spanish army still pursuing Vicente Guerrero and the remaining rebels. Convoluted events in Spain involving the king and the rise of republicanism made him realize that independence from Spain best served the *criollo* class he represented. He then had a truly brilliant idea. He proposed a compromise that could satisfy the special interests of Mexico's powerful but disparate factions. He had his army behind him, but even more, he had the ability to sell his idea. He convinced the faction leaders, at least those with some remaining power, to agree to a set of conditions he labeled the *Plan of Iguala*. Despite reservations, everyone realized this was the best deal they could get—the Church, the *criollos*, and the remaining rebels.

The *Plan de Iguala* had three parts or "Three Guarantees." It is important to outline these because, despite some "liberal" features, the Guarantees became the basis for the conservative side of the liberal/conservative struggle that characterized and disrupted Mexican politics for the rest of the 19th century and into the 20th. Even today they are intertwined in Mexico's political debate. The first part guaranteed freedom from Spanish rule but under some form of a monarchy. Throughout almost a decade of bloody revolution, the mystique of the monarchy, rule by an absolute king or emperor, waned but never died. Revived at the end of the War for Independence, it became a tenet of the conservatives. A Mexican monarchy would give the *criollos* freedom from direct Spanish rule under a system they understood.

The second part guaranteed all former privileges to the Roman Catholic Church and to the military. Long past was the era of the dedicated padre carrying the cross alongside the conquistadores' sword into the remote frontiers of New Spain. The Church owned much property and had become rich, even corrupt in their dealings with their still-faithful congregations. A more progressive section of this guarantee was freedom of religion, which helped with the liberals. The guarantee of privileges for the army established a base of power for barracks revolts and coups for the next several decades.

The third guarantee established equality between the *criollos* and the Spanish-born *gachupines*. Clearly, this step toward class equality omitted the Indians, about half of the population and the mestizos, about twenty-five percent, depending on who was counted and who did the counting.[128] Still, it was a step, and it effectively eliminated the legality of the *casta* system that had been so rigorously enforced under Spanish law. Social discrimination persisted, but a few decades later a Zapotec Indian became Mexico's most revered president.

The three-colored panels of the Mexican flag, reputedly designed by Iturbide himself, represent these three guarantees. He placed the ancient Aztec symbol of eagle, snake, and cactus in the center to link Mexico's ancient empire to the new. Soon after independence, Iturbide satisfied those who yearned for a monarchy by crowning himself Emperor Agustín I.

After acceptance of the Plan of Iguala, the war wound down almost bloodlessly. The last viceroy accepted the Plan, and Spanish troops left Mexico City. Like a knight in shining armor Iturbide rode a black charger at the head of a grand parade into the center of Mexico City on September 27, 1821 to the cheers of an adoring mob. Unfortunately for him and for the fledgling country, his genius for creating a coalition to end the war did not extend to nation building. Preoccupied with the expensive trappings of royalty, when the impoverished nation could not pay its army, let alone meet other government obligations, Agustín's reign lasted less than ten months. Some of the old Spanish provinces wanted no part of the new country. Central America south of Chiapas broke away and formed their own country, which eventually separated into five republics. The huge area of Texas had too few people to form any kind of resistance. That would come a decade later.

The liberal opposition that Iturbide tried to suppress found an unusual but effective forum in the secret meetings of the Freemasonry fraternal organizations that surfaced in Mexico during the War of Independence. Organized resistance arose out of these meetings so quickly that the Emperor hardly had time to enjoy himself before he was ousted and on a ship bound for exile in Europe.

Perhaps if Iturbide had seen beyond personal aggrandizement, and had someone with Morelos' skills at his side, Mexico's history would have taken a different turn. As it was, the stage was set for decades of political turmoil, war with the United States, loss of territory, more "plans," more constitutions, civil war, capped by invasion from France in 1862. Between 1824 and 1862, Mexico had 31 different individuals serve as president, many returning after being ousted. This revolving-door executive does not count the reign of General Antonio López de Santa Anna, who assumed the presidency no less than eleven times in 22 years. This flamboyant, cunning, opportunist took advantage of the turmoil and became Mexico's dominant figure during much of the first half of the 19th century. There are no monuments honoring his memory unless one counts the 567-foot column at the San Jacinto Battlefield near Houston that marks his defeat by the Texas independence army in 1836.

Meanwhile Back in Chihuahua

The authorities in Nueva Vizcaya remained conservative and staunch supporters of King Ferdinand until the very end of the War of Independence. In 1814, the crown had appointed Alejo García Conde, a former quartermaster in Nueva Vizcaya, as governor of the Provincias Internas and then four years later promoted him to the highest position, commandant general. In mid-century, one of his three sons, Pedro García Conde, would head the Mexican commission negotiating the new boundary with John Bartlett after the Mexican-American War.

Comandante García Conde did not know he would be Nueva Vizcaya's last head of government. He remained loyal to the Spanish Crown, almost to the end. As Iturbide was consolidating his position in Mexico City, Chihuahua conservatives raised enough money for the comandante to send a small army marching south to aid the Spanish cause. In route, the troops heard the news and declared for Iturbide's *Plan de Iguala* and independence. The officer in charge ordered an about face, and they marched back to Ciudad Chihuahua. García Conde realized he had no choice but to accept the reality of independence.

In Durango, it took a battle to convince the residents there that they could no longer look to the Spanish Crown for governance. Iturbide had to send another army to Durango. After skirmishes, artillery bombardment, and considerable loss of life, the defenders surrendered, and the town council officially accepted the reality of independence.[129]

The Chihuahuan people accepted the reality as well. Two years later, the same citizens that had funded the small royalist army, and who had watched passively as Hidalgo was marched to the scaffold, now subscribed donations for a monument in their city honoring Hidalgo.

On September 1, 1821, the day after Durango capitulated, a young officer rode into the Janos presidio with the news. As of that date, the Apaches and the settlers in Janos and the Casas Grandes Valley had managed a wary, "bad peace" for 30 years. Adequate food supplies and severe reprisals formed the two supports for this fragile relationship. Enough time had passed to allow long-serving soldiers to end their military careers and retire to nearby ranches and farms.

Given the long distances and slow communications, little changed politically in Nueva Vizcaya during the first years of independence. Iturbide assigned new officials, but their titles and the political structure remained more or less the same as did the province name. The deposed commandant, Alejo García Conde, survived to become a brigadier general in the Mexican Army.

One significant symbolic event did occur. In August 1822, the bodies of Hidalgo and his three fellow martyrs were disinterred and taken with full honors to Mexico City. A solemn parade followed the highly decorated urns through Ciudad Chihuahua. A military guard then escorted them to Mexico City, where thousands greeted and cheered the entourage. The bodies were reunited with their respective skulls from the Guanajuato Alhóndiga de Granaditas and reinterred in a church with great ceremony. They came out again a century later in 1925 to be placed in Porfirio Díaz's Ángel de Independencia monument that had been expanded into a mausoleum. Never at rest, they were disinterred again or at least the skulls were taken out in 2010 and put on display in the mausoleum to inspire school children and other visitors and remind them of their heritage.[130]

The following year, 1823, the garrison at Durango joined the expanding movement to overthrow Iturbide. Apparently for those in Durango, a Spanish monarchy was fine but not one created locally. The pendulum had swung to the liberal side for the fledgling country. In Mexico City, a democratic government was established with the classic three branches within a federal and state framework. This "Federalist" system was sound, but it set up a power struggle between the states and the central government. As happened in the United States, this struggle contributed to civil strife and rebellions.

The former revolutionary and follower of José Morelos, Guadalupe Victoria, became Mexico's first president. He was a good choice, and the many monuments and place names throughout Mexico bear witness to that. Victoria served his full four-year term, the only president to do that for the next 40 years.

Part of the massive government reorganization was the creation of states to replace the old Spanish provinces. Initially it was the intent to create one state out of the province of Nueva Vizcaya. However, the newly enfranchised voters elected two sets of congressional deputies, one complete set each from Durango and Chihuahua. Both groups insisted their city be the state capital. The new congress wisely amended their new constitution, cutting the baby in half to create two states. Nueva Vizcaya was no more. In another twist of irony, Chihuahua's first governor had been a member of the tribunal that had condemned Miguel Hidalgo to death thirteen years before.[131]

The Spanish had used another tier of government, the *municipio*, a concept roughly equivalent to a county in the U.S. The Mexicans continued this system. Both Janos and Casas Grandes became municipio seats, charged with governing the surrounding designated area. The official founding date for each municipio is 1820, just before independence. That Casas Grandes qualified for this designation indicates enough settlers were comfortable with the relatively peaceful conditions to move into the valley and create a substantial community. The *municipio* system survived Mexico's political turmoil. Today the town of Casas Grandes remains the *cabecera* or seat of the municipal government that includes Mata Ortiz.

A large cross dominates the center of the Casas Grandes coat of arms or *escudo*. This represents the large prehistoric cross laid out on the grounds of Paquimé, one axis pointing to the setting sun on the days of the equinox. To the ancient people, it might have represented earth, sun, air, and water or perhaps the four seasons. Regardless, Paquimé and its mysteries were a source of pride worthy of being the central feature of the escudo. The smaller cross in the upper left quadrant represents the Order of Santiago, an elite military/religious group (similar to the Order of Calatrava to which the Red Captain, Hugo O'Conor, belonged). Francisco de Ibarra, the first European to see Paquimé, and first governor of Nueva Vizcaya, was a member and entitled to wear the black robes of the order bearing the Cross of Santiago. At the top of the escudo is the date Ibarra's expedition entered Paquimé. The fleur-de-lis in the upper right quadrant represents the nobility

Casas Grandes coat of arms

of the people. The bottom quadrants show the products of the land, cattle, wheat, and pine trees on the left and an apple, peach, and pear on the right. A Mata Ortiz pot might have been part of the escudo if it had been adopted a few years later.

While the basic structure of state and municipio persisted to modern times, the vague boundaries and property titles of the frontier era became even more confused during the decades of changing administrations, war, revolution, and land reform. The properties included municipios, ejidos, private property, and government or unclaimed land called *baldíos*. Conflicts that began in 1927 over land between the Ejido Casas Grandes and the municipios of Casas Grandes and Nuevo Casas Grandes were not resolved until 2016, when Beto Baca of Mata Ortiz was president of the Casas Grandes municipio.[132]

A Traveler's Observations

Few details exist about how people actually lived in the Casas Grandes Valley at the time of Independence and after. The English Navy Lieutenant, R.W.H. Hardy, R.N. in his book about his travels between 1825 and 1828

provides some descriptions. On his way to Mexico City after his exploration for pearls in the Gulf of California, he stayed four days at the Hacienda
Carretas at the base of the pass he had just crossed from the Bavispe Valley. He said the area had "wood, water, and pasturage." His host was Don
Manuel Samaniego, the brother of the leading citizen of Bavispe, who had
been Hardy's host a few days before. Another brother, Tiburcio, spoke fluent Athabascan and could converse easily with the Apaches. This enabled
the Samaniego brothers to establish a good relationship. The Apaches left
their cattle and other stock alone, at least for a while. Six years later in
April 1833, the Apaches ran off a large herd of cattle, horses, and mules.
Raiding had increased in part because the recently independent Mexican
government was unable provide the rations specified in past agreements.[133]
References to earlier attacks indicate that a functioning "hacienda" existed
at Carretas at least as far back as 1770.[134] The mission had been destroyed
in the Great Southwest Uprising in 1684, but apparently a cattle operation
survived or was established later. At the time of Hardy's visit, Don Manuel
Samaniego operated a very profitable *mescal* still, which Hardy described
in detail. He also noted that for five or six years enterprising (and brave)
entrepreneurs from Missouri hauled wagonloads of dry goods to the Casas
Grandes Valley to trade for mules. There was a demand for the animals
in the Midwest and the profits high, if (a big "if") they could be delivered
safely through Apache country back to Missouri. This trade was clearly
important to remote Chihuahua settlements.

Another feature of this faraway region was the primitive medicine
and health care. Lt. Hardy's guides viewed him as a kind of doctor. He
had a large supply of charcoal pills which he dispensed liberally to various
"patients." According to him the pills worked wonders.

It took Hardy's party two days to reach the Janos presidio. He stayed
with the local priest, who had a houseful of "nieces." According to Hardy,
celibacy was not widely practiced among the priests of Chihuahua. He did
not think much of Janos, finding it small and the inhabitants "sufficiently
wretched."

Traveling through Sonora, his party had found no blacksmiths or
horseshoes anywhere and so far, none in Chihuahua. They tied pieces of
hide on the mules' hooves as some protection from the rocky trails.

The route south from Janos led to an intersection, one branch going northeast to El Paso and the other south to Ciudad Chihuahua. They passed through Ramos, which had good grass, and arrived in Casas Grandes, a town he thought to have about 300 people. The party stayed in what he described as an old round tower. That might have been a section of the town's defensive wall. He was impressed by the Paquimé ruins, but not the town, finding the people to have "a very indifferent character for honesty." He did note the fertile soil and the abundance of water and wood.[135]

He crossed a plain full of prairie-dog holes and continued into the Santa Maria Valley and the presidio town of San Buenaventura. With a population of 1,400, San Buenaventura appears to have been the most important town in northern Chihuahua in the late 1820s and to Hardy, the most attractive. He continued to Ciudad Chihuahua, Mexico City, and to Veracruz, where he embarked for Norfolk, New York, and finally back to England.

Conflicting Agendas

In Mexico City, the capable Guadalupe Victoria could not quite meet the challenge of the conflicting forces that swirled through Mexican society and politics following independence. Everyone had an agenda. Even Iturbide attempted a comeback and returned to the shores of Mexico. This was a fatal miscalculation because in absentia, his sentence had been changed from exile to execution by firing squad. Instead of being welcomed as a hero, he was arrested, tried, and shot. The liberals had divided into two quarrelling factions of radicals and moderates. The conservatives, led by General Santa Anna, lurked in the background, disrupting the moves to democracy and waiting their chance. An empty treasury was an immediate problem. The revenue system, such as it was, provided only about half of what Victoria needed to cover the leanest of budgets. Much of New Spain's economy was based on mining. The War of Independence and the exodus of the Spanish had effectively shut down many mines. It would be years before production revived. Victoria borrowed from European banks, a start down a slippery slope that set up the rationale for the invasion by France in 1861. Well intended policies to open Texas to foreign immigration to offset the Comanche Indian threat, plus the abolition of slavery in Mexico in 1829, set the stage for the Texas Revolt in 1835.

In northern Chihuahua, the Mexican government tried to carry out the established Spanish policies in dealing with the Apaches but simply did not have the resources. Presidio garrisons deteriorated as did the food distribution system to the tribal members. As the distribution from the Janos presidio declined, raiding increased proportionally until by 1830 the "bad peace" was over.

It is almost impossible to follow the convoluted machinations, treachery, massacres, and peace attempts of the next decades in the north, centered at Janos. One example illustrates the times. A vengeful troop of Mexican soldiers from a presidio in Sonora rode over the passes to Janos one night and massacred a group of still-peaceful Apache families under the noses of fellow soldiers sleeping in the nearby Janos presidio. This sabotaged any chance the Janos commander had for maintaining a semblance of peace in his jurisdiction.[136] Also, North American freebooters and scalp hunters became involved as did Comanches, crossing the Rio Grande to take advantage of the unstable situation. This was serious as even the hard-bitten Apache warriors avoided the Comanche.

Toward the end of the 1830s, most of the soldiers were gone from the presidio, and conditions around Janos had deteriorated to the point that the settlers were abandoning their hard-won properties and going south to what were considered safer places such as the growing agricultural hub at Casas Grandes and the mines near Corralitos.[137] Not that these places were totally safe. Apaches raided Casas Grandes in the summer of 1835, killing a captain and five soldiers.[138]

In 1839, Chihuahua Governor Ángel Trías Álvarez hired groups of freebooters as mercenaries to campaign against the Apaches. One of the most notorious was James or Santiago Kirker, who raised a mixed company of 200 Mexicans, Americans, Shawnee and Delaware Indians. He based his force in Casas Grandes and rode out to kill Apaches. Armed settlers, *vecinos,* sometimes rode with him.[139] It is not recorded how the people of Casas Grandes felt about Kirker's professional killers camping in their community. Presumably, they approved because for a while in 1840, his was the only force in the field against marauding Apaches. The problem was that the governor paid for these services by the scalp. Kirker and those who followed him—this policy in one form or another stayed in effect for decades—did not distinguish one Indian scalp from another. He killed everyone with black hair he could find, men, women, children, whether they were living peacefully, involved in peaceful negotiations, or even from the Apache tribe. While effective in the short-term, the net effect was to turn trading and raiding into a war of vengeance and vicious retaliation.

Governor Trías appears in Cormac McCarthy's popular novel, *Blood Meridian*. Just as he did in real life, the fictional Trías hires a gang of scalp hunters, led by the bloodthirsty John Glanton, a real-life competitor of John Kirker. Larry McMurtry also featured Kirker briefly in *Deadman's Walk*, the first of the *Lonesome Dove* series.

Governor Ángel Trías' part, both real and fictional, in this dark episode of scalp hunting obscures the central role he played in Chihuahua's history for two decades. A cultured man, educated in Europe, he owned several huge haciendas covering a significant portion of Chihuahua. During an era of unrest and revolving-door politicians, Trías occupied Chihuahua's governor's chair for eight terms.[140] Despite losing the two major battles fought under his command against U.S. invaders, his fierce loyalty to Chihuahua, his anti-North Americanism, anti-monarchism, and anti-Protestantism caused him to remain popular with his constituency and their particular Chihuahuan mix of conservative and liberal views. Conflict of interest was not an issue as his haciendas covered a significant portion of the state he governed. One of the largest was Hacienda Encinillas, an important holding estimated to cover 526,100 hectares (1,300,000 acres).[141]

In 1868 a year after Trías death, Encinillas became a major part of Luis Terrazas's empire. The Apache Victorio, whose defeat by Joaquín Terrazas and Juan Mata Ortiz (the village's namesake) began the final chapter in the Apache Wars, was said to have been born at Encinillas.

As would be expected of a large *hacendado*, Trías held conservative views. He always supported President Santa Anna, a fact that historians do not fully understand, given that the erratic president paid little attention to the northern states.[142] However, Trías strongly opposed Santa Anna's sale of northern land to the U.S., the Gadsden Purchase. He had to be ordered to comply with the terms of the sale. Surprisingly he later became a liberal when Benito Juárez emerged as the progressive leader of Mexico.

The Second Lieutenant

Farther north at Janos, another important player of this era, an obscure thirty-five-year-old officer, reported for duty at the presidio in October 1840. The first inspections by Second Lieutenant José Baltazar Padilla revealed that he had inherited a real mess. The garrison as a fighting force was almost nonexistent and morale was bad. No clear impression of Lieutenant Padilla emerges from the old records. He was a twelve-year veteran from San Elizario, but we don't know what he looked like or if he had a family. The picture that does emerge is of a dedicated soldier, brave and doggedly determined to do his duty. Less flamboyant than the Red Captain, Hugo O'Conor, he appears to be from the same mold, living a life on horseback, pursuing, fighting, or trying to negotiate with a hostile people of another culture. He clearly believed in and preferred negotiated peace however fragile. Old correspondence and reports from the Janos presidio reveal his painstaking efforts to cobble together peace arrangements. When these fell apart, and raiding canceled trading, he never hesitated to take the field and lead his men into combat to reclaim stock, to free captives, and to punish. He often came in conflict with superiors, who advocated the harsher, scalp-hunting methods that he knew would lead to vicious retaliation. He served and survived eighteen years in this remote outpost before disappearing from the historical record.

After arriving at Janos, Padilla set about rebuilding the garrison troops to a point where they again could take the field. Authorities in Casas Grandes, Corralitos, and Barranco sent him prisoners who had been sentenced to military service. With these additions to his force, however dubious their origins, he actually negotiated periods of peace, shaky periods but peace, nevertheless. Apaches gathered and lived around Janos. Cochise, destined to be one of the Apache's greatest leaders was listed on the Janos ration list in 1842 and 1843.[143]

This could not and would not last. Great events overtook the entire country and drained away Padilla and the entire garrison, leaving no military presence at the Janos presidio. Governor Trías, now commanding the army in Chihuahua, ordered Padilla and his men to the capital to join the Chihuahua Cavalry.[144] War and invasion loomed on the northern horizon.

Santa Anna, Revolt, and War

On the national scene, the 40-year career of Antonio López de Santa Anna was remarkable for its inconsistency and yet its resiliency. Santa Anna always seems to return to the center of Mexico's politics, regardless of the previous disaster. There are parallels with Iturbide. Like "Emperor" Iturbide, he was born into a prominent, conservative *criollo* family. Also, like Iturbide, he was a career army officer, and he derived most of his power from the army. References describe him as a capable military commander and a cunning politician. These descriptions fall short of presenting a full picture of this charming, mercurial man, who regardless of his betrayals and gross failures, always seemed to be welcomed back to lead the country, usually to another disaster. He not only changed sides as the political winds blew, but he also often created his own wind, backing or leading factions, sometimes conservative, sometimes liberal, betraying them when convenient.

When the War of Independence erupted with Hidalgo's Grito, sixteen-year-old Santa Anna had just become a cadet in a unit of the Spanish Army in Veracruz. He went into combat against the insurgents and received a wound in the hand, just after turning seventeen. He rose rapidly through the ranks. When Iturbide concluded the War, he made Santa Anna a general, a mistake as it turned out. Santa Anna went back to his home state of Veracruz and turned it into a stronghold with him as war lord or *caudillo*. With Veracruz as his power base, Santa Anna turned on Iturbide and became a major factor in forcing the emperor into exile. Santa Anna went on to support the establishment of a Mexican republic, which led to the election of Guadalupe Victoria.

After Victoria's term ended in 1828 another freedom fighter, Vicente Guerrero, was installed as president after Santa Anna lead a coup to oust the duly elected successor to Victoria. Guerrero lasted less than a year before being executed after another coup. Two presidents later in 1833, Santa

Anna became president. He liked the title, but not the governing part. He turned everything over to his liberal vice president Valentín Gómez Farías, who enacted many reforms particularly limiting the army and Church (including shutting down the mission system in California). Many of these reforms, while repealed, restored, and repealed again, became the basis for action by future liberals including Benito Juárez. The immediate reaction to the reforms by the army, Church, and Santa Anna himself was to force Gómez Farías into exile.

By 1835, Santa Anna was effectively the dictator of Mexico, centralizing power at the expense of the states. All of these political machinations had been accompanied by protests, riots, revolts, and executions. At least eleven states wanted no part of Santa Anna. While Chihuahua remained conservative, other states declared independence and formed their own armies. Santa Anna himself led the Mexican Army against strong secessionist forces in Zacatecas, defeating them in battle and squelching that rebellion. Another rebellion was put down in Oaxaca, and both states remained part of Mexico. Texas turned out to be different.

The policy of encouraging foreign settlement in Texas, started by Victoria, had attracted many North Americans looking for cheap land. In less than ten years, the population had risen to over 20,000.[145] Some brought slaves to work their new fields. Mexican government officials realized they had made a mistake. They passed laws to restrict immigration and imposed duty fees at the border. Attempts to enforce these new laws and antislavery laws created incidents, and the incidents led to rebellion. Santa Anna sent an army north to San Antonio, and the Texans, also called "Texians" drove it out. It should be noted that the Texians represented both former North Americans and Mexicans, who wanted nothing to do with rule from Mexico City. Santa Anna himself then organized a larger army and marched to San Antonio to confront the rebel Texans behind the walls of the former Misión San Antonio de Valero, a fortress now called the Alamo. Movies in the U.S. about the ensuing battle show Santa Anna's troops advancing on the fortress wearing spotless uniforms and boots. In fact, he had raised a ragtag, barefoot army, poorly equipped and poorly fed for a winter campaign. Many were Indian conscripts who did not speak Spanish. Nevertheless, he had over 3,000, which proved enough to overcome and eventually slaughter the 150 Alamo defenders. This battle solidified the Texans' resolve and provided a battle cry.

An overconfident, overextended Santa Anna pushed eastward. Under Sam Houston, the Texas volunteers retreated, reorganized, and suddenly struck a surprised Santa Anna at San Jacinto, today a memorial site near the city of Houston. Santa Anna was captured. He bought his freedom with a promise of Texas independence. The government in Mexico City disavowed his agreements, setting the stage for a much bigger war less than a decade away.

In spite of the common border, the events before and after the establishment of the independent Lone Star State had little impact on the people of northern Chihuahua except to increase animosities between Chihuahua officials and the increasing numbers of U.S. traders bringing goods across the border. Arbitrary changes in regulations, fees, and tariffs infuriated the North Americans, who wanted to trade as they pleased. Violations, actual and perceived, led to imprisonments and seizure of goods. Chihuahuans resented what they viewed as the excessive aggressiveness of the North Americans. Worse, they objected to ideas and philosophies accompanying the North Americans, particularly Protestantism and Freemasonry. Freedom of religion was official policy, and various rites of Masonry continued to be part of the political scene in central Mexico, but not in Chihuahua, not yet. The former supporters of King Ferdinand remained conservative.

At the same time, many Chihuahuans were unhappy with the central government. They blamed officials in Mexico for the Apache upsurge. A fledgling separatist movement actually got underway instigated by settlers who felt they could better combat the Apache by joining with the United States. The invasion of Chihuahua in 1847 by the U.S. Army quickly aborted that movement. Regardless of their feelings toward their central government, Chihuahuans did not take lightly any kind of invasion, whether Apaches, North Americans, or as it turned out later, the French.

The Mexican-American War

Ángel Trías was the governor and military leader of Chihuahua at the time of the Mexican-American War. Don Ángel disliked, maybe even hated, what he considered the uncouth North Americans and their ideas. As had been so often the case in Mexican history, Chihuahua remained a sideshow during the Mexican-American War. Regardless, blood was spilled, property destroyed, lives lost, and hatreds compounded.

Border irritations and confrontations grew into open hostility. The tipping point occurred when the United States Congress voted to annex Texas as the 28th state. Mexico had never accepted Santa Anna's deals and had warned the U.S. government that annexation of Texas would mean war. Mexico had launched at least three military expeditions across the Rio Grande capturing territory that included San Antonio, but the effort ultimately fizzled out. The boundaries to Texas in that era included almost half of New Mexico and parts of Oklahoma, Kansas, Colorado, and Wyoming. With some significant exceptions in the border areas, most of the inhabitants of this vast area did not want to be ruled from Mexico City.

The boundaries of thinly populated California included all of Nevada, most of Arizona, and parts of New Mexico, Colorado, and Wyoming. The Hispanic Californios had benefited enormously when Gómez Farías had shut down the missions and caused the mission landholdings to be distributed. Most Californios resented Mexican rule and had actually fomented their own unsuccessful rebellions. Leaders in California were beginning to think their future lay with the U.S. A more diplomatic, less heavy-handed approach by the United States government might have averted war in California and accomplished the same result. As it was, the aggressive administration of President James K. Polk appeared to welcome war.

In Mexico City, the struggling government seemed willing to make some accommodation until Gómez Farías again became president in 1846. He would not accept any compromise. However, he faced a serious problem. Who could raise an army and lead it against the Americans? He did not trust Santa Anna, who had betrayed him once, but he had no choice. That high-risk general was the only one with the charisma, energy, and experience to take on the job. The problem was he had been exiled to Cuba, now blockaded by the U.S. Navy.

This set off an almost unbelievable sequence of events. Santa Anna tricked the Polk administration into allowing him to slip through the blockade by promising to negotiate a peace favorable to the U.S.[146] Back in

Mexico, he then raised an army, marched north into Coahuila and fought a battle against a force under Zachary Taylor at Buena Vista, near Saltillo, the state capital. Both claimed victory, Taylor in such a convincing manner to the American public that it led to the U.S. presidency after Polk in 1849. For General Santa Anna, the battle led to the presidency as well. He betrayed Gómez Farías again and became Mexico's president for the tenth time. Soon after, General Winfield Scott landed a force at Veracruz and marched west on Hernán Cortés' old route of conquest from Veracruz to the Valley of Mexico. Realizing the danger, competing factions, both liberal and conservative, rallied behind Santa Anna. This was probably his finest hour as he effectively organized the army and prepared the defenses for Mexico City.

Earlier in August 1846, General Stephen Watts Kearney and his Army of the West had occupied Santa Fe. He divided his command into three parts. Leaving a garrison to hold Santa Fe. A second unit of 300 troops led by Kearney would march on through the mountains and deserts to California. He ordered the remaining troops, a regiment of Missouri Volunteers under the command of Colonel Alexander W. Doniphan, to march south via El Paso and take Chihuahua. Kearney, guided by scout Kit Carson, made it to California and was immediately defeated in the biggest battle ever fought in California at San Pascual in what is now northern San Diego County. Fortunately for Kearney, reinforcements arrived from San Diego and rescued him. After a few other confrontations involving Kearney, Commodore Stockton and John Fremont, the-not-too reluctant Californios capitulated.

The Battles of Sacramento and Santa Cruz de Rosales

Colonel Doniphan had been a prominent lawyer in Missouri and a friend of Abraham Lincoln. He turned out to be a capable officer, keeping his obstreperous Missourians in line and leading them successfully in battle. For this campaign, he received unexpected but welcome support. Scalp hunter James Kirker and his followers thought they were being treated poorly by Governor Trías, who had suspended payment for scalps because the scalp-hunter gangs had ratcheted up to killing anyone with black hair. Kirker changed sides and joined Doniphan's command. His men may have been an unsavory lot, but they knew the country and they could and would fight.

Colonel Doniphan had orders to coordinate the Chihuahua attack with General John E. Wool, who was supposed to come from San Antonio. There was a mix-up, and Wool never communicated his change of plan to Doniphan. Instead of converging on Chihuahua, Wool marched south from San Antonio and attacked Saltillo. Doniphan, following his orders, left El Paso on February 8, 1847, with 924 soldiers and six cannon plus 300 civilians, including traders with 315 wagons full of goods. He pushed the somewhat motley array down the Chihuahua Trail, the old trade route from Santa Fe, today traversed by highway 45. They crossed the treacherous soft sand of the Samalayuca Dunes, *Los Medanos de Samalayuca*, losing men, animals, and supplies. They saved themselves from a prairie fire by rushing into bogs around Laguna Encinillas, north of Ciudad Chihuahua.

Governor Trías organized defenses for the capital along a line on the Sacramento River about 15 miles north of Ciudad Chihuahua near the Hacienda Sacramento. On a plateau in front of the river, his men built 28 trenches and placed their cannon facing the road to the north. This was the obvious attack route for the North Americans.

On February 28, 1847, Second Lieutenant Padilla from Janos sat his horse on the hill with the Chihuahua Company of the Mexican Cavalry, over 800 troopers. They watched the foreign invaders advance. He and his Janos veterans had fought many running battles with Apaches. They had fought those tough, vicious warriors hand to hand, on foot and on horseback. Never in all their combat experience had they faced ranks of advancing infantry across a battlefield, backed by massed artillery fire. General Doniphan did not take the obvious route. He left the road and made a flanking movement to his right in rough terrain. The Missourians had to drag the cannon through an arroyo and up the cliffs of the plateau. After enormous effort, they made it and set the cannon to enfilade the Mexicans' unprotected left.[147] Colonel Doniphan's skillful use of the cannons, pulled 300 miles from El Paso, enabled his infantrymen to storm the trenches and carry the day. Trías ordered the cavalry to charge, but Doniphan's artillerymen loaded their cannons with canister shot and scattered the charging troopers. Don Ángel Trías had no option but to surrender. He managed to escape south with his government officials and the remnant of his army including Lieutenant Padilla, who had survived the Light Brigade-like charge into the cannon fire.

Another in Trías' ranks who survived that day was Luis Terrazas's father. Juan Terrazas. He returned to his family and businesses in Chihuahua, only to be struck down by cholera two years later.

Doniphan collected his troops, reformed, and marched the few miles from the battlefield into Ciudad Chihuahua. The Missourians occupied the city for two months, not exactly sure what they were supposed to do. Doniphan sent a few troops to occupy Galeana, Corralitos, and El Barranco.[148] They finally received orders to march to Saltillo to join General Wool. This they did, struggling for 450 miles through harsh country and fighting Indians on the way. General Wool reviewed the now ragged regiment and sent them off to Veracruz 750 miles away. They marched those miles to the port city, boarded ships and sailed to New Orleans, where they were mustered out. The First Missouri Volunteers had done everything asked of them and more. They returned to their homes with a lifetime of stories or at least enough to last until the American Civil War, now just fourteen years away.

It is unclear what this battle and brief occupation of the capital accomplished in the whole scheme of the Mexican-American War. Hostilities would drag on for another year with terrible battles fought in Mexico City, culminating in the heroic stand by the Mexican soldiers and cadets on the hill of Chapultepec Castle. Five of those cadets, ages 13-19, and their lieutenant, have been immortalized in Mexican history for refusing the order to retreat and sacrificing themselves to protect the Mexican flag. The Mata Ortiz middle school, *Telesecundaria #6038*, bears the name of the *teniente*, Juan de la Barrera.

The two neighboring countries ended their war with the signing of the Treaty of Guadalupe Hidalgo on February 2, 1848. The U.S. Congress ratified it on March 10.

While the war was still going on, and after General Doniphan left Chihuahua, Governor Trías and his officials returned to the capital and resumed governing. He retained what was left of his army in the capital including Lieutenant Padilla and the Chihuahua Cavalry. As it turned out there was one more battle to be fought, and lost, even after the war ended. That battle clearly accomplished nothing at all except to kill some brave Mexican and U.S. soldiers.

General Sterling Price, another general from Missouri, had taken command of the Army of West and was the military governor of the large, undefined area called New Mexico. Price would gain fame in the Civil War as a Confederate general, losing several key battles to Union forces. He got the idea that a Mexican army was on the move and threatened New Mexico. In spite of orders limiting his authority to enter Chihuahua and in spite of the fact that the formal Treaty of Guadalupe Hidalgo had been signed the month before, Price with three companies of cavalry and four companies of infantry left El Paso on March 1. Governor Trías met them at the Battle of Sacramento site. He informed Price that the war was over. The general from Missouri thought it was a trick and marched to the capital. Trías ordered his men out of the way and retreated fifty miles south to the town of Santa Cruz de Rosales. General Price called for a unit of artillery from El Paso. When it arrived, he went after Trías, pushing on to Santa Cruz de Rosales. Trías again sent a message saying in effect, "The war is over, you won!" Price had an army and a perceived enemy in front of him. He wanted a battle. On March 16, he gave the order to attack. The Mexican defenders fought well. A small unit of cavalry, perhaps including Lieutenant Padilla, attacked the rear, briefly delaying Price's advance. The Americans then attacked from three directions and overwhelmed the defenders. The Mexican officers were held captive for short time then pardoned. When the Secretary of War heard about Price's action, he sent orders to him to release all confiscated property and immediately return to the U.S.

The battle, as unimportant as it was except to the families of the slain, had the strange effect of solidifying the two commanders with their constituencies. The loser, Don Ángel Trías, became even more popular with the Chihuahuans. He remained in politics at the state and federal levels until his death in 1864. General Price, while somewhat disgraced in Washington, became so wildly popular in Missouri that they elected him governor in 1852.

The Treaty of Guadalupe and the Gadsden Purchase

While the battles in Chihuahua were sideshows, the overall war, its treaty, and the subsequent Gadsden Purchase had an enormous effect on the future of the two countries and specifically on northern Chihuahua and the Casas Grandes Valley.

Under the terms of the Treaty, General Santa Anna ceded a vast, mostly empty land, for 15 million dollars (about $4.5 billion in today's dollars). Most of the few people who lived in the ceded land preferred the change of government, particularly those in Texas and California. The entire non-native population in California (which included Nevada and parts of Arizona) was less than 8,000. Texas, of course, had already revolted and established itself as an independent country 12 years before. Santa Anna and other Mexican authorities may not have thought they lost all that much. It was certainly a blow to their pride, and mines and agricultural resources were lost. However, six years later, Santa Anna sold even more empty land in a transaction called the Gadsden Purchase in the U.S. and *La Venta de la Mesilla* in Mexico. Some historians look back through time and see the purchase as another example of the U.S. taking advantage of Mexico. Another view suggests Santa Anna and his government were frustrated by their inability to control the northern regions. It made more sense to sell the violence-plagued land than to continue to try to defend it. Besides, they needed the money.[149]

Mexico received an important concession. The U.S. agreed to control the Apache raiding across the border—a near impossible task that affected border history for the next forty years.

On the last day of 1854, James Gadsden, the ambassador to Mexico, signed the deal that that bore his name. The border was pushed south past the Tucson Presidio (population 760), encompassing all of today's southern Arizona and what became the boot-heel of New Mexico. The sale included a significant portion of the Janos presidio's former jurisdiction. Santa Anna's government received a much needed 10 million dollars (about $3 billion in today's dollars). This agreement and subsequent boundary surveys settled most of the border delineation problems that had plagued both governments since the war's end. It also provided a southern route for a U.S. transcontinental railroad. Today, Interstate 10

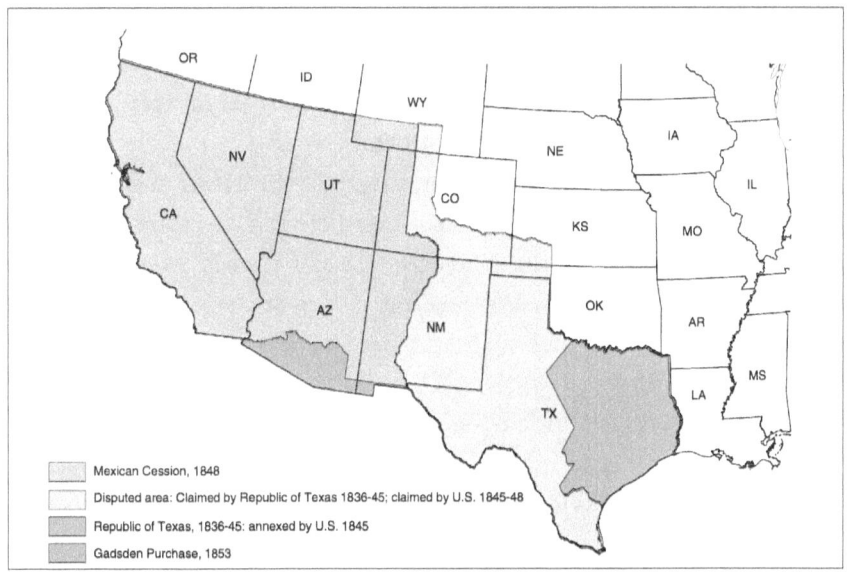

The Treaty of Guadalupe Hidalgo and the Gadsden Purchase or Treaty of Mesilla.
Map: Courtesy of the U. S. Geological Survey

parallels that railroad for mile after mile with little to break the traveler's view of the endless basin and range desert but palo verde, ocotillo, and mesquite framed by distant mountains.

Picking Up the Pieces

In late 1848 or early 1849, Second Lieutenant Padilla, now pardoned by the U.S. Army and released from duty in Ciudad Chihuahua, rode north up the Santa Maria Valley, through San Buenaventura, Galeana, over Chocolate Pass, then northwest to the Casas Grandes River and his duty station at Janos.[150]

Once again, Padilla set to work to reconstitute and reorganize the garrison. New unexpected challenges made his task even more complicated. Local conditions had changed dramatically. The border was now much closer. For as long as anyone could remember, the presidio's jurisdiction had extended north endlessly into wild empty land. Now another country was only a day's ride away, a country Padilla's soldiers technically could not enter. The Apaches could raid across the border and make it back, even with slow-moving herds of stolen stock before pursuers could catch up. The North Americans' inability to prevent cross-border raids led to draconian measures by the Mexican authorities.

Just after Padilla left for Chihuahua in 1847, the Mexican government established a new layer of administration between the state and *municipio*, called the *cantón*. The Janos and Casas Grandes *municipios* were part of the Galeana *cantón*. The new *jefe político* of Galeana, Captain José María Zuloaga, had established his headquarters at the family's Hacienda Corralitos.

The most famous or infamous land owner/entrepreneur/ politician in Chihuahua history is definitely Luis Terrazas. He served six times as the governor, apparently taking over the office or leaving it to others at his convenience. At the height of his power, he owned 7 million acres, banks, mines and every kind of commercial enterprise. No one ever equaled him, but the Zuloaga family was not far behind. The family patriarch, Carlos Zuloaga, bought the Corralitos Hacienda and its vast lands from the Azcárate heirs in the late 1830s.[151] He had four sons, José, Luis, Tomás, and Félix. Carlos must have been a proud father because all of his sons played important roles on the state or national scene in virtually all fields—economic, military, governmental, and judicial. Félix served as the country's president three different times.

The eldest, Captain José Zuloaga, a retired army officer, served briefly as Chihuahua's governor, but for most of the twenty-year period between 1847 and 1868 he held the position of jefe político for the Galeana cantón. His experiences as a frontier army captain, fighting the Apache, had left him with hatred so bitter that he advocated any measure to protect the family property and workers at Corralitos, including genocide.

Hacienda Corralitos, the First Hundred Years

Hacienda Corralitos is the longest continuously operating rancho in the Casas Grandes Valley. Even Captain Francisco Ramírez' older Hacienda Ramos must take second place because for many decades it was either abandoned or just a part of Corralitos.

Information about the early history of the ranch is a hazy mixture of human recall of long past events and scanty documentation. Sometime around 1775, the father of an El Paso merchant named Juan Azcárate, received a grant from the Spanish Crown that conveyed to him a large tract in the Casas Grandes Valley, El Rancho del Corralitos. Juan Azcárate's mother came from the powerful Ponce de León family, who owned a grant on the north side of the Rio Grande in the El Paso del Norte area. Most of the development of that important town had occurred on the south side of the river. After the boundary was established in the 1850s, subsequent to the Mexican-American War, El Paso expanded on the U.S. north side. Nine hundred acres from the Ponce de León grant became a core parcel of the new town. Two El Pasos was obviously confusing and the south side in Mexico became "Ciudad Juárez" in 1888.

Juan Azcárate inherited the Corralitos property in the early 1800s. He received significant returns from the mines and ranchos, enough that he and his wife Eugenia decided to move to the Spanish village of Corralitos, shaded by old cottonwood trees, along the east side of the Casas Grandes River. The little town lay about 150 miles southwest of El Paso. The name came from pens used by sheep herders. The Azcárates built a house they called Casa de Amo, House of the Master. This thick-walled structure is likely the ranch headquarters and owner's home that remains today. The couple had six children.

In 1828, a daughter, Juana María, married Hugh Stephenson a trader and miner from Mesilla, New Mexico. The record is not clear, but Stephenson apparently acquired from his Azcárate brothers-in-law mines in the Capulín Mountains near San Pedro Peak, eighteen miles east of ranch headquarters. He transported the ore to a smelter built just east of the Corralitos ranch-house compound. There he minted unique small-silver bars with his name and the value stamped into the surface. Although the Stephensons made a great deal of money from the mines, the family sold the ranch and mines to Carlos Zuloaga in the late 1830s.[152]

Captain José María Zuloaga took over Corralitos and made it his headquarters when he was appointed jefe político for the newly formed Galeana Cantón. For three decades he managed the hacienda and acted as genial host for travelers passing through or seeking refuge.

Throughout his stewardship, he fought, murdered, enslaved, and traded with Apaches. In that era of trading and raiding, he was often in conflict with Lieutenant Padilla, his tough subordinate at the Janos Presidio.

Mining had been conducted for a long time on Corralitos land. Miners Ángel and Mariano Aguirre had been working the old Spanish diggings and perhaps Stephenson's mines near San Pedro Peak when they discovered new high-quality silver ore. It is unclear what right the Aguirres had to prospect on Corralitos land, but in 1839 just after the Zuloagas bought Corralitos, the Aguirres sold their interest in the mine to the new owners.

The timing was good. Since the early 1800s, the operators of the Santa Rita del Cobre mine, east of today's Silver City, New Mexico, had shipped crudely smelted copper by mule train on the trail from New Mexico through Janos to the smelter at Corralitos. After further refining, the copper continued down the trail to Ciudad Chihuahua or on to Mexico City. How the Corralitos smelter owners were compensated is unknown. At about the same time, Apache attacks on Santa Rita and the mule trains completely shut down the mine, the trail, and the source of revenue to Corralitos. To offset the loss, Captain Zuloaga hired in 1838 the former leasee and manager of the Santa Rita Mine, Robert McKnight and his partner, the Frenchman Stephen Courcier, to operate the new San Pedro mine. McKnight, originally from Virginia, came west to Taos in 1812. Although New Mexico was far from the centers of the Mexican War of Independence, Spanish authorities were nervous and immediately arrested him as a spy. This could be dismissed as an act of petty xenophobia, but it might be true. McKnight was later charged in Chihuahua for selling guns to Apaches and trading for stolen stock. He associated with the infamous scalp hunter James Kirker, which was not a character recommendation. Whatever the truth, McKnight served almost nine years in prison. He was released, perhaps after Mexican authorities replaced the Spanish in Taos. McKnight eventually returned to New Mexico, became a Mexican citizen, and married Brigida Tigeros from Durango. Starting in 1828, he and Courcier had operated the Santa Rita mine successfully for nearly ten years.[153]

In spite of his dubious reputation, McKnight along with Courcier knew how to make a mine profitable. Not only did they develop a revenue source

Slag pile from the 19th century Corralitos smelter. Photo: 2018

for Zuloaga at San Pedro, but they also opened their own mine and built six smelters at Barranca Colorada four miles south of Corralitos.

Robert McKnight died in 1846. His son-in-law Lewis Flotte, who had worked for McKnight and married his daughter Refugio, took over the mine and smelters. John Russell Bartlett, the U.S.-Mexico boundary surveyor, visited Corralitos and Barranca Colorada. He wrote that Zuloaga and Flotte did not get along.[154] The frustrated Flotte was considering selling out, although he and Courcier had made a great deal of money. What happened to Flotte, Courcier, or their town and smelters is not known. Barranca Colorada disappeared. Local historians have located the site, but nothing remains of the community or the once prosperous smelting operation.[155]

The mining and cattle business at Corralitos continued to produce and grow. Captain José María Zuloaga can be criticized for his politics and his harsh techniques, but he managed to prosper during the era of the Apache wars when others failed. Most large land owners abandoned their properties and sold for low prices to Zuloaga or Luis Terrazas. When Captain Zuloaga died in 1868, he had expanded Corralitos to 1.5 million acres. His son, Carlos, named after the grandfather, assumed control.

Slavery had been outlawed in Mexico and it is not clear how much that abominable institution remained a part of the mid-19th century trading and raiding culture. Apaches still needed young men to replace fallen warriors, and all settler economic activity still depended on working hands. The role of captives and the trading of slaves to supply these needs may have diminished. However, there is little doubt that Zuloaga used prisoners captured by the scalp hunters to work his mines and smelter.[156] An eyewitness account from an odd source bears this out.

The Spy

The source was another unusual character, who arrived on the Casas Grandes scene during the postwar turmoil. Philippe Rondé was not a soldier, warrior, rancher or settler. He was a French artist, whose specialties were landscapes and church interiors. This unlikely candidate for the rigors of the Chihuahuan frontier decided to travel the world finding, painting, and recording obscure regions. Nowhere could have been more obscure (or dangerous) for a Parisian artist than the high plains of northern Chihuahua in 1849. Rondé and his companions suffered the expected physical hardships made worse by the constant fear of Indian attack. Their fears were realized at least once while camped on the Gila River in New Mexico. A few of the Apache leader Mangas Coloradas' warriors suddenly attacked. The surprised campers fought back, and when Mangas Coloradas came on the scene, he saw a small battle in progress. For reasons of his own, he called off his warriors. After a parlay, he ordered Rondé and his party out of the area, and they hurried south to Janos.[157] The near-death experience did not deter the artist.

Historians don't know quite what to make of Philippe Rondé. He wandered around the rugged country, seemingly without motive. A sufficient number of drawings and written reports have survived to give a good idea of where he went but little to explain why. Professor Jesús Valdés Vargas thinks Rondé might have been a spy for the French government. The French, British, and Spanish had a great interest in Mexico. Not only did these colonial powers have expansionist ideas, Mexico owed them a great deal of money. It makes a wonderful, romantic story to think of a French artist filing intelligence reports from remote corners of Chihuahua. France did invade Mexico ten years after Rondé left. What is known is that Rondé spent 25 years tramping the backcountry throughout the world and survived. With the eye of an artist (and perhaps of a spy) he left behind a rare word picture of the Hacienda Corralitos, a snapshot in time of the place and people.

In early August 1849, Rondé and a French companion were traveling along the Casas Grandes River when someone tried to steal their mules and they sought refuge at Corralitos. Captain José Zuloaga greeted them with the open hospitality of the Mexican ranchero. He had their mules cared for in his large stable and then invited the French travelers into his home. Zuloaga was 55 years old and the *patrón* for a town of about 400 vaqueros, miners, and their families. The town was laid out with four street entrances, north, south, east, and west, designed to discourage invaders. The main house was surrounded by a moat fed by the Casas Grandes River. Rondé said, "Like all haciendas of northern Mexico, Corralitos looks like a fortification ..." As the jefe político, Zuloaga had insisted that Lieutenant Padilla assign to him five soldiers and a sergeant. Rondé noted this must have weakened an already depleted garrison at the Janos presidio.

On the east side of the main house was the smelter, the "silver factory," as Rondé called it. There he saw five Apaches in shackles breaking up the silver ore. While they seemed to have adequate food and tobacco, they clearly were slaves. As described by Rondé, they represented a cross-section of Apache men of the era. One was docile and childlike, another crafty and deceiving, and a third an impassive, humorless warrior. The threat of incarceration in a nearby dungeon kept the Indians and presumably the other workers in line.

In describing the other workers, Rondé did not distinguish between mestizos and Indians living peacefully and working at Corralitos, referring to all as "peons." He did describe the feudal conditions of the haciendas, the absolute mastery of the patrón, and the life-long indebtedness of the peon to the "company store." The quality of their life depended on the personality of their patrón. Some he had observed in other places lived a miserable life. However, he said, "Mr. Zuloaga was loved by his workers; he had hired a schoolteacher and offered prayer in his church on Sundays."[158] Captain

Zuloaga appears to have had many approaches in his dealings with people from benevolent despotism to genocide. However, he was a generous host, and Philippe Rondé seems to have enjoyed his hospitality before deciding to move north on an unexplained mission.

The Reluctant Surveyor

Almost exactly three years after Rondé's departure, another traveler arrived at Corralitos to enjoy Captain Zuloaga's hospitality. This time it was a North American. John Russell Bartlett had been appointed by President Polk to head the Mexican-United States Boundary Commission, established in accordance with Article Five of the Treaty of Guadalupe Hidalgo. The article called for a Commission to conduct surveys and reach an agreement with Mexican counterparts to define the specific geographic location of the new international boundary. Bartlett was a well-known historian, linguist, ethnographer, bibliographer, and politician, but not a surveyor. This was strictly a political assignment. It was his connections with the Whig party that secured the appointment. The expedition included soldiers, surveyors, engineers, scientists, supplies and relevant equipment. The expedition had what it needed, but Bartlett's tenure as commissioner was characterized by dissension and poor results.

The thirty-man party left New York by ship on August 3, 1850. They landed at the now-abandoned port of Indianola, Texas twenty-seven days later and proceeded overland to El Paso. There, with General Pedro García Conde, the Mexican commissioner, they began work on December 3. García Conde was the son of Alejo García Conde, who had played such a significant role as the last commandant of Nueva Vizcaya in the Spanish era.

The survey efforts were not successful. The final Conde-Bartlett report placed the boundary several miles north of El Paso. This of course favored Mexico. General Conde had done his job, but it appears Bartlett was inattentive and had not. Congress and all other involved U.S. officials rejected the report out of hand. It took six more years of commission surveys and negotiations to settle the boundary location. Bartlett was relieved and replaced by a Democrat appointee from the Fillmore administration.

While the surveying work was taking place, Bartlett had a wonderful time traveling at taxpayer expense, painting and writing about matters unrelated to the survey. That turned out to be his legacy. He wrote a two-volume work about the geography, flora, and fauna of the U.S. southwest and Mexican northwest that has stood the test of time.[159] Nineteenth-century travelers through the region used it as a guide, and scientists and historians ever since have found it useful. It is ironic that Bartlett's name is always associated with the Mexican-American boundary survey while the names of those who did the real work are obscure historical footnotes.

On one of his diversions away from the survey work, Bartlett and his companions, including artist Henry Cheever Pratt (30 prints of his paintings appear in Bartlett's volumes), headed southeast across a broad plain toward a row of cottonwood trees that marked the Casas Grandes River. He noted the rich farmland near the river, which was fallow due to the shortage of oxen to cultivate the fields. He did not explain, but Apaches presumably ran off the stock. It was the rainy season and the river was about one hundred yards wide. They found a ford and crossed their animals without mishap. They rode on to the Corralitos, where they camped for the night. Captain Zuloaga was away, but in the morning, his superintendent graciously showed him the town and smelter. The superintendent said that three weeks before three men had been killed by Apaches while driving a herd of mules and cattle. The herd was stolen, but there was no one available to pursue.

Bartlett described the town much as Rondé did with the same estimate of population. However, he said most of the residents were dependent on mining as the fields lay untilled. The streets were full of muddy holes and wallowing pigs. The people looked sickly. He attributed this to the arsenic fumes from the smelter that pervaded the area. Although the smelter seemed primitive, it produced a great deal of silver from ore brought in carts from the San Pedro mine, eighteen miles away. The smelter workers stoked the furnaces with mesquite roots, the only available fuel.

In the afternoon, the Bartlett party rode four miles south along the river to Barranca Colorada. This was the village with six smelters started by Robert McKnight and Lewis Flotte, his son-in-law. McKnight had died and Flotte was in charge. Bartlett was impressed with Barranca Colorada's more extensive smelters. He noted that the large bellows pumping air into the six furnaces were powered by machinery driven by mules perpetually walking in a circle, a *rastra*.

They stayed in the area a few more days, making an excursion, August 10, 1852, to Casas Grandes and Paquimé. He made revealing observations about Casas Grandes and the people living there. The town had about 400 inhabitants. He emphasized they were strictly farmers, with fields of corn and grain and orchards around the town. They shipped their products to El Paso and Ciudad Chihuahua. The people were industrious and physically in much better condition than those breathing arsenic fumes near the smelters.[160] Apaches still raided and Bartlett saw graves of their victims along the trail to Corralitos, The settlers of Casas Grandes were surviving but things would get worse.

The Fifth Law

One of the draconian measures adopted by the Chihuahuan government to address the Apache problem was the Fifth Law. No one knows exactly where Governor Trías stood on the matter, but Captain Zuloaga had enough political influence to convince the Chihuahua legislature in May 1849, to enact what became known as the "Fifth Law." This law legitimized and codified scalp hunting as official state policy. It provided a schedule of payments for the scalps of men, women, children and prisoners. Zuloaga's headquarters at Corralitos became one of the receiving and payment stations. The notorious James Kirker and his cohorts were back in business with legal sanction.

Lieutenant Padilla, senior officer at the Janos Presidio, now reported to el jefe político Zuloaga and they immediately came into conflict.[161] Padilla preferred to negotiate whenever possible even if the Apache negotiators were not sincere. Buying time with "bad peace" was better than the brutal tactics of the Fifth Law that brought stepped-up levels of revenge. Besides, most of the settlers still needed to trade, particularly for stock.

The Apache were the main supplier of horses and mules in the Casas Grandes and Santa Maria Valleys. Some of these animals had been through so many owners legally and illegally that their branded sides must have looked like graffiti on a wall. Even Zuloaga traded when he found it to his advantage. He still forbade Padilla to negotiate and ordered indiscriminate killing, and capture. After decades of trading and raiding, some Apache individuals and families were content to live peacefully near the presidio in settlements called *rancherias*. The degree of sincerity for genuine peace varied but nevertheless existed. Padilla understood these subtleties. Captain Zuloaga and enforcers such as Kirker did not or did not care.

Not surprisingly, these policies led to a change in the attitude of Apache leadership. The Apaches had always distinguished between raiding for necessary economic purposes and warfare based on revenge.[162] The more they felt the pressure of the Fifth Law, the more the Apaches attacked for pure revenge and their revenge was as brutal as the scalp hunters.

Mangas Coloradas

Lieutenant Padilla and his garrison now faced a new generation of leaders with Mangas Coloradas one of the most formidable. He hated Mexicans and they hated him, all with good reason. Just after Lieutenant Padilla and the garrison company left for Ciudad Chihuahua in July 1846, to fight the U.S. invasion, Zuloaga organized a group of volunteers from Janos, Casas Grandes, and Corralitos, all who felt they had scores to settle with the Apaches. There were reports from Galeana that the Apaches had paraded in town wearing jewelry and bloody clothing that residents recognized as belonging to recent victims. Zuloaga's group joined James Kirker's band of scalp hunters and rode to a rendezvous near Galeana. Local residents lured over 100 Apaches living nearby into town with promises of food and alcohol. The Indians had a grand fiesta, dancing and drinking themselves into a stupor. At dawn, when they were virtually helpless, Zuloaga and Kirker gave the order. Vengeful settlers and professional killers surrounded the Indians and opened fire. Not bothering to reload, they charged into helpless mass, stabbing and clubbing men, women, and children indiscriminately. The literal smashing of a baby in a nearby church became a particular point of vengeance for Mangas Coloradas when he heard the news from the few survivors who had straggled back to his camp.

After the funeral rites and days of mourning, Apache leaders met for several days with Mangas Coloradas to hear the survivor stories and to plan the inevitable retaliation. They planned well, ensuring their warriors were adequately armed and stimulated by war dances and even a mock battle. In late fall they fell on an unsuspecting Galeana, shooting as many residents as possible as they emerged from their houses and running down others on horseback and stabbing them with lances. Predictably, many died or suffered terrible wounds, and of course Zuloaga and Kirker were not present (James Kirker actually died in bed in Contra Costa, California in 1852, a respected citizen of his community). The Apaches had their revenge, and everyone prepared for the next cycle of violence. Several young warriors distinguished themselves in the battle/massacre including Mangas Coloradas' son-in-law Cochise and a warrior known in later years as Gerónimo.[163]

This example of pure vengeance warfare is particularly egregious, but it graphically demonstrates the situation Padilla found when he brought the remnants of his cavalry company back to Janos in early 1849. For the next eight years, he did the best he could with what he had. The central government in Mexico could not finance many soldiers, and not many wanted to be posted to this remote, dangerous land. Desertions were common. For the tenacious Padilla there was one consolation. In November 1854, after 26 years of active, arduous combat service, Lieutenant José Baltazar Padilla was promoted to the rank of captain. He was 49 years old.

While the cycle of trading, raiding, and negotiation repeated itself, the pendulum had definitely swung in the direction of the Apaches. The major settlements in the Casas Grandes and Santa Maria Valleys hung on, but many properties were abandoned. In 1855, Padilla, while chasing Apaches, rode through Hacienda de Ramos and found it totally abandoned.[164]

Since about 1850, Mangas Coloradas had emerged as the overall leader of the diverse bands of Chiricahua Apache. A huge man, said to have been six feet six inches tall, he commanded respect from the fiercely independent Apaches. As a fighter against enemies on both sides of the border, he was one of the great Native Americans. He orchestrated several raids that were almost military expeditions, riding with his warriors deep into Sonora as far as Hermosillo and back through the mountains into Chihuahua. He usually left Janos and the Casas Grandes Valley unharmed, perhaps because Gerónimo and the warrior Juh at the time camped near Janos with their families.

During his wide-ranging excursions north of the border in the U.S., he observed miners, fur hunters, and soldiers on the trails, and he sometimes met with them. Once he encountered General Stephen Watts Kearny and his expeditionary force on the way to California. The arms and discipline of the U.S. troopers impressed Mangas Coloradas.

Just after the war, the discovery of gold in California stimulated a mass migration of would-be miners. Some tried to reach the gold field by following the old trails across Chihuahua. They were easy prey, but he had little interest in them. His hatred was directed toward Mexicans. He seems genuinely to have wanted peace with the North Americans.

The sticking point that ruined any chance of agreement was raiding across the border into Mexico. In his mind, any peace agreement with the North Americans should permit the Chiricahua to attack their mutual enemy across the new border and retreat comfortably back to safety. The Apaches would leave North Americans alone, and everyone wins. He was quite willing to accept the U.S. Army's long list of conditions except one. Army negotiators insisted on enforcing Article Eleven of the Treaty of Guadalupe, which guaranteed Mexico protection from Indian assault. To Mangas Coloradas, this made no sense. Hadn't the U.S. Army just defeated the Mexicans? They were the enemy. This misunderstanding between the two cultures soon became a source of death and destruction on the U.S. side of the border and opened the final chapter of the Apache wars.

By the start of the U.S. Civil War in 1860, all thoughts of a negotiated peace were over. The Chiricahua Apaches were engaged in serious attacks on towns, mines, ranches, stage coaches, and mule trains in southern Arizona. Led initially by Mangas Coloradas and later by son-in-law Cochise, aided by a new generation including Victorio, Juh, Nana, and Gerónimo, they literally drove the settlers of all races out of what they considered Apache land in southeastern Arizona. Settlers, miners, and ranchers simply abandoned towns, mines, and ranches, leaving the Apache in full control.

On July 15, 1862, in one famous battle in Apache Pass, north of the Chiricahua Mountains, Mangas Coloradas, now in his seventies, organized an ambush of U.S. Army soldiers. This was a detachment of a regiment of California volunteers that had marched to New Mexico to combat a takeover by Confederate rebels. A desperate trooper firing from behind his dead horse hit Mangas Coloradas in the chest. The warriors now became more concerned about their badly wounded leader than the fight even though the battle lasted the rest of the day and into the night. The well-trained soldiers, after the initial shock and the loss of several men, had retreated to defensible positions in the rocks. At daybreak, they brought up two small cannon. The additional heavy fire broke up the attack.

The warriors knew of a Mexican doctor in Janos. Getting Mangas Coloradas to that doctor became their objective. Somehow, these resourceful nomads transported their wounded chieftain through the southern Arizona desert into Sonora and across the mountains to Janos. They rode into town and took all of the surprised residents as hostages. The doctor appeared and they made it clear to him that he must save their leader or everyone in town would die. With this incentive, he extracted the bullet, and dressed the wound. The old warrior survived.[165]

This unusual story offers hints about life in the remote presidio town and raises questions. It appears that a competent doctor lived and worked at Janos. Who was he? Were trained doctors common at the frontier presidios? Captain Padilla did not list him on his rosters, which suggests he was not military. There undoubtedly was a great need at Janos for treating wounds and setting bones of the soldiers and settlers. Did he treat Apaches regularly? The Arizona warriors seemed to know him and made an extreme effort to get their wounded leader into his care.

However interesting it is to contemplate these questions, the fact is that Mangas Coloradas survived but not for long. Back in Arizona, he tried to negotiate with the U.S. Army commanding officer at Pinos Altos, one of the few towns the Army still controlled. The officer was in no mood for talk with one he regarded as a killer. He ordered the old man put in the fort's prison cell where the guards mistreated and eventually shot him.

Mangas Coloradas was indeed a killer, but he possessed remarkable qualities and was a great leader of his people. This was a shabby ending for such a man.

6

—

National Politics and
The End of the Apache Trail

The Last Muster

On April 1, 1858, Captain José Baltazar Padilla mustered the Janos Presidio garrison for the last time. He left no record of his thoughts as he reviewed the remnants of the command he had served for eighteen years. He did leave a carefully prepared muster list of the 30 officers and men present and accounted for, including a bugler and an armorer. He noted the names of thirty-two additional soldiers that had recently left military service to avoid the political coups brewing in Mexico City. The garrison had been ordered the previous month to leave the presidio and march in support of one of the conservative factions quarrelling with the liberals in the capital. Half of the Janos troops opted out.[166] Most in Chihuahua were sympathetic to these former soldiers. What happened in Mexico City did not concern them. Those in power in the center of the country, safe for centuries from Indian attack, had never paid sufficient attention to those living under the constant threat of violence. The Chihuahuans had enough on their hands to care about coups and counter coups in the capital hundreds of miles away.

The jefe político, José Zuloaga, did not share these feelings for good reason. His brother Félix had engineered the coup and was now president. Zuloaga obeyed the order, assembled the remaining loyal troops and left for Mexico City. Presumably Captain Padilla rode at his side. The Janos presidio closed. When Félix Zuloaga was ousted by a second conservative coup, José Zuloaga returned to Corralitos in 1860 to resume his duties but Captain Padilla did not. After years of loyal service, this capable soldier disappears from the pages of history.

In retrospect, perhaps the Chihuahuans should have paid more attention to central politics. Their presidio at Janos was gone along with its soldiers. However, the local people of the Casas Grandes Valley had been dealing with the Apaches for a long time. Armed settlers, *vecinos*, some former soldiers, filled the gap left by the Mexican military. Captain José Zuloaga at Corralitos was still in command as jefe político of the Galeana Cantón. Other leaders emerged from the armed settlers, including Juan Mata Ortiz. Another was Joaquín Terrazas, a cousin of Luis Terrazas. Juan Mata Ortiz came from Galeana in the Santa María Valley. He had been fighting Apaches since his teens. After José Zuloaga died in 1868, he became the Galeana Cantón jefe político.

The State of the Union

Politics in Mexico City remained in a convoluted standoff between extreme conservative and liberal interests, overshadowed by a consistently empty treasury. Little of substance could be accomplished. When one of the many presidents took action, it usually had unforeseen consequences that made matters worse. The Church retained vast power and owned a significant amount of the productive land. In spite of recent setbacks, the army retained power and privileges beyond the control of civil authority.

When war with the U.S. ended in 1848, Santa Anna went into exile and liberals took over the central government. They tried to govern responsibly, but entrenched special interests, huge debt, and open rebellion in various corners of the country overcame their best intentions. The conservatives, made up of Church leaders, army officers, wealthy *criollo* landowners, and the holders of government debt, pushed hard for a strong, authoritarian central government. They even talked of bringing back a European king. Finally, and hard to believe, they opted once again for General Antonio López de Santa Anna.

Once again, the Mexican people looked to this charismatic purveyor of many of their worst disasters. Santa Anna received the word in Venezuela, where he was living in exile on a hacienda. He took a ship to Veracruz, arriving to great fanfare at the port city in April 1853. The conservatives already had forced out the liberal president, and Santa Anna assumed duty as president/dictator with sweeping powers. This, his last run at managing the country, was predictable. He centralized the government, reducing the power and independence of the states. He enlarged the army, and clamped down on liberalism in any form, including the press. His most famous act during this period was the sale of southern Arizona to the U.S., the Gadsden Purchase. This put much-needed money in the treasury, but he proceeded to loot the proceeds for his own self-aggrandizement. A serious issue for him was his own title. After careful consideration, he decided that His Most Supreme Highness was appropriate. After less than two years, the enthusiasm for Santa Anna had vanished along with the money. Rebellion again swept the country. This time it would be different.

The criollos, Church, and military had co-opted the War of Independence thirty-five years before. Liberal thinkers and leaders starting with Hidalgo and Morelos had ended up in front of firing squads, but their ideas survived. A new generation, now mostly from the mestizo classes and including some Indians, began to clamor for reform. Their ideas covered the entire list of liberal-democracy concepts that philosophers and politicians had been fomenting since the Enlightenment. Some of the thinking was sound and some completely idealistic and impractical for a largely illiterate agrarian society. One common thread was racial equality and even a glorification of Aztec ancestry. This was in a society still gripped by the old Spanish casta prejudices. Also basic to the calls for reform were confiscation and redistribution of Church lands and subservience of the army to civil authority. Various opposition leaders emerged after the last conservative debacle with Santa Anna. Among them was a Zapotec Indian lawyer from Oaxaca named Benito Juárez.

Plans, Proclamations, and Constitutions

While Santa Anna ruled, two liberal leaders, Juan Álvarez, a follower of Morelos, and Ignacio Comonfort, a famous guerilla leader and key figure in the opposition to Santa Anna, prepared a plan. They wanted to temporally reorganize the government until another constitutional convention could be held and a new constitution drafted. Their Plan of Ayutla became a widespread rallying cry. Santa Anna made half-hearted attempts to quell the rising rebellion. But he knew how the system worked. In spite of his flaws, His Most Supreme Highness was a canny manipulator, a political survivor, and he knew it was time to get out. In August 1855, he wrote out his abdication and slipped out of the country on a steamship back to Venezuela. The era of General Antonio López de Santa Anna was over. He lived twenty more years, always trying without success to reinsert himself back into the political scene. He died in 1876, an event ignored by the Mexican people.[167]

His sudden departure left a temporary vacuum that was quickly filled. At a meeting in Cuernavaca, chaired by the liberal elder statesman, Gómez Farías, Juan Álvarez was named president. He had been a leader in every liberal rebellion for 40 years and was revered as a champion of the lower castas. As a sign of the times, he made the traditional grand entry into Mexico City escorted by a contingent of Indians (not Apache). It was a fine gesture as Indians from all parts of the country still represented almost half of the population. As with so many of the liberal actions of this time, the unintended consequence was to frighten the well-off criollos and mestizos and solidify their opposition.

As had many before him, Juan Álvarez soon found it was easier to rebel than to govern. Shortly after reaching the capital in November 1855, he turned the presidency over to Ignacio Comonfort. This selfless man and his new administration went to work. They issued a proclamation that became known as *Ley Lerdo*. The intent was to strip the Church of its haciendas and other vast landholdings. Benito Juárez, the new Minister of Justice, issued another proclamation abolishing the long-held independent judicial powers of the Church and army. Juárez not only could issue proclamations, he was also a tough administrator. He immediately began to enforce what became known as *Ley Juárez*. A constitutional convention, made up mostly of criollo and mestizo intellectuals, began to work. After more than a year of meetings, the idealistic result produced in early 1858, antagonized most everyone.

Despite the best of intentions by the new reformers, the almost insurmountable problems that had made Mexico dysfunctional since independence had not gone away. The conservatives remained intransient, willing to go to war rather than compromise. The proclamations and *leys* incorporated into the constitution made sense in a perfect world but often made matters worse in the decidedly imperfect Mexican political scene. The idealistic constitutional convention members wanted to limit executive power at a time when a strong executive was crucial to holding the nation together. The attempt to strip the Church of its lands had the unintended result of allowing large estates to pass into the hands of foreigners and to hacendados already rich with land.

One particularly grotesque unintended consequence resulted from language in the *Ley Lerdo* regarding taking property from the Church. This language could be construed to apply to communal *ejido* and Indian lands as well. Unscrupulous local politicians used the *ley* to take lands that had been held in common, in some cases for centuries. The very people the reformers vowed to protect were protesting against the reforms and threatening to take up arms against the government.

The powerful hold the Catholic Church still had on the Mexican people at all levels remained a major obstacle to real reform. The Church wielded the threat of excommunication, a terrible weapon that affected even many liberals. Executives and congress waffled when it came to enforcing the *leys* against the Church.

Conservative reactionaries saw their opportunity. Through a set of convoluted machinations, Comonfort was forced into exile. Benito Juárez was declared president but was driven out and barely escaped with his life. After a long run through Mexico, Panama, and the United States, he ended up in the liberal stronghold of Veracruz. In Mexico City, Félix Zuloaga, with the support of his powerful Chihuahuan family, declared himself president. This was early 1858. The country now had two presidents and a civil war—The War of Reform.

War of Reform

The history of Mexico is laced with ideological, racial, economic, and social conflicts that degenerated into bloody civil wars. Many detailed accounts have been written about some of these including the War of Independence, the French Intervention, and the Revolution of 1910. Not as often covered by historians but of comparable importance to the evolution of Mexico as a nation, were the terrible years of the War of Reform, also known as the Three Years War.

Ideas that began in the Enlightenment and were nurtured and expanded by 16th-18th century French and English philosophers, Thomas Jefferson, and the leaders of North American, French, and South American revolutions, gained traction in Mexico. These ideas ran headlong into an entrenched feudal-like society. Although the three years of war became a confused mess of conflicting adversaries and factions, the basic objectives were clear. Conservatives fought to preserve an old-world order that had existed for centuries. Liberals, taking up the cause of the common man, fought for change and a new way of life. It was a defining moment in Mexico's history and the country would never be the same.

The war set a new standard for brutality, including mass killing of prisoners, unusual even to a country somewhat numb to the horrors of internal warfare. Better led, better armed, and better financed, the conservatives won decisively most of the pitched battles in the various states. They controlled the towns but faced intensive guerilla action in the hostile countryside—a situation that has confounded aggressors worldwide for all time. And the liberal armies always returned. Their commander, General Santos Degollado, became famous as the "hero of defeats." After each, he always reorganized and came back for more.[168] This persistence became a hallmark of the new liberal leadership, particularly of Mexico's most revered leader of all time, Benito Juárez. Historian Henry Bamford Parkes describes him eloquently:

"In this crisis, Benito Juárez, who had become the symbol of constitutional government, began to display a moral grandeur unequalled by any other Mexican before or since. He was surrounded by men of greater intellectual brilliance. Juárez, the small dark-skinned Indian from the mountains of Oaxaca, relied on them for advice, distrusting his own intellectual capacities; he spoke rarely and with hesitation. Yet he had, in a superlative degree, what Mexico supremely needed: undeviating honesty, and an indomitable will which never would accept compromise or defeat. To the European ideology of liberalism, he brought an Indian simplicity and persistence, and the unending courage with which, three centuries before, Cuauhtémoc had resisted Cortés."[169]

The quotation describes in a few words the social force that defeated the conservatives and changed Mexico.

The Church financed the conservatives, but as the war wore on, the centuries-long accumulation of gold, silver, and precious stones was dissipated. The liberals, some responsible to the Juárez government and others no more than opportunistic looters, plundered the Church properties to either help pay the bills or enrich themselves. Juárez issued the Laws of Reform of July 1859 that authorized confiscation of all Church property except the actual church structures. Starting with implementation of the *Ley Lerdo* (Miguel de Lerdo de Tejada also drafted the new Laws of Reform) Church lands, wealth, and power diminished dramatically. The new Laws dealt the final blow. Mexico would remain a primarily Catholic country to the present day, but the distinction between church and state had been made.

Worn down, out of money, and constantly pestered by guerillas, the conservative armies began to lose battles. One particularly effective guerilla leader in the south was a young, former law student from Oaxaca named Porfirio Díaz. Finally on December 22, 1860, at San Miguel Calpulalpan northwest of Mexico City, the last conservative army was routed by General Jesús González Ortega, who had replaced General Degollado, now retired with his record of defeats intact. Following tradition, General González Ortega, resplendent in a dress uniform, led the victorious liberal army in a grand procession through the cheering mobs of Mexico City. A few days later, President Benito Juárez, wearing a plain black suit, rode quietly into the city in a black carriage.

Reform in Chihuahua

To the settlers of the Casas Grandes and Santa María Valleys, the fact that much of the country had torn itself apart in the War of Reform was largely irrelevant. They still were consumed by their own wars with the Apaches. Politics in the state capital, Ciudad Chihuahua, had remained conservative. Except for the ten-year term of Don Ángel Trías, the governorship had been a revolving door of short timers similar to the presidents in Mexico City. Those growing up in the northern valleys looked to themselves not the government for the resources to survive. From this, a new, frontier style of liberalism began to grow. Young influential Chihuahuans like Luis Terrazas and his cousin Joaquín Terrazas resented the oppression of the Church and army as much as the followers of Benito Juárez. Also, they resented invaders from anywhere. This new Chihuahua-style liberalism surfaced when a fanatically religious conservative general from the state of Durango marched into Ciudad Chihuahua. The Chihuahuans reacted violently. Vecino guerillas, led by Juan José Méndez, Luis Terrazas, and Joaquín Terrazas entered the city, fought through the streets, virtually annihilating the Durango force.

Chihuahua would never be considered radically liberal, but reform ideas entered the mix. Old conservatives like Don Ángel Trías, who even supported Santa Anna, turned to the Chihuahua version of the liberal cause.

In 1860, the federal government appointed Luis Terrazas at age 31 as Chihuahua's governor. While he had been promoted to the rank of colonel, he was technically too young to be governor. Benito Juárez 's congress made an exception. Exceptions would become the trademark for Terrazas's remarkable career. He would dominate Chihuahua for the next 50 years and become the second most famous name in Chihuahua history. The most famous would be a bandit/rebel, who became Terrazas's mortal enemy.

The Constitution of 1857 gave the federal government the power to select and depose the state governors.[170] This meant the new governor served at the pleasure of Juárez. Like virtually all of those sitting in Mexico City since Independence, Juárez ignored Chihuahua and its requests for help. He even criticized the northerners for not dealing adequately with the Apaches on their own.

Juárez did have other immediate problems that dominated his attention. The French had invaded and were in the process of making an Austrian archduke the Emperor of Mexico. In 1864, Juárez ordered Governor Terrazas to send him 2,000 men. Faced with Apaches probing Chihuahua's every weakness, Terrazas could not raise or send away a force that large. Apaches were not Juárez 's problem. He removed Terrazas and appointed the reliable but somewhat conflicted Don Ángel Trías again as governor.

As part of his orders, he had to confiscate property belonging to his friend Terrazas.

The French landed at Veracruz and marched on Mexico City forcing President Juárez to flee again, this time to the north. In another of the ironies of northern Chihuahua history, the president, who has provided no resources, only criticism to the north, now sought refuge among its people.

In Ciudad Chihuahua, they welcomed him with a parade route decorated with flowers and flags. An honor guard led by Joaquín Terrazas preceded the simple, black presidential carriage. Cousin Luis, out of political favor, was hiding out in El Paso. A brief, quiet speech at Hidalgo's monument solidified Juárez's hold on the people. Even though he had ignored their problems, lost most of the country to the French, and was a fugitive, he was their president. The day was October 12, 1864, a date destined by ironic coincidence to become *El Día de la Raza* in Latin America and Columbus Day in the U.S.

Juárez and his cabinet established their government-in-exile in Chihuahua in a building known today as Juárez 321. They governed and guided the resistance as best they could from there or from a refuge in El Paso for the next two years.

Another Emperor, Maximiliano

All through the battles between conservatives and liberals, dreams of monarchy had never gone away. Certain clergymen, upper casta members, and followers of Santa Anna worked quietly to convince the governments of Europe that Mexico was ready to be ruled by a European monarch. Britain, France, and Spain felt free to meddle, because Mexico owed them a great deal of money. When President Juárez, with nothing in the treasury, suspended payments, the three countries reacted by occupying Veracruz in a joint operation in January 1862. Confederate forces had fired on Fort Sumter the previous April. It is unlikely the three European powers would have so blatantly challenged the Monroe Doctrine if the United States was not so preoccupied.

Britain and Spain wanted bond payments resumed and a long list of other claims resolved. Somehow, they thought occupation of Mexico's major port and source of custom revenues would secure their position. France had other ideas.

Napoleon III, emperor of France, wanted to occupy Mexico. Influenced by Mexican monarchist exiles, he believed he could create in Mexico a monarchy headed by a European prince under his control. His motive was partly the classic political use of foreign intervention to divert the people from problems at home and partly to control Mexico's trade and assets. Napoleon was particularly interested in Mexico's still productive silver mines. He selected Archduke Ferdinand Maximilian as the future emperor, the younger brother of Franz Joseph of the Hapsburg Austrian Empire. Napoleon considered this a brilliant choice. Maximilian and his wife Charlotte (Carlotta), daughter of the King of Belgium, made an attractive couple with impeccable royal credentials. Hapsburg kings of Spain had colonized Mexico, and this would return a golden age. More practically, use of the Austrian prince as a surrogate would solidify Napoleon's sometimes shaky relationship with Austria. When the British and Spanish realized what Napoleon was doing, they left Veracruz.

Undeterred, the French landed 6,000 battle-tested troops at the port. They marched west following Cortez's route to Mexico City. The commanding general was led to believe that a show of force would cause the people to rise up and join him against the Juárez government. On the way, he had to subdue the major city of Puebla. Juárez put Ignacio Zaragoza, his Minister of War, in charge of the city's defenses. Zaragoza had risen through the ranks to become an effective general for the liberal cause. He prepared well, turning every church into a fort manned by a hodgepodge of Mexican troops, numbering only 4,000.[171] In another twist of history, Zaragoza's artillery consisted of cannons captured by the British from Napoleon I at Waterloo in 1815. Mexico bought them from the British in 1824 just after Independence.[172] They were old but still worked. The French general ordered a direct assault. His experienced troops, thinking this would be easy, charged into a storm of fire from the old cannons. As they fell back, Zaragoza counterattacked. His cavalry, all skilled Mexican horsemen swinging their swords, rode into the flank of the retreating mass of French soldiers before they could reform. Estimates of French losses vary between 500 and 1,000. Whatever the figure, it was a rout. The Mexicans lost eighty-six. One of the cavalry leaders, a young general named Porfirio Díaz, gained personal fame from this legendary charge.

Eleven months later, a French army of 30,000 with a new general laid siege to Puebla and forced the starving defenders to surrender. A few Mexicans escaped including Porfirio Díaz, who took command of the resistance in Oaxaca. On June 10, 1863, the French army marched into Mexico City unopposed. Napoleon's forces controlled the central government.

Napoleon's initial defeat and subsequent victory at Puebla exposed to the world the defects of his plan and set up ultimate defeat.

Puebla helped unite a dispirited war-weary people behind a single cause—repel the invader. Ignacio Zaragoza died of typhoid fever not long after the battle. The country hailed him as one of the great heroes in Mexican history. Countless plazas, streets, and communities bear his name, including at least two northern Chihuahua towns. The battle also elevated Porfirio Díaz to national prominence, opening the way for his later moves to political power.

This was the time for Napoleon to back away and cut his losses. Maximilian himself wavered, not sure of the plan. He had not yet left Austria. Had he backed out, he probably would have lived a long, contented life with Charlotte, ruling some small kingdom. National pride and misinformation caused both Napoleon and Maximilian to continue the takeover of Mexico. They made the mistake governments would repeat through the next century—trying to occupy and rule a country where they were not wanted.

Maximilian, now *Maximiliano,* did the best he could, which was considerably short of good enough. He did not actually arrive in Mexico City until June 10, 1864. The French army continued to spread its control over the country. Their difficulty came when the occupying troops moved out of a subdued city or region, Juárez 's people moved right back in, displacing whatever local monarchial administration the French had left behind. Also, it turned out that the new Emperor was quite progressive. He believed in the common man, and he refused, among other things, to return the estates and control of the school system to the Church. He already was at war with Juárez and the liberals. Now he alienated the conservative elements that had engineered his monarchy. Then came a crippling blow.

General Lee's surrender at Appomattox ended the Civil War and allowed Lincoln to turn his attention to Mexico. He forcefully suggested to Napoleon that this would be a good time to leave Mexico. The French emperor did not want a fight with the U.S., and he had had enough of Mexico anyway. He gave the order. Throughout 1866, French units withdrew from occupied areas and embarked for home. There were complicated machinations involving other European governments, but essentially Maximilian was left holding the bag. He should have abdicated, but he struggled on for another year. He did have a Mexican army led in part by Belgian and Austrian officers that had some success. It was not enough. Backed by U.S. arms shipments, the Mexican resistance, led by the relentless Juárez, grew stronger, controlling more territory and gradually closing in on Mexico City. Porfirio Díaz organized an army that captured Oaxaca. Gaining more fighters, he marched north on Puebla. As Juárez's forces closed in, the young emperor went to Querétaro and personally and bravely led the remnants of his army in a last battle. After making a final stand on a rocky hill, *El Cerro de las Campanas*, the Hill of the Bells, he and a few loyal officers were captured.

Heads of state around the world sent messages to Juárez asking that Maximilian be spared. The unrelenting president was adamant. A clear message must be sent to every world power to never again consider intervention in Mexico. On June 19, 1867, the second emperor of Mexico stood before a firing squad on El Cerro de las Campanas not far from where he was captured. The site is now a national park.

For the second time, President Benito Juárez wearing his black coat rode through the streets of Mexico City in a black carriage.

The Battle of Chihuahua

Two years before, in the spring of 1865, French troops arrived and occupied Ciudad Chihuahua. Juárez, who had been operating his government-in-exile there, fled to El Paso with his cabinet. French occupation of Mexico never extended much farther north than Ciudad Chihuahua. Maximilian knew if the U.S. took sides against his monarchy, it would be a serious problem. He ordered the army not to go more than a day's ride north of the city to avoid any antagonizing border incidents.[173] The clergy and a group of monarchists greeted the French as saviors, but most Chihuahuans deeply resented the invaders. Initially they did not resist. They were too preoccupied with the Apaches, and the French had a strong force.

During the first years of the French intervention Joaquín Terrazas and Juan Mata Ortiz led citizen militias on campaigns against the Apaches. With the death of Mangas Coloradas, Cochise had emerged as the dominant leader of the Chiricahua. Even though Cochise raided mercilessly through the decade of the 1860s, often accompanied by the tough, stocky Juh, he usually left the Casas Grandes Valley settlements alone. He preferred to steal stock in other regions, particularly Sonora, and drive the animals to Janos, Corralitos, or Casas Grandes to trade for what they needed including bullets and powder. The settlers then would sell the stolen stock across the border to North Americans. Trading ammunition was a big issue. Sonorans and North Americans complained about this trade. A U.S. Army colonel, chasing Apaches south of the border, confronted José Zuloaga at Corralitos about it. Zuloaga, who, depending on the circumstances, was happy to kill, enslave, or trade with the Chiricahua, denied everything.[174]

During 1864, Joaquín Terrazas stopped campaigning against the Apaches and began re-assembling his vecinos into an army to resist the French. Somewhere, he obtained artillery pieces, probably from the U.S. Abraham Lincoln admired Benito Juárez and always was sympathetic to the Mexican resistance as was his Commanding General Ulysses S. Grant. As the Union Army developed a surplus of arms toward the end of the war, Grant suggested to General Philip Sheridan, the commander in Texas, that he might "lose" some of the surplus arms along the border.[175] Juárez bought many more modern weapons as they became available in the U.S. Whether any of these "lost" weapons left along the Texas-Chihuahua border fell into the hands of Terrazas's force is unknown.

The French occupation troops left Ciudad Chihuahua in February 1866, leaving control of the city and region to a small army of Mexican monarchists. Luis and Joaquín saw this as their time to openly resist and take back their state and its capital. Luis assumed the title "general" and took command of the 550 armed men assembled by Joaquín.

The hill in Ciudad Chihuahua called Cerro Grande today features a large, white cross as well as a grand view of the city. In 1866, it had a grand view of the monarchist position in the center of town. Joaquín was able to drag his cannon to the top without opposition. Another commander mounted cannon on high ground near the Chihuahua aqueduct. They opened fire, scattering the monarchist troops. A few retreated to the Cathedral tower but surrendered when a cannon ball hit a large bell.

Juárez and his cabinet returned to the city for yet another time. They remained there until December 1866, when Juárez moved to Zacatecas. General and again Governor Luis Terrazas and a chihuahuense honor guard escorted him to the border.

The Beginning of the Porfiriato

The terrible struggle against Maximilian's empire had the positive effect of uniting Mexico as never before behind one man. Benito Juárez's single-minded focus had enabled a fractionalized citizenry to rally and defeat the foreign occupation. However, like so many predecessors, he soon faced the difficulties of governing and maintaining peace. Many of his most effective supporters, especially Porfirio Díaz expected more from him and, feeling ignored, began to challenge him.

Nevertheless, the indomitable Indian president controlled the government for four years. He instituted many reforms, establishing a nation-wide education system separate from the Church and preventing ejido takeovers in spite of the Ley Lerdo's unintended provisions. His prestige, reforms, and military successes in the field against armed rebellion enabled him to overcome direct opposition from Díaz and other former supporters. Reelected for four more years, he suddenly died of a heart attack on July 18, 1872.

His successor was Sebastián Lerdo de Tejada, younger brother of Miguel Lerdo de Tejada, the author of the infamous Ley Lerdo. The younger Lerdo had been a member of Juárez 's roving cabinet-in-exile. He proved to be a capable vice president, carrying out Juárez 's policies and suppressing armed rebellions that still plagued the country. However, it had been impossible not to make enemies. The disaffected Porfirio Díaz had been soundly defeated in earlier attempts to topple the government, but he kept trying. Out of a controversy surrounding Lerdo's reelection in 1876, Díaz saw opportunity. He produced a manifesto, the *Plan de Tuxtepec*, which proclaimed among other things that Mexican presidents should not serve more than one term. Using the "no reelection" slogan, he enlisted the support of dissidents in no less than twelve states. Díaz's ambitious plan to control the central government was out in the open. He assembled troops and began an armed campaign.

Cochise and the U.S. Army

While Porfirio Díaz angled for power in Mexico City, Governor Terrazas tried to deal with his own problems in Chihuahua. The treasury as usual was empty, and Apaches continued to raid across the border. He authorized Captain Cayetano Ozeta to establish a unit of armed volunteers at Janos in early 1868, the first garrison at the presidio in ten years. Except for this garrison, armed civilians, under local leaders remained the only defense against Apache raids.

The venerable Captain José Zuloaga died later that same year. This old campaigner, who embodied in one person all of the virtues and sins of the Apache-war era, was the last local commander to remember Spanish times. Juan Mata Ortiz in Galeana took his place as jefe político.

The Apaches also had problems. Cochise, perhaps feeling his age, realized the North Americans eventually would overwhelm him and his people. He is quoted as saying "Americans are everywhere."[176] He intensified his attacks to establish a strong bargaining position, and then asked for peace negotiations. The U.S. Army was well aware that Cochise was a powerful leader with direct control or influence over many different Apache bands. A peace agreement with him was important. Unfortunately, they insisted he relocate from the mountains of southern Arizona to a reservation in New Mexico. Cochise adamantly refused, causing more delays and more bloodshed, particularly in Arizona. Both sides were frustrated and distrustful. Cochise would disappear for long periods. After spending a few peaceful months at Janos, he realized he could not stay in Mexico.[177] In October 1872, he and representatives of the U.S. Army finally entered into a peace agreement. It took time to sort out the details, but Cochise and his followers settled where he wanted in the Dragoon and Chiricahua Mountains of southeastern Arizona close to the Sonora border. The U.S. representatives agreed to supply regular shipments of food. As with Mangas Coloradas, the sticking point was the ongoing raiding into Mexico. Peace was established in southern Arizona, but Cochise's people had a long bloody history south of the border, particularly in Sonora. They considered Mexico fair game regardless of their agreements.

Cochise died two years later in 1874, perhaps of stomach cancer. By making peace with the North Americans, he understood what successor leaders, Gerónimo, Juh, Victorio, Nana, and Loco, did not or would not. They could not fight or maintain their raiding lifestyle against the relentless march of settlement into the Southwest.

Díaz Prevails

In June 1876, Luis Terrazas ordered Joaquín Terrazas to muster all of the detachments together and prepare to ride south to confront a force of Díaz rebels. As supporters of Juárez and his successor Lerdo, the Terrazas cousins had no use for the usurper Díaz. They had confronted him before and told him never to return to Chihuahua.[178] Juan Mata Ortiz with the Galeana detachment caught up with Joaquín after returning from a pursuit of Apaches. Together, they met the rebels at Rancho de Ávalos, southeast of Ciudad Chihuahua. Ángel Trías Ochoa, the son of the former long-term governor, had changed to Díaz's side. He commanded the rebels, and like his father before him at the Battle of Sacramento, he lost. He and his troops were expelled from the state.[179]

Things were always a bit different in Chihuahua, and this victory was no exception. Díaz prevailed over Lerdo in almost all armed confrontation in the other states. Lerdo had made a fundamental error. He alienated powerful financial interests in the United States. The issues were complex, but simply put, Lerdo defaulted on bond interest and principal payments and he refused to allow U.S.-financed railroads to be developed in Mexico. The Juárez government had paid for munitions that helped oust Maximilian with bonds, payable by the government with interest. The financiers knew

the bonds were risky, but they were looking for future concessions as possible payment. In the best interests of Mexico as he saw it, Lerdo refused to
pay or to make concessions, especially for railroad building in the north.[180]
What little money left in the treasury was desperately needed for other projects, and Lerdo and many others feared concessions would allow the U.S.
to dominate their country. Also, Mexican officials could not reconcile the
amounts the financier's claimed with the accounting of goods received. The
desperate Mexicans probably had been overcharged and many arms shipments probably had not reached Juárez 's troops. The tragedy was that millions were spent, and the government was left with huge debts.

Porfirio Díaz catered to the financiers. They saw in him their opportunity to gain concessions, recover their investments, and to move freely as
entrepreneurs in Mexico. They and other special interest groups along the
border also saw him as a strong leader, capable of stabilizing the fractious
country. They turned out to be right. Arms and money to pay his troops
began to flow to Díaz. These resources enabled him to overthrow Lerdo's
government, striking the final blow on the battlefield at Tecoac on November 16, 1876, in the state of Tlaxcala.[181] The following May, he was declared
president. This began the *Porfiriato*, 35 years of control by the most powerful man ever to head the Mexican government.

Díaz appointed Ángel Trías Ochoa (the loser to the Terrazases at the
battle at Rancho de Ávalos) governor of Chihuahua, a position he held for
two years. Luis Terrazas quietly retired and bided his time as did his cousin
Joaquín and Juan Mata Ortiz.

Trías did not have his father's governing (or survival) skills and soon
alienated everyone. The Chihuahuans rebelled, removed Trías and rein-
stalled Luis as governor in November 1879. Instead of trying to quell the
rebellion in Chihuahua by force, Díaz followed a politically clever technique that he devised to control Mexico's diverse regions. He instituted
policies that made governors, chieftains, and *caciques* very wealthy but
reduced their political power. Díaz saw that the best way to keep Chihuahua in line was through Terrazas, and Terrazas realized, in spite of his earlier resistance, that the future of the country as well as his own lay with
Díaz. He eventually became so identified with the Díaz regime that it led to
his downfall. That would be decades into the future.

In the meantime, it was business as usual in Chihuahua. Joaquín Terrazas and Juan Mata Ortiz were again on the trail chasing Apaches. This time they had a specific objective, Victorio.

The San Carlos Reservation Plan

After making the deal with Cochise, the U.S. government broke it four years later. Representatives of the Army and government were frustrated as other Apache bands, not under Cochise's direct control, continued to raid. Also, the terrain of Cochise's mountain reservation made it difficult to transport all of the food necessary on a regular schedule to the Apache families. Those representatives should have tried harder. Instead, in 1876 they devised a one-size-fits-all plan that would relocate all Arizona Apaches, regardless of band affiliation, to one place, the more accessible San Carlos Reservation in Arizona. Four years before in 1872, the same year as the agreement with Cochise, President Grant had signed the bill creating San Carlos. General George F. Crook, who had been assigned as the commanding officer of the U.S. Army Division of Arizona the previous year, worked to pacify and relocate Apache bands from northern and eastern Arizona.

Crook, a West Point graduate, had gained valuable experience dealing with Indians in California and the U.S. Northwest both before and after serving in the Civil War. For the times, he took an enlightened but practical approach to dealing with Indians. He respected them and learned their languages. He employed effective techniques to control their depredations such as using Apache scouts as guides for Army patrols and to track down renegades. Apache policemen were organized to keep order on the reservation. Unfortunately, Crook was reassigned the year before the new plan could be put into effect for San Carlos. As flawed as it was, the plan might have worked with less violence had it been implemented by Crook's steady hand. Left to lesser men, even some with good intentions, the effect of the forced move to San Carlos ranged from reluctant acceptance to outright rebellion and seven years of warfare.

Initially, about half of the affected Apaches moved. This included Cochise's old band, whose members trekked north from their mountains out onto the hot, dry plains of the new reservation. Some, including Victorio and his band from New Mexico, moved to San Carlos for a short time and left frustrated by the miserable conditions and erratic food supply. Compounding this frustration was the offensive idea of being lumped together with other unfriendly bands with whom they had grudges and blood feuds.

Juh would have nothing to do with San Carlos. He left immediately for Mexico. In June, 1876, he led a large band into the Sierra Madre to a secure stronghold on a high mesa west of Casas Grandes on the border between Sonora and Chihuahua. There, he controlled Carretas Pass, forcing east-west traffic north to Púlpito Pass.[182] This was the same month that Joaquín Terrazas and Juan Mata Ortiz led all available fighters south, away from the valley, to confront the pro-Díaz force at Rancho de Ávalos.

When Díaz came to power shortly thereafter, Terrazas and Mata Ortiz were out of favor and not campaigning, leaving Juh a free hand to plunder. Communities in Sonora suffered, but he appears to have left the vulnerable Casas Grandes Valley alone for almost two years, preferring to trade there. The story told locally is that Juh was raised by the Varela family in Casas Grandes. True or not, the warriors routinely spared the town.

Even this local peace was short lived. In a few months, the entire region from Arizona and New Mexico to northern Sonora and Chihuahua exploded into seven years of violence unprecedented even in this historically violent land.

The Big Picture

By the 1870s, Mexico and the United States were following two distinctly different policies toward the Apaches. The U.S. had committed to the reservation system. The history of the acceptance and rejection of this policy throughout the west is well known. Setting aside basic morality issues, the reason for lack of acceptance by certain Apache bands and the resulting terrible massacres and battles can be laid to deceit, greed, ineptness, and lack of faith on both sides. The role of the U.S. civilian officials in this sad story is well documented. It is also clear that often the Apache leaders had no intention of living up to their agreements. When the weather turned cold and the grass thin, they would negotiate and agree to return to the reservation. By spring they would be gone, often into Mexico to avoid the pursuing U.S. soldiers. The Apaches have been quoted as saying that all they wanted was to be left alone to live as they had always lived.[183] This was certainly true for many, but for others the old ways included raiding their neighbors, stealing livestock, and sometimes killing. One reference states it clearly, "An Apache was born into a ritualistic and complex culture geared toward preparing him for war and raiding, if a boy, or for being the wife and mother of warriors, if a girl."[184]

There was no reservation system in northern Mexico; the policies, official and unofficial, ranged from assimilation to extermination. Slavery was illegal, yet the Chihuahua state government still paid a bounty for Apache scalps in the 1880s. Apache families would settle peacefully in encampments, *rancherias*, around Janos, Casas Grandes, and Ramos only to be attacked viciously by soldiers and vecinos from Sonora in retaliation for crimes committed by other Apaches in their faraway communities. The Apache survivors retaliated in turn. The brutality on both sides generated a mutual hatred between Apaches and Mexicans that exceeded that north of the border.

Victorio's Breakout

What restarted the cycle of violence in Chihuahua as well as in Arizona, New Mexico, and west Texas in 1879 was Victorio's escape from the New Mexico's Ojo Caliente Reservation in August. Some Apaches had lived contentedly in Ojo Caliente area on the eastern edge of the Black Mountains for a long time. The Department of Indian Affairs had briefly established Ojo Caliente as a reservation for all of the southern New Mexico Apaches. Located east of Arizona's San Carlos Reservation over the Black Mountains on New Mexico's Alamosa Creek, the Apaches liked it there. The abandoned site today is in a remote area near the junction of state highways 54 and 142.

When the Department of Indian Affairs (later the Bureau of Indian Affairs) decided to close the reservation, trouble began. Victorio had left San Carlos two years earlier and refused to return. He had come back to New Mexico and agreed to stay at Ojo Caliente. He was wary and did not trust the Indian agents who were getting mixed signals from their superiors at the Department. Victorio became convinced that his people would be forced back to San Carlos. The tipping point came when civil authorities in Grants County charged Victorio with murder and horse stealing (which was worse?). Before the sheriff could arrive to arrest him, he, along with Nana, ran for the border with 75 warriors and 375 women and children. They first camped in the Sierra de la Candelaria, north of the swampy area above Laguna de Guzmán, the terminus of the Casas Grandes River. He sent scouts south of the Laguna to the old presidio town of Carrizal to assess the situation. When the scouts returned, he set an ambush. Eighteen Mexicans, following the scouts' trail, rode straight into the trap. Apaches rose up in front and opened fire. When the Mexicans tried to retreat, more Apaches rose up behind and killed the survivors. Victorio and Nana waited. When the news reached Carrizal, another thirty-five men rode out in pursuit. When they found the massacre site, they stopped, dismounted, and began to bury the victims. While they were working, the waiting Apaches opened fire and killed fifteen more. The rest ran on foot, leaving for Victorio badly needed horses, guns, and ammunition. This began a series of similar massacres, including attacks on ranches, stagecoaches, sheepherders, travelers, and Army patrols on both sides of the border.

Luis Terrazas, once again the state governor, now had Federal troops available to him under the command of Colonel Ponciano Cisneros. The Governor, who incidentally had lost several hundred horses to the raiding Apaches, put Joaquín Terrazas and Juan Mata Ortiz under Cisneros' command. The soldiers and armed vecinos spent the rest of the summer crisscrossing from the Sierra Madre to Laguna Guzmán, without ever sighting the Apaches. At the end of the year, the campaign was over, and the tired troopers went home.

Victorio lost warriors but other renegades joined him. For a short time, his effective fighting force actually increased. All U.S. Army units were on alert. Arizona alone had 13 posts and two supply depots, including four companies of Apache scouts. Brevet Major General Edward Hatch commanded the Division of New Mexico, which included the 9th Cavalry, one of the regiments of the famous Buffalo soldiers. Hatch had been the first commanding officer of the 9th. He ordered all units to the southern part of the state and took personal command of the pursuit. There were bloody clashes, ambushes, massacres, and countless fruitless pursuits by the hard-riding cavalry. For a year and two months, Victorio's small band of approximately 75 warriors, encumbered by three times as many women and children, eluded an army of over 1,000 troopers.

Caches of supplies in the Black Mountains, Sierra de la Candelaria, and elsewhere replenished what the Apaches lost on the trail or fighting. Hidden caves provided shelter for the women and children while the warriors carried out attacks.[185]

As the months went by, mounting pressure on Victorio took a toll. The soldiers and their officers learned how to fight the skilled guerilla leader. They blocked trails, set their own ambushes, and placed well-armed guard details near water holes. Several clashes occurred around water holes with both sides desperate for water. By late spring, 1880, Victorio himself had barely escaped some hard-fought skirmishes and he had lost men and stock. In July, he crossed back into Mexico to escape the soldiers. Governor Terrazas the previous month had ordered Juan Mata Ortiz to call up his volunteer vecinos and patrol the northwest part of the state. Colonel Adolfo Valles, who had replaced Colonel Cisneros, was already patrolling the northeast to the Rio Grande and along the Texas border.

Victorio did not stay in Chihuahua long. Instead, he led his band northeast across the swollen Rio Grande into west Texas. Why he moved into this unfamiliar territory is unclear. In hindsight, he should have continued in the opposite direction, southwest, to Juh's stronghold in the Sierra Madre. Perhaps he was uncomfortable with Juh. While they had campaigned together, they were from different bands. The move was a tactical mistake. In the west Texas hills, U.S. Army units caught up, and he lost men and animals in skirmishes with them. Worse, Colonel Valles stumbled into him, and he lost more men in a vicious fight with the much larger Mexican federal force. The fight in the Sierra de los Pinos near the Rio Grande on the Texas side cost Valle six men. That was enough for the general.[186] He ended his campaign and returned to his garrisons, the cavalry going to Carrizal and the infantry to El Carmen.

Victorio
Photo: Lot 24 SPC Sw Apache NM ACC 20263
Cat 129781 #9-49 02040900, Courtesy of
the National Anthropological Archives,
Smithsonian Institution

Victorio had not been defeated but he had lost thirty to fifty percent of his warriors.[187] Hard pressed by the U.S. Army, Victorio led the remaining men, women, and children, and their stock back across the river into Mexico for the last time. They went west to hideouts in the Candelaria Mountains.

Through August 1880, Victorio's people rested. At the end of the month, Victorio sent out a raiding party, and they returned with a large herd of horses from a ranch belong to Dr. Mariano Samaniego, a very prominent citizen of the state. He had been one of the first doctors in the area, and he had served briefly as acting governor in 1876. Apparently, he was well informed on the Apache movements in northeastern Chihuahua and had sent information to the U.S. Army in the past.[188] Dr. Samaniego would be Victorio's last victim and inadvertently the supplier of horses for the infamous Apache's last run to freedom.

Victorio had been driven from U.S. soil, but many were not convinced. The press hounded the Army as did officials from the Southern Pacific Railroad then in the process of building the second transcontinental railroad. The Army concentrated resources into a large force and marched across the border toward the Sierra de la Candelaria. They were joined by Texas Rangers and other civilians eager to be in on the kill.

Joaquín Steps Up Again

On August 22, 1880, Governor Terrazas called General Valles and his cousin Joaquín to Ciudad Chihuahua. Victorio was back in his jurisdiction, and he wanted action. He ordered Valles to take the field supported by Joaquín Terrazas. The general politely but adamantly refused. He had many good reasons, but it was clear he had had enough of Victorio. Not so Joaquín. When Don Luis turned to him, he agreed to raise a force of vecinos, armed civilians, and seek out Victorio. As a recruiting inducement, Don Luis agreed to pay (from the almost empty state treasury) four pesos per day for those without a horse and a two-peso bonus per day if they brought a horse. Amounts for warriors' scalps would be paid in accordance with existing state law; a version of the Fifth Law was still on the books. Two thousand pesos would be paid for Victorio dead or alive.[189] Joaquín left with a small escort and four white horses, a habit that

Joaquín Terrazas about 1920

170

always ensured he had a fresh mount. He rode hard for almost a month, visiting communities to raise recruits.

Joaquín Terrazas carried the rank of colonel, although he usually led vecinos, and not federal troops. Born in Chihuahua, he was now fifty-one years old and had been fighting Apaches all of his life. He was tall, thin, and one of those few born to command. He had fought for Benito Juárez in the War of Reform, against the French monarchy, and against the usurper Porfirio Díaz. In between those battles, he fought Apaches. His second in command on this campaign would be his old comrade-in-arms Juan Mata Ortiz from Galeana, who already had received his own orders from the governor to organize his vecinos and take to the trail.

Who was Juan Mata Ortiz?

Juan Mata Ortiz is obviously important to this story because unknowingly, and long after his death, he lent his name to the little village that became so famous for its pottery. His name is also on that list of hard-riding

Juan Mata Ortiz

171

The granddaughters of Juan Mata Ortiz hold the original portrait. Photo: 2009

Chihuahua characters that stretches back through the history to Captain Francisco Ramírez. Like Joaquín Terrazas, he was born in Chihuahua, probably in Galeana, in 1836 to parents Felipe Ortiz and Josefina Mendoza. Unlike the lean Joaquín, he was heavyset, known to the Chiricahua as "Captain Gordo." With the life he led, it is hard to believe he was very fat. The description suggests a physically large man. Also, unlike Joaquín, he did not survive the Apache Wars to write his memoirs. The fragmented details of his life can be pieced together only through comments in official reports and one large picture hanging in his still-existing home on the main street of Galeana, where he lived with his wife Juana Carbajal.

He must have been impressive and capable even when young. The infamous scalp hunter James Kirker claims to have met him when he was ten years old, just before the first of the double Galeana massacres in 1846. Kirker said the young Mata Ortiz was already helping organize expeditions against the Apaches. Ten seems very young, but it is clear that Mata Ortiz was an effective leader of men from a young age. He held the civil and military position of jefe político of the Cantón of Galeana from 1868 until his death in 1882.

The Battle of Tres Castillos

After receiving his orders, Mata Ortiz sent couriers to the cantón settlements asking volunteers to rendezvous at Corralitos. A month later, he had 119 armed and ready men, about one third from Galeana, the rest from the Casas Grandes and Santa María Valleys. Joaquín came to Corralitos with 50 men. The contingent from Casas Grandes was commanded by Eleuterio Arellano. Tarahumara Indians also joined led by Mauricio Corredor, reputed to be a crack shot. These Indians were anxious to fight and to put an end to the Apache wars. They had suffered in two ways—from direct attacks by the Apaches and from murders by scalp hunters wanting their long black hair.

The combined force went east to Carrizal, where more volunteers joined, bringing the total to about 350. Joaquín divided the force, sending Mata Ortiz north to intercept and escort a much-needed train of supply wagons ordered from El Paso. Joaquín led the other column eastward looking for Victorio's band. Scouts sent in various directions reported no sign of the Indians. When Mata Ortiz rejoined Joaquín in the Sierra de los Pinos on the Texas border, near the site of General Valles' battle, the commander had no idea where Victorio had gone. Joaquín himself had already been on the trail for many weeks, covering hundreds of miles, first recruiting and now pursuing, but he was relentless. He and Mata Ortiz sent their men scouring the hills and ranges to the south until on October 7, a scout reported Victorio's Apaches moving southwest toward a place called Tres Castillos. Joaquín and Mata Ortiz turned their two columns to the southwest.

By now, the two commanders had time to evaluate their men. Joaquín dismissed ninety he considered useless. He also dealt with another delicate matter. The large U.S. Army force with Texas Rangers and eager civilian vigilantes had crossed the border and were moving west to Victorio's old area between the Candelaria Mountains and Laguna Guzmán. Joaquín must have been a good negotiator because through courier messages and direct meetings, he convinced all of the North Americans to withdraw.

Joaquín did not trust the Apache scouts used by the U.S. Army, although he probably could have used them on this campaign. Of more importance was his fear of a large U.S. force probing deep into Chihuahua. It is not known whether he received orders or this was his own idea. Either way, he rejected the involvement of North Americans, and they retreated across the border.

The Tres Castillos site is a geologic anomaly. Two rocky extrusions rise out of the flat Chihuahua plain. The larger to the north has two peaks. These two in conjunction with a separate smaller peak a few hundred feet to the south form the "three castles" Eons of wind and weather have turned the extrusions into a jumble of boulders, caves, and jagged outcroppings—a natural fortress. Visibility extends for miles in all directions. Broad, shallow seasonal lakes turn the adobe soil into a sticky gumbo, limiting the approaches. The Apaches had roamed this area for years and had built fortifications and hidden corrals on various levels in the mass of rocks. It made a formidable defensive position, but with no avenue of retreat.

Most of the rock forts are just below a notch in the south peak. Terrazas and Mata Ortiz approached from that side.

Like many stories of heroics in battle, versions vary as to what exactly happened on October 14, 1880. The Apache band traveled in three groups.

Tres Castillos. Photo: 2008

The first two under the direct command of Victorio retreated to the smaller southern peak when they saw the Mexican troopers. Nana, with the third group, either rode off to hunt or saw the dust from the two columns and galloped to safety. At dusk, the Mexicans approached the south peak. Each column had ten men in front including Tarahumara to make the force appear smaller. Perhaps this ruse worked because Victorio and mounted warriors sallied out, whooping and creating a great cloud of dust. Joaquín halted the columns, but two Tarahumara, the captain, Mauricio Corredor, and another named Roque, ran forward on foot. The Apaches charged screaming. Mauricio and Roque stopped, raised their carbines, and fired pointblank. Victorio fell dead from his white horse. His shocked warriors retreated. Joaquín led his column left around the south peak. Mata Ortiz led his column to the right, firing at the Apaches and cutting off a group trying to escape. Other warriors made it back into the rocks where their women and children waited behind the redoubts. Joaquín's men tried to follow, but it was too dark. Night had fallen. Cries, chants, and occasional shots broke the stillness through the night. At dawn the battle resumed in earnest. Joaquín placed sharpshooters on the north peaks. With their

Apache Rock Forts, South Peak, Tres Castillos. Photo: 2008

44-40 rifles they shot at anything that moved among the rocks to the south. The Apaches in a good defensive position returned the fire, holding back the advance until they ran out of their already short supply of bullets. By midday, the Mexicans had worked their way up into the redoubts, grappling hand to hand with the remaining warriors. One by one the warriors were killed or were too badly wounded to continue the fight. The Mexicans began to hear women crying out for mercy for their children. One young warrior with a supply of bullets climbed high in the rocks and held out until several volleys from crack shots ended his brave fight. Two others held out in a narrow cave, refusing pleas to surrender until they too ran out of ammunition and were killed. The battle was over.

Victorio's death marked the beginning of the end for the free-raiding Apaches. Seventy-eight Apaches were killed. Sixty-eight women, children, and wounded men were taken prisoners. Terrazas lost three men killed and ten wounded, four seriously. These numbers as well as other details of the battle vary according to the source. The prisoners were bound and either rode or walked across the desert to Ciudad Chihuahua, about 100 miles. The victors rode alongside with the scalps of the dead men hanging from their saddle horns. They crossed the Chuvíscar River and rode down

Joaquín Terrazas and Juan Mata Ortiz triumph over Victorio. Mural in the portico of the Galeana District office. Terrazas stands over Victorio's body in foreground. Mata Ortiz astride his white horse raises his rifle.

Avenida Juárez between cheering crowds, displaying their trophy scalps on "long poles" like pagan warriors of old.

Joaquín Terrazas and Juan Mata Ortiz were hailed as heroes and covered with glory. In his official report Terrazas cited Mata Ortiz and Mauricio Corredor for gallantry. Corredor was given a special suit of clothes and a nickel-plated Sharps rifle. Joaquín Terrazas received most of the attention and accolades. A large, impressive monument was erected in his honor, which still stands on the outskirts of Chihuahua. A monument for Juan Mata Ortiz would need to wait.

It is not clear if any of the wounded warriors survived or what happened to them. Women over the age of thirteen were put in the city prison. Their fate also is uncertain. Children were taken into the homes of the local Chihuahua citizens, presumably to be raised as servants or workers. Governor Luis Terrazas took a boy and a girl. Some may have run away. Those who survived would have grown up and disappeared into the mestizo culture.[190]

An Incredible Affair

The battle at Tres Castillos and the demise of the great leader Victorio was a major victory in the 200-year long struggle with the Apaches, but it was not quite over as some newspapers reported. Juh, Gerónimo, and Nana still rode free, and they wanted revenge. Nana with the remnants of Victorio's band that had escaped the battle rode north. He caught and killed nine Mexicans, who probably had fought at Tres Castillos as one was mounted on Victorio's saddle. Whoever he was, he died badly.

Nana, described as a physically powerful man, was nearing 70 years. With about 30 warriors and their women and children, he crossed the border into Arizona's Mogollon Mountains for the winter. When spring came, he left the women and children hidden there and crossed back to Mexico, where he raided mercilessly. Mata Ortiz and his men went after him and chased him into New Mexico. In two months of raiding there, his small band attacked twelve ranches and towns, killing five soldiers and thirty settlers in spite of the large U.S. Army presence. They met soldiers in combat seven times. Nana eventually gathered his people from their hiding place and retreated to Juh's Sierra Madre stronghold.[191] Juh and Gerónimo were not there.

Earlier, after some serious raiding and killing of their own on both sides of the border, Juh and Gerónimo negotiated a deal with the commander of the U.S Army Division of Arizona, Colonel Orlando B. Willcox (for whom Willcox, Arizona is named) to return peacefully to San Carlos. Some of his subordinates strongly objected, but the colonel approved the deal.[192] These two notorious Apache leaders moved their bands north to the reservation sometime in early 1880 before Tres Castillos. Many other Apaches already had accepted the inevitable and were living in San Carlos, including their old raiding companion Chief Loco. They stayed almost two years. Then, amidst political turmoil on the reservation (not of their making), the Indian agent threatened to send them to Oklahoma. The two warrior chiefs gathered their hidden weapons, organized their people and stock and ran for Mexico. Chief Loco refused to join them. As soon as he got the word, Colonel Willcox sent four cavalry companies "in the most vigorous pursuit."

Gerónimo has come through history as the most famous Apache. His name remains a household word, and there is no question that he was an important leader and the ultimate survivor. He appears to have been the spokesman because Juh stuttered. However, when it came to battle and tactics, Juh was in command.

Leading his band of men, women, and children through Arizona's basin and range country into Sonora was an incredible feat. The warriors killed everyone they encountered including telegraph linemen, teamsters and a telegraph operator. Two companies of troopers caught them south of the Gila River, but Juh's tactics, including an unexpected night diversionary attack on the soldiers' flank, enabled the warriors to lead the women and children through the mountains and arroyos across the border.[193] They joined Nana in the stronghold above Casas Grandes.

The guerilla-fighting skills of these Apache leaders and those before them are legendary. The discipline and tactics necessary to move a large group across hundreds of miles of territory crisscrossed by Army patrols cannot be overemphasized. Now Gerónimo, Nana, and Juh, sitting in council meetings around a fire with their subchiefs, came up with the most audacious scheme of all to test these skills. They would ride to San Carlos and kidnap all of Chief Loco's people, some 400 men, women, and children and bring them to their Sierra Madre stronghold. They almost succeeded.

Loco now led a group that had no intention of leaving San Carlos to join a band of renegades. Sources disagree on the motives of the three schemers in the Sierra Madre. One source says the constant warfare had taken its toll and they needed more fighting men. The warriors by then consisted of a mixed group of Chiricahua, New Mexico Apache, a few Navajos, and young Mexican and white warriors, captured as children. Another source disagrees stating that of the 400 in San Carlos only 75 were potential warriors and the other 325 represented noncombatant mouths to feed.

At least two eyewitnesses recorded their experiences. James Kaywaykla was a child, part of Nana's band living in the stronghold.[194] Jason Betzinez was an older boy not quite of warrior status. He and his family were living in San Carlos in 1882 and were kidnapped. Their accounts are similar, but they disagree as to the willingness of those with Loco to break out. Part of the plan may have been to reconcile families split apart by warfare and outbreaks from the reservations.

Juh, Gerónimo, and Nana seemed to have been genuinely concerned about the well-being and even the survival of Loco's band in San Carlos. Apparently, they had been located in a particularly hot, unhealthy, and unproductive area.

In April 1882, Juh and Gerónimo took a contingent of warriors north, leaving Nana in charge of the stronghold. Unopposed, they reached Loco's settlement, 200 miles from the border. The site is now San Carlos Lake, a large reservoir created by the Coolidge Dam on the Gila River.

In the early morning without warning, they rode through the lines of teepees ordering everyone out and to immediately start walking south or be killed. According to Betzinez, they grabbed what they could and in a long straggling column followed Gerónimo east along the Gila River into the Gila Mountains. A rearguard of warriors killed two San Carlos Indian policemen, who had ridden up to investigate the commotion. Now Juh, Gerónimo and their subchiefs had to guide and feed some 400 unwilling and unprepared people through 200 miles of a thoroughly alarmed territory while being chased by over 1,000 soldiers. If they eluded the soldiers and reached Mexico, they thought they would be safe.

As the reluctant men, women, and children plodded south, they stayed in the up-tilted mountains of the basin and range country for protection. The warriors raided far and wide attacking ranches, herders, and wagon trains. In the first few days, they killed over forty people taking weapons and stock. The people from San Carlos had no time to gather their own horses, and mounts were needed to get the column moving faster. Betzinez describes the warriors driving a herd of sheep into their mountain camp-site, which the hungry families butchered and cooked in fires of brush. They continued south through the Dragoon, Chiricahua and Peloncillo Mountains along the New Mexico border. They usually moved at night, staying high whenever possible. U.S. Army Companies caught up to them three times, twice in the Peloncillos just south of the newly constructed Southern Pacific railroad tracks at Horseshoe Canyon and Stein's Peak, both roughly 25 miles southeast of present-day Lordsburg. After fire fights, Juh, Gerónimo, and Chief Loco, now resigned to his fate, managed to extract their people from the battle areas and continue running. After ten or twelve days, they crossed the border somewhere east of Douglas, prob-ably south of Cloverdale, New Mexico.

They had made it, or so they thought. They camped about 25 miles northwest of Janos near a marsh that provided water. The leaders gave ren-dezvous instructions as to where to meet in the mountains in case they became separated. Otherwise, they celebrated. What they did not know was that two companies of the 6th Cavalry and one company of Apache scouts had crossed the border.

The pursuers surprised the Apaches, who had become uncharacteristi-cally careless, and ran off most of their mounts. The Apaches retreated into rocks of a nearby butte protruding from the plain. From this position, they fired at the soldiers. After several hours of shooting back and forth, four young warriors worked their way behind the soldiers and fired at them. This distracted the cavalry long enough for the able-bodied men, women, and children to sprint from the butte to nearby rugged hills. Most made it and the casualties were surprisingly light, but they had lost their meager belongings and their animals.

They continued south toward Sierra Huachinera, a northern spur of the Sierra Madre. Along an arroyo west of Janos near the San Pedro River and the road to Púlpito Pass, they walked into a trap. Waiting for them were troops of the Mexican Sixth Infantry Regiment, commanded by Colonel Lorenzo García, plus units from Sonora militias. The soldiers rose from nearby ravines and fired at short range into a line of people walking in the arroyo. This time it was every man, woman, and child for themselves. Fast runners like Jason Betzinez eluded the rifle fire and lived to tell their stories. Gerónimo rallied about thirty warriors in a deep arroyo, and they made enough of a stand to enable some of the less swift to survive. When night fell, they too fled into the mountains. About 100 were killed or captured. The others eventually found their way to Juh's stronghold, arriving with nothing but the clothes they wore.[195]

Bringing the people from San Carlos 300 miles to the Sierra Madre under constant pursuit was a remarkable military feat but falls short of being "incredible" as it is called by one historian.[196] It falls short because Juh and Gerónimo made two miscalculations, one almost fatal. They assumed the U.S. Army would stop at the border. While this was a serious error, the escapees survived the Army's attack reasonably well. What these two experienced leaders failed to comprehend was how far the Mexican authorities now were willing to go to end the Apache menace. The days of trading and raiding were over. The pendulum had swung and would stick on the Mexican side, but the end would be messy.

Massacre at Casas Grandes

Why Joaquín Terrazas and Mata Ortiz did not participate in García's ambush is not known. Ten times in 1881, they and their men rode out in pursuit of Apaches with the full support of the federal and state governments. Terrazas's orders were clear—capture and kill Juh and Gerónimo.[197]

The Apaches still had a large group in the Sierra Madre in spite of losses in the combined bands of Gerónimo, Juh, and Loco. Periodically, they needed to move from their overgrazed and over-hunted hideouts in the deep canyons. For a while, they were bold enough to move out onto the open prairie on the east side of the Palanganas River to take advantage of the tall grass. From Betzinez's description, one of the large campsites must have been very close to the Pearson/Mata Ortiz town site.[198] They avoided contact with the Mexican forces.

In May 1882, a great council was held, and the chiefs and subchiefs decided that at least some of the Apaches would seek peace and trade at Casas Grandes. By now, Casas Grandes had emerged as the most important town in the Valley. Joaquín Terrazas used it as his base, and soldiers were stationed there part of the time. As clever as they were, the Apache leaders apparently did not understand that times had changed. The days were over when the Mexican settlers, glad for any relief from attack, would accept offers of peaceful trade. As the historians Lister and Lister so neatly put it, the Mexicans had "handed out food and clothing with one hand and crossed themselves with the other."[199] As much as they benefited from the trade, the Mexicans now had other ideas.

Following a decades-old procedure, the Apaches sent an old woman to Casas Grandes with a message for Terrazas stating their peaceful intentions. At first, the Apaches were suspicious. Reassured by the Mexicans, about 250 Apaches, 70 warriors and the rest women and children came in and camped southeast of Casas Grandes at *La Boquilla,* near the junction where the Palanganas and Piedras Verdes Rivers form the Casas Grandes River. This is just north of the Hacienda San Diego compound. All was calm. One story is that Colonel Terrazas sent a wagon load of mescal to the camp. Whatever the source, by the second day, many began to drink. One theory is that Gerónimo liked to drink, and that was the incentive to come in. Young Betzinez was there and very critical of the drinking. Before dawn on the third morning, many lay about in a stupor.

Terrazas and Mata Ortiz had devised a plan in which Terrazas would lead a column from Casas Grandes around Cerro Moctezuma into the San Diego Valley and attack the camp from the south. Juan Mata Ortiz would lead a second column due south and attack from the north. The objective was to kill as many warriors as possible and capture the women and children. It was a good plan except Terrazas's column had to ride about thirteen miles. Mata Ortiz arrived first and some of his excited men opened fire. Surprise lost, they charged into the groggy but aroused Indians. Terrazas's men arrived shooting and grabbed as many women, and children as they could. The Apaches scattered, many climbing the cliff to rocks above the camp and set a defensive position. Others escaped into arroyos that paralleled the Palanganas River and went south behind Cerro de la Bandera and El Indio above the Pearson/Mata Ortiz site. Still others lit the grass afire to create a smoke screen to hide their escape.

The best estimates are that at least 20 warriors were killed and 35 women and children captured.[200]

Young Betzinez's fast feet saved him again. Cold sober, he ran for his life. Juh and Gerónimo also escaped, but not before screaming taunts of revenge at Captain Gordo. He would die by fire, they raged.

When the survivors finally found each other, they rendezvoused near the future train station of El Rucio, south of the Pearson/Mata Ortiz site. They divided into two bands headed by Juh and Gerónimo. With Terrazas and Mata Ortiz hunting them, they crossed the San Diego Valley and moved deep into Sonora for the summer. They reunited in the fall and sat down with their subchiefs to prepare their plan of revenge.

The Death of Captain Gordo

The old town of Galeana lies twenty-seven miles south of Nuevo Casas Grandes along today's highway 10. This route has been a main north/south thoroughfare since Spanish times. On November 13, 1882, a small band of Apaches rode into the town in broad daylight and drove off horses belonging to the townspeople. When he heard the alarm, Juan Mata Ortiz immediately organized twenty-one of his vecino militiamen, mounted, and rode in pursuit. With all of his experience, he probably should have been wary as the Apache were more brazen than usual. After fourteen miles, Mata Ortiz and his men approached *Puerto Chocolate*, the pass through the low hills separating the Galeana municipio from Casas Grandes. Suddenly from the arroyos along the road, two hundred Apaches leaped up and attacked the soldiers from all sides. They had waited until the decoys passed. The trapped Mexicans ran to the top of the rocky outcrop of Chocolate Hill, since known as *Cerrito Mata Ortiz*. They quickly stacked rocks as protection and maintained a steady fire. Although they had the high ground, they were completely surrounded. The Apache warriors crawled close to the top of the outcrop, pushing boulders in front of them as shields. They charged as the defenders one by one fired their last bullet. In the final hand-to-hand fight with knives and rifle butts, the Apaches killed every man except one. Gerónimo gave the order to allow the last man alive to escape to spread the word of Apache vengeance.[201]

No one knows exactly how Mata Ortiz died. The most gruesome accounts state that Juh and Gerónimo carried out their threat and burned the hated "Captain Gordo" alive on top of the hill, each warrior bringing one piece of wood to add to the pyre. Others disagree. The memory of their hero remains strong among the people of Galeana more than 125 years later. In 2009, volunteers cleaning the Galeana Catholic church pointed exactly to where his presumably intact body lay buried under the sidewalk. To their annoyance, a former priest with no sense of history, had cemented over the church entranceway and the nearby grave. The consensus seems to be that the Apaches may have mutilated Mata Ortiz in their rage, but he was not burned. Good stories die hard, and the tale of the burning pyre persists.

The Battle of Tres Castillos monument honoring Joaquín Terrazas still stands in Ciudad Chihuahua, but for over one hundred years no monument or plaque existed recognizing Juan Mata Ortiz. The people of Galeana did

Zócalo in Galeana. The monument placed in 1990 honoring Juan Mata Ortiz and the troopers killed in the fight at Chocolate Pass is the pyramid structure on the right.

name the little plaza in front of the church for him, but even his gravesite, remained unmarked.

Over a century after the fight in Chocolate Pass, the omission of a monument and plaque was rectified. On November 13, 1990, the Galeana municipio placed a rock pyramid with a large plaque in the plaza memorializing Mata Ortiz and the troopers who died protecting their town that same day 108 years before. The church is on the west side of the plaza and the monument is on the east side facing Mata Ortiz's house across the main street.

He was honored in another way in 1925. An early source noted, "Today a railroad settlement south of Casas Grandes perpetuates the memory of the Indian fighter of Galeana."[202]

The plaque states that 29 troopers plus Mata Ortiz
were killed, but only 22 names are listed.

It is interesting to conjecture as to how much the growing fame of the pottery village, that former "railroad settlement" bearing Mata Ortiz's name, influenced the citizens of Galeana to place a monument so long after his death. In the normal course of events, his name probably would have faded from memory and remained an obscure reference if it had not been placed on the now-famous village. In a peculiar accident of history, the name of this rugged old Apache fighter now graces a unique ceramic art form, known, collected, and talked about throughout the world.

General Crook Commands

After taking their revenge at Galeana, the Apaches rode west to their hide-outs in the Sierra Madre. To avoid Joaquín Terrazas's patrols in the more populous areas, they probably took a trail over the Sierra America, such as the one through San Joaquín Canyon to the Palanganas River near the Mata Ortiz town site. At night, they would have crossed the open plains to San Diego Canyon to enter the Sierra Madre. In the mountains, the band split again; a few stayed with Juh and the rest with Gerónimo. Juh later had two bad encounters with Mexican soldiers, losing his wife, other family members, and a few, now irreplaceable warriors. He retreated deeper into the canyons. Curiously, some of his people still seemed able to trade in the Casas Grandes stores. Today, a building still stands where the Apache reputedly traded for goods.

In November 1883, Juh himself came in and bought whiskey. Drunk, he rode with his two sons back up the mountain trail. On a rim of a steep bluff, his horse slipped, and horse and rider fell over the edge into the river below. His sons scrambled down, but Juh was too big to lift out of the stream. They held his head up until others came to help carry him to the bank. There the great Apache warrior and chieftain died. Like Mangas Coloradas before him, a legendary leader came to an inglorious end.[203]

During the previous year on July 29, 1882, the U.S. and Mexican governments put aside their mistrust and took a significant step to address the "Apache problem." They signed a reciprocal agreement that permitted regular troops of either army to cross the border in "close pursuit of 'a band of savages."[204] The agreement had specific conditions, but the net effect eliminated the Apaches' decades-long ability to raid in one country and find sanctuary in the other. This reduced the Apache's options, forcing them deeper into the Sierra Madre to avoid the expanding patrols on both sides of the border.

In September 1882, General George Crook again assumed command of the U.S. Army Division of Arizona, inheriting serious problems. The Indians on the reservations were close to open rebellion over ration shortages and other bad conditions, created in part by corrupt civilian agents. Renegade Apache continued to raid and kill on both sides of the border.

Crook had the military and administrative skills along with the personality to deal with these problems firmly and humanely. The government had wisely given him authority over the reservation police and the distribution of food, thus eliminating two areas of constant conflict when administered by the Department of Indian Affairs agents (unfortunately, this sound arrangement changed and broke down later). He took extraordinary measures, personally visiting Apache leaders in hiding to hear and record their grievances. He removed miners and other squatters from the reservations, relaxed onerous rules, and installed a measure of self-rule through the Apache police and courts. He had devoted junior officers, of whom at least three played significant roles over the next four years. These three were capable and intelligent, respecting the Apaches both as enemies and as their charges on the reservation. All became effective in dealing with the Apaches as fighters and negotiators. Captain Elliot Crawford, a veteran of the Civil War and the Sioux Wars, was detached from his 3rd Cavalry regiment by Crook and given special duty as the commander of the San Carlos and Fort Apache Reservations. Crawford fully subscribed to his commanding officer's belief that developing effective Apache Scout units was the only way to combat and subdue the renegade Apaches. He understood that it would take the scouts' extraordinary endurance and tracking skills just to find the hostile Apache in their rugged retreats. Under Crook, he was key figure in expanding and leading the scouts.

Lt. Charles B. Gatewood, a West Point graduate, was made commander at Fort Apache, reporting to Crawford. Of the three, he initially was the only one with Apache experience, having ridden many patrols during the Victorio campaign. The others by necessity learned quickly.

The third officer and one especially important for this story was Lt. Britton Davis, who had graduated from West Point just three months before Crook assumed command. He was detached from the 3rd Cavalry and assigned as assistant to Crawford. Davis' father had been the governor of Texas and was a friend of E.B. Morgan, the head of the Wall Street syndicate that purchased Hacienda Corralitos in 1880. Lt. Davis left the Army in 1886 and became manager of the Corralitos ranch and mines, which brings him back into this story later. Davis wrote a book detailing his experiences in the Apache Wars. This often-cited reference provides an eye-witness account from the Army point of view as a counterpoint to Betzinez's outlook as an Apache warrior. Among other things, Davis describes one of the soldiers' recreational activities—baseball.[205]

A friend of Davis was Lt. Franklin West. While campaigning with General Crook in the Sierra Madre, West took a particular interest in the numerous ruins in the Bavispe Valley. The following year, he ran into Adolph Bandelier at Fort Huachuca and while walking together, he passed on his observations. These apparently were important clues for Bandelier because he referred to West several times in his journal.

Gerónimo had established his base camp on the rim of a deep canyon near the headwaters of Bavispe River. His band stayed there quietly for many months. In March 1883, he began raiding Sonoran communities for stock and ammunition. By this time, the Indians had accumulated U.S.-made, sixteen-shot 1860 Henry rifles and perhaps even Winchester 73s. These were sophisticated weapons, but the warriors chronically lacked ammunition. A sub-chief named Chato led a small group of warriors north across the border, primarily searching for cartridges that fit their guns. They rampaged for six days killing twenty-six people. General William Tecumseh Sherman, Commanding General U.S. Army (equivalent to the Chief of Staff U.S. Army after 1903) ordered General Crook to pursue the warriors into Mexico in accordance with the border agreement.

Crook went by train to personally confer with Mexican authorities in Sonora and Ciudad Chihuahua and notify them of his proposed action. He returned to mobilize a force consisting of forty-five Sixth Cavalry troopers, six officers, including Lt. West, and 193 Apache scouts, commanded by Crawford and assisted by Gatewood. Crawford's Chief of Scouts and interpreter was the legendary gunslinger, Tom Horn. Steve McQueen portrayed him in the movie *Tom Horn*. The eager Apache scouts all wore red bandanas to distinguish them from the renegades. One scout, who was also an interpreter, was known as Mickey Free. Half Mexican and half Apache, he had been captured as a boy from an American ranch in Arizona, where he lived with his Apache mother. He was raised as an Apache warrior, an example of the cultural and DNA mix occurring in northern Chihuahua and the borderlands.[206] The expedition rendezvoused at San Bernardino Springs on the Arizona side of the San Bernardino Valley. The famous Arizona lawman John Slaughter bought the huge surrounding ranch later that year. It is now a National Historic Landmark.

With General Crook in personal command, the detachment crossed the border into northern Sonora on May 1, following the San Bernardino Valley through the devastated settlements of the Sierra Madre's Bavispe Valley to Huachinera. The scouts trotted ahead on foot, carrying rifles and spare moccasins dangling from their gun belts. Explorer Adolph Bandelier would follow the same route less than a year later in February 1883. Near Huachinera, the scouts found a trail of the Apaches going southeast into a particularly rugged series of gorges and ridges, where the Bavispe and Aros Rivers join to form the Yaqui River. The Spanish explorer Francisco Ibarra became terribly lost here 300 years before. The steep, dangerous trail slowed the troopers, and Crook sent Crawford, Gatewood, and the scouts forward. A runner returned saying they had surprised and subdued a large Apache camp. When Crook caught up, he discovered the advance party had captured the women, children, and old people of Gerónimo's main band.

At almost the same time, while Crook was mobilizing his troops, Gerónimo led his warriors rode out of the mountains on raid east across the plains and the Palanganas River somewhere south of the future site of Mata Ortiz.[207] They went as far as the Santa María River near San Buenaventura, capturing five Mexican women, wives of soldiers stationed at Casas Grandes. Gerónimo's plan was to trade the women for Apache family members held at Casas Grandes since the massacre the previous summer. He still thought he could establish a peaceful trading relationship there.

At his campsite one night, Gerónimo had a vision. According to the young Betzinez, who was at his side, Gerónimo somehow suddenly knew his people back in the mountains had been captured. Abandoning the raid, but keeping the Mexican women, Gerónimo led the warriors back into the Sierra Madre. Whether spirits spoke to him or a shrewd guess, Gerónimo was right. Most of the women and old men left behind had surrendered to General Crook. After years of running, they had had enough. This included the old chiefs such as Loco and even Nana. Gerónimo watched the camp from a height, then rode down to confer with the general. Betzinez said the Apaches trusted Crook and in later years still thought highly of him. Crook laid out the options to Gerónimo, which essentially were to come to the reservation or be killed by either Mexican or U.S. troops. Gerónimo agreed but asked for time to collect those of his band still hiding in remote areas. The wily chief actually wanted time to raid and accumulate a herd of cattle and horses to sell to the Indians in San Carlos. The general really had no option. He and his troops had a large, potentially hostile, group to control. Had he taken Gerónimo by force, the others would have scattered. He accepted Gerónimo's promise to come to San Carlos in two months and gave orders to his troops to depart.

A long column of scouts, cavalrymen, and 375 Apache men, women, and children followed him out of the mountains, across the plains, and over the ghastly bone-strewn site near Janos where General García's Mexican soldiers had ambushed the escaping Apaches the previous year. In route, the captive Mexican women were returned to their families in Casas Grandes. The column crossed the border, camped in the Peloncillo Mountains, and continued to the San Carlos Reservation. Betzinez said their first location was not a good place, and the resident Apaches did not want them there. After a year, Crook had them moved north to the Fort Apache Reservation in the White Mountains. They were assigned an area called Turkey Creek about 15 miles from Fort Apache itself. Crook put Lt. Britton Davis in charge. The young officer rode to Turkey Creek and pitched his tent near the Apache encampment.

Other bands, led by various subchiefs straggled out of Mexico to the border and were escorted by Army soldiers to San Carlos or Fort Apache. Gerónimo did not arrive until February 1884, many months after he promised. Lt. Davis was ordered to the border to meet and escort him to Turkey Creek.

That same month Bandelier reported seeing fires in the Sierra Carcay set by Joaquín Terrazas's men patrolling for Apaches.[208]

Apparently Gerónimo thought he could re-enter the United States with his people and a stolen herd on his own terms. He did not understand the complexities of the world he was about to enter.

In spite of being hailed as a hero after the campaign, including a banquet in his honor given by the mayor of Tucson, General Crook received and continued to receive severe criticism from those with their own agendas. Many local people backed by sympathetic territorial newspapers did not want the renegades repatriated to the Arizona reservations, an early example of "not in my back yard." A significant number of Apaches from other bands already living at San Carlos had their own reasons for hating the Chiricahua and wanted nothing to do with Gerónimo or his people. News editors railed at Crook's so-called permissiveness. In spite of policies specifying their reservation authority, Crawford and his officers constantly clashed with the sometimes corrupt and often inept Department of Indian Affairs agents over jurisdiction, ration distribution, policing, and punishments. Federal and local civil agencies claimed jurisdiction, charging individual Apaches with murder and other crimes, despite amnesty agreements between these Apaches and the U.S Army. Mexican officials came across the border to re-claim stolen stock in accordance with diplomatic agreements. U.S. Custom officials wanted to confiscate this same stock until custom duties were paid. To top it all, Mexican soldiers still had the right under the mutual agreement of 1862 to cross the border and attack the Apaches.

Lt. Davis avoided all of these pitfalls and successfully shepherded a balky Gerónimo and his slow-moving herd through 200 miles of hostile Arizona to Turkey Creek. Crook would not permit Gerónimo to keep the herd. Mexican agents arrived, audited the brands on each animal, and drove them back across the border to the owners. No doubt, a beneficiary of this action was Luis Terrazas, who was acquiring large ranch properties. Gerónimo did not understand the diplomatic niceties of the U.S. government returning "his" stolen cattle and was enraged. Lt. Davis said he never got over it and his loss contributed to the events that followed.

In his book, Betzinez suggests the Apache were adapting to life at Turkey Creek. He does note that there were troublemakers. Lt. Davis had another view. He saw the Chiricahua as indifferent farmers who should have been given sheep and cattle to herd rather than the seed and plows the Department of Indian affairs insisted on providing.[209] Davis, living in his tent nearby, made an effort to know and understand his neighbors and charges. Gerónimo and a few other subchiefs remained aloof camping away from the main settlement. Davis worked hard to establish relationships with the individual Apaches, but he never liked Gerónimo. Davis saw him as vicious, intractable, and treacherous.

The Gerónimo Campaign

Negative political and bureaucratic factors combined with the actions of renegades who would not or could not live peacefully for any length of time, created a volatile mix that exploded in May 1885. While the Apaches had legitimate complaints, the catalyst was a clash of cultures. General Crook had forbidden brewing *tiswin*, a fermented drink made from sprouted corn.[210] It is similar to *tesgüino*, the Tarahumara drink prepared sometimes in Mata Ortiz for the Matachines dances. Another cultural issue was Crook's prohibition against wife beating and nose mutilation, the traditional Apache punishment for adultery. After a forbidden tiswin all-night drinking bout, the grim group of chiefs and subchiefs with their warriors stood at sunrise outside Lt. Davis' tent. They wanted to talk. Scouts stood by under trees watching. Davis invited them into his tent. The basic message was while they had agreed to surrender, they had not agreed to change the way they lived. Old Nana made a speech, stating emphatically that he was not a child and could eat or drink whatever he wanted. Further, his women were not mistreated if they behaved. He stalked out of the tent.[211]

The council was not a success. Davis could not rescind Crook's orders. After the Apaches left, he sent a courier to headquarters for instructions, but before a response came, Gerónimo, Nana, and other subchiefs heard that Lt. Davis and Chato, a Chiricahua raider turned Army scout, had just been killed. It was not true but it alarmed the chiefs because of the consequences they would suffer from such a murderous act. Their only alternative was to run. They gathered their bands, stole cavalry horses, cut the telegraph wire and broke out. For Gerónimo, it would be his last.

Many refused to follow. Loco with his people stayed as did young Betzinez, changing his mind at the last minute. The fugitives ran hard for the border, one group covering 90 miles in a single grueling nonstop stint. When Lt. Davis took muster, thirty-five warriors, eight boys not quite warriors, and 101 women and children were missing.[212]

It is hard to believe, but after all of this time and effort, Apaches were again raiding and killing across the border. Following the breakout, one particularly audacious group raided deep into Arizona, clear to Fort Apache, killing everyone they found, white or Indian, and carrying off women. They continued to raid even turning to attack patrols chasing them in hot pursuit. They re-crossed the border after four weeks of killing and mayhem, virtually unscathed.

To complicate matters General Philip Sheridan, Sherman's successor as General of the Army, the country's highest ranking army officer, arrived in Arizona to straighten things out. He opposed Crook's use of Apache scouts and advocated moving the troublesome Chiricahua Apaches and their families to Florida. To do this, the Apache first had to be caught. Sheridan wired authorization to Crook to pursue the renegades into Mexico.

Captain Crawford had become disgusted by the constant bickering with civilian Indian agents and had requested reassignment back to his former regiment. Crook immediately recalled him and sent him and Lt. Davis across the border with a large force of scouts. Lt. Gatewood followed with more scouts and units of the 4th Cavalry. They followed Gerónimo's trail deep into the same rugged canyons of the Bavispe River as Crook's 1883 expedition.

The large force found some of the women and children but rarely glimpsed the renegade warriors. After days of frustration, Crawford ordered Lt. Davis to take a smaller troop of forty scouts and follow newly discovered renegade tracks east. These eventually led out of the mountains. Based on Davis' description, the Apaches probably descended the San Diego Canyon route west of the Mata Ortiz site and crossed the plains and the Palanganas River. Davis and his men followed the trail over the Sierra America through San Joaquín Canyon to a campsite on the Santa María River, twelve miles north of San Buenaventura.[213] A few days later from a ridge, they sighted Gerónimo's band about fifteen miles away. The renegades now were going north after a raid for fresh horses on Luis Ter-razas's Hacienda Santa Clara, west of Namiquipa.[214] Davis' troops were too far away, but they followed anyway until they met a force of Mexicans. The Colonel in command informed Davis that he too was on Gerónimo's trail "seeking the same quarry." Under terms of the agreement the U.S. Army had to withdraw across the border.

By this time Davis' command was out of food, and the scouts were walking barefoot, having worn out their spare moccasins. After 24 days and 500 miles of mountain country, plus frustrating confrontations with uncooperative Mexican authorities, they ended up walking the last 75 miles along the railroad tracks to El Paso.

Davis went no farther. He resigned his commission and went to work as the manager of Hacienda Corralitos. In 1929, he wrote his book, *The Truth About Gerónimo* that gives many details and insights to the era. He dedicated the book to Captain Crawford and Lt. Gatewood.

Crawford returned to Arizona to refit. He re-entered Sonora in December with a much smaller, more effective command, mostly scouts and a pack train. Back in canyon country, his scouts found Gerónimo's camp. The Indians had vanished so suddenly that they left their supplies, food, and horses. Gerónimo, hiding nearby, sent a message that he would come in and talk with Crawford the next day.

At dawn, a group of Mexican scalp hunters (warrior scalps still brought 200 pesos), led by Santana Pérez and his second-in-command Mauricio Corredor, the Tarahumara hero of Tres Castillos, approached Crawford's sleeping camp and opened fire. They probably saw only Apaches and not U.S. Army Apache scouts. Crawford called out their identity in Spanish. When he stood up to wave a white handkerchief, someone fired and hit him in the head. Another bullet hit Tom Horn in the arm. The scouts went crazy and would have massacred the Mexicans if not restrained by the other officers. They already had shot dead Pérez and Corredor along with four of their men. It might be an embellishment to a good story, but it was said that Corredor shot Captain Crawford with the nickel-plated Sharps rifle given him six years earlier for killing Victorio. From a nearby ridge, Gerónimo and his warriors quietly watched.

Captain Crawford, wounded and unconscious but not yet dead, was carried north by his faithful scouts. He died a few days later near Saguaripa, where Francisco de Ibarra had fought the Ópata. They buried him, but a few months later a packer under Army orders exhumed the body and carried it on a mule to a Southern Pacific station in Arizona. It was loaded on a freight car and shipped to Kearney, Nebraska. Crawford was reburied there with one of the largest funerals ever held in the state. He still did not rest in peace. In 1908, old comrades, some now generals, ordered his body exhumed again and sent to Arlington National Cemetery for burial with full military honors. His grave is marked by a marble obelisk down the hill from the tomb of General Crook, his commanding officer.[215]

What became known as the Crawford Affair caused an international incident. The U.S. government formally protested and the Mexican government held an inquiry in Ciudad Chihuahua. The U.S. Army also held an inquiry. Nothing came of either and the issue between the countries faded. The publicity did not. To honor Crawford, two new communities were named for him later that year, Crawford, Nebraska and Fort Crawford, Colorado. These naming events not only honor Crawford's memory but illustrate the attention being paid to the details of the Apache Wars throughout the country at that time.

After this episode, Gerónimo agreed to meet with General Crook. In late March, the skittish Apache did show up for the meeting in remote Cañón de los Embudos (funnels) in northern Sonora about twenty miles southeast of the border town of San Bernardino.[216] The canyon remains difficult to access today, even with four-wheel-drive vehicles. Crook was well aware of the accusation of being soft on the Apaches. At this meeting, he made it very clear through his interpreters Tom Horn and Mickey Free that this was Gerónimo's last chance. Public pressure, starting with President Cleveland, was so great that exile and imprisonment were now part of the negotiations. Many wanted to hang Gerónimo and he knew it. The two adversaries finally agreed that Gerónimo would be sent to prison in Florida and then return to Turkey Creek. General Sheridan flatly rejected the agreement, citing President Cleveland's insistence on unconditional surrender.

For Crook this was the end of eight years of struggle. He submitted his resignation and was reassigned. Meanwhile, the suspicious Gerónimo, goaded by an unscrupulous whiskey trader that had been following Crook's detachment, decided he had been tricked and ran with a small group. Others, even old Nana, one of the hardest of them all, surrendered and submitted to escort across the border to San Carlos.

General Miles Takes Credit

General Nelson Miles, who had lobbied for the job for years, succeeded Crook. He did not believe in his predecessor's methods and made many changes, reducing the number of scouts, returning Lt. Gatewood to his regiment, and increasing the regular-army soldiers stationed at Arizona posts to 5,000, a fourth of the entire U.S. Army. He has been called pompous, arrogant and self-aggrandizing.[217] Justified or not, he did not have Crook's empathy for the Apaches or understanding of the tactical situation. What he did have was the complete backing of Sheridan, the Secretary of War, and the President, with access to unprecedented resources to capture or kill about three or four dozen Apaches.[218] After four fruitless months of the hardest kind of pursuit by regular soldiers, General Miles reluctantly agreed to recall Gatewood, the only officer left that Gerónimo trusted, and let him attempt to find the renegade and negotiate a surrender. Gatewood accepted his orders and took the field once again; this time with only two scouts, interpreter Tom Horn, and a small escort of soldiers. Although Gatewood was sick, he rode with his detachment 200 miles from the border through the Sierra Madre until his scouts picked up the trail near Fronteras, Sonora. The two scouts followed the trail for three days, carrying a flour sack on a stick as a flag of truce. The trail led to the foot of a ridge with a promontory called Torres Peak at the bend in the Bavispe River where it turns from north to south near the Sonora border. Gerónimo had been watching. He hailed them and invited them up to parlay. Not knowing if they would be shot, the two scouts climbed the ridge. Gerónimo stood there with a small group of warriors. They began to talk. After much conversation, the scouts convinced the warriors, if not Gerónimo, that if they ever wanted to see their families again, they must surrender and go to Florida. The renegades knew and trusted Gatewood and agreed to meet him the next day.

Still sick, the lieutenant rode to the designated place along the river and waited in a clearing. He sat, wondering if he would be killed. Warriors came individually or in small groups and stood by. Finally, Gerónimo himself stepped from the bushes. He sat down with Gatewood, commented on how thin the officer appeared and asked for whiskey. Gatewood had none, but he did have General Miles' simple terms—surrender and be sent to Florida to await the decision of the President as to their final disposition. Gerónimo flatly refused, insisting that they be allowed to go back to the reservation with full immunity. Gatewood told Britton Davis years later that Gerónimo looked him in the eye and said, "Take us to the reservation or fight." For the rest of that day and the next, Gatewood sat and listened to Gerónimo's harangues. He answered the same questions over and over. The few remaining warriors were tired and wanted to be with their families. One by one they stood and accepted the terms. Gerónimo, virtually alone, finally agreed to surrender to General Miles. Lt. Gatewood, an obscure, dedicated, and brave junior officer with two anonymous scouts had successfully negotiated the deal that effectively ended the Apache Wars and two centuries of conflict. [219]

The next step was to get Gerónimo and his band safely out Mexico. The Mexican Army had many troops in Sonora looking for them. On August 26, Gatewood and the Apaches joined with a small Fourth Cavalry detachment and started for the border. They had not gone far when the Mexican commander of the Fronteras garrison with 200 troops blocked the trail. They wanted Gerónimo or at the very least to be part of the surrender process. It was an explosive situation. The U.S. Army had official permission to be in Mexico, but the Mexicans deeply resented and outnumbered them. To make matters worse, the Apaches still carried their guns. Gerónimo had insisted they retain their arms until the border, knowing Mexican regulars and irregulars were after him with sharp scalping knives. He foresaw this confrontation. With his hand on his pistol, he became very excited, insisting he would have nothing to do with the Mexicans. Before the situation blew apart, Gatewood diverted Gerónimo and moved the Apaches down the trail while the Fourth Cavalry officers negotiated a compromise. They agreed that a Mexican officer could witness the meeting with General Miles and confirm for his government the final surrender.

Now Gatewood had the problem of getting General Miles to the meeting.[220] The general kept finding excuses, but finally reluctantly met and accepted the formal surrender of the Apaches with Gatewood on September 3 in the now famous Skeleton Canyon in the Peloncillo Mountains of southern Arizona. A monument stands commemorating the event of September 4, 1886, close to a rest stop off State Route 80 and Skeleton Road, near the New Mexico border.

The End of the Trail

After the surrender, Chiricahua Apache history diverges from events in and around the Casas Grandes Valley. In summary, General Miles lied to Gerónimo and the other Chiricahua, and he lied to his superiors about the agreement terms. He took credit for "capturing" Gerónimo and did his best to keep Lt. Gatewood out of the spotlight. He refused to let Gatewood attend a Tucson banquet honoring the Lieutenant, instead going himself and accepting the honors. In spite of ill health, Gatewood served ten more years in the Army in the Sioux Wars and Wyoming's Johnson County War, receiving serious wounds, and finally dying of cancer in 1896. He never was promoted to captain.

The Chiricahua, about 400 including those living peacefully at San Carlos, and more egregiously all of the U.S. Army scouts, were exiled to Florida. Civil authorities in Arizona and New Mexico wanted to try them all for murder. Instead, they were officially designated prisoners of war and removed. Women and children initially were separated from the men and sent to different locations at Fort Marion and Fort Pickens, a specific violation of the agreement. Eventually all were moved together to Mt. Vernon Barracks in Alabama. General Crook, in his new assignment as commander of the Division of Missouri, spent the rest of his life attempting to rectify this mistreatment of his former enemies. He died suddenly in 1890 with little being done other than reuniting a few Apache families. Four years later in 1894 and over eight years after shipment to Florida, the

341surviving Apaches, still prisoners of war, were moved to Fort Sill in the Indian Territory in what is now Comanche County in southeastern Oklahoma. They lived in rancherias around the post, farming and raising cattle.

The ultimate survivor Gerónimo took up farming and cattle raising, but more amazingly the Army gave this most-famous Indian desperado permission to participate in activities such as Pawnee Bill's Wild West Show. He also attended the St. Louis 1904 World's Fair, both as a visitor and an attraction, and rode the Ferris wheel. To cap these experiences, he rode in Theodore Roosevelt's inaugural-day parade in Washington DC in 1905. Unfortunately, like Mangas Coloradas and Juh before him, he had an ignominious end.

In 1909 at age 90, he indulged his taste for whiskey in a nearby town. Returning home, he fell off his horse and lay in the cold grass all night. That was too much even for the old warrior. He developed pneumonia and died in the Fort Sill Indian hospital on February 17, 1909.[221]

Gerónimo's legend was established long before his death. Dime novels and lurid newspaper articles titillated readers with his exaggerated exploits in the Wild West. This made him an attraction as people lined up with nervous anticipation for a glimpse of the murderous savage.

General Nelson Miles successfully climbed the political ladder and became Commanding General of the U.S. Army.

Jason Betzinez went to Carlisle Indian School in Carlisle, Pennsylvania, where he earned an Anglo name and learned to be a blacksmith, a trade he worked for 32 years. While in his 90s, he wrote his book that has become a basic source for historians.

In Chihuahua, Joaquín Terrazas quietly retired. Local historians still revere his memory, most dramatically in murals on government buildings in Ciudad Chihuahua, Galeana, and Casas Grandes.

Broncos and the Apache Kid

People of a fiercely independent raiding culture do not just disappear. Gerónimo's surrender ended the Apache Wars, but a few refused to follow him out of the mountains and a few could not. They remained hidden, some for decades, in the Sierra Madre's deep-canyon terrain. Their survival skills made them almost impossible to find. They occasionally stole stock and a few times committed grisly murders and kidnapped children. Renegades, known as "broncos," from Arizona and New Mexico joined them. Bronco outlawry lasted into the 1930s.

One of the most notorious broncos was a former Army scout known as the Apache Kid. In 1889, about to be imprisoned for a tiswin-induced murder, he killed his guards in route to the Yuma Territorial Prison. He raided across the southwest and into Sonora, becoming such a legend that at least four stories of his death exist. Three are violent. The fourth is that he died of tuberculosis in the mountains.[222] Verified sightings of the Kid were reported years after his death.

Most bronco action took place in the mountains on the Sonora side of the Continental Divide. On the Chihuahua side, the most famous event was the Hans A. Thompson family massacre in September 1892. Thompson with his wife and children had a farm and dairy near the LDS settlement of Colonia García in a mountain valley thirty miles west of Colonia Juárez. While he was away with his older sons working a part-time threshing job, his wife, two teenage boys and a six-year-old daughter did the chores. Eight Apaches came into the farmyard. They raised their guns and shot both boys and their mother. Ignoring the girl, they ransacked the house, loaded household goods on the two Thompson horses and left. One of the boys named Elmer, though wounded badly, survived as did his little sister Annie. Carl Lumholtz heard this story when he explored Cave Valley two years later. As was usual, the attack was blamed on the Apache Kid.

Apache Aftermath

Stories of Apache sightings persisted into the 1930s in the mountain towns such as Pacheco. True or not, these were the exceptions. The Apaches were effectively gone from the Casas Grandes Valley and all of Chihuahua. Bronco outlaws continued to raid from Sonora into Arizona. Vigilantes tracked them down. In November, 1935, a vigilante party ambushed and massacred two men and several women as they attempted to steal cattle staked out as a trap. This pathetic event was the last Apache fight.[223]

The Next Era Defined

The Apache Kid and his fellow outlaws committed horrible crimes, but their actions were more a nuisance than a deterrent to development in the Casas Grandes Valley. The elements that defined the previous 200 years, the Apaches and the erratic politics of the central government, had faded even before Gerónimo's surrender officially closed that era.

Different elements would describe the late 19th century and the first decade of the 20th. Porfirio Díaz claimed the presidency and remained the president/dictator for 37 years, an era known as the *Porfiriato*. His tight control resulted in an unprecedented period of national peace and stability. In contrast to his predecessors, he encouraged foreign investment, which led to the rapid development of railroads and other infrastructure to support expanded mining, ranching, lumber, and oil production. The land was concentrated into great haciendas owned by foreign corporations and wealthy Mexicans. Díaz also encouraged emigration and welcomed religious groups and any others seeking a new life.

With the Apaches gone and with a stable government, the defining elements for northern Chihuahua and Casas Grandes Valley became the arrival of the LDS settlers, the control of property and business by one man, and the development of resources by foreign capital. One side effect of the foreign investment would be the creation of a new town in the Casas Grandes Valley. They called it Pearson.

7

—

"I'm not from Chihuahua; Chihuahua is Mine" Luis Terrazas

The Portrait

In the salon of the Hacienda Agua Nueva hangs a portrait of Don Luis Terrazas. The standing figure looks out passively at the viewer. Other than the physical characteristics of a beard and balding head, the painting reveals little of its subject; the person who became Chihuahua's most powerful and second most famous man ever. He was said to be, among other things, the largest landowner and cattle rancher in the world. He may have been. Such superlatives are difficult to verify, but if Don Luis was not the very largest, he was competitive for that title. Between 1868 and 1910 he accumulated seven million acres. To put that in perspective, the famous King Ranch in Texas has 825,000 acres, and the largest ranch in the world today, an Australian sheep station, has six million acres. Much has been written about the number of acres, cows, haciendas, banks, factories, and businesses Terrazas owned. No clear picture of the man himself emerges from behind the statistics.

Don Luis physically was not a large man, although those who knew him, even in later life, described him as "sturdy" and "robust."[224] He was said to have a certain elegance without being flamboyant in spite of his

Luis Terrazas, largest land owner
and cattle rancher in the world.

wealth. As with the painting, nothing in his photographs—clothing or demeanor—suggests vast wealth or power.

The Debate

This contradiction is best illustrated by a contentious debate between two respected historians, Francisco R. Almada and Guillermo Porras. It started with a chapter about Terrazas in a book written by Almada in 1950 called *Gobernadores del Estado de Chihuahua*, chapter 39 to be specific. Almada's criticism of the great Chihuahua patriot of many titles, Don, Señor, General, and Gobernador Luis Terrazas caused a storm of controversy. Memories of the Revolution and the difficult years afterward were still vivid and divisive. Many weighed in on both sides, culminating in a four-month series of competing articles by Almada and Porras in two newspapers *El*

Heraldo and the *Tribuna*.[225] The two historians represented the classic sides of Mexican politics and culture—liberal and conservative. The fact that their debate existed at all may be because Terrazas was a contradiction exhibiting both liberal and conservative biases in his actions and associations as he built his empire and gained control over Chihuahua.

As a Liberal, Almada (1896-1989) was well qualified for his role as a revisionist historian. His own biography should be written. Described as a historian, professor, and politician, his books provide important references, particularly about Chihuahua. He started his political career as a *municipio* president and went on to serve in Chihuahua's state legislature, the federal legislature, and other political and academic positions. The most dramatic incident of his political life occurred when he was appointed Chihuahua's acting governor. An opposing faction tried to remove him physically from office. Shots were fired, killing the chief of police and a second man. It took federal troops to restore order. Almada survived the coup and was reappointed.

His literary opponent, Guillermo Porras (1917-1988), was also well qualified to enter the debate. More conservative than Almada, he studied in Jesuit schools becoming a lawyer and historian. After receiving a canonical doctorate in Spain, he was ordained. A unique fact in his history was his service as chaplain at Harvard University for seven years. His book *Haciendas de Chihuahua* is an important reference for historians.

The key points of disagreement concerned Terrazas's actions on four widely separated issues. The first concerned his conduct during the Battle of Tabalaopa, a minor episode during the terrible strife to retake Ciudad Chihuahua from the Conservatives during the War of Reform. Luis Terrazas and his cousin Joaquín Terrazas led a small force against a conservative position in a hacienda outside the city. Liberal leaders pressed more attacks on the city, and after a series of battles and guerrilla action, ultimately drove out the conservatives. Luis Terrazas received much of the credit and emerged as the man of the hour. At age 30, he was appointed state governor. According to Almada, the successes in battle claimed for Terrazas were fraudulent, and he actually lost the one skirmish he led at Tabalaopa. His cousin Joaquín, a hardened battle commander, openly confirmed their defeat. Almada makes much of this, using it as an example of Terrazas's self-aggrandizement.

What is more interesting about this incident is not the glorification of a defeat in battle since that has been going on throughout history. The fact that Luis Terrazas at age 30, with no military training, was given the authority and was able to raise and command an armed force, says a great deal about him and how he was regarded.

Another of Almada's criticisms had to do with the distribution of confiscated Church properties and use of the resulting funds. There is no question that Benito Juárez and the liberals destroyed the financial power that the Catholic Church wielded for more than two centuries. The net effect was to transfer Church land to a class of large landowners, *hacendados*, throughout Mexico. One powerful, privileged class was substituted for another, bypassing the general public that liberal policies were designed to benefit. Almada maintained that Terrazas was complicit in this transfer and he benefited personally. He goes on to say that when Terrazas first became governor in 1860 and was responsible for administering the disposition of Church lands, he not only sold Church properties to friends for low prices, he also retained the proceeds in the state treasury, contrary to federal instructions.

Terrazas rose to power by developing a complex network of family, friends, debtors, and officeholders beholden to him. He began by exploiting the important contacts within his wife's family and to expand them on a scale almost too complicated to comprehend. His four surviving sons became businessmen or held key governmental offices while his eight daughters married into other important families both liberal and conservative. One son-in-law, Enrique Creel, became a prominent banker, landowner, state governor, ambassador to the U.S., cabinet member, and an advisor to President/Dictator Porfirio Díaz.

Beyond his family, Terrazas as governor made sure the confiscated lands were sold to useful friends and office holders. For example, in 1886, he sold no less than five hacienda-size properties to José Cordero, a very rich merchant and former governor, who controlled a significant Liberal faction in the state.[226] With this type of ally, Terrazas was able to maneuver through the web of fractionalized liberals and intransigent conservatives that made up the Chihuahua political scene. He put at least part of the proceeds of the sales in the state treasury to pay state bills and refused to remit the required amounts to the federal government.

Almada's allegations were therefore at least partially correct. However, it must be noted that Terrazas does not appear to have personally gained financially during this first term as governor. The term ended in 1864 and he did not acquire his first property until 1865, and that property was very small by Chihuahua hacienda standards. What he did acquire during that period was a network of contacts and people beholden to him.

Almada's third charge criticized Terrazas's handling or mishandling of custom duties at the Chihuahua border points of entry, particularly El Paso. This was important revenue to the federal government, and like the Church property sales, too much stayed in the state treasury.

The fourth charge concerned financial dealings of Terrazas's Banco Minero. Guided by Enrique Creel, the Terrazas family created a powerful banking conglomerate, headed by Banco Minero. By granting or withholding credit, they controlled who did business in Chihuahua. In addition to this use or abuse of power, Almada complained that the bank issued fraudulent paper of some sort in the early days of the Revolution. He may have been right. Given the times, it is almost impossible to determine what actually happened, let alone assess motive.

Guillermo Porras counters the charges in his published responses. He stated emphatically that Luis Terrazas was the greatest man Chihuahua ever produced.[227]

The Young Luis

The variety of issues debated by the two historians illustrates the complexities and contradictions of Terrazas's story. From boyhood in Ciudad Chihuahua, he moved rapidly into prominent positions. Born on July 20, 1829, he was baptized four days later in the great cathedral on the city's central plaza, a structure that would play other roles in his life. His father was Juan Terrazas and mother Petra Fuentes. The Terrazas extended family had been in Chihuahua for a long time. Luis's great grandfather, Lucas Terrazas y Soto, a cattleman, lived in an area called Labor de Dolores. Later the named changed to Labor de Terrazas. Lucas had thirteen sons.[228] This significant procreation resulted in several Terrazas family lineages in Chihuahua. In later decades, distant cousins of Luis, like the soldier

Joaquín Terrazas, supported him while, others, like newspaperman Silvestre Terrazas opposed him.

Two men influenced Luis in his youth, which gives some insight to his character. The first was his father, Juan José Terrazas, a religious man, who owned a butcher shop and other small businesses and was successful enough to send his son Luis to the Instituto Científico y Literario, a secondary school on the plaza across from the cathedral. The school founder, Padre Luis Rubio, was the other significant influence on young Luis. In spite of Terrazas's anti-Church position at the political level, Padre Rubio remained a part of his life, officiating at family baptisms and marriages.[229]

The plan was for Luis to become a priest. However, cholera made one of its periodic sweeps through Chihuahua in 1849 and took Juan Terrazas. At age twenty, Luis took over the butcher shop. He already had some experience working with his father, and now as the proprietor, he learned all aspects of the meat business, practical lessons that would serve him well. Two years later at age 22, Luis came to the attention of Governor Urquidi, who gave him his first public employment as *guardia fiscal* of the Administración General de Rentas, essentially an auditor for the tax collector.

He also started a family. On February 2, 1852, he married Carolina Cuilty Bustamante, age 19, the daughter of Col. Gabino Cuilty. Whether the marriage was a romantic liaison or arranged is unknown, but it was fortuitous for Terrazas. Not only did the marriage last for 67 years, producing 14 children, but Carolina was politically and socially connected. Luis used these connections skillfully as he began to build his empire.

It may be that Luis fathered 14 children, but Carolina bore only thirteen. Rumor indicates that one girl, Guadalupe, was Luis's illegitimate daughter.[230] If true, this bit of historic gossip confuses the understanding of Terrazas's character. As a young man, he studied to be a priest. Virtually all his biographers describe him as a family man, a hard worker, and man of simple pleasures not susceptible to the usual temptations of vast wealth. Whatever happened, the marriage lasted a very long time, and all reports indicate he was devoted to Carolina. If Guadalupe was the result of a casual encounter, Luis took responsibility and raised her.

Carolina's father had acquired a huge property in the Cuauhtémoc area of Chihuahua that became the Hacienda Bustillos. This came about because of the family relationship with Anastasio Bustamante, a military leader during the War of Independence. Later Bustamante served as president for brief periods during the post-Independence era of revolving-door presidents. He was in office at least long enough to see that Colonel Cuilty got the hacienda.

By 1845, Cuilty had already passed the property to another son-in-law, Pedro Zuloaga, who, with several brothers, made up one of Chihuahua's most powerful conservative families. Pedro married Carolina's sister Luz.[231] Pedro's brother José owned the Hacienda Corralitos and was a major player in the mid-19th century history of the Casas Grandes Valley. The genealogy is complicated, but the underlying point is that Luis at 22 was now on the inside circle of powerful Chihuahua families. The genealogy became an integral part of an even more complicated political scene. Luis Terrazas's meteoric rise occurred and was part of one of the most turbulent times in Mexico's turbulent history. The rebellion against His Most Supreme Highness General Santa Anna led to the War of Reform. That was the tipping point in Chihuahua as many turned from supporting Santa Anna to the liberal side, at least to a Chihuahua style of liberalism. The Chihuahuans opposed the Church's privileges, wealth, and excesses while remaining loyal to the Catholic religion. They fiercely resented and opposed invaders of any kind. Some remained conservative including the Zuloaga brothers, while others like oft-times Governor Don Ángel Trías became staunch liberals. Terrazas identified with the liberals but began a long career of liberal and conservative actions and associations that built his empire and confounded his contemporary opponents and later historians.

After fulfilling his three-year obligation with the Administración General de Rentas, Terrazas successfully ran for the council of the Ciudad Chihuahua municipio. A year later in 1856, he joined with his wife's brother-in-law, the ultra-conservative Pedro Zuloaga, to bid successfully on the meat delivery contract for Ciudad Chihuahua.[232] Luis had learned his father's lessons well and was now in a lucrative meat business.

In 1859, he was reelected to the council but before he could complete his term, the old-time conservative-turned-liberal, Ángel Trías, appointed Terrazas as jefe político of the Iturbide District that included Ciudad

Chihuahua. Trías was between governorships and the comandante of Chihuahua's armed forces. Terrazas's position as jefe político made him the military commander of the city with rank of colonel. He was also elected an alternate deputy to the state legislature.

In the War of Reform, the conservative forces initially overwhelmed the liberals in Chihuahua, occupying the capital and installing a governor. When the liberals ultimately prevailed, Terrazas emerged as one of the heroes (right or wrong as debated by Almada and Porras). Benito Juárez's government, back in power in Mexico City, appointed Terrazas governor of the state. He was just 30 and unprepared for the job. As capable as he was, he inherited an insolvent government faced with raiding Apaches in the north and implacable conservative enemies everywhere else. To cap his difficulties and the difficulties of his nation, the French landed troops in Veracruz in early 1862. This led to the rift with Benito Juárez over Terrazas's refusal to provide men to leave Apache-ravaged Chihuahua to fight the French. Terrazas lost his position and had to flee across the border to El Paso. That he was able to mend the rift and reestablish himself with the typically intransigent Juárez reveals something of Terrazas's character and ability. Also, the two master politicians needed each other during those desperate times. Juárez with his government in exile tried to lead the resistance from Ciudad Chihuahua. He reinstated Terrazas as governor but only briefly because troops loyal to the new Emperor occupied the city. Juárez and his government members retreated to El Paso.

The indomitable spirit of their Indian president-in-exile began to unite the country. The Emperor's army struggled to maintain control, especially in Chihuahua. In February 1865, the French occupation troops were assigned elsewhere, and the city was left with a contingent of pro-Maximilian Mexican troops. Luis Terrazas and his cousin Joaquín saw their opportunity. Luis by now had been promoted to "general." The two organized 550 men and attacked the city with a pincers movement that forced the defenders into the cathedral. After a few cannon balls were lobbed into the cathedral, one hitting a bell, the garrison surrendered. Maximilian's forces never returned. Juárez moved his government back to Ciudad Chihuahua. In December 1866 with Maximilian about to fall, General Terrazas rode in the honor guard that escorted Juárez to the Chihuahua-Durango border.

Juárez asked Terrazas to join his government in Mexico City, but Luis knew his fortunes lay in Chihuahua.

Porfirio Díaz Becomes President

Díaz, hero of the Battle of Puebla and a former supporter of Benito Juárez in the struggle to oust Maximilian, turned on and challenged Juárez at the time of the latter's reelection in 1872. Díaz was unsuccessful, actually losing against Juarista forces at Cerro de Bufa near Zacatecas, close to where Pancho Villa would later win a major battle in the Revolution. When Juárez suddenly died of a heart attack on July 9, 1872, Díaz renewed his challenge against Vice President Sebastián Lerdo de Tejada, Juárez 's successor.

Lerdo de Tejada proved to be no pushover. An experienced politician, he probably was Juárez's closest advisor. He worked hard to carry out Juárez's policies and capably administered the still-fractionalized country for an entire term. Regional *caciques* or war lords were neutralized and beginnings made to restore and modernize the country's devastated infrastructure. He oversaw the completion of Mexico's first railroad, a line between the port of Veracruz and Mexico City.

Luis Terrazas as governor of Chihuahua supported Lerdo de Tejada and opposed Díaz. When Díaz made a move in Chihuahua, Terrazas confronted him and personally escorted the humiliated usurper to the state border. This did not stop the ambitious Díaz. Over the next five years, he gained allies around the country. When Lerdo de Tejada was reelected in 1876, Díaz defied him, claiming he violated the no re-election laws. When Lerdo de Tejada tried to enforce his legitimacy with federal troops, he lost in battle against Díaz supporters at Tecoac in the state of Tlaxcala, north of Puebla. Lerdo de Tejada went into exile in New York City, and Porfirio Díaz took over the government in Mexico City. In spite of his widely publicized no re-election campaign, he managed to stay as head of the country for the next 35 years.

Through a policy of patronage and force, termed *pan o palo*, "bread or club," Díaz gained allegiance from most of the state leaders and caciques throughout the country, but not Chihuahua.

In 1884, Díaz tried to exploit the regional factions there by officially removing Terrazas as governor and replacing him with people from Guerrero, a Chihuahua District south of the Casas Grandes Valley, hostile to the Terrazas family. Many appointees followed. Ángel Trías Jr. even served as governor briefly. Don Luis was out of office for 19 years as Porfirio Díaz used all of his skills to marginalize the Terrazases. He met his match. The combined efforts of Díaz at the federal and the *Guerreristas* at the state level could not take Terrazas down. The story is a complicated tangle of regional alliances, political power plays, and economic control. Don Luis was a master in this arena. His family remained entrenched and actually prospered during the next twenty years, as they deflected opposition moves and co-opted former enemies. Even early in Díaz's regime, when his attacks on Terrazas were intense, the family was able to diversify, building a textile mill and the first modern flour mill in Chihuahua. Their cattle empire continued to grow as did their influence. According to historian Mark Wasserman, by 1910, most of the leading families of Chihuahua were related to the Terrazases by blood, marriage, or business.

Terrazas's Haciendas

In 1865, the same year that Maximillian's forces were driven from Chihuahua, Terrazas bought his first property, the Rancho Ávalos just south of Ciudad Chihuahua.[233] He bought it from a widow and paid over two years. Not long after, he acquired an adjacent property called La Cañada. This piece had sentimental value because his father had run cattle there.[234] The combined properties became known as Ávalos y Anexos. Compared with future acquisitions, it was very small, 17,712 acres (7,168 hectares). These purchases just hinted at what was to come.

At 36, Luis had risen to prominence through tumultuous times. He understood how to make the dysfunctional system work to his benefit. The corruption of President Benito Juárez's liberal land policies, intended to strip the Church of its vast holdings, also opened the door to confiscating communal land of small communities. People the policies were supposed to protect lost their properties. Throughout Mexico, administrators at the state level granted land to friends and those in power. Even Juárez could not head off these unintended consequences and the process began of converting much of Mexico's productive land into large haciendas owned by a few powerful families. This occurred in the north but, at least initially, in a different way.

Many landholders, large and small, had already left Chihuahua. Vast amounts of property had been simply abandoned because of the ongoing Apache menace. Land was cheap, and while the Apache would remain a threat for fifteen more years, the time to acquire property was now. The right man with a little capital and a great deal of courage could make a fortune. Luis Terrazas was that man, not the only one but the most successful. He bought from those willing to sell at low prices, often with payment terms of two to three years to leverage his capital. One title after another was recorded in the Palacio de Gobierno in Ciudad Chihuahua.[235]

His next acquisition was much larger than Rancho Ávalos y Anexos, the Hacienda Agua Nueva (sometimes Aguanueva). The full name was and is the Hacienda Nuestra Señora de Guadalupe de Agua Nueva. It still exists as an operating rancho 150 miles south of Ciudad Juárez on the east side of Highway 45. When Terrazas bought it in 1867, the property covered

Hacienda Agua Nueva

270,294 acres (109,384 hectares). He added more in 1875 and 1901. Text on a glazed-tile plaque in the entryway of the main house states that Luis Terrazas remodeled the house adding corridors and stonework. He used the finest building materials throughout. Even the horse troughs in the stable just behind a central patio were made of marble. He turned this estate over to Enrique Creel, his son-in-law.

To complicate the relationship, Creel was the son of a North American, Reuben Creel, who had married a sister of Carolina Cuilty, Luis's wife. The government confiscated the property after the Revolution, but a member of the Creel family was able to buy it back. A Creel descendant owns it today. The main house has been beautifully restored. The stable stalls now are modern guest rooms, each featuring a marble horse trough along the back. Beyond the manicured front lawn, the Chihuahua desert stretches northeast toward Tres Castillos. The tile plaque in the entryway also says that in 1880, Joaquín Terrazas and Juan Mata Ortiz brought the Apache prisoners here after the Battle of Tres Castillos.

Not many of the haciendas have retained their glory like Agua Nueva. The main house for the Hacienda El Carmen, acquired in 1877 and 1892, now is a well-used middle school in the town of Ricardo Flores Magón (named for the early radical revolutionary, whose inspiration helped bring down the hacendados). The run-down building has an impressive façade, and the tile floor and architectural flourishes around the doors and windows of the entry corridor hint at former grandeur.

The main house of Hacienda San Lorenzo, acquired in 1872, has not been converted for any reuse. Where it once overlooked 246,464 acres (99,740 hectares), it now stands vacant and crumbling amongst other buildings on the main street of the town of San Lorenzo. A gap shows around a door where an elaborate wooden door frame was purloined. It now decorates the entrance to a house on Buenaventura's plaza.

Terrazas's largest acquisition was Ángel Trías' old spread, the Hacienda Encinillas. The property dates to Spanish times and the first silver strike at Santa Eulalia. After the original Spanish grant or *mercedes*, the hacienda passed through several hands and was expanded until it contained over 1,300,000 acres (526,091 hectares) by Ángel Trías' time. Don Ángel Trías, one of the more stable characters in the chronically unstable Chihuahuan political history, lost much of his property after his two defeats defending Ciudad Chihuahua during the Mexican American War. The dedicated commander had personally raised and financed the defending army. Although he retained political influence until his death in 1867, he never recovered his properties. His son Ángel, Jr. concentrated on his military and political career and never rebuilt the family fortune.

The hacienda became the property of Dr. José Pablo Martínez del Río Castiglione. This prominent doctor and professor of obstetrics was part of a Spanish family that had established businesses in Panama before moving to Mexico. They were ultraconservatives and monarchists, part of the European-oriented elite that welcomed Maximilian to Mexico. Dr. Martínez del Río was actually the spokesman for the Mexican delegation that offered the crown to the new emperor.

The Encinillas property extended for miles south of the town of Ahumada on the main road between Ciudad Juárez and Chihuahua (Highway 45). Because of its location, the hacienda had served as a major stopover for travelers as well as a major target for Apache raids since the late 17th century. Repeated raids made it difficult to raise and sell cattle profitably, and Dr. Martínez del Río was not interested in hands-on management. He leased the property to Terrazas and a partner, Enrique Müller, for a low price. They took a business risk, managed the operation well enough to meet expenses and were able to hold on through the French occupation. After Maximilian's fall in 1867, Benito Juárez's government exiled sympathizers like Martínez del Río and confiscated their properties. Somehow through the political machinations, Müller emerged as the hacienda owner. The next year, 1868, Terrazas bought 965,000 acres (390,521 hectares) from Müller.[236] In 1905, he bought the remainder from Müller's heirs.

The rest of Dr. Martínez del Río's story illustrates the shifting alliances, influences, and contradictions of the era that Luis Terrazas understood so well. Totally discredited as an imperialist collaborator, Martínez del Río and his family lived in exile in Europe. In 1870, inexplicably, Juárez, who had refused to spare Maximilian's life, granted amnesty to many he had banished. Dr. Martínez del Río not only returned to Mexico with a full pardon, he recovered some of his property (not Encinillas) and lived out his life as a distinguished vice president of Mexico's National Academy of Medicine.[237]

Francisco Almada and other critics claimed Terrazas obtained properties through shady practices. There is no question that he paid low prices.
However, more than half of his holdings were acquired while the Apaches
were still active. He took the risk that enough cattle would survive each
year in the ravaged regions to be sold to meet expenses. He was an astute
businessman and exploited the laws as they were written. If he did anything illegal according to those laws, no one ever proved it, no matter how
loud their condemnation.[238]

Not long after the Encinillas purchase, he bought Hacienda Sauz,
another old Spanish property, located south of Encinillas not far from
Ciudad Chihuahua. Today a road lined with pecan groves extends east
from Highway 45 to the old hacienda compound. By the 21st century, the
buildings lay in ruins. The Municipio of Chihuahua acquired the central
compound and restored the manor house into a museum honoring the
Apaches, an ironic 21st century touch for a place that had had fought the
Apaches for 200 years.

Terrazas managed his ranching operations with meticulous care. He
studied the topography to use the land to its best advantage for crops, pasture, or rangeland. His people dug wells and built windmills to pump water
to earthen cattle-watering tanks. Farm plots provided corn, wheat, and
other products for his workers' tables. There is no question that most hacienda workers were little more than serfs, tied to the land by tradition, debt,
and lack of alternatives. Terrazas treated his workers better than most. The
least of his laborers were safe and relatively comfortable.[239] He particularly valued his vaqueros and often rode with them as they tended his vast
herds. They received good wages and in some cases their patrón permitted
them to run a few of their own cows on his range. One story is still told in
Chihuahua. President Díaz late in his reign visited his old adversary Terrazas at Casa Carolina, the mansion Luis built for his wife on the outskirts
of Ciudad Chihuahua. The two stood and looked out from the balcony at
the well-dressed crowds that had been summoned to honor the president.
Díaz asked where the workers were. Terrazas replied that these were the
workers. Díaz said he would never have to worry about rebellion in Chihuahua with such contented people.[240] The soon-to-be-deposed president
was wrong of course, but the story, true or apocryphal, makes the point.

Paz Porfiriana

Part of Don Luis Terrazas's spectacular success was timing. He personified the old expression that defines luck as "preparation meeting opportunity." At the beginning of the last quarter of the 19th century much of Chihuahua was in shambles. Decades of warfare had decimated the infrastructure of ranchos and farms—wind mills, acequias, corrals, and barns. Most mines were closed, some flooded with machinery rusting and inoperable. Little credit was available to promote business since the Church, the source of capital for centuries, had lost most of its assets. No trains or telegraphs—the modern communication systems of the era—operated. President Lerdo de Tejada brought some stability to the nation and encouraged development during his term. Porfirio Díaz built on that beginning. The positive features of his long period of rule were stability and economic development. The era of calm, so unique in Mexico's stormy history became known as the *Paz Porfiriana*, Porfirio's Peace. He restored public order and maintained it with his pan o palo technique, inducements and enforcement exercised by his personal police force, the *Rurales*.

Lerdo de Tejada had used his own version of these techniques. The two differed, however, on foreign investment. Lerdo de Tejada said, "Between strength and weakness—the desert," meaning he wanted barriers between the economic strength of the U.S. and relatively weak Mexico. Díaz saw it differently and welcomed U.S. and European investment.

By 1884, the Apaches were almost finished in northern Chihuahua. The country was stable. Foreign entrepreneurs, especially North Americans, were seeking concessions to invest in capital projects such as railroads and to develop Mexico's natural resources. The rising industrialized countries wanted the products Chihuahua could produce. All of these factors came together to provide the opportunity that Luis Terrazas had been preparing for since he took over his father's butcher shop.

The *Ferrocarril Central Mexicano*, the Mexican Central Railroad, incorporated in Massachusetts in 1880, completed a line from Ciudad Chihuahua to Ciudad Juárez in 1884. The line was extended south to Mexico City two years later. The new tracks crossed the river at El Paso and connected to the Southern Pacific, Santa Fe, and other U.S. lines. Governor

Terrazas happily drove the first spike into the rail of track that would pass through Hacienda Encinillas and near other of his haciendas. As the market was strong for Mexican cattle and minerals, the governor and the other surviving ranchers experienced a boom. For those who had not survived, Terrazas had ready cash to buy their properties. Again and again, he was accused of shady dealings by contemporary opponents and historians such as Almada. He did take advantage of the later laws that forced the sale of communal lands. Yet the sales records always seemed to name a seller. Who these sellers were often is unknown. Some were probably friends of Don Luis or influential people to whom he sold confiscated Church properties in the 1860s. Whoever they were, they had abandoned the land and sold for whatever they could get. Guided by Enrique Creel, the family had branched into banking. With his old conservative partner, Pedro Zuloaga, Luis and Enrique took over the Banco Minero de Chihuahua and built it into one of the most important banking institutions in Mexico. Creel became the leading banking figure not only in Chihuahua but the entire country.[241] Members of the Guerrero faction, old Terrazas enemies, had started the bank, but they could not withstand the economic pressure and lost it to the man they had pledged to destroy.

As governor, Terrazas steered the state's deposits to Banco Minero, conflict of interest being an unrecognized concept. The bank provided credit but only to enterprises approved by him. Although no longer governor, he continued to maintain tight control. Any foreign or local entrepreneur that Don Luis did not want found himself blocked by bureaucrats, the courts, or even the police. For those enterprises that did meet his approval, Don Luis and family members usually participated or benefited in some way as they did with the Mexican Central Railroad. The Guggenheim family, owners of huge mining and smelting company ASARCO, were close to Porfirio Díaz, but to start their smelter near Ciudad Chihuahua they had to buy the property and a state concession from the Terrazas family and turn the company store operation over to Luis' son Juan Terrazas.

Most of the Terrazas properties lay well to the east and south of the Casas Grandes Valley. One however, San Diego, was located in the center of the valley and is very important to the Pearson/ Mata Ortiz story.

Another was San Miguel Babícora, directly south of San Diego and extending into the San Buenaventura municipio.

Hacienda de San Diego

The highway going west from Casas Grandes makes a few winding turns in the low hills of Pasa de la Morita (also called Pasa de la Tinaja) just north of Cerro Moctezuma. Past a solitary packing house, the highway divides, one branch continuing west over the hills to the Latter-day Saints town of Colonia Juárez. The other turns south to Mata Ortiz. Past a bridge over the Piedras Verdes River, a large highway sign indicates a left turn to San Diego. After the turn, the pavement continues a short distance before the road turns to dirt. A few houses line the road. Three large buildings can be seen over the fields. On a slight rise above the arroyo stands the manor house of Hacienda San Diego.

The first view is of a large, single-storied structure, tall and imposing, in part because of the fifteen-foot interior ceilings and in part because the main floor is raised several feet above ground level. A broad staircase across the front leads through an arched portico to the main entrance. The house faces east making it photogenic in the morning sun and a dramatic evening scene as the sun sets over the Sierra Madre behind.

There is no question who built and owned the house. The initials LT stand out clearly carved in the stone façade above the portico entrance. Within the thick adobe walls are 18 rooms, two baths, and seven fireplaces. Rows of water pipes heated by a large wood-fired oven provided hot water to the baths, an advanced system for the time.[242] Construction began in 1902 and was finished two years later. The beginning date also is carved above the portico. The exterior window frames and the façade above and around the portico are made from *cantera,* a local volcanic stone. Durable, light weight, pale pink-orange in color, it can be carved into decorative shapes. The central patio featured a cantera fountain with a rearing horse of the same material. Someone broke in and stole the horse many years ago. A well-made replica was installed in 2004. Stone cutting must have been a respected skill because cutters left their mark etched into the stone work.

At San Diego Don Luis used architect Pedro Ignacio Irigoyen, who had worked on many of his projects. In 1881, during one of the periods when he was governor, he hired Irigoyen to build the Palace of Governors on Ciudad Chihuahua's main plaza. Irigoyen had been head of the Instituto Científico y Literario during 1850-51, the same school that Luis left to take over his father's butcher shop. Clearly, Terrazas admired Irigoyen's work. There are similarities between San Diego, one of Terrazas's late projects, and the main house at Encinillas, one of his earliest. San Diego differs in one distinct way in that there are no protective walls. The Apache Wars were over, ending the need to make ranch buildings into forts. Beyond the house to the south stands a large store house, *la bodega*. In addition to storage for grain, this edifice contained stables, offices, and a blacksmith shop. Down the gentle slope a short distance on the front side of the house stands a low rectangular building consisting of a series of rooms surrounding a large patio. These were quarters for at least some Terrazas employees. They called their quarters *las cuadras*, "the blocks." About 100 people lived there.

Near the employee compound was a stone corral. It still stands and is used each October 12 for a *jaripeo*, a calf roping and bull-riding contest.

Guillermo Genaro "Willy" Acosta Gutiérrez and his wife Sara Ramírez raised their three children, Diana, Denisse, and Daniel, in the manor house. Willy grows crops, mainly alfalfa, on farm plots, *labors*, on the rich bottom land near the junction of the Río Piedras Verdes and Río Palanganas. Willy has been on the property his entire life. He traces his family back through three generations of San Diego administrators to Jacobo Anchondo, Don Luis' manager.

In 1779, Padre Juan Agustín de Morfi saw the land called San Diego, when he accompanied Comandante General Teodoro de Croix of the Provincias Internas on an inspection trip. He recorded the name but made no mention of any settlement.[243]

In 1843, Torre, an Apache chief, made a request to the Janos presidio commander for farm land at "Rancho San Diego." Torre claimed his right to the land because his father, a prominent chief in the early 1800s, had "owned" the property. This might have referred to plots assigned around

Janos in 1802-03 during a peaceful time when some Apache bands agreed to try farming.[244] There is no indication of what happened to the request. A report of an Apache raid on "Haciendas" San Diego and San Miguel suggests there was active ranching in 1832,[245] but a later notation in a presidio report said San Diego was vacant in 1843. Other fragments in the historical record indicate someone tried to operate the rancho between 1843 and about 1867. In May 1884, Adolph Bandelier camped among what he described as the ruins in San Diego. He observed that the rancho must have been an "important concern" based on the number of buildings. However, the entire place had been abandoned for 25 years because of the Apache threat.[246] President Porfirio Díaz declared the land vacant in 1884 and sold or awarded Rancho San Diego to Domingo Leguinazábal in 1885.[247] Don Domingo with his unusual surname was a prominent merchant and member of an old Spanish family in Ciudad Chihuahua.[248] Six years later, a North American named Mr. Galvin (no first name given) was leasing the ranch according to Carl Lumholtz. Galvin let Lumholtz and his crew camp on the ranch and excavate anywhere they wanted. By this time Luis Terrazas may have owned the San Diego rancho. If so, he leased all or some part to Galvin.

Terrazas put together five parcels to create the Hacienda San Diego. While specific information is available for most of Terrazas's acquisitions, the references do not show the exact dates for San Diego. The timeframe can be narrowed down to between 1886 and 1901. The names of the previous owners are known, but circumstances of the sales are not. All of the five transactions create questions.

Don Luis acquired the first parcel from Señora Josefa Leguinazábal y Loya, who Terrazas probably knew. The Señora was the widow of Domingo Leguinazábal and perhaps wanted out of what to her was useless property. The fact that the word *cesión*, assignment, is attached to the sale reference, suggests that Don Luis and la Señora had a property-transfer arrangement different from a conventional sale. However it was accomplished, this transaction included the core rancho property. The land extended south to the northern boundary of Hacienda San Miguel Babícora. That boundary crossed the future Pearson/Mata Ortiz site through what is now Barrio López.

Alfonso Lancaster Jones sold the second parcel. Jones also owned Hacienda Tapiecitas, a 191,000-acre (77,295 hectares) property northwest of Casas Grandes that he sold to Terrazas in 1898.[249] Jones received Tapiecitas from Díaz's government in late 1886. His motive for selling is unknown, but it may have been nothing more than a speculative investment. Jones was a very prominent citizen in late 19th century Mexico. It is unlikely he would be a party to transaction that put him at a disadvantage. Trained as a lawyer, he served terms as both a senator and deputy in both houses of the national congress and rose to be president of the Chamber of Deputies. Porfirio Díaz appointed him Special Envoy to Great Britain to attend the coronation of Edward VII, after which he became ambassador.[250] If he had other motives for acquiring and selling Chihuahua land for other than speculative investment, it is not known.

Why General Carlos Fuero, the third seller, sold his parcel or ever acquired it in the first place also is not known. Historian Philip Stover has done considerable research on General Fuero and found nothing in his background that indicates he dealt in land. General Fuero is described as trustworthy, powerful, and highly respected in Mexico. His name even came into the common vocabulary as synonymous with honesty and a man of his word. He fought for Lerdo de Tejada against Díaz. After Díaz prevailed, instead of punishing his enemy, the new president offered the general a high position in the army administration. Fuero held several important commands, fought Apaches, and had the unusual distinction of being governor of four different states. He is most famous in northern Chihuahua for ordering the colonists of the Church of Jesus Christ of Latter-day Saints (LDS) to leave Mexico in 1885 while he was acting governor. He did not like foreigners and did not want them in his state or country. Over his strong objections, the LDS colonists appealed to Díaz, who overruled Fuero. The general was not happy, and as soon as a military position opened up elsewhere, he resigned as acting governor and left Chihuahua.[251] Why he acquired the property that the record shows he sold to Terrazas is unknown.

The fourth and fifth sales involved the LDS colonists and were even more mysterious. The record shows that parcels were transferred to Terrazas from the Mexican Colonization and Agricultural Company,

Hacienda San Diego
Photo: 3635866_AZSW Courtesy of
the University of Arizona Libraries, Special Collections

represented by Anthony Ivins.[252] The LDS Church had set up the company to hold its Mexican lands in trust.

Elder Anthony Ivins was a very important LDS leader, who later became an Apostle of the Church. He first came to Mexico in 1875 when Brigham Young sent a group from Salt Lake City to seek converts and find land for settlement. Their trip took them to Ciudad Chihuahua and through the Casas Grandes Valley. They found converts but no land. Ten years later after a great deal of effort, the LDS colonists obtained land for settlement. The question is why did Elder Ivins transfer parcels back to Terrazas? It may have had to do with the boundary-line confusion that occurred when the LDS colonists purchased land that became Colonia Juárez during the same time period that Terrazas was acquiring the Leguinazábal parcel.

Whatever the circumstances behind the five land transfers, Terrazas put together a major property totaling 122,000 acres (49,371 hectares) that became Hacienda San Diego.[253]

Jacobo Anchondo, a brother-in-law, managed San Diego for Don Luis.[254] The village of Anchondo on the road between San Diego and Casas Grandes, Camino de la Boquilla, was named for him. He must have been well compensated because he lived in a large, hacienda-style house called *El Refugio* in Casas Grandes that exists today, fully restored.

Anchondo appears to have managed San Diego as best he could during the Revolution. Rebel factions, led by various leaders, Orozco, Castillo, Salazar, and most notoriously Pancho Villa, roamed the valley.

The conflict between the hacendado Terrazas and rebel chieftain Villa was a central theme of the Revolution in Chihuahua. One of Villas' tactics was to drive off the herds from Terrazas's various haciendas. San Diego suffered losses, whether by Villa's men or others. The blame routinely fell on Villa for the actions of other rebel bands. Old timers told stories of seeing Villa at San Diego, or of knowing someone who saw him. In the vast number of photographs taken of Villa, none show him there.

Squatters caused other problems. Not all rebel leaders believed in land reform, but some like Máximo Castillo encouraged dispossessed local people to move on to hacienda property, plant crops, and take irrigation water.

After the Revolution, Terrazas reacquired Hacienda San Diego, and Anchondo continued as manager. His successor, Genaro Andazola Parra, was Willy Acosta's uncle. Another uncle, Ricardo Chávez followed Parra. After Chávez was Willy's father, Tomas Acosta Andazola.

When the hacienda lands were broken up, starting in 1920, 11,363 hectares (28,079 acres) were assigned to the old Casas Grandes ejido.[255] The hacienda managers became ejidatarios with rights to parcels designated for farming. Willy Acosta retains the ejidatario status and these rights.[256]

The manor house stands as a magnificent, crumbling monument to another era and to the man who dominated that era. The Acosta family members are proud of this history and proud of the building that is their family home.

Hacienda San Miguel Babícora

Luis Terrazas generally treated his vaqueros and field workers well by the standards of his time. Even his critic Francisco R. Almada did not complain about Don Luis as the patrón of thousands of employees. Conditions were different at San Miguel Babícora. Terrazas bought the property from Jesús Muñoz in 1874.[257] It was an old property with a trail of titles that went back to 1720. It was also very large, covering over two million acres. It extended from the southern boundary of San Diego up the Palanganas and

San Miguel Rivers over the mountains to the southeast to the southern end of the Galeana Cantón and into the Namiquipa Municipio of the Guerrero Cantón.

According to Edmund Otis Hovey, the noted geologist who carried out research in the area in 1903, the land had particularly fine grass with plenty of water, on a high plateau of the upper San Miguel River called *Llano de Cristo.* The hacienda manor house was there near the river. Hovey said it was built like a fortress to withstand Apache attacks.

Trouble started ten years later when Don Luis used the Law of Vacant Lands to add to his hacienda. He took over communal lands of a community called Cruces, part of Namiquipa Municipio. It was a remote area and the people who worked the land were fiercely independent. They now worked for Terrazas and bitterly resented it. He had to use the local authorities to keep them in line. Many became so deeply in debt to the company store that they were virtually wage slaves. It also was reported that the hacienda foremen used wedding-night rights with the workers' brides. It is no wonder that these disaffected vaqueros and workers at San Miguel were among the first to join the rebels.[258]

The New Century Begins with a Boom

Luis Terrazas and President Porfirio Díaz remained at odds until the 1890s. This may have been more personal than practical. Although the two were considered liberals as they rose to power in the tumultuous times of Benito Juárez, they became identified with everything the conservatives stood for, even the resurgence of Catholic Church power. Their interests converged, and with the encouragement Enrique Creel, they came to an understanding. Creel had become increasingly influential. In 1891, he became part of the *científicos* an important group of technocrats that advised President Díaz and who became a symbol of his regime. This was a valuable connection, and Don Luis saw clearly that it was not in the family's best interest to further jeopardize the relationship with Díaz, whether he liked him or not. He actually supported Díaz for reelection in 1892, heading the state organization.[259] Díaz still controlled Chihuahua's governorship, but in 1892, he selected Miguel Ahumada, a man acceptable to Terrazas. Ahumada turned out to be a capable administrator, and served ten years, an unprecedented length of time for any Chihuahua governor not named Terrazas.

The expanding railroads plus Díaz's 1885 law privatizing communal lands created an economic boom in Chihuahua. Foreign entrepreneurs encouraged by Díaz and Terrazas from their respective pinnacles of power, invested heavily especially in mines, railroads, and timber.

By 1909, U.S. and British companies owned 75 percent of Chihuahua's mining production. The American Smelting and Refining Company, ASARCO, alone owned 25 percent and had monopolistic control of smelting rates.[260] ASARCO bought and reopened mines in the old mining area of Santa Eulalia just a year after Apache raids had shut down operations. Ranchers now could ship their cattle by railroad car to expanding markets north in the U.S. and south to central Mexico, eliminating the long drives. Railroad construction required many workers. When the local supply ran short, contractors imported Chinese laborers. The need for workers coincided with the Chinese Exclusion Act signed into law in the United States by President Chester Arthur in 1882. Many Chinese had experience working on railroads in the U.S. These hard-working, thrifty men brought with them a work ethic and small-business skills. Saving their wages carefully, they would accumulate enough capital to leave the labor gangs and buy handcarts to sell goods or to open vegetable stalls. More savings led to small stores, laundries, truck farms, larger stores, and a significant role in the local economy. These Chinese joined the mix of Indians, Spaniards, Africans, and north Europeans that make up the Chihuahua mestizo, one of the *Siete Culturas* of the northern state.

Two other phenomena occurred as the old century turned into the new. It is no surprise given their political and economic control that the rich got richer. The hacendados, dominated by a few families in each of the state's districts, usually with ties to the all-powerful Terrazas clan, acquired more land, banks, factories, and commercial properties. Foreign companies expanded and continued to invest. In the early 1900s, Don Luis had a completely vertical meat-producing operation, starting with breeding cattle on the range, through feed lots, slaughter and packing houses, brokering, shipping and delivery.

The second phenomenon was the growth of the middle class. Despite the dominance of the hacendados and foreign companies, prosperity allowed more and more workers to be upwardly mobile. Expanding markets and good prices made room for small entrepreneurs and stimulated the upward movement. The Chihuahuans, particularly those around the presidio towns like Janos and Namiquipa, had always been fiercely independent. Neglected by the government during the Apache Wars, they depended upon themselves to survive. Those survivors carved out small ranches and mining operations. With the coming of the railroads, they could readily ship cattle to market and ore to the smelters. With the boom in railroad construction and the opening of new mines, experienced workers moved into foreman and supervisor positions. Mule packers opened freight lines to haul goods to and from the train stations. Tradesmen and craftsmen in the towns and cities opened stores and shops to provide goods and services to a clientele with money to spend.

Education played a significant role in this move to the middle class. For centuries, the Catholic Church had provided what little education that existed. Benito Juárez closed Church schools as part of his liberal program. In 1875, he mandated universal public education, even on the haciendas. While the quality of teaching obviously varied, many children learned the basics. Some used the opportunity to go on to higher education becoming professionals such as teachers, lawyers, and accountants. They found white-collar jobs in the expanding government agencies, in banks and company offices.

There is no question that hacendados and foreign companies held all the advantages, including tax exemptions, shipping rebates, business monopolies, political connections, and access to capital. Also, Porfirio Díaz's land laws took away much of the communal land that supported the small rancheros. Still, a parallel system emerged with the hacendados and foreign companies coexisting alongside a growing, educated middle class. That system crashed when the economy collapsed in 1907. The financial meltdown exposed the naked power of the privileged and the latent frustrations of the emerging middle class.

There were many causes of the Depression of 1907. The overheated economy created higher shipping and smelting costs. As world-wide mineral prices dropped, costs exceeded revenue. The stock market crash and the run-on banks in the U.S., known as the Panic of 1907, impacted Mexican banks and financial markets. These and other factors contributed, but the biggest problem was that the capitalist free enterprise system had been corrupted into a mix of monopolies, special privileges, and price fixing. The response by those in control of government and business was to raise taxes and prices even higher. Small companies began to fail as costs rose, revenue declined, and credit sources dried up. Small mines and ranches closed as did stores and freight lines. A tax was levied on each pack animal used by the freight lines, which in combination with reduced business, drove muleteers like Pascual Orozco, a future rebel general, into the front ranks of the upcoming Revolution. Some U.S. companies simply fired all their employees and left. Large companies like ASARCO fired many, reduced the wages of the remainder, and chose to wait for better times. It turned out those large-company managers made the right decision. The depression ran its course, and by 1910, business returned almost to pre-depression levels at least for the hacendados and foreign companies. Most in the fledgling middle class lost their jobs or assets and found it difficult to start again. It was business as usual for the elite but not for long.

Twilight of an Era

Regardless of the merits of the arguments in the debate between Almada and Porras about the character and tactics of Luis Terrazas as an individual, the Terrazas clan continued to acquire more and more land, sometimes ruthlessly, and they seemed omnipotent. But the corrupting effects of absolute power blinded family members to realities around them. Cracks, at first not noticed, began to appear in the apparently impregnable Terrazas façade.

Enrique Creel had gradually taken over the day-to-day operation of the family empire. In 1903, the Díaz-Terrazas reconciliation had gone so far as to allow Don Luis at age 74 to be nominated and elected governor after a 19-year absence. Assuming this was an honest election, the honor of being reelected may have been the high point of Don Luis's long career. It also was one of his few big mistakes. He was now identified with the Díaz regime.

The election was largely ceremonial. In a few months, Don Luis turned the governorship over to Creel, who finished the term and was reelected in 1907, serving until the outbreak of the Revolution.

Enrique Creel was a brilliant businessman and very comfortable in the commercial and governmental halls of power. Díaz appointed him ambassador to the United States, and he was the translator for the famous meeting between President William Howard Taft and President Díaz in Ciudad Juárez in 1909—the first time an American president ever visited Mexico.

Enrique moved easily in high circles, but he lacked Don Luis's common touch. The old man had been a leader of men of all classes. Many of his associates and supporters had shared campfires with him as they prepared for battle. He had ridden with them and he understood their problems. He was not just a patrón, he was their *patrón*. Creel by contrast conducted business in a high-handed, sometimes ruthless style. To his credit, he instituted many progressive reforms in government, education, and infrastructure. Unfortunately, his top-down mandates ignored the local autonomy that the Chihuahuans had maintained for centuries, particularly in the Casas Grandes Valley and the other communities in the Galeana District (formerly Cantón). Creel even tried to centralize local governments by appointing the traditionally elected municipio presidents. The independent Chihuahuans bitterly resisted that move. They already disliked Creel, in part because they considered him a North American because of his father. North Americans now were seen as exploiters and unfair competitors. The simmering resentment focused on Creel, the Terrazas clan, and increasingly on the old patrón himself.

Enrique Creel's Big Mistake

Another factor in that late 19th century mix was Porfirio Díaz's attempt to eliminate the communal land systems of the ejidos and municipios. The result was a transfer of millions of acres from community to private ownership. It is difficult to assess how complicit Don Luis was in some of the more ruthless land grabs that resulted. He and the family certainly took advantage of the land laws as interpreted and promulgated by Porfirio Díaz. The privatization of communal land was especially hard on small ranchers and farmers. When Enrique Creel later became governor in 1905, he made a bad situation worse.

President Díaz had decided that Benito Juárez's Reform Laws of the 1850s made communal lands illegal. This was a significant change. From Spanish times, local governments, municipios, such as Casas Grandes, held communal land for use by *rancheros*, defined as small independent ranchers and farmers at the edge of the middle class. The lands also were used by a poorer class of subsistence rancher/farmers or sharecroppers called *medieros*. The local rancheros and medieros also had the use of empty lands under *usufructo*, a traditional right-to-use concept. This was particularly important to the settlers in the vast Galeana District, including Casas Grandes.[261] Those belonging to the communal ejidos, the *ejidatarios,* had rights to that common land. Some of this communal land had been granted by Teodoro de Croix, the charming comandante general of the Provincias Internas, in 1778. A *bando*, an edict, signed by de Croix on November 15, 1778, still existed.

In 1883, Díaz ordered nation-wide surveys of all common lands. This led to the Executive Decree on Colonization and Survey Companies, often called the Law of Vacant Lands. The surveying companies would receive one third of the land they determined to be "vacant." One third would be sold at low prices, presumably to small rancheros, and one third would revert to the national government. Each ejido had always been restricted to 112,359 hectares (277,645 acres). The Decree cut that historic maximum to 28,080 hectares (69,387 acres). The surveyors declared the remaining 84,279 hectares (208,258 acres) to be vacant lands or *baldíos*. Towns and communities with land grants dating to the 18th century found themselves in court unsuccessfully defending their rights before judges beholden to the power structure. The net result was the transfer of even more land to insiders, foreigners, and hacendados.[262] The Decree enabled the LDS settlers to establish their first colonies in the Casas Grandes Valley, and for the North American-owned Corralitos Company to acquire 278,000 acres (112,503 hectares) of land that formerly belonged to the ejido of Casas Grandes.

It is too simplistic just to say that the Decree transferred the common lands from the poor to the rich and powerful. Small ranchers and businessmen with connections and available cash also took advantage of the new law, especially in Casas Grandes. An example is Silvestre Quevedo, one of the patriarchs of a local family that traces its ancestry to the establishment of the ejido in Teodoro de Croix's time. The year the law was passed, 1884, Silvestre Quevedo finished his term as jefe político of the Galeana District (also Luis Terrazas's last year as governor). The following year Quevedo became president of the Casas Grandes municipio. Men like him represented a growing, prospering middle class. The privatization and sale of communal lands enabled them to buy productive land at low prices.

The rancheros and medieros without cash lost the use of much of the ejido, municipio, and usufructo lands. Their loss was offset somewhat by the demand for workers on the railroad and in the expanding mines, smelters, and mills. As these enterprises grew, experienced workers moved up to higher positions and became part of the new middle class, an important class, but very vulnerable to slumps and recession.

At the turn of the century, ejidos still had some of their original land under the terms of Díaz's Land Law. The municipios also retained common land that provided resources for the usual governmental functions including administration, schools and for some towns, military installations. Portions of the municipio land remained for grazing and farming. House lots and government buildings had a special designation called *fundos legales*.[263] For Enrique Creel, even this amount of communal land was too much.

After Creel succeeded Luis Terrazas as Chihuahua's governor, he promulgated the Municipal Land Act of 1905. On the surface, the wording appeared to streamline Chihuahuan land policies and help small landowners. What it really did was accelerate the exclusion of rancheros and medieros from the land sometimes including their own homes. The last of the remaining communal land in the Galeana District was appropriated and subdivided. This included long-used lands around the old presidios like Janos, the economic last resort for poor medieros. The divided plots were available through a process called *denuncios*. An individual would "denounce" a particular plot, pay the established price, and receive a private title.

A particularly onerous section of the Land Act required all land holders to verify their *títulos individuales* and pay a *modesta cuota* to legalize the title. This applied to all homes (known as fundos legales) as well as pastures and other holdings. The Act established a short time line for the legalization process. The "modest fee" turned out to be about 25 pesos for homes in Casas Grandes and the other Galeana District towns. Many found the old, faded documents that gave them title to their homes, and were able to provide the needed funds. For others, working as laborers for 75 centavos a day, the fee was beyond their capacity. They and their families soon were out on the streets, their homes claimed by someone else who could pay the fee. At least one small rancher and miner named Manuel Orozco lost the house he grew up in as well as the family grazing land. Local police evicted him. The municipio council ignored his protests, finally jailing him for *insultos a autoridad*.

Enrique Creel was a brilliant financier, but blind to the social implications of these political decisions. His Municipal Land Act of 1905 exposed and significantly aggravated the underlying tensions in Chihuahua. Its implementation stimulated the rise of revolutionary rhetoric. The frustrated and dispossessed joined subversive groups and soon were in the ranks of fighting rebels. The Land Act, when added to the depression two years later, created the catalyst that exploded into revolution. This was Enrique Creel's big mistake.

Don Luis had remained a reasonably popular figure in Chihuahua attested by his election as governor in 1903. However, the depression and the land act destroyed his remaining credibility. As the leader and symbol of the clan, he and his old enemy Porfirio Díaz were identified together as oppressors. Creel remained in office until 1910, the year the depression ended. Four years later, a Revolutionary general named Pancho Villa sat in the governor's chair.

Casas Grandes at the Turn of the Century

In the second half of the 19th century, Casas Grandes as a town, municipio, ejido, and agricultural region emerged as the most important entity in the Galeana District. Janos declined after the presidio closed. The railroad was much closer to Casas Grandes than to the other major towns, and Galeana itself had a malaria problem because of nearby swamps. Casas Grandes Valley land was rich with water available from the river system and flowing springs. While Casas Grandes and nearby ranchos had their share of Indian attacks, Apaches in the later years, especially Juh, preferred to trade there rather than raid. The town's population rose rapidly during the Maximiliano era as dispossessed families from battle-ravaged regions farther south migrated north looking for refuge. Several, such as the Quevedos, Hernándezes, Fernándezes, and Aguilars, came with sufficient assets to build homes and commercial businesses.[264]

The oldest houses on the central plaza date to this era of the 1860s. The two-story buildings reflect the French style that was popular during Maximiliano's time in spite of the resistance to his reign. Early houses line a segment of the Camino Real that connected Mexico City with northern Nueva Vizcaya and New Mexico. This street is just west of Avenida Independencia. Today it dead ends just before the Casas Grandes-Nuevo Casas Grandes highway. The houses on the west side of the rough, unpaved road are very high and face away from the road. The high walls and small windows may have been for defensive purposes, or they may just reflect the sloping terrain. Houses on the east side face the street.

On the west side of the town's central plaza, adjacent to the old school, is the government building, constructed in 1903, still serving the municipio. The Salon de Actos across the street to the north came later. General Rodrigo M. Quevedo as governor ordered it built it 1935. Adjacent to the salon is the San Antonio Restaurante, which used to be a movie theater. The small entryway to the restaurant was the box office.

The restored home on the south side of the plaza was the original bank in the region, established by Francisco Malpala and Julián Aguilar. A man named Galindo married an Aguilar daughter and the house remains in the Galindo family today.[265]

Historian Jane-Dale Lloyd in her book *El Distrito Galeana en los Albores de la Revolución* describes in detail the effects of the Díaz and Creel land laws on the five major towns of the Galeana District. In doing so, she provides a historic picture of Casas Grandes and its people leading up to the Revolution.[266]

In 1904, Casas Grandes consisted of municipal lands, the remaining ejido land, and the fundos legales. By 1910, all of this land was privatized except the central plaza, the school, and the municipio government building. Even a nearby hill, where householders cut firewood to heat their houses in winter, was off limits. The best irrigated properties were taken first. These included the northwest barrios of San José and San Isidro that received water from the productive spring Ojo de San José; lands to the southwest of town served by the Ojo Vareleño, that had provided water to Paquimé in prehistoric times; and the Labors de Guadalupe and La Riqueña, areas that received water from *acequias* directly connected to the Casas Grandes River northwest of town. These last were considered some of the best land and a significant amount already was in private hands since Díaz's 1884 decree. The new 1905 law took the remainder.

Local businessmen/ranchers, who had done well during the economic boom of the late 19th century, took advantage of the new law. By the time the 1905 law was promulgated, Silvestre Quevedo's sons, Mauro and Silvestre, Jr., ranked among the most prosperous in Casas Grandes. The younger Silvestre was Rodrigo M. Quevedo's uncle. They owned pasture land and a small hacienda of 4,300 acres, a part of an old ejido called Arroyo Seco.

Mauro, the elder son, had a store in Nuevo Casas Grandes. Through the denuncio process they bought land in La Riqueña. They had money and the approval of the Terrazas family. It did not hurt that Silvestre was the suitor of Jacobo Anchondo's daughter and that Jacobo was Luis Terrazas's brother-in-law. They "denounced" and paid for land at El Rucio, located along the river (and future railroad) south of the Pearson/Mata Ortiz site.

Foreigners saw opportunity. One of the most aggressive and successful was Lewis Booker of El Paso. He already owned property in Janos and Ascensión. By 1909, he owned over 440,000 acres of grazing land and timber land, for much of which he paid twenty cents an acre. One of his ranchos, Palotado, was located northwest of Janos.[267] Booker would later attempt to build a railroad up the steep San Diego canyon to Pacheco in the mountains west of Pearson. The route became known as the *Caracol* or snail.

Jacobo Anchondo took several parcels in the Cantarranas and Moctezuma barrios southeast of town. In contrast to the north and northwest, this was marginal, rocky ground used by the poorest medieros. Anchondo probably took the land because it was adjacent to his Hacienda Anchondo (later El Refugio). The displaced medieros went to work as cowboys or laborers for him and for whomever else would hire them.

Several other Casas Grandes middle class businessmen and ranchers "denounced" property and houses. Don Genaro Galaz, the owner of a guest house and wholesale business, joined with family members to claim and buy parcels. Don Genaro's family remained prominent in Casas Grandes in spite of the hard times to come. The lives of his descendants intersect with other important events in local history. One of his daughters, Olaya Galaz, married Colonel Ignacio Campos, a member of Porfirio Díaz's *Guardias Presidenciales*, a military unit established by law to protect the president. The couple lived in her father's house on Independencia Street in Casas Grandes. That old family home now is occupied by Don Genaro's great-great grandson Carlos Quevedo Campos. His grandfather was a brother of General Rodrigo M. Quevedo from Casas Grandes and later governor of the state. Don Genaro's nephew was president of the Casas Grandes municipio during Charles Di Peso's excavation of Paquimé.[268]

Another entrepreneur, Hermenegildo Parra, already had acquired land under Díaz's law. He owned the largest general store in town, a guest house, a liquor store, and a wholesale seed business. One of his business associates was J.C. O'Bannon, an assayer in Ciudad Chihuahua. Together they owned a carbonated water factory. O'Bannon was close to the Terrazas family.

The Miranda brothers, Teodoro and Santa Cruz, traced their lineage back to one of the four families that Teodoro de Croix had encouraged to return to the abandoned Casas Grandes site in 1778. The family worked land for generations in La Riqueña and Labor de Guadalupe areas to the northwest. How they previously held the land is unknown, but in 1907 they apparently established clear title and added more from ejido land. Julián Aguilar, the banker, acquired 740 acres in Labor de Guadalupe.

To the north and northeast, the LDS colonists had established Colonia Dublán, and they used the law to secure more land, some of which had never been cultivated and, which they irrigated with a new acequia. The other acequia that served the region was owned by the Rio Grande, Sierra Madre and Pacific railroad. The company also denounced land south of the town.

LDS member Joseph Jackson came to Casas Grandes from Utah with his second wife to escape problems with his first wife. He claimed land surrounding Ojo de Varela that included an abandoned mill.[269] The ancient acequia had provided water to local farmers since prehistoric and Spanish times, but Jackson would supply only LDS-owned farms. Two of the oldest families, the Mirandas and Varelas, contested the action. The LDS Church representatives prevailed, but these conflicts created deep antagonisms over property and water rights that have never been completely resolved and still flare up today.

Luis Terrazas claimed at least five parcels of rich farmland in 1905 that he incorporated into his Hacienda San Diego. Historian Jane-Dale Lloyd thinks he may have acquired even more. Rebels later destroyed archives in the Galeana District offices, and a 1957 fire burned many property records in the Casas Grandes Municipio government office. Lloyd walked the San Diego property and noted that Terrazas's old stone walls extend farther than the presently recognized boundary. This is more than a historical curiosity as it adds to the ongoing confusion and conflict today among the municipio, ejido, LDS Church, and private-property owners.[270]

In 1907, Terrazas took former ejido land near the Hacienda Tapiecitas, which Don Luis had acquired in 1898. The Jeffers family now owns part of the old hacienda. That same year, Terrazas took the forested area used by the ejidatarios for firewood and lumber, including the traditional firewood hill. The wood was now for sale. The Flores Magón brothers seized upon this and wrote scathingly about it in their revolutionary newspaper *Regeneración.*

Historian Lloyd wrote in the conclusion of her book that, right or wrong, the expropriation of the communal property converted land use in Chihuahua to a capitalist system. Land was now a form of merchandise that could be bought and sold on an open market controlled only by supply and demand. This conversion had social implications. Lloyd used the terms "vertical" and "horizontal" to describe the changing social structure. Vertical refers to a multilayered structure from a low class up through middle class layers to an elite class. Horizontal implies broad equality with few layers between the lowest and highest in the local society. For centuries, the common menace of the Apaches had created a horizontal society in the Casas Grandes Valley and the rest of northern Chihuahua. Class distinctions based on the old Spanish casta designations lost their legitimacy in the face of a charging enemy. Various ethnic groups melded into the classic mestizo. With the advent of capitalism,

new class distinctions developed within a very short time creating a vertical society—high to low. By 1907, middle class ranchers and businessmen
were identifying with the hacendado class as their interests merged. The
medieros became a landless under class. Mediero resentment accelerated
as the classes polarized.[271]

The recession of 1907 and the resulting high tax laws, compounded
by a drought, exposed the fragility of the middle class. Many lost everything and turned to the revolutionary movement, providing experienced
leadership to an already disillusioned underclass. The conservative/liberal
issues of capitalism versus land reform—free enterprise versus communal
ownership—would haunt Mexico, particularly Chihuahua, through the
Revolution, Post-Revolution, and into modern times.

The Seeds of Revolution
The Battle of Tomochi

The absolute power of families like the Terrazases, the disenfranchisement
of the people from the land, and the dissolving middle class can all be seen
in retrospect as seeds of the Revolution. A less obvious spiritual side had
great influence on the mystically minded Mexican people. An example was
the Tomochi Massacre, 19 years before Madero's call to arms.

In the mountains southwest of Ciudad Guerrero, the little town of
Tomochi (sometimes Tomochic) sits astride Highway 16, the main route to
Basaseachic Falls, the highest in Mexico and a famous tourist attraction. In
the town, adjacent to the highway, a large mural on the side of the building
depicts the terrible events that occurred here in 1891-1892.

One of the frustrating and contradictory features of the Porfirio Díaz
regime was the re-emergence of privileges for the Catholic Church. The fractionalized liberals had always agreed on at least that one thing—breaking up
the economic and political powers of the Church. However, with Díaz's tacit
support, some of the old abuses reappeared. For some villages like Tomochi,
the traveling padre began charging higher fees for marriages, baptisms, and
funerals. In Tomochi, the padre took the painting of Our Lady of Guadalupe from the church and gave it as a gift to Governor Lauro Carrillo, one of
Díaz's appointees.[272] In their fervor and frustration, the townspeople turned

to a mystical sect that followed a young charismatic spiritualist, a *curandera*, Teresa Urrea, known as Santa Teresita de Cabora. The prominent author Luis Alberto Urrea, a distant relative of Teresita, wrote "The Hummingbird's Daughter," a fictionalized version of her life and influence on the Revolution. Urrea's narrative paints a vivid picture of 19th century hacienda life and how peasant people turned for solace to quasi-religious sects. Teresita became a focus of revolutionary zeal in northern Mexico.

When the townspeople placed a painting of her in the Tomochi church, the padre complained to Governor Carrillo, and he sent a battalion of soldiers to quiet the little town of 35 families. In the resulting mayhem, the soldiers killed every man and older boy in the village.

It is said that Luis Terrazas encouraged the Tomochi uprising from behind the scenes, reflecting years of political battle with Porfirio Díaz's supporters and governor appointees from Guerrero.[273] It might be true. The Tomochi Massacre helped sully Díaz's name and became a kind of spiritual rallying point for the agitation and eventual revolt against him. Unfortunately, Terrazas's name became irretrievably linked with Díaz and tyranny.

Throughout Mexico, the name Tomochi remains linked to the spirit of resistance against oppression.

Magonistas

The Mexican Revolution did not begin overnight. In the years leading up to 1910, there had been abortive uprisings that set the stage for the Anti-reelectionist *Plan de San Luis Potosí* and Madero's declaration for rebellion on November 20.

Some of the most influential rebellious actions prior to 1910 included the work of Ricardo Flores Magón from Oaxaca, his brothers Enrique and Jesús, and a young follower Práxedis Guerrero. Often called anarchists, they started in their student days advocating the overthrow of Porfirio Díaz. Ricardo in particular promoted the cause through his writings and speeches. He helped found the Mexican Liberal Party (PLM), which formed a rallying point for disaffected Mexican liberals. The brothers were called the intellectual heart of the early radical movement.[274] The term Magonism, *Magonismo,* came to mean radical thought and activity, even into modern times. In 1994, the Zapatista Army of National Liberation used the term when they took up arms in Chiapas. Ricardo spent much of his life in exile in the U.S., in and out of jail for radical activities. From far away across the border, his revolutionary spirit infected many Mexicans. Today, he is considered one of the great revolutionaries. Towns, streets, and schools throughout Mexico bear his name. Ricardo's numerous articles and those of his brothers were the most important writings leading to the Revolution.[275] Always on the move from town to town, meeting with Anti-reelectionists and PLM party cells, the brothers tried, not always successfully, to keep ahead of authorities on both sides of the border.

They may have met with Anti-reelectionist or PLM groups in Casas Grandes. On a side street in Casas Grandes, there is an old wall, a remnant of a fronton court where the federal garrison soldiers played *pelota* when off duty. The local conspirators, whatever they called themselves—Anti-reelectionists, PLM, *Magonista*—also played there, holding secret meetings during their games.[276]

Included in the games was young Rodrigo M. Quevedo, a member of the prosperous Quevedo family, whose history in Casas Grandes stretches back to 18th century. Born in Casas Grandes, he attended the town schools and perhaps the LDS Academia in Colonia Juárez.[277] An early revolutionary and member of the PLM party, he became a career army officer, first fighting in the Madero Revolution as a young lieutenant. He went on to fight for and against most of the major factions as the Revolution disintegrated into civil war. Unlike many of the early officers, he survived the Revolution and had a long and successful military and political career. He held several post-revolution military commands, served as Chihuahua's governor from 1932 to 1936, and as a senator from 1958 to 1964.[278] His image appears prominently in the history mural inside the portico of Casas Grandes' Salon de Actos, and a town south of Galeana now bears his name. In 1908, he was a young unknown activist, right out of school, anxious to right the wrongs of an oppressive regime.

Another attending the clandestine fronton meetings was journalist/soldier Práxedis Gilberto Guerrero. As a young writer, he worked for several newspapers. He also enlisted in the federal army reserve, becoming a lieutenant. After the army was ordered to fire on demonstrators in

Mural by Alonso Enríquez Blanco in the portico of the Salon de Actos, Casas Grandes. From left, Inocente Ávalos Hijar, Homobono Reyes Almanza, Roque Gómez, Ricardo Flores Magon, Praxedis Gilberto Guerrero

Monterrey, he resigned his commission and concentrated on journalism, working more and more for radical newspapers. He became a follower of the Flores Magón brothers and submitted articles to their popular radical newspaper *Regeneración*. As a PLM member he led or participated in unsuccessful pre-Revolution uprisings in Chihuahua and Coahuila.

When Madero called for the Revolution to begin on November 20, 1910, Práxedis was in the United States. He immediately traveled to El Paso. There, the former army officer raised a platoon-sized unit of 30 men ready to fight. They crossed the border on December 22, just a month after Madero's call. They raided a hacienda, then commandeered a train and rode west, pausing to destroy bridges behind them. At Corralitos they demanded horses and supplies. Their plan was to attack Casas Grandes. When they arrived, they found the garrison too strong. The alternative was Janos.

They rode to Janos and attacked the weak force there and briefly captured the town. Federal re-enforcements arrived and in the renewed battle, Práxedis apparently stood up to observe and was shot. He became one of the first heroes of the Revolution.

Why the Casas Grandes Anti-reelectionists picked the soldiers' fronton for their meetings is unknown, but the obvious happened. Someone pointed out the conspirators batting the ball against the wall and they were arrested. Práxedis Guerrero and Rodrigo M. Quevedo either were not present or somehow evaded arrest. At least three did not. Inocente Ávalos,

Homobono Reyes, and Roque Gómez spent two years in San Juan de Ulúa prison in Veracruz. They were released from jail in 1910 and given *salvo conductos*. Historian Miguel Méndez García has one of these original safe-conduct documents in his collection in Nuevo Casas Grandes. Homobono lost a leg, but he was able enough after he returned to deliver mail between Chihuahua and Sonora. Portraits of all three are part of the Salón de Actos mural along with Práxedis Guerrero and Rodrigo M. Quevedo.

Whether in Mexico or the U.S., incarcerated or on the run, the Flores Magón brothers' revolutionary spirit reached the Mexican people through their writings in an era when newspapers were the only means of mass communication.[279] U.S. authorities finally caught and arrested Ricardo Flores Magón as a subversive. He died in Leavenworth Penitentiary, Kansas, in 1922.

Tomochi, the work of the Flores Magón brothers, the establishment of the PLM, and games at the fronton wall set the stage for Francisco I. Madero.

Revolution in Chihuahua

Another irony of Chihuahua's history concerns the leader of the initial phase of the Revolution. Francisco I. Madero was not an oppressed worker or even a disaffected member of the new middle class. This visionary, who rallied the people in Chihuahua to start Mexico's Revolution, was not even from the state. He was a wealthy member of the elite class of hacendados in the state of Coahuila. As a matter of principle, he strongly opposed Díaz's bid for a sixth term as president in 1910. To promote his ideas, he wrote a book with the prosaic name, *The Presidential Succession of 1910*. The book touched a raw nerve of frustration throughout the country. Madero's message led to the formation of Anti-reelectionist clubs, encouraged and supported by him. These clubs found a ready membership and became cells of revolutionary thought and organization in almost every state.

In Chihuahua, Governor Enrique Creel at first ignored them and then tried to crush the movement. He used his full power, including troops, Rurales, and local police to threaten, arrest, and even physically attack those he perceived to be enemies of the state. Club membership only grew stronger and more influential.

Creel ran up against an old enemy, Abraham González from Guerrero, the district that contained many Terrazas-clan opponents. Like Madero, González was well educated and came from a wealthy family. He attended Mexican universities and the University of Notre Dame in the U.S.

In the late 19th century struggle for political control of Chihuahua, the González family, along with other powerful families in Guerrero, had lost out to the Terrazas family after Luis made an accommodation with Porfirio Díaz.

An intelligent leader, Don Abraham was a natural to head Chihuahua's Anti-reelectionist Club, based in the capital. He expanded branches into other communities, including Casas Grandes.

Madero's popularity grew to the point that he became an opposition candidate for the presidency. Even with his rising popularity, particularly with the radical left, his main objective was not high office. Rather, he wanted to end Díaz's multiple terms and return to a one-term policy. He took a moderate approach and attempted to negotiate with Díaz. The old president refused to step aside. He reacted with a campaign that was more of a crackdown. Madero became even more popular. Two weeks before the election date of June 20, Díaz had Madero arrested as a subversive and placed under house arrest in San Luis Potosí, capital of the state with the same name north of Mexico City. After Díaz's "victory," which everyone recognized as rigged, Madero either escaped or more complacent Díaz authorities paroled him. He went to San Antonio, Texas, where he and a cadre of devoted supporters set up a government in exile.

It was common in Mexico for challengers to the presidency to issue "Plans." While in exile in San Antonio, Madero published his own version, written while under arrest, called The *Plan de San Luis Potosí,* dated October 3, 1910. He abandoned his earlier moderate approach and declared Díaz's election as fraudulent and that he, Francisco I. Madero, would be the provisional president until a legal election could be held. In previous writings, he advocated change through a peaceful electoral process. Now he chose a specific date, November 20, for all of Mexico to rise and take up arms against Díaz, Terrazas, and all oppressors. That date is memorialized in Mexico as Revolutionary Day.

Madero attracted educated, capable people to his cause including his brother Raúl and Abraham González. He and his close supporters organized a cabinet with officers responsible for various functions of government. Supporters raised funds to buy arms. Surreptitiously, they maintained contact with Anti-reelectionists and like-minded groups throughout the country. They provided copies of the Plan of San Luis Potosí and whenever possible arms and ammunition.

Madero appointed Abraham González as the "governor" of Chihuahua to organize rebels there. Madero also funneled funds to González in El Paso to purchase arms and smuggle them across the border.

It was not nearly enough. November 20 came and Madero's grand idea of a nation rising up and overthrowing the oppressors fizzled out almost before it began—with a few notable exceptions.

Porfirio Díaz had made a career of suppressing resistance to his regime. In most states, in spite of all the rhetoric, the Anti-reelectionist leaders were ill prepared and easily crushed in preemptive strikes by Díaz's troops, local police, and Rurales. Rebel resistance survived in only a few places. One was Chihuahua where Abraham González had recruited some unlikely local men, who proved to be very effective rebel leaders, especially Pascual Orozco and Francisco "Pancho" Villa.

Orozco, a middle-class store keeper, mule-train freight operator, and arms smuggler, organized a few hundred men and drove out the government officials from his hometown of Ciudad Guerrero. He, Villa, and other leaders of small rebel bands scored newsworthy victories in firefights against regular federal troops. They developed a hit-and-run guerrilla strategy that frustrated and wore-down the more numerous and better-armed federals. By avoiding direct combat unless the odds and element of surprise were very favorable, Orozco soon became one of Chihuahua's most effective rebel generals during the Madero phase of the Revolution.

Francisco Madero proved this point by once deviating from the guerrilla strategy to seek a grand battlefield victory. He decided to take command personally and lead an all-out attack on Casas Grandes. Until this decision, Ciudad Juárez, one of Mexico's most important ports of entry, always had been the main objective. Through harassment, ambushes, and railroad destruction, Orozco had gradually isolated Ciudad Juárez, setting up a future attack on a weakened garrison. Something happened between Orozco and Madero. Orozco pulled back from Ciudad Juárez and returned with his men to his home district of Guerrero to harass federal troops, who had reoccupied some of the area in his absence. He was not present at the Battle of Casas Grandes.

Madero's Revolution had focused world-wide attention on Mexico. Adventure seekers and fortune hunters sought him out in San Antonio and joined his growing force of disaffected Chihuahuans of all classes, who were eager to fight against Luis Terrazas, Díaz, and everything they represented.

In February 1911, Madero marched his small army of about 500 men across the border and through the desert to Rancho Anchondo, just south of Casas Grandes near the Paquimé ruins. On March 6, Madero ordered a dawn attack on the garrison In this, his first and last battle as field commander, he was routed after federal reinforcements counterattacked.

Wounded in the arm, his bodyguard, Máximo Castillo, a future revolutionary general, rescued him and took him back to the house at Rancho Anchondo. Jacobo Anchondo, the rancho's owner and the administrator for Luis Terrazas's Hacienda San Diego, was away on business in El Paso. His workers, sympathetic to the rebels, gave refuge to Madero. Nothing could be done for his wound there, and they were vulnerable to pursuit. Castillo and his men moved him a few miles to the manor house at Hacienda San Diego. Again, sympathetic workers let them in along with several of Madero's key supporters that had survived the action. Afterwards, the name of Rancho Anchondo was changed to *El Refugio* to commemorate Madero's brief stay.

Some sources say Madero was first taken for treatment to a school on the central plaza.[280] The building is still there on the southwest corner. Casas Grandes' official historian, Leopoldo Horacio Chávez, disagrees. He points to the mural on the west wall of the Salon de Actos, where a portrait honors Manuel Gutiérrez Sáenz, whose revolutionary career covered most of the history of the Revolution. He grew up at Hacienda San Diego, where his father and uncle were employees. His mother was Mercedes Sáenz, who still lived at San Diego when Chávez knew her. She is Willy Acosta's great grandmother. Chávez relates how Castillo carefully transported the wounded Madero to San Diego, where Señora Sáenz and other sympathetic workers allowed them to enter. Inside, Mr. Kingo Nonaka, a trained nurse who was visiting a friend named Nakamura, tended Madero's wounded arm. He had no bandages, but Señora Mercedes Sáenz had a new baby. She gave Nonaka clean diapers to bind the wound.

Señor Chávez said federals later used the school on the corner of the plaza as a hospital, which may have led to rumors that Madero was treated there.

Several of Madero's loyal followers, men of distinction who had fought with him, also crowded into the hacienda. While at San Diego, this

Mural by Alonso Enríquez Blanco in the portico of the Salon de Actos, Casas Grandes. Manuel Gutiérrez Sáenz at left in uniform. At right is Melquíadez Álvarez, a Casas Grandes rancher, store owner and distiller of sotol, was the first from the area to be jailed as a Magonista conspirator. The sheet music, lower right, represents the corrido "Siete Leguas" about Pancho Villa's favorite horse. The building is Hacienda San Diego. Colonel Gutiérrez, an officer with Máximo Castillo, participated in the Battle of Pearson and was one of the suspects in the Cumbre Tunnel Massacre.

impressive group, still filled with revolutionary fervor even after defeat, proclaimed Madero President of the Republic of Mexico and "National President of the Revolution." Cheers went up and photographs taken. This act made San Diego the First Palace of the National Revolution.[281]

Revolutionary fervor aside, even San Diego was too close to the victorious federal troops, who had conducted a victory parade around the Casas Grandes plaza. Madero and his supporters, with what scattered rebels they found or found them, moved south to Bustillos, a town in the Guerrero District on the railroad line between Ciudad Chihuahua and Ciudad Guerrero. There Pascual Orozco regained control, and he and Madero came to an accommodation. Orozco again commanded.

In another ironic twist, the country viewed the Battle of Casas Grandes as a kind of victory and incentive to rebel. Madero's return to Mexico, win or lose, acted as a catalyst. The people rallied to him, and Orozco's ranks grew.[282]

In April, General Orozco, aided by Pancho Villa, laid siege to Ciudad Juárez. Díaz tried his old *pan o palo* negotiating technique on Madero. The moderate Madero actually fell for it, agreeing to Díaz's concessions and ordered the assault withheld. Orozco and Villa would have no part of it. On May 7, they attacked. After three days of house-to-house fighting, the federal garrison surrendered on May 10.

Nine days later in Morelos, Emiliano Zapata defeated a federal army at the Battle of Cuautla. Suddenly it was over. The all-powerful Porfirio had nothing left. On May 21, 1911, he signed the Treaty of Ciudad Juárez in which he agreed to abdicate in favor of Madero. Three days later he was on a ship for France and exile.

Japanese Revolutionaries

Seldom acknowledged in the accounts of the early days of the Revolution is the unusual story of Japanese migrant participation. As noted, a nurse, Kingo Nonaka, treated Francisco Madero's wounds at San Diego after the Battle of Casas Grandes. Who was he, and where did he come from?

The first Japanese workers came to Mexico in the late 1800s and early 1900s. A small but steady flow continued into the 1920s. By 1910, at the start of the Revolution, the numbers were not large, about 10,000.

The Japanese government encouraged this migration and the workers were lured by "contracts" that promised good wages and possibility of eventually acquiring their own land. They arrived in Chiapas and in Oaxaca to work on tobacco, sugar, and coffee plantations. Reality there consisted of low wages, squalid living conditions, and back-breaking work in torrid heat. Added to this mix was disease, particularly malaria. Kingo Nonaka was one of those workers and his story is similar to the other Japanese migrants with some unique twists.

Nonaka grew up in the Fukuoka Prefecture on the island of Kyushu. He worked in the fields and as a pearl diver until he heard about the opportunity in Mexico. At 16, he and an uncle signed contracts and boarded a ship for Mexico and a coffee plantation in Oaxaca. They found the working conditions unbearable. The uncle contracted malaria and died. After this, Nonaka, like many other disillusioned workers before and after him, took his meager savings and bought a train ticket to the north. Several Japanese who made the trip north at various times ended in the Coahuila coal mines where working conditions were different but also terrible and often dangerous.

Nonaka tried to get into the U.S. but was denied entry. He ended in Ciudad Juárez. A family there helped him, and he opened a small feed and seed store that he operated until the disruptions of the early stages of the Revolution. Needing some kind of a job, he went to work as a nurse in the city hospital. His timing was perfect as there was a great demand for medical care. The wounded poured in and Nonaka learned quickly. Soon he assisted with surgical procedures and care beyond the typical nurse and far beyond any reasonable expectation, based on his limited training and experience.

After Nonaka treated Francisco Madero's arm wound, he was recruited by the rebels and joined Madero's movement. Two months later, he was at the Battle of Ciudad Juárez, helping to treat the wounded. After that decisive battle convinced Díaz to resign, the new President Madero had Nonaka appointed chief of nursing at the Ciudad Juárez hospital.

After 1914, when Pancho Villa consolidated the revolutionary forces in the north, he organized his army into *La División del Norte*. To treat the wounded of this great force, he created the most modern hospital train ever seen in Mexico. Called the *Batallón de Sanidad de la División del Norte*, the train followed Villa's División del Norte into battle. More than 60 North American and Mexican doctors cared for the wounded. Auxiliary trains took the extreme cases to hospitals in the closest cities.

General Villa promoted Nonaka to captain and put him in charge of all "nursing" on the train. Villa respected and liked Nonaka, and the newly promoted captain had direct access to the general. One of the most famous of the many photographs of Villa show him at the head of a column rearing back on his horse, *Siete Leguas*. Next to him, driving an ambulance wagon is Kingo Nonaka.

Nonaka survived fourteen great battles, and after the fighting stopped, he joined other Japanese in northern Baja California. There he became a noted photographer. After Pearl Harbor was attacked in 1941, Japanese-Mexicans were forced by presidential order to move inland, in a manner similar to the Japanese-Americans in California. Years later in 1967, the same Mexican government honored him for his service to the Revolution

Pancho Villa riding Siete Leguas with Kingo Nonaka driving the wagon.
Photo: cph 3a55041 //hdl.loc.gov/loc.pnp/cph.3a55041
Courtesy of the U. S. Library of Congress

and awarded him a medal. He passed away in 1977 at age 88. For a migrant worker from Japan, he served his adopted country well, but he was not the only one. Many joined the revolutionary forces for a variety of reasons, some willing, some with no other option. They performed well. Examples include Tsuruo Nisho, a personal cook for Pancho Villa; Shunzo Harada a judo instructor; and Zenzo Tanaka, who rose through the ranks to become a cavalry officer.

It seems strange that Villa and others respected the Japanese, while their hatred for the Chinese reached Sinophobic levels. Part of the answer lies in the military careers of soldiers like Harada and Tanaka. Japan had defeated the forces of China in 1894-95 and of Russia in 1904-05, giving the Japanese a reputation as great warriors. Whatever their actual limited military background might have been, the stellar performances of these migrant workers during the Revolution only enhanced this reputation.

It is not known whether Kingo Nonaka ever returned to the Casas Grandes Valley. His hospital train must have passed through Pearson, but there is no record.

After the Revolution and World War II, most Japanese immigrants concentrated in northern Baja California, Guadalajara, and Mexico City. A few remained in northern Chihuahua adding to the mix of cultures.[283]

The Last Years

Luis Terrazas was 81 years old when the Revolution began in 1910. Although now identified with Díaz, he made no effort to support his old enemy. He, like Díaz, attempted to reconcile with Madero, but it was too late for any moderate approach. Revolution was unleashed. Radicals such as Máximo Castillo encouraged people to take the land and holdings of the hacendados. Squatters swarmed over Hacienda San Diego, San Miguel Babícora, and other Terrazas properties.

The family did their best to hold back the radical tide. Professor Jesús Vargas Valdés, noted Chihuahua historian, described Terrazas as a good *patrón* who treated his workers well. When the Revolution came, they did not leave to fight, at least not immediately.[284] Certainly many, especially his *vaqueros*, remained loyal on several haciendas. On other properties, such as San Miguel Babícora, the enmity against the Terrazases was too strong for anything but rebellion.

Don Luis and Enrique Creel held their crumbling empire together for another year, but in 1912, they made a serious miscalculation. Pascual Orozco, frustrated by not being named as Minister of War and by Madero's moderate approach, rebelled against the new president, creating a revolution within a revolution. Don Luis financed Orozco, This time the shrewd old politician bet on the wrong man. Madero's forces drove Orozco out of the country, and Don Luis and family members had to leave as well. In 1913, a long caravan, dramatically called *la caravana de la muerte*, followed the old road northeast across the desert to El Paso.

He lived in El Paso for seven years. His son Alberto stayed behind to fight for the federals, finally leaving in 1914 after receiving a bad wound in a battle against Pancho Villa at Ojinaga. Don Luis had to endure the kidnapping and early death in 1917 of another son and namesake, Luis, Jr. Enrique Creel moved to Los Angeles and worked to maintain business and political contacts in Mexico. In 1919, Luis' beloved Carolina died, and he suffered a stroke that left him partially paralyzed. That year, he moved to Los Angeles, California and for a while lived in Long Beach in the Virginia Hotel.

By 1920, the revolutionary turmoil had calmed enough for him to return to Chihuahua. Creel followed shortly after. With whatever strength he had left, Don Luis began to reassemble his holdings. The family had assets as Terrazas had taken a considerable amount of money into exile.

Venustiano Carranza emerged from the messy warring factions as the overall leader of Mexico and assumed the presidency in 1917, with the blessings of the United States. Even after all of the bloodshed to end oppression, Carranza felt it was in the best interest of the country to restore hacendado assets. Like Madero before him and Obregón after him, land reform was not high on his revolutionary agenda. These men were capitalists, believing communal and small land holdings to be inefficient and economically regressive. In 1919 before he had even returned to Mexico, Terrazas's son Alberto had applied to the government for restitution and received back most of their expropriated lands.[285] Chihuahua Governor Ignacio C. Enríquez, who rotated in and out of the governor's chair into the post-revolutionary era, expedited the recovery for Terrazas.

Enrique Creel returned to become an advisor to General Obregón and seemed to have had influence. Obregón, who assumed the presidency in 1920 after Carranza was assassinated, had been the Revolution's most successful general, defeating Villa in several battles, paving the way for Carranza. He later turned on Carranza, was elected president, and oversaw a bizarre set of events that took away the Terrazas family land holdings while adding a fortune to their substantial remaining assets.

Arthur J. McQuatters, a North American entrepreneur representing a group of New York bankers, negotiated with the Terrazas family to buy virtually all of their reinstated landholdings, 5.7 million acres at $2.50 an acre. San Diego was one the 13 haciendas included in the proposed sale. The Revolution was barely over.

Governor Enríquez, trying to restore his shattered state and specifically to build irrigation projects with an empty treasury, saw in McQuatter's plan a way to finance his projects. McQuatters had a great deal of experience in Mexico, and he worked hard for two years on this transaction. He hired engineers to conduct surveys and detailed studies of the land and water sources. The plan called for extensive irrigation systems and other infrastructure projects including schools. When all was in place, the land would be sold in small parcels to the people, the displaced rancheros and medieros. Part of the plan was to create a bank to provide credit. For this he wanted tax breaks and exemption from the new land laws.

Many politicians at the state and federal level were very enthusiastic. Restoration and development would occur at no cost to the defunct treasuries. The project went to the desk of President Obregón and he granted approval, at least initially. When word got out, a storm of criticism from all parts of the country landed on that same desk.

For a great many, this was not what the Revolution was about. They had fought to rid the country of foreigners and for land reform. Even Pancho Villa, who had retired to his own large rancho, sent a letter suggesting that sale might incite violence. "Bullets will fly," he said.

Earlier, after the defeat of the usurper Victoriano Huerta, Venustiano Carranza needed to consolidate his position as head of state and to offset policies and influence of Villa and Zapata. In an appeal to the campesinos, many still fighting, and under pressure from subordinates, he approved the

Agrarian Law of 1915. This was not a radical law, but it opened the official door to land redistribution. The next step was a new constitution.

By 1917, although fighting continued, Carranza had established himself in Mexico City, and his government had been recognized by the U.S. He knew he still had to deal with the large segment of the people that ranged from progressive to radical. A necessary move would be the replacement of the sixty-year old Constitution.

Therefore, Carranza permitted the organization of a constitutional convention in 1917. He did not attend but thought he could control events. The result was somewhat different from what he intended. The attendees represented the new middle-class politicians. The old hacendado políticos were excluded. The Constitution of 1917 that evolved had some defects and ambiguities, but it has guided the country for over one hundred years. Modifications have been made but no radical changes until 1992 during the presidency of Carlos Salinas de Gortari.

One article of the new Constitution that became famous, Article 27, recognized the right of private property but emphasized that the government controlled the nation's land and water distribution. Policies should benefit all of society, not just the individual. This set the stage for land distribution to communal entities and small holders whether Carranza, Obregón, Governor Enríquez, or anyone else felt it economically efficient. It was Article 27 that the liberal presidents such as Lázaro Cárdenas, used to break up large land holdings and create ejidos. The first of the three parcels of the new Pearson/Mata Ortiz ejido was allocated in 1923.

Obregón could not withstand the reaction to the proposed sale to McQuatters. Yet he could not just appropriate the Terrazas lands under Article 27. For one thing, he was desperately trying to curry the favor of the U.S. Government, which was unhappy with the rebellion against Carranza and the expelling of U.S. businesses. If he vetoed the sale, the conservative administration of President Harding would accuse him of Communism. A compromise was worked out that affected land polices for decades.

The federal government created an agency to take ownership of land, *La Caja de Préstamos para Obras de Irrigación y Fomento de la Agricultura S.A*, known simply as *La Caja*. This agency bought the Terrazas properties. The price was less than the McQuatters' offer but still over seven million in

U.S. dollars. Social reform had triumphed over capitalism, but the Don Luis touch, the ability to turn disaster into fortune, lived on. McQuatters also did reasonably well, receiving between $400,000 and one million dollars.[286]

La Caja paid ten percent down to Terrazas and the balance over 10 years. With these proceeds and the money Don Luis had taken to the United States, his grandchildren and great grandchildren became ranchers, industrialists, and politicians. In the 21st century, their descendants carry on Don Luis's legacy.

The patriarch died June 18, 1923, in El Paso at age 94. Adding to the list of Chihuahuan ironies, Pancho Villa was assassinated almost exactly one month later on July 20, 1923, one crime that could not be blamed on Terrazas.

The family reverently transported Don Luis' remains to Ciudad Chihuahua, the place of his birth. They buried him next to Carolina in the churchyard of Our Lady of Guadalupe.

Photos of the old man in his declining years, like the painting of the younger man, reveal little of Don Luis' personality or character. With a plain dark suit and white beard, he could be the patriarch of any prosperous family.

Historian Héctor Chávez Barrón tried to describe Terrazas by using a Castilian proverb, *genio y figura hasta a la sepultura.*[287] The old expression is subtle. In one sense, it means "genius and character from cradle to grave." In another, it is similar to "the leopard cannot change its spots." Chávez amplified this, saying that Don Luis was a successful 19th century man, who conducted himself by the standards and morals of that era. What set him apart was his unbreakable will and courage to resist, to resist against family tragedy and attacks from all sides, business and political.

8

Colonies for the Saints

A Place of Refuge

Colonists of the Church of Jesus Christ of Latter-day Saints (LDS) first arrived in the Casas Grandes Valley in 1885, just after the Apache threat finally faded away. These hard-working people made a significant impact on the region. They brought their own version of religion, education, farming and business techniques that they integrated into the mix of northern Chihuahuan cultures. They and their descendants were consummate historians, leaving behind dozens of books and memoirs of their pioneering experiences. These often-poignant accounts record years of back-breaking work, good times and bad, supported by a strong faith and sense of family. One young mother wrote, "We lost all we had three times."[288] This overview starts with LDS President Brigham Young in 1875, ten years before the first colonists arrived in Chihuahua.

That year, he called for missionaries to go to Mexico to proselytize and also to look for land suitable for colonization. This was part of his broad plan to establish LDS colonies throughout the southwest. A second group of missionaries followed the next year. All gave favorable reports about the land potential but no action was taken, partly because of the ongoing Apache threat. Brigham Young died in 1877 and his successor as Church president, John Taylor, continued to send missionaries to Mexico, some of whom stayed permanently in Mexico City.

This was a time of great disruption for the Saints in the Utah, Arizona, and New Mexico Territories. The issue was plural marriage (polygamy). Congress had passed legislation banning such marriages as early as 1862 during Abraham Lincoln's administration. Brigham Young negotiated a deal with Lincoln to keep Utah out of the Civil War, and the law was not enforced. The issue surfaced again in the form of the Edmunds Anti-Polygamy Act of 1882. This placed severe penalties on plural marriage, which included imprisonment and loss of citizenship rights such as voting or holding public office. The loss of rights could be imposed on those who believed in plural marriage, whether they practiced it or not. This time the law was strictly enforced. More than 1,300 men spent time in jail. In 1890, the LDS leaders accepted the law and advised members to refrain from the practice in the U.S.

As the process leading to acceptance of the law unfolded, LDS President John Taylor recognized that many still would adhere to plural marriage and to their responsibility, legal or not, to support and nurture their multiple families. He developed a plan for immigration to Mexico. In a December 1884 letter to the president of the St. Joseph Stake in Thatcher, Arizona, President Taylor wrote that an effort must be made to find "a place of refuge under a foreign government to which our people can flee."[289] (a "stake" in the LDS organizational structure is made up of five or more congregations or "wards").

The word spread that the Church was making ready a "place of refuge" in Mexico.

Two expeditions explored the Yaqui River/Bavispe River area of Sonora looking for land without success. A third party, led by Alexander F. Mac-Donald, a prominent Church member, entered Chihuahua via El Paso to buy land. When MacDonald received the call to go to Mexico, he already had served six months in jail for polygamy. He had three wives. Incarceration did not slow his appointments and election to higher offices both civic and church throughout Arizona. Under the law, it was a crime for him to hold public office. After the citizens of Mesa, Arizona, elected him mayor, federal marshals descended on the town intending to arrest him again. Before they arrived, he left for Mexico with orders to find land for plural families. He had already participated in the two earlier expeditions to Sonora. In January

1885, under the direction of Apostle Moses Thatcher, he left for Chihuahua. Elder Thatcher was one of the Quorum of Twelve, the highest governing body under the LDS president. The Apostles were addressed by the honorific "Elder." He would become a significant player in the development of the Mexican colonies. He later owned Cave Valley and was the one that gave archaeologist Carl Lumholtz permission to excavate there.

MacDonald and three companions met with landowners and real estate agents in El Paso to review maps and learn of land possibilities in Chihuahua. MacDonald may have had surveying experience that aided him in this task, and it could have been part of the reason for this assignment.[290] Crossing into Ciudad Juárez, he and his companions took a train of the just-completed Mexican Central railroad to the San José station (on some maps, the Gallegos Station), 52 kilometers south of Ciudad Juárez. Close by was the Samalayuca hacienda of Dr. Mariano Samaniego, a lawyer/physician/ politician, Luis Terrazas ally, and patriarch of the most powerful family in Ciudad Juárez.[291] This knowledgeable man welcomed the LDS delegation and gave them excellent advice on all phases of acquiring land in Chihuahua. He lent them his buggy to continue the journey.

From the ranch, they followed a trail through the town of Ascensión into the Casas Grandes Valley and liked what they saw. They previously had made contact with the García brothers, who controlled vast tracts near the Casas Grandes River and in the nearby mountain valleys. However, negotiations failed to secure any property except for 300 acres they rented at Corralitos. After four weeks on the trail, MacDonald returned to Ascensión on March 1 and was surprised to find LDS members camped nearby, led by William C. McClellan. President Taylor's word about colonies in Mexico had spread quickly, and people were arriving prematurely looking for the "place."

McClellan was a man honed by the hardships of the LDS experience. At age thirteen, he was solely responsible for an ailing family. He helped them escape during the First Exodus, when LDS members left founder Joseph Smith's settlement at Nauvoo, Illinois. The young McClellan joined the Mormon Battalion during the Mexican-American War and participated in the early development days of Salt Lake City. When the Saints resisted the entrance of the U.S. Army into Utah Territory during the Utah War of

1857-58, young McClellan joined the "Nauvoo Legion" that harassed the U.S. troops.

Heeding President Brigham Young's call for expansion, he had pioneered settlements in New Mexico and Arizona. He now led a group that had heard President Taylor's words and had assembled in Snowflake, Arizona, in early 1885, ready to cross into Mexico.

Snowflake, located about 25 miles south of Holbrook, was founded by Apostle Erastus Snow and William Jordan Flake, both prominent LDS pioneers in Arizona. Apostle Snow played an important role supporting the LDS colonists in Mexico.

McClellan's group crossed the border on February 22, 1885, and suffered through the unfamiliar customs inspection, taxes, and entry fees on their own at Ascensión port of entry. They expected that an advance party from the Church would meet them and direct them to their property. No one came. They did not know what to do other than set up camp and wait.[292] When MacDonald arrived a few days later, he was dumbfounded to find people already there. He had to explain that he had not yet purchased any property. All he could do was to direct the expatriates to make a more permanent camp along the river about two miles north of Ascensión and continue to wait. On March 7, an even larger group came in from Snowflake, and then more began arriving. McClellan's camp swelled to 350 would-be colonists.

MacDonald hurried back to Arizona and reported to Elder Moses Thatcher. The two with an additional party of colonists from St. George, Utah, immediately returned to Ascensión to reassure their restless people. These farming folks felt the oncoming spring and knew the time to plant was approaching.

MacDonald and Elder Thatcher met with the García brothers, Telésforo and Mariano. These two were official surveyors. Under Porfirio Díaz's Law of Vacant Lands, they platted so-called abandoned lands, the baldíos. Much of the baldío land had been communal land that the law privatized. The surveyors received one third for their work and were in a position to purchase the surveyed parcels at low prices. The Garcías became speculators, purchasing the surveyed parcels at low prices to resell.

The LDS agents thought they had a deal with the Garcías for land near Ascensión in the area of the Mormon encampment, now referred to as Camp Díaz. They liked this location because of its proximity to the border and to an established town but the Garcías raised the price. Frustrated, MacDonald and Elder Thatcher continued to look elsewhere, but March turned into April.

Colonists with enough cash rented fields from local Mexicans and planted a crop. A few others plowed and planted seed on the 300 rented acres at Corralitos. Isaac Turley led eleven families five miles north of Casas Grandes to rented land at Tres Alamos, also called San José (not to be confused with the San José Station south of Ciudad Juárez), that became known as Camp Turley. They were able to plant one crop. The site was west of the later Colonia Dublán across the Casas Grandes River. An obelisk with a missing plaque marks the Camp Turley site.

While there was some contact with Mexican citizens involving supply purchases and land rentals, most locals in Casas Grandes and Ascensión had no idea who these foreign people were or their intentions. Many, who grew up listening to the stories of the Mexican-American War, disliked North Americans, and resented this intrusion. Local officials felt the same way, including the jefe político of the Galeana Cantón, Silvestre Quevedo, Sr. The successor to the late Juan Mata Ortiz. Quevedo came from a prosperous Casas Grandes family. The news that Elder Moses Thatcher had letters of recommendation from Chihuahua Governor Carlos Pacheco Villalba had not reached the jefe político or even the government in Ciudad Chihuahua. The lack of communication probably was due to the fact that Governor Pacheco was also President Díaz's Secretary of Public Works and spent most of his time in Mexico City. Pacheco had been installed as Díaz's man to replace Luis Terrazas as Chihuahua's governor during the height of the conflict between Díaz and Terrazas. Because Pacheco was in Mexico City, an acting governor, General Carlos Fuero conducted the state's day-to-day business. General Fuero was mentioned earlier as one who sold a parcel to Luis Terrazas that became part of Hacienda San Diego. The General was capable and well known for his integrity, but he did not like North Americans or any other foreigners in his country. These strong feelings were in part due to the fact his father had been badly wounded in the Mexican-American War.[293]

On April 9, Alexander MacDonald received a letter delivered by the Casas Grandes municipio officials. He was shocked when he opened it and read an order, signed by General Fuero, directing the LDS immigrants to leave Mexico within 16 days. MacDonald immediately rode to Corralitos to notify Apostle George Teasdale, who had just arrived with Miles P. Romney to take charge of the LDS colonies. Word was sent to Apostle Thatcher, who was in Salt Lake City. Everyone galvanized into action. Elder Thatcher sent a message to LDS missionaries in Mexico City that he and Apostle Brigham Young, Jr. were on their way to the capitol. A team headed by MacDonald took a Mexican Central train to Ciudad Chihuahua to confer with General Fuero but got nowhere. He was adamant they leave.

Elder Thatcher and Elder Young fared better in Mexico City. They arrived May 9 and were well received once the issue was understood. Both Carlos Pacheco and President Díaz in person assured them that the LDS settlers were welcome and the government would help them. The expulsion order was rescinded. General Fuero took the first available military command and left Chihuahua in disgust. The crisis passed, but local resentment persisted and the would-be colonists still had no land.

Those familiar with northern Chihuahua know how miserable the wind can be that blows across the high plains in spring. One woman wrote about living and cooking in her tent, "... if I could find a place to put all of the sand and dirt which blows in, we would have ample land without buying it."[294]

Spring stretched into summer. Some of the colonists became so discouraged they packed what they had and left for the U.S., feeling arrest by U.S. marshals to be worth the risk. More Church officials came to assess the situation and offer encouragement, including Apostle Erastus Snow. The fact so many Apostles and other high officials were involved underscores the high priority the Church placed on the concept of Mexican colonies. Elder Snow spent most of the rest of his remaining years in the Casas Grandes Valley, becoming an emissary for the various colonies, traveling extensively, sometimes to Mexico City to meet with officials as high as Porfirio Díaz. He built a large home in Colonia Juárez but died in 1888 before he could use it. The house still stands. Early leaders including Apostles Thatcher, Teasdale, and Ivins lived there.[295]

It was not until January 1886 that Alexander MacDonald finally came close to acquiring land. He and Elder George Teasdale in Mexico City negotiated to purchase 49,400 acres along the Piedras Verdes River, just west of the river's junction with the Palanganas River and adjacent to the old San Diego rancho property. This site became Colonia Juárez. They also obtained 7,000 acres north of Ascensión that became Colonia Díaz, and 60,000 acres of mountain timberland in an area called the Corrales Basin, where Colonia Pacheco and other mountain colonies would be located. They closed the deal on February 12, 1886. The Church paid $12,000. It is not clear whether this was the final price. Others may have added funds to the Church contribution.[296] It is also unclear from whom the property was purchased. Some or all of the land may have belonged to the García brothers. Three other names surfaced during legal quarrels several years later. A lawyer claimed that Ignacio Gómez del Campo, Luis García Teruel, and Ramón Guerrero had sold the property illegally.[297] Del Campo, a surveyor was involved, but the negotiations appear to have been with federal officials in Mexico City. The government reaffirmed the LDS's rights to the land in 1893. The parcel purchased north of Ascensión may have been Camp Díaz or another in the same area.

Several local Mexican residents deeply resented the sale of the Colonia Juárez 49,400 acres. As far as they were concerned, this property had belonged to them since Teodoro de Croix and Spanish times and had been stolen by Díaz's baldío laws. The first of many lawsuits was filed to no avail. Resentment over land would plague the relationship of local Mexicans and Anglo-LDS residents to the present day.

Whatever the source of the land, the LDS Colonists were ready with an organizational plan. By popular vote, they agreed to create a company that would hold the land in common and provide capital for development. After a few changes, this entity became the Mexican Colonization and Agricultural Company. Its first president was Elder Moses Thatcher and the manager Alexander F. MacDonald. Elder Erastus Snow represented the president of the Church in Salt Lake City. LDS members in good standing with the Church could apply and lease land for a minimal amount. If a member lost his good standing, he could be evicted following a mediation process. Provisions in the contract permitted the leasee to purchase the land, and over time most ended in private hands.

As part of the purchase negotiations in Mexico City, the colonists were allowed to move on to their designated parcels beginning in November 1885, prior to the final agreement. MacDonald surveyed the properties and laid out the towns. The colonists had waited a longtime but finally had found their "place." They named the community near Ascensión Colonia Díaz to recognize their benefactor in Mexico City. Colonia Juárez was named after Mexico's greatest hero, Benito Juárez.[298]

MacDonald laid out the town carefully, following a specific guideline devised by Church founder, Joseph Smith, Jr. Called the Plat of the City of Zion, it was a grid plan designed to concentrate the houses yet give each one a sense of privacy. The land was laid out into square blocks with wide streets. Each block was divided down the center, and each side of the dividing line was further divided into three to five lots. The houses were built in the center of each lot. A unique aspect of the Plat was each block was always perpendicular to the adjacent blocks. Thus, each house looked across the street at the side of his neighbor's house rather than at the front, enhancing privacy. Each lot had a fence denoting what was private inside and public outside. As a result, lot sizes were equal.[299] Each lot had access to water. The farms outside of the town were places to work not live. Joseph Smith based his urban planning design on the concept that concentrating people would enable them to develop community educational, cultural, and religious opportunities, not available to people scattered on remote farms. This worked particularly well for Colonias Juárez, Dublán, and Díaz. Today, the broad tree-lined streets of Dublán, now, an upscale neighborhood of Nuevo Casas Grandes, serve as a reminder of the original Plat of the City of Zion.

Even with the incentives of urban living, there were those who chose to live on remote ranches or in tiny settlements, particularly in the mountains. Church leaders often tried to dissuade these people, but they either preferred that lifestyle, or the remote place offered the economic opportunity they sought.

A Surveying Error

Apostle Teasford appointed George W. Sevey as presiding elder. On December 7, 1885, Elder Sevey led ten families from Camp Turley to parcels along the banks of the Piedras Verdes River in the San Diego Valley. Months of uncertainty were over, but they now faced the winter. Their first shelters were caves dug into the riverbank. Fires at the entrances provided heat. In a few days, more families arrived, and parcels were assigned.[300]

With shovels and with horse-drawn scrapers, called "Fresnos," a mile-long canal was dug from a dam upstream to the prospective fields. The next project was a meeting house. They constructed walls of vertical poles with interwoven willow branches sealed with adobe mud plaster. The result was a space for their church, school, and social events. And they did have social events. On March 21, 1886, Benito Juárez's birthday, they celebrated the establishment of their new home. Fiddlers played, orators spoke, cannons fired, and everyone shouted "Viva Colonia Juárez," "Viva Mexico." A "sumptuous repast" was served. Finding the ingredients for anything called a sumptuous repast shows the resiliency of these hard-pressed but optimistic people. They even invited the new jefe político Don Urbano Zubía and the local Catholic priest to attend and speak. Apparently, Don Urbano had a different attitude toward the colonists than his predecessor Silvestre Quevedo. Whatever his feelings toward his hosts, he appeared to have had a good time, giving a speech, and partaking of the repast. The Catholic priest from Casas Grandes also spoke. What he said to the LDS members was not recorded.

Shortly after the celebration, it was warm enough to plow and plant. Between sessions in the fields, the men worked on building houses and planting trees. By summer, crops had grown tall and for the first time the future looked secure. That optimism was crushed when the colonists received word that there had been a "surveying error." Their Colonial Juárez site was located within not adjacent to the Rancho San Diego. The property they were supposed to have purchased for farms and the town-site was two miles north up the Piedras Verdes River on a comparatively desolate rocky place. Luis Terrazas would allow them to harvest their crops in the fall, but then they must move without any compensation for their improvements—dam, irrigation system, and buildings. Terrazas did not own the land, although he purchased it a few years later. Apparently, he controlled it under some arrangement with the owner Domingo Leguinazábal.

At first glance, it is hard to accept the "surveying error" excuse for forcing the move. Exact property lines always have been an issue in the Casas Grandes Valley, and the Colonia Juárez property covered 49,400 acres. The land had been surveyed originally by the García brothers, and they must have been aware of rich parcels along the Piedras Verdes River, adjacent to the old San Diego Rancho. Elder Erastus Snow had joined Alexander F. MacDonald and the other negotiators in Mexico City. After the others left, Elder Snow stayed several more days to "get copies of deeds, and regulations and instructions from the government to the custom house officials on the frontier relative to the admission of our colonists and their effects free of duty under the colonization laws."[301] Snow also obtained an order directing the jefe político and judge of the Galeana Cantón to conduct an official survey of the newly purchased lands. It appears an experienced surveyor had been involved in every step of the prolonged purchase negotiations.

The surveyor Ignacio Gómez del Campo had advised MacDonald and provided him with a survey map. Gómez del Campo also claimed land ownership, and land he supposedly owned may have been part of the transaction

Elder Snow did everything he could to reverse this disaster. A sympathetic Governor Carlos Pacheco wrote a letter to Luis Terrazas asking him to use his influence to convince the owner of the disputed parcel. Terrazas graciously introduced the LDS leaders to Señor Domingo Leguinazábal. Don Domingo was "incorrigible" as Elder Snow put it and would not sell.[302] This transaction is interesting, somewhat mysterious, and often misunderstood by authors writing on the subject. They blame Luis Terrazas for conniving to cheat the colonists. It was said that Elder Erastus Snow was particularly bitter over what he considered Terrazas's betrayal.[303] However, Elder Snow's own letters show clearly he knew that Terrazas did not own the disputed original site. He blamed McDonald for the error.

In a letter, dated June 22, 1886, to his son-in-law Moses Thatcher he wrote "(His (MacDonald's) blunder in buying from an unreliable map and guessing at distances with his head half turned around ..."[304]

Don Luis remains a controversial figure, but he was not known for cheating people. Most likely Alexander MacDonald naïvely trusted Gómez del Campo, who provided erroneous information. It is clear that Domingo Leguinazábal owned the land and had no intention of selling. Born in Spain, Leguinazábal was a well-known merchant in Ciudad Chihuahua, who gained fame by leading a group of armed storekeepers against looters when the French occupied Ciudad Chihuahua. He lived several more years and died in 1899.[305] His widow sold the land to Luis Terrazas in 1901.

However it happened, the colonists were forced to relocate. They completed the harvest and prepared to leave behind the product of their hard work and cash investment—houses, canal, and irrigated fields—and start over.

The colony and Church leadership remained steadfast. Alexander MacDonald laid out the new town's grid, retaining the original name. The term "Old Town" afterwards referred to the first site. It is now called Cuauhtémoc, an ejido community of about 300 Mexican residents on the road from Colonia Juárez south to Mata Ortiz

MacDonald also surveyed a route for a new canal, this time three miles long. Another dam was built, but the Piedras Verdes River ran low in this part of the valley. Even with the dam, adequate water for irrigation was a serious matter. There was nothing to do but forge ahead. Apostles Thatcher and Snow dedicated the site on January 1, 1887, and the move began under the direct leadership of George W. Sevey. Town-lot and field allocations were made again, the canal built, fields cleared and plowed, and adobe houses begun. A road, twelve miles long, connected Colonia Juárez and Casas Grandes. Rocks had to be cleared from the fields. Children with little wagons spent their days picking up rocks and hauling them to the edges of the fields.

Water flowed in the new canal until the river level began to drop. The steady decrease seemed to be another catastrophe for the beleaguered colonists. Without water, their colony was doomed.

On the morning of May 3, 1887, the ground began to shake. People rushed outside as the land seemed to rise and fall around them. The schoolteacher, Annie W. Romney, hustled the children out into the open, fearing their "stockade building" of vertical poles would collapse. Clouds of dust rose in the western foothills, then smoke from burning trees. The earthquake had started a fire that spread east into the tall grass and across the plains to the edge of the settlement. Everyone turned out with shovels and rakes to stop the flames before any buildings caught fire. Scholars studying the ground later, estimated the quake magnitude at 7.4 at the epicenter in northern Sonora.[306] Widespread damage occurred from Galeana in Chihuahua to Bavispe in Sonora. Forty-two people died in Bavispe, a town of 600, when log roof joists separated from the shaking adobe house walls, allowing the roofs to fall on the occupants. For most, this huge earthquake was a disaster. But in Colonia Juárez after the fire was controlled, men inspecting their properties found new springs along the river. Shortly thereafter, they noticed the river rising. Higher and higher it rose until the flow reached a level greater than anyone could recall.[307] For people steeped in religion, this geological event had significance at many levels from the spiritual to the practical. At the practical level, the irrigation canal ran full, providing water for years of prosperous farming.

Over time, the colonists and their descendants built substantial brick homes in a Midwestern-American style. By 1894, ten years after they had crossed the border, the Colonia Juárez colonists could point to many accomplishments. They had built a cooperative cannery, as they found the land and climate suitable for fruit-tree cultivation. The town also boasted a flour mill, sawmill, planing mill, cheese factory, tannery and general store, all run on a cooperative basis. The leather produced by the tannery was good enough for shoes, which led to the formation of a shoe factory. This had a positive impact on the local economy. Instead of the colonists spending their limited cash for this mundane but crucial product, the factory produced enough shoes to sell and generate cash. The cannery also generated cash, shipping canned fruit and tomatoes throughout Mexico with the expansion of the railroads.

A visiting Church official gave high marks on the moral condition of the community, reporting no instances of drunkenness and only two young men using tobacco.[308]

In June 1887, Colonia Juárez became a ward with George Sevey as Bishop and Miles P. Romney and Ernest L. Taylor as the two Counselors in accordance with standard LDS organization. Bishop Sevey was described as "… warm-hearted and congenial, and full of compassion for the erring…"[309]

The Juárez Stake was officially established on December 9, 1895, with the headquarters in Colonia Juárez. The Church called Apostle Anthony W. Ivins, then living in St, George, Utah, to be president. Ivins was a well-known leader in the LDS world. His only wife, Elizabeth Ashby Snow, was the daughter of Apostle Erastus Snow.

Elder Ivins had been with the first group of missionaries sent by President Brigham Young in 1875 to search for possible sites for settlement. Elder Ivins served as stake president longer than anyone since.

A distinguished-looking man with sharp features, he used persuasion rather than command to exercise his authority. As a result, he was well-liked both by workmen as well as those at the highest Church levels. He spoke Spanish fluently, and although he was reluctant to leave his home in St. George, he accepted the call. Elder George Teasdale retired.

The LDS colonies did not have a typical local-government structure. They were within the Casas Grandes municipio, the Galeana Cantón (later district), and the state of Chihuahua. They responded to those external authorities and to all levels of Mexican laws and regulations. Internally, they were for the most part self-governing. For the first few years, there was no city council, judiciary, or police force. The bishop of each ward and his counselors managed most of these civil functions as well as tending to the colonists' spiritual needs. The bishops reported to the stake president and his counselors, who were the overall administrators and ultimate arbiters of disputes. The municipio did assign a *Comisario Policía* to each colony as was done for each Mexican town. The appointee was responsible for various administrative duties from maintaining law and order to performing civil marriages.[310] The LDS leaders worked closely with these Mexican magistrates to ensure minimum conflict with Mexican law or authority.

For twelve years, Stake President Ivins worked tirelessly for his constituents. He drove his buckboard over the rough roads from colony to colony to resolve disputes, work on administrative issues, officiate at ceremonies, and help the needy. Externally, he dealt with Mexican authorities at all levels, resolving bureaucratic issues, claims, and land title, water, and personal disputes. He often was in Ciudad Chihuahua and Mexico City, where he earned the respect of the state governors and of Porfirio Díaz himself.

The Ivins years turned out to be prosperous years for the colonies. After ten years of grinding hard work and disappointments, the colonies flourished in the next decade under President Ivins' management. Dramatic improvements were made from house building to education. Colonia Juárez emerged as the ecclesiastical, educational, and economic as well as the geographic center of the colonies. They even had electric and telephone service using power supplied by a water-driven dynamo. The river divided Colonia Juárez, which caused serious access problems during heavy rains. Elder Ivins solved this by hiring Samuel E. McClellan, the son of William C. McClellan, the leader of the first group of colonists, to build a bridge. The concrete pillars that McClellan installed still support the single-lane concrete bridge used today.[311]

In 1904, LDS President Joseph F. Smith in Salt Lake City promulgated the "Second Manifesto." This made clear that plural marriages were not to take place anywhere in or out of the United States, including Mexico. Those who participated in or conducted a plural wedding did so under the threat of excommunication. It was the responsibility of Juárez Stake President Ivins to carry out this official declaration. Enforcement was erratic as a few Apostles, traveling back and forth to Mexico, continued to perform plural marriages, at least through 1904. Others refused. A few high-ranking LDS members living in the U.S. maintained one or more plural families in the colonies, which led to at least one high-profile excommunication.[312] It is not clear how plural marriage phased out after 1904, but by 1912, when so many returned to the U.S. during the Exodus, it appears to have not been an issue.

Some individuals with influence over small groups openly refused to accept the manifesto. After excommunication, they formed a variety of fundamentalist sects. Members of a few of these sects live today in Colonia LeBaron, a community of about 1,000, eight miles south of Galeana The town was named after Alma Dayer LeBaron, a radical fundamentalist and former Colonia Juárez resident.

In October 1907, President Ivins became an Apostle in the Quorum of Twelve. He left the Stake presidency on March 7, 1908, and Junius Romney assumed his duties.

The Romney Family

The numerous members of the prominent Romney family trace their lineage to Miles Park Romney, one of the original colonists. His English grandfather converted to the LDS faith after hearing one of the first missionaries sent to England by Prophet Joseph Smith, Jr. Totally committed, he and his family booked passage to New Orleans and eventually to Nauvoo, Illinois, where Miles Park was born. In 1850 at age seven, his family made the 2,000-mile trek with Brigham Young to Utah Territory to found Salt Lake City. He grew up with the new city, following the family tradition of carpentry, architecture, and occupying important Church positions. He followed President Young's admonition to marry young, and he eventually had five wives. Hannah Hood Hill, his first wife, gave birth to their son Gaskell in 1871 in St. George, Utah.

By 1885, the enforcement of the plural marriage laws caught up with Miles Romney and he moved with the early immigrants to Mexico. After successfully surviving the early trials of the colonists, he emerged as a

Birthplace of George Romney, former governor of Michigan, Dublán, Chihuahua.

religious and social leader. Apparently, he was a talented actor and producer of plays. He created a drama association that became very popular
with the entertainment-starved colonists.

Gaskell was fourteen when the family immigrated. He followed in his
father's footsteps as a Church, community, and entertainment leader. In
Dublán, he had a large house constructed for his only wife, Anna Amelia Pratt. The builder was a Danish colonist named Jens Christian Larsen
Reinhold, a skilled mason, who constructed houses for many prominent Dublán residents. George Romney, later the governor of Michigan,
1963-1969, was born in that house, which still stands on Dublán's main
boulevard.

Junius Romney was born in 1878, to Miles Park Romney's third wife,
Catherine Cottam. He was eight when that branch of the family came to
Mexico. At sixteen, he went to work for Henry Eyring's Mercantile Cooperative. This was his practical education even though he did attend the Academy in Colonia Juárez. He learned merchandising, bookkeeping, Mexican
customs, Mexican law, and to speak Spanish. All valuable attributes as he
moved through stake ranks to become president.

La Academia

Education was a high priority from the beginning. Even though children
were needed as workers from a young age, with boys of seven plowing fields
behind mule teams, time was set aside for school. Teachers held classes in
homes or in primitive buildings until more substantial schools could be
constructed. Annie M. Romney, the fifth wife of Miles P. Romney, whose
quick thinking during the earthquake saved her students, is credited with
being the first teacher, at least the first paid teacher, in Colonia Juárez. Her
first class of 60 students sat on split logs and wrote on slate boards with
chalk. They had no pencils, paper, pens or ink.

Elder George Teasdale, the Apostle in charge of the Mexican colonies,
believed that "a man cannot be saved in ignorance." In the late 1880s, as life
in the colonies began to stabilize beyond the survival level, he led an effort
to build a substantial community building in Colonia Juárez that would
serve for meetings, school classes, and religious instruction. He convinced

La Academia, the Colonia Juárez Academy.

the citizens to bear the cost, each family head contributing fifty dollars and each single man twenty-five dollars. This was an enormous sum for that era, particularly for the cash-short colonists. Fourteen hundred dollars was raised and a substantial adobe building constructed that measured 24 by 40 feet, the standard size for many modern classrooms. Additions were made in subsequent years, which permitted students to be organized by class and ability through the eighth grade. They named the school the Juárez Academy. Colonists built similar schools in Díaz and Dublán. In the fall of 1892, church officials in Salt Lake City incorporated the three schools into the General Church System and appointed a Board of Education for all of the colonies and local boards for each ward.[313]

Education took another major step with the arrival of Stake President Ivins in late 1895. Shortly after settling into his new position, he held a meeting and presented a comprehensive educational plan, which included a high school that would serve all of the colonies. The residents were enthusiastic about secondary education, and Ivins' low-key but persuasive style convinced the colonists not only to build the school but to pledge eight percent of their income to cover the cost. The Juárez Stake Academy with six classrooms, auditorium, office, and prayer room was completed in less than a year and ready for the September 1897 class of 291 students. President Joseph L. Smith traveled from Salt Lake City to attend the dedication.[314]

By 1903, they needed more space as the Academy had expanded to a four-year high school with a broad range of classes. Stake President Ivins held another meeting. This time he had even a grander plan. He proposed a large two-story complex of buildings on a landscaped campus. He talked of his dream to see such a school from the first day he arrived. To emphasize his commitment, he donated a five-acre site. As before, his plan was met with enthusiasm and pledges. The Church and other wards also contributed and the cornerstone was laid on January 8, 1904. The buildings were ready for the opening of school in September 1905.[315]

The main building remains today, a two-story brick structure with two dormers and a short, pointed tower over the entrance. A carved-stone portico features the Mexican eagle. Marius Mickelson, an immigrant sculptor from Denmark, did stonework for the portico as well as for other homes being built in town.[316]

The Juárez Stake Academy became and remains a center for education, attracting Mexican students as well as the colonists' descendants. Classes have been held continuously since 1897 except for one year during the Revolution. Everyone pays tuition. The elementary school is now a government school with the required curriculum and rules. The middle and upper schools are run by the Church. At that level, Church members pay a reduced fee. Classes are taught in Spanish and English, and students graduate fluent in both languages.

The dual-language program is relatively new. For years, teachers taught only in English. Dr. Ernest LeRoy Hatch, who was born in Colonia Juárez in 1911, and who served the medical needs of the people of the Casas Grandes Valley for decades, attended all-English classes at the Academy. English was spoken both at home and in church. He later said he had little contact with local Mexican people and had to study hard to learn Spanish when called on a mission to a Mexican community.[317] As with language, the Academy curriculum has moved with the times. Graduates today qualify for both U.S. and Mexican universities.

Colonia Díaz

Colonia Díaz is considered the first permanent LDS colony in Mexico. After the long wait in tents at Camp Díaz, the impatient settlers rushed to occupy the newly purchased 7,000 acres in 1885. The land proved to be fertile and adaptable to almost any crop, vine, or fruit tree. The location was good, 200 miles from El Paso, 90 miles from Deming, New Mexico, and 250 miles from Ciudad Chihuahua. Supplies and equipment could be purchased from Deming, but the settlers had to be careful as border tariffs constantly changed and often were prohibitive. Alexander MacDonald laid out the town's grid system. Lots were assigned for houses and shade trees planted along the wide streets that he platted. At Díaz, the water table was high, only eight to ten feet below ground level, well within the reach of pumps driven by windmills and the ever-present wind. In 1888, to supplement the well water for irrigation, the colonists constructed a dam on the Casas Grandes River and dug a four-mile canal. Later, when they acquired more land, they dug a 25-mile canal to a group of springs. Crops included sugar cane. Women needed sugar for canning, but someone had a recipe for candy that could be mass produced. In 1887, they built a cooperative candy factory to produce this universally desirable product. Candy shipped easily and the sales generated much-needed cash.[318]

The natural resource they lacked was timber, particularly roof shakes. The other new colonies to the west in the Sierra Madre had yet to set up sawmills, and the combination of price and tariff made large purchases from Deming prohibitive.[319] As a result, the first Díaz houses were a ramshackle combination of wagon boxes, canvas, and willow poles until the western-colony mills could begin to provide lumber.

The acquisition of more land came about after John W. Young, one of President Brigham Young's sons and a land speculator, bought 60,700 hectares (150,000 acres) north of Colonia Díaz for $110,000. The price per acre was small but the total cash outlay was substantial for that era. In 1889, the Mexican Colonization and Agricultural Company bought 28,000 acres from Young to add to Colonia Díaz's original 7,000.[320]

Most of Díaz colonists arrived on their new land impoverished. Frequent moves in U.S., jail time, and the long wait for their "place," had eroded most of their assets. When the Díaz settlers finally received their house lots, they built simple houses with whatever material was at hand. Dirt floors were covered with hand-woven rugs. Boxes served as tables unless the family had carried furniture pieces in their wagon over the long trail. Mattresses were straw ticks, essentially a flat sack stuffed with straw or corn husks. Candles or kerosene lamps provided light, and water was carried in buckets to the house from wells or irrigation ditches. The land had to be cleared before crops could be planted. Around Díaz, the thick mesquite bushes had to be cut and the heavy roots grubbed out one by one with shovel, crowbar, and a team of horses harnessed to the multiple trunks. If a family had to sell its team of horses to buy food or if their animals were too old or lame to pull a plow, the family would try to borrow or rent a team from neighbors. Lacking a team, they tilled the soil with hoes, chopping the hard earth into furrows for seeds and water.

The Church provided the organizational structure and hierarchy that made the colonies function. Each community eventually became a ward with a bishop and counselors in charge. William Derby Johnson Jr. served as Colonia Díaz's bishop for most of its existence. Johnson had a college degree, having attended the University of Deseret in Salt Lake (later the University of Utah). He held several business and education positions in Utah before Apostle Erastus Snow insisted he take his four wives to Mexico to avoid arrest.

Most land as well as commercial and industrial enterprises were held in common until the community as a whole was economically stable. Gradually individuals were able to buy their land or enterprise on an easy installment plan. This of course was always contingent upon the family head remaining in good standing with the Church.

Children attended elementary school in all of the colonies for at least three months during the winter. By 1895, Colonia Díaz had constructed a substantial adobe building and started the Díaz Academy for secondary students.

Relief Societies established by women had existed since the early days of the LDS church. These continued in the colonies to aid the poor, teach useful crafts, and promote mental and physical health. After the town of

Pearson was established in 1909, LDS mill employees built a Relief Society building there. In early 1913, federal troops used it as a barracks.[321]

Social clubs, organizations, Sunday schools, and religious sessions all kept morale high and provided diversion from the numbing work. Also, the colonists loved parties. All holidays, U.S. and Mexican, were celebrated. Folk dancing and square dancing were very popular. Violins, flutes, harmonicas, accordions, and even organs had survived the trail and their players were in great demand.

By 1900, Colonia Díaz had a population of 623, with most engaged in farming and ranching. In addition to the candy factory, they had a broom factory, and flour mills, the first one driven by windmill power. Population growth from the typically large families was offset by deaths from a myriad of diseases against which the colonists had few remedies.

They met the challenge of disease like all the other hardships they faced, and in ten years, substantial houses lined the shady streets as symbols of their success. A highpoint for Colonia Díaz came in 1896, when the colonists held a farmer's fair to show off their products. President Porfirio Díaz, for whom the colony was named, sent a letter praising their accomplishments. Chihuahua governor Miguel Ahumada came in person and delivered a long speech echoing President Díaz's written praise.

Ernest Romney succeeded William Johnson as bishop on July 11, 1911, just over a month after Francisco Madero's Revolution forced President Díaz to abdicate. Beginning that year, the Casas Grandes Valley became a thoroughfare for raiding parties and rogue generals for a decade as the Revolution degenerated into civil war. The attacks on LDS colonist property, theft of goods and stock, threats, and physical assaults forced in 1912 yet another Exodus in the 80-year Mormon history. Colonia Díaz did not survive.

Colonia Pacheco

The first settlers to drive their wagons to the mountain timberlands purchased by MacDonald, arrived in a high valley in April 1887. A logging road had already been constructed up the steep walls of San Diego Canyon to the Corrales Basin.[322] At 7,000 feet, the growing season was short, but the newcomers eventually found they could grow enough sorghum, oats, corn, potatoes and a variety of other vegetables to support a small colony and leave a surplus to sell. They grazed cattle, goats, and sheep but the main industry became timber cutting and lumber production.

The settler/foresters felled trees with two-man crosscut saws, trimmed the branches with axes, and cut the logs into lengths that would fit their mule-drawn wagons for the trip down to the mill in Colonia Juárez. Depending on the circumstances, logs also were dragged to portable mills set up near the logging sites. Portable sawmill technology was available and at least some colonists had experience with it. Ten years before coming to Mexico, they had heeded President Brigham Young's call in 1876 to establish colonies in Arizona and New Mexico. Where they found stands of pine, they set up portable steam-powered sawmills. Use of steam engines had expanded rapidly in the 19th century. By 1875, at least one manufacturer, the Frick Company of Waynesboro, PA, marketed a portable steam sawmill. Such a mill could be assembled on site in four or five days.[323]

For lumbermen, the question has always been whether to bring the logs to the mill or bring the mill to the logs.

Local historians continue to debate the location of the very first mill. Was it in Colonia Juárez or in the mountains?[324] Whatever the answer, it is clear the settlers had mills in operation in both areas very early. Whether logs were hauled down the mountain or sawn on site depended on the situation just as it did over a century later when diesel trucks crawled down the rugged dirt road loaded sometimes with logs and other times with cut lumber. At night their headlights could be seen from Mata Ortiz, moving back and forth down the mountain switchbacks.

Joseph James was one of the colonists with experience in the forests of Arizona. With his 25 children, he settled and eventually prospered in Hop Valley (Jovales) near Pacheco, farming, and running a dairy and a sawmill. He must have been a character because anecdotes of his humor abound. He told one story about Mrs. Crow, a Colonia Pacheco woman who tended to neighbors' wounds. When she sewed up his badly cut leg, he said he only paid her half of her fee because the wound only cut through half his leg. His demise, however, was not a joke. Frustrated by carrying logs down the difficult roads, he, his sons, and Mexican workers built a flume down a steep canyon to the valley. With great effort, timbers and thick boards were prepared and a long flume constructed. Water was diverted into the flume to carry the logs. On the day of first test, a crowd gathered at the bottom. A son at the top hoisted a log into the flume and let it go. It careened down the slick surface gathering speed. Almost at the bottom, it flipped over the side into the watchers, killing, as if by retribution, the flume-builder James and one of his workers.[325]

MacDonald surveyed Colonia Pacheco into blocks and then into one and a quarter acre house lots bordering wide streets. Down the middle of each block at the back of the lots, he laid out alleys for access to corrals and barns. The first homes were built of logs, with the entire community turning out to cut the logs, notch the ends, raise them into place, and fill the cracks with mud. In 1890, Albert S. Farnsworth, a skilled builder who worked on many of the house projects, started a small sawmill in Colonia Pacheco operated by his brother Alonzo. A steam engine produced the power for the saws that cut home-construction lumber, fence posts, railroad ties, and mine supports. By the early 1890s, lumber to sell was hauled to places as far away as Bisbee, Arizona.[326] This continued through the 20th century with much activity during the 40s and 50s. Today's topographical maps show a maze of mountain logging roads in the mountains above Mata Ortiz. At least one mill still operates in Jovales, flume-builder Joseph James' former settlement, now an ejido.

Life was hard in Pacheco. A drought in 1891 caused the corn crop to fail and cattle starved. Plow horses had to be sold just to buy food. Some settlers left, but most survived, possibly because of the LDS policy of always keeping (or at least trying to keep) a year's supply of food on hand.

Hunting, particularly bear hunting, became a source of cash income. When word spread about bears in the Sierra Madre, big-game hunters from the U.S. and Europe undertook the long journey made possible by the railroad. Several lines ran from the East Coast to El Paso. After 1897, aspiring hunters could ride the Rio Grande, Sierra Madre and Pacific railroad to Nuevo Casas Grandes. That took about one day. Skilled guides, like George Lunt, met them at the station and took them by wagon for two days across the plains and up the steep canyon road to Colonia Pacheco. From there they rode horses into the rugged bear country. The Lunt family built a nine-bedroom brick guest house for hunters and other boarders. They

Pacheco Cemetery

found local clay that could be fired in a makeshift kiln and made 62,000 bricks by hand. The house was finished in early 1902 and hosted many distinguished guests. Colonel William Greene, the copper magnate, once brought a group of U.S. Senators and mayors to hunt.[327]

With the cycle of planting and harvesting crops, felling trees, sawing logs, and guiding hunters, Colonia Pacheco rose from day-to-day subsistence living to relative prosperity that lasted until the Revolution and the Exodus of 1912. The old cemetery has become a place of pilgrimage as the headstones bear some of the most prominent names in the colony's history.

Colonia Chuichupa

In 1893, Alexander F. Macdonald, Henry Eyring, and Meliton G. Trejo (Spanish translator of the Book of Mormon) were directed to secure more land for the colonies.[328] MacDonald by now had considerable experience dealing with the García brothers, and this time he negotiated an agreement that enabled the Mexican Colonization and Agricultural Company to buy

2,530 hectares (6,250 acres) of potential farm and ranch land within the high mountain forest of the Chuichupa Valley.

Chuichupa lay almost 85 miles southwest of Colonia Juárez, near the Sonora border, a long trip over a rough mountain road to sell products or buy supplies. Even Pacheco was 45 miles away. But the valley was good dairy country, and potatoes and vegetables could be profitably raised in spite of the short growing season.[329]

The first settlers arrived from Colonia Juárez on April 11, 1894. By 1911, the settlers had built sturdy brick homes along wide streets lined with newly planted cypress trees. A small sawmill and shingle mill operated nearby. As lumbering grew, sawmill operations supported by tiny communities extended deep into the forest.

By the spring of 1912, the railroad had been extended south from Pearson 60 miles to Chico Station, just 20 miles from Chuichupa. Suddenly, the most remote colony was only a few hours by wagon from modern transportation. A telegraph line ran from station to station on the railroad. It is not clear, but a line may have run from the Chico station to Chuichupa, providing the residents instant communication with the large colonies in the Casas Grandes Valley.

Visitors in the 21st century still comment on the natural beauty of the Chuichupa setting in the little valley surrounded by pines. Chuichupa became a branch of the Colonia García Ward and a separate ward in 1900.

Colonia García

In March 1894, Alonzo L. Farnsworth, brother of Albert S. Farnsworth, left his sawmill job in Pacheco and moved his three wives and families ten miles to a lush valley called Round Valley. As a young man, Farnsworth had been sent by President Brigham Young to Tuba City, Arizona, to "make peace" with the Indians. After a few years in Arizona, he moved his growing plural family across the border. More settlers followed and the valley became known as Colonia García.

The arrangement Farnsworth made with the García brothers is not clear. In 1898, MacDonald and Elder Ivins, by then the Juárez stake president, negotiated with Telésforo García in Mexico City to pay the balance owed and transfer the land to the Mexican Colonization and Agricultural Company for the benefit of Farnsworth and the 43 families living in the valley.

Cave Valley

In 1887, a few settlers from other colonies decided to move to a small but attractive site called Cave Valley, close to the now-famous Cave of the Olla. They laid out a small town adjacent to a creek that flowed into the Piedras Verdes River a short distance away. Elder Moses Thatcher had purchased the land for the timber and to raise cattle. His financial arrangement with the settlers is not known. They attempted a communal style of living, the Church of the United Order. The United Order failed here as it did elsewhere. Many left and by 1894, when Carl Lumholtz began his excavations around the Cave of the Olla, only ten families remained.

By the 1980s, only two or three Mexican families lived on the site that was written phonetically on maps as *Quebale*. The main community in the area now is a logging town a short distance to the northeast. The official name is Ignacio Zaragoza, but it is known as El Willy. Local lore attributes the name to a bootlegger named Willy, who ran a still nearby. The still did exist, and its rocky remains can be found north of town.[330] The much-more mundane source of the name was the Williams Ranch north of the town. George Calvin Williams came to the Cave valley region in the late 1880s and established the ranch. It was to this ranch that the surviving little girl of the famous Thompson Massacre ran with her sad message, "The Indians are real bad over at our place."[331]

Logging has been an on and off affair at El Willy. When Adalberto Pérez Meillón arrived as a new teacher in the tiny community in 1980, the mill was closed. It reopened in 1986 for a few years, after converting from a circular saw to band saw. The Ejido Ignacio Zaragoza ran the mill.[332]

In the 1980s, Raúl and Cuauhtémoc López owned Casa Blanca, a substantial old house formerly owned by an LDS settler. The house stood at the head of the pasture through which visitors had to drive to access the Cave of the Olla. The house later burned down. Javier, another brother, still looked after the property and ran the store in El Willy in 2019.

Colonia Dublán

The last major LDS colony town established in Chihuahua was Colonia Dublán. Settlers living in the other colonies had noted the rich cultivated fields along the Casas Grandes River north of Casas Grandes. An attempt was made to buy 29,540 hectares (73,000 acres) northeast of Casas Grandes from Lewis Huller, a Mexican resident of German descent, who appears to have been a land speculator. During the negotiations in late 1888, George Lake, who had lived in Colonia Juárez and Casas Grandes moved onto a parcel and began farming. Approximately 500 others followed during the spring of 1889. It turned out to be another bad deal. Huller became insolvent and could not deliver clear title. It was planting time, and the settlers that stayed in the area were forced to buy or rent parcels, *terrenos,* from Mexican owners. A terreno in this area was defined as a parcel extending back a mile or two from the river to a surveyed line running through the Casas Grandes Valley. This was not raw land to be broken by plow the first time. Most had been cultivated for decades, and some dated back to Spanish times.

Elder Lake had enough money to buy a parcel. He was destitute when he first arrived in Chihuahua with two of his three wives. Before Mexico, he had lived a peripatetic life in Utah, Idaho, and Arizona as a teacher, missionary, farmer, and even a stake president in two different locations. Somewhere he developed medical and surgical skills, once saving the life of an Indian by removing a bullet from his abdomen. The Indian became his friend for life. While living in Casas Grandes, Elder Lake began treating the sick and injured. Apparently, he did more good than harm because Apostle Erastus Snow designated him the area doctor. He spent the rest of his life traveling from settlement to settlement tending to the medical and spiritual needs of the colonists. Gun shots must have been a specialty because his second patient was a local Mexican with a bullet in his leg. While the designated doctor was making extended house calls, his sons ran the farm.[333] Colonia Huller was first name of the settlement.

In spite of the setback acquiring land, the colony grew steadily, reaching 1,200 residents by the early 20th century. Eventually, the original Huller tract came under LDS ownership. Most of the economy was based on farming and dairy production until a U.S. syndicate constructed the Rio

Grande, Sierra Madre and Pacific railroad from Ciudad Juárez through Dublán to Nuevo Casas Grandes, the last station on the line.

The proximity to relatively inexpensive rapid transportation made Dublán the mercantile center of the region. Storekeepers bought merchandise of every description and shipped it throughout Mexico. By the turn of the century, the town had a prosperous air with large brick or rock homes along broad shady streets.

A major project was converting two large dry lakes that may have been pre-historic reservoirs into storage areas for surplus water from the Casas Grandes River during the rainy season. An entrepreneur named Elder Henry Eyring Bowman had come late to Mexico, settling in Dublán in 1897. He was instrumental in establishing various enterprises including consolidating the stores in Dublán and Colonia Juárez into one cooperative, the Union Mercantile, S.A., Ltd. Bowman managed the cooperative.

When Colonel William Greene acquired the Rio Grande, Sierra Madre and Pacific railroad from the original U.S. syndicate and began to expand the line beyond Nuevo Casas Grandes, many local LDS men went to work

Union Mercantile, Dublán, Chihuahua
Photo: Brigham Young University Library Archives,
L. Tom Perry Special Collections

for him. His company ran up huge bills at the cooperative store. When the venture failed, Bowman took in payment all of Greene's, tools, Fresno scrapers, camp equipment, wagons, harnesses, and 200 mules.

With this equipment the Dublán settlers dug and scraped a thirty-foot wide canal six miles long from the head gate at the river to the lakes. From these new reservoirs, small canals connected to the fields. Bowman took charge of the newly created Laguna Water Company.[334] The system opened hundreds more acres to farming. Much of the infrastructure still exists, and the lakes, due east of Nuevo Casas Grandes, are used for recreation and are a popular destination for birders.

The main lake, Laguna Rodolfo Fierro, gained notoriety and its name from a famous incident in the Revolution. Fierro was one of Pancho Villa's most important generals. He also was a sadistic killer, nicknamed "the Butcher." In October 1915, he was helping Villa lead an army into the Casas Grandes Valley with the intention of crossing the Sierra Madre through Púlpito Pass to confront Carranza's forces at Agua Prieta. He arrived at the swampy shore of the lake, and impatiently decided to ride across what he apparently viewed as a shallow swamp, rather than ride all the way around. His men declined to follow. Fierro urged his horse forward into what turned out to be deep water with a very soft sandy bottom. The horse foundered, and Fierro, loaded with pistols, ammunition bandoliers, and a money belt stuffed with gold coins, could not keep his head above water and drowned. Villa, preparing to go into battle, lost his second-in-command at a crucial time, but few if any of the troops mourned.

By 1890, the community had been designated a ward, and the name changed from Colonia Huller to Dublán to honor Manuel Dublán, President Díaz's finance minister, the *Secretaría de Hacienda* (the town also was known locally as Laketown and San Francisco).[335] This followed a practice of naming the colonies after prominent officials in the Díaz regime (other than Juárez) that alienated the revolutionaries after 1910.

Dublán became a separate stake a 100 years later in 1990. The town remained within the Casas Grandes municipio until 1923, when it was incorporated into the Nuevo Casas Grandes municipio.

There is only conjecture as to why the railroad line was terminated just south of Dublán at Nuevo Casas Grandes and not extended to Casas

Grandes, the main town of the era. Financing could have been the issue since an expensive bridge would have been necessary over the Casas Grandes River. Whatever the reason, the station at the end of the line planted a seed that grew into the major city of the region. Colonia Dublán eventually became the northern neighborhood of Nuevo Casas Grandes.

Three Colonies in Sonora

From the days of their first explorations, the LDS leaders had always liked the country along the Bavispe River in Sonora. Indian troubles and other issues kept them from acquiring land until 1892 when a group from the mountain colonies bought 200 square miles along the winding river for $35,000.[336] They located their town, called Oaxaca after Porfirio Díaz's birthplace, a few miles west of the entrance to Púlpito Pass that led to the Casas Grandes Valley. The local mines provided a ready market for the colony's products and the settlers did well. Then as had happened so many times, disaster occurred.

In 1905, heavy summer rains caused the Bavispe River to flood and completely destroy the town and all of the improvements. Even the topsoil from the fields washed away. The colonists barely escaped and most never returned. The Oaxaca cemetery remains as an attraction for those who haunt old cemeteries.

Other LDS settlers bought a site twenty-five miles farther north in 1898. The laid out a town named José Morelos after Mexico's great hero in the War of Independence against Spain. Others not finding available land established a third colony, San José de Rosebello, upriver from Morelos. New LDS colonists came south from Arizona and staked out the raw desert land. These people knew how to build and very quickly had a church, meeting house, and productive fields irrigated by a system organized as the Gabilondo Canal Company. Young men found jobs in the many mines in the area as far away as Colonel Greene's Cananea or closer at El Tigre on the Bavispe River. The settlers enjoyed the results of their hard work for only a few short years. By 1911, the men went to their fields carrying rifles.

The Exodus

For 28 years, the LDS colonists in Mexico had overcome adversity and catastrophe, both human and natural. Fire, flood, earthquakes, hunger, disease, punishing labor, bureaucratic interference, murder, long separations, and heartbreaking losses of family members did not deter them from building prosperous lives. Their very success ultimately led to their defeat.

From the beginning of their immigration, the LDS colonists tried to achieve a certain level of rapport with the local population. They celebrated Mexican holidays, honored government figures, obeyed the law, and recruited converts. Much of this was superficial. The Church discouraged intermarriage, and most colonists lived in separate towns with their own church, municipal, and educational institutions. They hired Mexican workers, developed business relationships, and even made friends, but remained far more separate than integrated. At the time of the Revolution, most did not speak Spanish. Separatism bred suspicion, resentment, envy, and lack of respect. There is evidence that some colonists looked down on the local population, particularly the poor.[337] It did not help that the colonists enthusiastically supported Díaz and the regime that had made their immigration possible. It also did not help that they represented a religion dedicated to seeking converts in the midst of a Roman Catholic society. And it did not help that the colonists had exploited Porfirio Díaz's federal land laws and Governor Enrique Creel's Land Law of 1905 to expand their holdings to almost 500,000 acres.[338] They had worked very hard but were perceived now as "haves" in a "have-not" society.

There is little discussion in the references of the effect of the 1907 economic recession on the colonies that so decimated the fledgling Chihuahua middleclass. It appears the colonists fared much better and achieved solid control of commerce and industry in at least the Casas Grandes Valley.

At the beginning of the Revolution, Church officials in Salt Lake City and Colonia Juárez had ordered their people to remain strictly neutral. This policy failed to save them. It failed them in part because of the deepset antipathy toward the LDS form of soft foreign invasion. Also, some rebels perceived them as supporting federals or other rebel factions.

After the initial phase of the Revolution that deposed Díaz, the moderate leader and new president, Francisco Madero, could not hold the more radical elements together. As groups broke away from Madero, led by rebel generals such as Pascual Orozco, the Revolution degenerated into civil war. Factions with different objectives fought each other and against whoever was in charge of the federal government.

The LDS colonies were clearly different, and most rebel chieftains riding through the Casas Grandes Valley did not regard them as serious enemies despite threats and rhetoric. What rebels wanted was what all armies through time have wanted, resources—guns, ammunition, horses, saddles, food supplies, feed, boots, money—all of the material necessary for an army on the march. Villa was known for his hatred of certain groups, particularly Chinese, but he liked North Americans and treated the LDS colonists with respect, at least initially.

Unfortunately, General José Inés Salazar and a few others felt differently. Salazar seemed to have a personal vendetta against his former LDS neighbors and treated them harshly, encouraging his troops to hassle them and plunder their homes, and threatening them far beyond what was necessary to confiscate supplies for his army.

Salazar knew the LDS colonists well, having grown up among them. He was born in 1884, some sources say in Casas Grandes, and others say on his parents' ranch near the town of Sabinal, northeast of Corralitos. Historian Philip Stover says that the consensus of local historians now is that the future revolutionary was born in Casas Grandes in the house of his well-to-do parents, adjacent to the plaza.[339] The Salazar family had considerable influence in the area. When the Rio Grande, Sierra Madre and Pacific railroad line was completed in 1897 between Ciudad Juárez and Nuevo Casas Grandes, the engineers laid the track in an arc between Ascensión and Corralitos to include Sabinal, instead of a straight-line south, a manifestation of Salazar's family influence.

In 1922, a group of about 500 "Old Order" Mennonites from Manitoba, Canada established a colony at the town of Sabinal. They lived a quiet, isolated existence as farmers and dairymen until 2018, when the government brought electricity to the town. This spilt the community, and several have moved to even more remote areas The old Salazar rancho nearby still exists as one of two that date back to Spanish times with original buildings intact and in use. Corralitos is the other.[340] To add to the historical ironies of the region, the Salazar rancho is now owned by LDS members.

Philip Stover has studied the voluminous reports and memoirs left behind by the colonists as well as other material in an attempt to understand Salazar and his motives. He found one unusual coincidence. Several of the leaders, including Salazar, that were particularly brutal to the LDS colonists, attended La Academia. Stover draws no conclusions from this other than to note that these rebel leaders closest to the LDS communities for whatever reason bore them the most enmity.[341]

Salazar, a big imposing man, was a friend of Pascual Orozco with whom he may have smuggled arms from the U.S. prior to the Revolution. He supported Madero and emerged as an early rebel military leader. As the Revolution progressed, he became known as the "Chameleon" for changing sides when it suited him. His first change was to reject Madero even before Orozco famously defected to start the Orozco Rebellion in March 1912. Antonio Rojas also declared against Madero. Orozco united these counter-revolutionaries and for a few months controlled Chihuahua. Salazar, as a subordinate to Orozco, established his headquarters in Casas Grandes, and harassment of the LDS colonies began. Orozco's troops carried large red flags. This caused the colonists and local Mexicans to refer to all rebel troops as Red Flaggers, at least until Pancho Villa became a factor in their lives.

The first incident against the colonists occurred a month before on February 12, 1912, when Enrique Portillo, jefe político of the Galeana Canton, which at the time had its offices in Casas Grandes, rode into Colonia Juárez with 25 armed men. In the name of General Salazar, he demanded a gun, horse, and saddle for each of his men plus food. The colony leaders stood up to Portillo, and he backed off. President Junius Romney informed the U.S. consul and wrote a stern letter to Portillo. In a meeting with Salazar and Portillo, Salazar appeared cooperative and issued a written order guaranteeing the neutrality of the colonies. It was a farce. Confiscation and plundering became widespread in all of the colonies. Local Mexicans, emboldened by the acts of the soldiers, stole stock and other property and in a few instances, physically attacked individual colonists.

Junius Romney had been stake president for only five years and now faced the worst crisis his people had known. Church officials in Salt Lake City, powerless to help, told him he was on his own to make whatever decisions he thought necessary for the safety of the colonists. Former Stake President Anthony W. Ivins did come back from Salt Lake City to help Romney. His considerable negotiating skills appeared to help initially with the rebels but not for long.

What precipitated the crisis was Salazar's demand on July 26, 1912, for all of the colonists' guns and ammunition. The overall situation was very tense. During July, several Red Flagger generals, fighting with Orozco against Madero's federals, moved troops into the Casas Grandes Valley. Salazar was at Casas Grandes. Máximo Castillo had 600 men at Hacienda San Diego, and General Antonio Rojas had just unloaded his men from a train in Colonia Dublán. All made demands on the colonists and allowed their troops to plunder. Elder Anthony Ivins managed to convince General Castillo to back off until Elder Ivins could return to Ciudad Juárez and consult directly with General Orozco. In Casas Grandes, Salazar could not be mollified. He ordered Romney to appear before him. What the colonist leaders probably did not realize was Orozco's Red Flagger rebellion was collapsing. Pascual Orozco himself was already on the run for the border. President Madero had appointed a veteran officer, General Victoriano Huerta, to command the federal forces. Huerta organized an effective campaign and defeated Orozco in three consecutive battles. Salazar and the other commanders in the valley were essentially rogues, short of guns, ammunition, and supplies, waiting to affiliate with whoever looked to be a winner.

On July 25, President Romney, accompanied by Henry Eyring Bowman entered Salazar's headquarters at exactly the time ordered. The General greeted them with a blast of rhetoric, stating that all of his former guarantees given orally or in writing were null and void. Further, all guns must be turned in immediately, that day. President Romney stood up to Salazar, stating he did not have the authority to order the settlers to give up their private property. Further, Salazar could do what he wanted with him, but he would not issue the order. The frustrated general turned nasty. He threatened to turn his men loose on the women and children, and to declare war on the colonists and attack them as enemies in their homes to get their guns. He said "Mr. Romney, our big guns are now trained on those beautiful homes in Dublán, unless you comply with my demands, those houses will be reduced to rubble. We will ransack the town and take whatever we want. This same course of action will follow through with Colonia Juárez and all the other LDS colonies."[342]

Romney realized he had no choice. He finally told Salazar that guns would be turned in. They agreed the Dublán and Colonia Juárez schools would be the collection places. The valley towns now had telephones, and he spread the word for everyone to bring to the schools their guns or at least some old gun to make a show. President Romney made sure the collection process was organized in Dublán and left for Colonia Juárez.

All of the Colonia Juárez men had gathered in the chapel for a meeting. Their first reaction, expressed by Bishop Joseph C. Bentley, was not to submit to Salazar. They were armed and wanted to fight. After the stake president arrived late in the evening and discussed the reality of situation, they realized, if reluctantly, that they were too few to successfully fight and must comply with Salazar's ultimatum or be killed. They also realized it was time to evacuate their women and children to the United States.

A group led by Bowman went to El Paso to organize special trains. El Paso became the default destination because of the railroad connection. President Romney wrote letters to each colony instructing ward leaders to assemble women, children, and old and infirm men for departure. Messengers rode hard to deliver the letters to the mountain colonies. The handwritten letters instructed the colonists in Pacheco and García to proceed to the station at Pearson, the new town nearby that had grown up around a large lumber mill. Those in Chuichupa should take the train from the Chico Station, and those from Dublán the Nuevo Casas Grandes station.

It happened quickly. The first refugees left the Pearson Station on the regularly scheduled Pearson to El Paso train on July 28, just three days after the meeting with General Salazar. There were not nearly enough seats for the 350 on board. It was hot and most windows would not open. They soon ran out of water, and much of the ride echoed with the crying of thirsty children. The train came into the El Paso Union Station at midnight. Elder Ivins and other LDS officials were there along with local El Paso citizens to help. Three more trains arrived the next day including one from Dublán, where the passengers had been badly mistreated and their trunks and bedding searched before they were allowed to depart. Special trains ran for the next three days.

The date of the first refugee arrivals, July 28, has been noted in El Paso celebrations as the day to honor the hospitality and care rendered to the exhausted, bewildered refugees. The citizens of El Paso responded well, providing food and water, but the situation was grim.

Dozens of memoirs have been written by the survivors and their descendants of this ordeal.[343] Even after reading many of these accounts, it is hard to imagine the trauma these people experienced. Within hours they were expected to pack a trunk, prepare bedrolls, organize children of all ages, and get all in a wagon to the train station, in some cases hours away. What to take? What to do with heirlooms? How long would they be gone? Where were they going?

Authorities in El Paso representing the government, both federal and local, along with the LDS Church, had done what they could within a very short time. Many of the women, children, and old men were crammed into an abandoned lumber yard building with each family assigned a few square feet. There was no privacy except for blankets hung on ropes between the families. Some tents were delivered and set up in the open yard. Five babies were born the first night in those miserable conditions.[344]

Other families were sent from the train station to a building near the El Paso Foundry. The rainy season added more misery, but when the sun came out, it was blistering hot under the buildings' metal roofs. Food was provided but was difficult to cook. One child, writing years later, said they ate mostly canned tomatoes. There is little mention in the records of washing or sanitary facilities, but these must have been extremely primitive. Soldiers from Fort Bliss built showers using raw lumber and pails with holes punched in the bottom. While the locals helped, they also viewed the refugees as a spectacle, peering at them through the fences. Overriding the humiliation and physical discomfort was their anxious fear for the future. They had no idea what would happen or when they would see their husbands and fathers again.

The men back in Dublán and Colonia Juárez soon realized that evacuating the women and children did nothing to alter the dangerous situation.

In Dublán, the rebels confiscated a train engine and boxcars and ran it to the Union Mercantile store. They loaded the entire inventory of food, hardware, and supplies of all kinds into the boxcars. Anson B. Call, one of the founders of the cooperative store, watched helplessly as the rebels drove the train down the track offering the contents to anyone along the way. A key LDS business, important to the entire region, was completely destroyed in hours.[345]

Faced with more plundering, confrontations, and physical threats, the men held secret meetings, which was difficult because of rebel patrols. The situation called for discipline and a clear plan. The colonies' ward structure that everyone understood helped these desperate men meet the emergency. After thorough discussions and all disparate opinions heard, they agreed on a plan. Under President Romney's overall leadership, they organized themselves into military-like units of five to eight men with each unit electing a captain. The "officers" included Bishop Thurber in direct command, Gaskell Romney (George Romney's father) as quartermaster, and Anson B. Call as Chief Sanitary Master. The latter position indicates the colonists were aware of the importance of personal sanitation for a large group moving from campsite to campsite. The officers devised an operating plan that all captains understood. The first step was to smuggle provisions and their remaining guns to a rendezvous location.

They chose a rugged canyon about seven miles northwest of Colonia Juárez known as the "Stairs." Rain and snow melt had eroded the canyon soil down to bedrock, which climbed up in a series of stair-like ledges. Other ledges lay high on the canyon sides. Only two trails led to the canyon, and steep bluffs to the east created a good defensive position if that should ever be needed. The site had plenty of water to sustain a large camp of men and horses.[346]

In the middle of the night, President Romney sent instructions by riders to the other colonies, detailing where and when to meet. A telegram was sent to Chuichupa.

Romney and the other leaders knew this would be an arduous trip. One of the storekeepers loaded food and supplies from his shelves into a wagon. In the night, he delivered his crucial load to the Stairs without detection.

As desperate as they were, some of these colony men wanted to save more than their lives. They wanted to save their community culture. In the late-night discussions, Colonia Juárez Bishop Joseph C. Bentley had been reluctant to leave, and he fully expected to return. To this end, he put all of the ward records and minutes into metal tins and loaded them into a wagon. He hauled them to the Stairs and placed them on the high canyon ledges. The wagon must have been full of tins. Bishop Bentley had been ward clerk and stake clerk as well as bishop, and the voluminous documents dated to the colonies' inception. This valuable historic resource was considered lost for over 70 years. But Bishop Bentley must have retrieved them sometime after the Exodus because the archivist for the LDS Church found them in the possession of a Bentley grandson. The documents are now on file in Salt Lake City.

When all of the preparations were made, President Romney gave the order on August 1, and the men left quietly in the night, avoiding the patrols, and leading pack animals and spare horses. Most arrived safely without incident, but not all.

In Dublán, dark as it was, the rebels realized everyone was gone. Armed riders quickly rode in pursuit, led by Manuel Gutiérrez. They caught the escapees and opened fire, wounding a young colonist in the leg. The pursuers did not realize the desperate colonists had not given up all of their guns during the turn-in charade. In fact, the retreating colonists were well armed. Bishop Thurber, in command, ordered ten men to stop, turn their horses, dismount and open fire. The surprised rebels reined back abruptly, wheeled their plunging horses, and galloped back to Dublán.

At the Stairs, everyone was present by August 3 except the men from Chuichupa. It turned out they had just left August 3 and had much farther to go. They almost waited too long. Just after they rode out, they looked back with binoculars from a ridge, and watched Red Flagger troops enter their town, break down doors, and fire shots at the pigs and cows. As a measure of their fear and desperation that day, the Chuichupa men elected to kill all their dogs, their beloved, highly trained companions that helped so much with the cattle and sheep. Barking was a security issue, and the men also felt the dogs would suffer on the long hot days ahead on the trail through mountains and desert.

After waiting at the Stairs campsite until August 5, President Romney and the main body decided they could not wait any longer. There were rumors of Red Flaggers ahead and behind them. Two hundred and thirty-five men with 500 horses (some sources say 1,000) left on August 7 for the border. With guard details in front and back, they rode through Tapiecitas, crossed the Janos River, passed through Colonia Seco, and Rancho la Palotada northwest of Janos. They crossed the border into New Mexico on August 10 (the same day the Chuichupa men arrived at the Stairs). Safe now, they pushed their weary horses on to the rancho at Dog Springs, a place no longer on the map but located about 11 miles east of Antelope Wells, *El Berrendo*, one of the most remote official crossings along the border. A small U.S. Army detachment stationed at the rancho saw them coming and almost opened fire before recognizing the tired escapees. They had covered up to 60 miles per day and needed to rest themselves and their horses, if only briefly. They pushed on to Hachita, then to El Paso, some by train and others by horse and wagon. The first few arrived on August 13 to an unimaginably joyous reunion with their families. The Chuichupa men reached El Paso safely later in the month.

In all, 2,500 LDS refugees came to El Paso. Some stayed, some left for other opportunities in Utah, Arizona, and New Mexico, while a small number returned to Mexico. Those who stayed in El Paso were organized into a ward six years later in 1918.

The Exodus occurred in different ways in other locations. At Colonia Díaz, the messenger with President Romney's letter arrived at 4:00 in the morning. After a meeting conducted by the bishop, the residents decided to take the women and children to Hachita, New Mexico. By 11:00 that same morning, 85 wagons were packed with trunks and bedrolls, the only belongings these settlers would ever see again from their experience in Mexico. The women and children with the few men with them camped at Dog Springs before going on to the old mining town of Hachita. After the remainder of the men evacuated, the Díaz exiles remained in Hachita in tents provided by the U.S. government until the families gradually dispersed to new lives elsewhere. They never returned to Colonia Díaz. Early in 1913, a structure caught fire, whether accidently or intentionally, is not clear. The entire town burned. For over a hundred years, it has been a ghost town, where visitors seek out pioneer names on the headstones in the cemetery.

In the Sonoran colony of Morelos, it was not the rebels but federal troops under General Agustín Sanjinés, the commanding general in Sonora, that caused the depredation at least initially. In July, Sanjinés moved 1,000-1,500 federal soldiers into Colonia Morelos and allowed them to take anything and do anything. Drunkenness, debauchery (there were plenty of camp followers), and property damage was rampant for the next few weeks.

Word came that Salazar with his army was marching to Sonora, not to attack the federals but to attack the colonists. With this news, the colonists organized an exodus of the women and children. On August 30, sixty lumber wagons loaded with 450 women, children, trunks, and bedrolls left Colonia Morelos in a heavy rain. They made it to Douglas, Arizona, where U.S. government representatives and local citizens looked after them. The men should have left then as well. When they did decide to leave a few days later, the federal troops had moved to Agua Prieta opposite Douglas on the border and Salazar's rogue army had arrived in Colonia Morelos. As the LDS men tried to leave, the rebel soldiers harassed them, taking their animals and belongings. One man was kidnapped and held for several days before being released to find his way to the border on foot with nothing. None of the Sonoran settlements survived as LDS colonies. The Church sold its interest to the Mexican government in 1921.

Approximately 4,500 LDS colonists left Mexico in 1912. They were not the only ones to have their lives disrupted and to be dislocated from their homes. War falls hard on ordinary people. Historians disagree on the numbers, but at least a million died during the Revolution and perhaps many more. Also during that decade, about the same number left Mexico for the United States and elsewhere. LDS colonists, North Americans, and other foreign businessmen and their families represented the most obvious evacuees, but hundreds of thousands of Mexican nationals also left. They left for a variety of reasons caused by the fighting and brutality, but they left, creating the first great migration of Mexicans into the United States.

Exodus Aftermath

In spite of the trauma, many of the exiled LDS colonists expected to return to their homes in Mexico. Some had not wanted to leave in the first place, but after protesting they accepted President Romney's instructions. From El Paso, President Romney wrote letters complaining to Mexican government officials and received back assurances that never could be met. He did receive permission to send an inspection party to the colony towns. When that party returned with a dismal report about the physical condition of the towns and fields, President Romney decided to go himself. The federal commanders, General Sanjinés, who had allowed the depredations in Colonia Morelos, and General José de la Luz Blanco, had moved their headquarters to Pearson. President Romney met them there. The federal generals disclaimed any responsibility for the colonists' plight and referred President Romney to the local municipal authorities. One of those was Felipe Chávez, the Comisario Policía of Colonia Juárez (Felipe Chávez, was the grandfather of Leopoldo Horacio Chávez, the current official historian for Casas Grandes). He and the president of the municipio, Porfirio Talamantes, appointed a judge from the Galeana District as an inspector to review the condition of the damaged properties. The official reports were shocking but little was done.[347]

Every house and store in Dublán had been looted of virtually all of their contents. Any furniture left behind had been smashed. Windows and doors were broken and holes punched in the floors and ceilings, presumably by looters looking for hiding places. The mountain colonies suffered the same damage. In addition, stock had been taken or shot and most harnesses and farm tools stolen.[348]

The reports did contain a few bright spots. In some fields, crops had not been ruined and could be harvested. Also, stray stock wandering in the hills could be rounded up. In Colonia Juárez the damage appears to have been less severe.

Bishop Joseph C. Bentley had not wanted to leave in the first place. After many meetings in El Paso, he and 60 men returned to Colonia Juárez just two weeks after the Exodus. At least some found their properties intact. Bishop Bentley's loyal Mexican employee, Cornelio Reyes, had protected and maintained everything belonging to the Bishop. In one story, Bishop Bentley, prior to leaving, had gone, after dark, to the house of Felipe Chávez, the Comisario, and requested that he and others watch over the LDS properties. He asked Chávez to explain to both federals and rebels alike that he, the local magistrate, was in charge of all of the properties, and they should not be touched.[349] This seems unlikely given the extreme secrecy of the exit plan. But the story does suggest that relations with the local Mexicans in Colonia Juárez was less hostile than in the other colonies.

The returnees rounded up stray cattle and prepared for the fall harvest. Bishop Bentley and others felt comfortable enough to notify their families in El Paso to return.

The town did not escape unscathed. Several returned to find burned-out homes and buildings. Many stood in ruins for years along the streets as constant reminders of terrible times.

The returnees were the intrepid ones. After many meetings and communications, official and unofficial, the U.S. government offered free transportation for the exiled families to anywhere in the country. Most took advantage of this generous offer, scattering across the nation and into Canada. A significant number went to LDS communities in the Southwest, some staying close to the border waiting for their opportunity to return to their Mexican homes.

In February 1913, Bishop Bentley led another group of 65 men, women, and children back to begin the rebuilding process. By the end of the year, about 300 Mormons lived in Colonia Juárez and Dublán. Those that tried to reestablish in Colonia Morelos in Sonora found the local Mexicans so hostile that most soon left.

A combination of factors led to the ultimate abandonment of the mountain colonies. Some did return, driven by the memories of their lives in the beautiful mountain valleys and by the practical idea of salvaging assets they had worked so hard to build. This would not be easy. Significant damage had been done, and the isolation of the mountain colonies made them difficult to rebuild and dangerous to defend. They also were a long way from amenities they had become used to such as quality secondary education.[350]

There were exceptions, A few mountain ranches remained in LDS-member ownership and are retained by family descendants today.

A small number of families tried to rebuild in Colonia García, but the extremes of drought and flood drove them back to the lower valley. Chuichupa did have a revival. In early 1914, it was reported abandoned by Anglo-LDS colonists. Later several returned in spite of the distance, helped by access to the railroad. The expansion of the lumbering industry by Dr. Fred Stark Pearson's companies created an economic base that attracted people, both Anglo and Mexican, to Chuichupa. In the early 1940s, well after the Pearson era, the town was described as having tall cypress trees along wide streets in front of sturdy brick houses still occupied by Anglo LDS members as well as Mexican families. The community was substantial enough to regain its status as a ward.[351] Gradually Mexican families bought the properties and the last Anglo family left sometime in the 1950s.

Some of the Exodus returnees found work in Pearson. The newly created Mexican North Western Railway had completed the loop of track from Ciudad Juárez over the mountains to a junction that connected to Ciudad Chihuahua and south to Mexico City. A large lumber mill was under construction and jobs were available there, on the railroad, and in the mountain timber-cutting sites.

A Land in Turmoil

The railroad and mill managers struggled to keep their operations running as Chihuahua slid into political turmoil during 1913. President Madero made another bad decision, this time a deadly one. His choice of General Huerta as commander had been good as far as effectiveness in the field against Orozco was concerned. While Huerta had established garrisons in the railroad towns, including Pearson and regained control, he had other ideas. Madero should have been more wary.

On February 18, 1913, in the same month that Bishop Bentley led the second group of returnees back to Colonia Juárez, Huerta, along with members of the old Díaz regime, staged a coup, forced Madero to resign, and murdered him as he "tried to escape." They also murdered Chihuahua's governor, Abraham González. Within hours of Madero's death, the conspirators manipulated the succession laws and Huerta was appointed president. He dissolved the legislature and established a military dictatorship.

Now the "generals" had to decide again who to support. Orozco, Salazar, and Rojas, previously all staunch revolutionaries, decided to join Huerta and become part of his oppressive federal regime. Other regional politicians and military chieftains would have nothing to do with Huerta. Venustiano Carranza, the governor of Coahuila, proclaimed himself "First Chief" and called for rebellion. Many rallied to him or at least to the idea, including Álvaro Obregón in Sonora, Emiliano Zapata in the central state of Morelos, and later Pancho Villa in Chihuahua. Carranza's allies were called "Constitutionalists," referring to Huerta's violation of the 1857 constitution regarding presidential succession.

As serious as these national events were, they caused little concern for the colonists in the Casas Grandes Valley trying to rebuild their lives. During 1913, a few incidents occurred, but overall, the situation remained relatively quiet until April 26, 1914. That day the colonists received a message from the Church president in Salt Lake City stating they should leave for the U.S. immediately.

The arrest of seven U.S sailors for trespassing in the gulf port of Tampico, combined with the exposure of a German shipment of arms to Mexico, grew overnight into an international incident. President Wilson either overreacted or acted deliberately to weaken Huerta. He sent in marines and armed sailors to occupy Veracruz, which resulted in clashes and shelling of the city.[352] Feelings ran high against North Americans, and newspaper headlines screamed of the danger to U.S. citizens in Mexico. Many left.

This started a second Exodus from the LDS colonies. Bewildered residents of Colonia Juárez and Dublán began to frantically pack.

The LDS president in Salt Lake City had responded to the hysteria in the newspapers. Most who left the colonies soon realized this and returned.

A third small-scale Exodus occurred in 1917 when colonists chose to leave under the protection of the U.S Army after the incursion into Mexico chasing Pancho Villa, but that would come later.

A few months after the Tampico/Veracruz Incidents, Huerta went into exile. Carranza assumed authority in Mexico City supported by General Obregón. Villa and Zapata did not trust Carranza or recognize him as First Chief. With the common enemy gone, they soon clashed with Carranza's forces led by Obregón.

Villa did not fare well during 1915, losing a series of battles against Obregón. Still formidable, he decided to invade Sonora, which he believed would fall easily. From the command post in central Mexico where he had retreated after his defeats, he commandeered 19 trains from the National Railroad and sent his troops, camp followers, horses, cannon, supplies, and all the paraphernalia of war north into the Casas Grandes Valley.

Of the hardships, the LDS returnees faced in 1915, one of the worst was fear. This was not new to them but threats, rumors, lack of accurate information, and direct confrontation took their fears to a new level. Most had no clear picture of what was going on. Before the Exodus, all depredations, no matter who caused them, were blamed on Red Flaggers and now all fell on Pancho Villa. In late September 1915, the rumor spread that Villa was coming north. Their worst fears were confirmed when Villa's 19 trains rolled into Colonia Dublán. Only 200 LDS returnees lived there, and this small group watched as 10,000 people with 8,000 horses piled off the freight cars and began setting up camp in the streets, fields, empty houses, and along every water canal and ditch. The camp followers and *soldaderas* started cooking fires with anything that would burn. They stayed for three weeks. Contrary to fearful expectations, General Villa gave strict orders not to physically molest the residents. Supplies, feed and particularly horses were confiscated, but Villa, who had always respected LDS members, allowed no physical harm. He even went through the charade of paying with currency he had printed during his brief reign as Chihuahua's governor.

On October 16, 1915, the army left for Sonora. Villa had perfected the logistics of moving troops by train, but no trains crossed the Sierra Madre from Chihuahua to Sonora (and would not until 1961). Villa commandeered every wagon that could be found. Frugality overcame the vow of neutrality for three Dublán wagon owners. They agreed to be drivers in order to ensure the return of their equipment. The camp followers and soldaderas were sent to Casas Grandes and not allowed to accompany their soldiers on the march to the battleground.

The departing army left behind piles of trash, garbage, and human waste. The residents had no idea how to clean up the mess, and they worried about disease. Then a thunderstorm unleashed heavy downpour, considered providential, that washed much of the filth into the river.[353]

Villa managed to get his army across the mountains but suffered a terrible, bloody defeat at Agua Prieta.

The three Dublán drivers hauled ammunition in their wagons to the front lines until they could see Villa was losing. They made a run for the border and safety.[354]

Tattered and frustrated, the defeated soldiers struggled back across the frozen passes from Sonora. Some looked for their families in the valley communities. Others searched for Villa, wanting to rejoin because they had nowhere else to go. Many simply tried to disappear, but all needed something to eat. Many of the exhausted, hungry men quietly accepted the generosity of the LDS and Mexican residents in the valley. Others used force.

In one account, about 20 mounted soldiers rampaged through Dublán at Christmas time. In another incident, Bishop Anson Bowen Call faced three rebels who broke into his house and threatened to kill him and ravish the female members of his family. Bishop Call stood his ground, denying access to the stairs to his family above. He was dragged outside and roughed up, but the soldiers left and never returned.[355]

Two-and-one-half months later, on March 17, 1916, the leading units of General John Pershing's 2nd Provisional Cavalry Brigade arrived north of Dublán. The week before, Pancho Villa had crossed the border and attacked the town of Columbus, New Mexico, killing civilians, U.S. soldiers, and burning buildings. Pershing's Punitive Expedition to find and destroy Villa was the U.S. response despite vigorous protests from Carranza in Mexico City. Eventually 14,000 U.S. troops arrived and passed through Pershing's main base north of Dublán. For the first time in five years, the colonists felt completely safe. Also, they had a huge market for their farm products, hay, leather, and lumber. The payments in U.S silver dollars helped restore their depleted assets. A few more exiles returned to their colony homes to take advantage of the U.S. Army business.

The period of prosperous safety lasted just ten and a half months. When Pershing and his troops left for Columbus, a long line of cars, wagons, and people on foot followed. These included LDS members, Mexicans, Chinese (particularly Chinese), the families of U.S. businessmen, and many of the businessmen themselves. All sought sanctuary from Villa's revenge. The fear was real. Anti-U.S. feelings had intensified during the Punitive Expedition.

José Inés Salazar by now had joined Villa. He had changed sides so many times, one wonders if he could remember why he was fighting. On February 17, 1917, he rode into Colonia Juárez at the head of a column of well-armed men. His second in command was Silvestre Quevedo, Jr. On the road they encountered three Chinese storekeepers making a delivery. They summarily shot the three for the provisions in their wagon. Two died. The third badly wounded man was found and taken to El Paso for treatment.[356] The rebels divided the stolen supplies as they made camp. The large bully Salazar, who had forced the Exodus of LDS colonists from their homes and fields, had returned.

After the shooting of the Chinese, Salazar ordered all men, Anglos and Mexicans to assemble at the flour mill. This was something different. Quevedo and the other rebels thought they had come to sack the town. Instead, Salazar, still a formidable man, harangued the assembled men, stating that Villa had ordered them all to join the fight against Carranza, Obregón, and the United States or be lined up and shot. According to LDS lore, Joseph Bentley, now the Stake president, stepped forward and looked up at the much larger man and made his own speech. He stated clearly and calmly that they were not in this country to fight for either side. The Mexicans were their friends. They had no intention of fighting for or against anybody. He described what they had accomplished and their respect for Mexicans. He said it was up to Salazar to decide whether to shoot them. If Villa came, he would tell him the same thing. Salazar's demeanor suddenly changed. He may have realized that for him, it was over. He agreed with President Bentley. They spoke quietly, shook hands, and the men returned to their homes.

The story has been told and retold, but whatever the exact details, this episode was the last major confrontation in Colonia Juárez, although rustling, thievery, and extortion demands plagued the town for the next two years.[357] In May, Salazar abandoned Villa. A mule may have kicked him in the head, or he might have suffered from depression. He may just have wanted to go to his family in El Paso. Regardless of his motive, he rode north with just three loyal men, perhaps including Manuel Gutiérrez. On July 26, 1917, they entered Rancho Nogales, northwest of Janos, a large holding of the Palomas Land and Cattle Company. The ranch foreman knew they were coming and who they were. He and his ranch hands set an ambush and killed all four, including the large general, who had so terrorized the LDS colonists.

The foreman now had a problem. Salazar remained famous and a revolutionary hero to many in spite of his chameleon-like tendency to change sides. To hide the deed from reprisals, the cowboys stuffed him down a well. Historians have not been able to determine the location of his body, which has become a bit of a historical mystery.[358] Salazar's great grandchildren have expressed interest in using ground-penetrating radar equipment at Rancho Nogales to search for his remains.[359]

In 2019, the Casas Grandes municipio council approved a proposal to place a monument to General Salazar in the town plaza.

Rejuvenation

Salazar's demise marked a turning point in the fortunes of the colonists. They still faced two more years of rebel activity, more banditry than revolutionary. By 1919, their population had increased to 630, still less than 15 percent of the total prior to the Exodus.[360] They continued their routine of working, planting and harvesting, but morale was not particularly high.

Villa remained active, but in May 1920, Carranza was assassinated (possibly suicide) after a dispute with General Obregón over presidential succession. Congress appointed Adolfo de la Huerta (not to be confused with Victoriano Huerta, the deposed dictator) as interim president until elections could be held. De la Huerta was a skilled administrator having served in a number of positions including governor of Sonora. In his short tenure, he instituted several measures to aid the transition from civil war. He opened negotiations with Pancho Villa, over Obregón's strong objections. In exchange for a 25,000 acre hacienda at Canutillo near Parral, Chihuahua, Villa agreed to lay down his arms and recognize the government. Two hundred and fifty of his loyal soldiers moved with him to the hacienda, all with government pensions. Obregón became president six months later.

In 1919, Elder Melvin J. Ballard, a member of the Quorum of Twelve Apostles was sent to inspect the Juárez Stake. His talks and sermons encouraged the colonists. Elder Ballard also stimulated their missionary efforts.

This stimulus, plus disenchantment with the Catholic Church brought about by the anticlerical agenda of the Revolution, began to increase the LDS Mexican population despite government restrictions on all church activity.

By 1921, the situation had calmed, and a few, anxious about their properties, felt secure enough to return to the mountain colonies. That year, 816 LDS members lived in Colonia Juárez, Colonia Dublán, and in the mountains.[361]

In the spring of 1922, W. Ernest Young, an Academy teacher, became Bishop of Colonia Juárez. He picked two other teachers as his counselors, and the three infused new energy into the ward. They promoted long postponed projects such as rebuilding the old bridge across the Piedras Verdes River. Fruit trees had always been grown, but they now encouraged planting orchards of apples and peaches on the land vacated during the rebellion. The world-wide Depression had little impact on the colonists. In 1932, Ernest Hatch shipped apples to a fair in Mexico City, the first crop exported from of the colonies since 1896.[362] These crops not only produced cash but led, years later in 1966, to the formation of a fruit-packing and marketing cooperative *Sociedad Local de Crédito Agrícola, Paquimé*. Mexican farmers participated, but this form of agricultural industry became a major factor in the prosperity of the Anglo-LDS community in the second half of the 20th century.[363]

Anti-Clericalism

In 1924, Plutarco Elías Calles, commander at the Battle of Agua Prieta, succeeded Obregón as president of Mexico. The next year, Calles began a harsh enforcement of anticlerical laws, based on the Constitution of 1917. Priests, ministers, and missionaries of all religions were severely restricted from performing their duties. Catholics throughout the country reacted violently. In spite of the long history of liberal reforms to control church power, Catholicism remained deeply ingrained in the Mexican people. Many Catholics took up arms and rebelled in what became the three-year long First Cristero War. War-weary Mexico was torn again by bitter fighting but not in Chihuahua. Instead of promoting rebellion, Roman Catholic

Bishop Antonio Guízar forbade any Chihuahuan participation in Cristero violence under threat of excommunication.

Few incidents occurred, the most significant was General José Escobar's retreat with his rebel Cristero army north through Casas Grandes. Federal forces had defeated him at a battle in Jiménez in southeastern Chihuahua, and he ran north for Púlpito Pass and Sonora.[364] The federals in pursuit caused some property damage, which was minor compared to the death and destruction in other parts of the country.

Calles' draconian laws applied to all religions, and the LDS members struggled to keep alive their formal church activity. Proselyting was banned for nine years. After 1934, the government relented somewhat, but all missionaries had to be Mexican citizens.[365]

In spite of the restrictions, LDS missionary work in Mexico, which began with President Brigham Young's order in 1875, has to be viewed as successful. Figures vary widely between official and semi-official sources. The Mexican census of 2010 counted 350,000 LDS members, a figure sources in Salt Lake City claim is low by as much as a million[366] In 2009, the Church reported 220 Mexican stakes and 1,989 wards and branches. The official numbers at any given time are immaterial. What is important is that while the number of Anglo members declined, the Church of Jesus Christ of Latter-day Saints has made an impact on the religious structure of Mexico. This is particularly true in northern Chihuahua, where most communities have an LDS chapel. Mata Ortiz is an exception, although several members lived there when the mill was under construction.

The colonies prospered during the relative peace of the 1930s. This resulted in part because of the acquisition of the productive land of those who did not return. Many sold at very low prices. This tended to concentrate large land holdings into the hands of a few LDS members, changing the colonies' socio/economic structure. In the pre-Exodus days, cooperative ownership and other community practices kept the colonists comparably equal. With the accumulation of property, the gap between rich and poor increased. Several of the pre-Exodus industries were never reestablished. The net effect was fewer opportunities for young people entering the job market. Also, the Mexican worker, in spite of all of the travails of the Revolution, emerged from the conflict with new rights and a new awareness of these rights. Mexican farmers, tradesmen, and laborers all provided increased competition.[367]

The Anglo-LDS population was about 1,200 in 1938.[368] World War II caused a decline as younger people moved to the U.S. to serve in the military or work in war plants. People moved back and forth after the war for family and economic reasons. In 1945 the number stood at 1,000 and 650 by 1950.[369] The issues of citizenship, dual citizenship, national military obligations and residency requirements are very complex. These evolved and changed in the postwar era, affecting movement back and forth across the border, particularly for younger people.

The Constitution of 1917 and subsequent additions had provisions regulating irrigation and conservation. The colonists as well as the local Mexicans in the Casas Grandes Valley adapted to these regulations without serious disruption. Some property was lost, usually because absentee owners failed to pay their taxes, and the land reverted to the government.

Also, the Constitution prohibited foreigners from owning land within 100 kilometers of the border. This provision and the failure to pay taxes caused the government to take the Colonia Díaz properties and form an ejido.

Enclaves of Anglo-LDS members remain in the town of Colonia Juárez and the Nuevo Casas Grandes neighborhood of Dublán. Most are descendants of Exodus survivors. Few have intermarried and most names on the historic listing of Colonia Juárez and Dublán stake presidents are Anglo.[370] A high point for these descendants as well as for all other LDS members in the Casas Grandes Valley was the dedication of their temple in 2000.

A White Temple on a Green Hill

The seed that grew into the idea for a temple was planted when LDS President Gordon B. Hinckley visited Ciudad Juárez for the Academia Centennial in 1997.

Temples, and the special activities held there, have always been an integral part of the LDS Church, dating to the first built in Kirtland, Ohio, in 1836. Colonists came to northern Chihuahua in 1885, but the first temple in Mexico was not built until almost 100 years later in 1983 in Mexico City.

The colonists held regular services in local chapels, but for special temple activities, they and their descendants had to travel hundreds of miles north to Arizona, or Utah and much later south to Mexico City.

President Hinckley arrived by air in El Paso and was driven for several hours to Colonia Juárez and to what he considered an extremely remote corner of his constituency. He seemed impressed by the two remaining colonies, Colonia Juárez and Dublán. Speaking frankly he said he would like to see everyone able to get to a temple without too much inconvenience, but with 5,000 members "there are not enough of you to justify a Temple." They would need four or five times the current membership, an impossible task in the vast, sparsely populated area.

Hinckley reflected on this problem riding back to the airport in El Paso. When he took the presidency, there were 47 LDS temples throughout the world, all large. This had been the pattern for over 150 years. Traveling along as he said later in a speech announcing a new policy, "The answer, we believe came bright and clear." The Church would construct small temples in remote areas.

On March 7, 1998 on a freezing Saturday, five months after this announcement, Church members broke ground on a hill above Colonia

The Church of Jesus Christ of Latter-day Saints Temple, Colonia Juárez.
Photo courtesy of Philip Stover.

Juárez. Construction began the following Monday. A Utah contractor constructed the building, but the temple grounds and hillside were landscaped by local members, who donated thousands of hours of labor. On some days, as many as 300 people of all ages worked on the site.

Almost to the day one year after the groundbreaking on March 7, President Hinckley made his second trip to Colonia Juárez to participate in the ceremonies dedicating the pure white structure on a green hill above town, the smallest temple in the smallest LDS temple district in the world.[371]

One of the Seven

The LDS colonists' culture that dropped into the Casas Grandes Valley in 1885 was almost completely alien to the mestizos that had evolved there over 200 years. Religion, morals, lifestyle, and economic skills totally differed. The edges of these sharp differences have softened somewhat over the decades. Mexicans have converted. The prosperity of the LDS agricultural and business enterprises provided jobs for local Mexicans and, perhaps more importantly, the incentive to emulate LDS entrepreneurship. The original reason for their immigration has disappeared, but those remaining found their "place" and stayed, becoming one of the Siete Culturas of the Casas Grandes Valley.

Differences, including social separation in civil and church affairs, do persist. Usually these surface over land-ownership issues. The Casas Grandes Ejido claims that over half of their communal land was taken illegally.[372] Lawsuits and negotiations continue and sometimes ugly confrontations occur. Many, but certainly not all, of the claims have been resolved. These issues do not alter the fact that the Anglo-LDS residents and the local Mexican population, LDS or not, have more in common than not. They live in the same towns, work in the same places, and often attend the same schools. For most in the Casas Grandes Valley, the mixture of distinct cultures has always existed. It is their normal.

9

—

Dr. Fred Stark Pearson

Almost Unknown

Just as the late 20th and early 21st centuries will be remembered as the great age of electronics, the late 19th and early 20th centuries are known as the great age of electricity. After centuries of flickering lamps and candles, inventions by such genius entrepreneurs as Michael Faraday, Thomas Edison, Nikola Tesla, and George Westinghouse literally lit up the cities and towns of the world. This happened in a remarkably short length of time.

Some of these technological pathfinders remain household names, readily identified in school books, on monuments, and on the logos of current-day companies. There were others of comparable status that for various reasons are less well known or even totally forgotten. Falling somewhere within these categories is the brilliant electrical engineer/entrepreneur Dr. Fred Stark Pearson.

Most do not recognize the Pearson name. The chemistry building at Tufts University in Massachusetts was named after him in 1926. Thousands of students and faculty have passed through Pearson Hall since without knowing the origin of the name. In Barcelona, Spain, a monument with a Greek-style statue stands in the center of Pedrales Plaza with the name "Pearson" on the base. Few other places honor the name of the man who was once called the greatest engineer in the world.

Visitors to Mata Ortiz top the rise above town and drive down across the track to the main street. Straight ahead stands an old adobe building covered with chipped white plaster. A faded sign in the plaster reads *Mercado Pearson.*

Everyone in Mata Ortiz, children and adults, know the name of their town used to be Pearson. They can point to the hill where his house stood.

One evening in 1984, Don Chuy López visited the home of Mata Ortiz potter Juan Quezada. Adults and children gathered around the kitchen table under a single bare light bulb, dangling from the ceiling, to hear his stories. Don Chuy came from Zacatecas and claimed to have witnessed the great battle there in 1914 between Pancho Villa's *Division del Norte* and the federal forces of President Victoriano Huerta. He also claimed to have seen General Pershing's airplanes flying overhead looking for Villa in 1916. He told of the early days of Mata Ortiz and of the English lord named Pearson who between 1909 and 1913 extended the railroad from Nuevo Casas Grandes past the railroad camp, called Pearson, and over the mountains to the connection at Madera and the rest of Mexico. The old man went on to describe the great lumber mill that Pearson built just beyond where they were sitting. Logs from the mountains were cut in the mill and the lumber hauled away by Lord Pearson's trains. But the *revolucionistas* blew up the trains and the great mill could never work at capacity. Pearson left Mexico, said Don Chuy as he finished his tale, and the English lord went down with the Titanic.

This was Don Chuy's story, not only his but the standard version in the village for years. Even such distinguished anthropologists and historians as Florence and Robert Lister repeated essentially the same version in their book, *Chihuahua, Storehouse of Storms.* They described Weetman Pearson—the British magnate with the title "Lord Cowdray," who dredged the harbor at Veracruz, built the Tehuantepec railroad, and developed the Tampico oilfields—as the builder of the Pearson lumber mill. They also agreed with Don Chuy that Pearson met his demise on the Titanic. This is the story ... except, there are discrepancies.

The Titanic hit the famous iceberg on April 14, 1912. On that date and for the next couple of years, Dr. Pearson was in Mexico connecting the last gaps in his rail line and powering up his lumber mill. The biography of Weetman Pearson, 1st Viscount Cowdray, *Member for Mexico*, by Desmond Young describes this Pearson's projects in Mexico but says nothing of any activity in Chihuahua. Young also states that Weetman Pearson died in bed in Cowdray Castle in England in 1927.[373]

Anthropologist, Dr. R. B. Brown, director of the pre-historic Paquimé site during the 1980s and early 90s, was troubled by these discrepancies. He checked local files and old books on railroading and discovered another Pearson—Dr. Fred Stark Pearson—a brilliant engineer known for projects throughout the Western Hemisphere, and also a major developer in Mexico.[374] Don Chuy and the Listers can be forgiven for the mistaken identity. Only five years apart in age, both Pearsons developed huge projects in Mexico at the same time during the Porfirio Díaz era. Dr. Fred Stark Pearson's most important legacy is the hydro-electric system bringing electrical power to Mexico City. Weetman Pearson's company, the Mexican Eagle Oil Company, *Mexicana de Petróleo el Águila, SA*, drilled the first successful oil well in Mexico and built the first refinery.

Dr. Fred Stark Pearson, 1861-1915
Photo: Courtesy of Fred Harwood and S.A Morse

It is hard to visualize in this time of instant accessibility through the internet to obscure publications and distant archives how arduous it was to research less well-known subjects just 25-30 years ago. Dr. Brown did the work and found the correct Pearson.

Dr. Fred Stark Pearson was not always so unknown. By the first years of the 20th century, Pearson, a New Englander and graduate of Tufts, had earned the reputation as the most important electrical engineer in the world. Demand for his expertise on hydroelectric and street railway projects extended through the Western Hemisphere from Brazil to Canada. His name gave credence to international financiers evaluating start-up ventures in these faraway places. Contemporaries included luminaries such as Edison and Westinghouse. Unlike them, Pearson's name did not remain in the public memory. The few existing references usually repeat the same errors. Some assume his name was Frederick. It was just Fred. He often is called a Canadian, probably because he completed major projects and incorporated several companies there. His birthplace was Lowell, Massachusetts. Others call him an Englishman because of the confusion with Weetman Pearson. Finally, Pearson did not go down with the Titanic. Although tragically, he and his wife did perish at sea.

In spite of the errors and lack of attention to Pearson in modern references, he was a most significant figure during that period of phenomenal industrial growth and technical achievement of the late 19th and early 20th centuries.

The Prodigy

Fred Pearson's astonishing memory and grasp of scientific subjects were evident as a boy. He was born on July 3, 1861, to Hannah Amelia Edgerly and Ambrose Pearson, a civil engineer on the Boston and Lowell Railroad (later the Boston and Maine). The falls of the Merrimack River flowing through Lowell provided waterpower to run the textile looms of America's first major factory-based industry. Lowell became known as the "Cradle of the Industrial Revolution." Pearson, who would develop massive electric power systems based on water power, was born into this environment. As a boy, abundant energy and insatiable interest in everything around him must have drawn him to the huge brick mills and the tall water wheels that, through a system of gears, drove the looms.

Today he might have been diagnosed as "hyperactive." He was often in trouble, devising technical tricks such as poking a hole in the ceiling above his school desk and running a string through the ceiling to another hole, and dropping the string to the handle of the coal shuttle. One tug from his desk and the coal shuttle upended with a satisfactory crash. On the positive side, he read scientific books on such subjects as metallurgy, checked out of the library at age eight.[375]

The family moved around New England as Ambrose Pearson worked on other railroad projects in this grand era of railroad expansion, fueled by the Civil War and the ongoing Industrial Revolution. Through his father, young Fred was exposed to the practical work of expanding railroads. In 1870, the family moved to Putnam, Connecticut where they became close friends with the William Ward family. Ward, a stonemason, may have done work for Ambrose on railway bridges. He had four daughters, the oldest named Mabel. Hyperactive Fred alternatively fascinated and terrified the Ward girls. William Ward, a strict Congregationalist, did not know what to think about this eager young man so full of what the sober Ward considered wild ideas. But Fred was an attractive man, tall and erect with a wiry build, and wavy dark hair. At family gatherings, he played the violin, taught everyone to dance the Schottische (a country dance popular in the Victorian era), and apparently charmed the elder Ward (as well as the daughters). A few years later, Ward quietly bought a suit for Fred to wear at graduation, something the young man did not have and could not afford. The friendship continued even after both families moved away. By 1879, the Wards lived in Lowell, Massachusetts.

In 1880, William Ward sent Mabel, his eldest daughter to Dresden, Germany, to study French, German, and music. Mabel remained in Europe three years, becoming an accomplished pianist.

After four years in Putnam, the Pearsons had moved to Wilton, New Hampshire, where Ambrose, the father, suddenly died. Fred was fifteen. Hannah, his mother, was a resourceful woman, but they had little money, and Fred was now the man of the family. He appealed to an uncle for help and was abruptly turned down. Fred never forgot the rebuff and vowed he would be richer than his uncle. The next year, at sixteen, he left high school and the family moved to Medford, Massachusetts. Hannah may have relied on her late husband's associates because Fred was hired as the stationmaster at the Medford Hillside Station of the Boston and Lowell Railroad. The track ran along the base of the hill where the station and the adjacent Tufts College (it became a university in 1954) were located. Fred was in charge of ticket sales, baggage handling, freight, mail, telegraph and the signal system.[376]

Professors going to and from their various assignments became acquainted with the boy who sold them tickets who was always reading. They talked with him almost as equal about his wide variety of interests, including philosophy, theology, and all phases of science. The college hired his mother as the campus postmistress, and the two became part of the school community. Then one adventure brought young Fred sharply to the attention of college and the railroad officials.

The Medford Hillside Station was a "signal station." Trains came through five or six times a day and only stopped when necessary for passengers, mail, or freight.

When an approaching train sounded a warning whistle, a signal arm had to be lowered manually to indicate whether the train should stop. At the sound of the whistle, Fred ran down a flight of wooden stairs, lowered the signal and ran back up the stairs to the ticket window to serve any last minute customers. As young and agile as he was five or six round trips a day became a chore and distracted him from his books. He devised a solenoid-tripping device that would raise and lower the signal arm. He ran wires from the solenoid to a switch in the station office and up the hill to a battery in the college chemistry building. At the sound of the whistle, he put down his book and reached from his chair to the switch. Boston and Lowell officials soon found out about Fred Pearson's labor-saving device. Instead of being alarmed, they embraced the concept. One of the historic roots of the modern automatic railroad semaphore system traces back to Medford Hillside Station and the young stationmaster.[377]

This is a good story and was told many times as Dr. Pearson gained fame for his pioneering engineering accomplishments. An article in Cassier's Magazine in 1900 had this version:

"As station agent of the Boston & Lowell Railroad, there were but few trains for which he had to sell tickets, but there were many trains which he had to flag…. This bothered young Pearson not a little; for this he had to leave his classes at the most inopportune times and repair to the little station under the hill. He set about to find a way out of this work, and accordingly rigged up an electrical appliance that did the work for him. After that young Pearson attended his classes in peace."[378]

This assumes Fred was already attending classes. Whether he was or was not, the faculty at Tufts had recognized his potential and encouraged him to enroll. In 1879, a loan from another, more sympathetic, uncle made it possible. That first year, he excelled in mathematics and chemistry. The following year, he transferred to the Massachusetts Institute of Technology for advanced chemistry. Hannah took over his duties at the station. Tufts' professors were breaking new ground in the sciences, particularly physics. But the chemistry facility was inadequate, a woeful situation, according to the complaints of several college presidents, that was not corrected until the Pearson Memorial Laboratory (Pearson Hall) was completed in 1923.[379]

Back at Tufts in 1881 and still an undergraduate at barely 20 years old, Fred became an assistant to Amos Dolbear, the leading professor in the Physics Department. Dolbear was an early electrical energy pioneer, whose experiments with speech vibrations transmitted by electrical current pre-dated Alexander Bell (and led to much litigation). For Pearson, it was a prestigious assignment.

Fred Stark Pearson comes through the reference pages not only as brilliant, but as a man of many enthusiasms. He loved philosophy and music as well as the sciences. He played the violin in the school orchestra, and he was a competent sailor. People liked him as he always seemed to approach life with optimism. He remained a handsome man, although by age fifty his thick, wavy black hair had turned white.[380]

He enjoyed life, but he had a strong work ethic, believing hard work and technical skill could solve any problem. His convincing manner enticed more sober men to share his enthusiasm if sometimes against their better judgment. As he became more affluent, he enjoyed mingling among the socially important in Canada, New England, Europe, and Latin America, wherever his projects took him. His optimism and faith in himself later led to some questionable decisions as the early 20th century degenerated into economic and political confusion, creating problems beyond his control.

Despite his bouncy enthusiasm, his health always was an issue. As a young man, contemporaries described him as frail, often suffering from unspecified "fatigue." Although the pace he maintained traveling from continent to continent and country to country would appear to have exhausted anyone.

He finished his bachelor's degree in Mechanical Arts in 1883 and his master's degree the following year. In his new suit, he threw himself into the graduation exercises, speaking, playing in the orchestra, and presenting a special graduation thesis on Class Day. Two of the Ward sisters attended. Mabel was still in Dresden. Fred obtained the music for the Mexican national anthem, which the school orchestra played in honor of a Mexican student in his class. Some researchers regard this as an indication of his respect for the Mexican people that helped open doors for him in his later work in Mexico.[381] The college granted him awards in mathematics and immediately gave him a job teaching in the Applied Engineering Department, which suggests he could have had a distinguished academic career. That would have too comfortable for Fred Pearson. He sought creative engineering challenges. His ability to redesign and adapt electrical components and the new inventions of others into practical electrical systems began his reputation as a problem-solver. Before graduating, he received his first consulting job at a Virginia gold mine. What he did there is unclear, but he always had a fascination for mines. In 1886, he left the university, but he retained close contacts with colleagues at Tufts, Harvard, and MIT. They provided friendship, technical advice, and direct services as employees on his many enterprises.[382]

The year he left Tufts, a Boston engineering firm hired him to go to Paris to investigate a sewer-system project. By coincidence, he booked passage on the same ship as Helen Ward, one of the Ward sisters, on her way to visit Mabel in Dresden. Mabel had completed her studies and taught for a short time at the Tilden Seminary in West Lebanon, New Hampshire. She did not care for teaching and returned to Dresden to study to be a concert pianist. Fred surprised Mabel in Dresden and then insisted on taking the sisters on a world-wind tour of Paris that included the sewers.

Fred and Mabel did not appear to have any sort of special relationship other than a mutual love of books and music. But after only a few months of piano study, Mabel decided to accompany Helen and Fred back home. After the passage, Fred announced to William Ward that he wanted to marry his daughter. The conservative New Englander acquiesced, and the wedding took place on January 5, 1887, in the Ward's large brick home in Lowell. The new couple moved to a house on College Avenue in Somerville, Massachusetts, a town so close to Medford that the Tufts College campus spread into both communities. There, a few miles north of Boston, they began a family, which grew to include two sons and a daughter—Ward,

Frederick, and Natalie. The family moved several times but stayed close to the Lowell/Somerville/Boston area for the next seven years.[383]

Mabel proved to be an intelligent companion, elegant hostess, and diligent caregiver for her strange, brilliant, and charming husband. In addition to these virtues, Mabel tirelessly accompanied Fred on his constant travels to consult on projects. Sometimes pregnant on the earlier trips, or with children in tow later, she was by his side. The marriage was a happy one.

The Engineer/Entrepreneur

In Somerville, Pearson and a few Tufts professors organized the Somerville Electric Light Company, SELCO, an early-day "high-tech startup." They installed a dynamo in an old grist mill on the edge of town driven by the same coal-fired steam engine that had turned the mill stones. The dynamo generated electricity that ran through copper wires strung on square pine-wood poles.[384] Elmer H. Capon, the first president of Tufts College became the SELCO president. Pearson was the general manager and initially the treasurer. It was said he did not write anything down but kept all the accounts in his head. As impressive as this was, the company soon hired a conventional bookkeeper. SELCO installed incandescent lights in Tufts College, one of its first customers. Two years later, the company built another powerhouse in the center of town with five dynamos.[385] SELCO became part of the Boston Edison Company in 1903. By that time Pearson was on to grander projects.

The original Tufts group had also organized the Woburn Electric Light Company in a nearby town. Community electrification was still in its infancy (Edison patented the light bulb only eight years before), and engineers from all over the country came to Somerville and Woburn to see Pearson-designed systems. What is commonplace today was new and exotic in the 1880s.

Lack of adequate equipment hindered the efforts of those engineers trying to replicate electric-power systems in their communities. To meet the problem, Pearson formed another company to build more powerful steam-driven generators. This ability to create or modify equipment to meet particular needs became one of Pearson's most sought after skills.

The Somerville and Woburn projects came to the attention of a syndicate of Boston railway promoters led by industrialist Henry Melville Whitney. His group of well-financed creative entrepreneurs had consolidated Boston's horse-car lines into the West End Railway, a system of 2,000 cars served by 9,000 horses. Even though only a few small, electrified street railways existed in the world, these shrewd men saw that the future lay with electricity. They had examined the system in Richmond, Virginia, designed by Frank Julian Sprague, another electrical pioneer, who gained fame for developing electrical systems to drive elevators in the new skyscraper buildings being built in the major cities. The Richmond Union Passenger Railway was the most advanced street railroad at the time, although it had only 40 cars and 12 miles of track. As brilliant as Sprague was, the technology he used was inadequate to move dozens of large, heavy cars on rails, powered from a single source. After their visit, Whitney and the syndicate members remained convinced, electricity was the answer. They invited Pearson to Boston, and after interviews, they took a business risk and hired the 28-year-old for $2,500 a year, the equivalent of about $65,000 today.

Pearson attacked the formidable technical problems with fierce energy. Relying on inventor William Stanley's recent theories on alternating current, Pearson designed a 500-kw generator, the largest at that time, plus motors and dynamos that would deliver unprecedented power to move heavily loaded cars. Engineers at Westinghouse, then the biggest producer of electrical equipment, said Pearson's specifications were impossible. Undaunted, he turned to the Thomson-Houston Company, a small manufacturer of electrical parts. Under Pearson's guidance, the company not only produced the requisite equipment for West End Railway but began receiving orders from all over the country. Later in 1892, Thomson Houston combined with other companies to form the General Electric Company. When Pearson finished the initial project for Whitney, he continued to manage the railway and expand the lines into more Boston neighborhoods.

The syndicate's risk paid off. The electrified West End Railway was a huge success, providing unprecedented service and financial return. Nine thousand horses left the city, which must have been another sort of public service.

The company paid a ten percent dividend, and Boston boasted the largest powerhouse in the world. The promoters did not forget who made this happen. When Pearson left Boston, his salary had risen to the equivalent of $324,000. In 1894, he was invited to New York City. He and Mabel left Somerville with the children and moved to the big city and new challenges.

The rapid electrification of so many towns and cities had left an ugly web of crisscrossing wires marring city streets. Streetcars were connected to live overhead wires by a "trolley pole" with a grooved wheel in the end. New Yorkers wanted streetcars and easy inexpensive transportation, but they were adamant about overhead wires. The mayor personally cut down a telegraph pole at the corner of Broadway and 23rd to make the point.[386] Somehow power must be provided underground to the streetcars in all-weather without electrocuting pedestrians. A horse had already suffered this fate in an earlier experiment. Safe technology did not exist.

Pearson worked with engineers of the new General Electric Company to design and produce a special conduit that was placed in a slot in the street between the two track rails. A special metal shoe mounted below the car fit into the slot and connected to the power source. The first line with the slot was installed on Lennox Avenue. It worked and was safe. Two years before the turn of the century, New Yorkers could ride fifty-seven miles of city streets without seeing an overhead wire. They loved the new system, called the Metropolitan Street Railway, and Pearson received many honors. Tufts College presented him the first of two honorary Doctorate degrees, Science in 1900 and Laws in 1905.[387] The famous "slots in the streets" were a New York City feature until they were paved over in the fall of 1950.

With a solid reputation established, the now Dr. Pearson became more than consultant or employee. With Whitney and other entrepreneurs, he founded large coal and natural gas operations in Canada to produce fuel for the Boston and New York power stations as well as the rest of the rapidly expanding electrification of the northeast. Not only was Pearson an officer and director of the Dominion Coal Company, he also designed the mining equipment, the railroad to ship coal to the port, and the piers and loading equipment to move coal from the railroad cars to the waiting ships. He continued as Chief Engineer with the Metropolitan Street Railway, as a consulting engineer in Boston and other new streetcar systems in the East and Canada.

By 1898 at age 37, Pearson began to suffer one of his spells of "fatigue." By any standard, he had been enormously successful. His combined projects paid him the equivalent today of two million per year but demanded all of his time and energy. He was worn out. Mabel wanted him to relax, and the two to live a more leisurely life. She convinced him to resign from Metropolitan and take a long European trip. His devoted employees and associates gave him a huge send off at Delmonico's, which lasted into the early morning. Many dignitaries spoke including William C. Whitney and his brother Henry Melville Whitney, Pearson's West End Railway mentor. William C. Whitney, a noted lawyer, politician, and former Secretary of the Navy under Cleveland, called Dr. Pearson the "greatest genius of the century."[388]

After their return from Europe, Pearson bought the Coronet, a 131-foot schooner that had gained fame winning a 3,000-mile trans-Atlantic challenge race two years after it was built in 1885. Purchasing a yacht was more of a boy-hood dream than an ostentatious desire to show off his financial success in that golden age of the nouveau riche. They sailed down the coast into the Gulf of Mexico, into Havana Harbor, past the wreck of the battleship Maine to their anchorage. The Spanish-American War had just ended, and entrepreneurs were already on the scene pursuing opportunity. Word got out that Dr. Pearson was in Havana. He was asked to consult on a street railway project, but at Mabel's urging, they sailed on to Santiago, where family members joined them for the trip back to New York.

These trips restored Fred's health. Mabel hoped they could now live a quieter life. Fred even talked of buying a farm. Mabel was to be disappointed. Her irrepressible husband turned in the opposite direction becoming even more of a peripatetic "techno-engineer" hopping from country to country. With swash-buckling Canadian financiers, used to pushing the edges of the lax Canadian corporate and finance laws, Pearson formed companies to produce coal for steam-power plants and other companies to develop hydroelectric power systems. Once electricity was available, he and his partners formed more companies to build and operate street railways and irrigation projects. On an even larger scale, Pearson formed companies to develop hydroelectric systems for Rio de Janeiro, Sao Paulo, Havana, Mexico City, and cities in Canada. Demand for capital was continuous. When he and his associates exhausted the Canadian and U.S. sources, they turned to London's financial markets.

Great Barrington Estate

Fred and Mabel Pearson built a house in Boston with enough land around for their three children to roam. Mabel liked it very much, but for Fred it was not close enough to the action in New York, where he established his main offices.[389] In 1894, they moved to the city, where they lived in a succession of houses and apartments.

Dr. Pearson did not spend much time in any one place, regardless of where he lived or worked. He traveled persistently looking at projects, always with a head full of ideas, plans, and calculations. The entire family often accompanied him, sometimes for months at a time but only in the summer. In spite of the demands on his time, Dr. Pearson adhered to the children's school schedule. Also with him were two young traveling secretaries, who scrambled to keep up with a constant flow of dictation to be typed and sent to project managers, financiers, prospective clients, and colleagues. Mabel tried to make certain that her husband, in his peripatetic enthusiasm, remembered to eat, sleep, and dress properly.

While Mabel did her best, Fred, not surprisingly, experienced bouts of "fatigue." Mabel urged him to find a permanent home, a place he would like and would go to restore his strength. The couple often went to London, a major financial center, and they had a house in the countryside of Surrey. Both loved it there, but in 1902 while attending a meeting of electrical engineers, Pearson discovered the Great Barrington area of the Berkshire Hills in western Massachusetts. Colleagues already living in the area included George Westinghouse and a great friend of Dr. Pearson, the inventor William Stanley, Jr. It was Dr. Stanley's ideas on alternating current that enabled Pearson to build the equipment necessary for the Boston street railway project.

Edgewood Estate, Great Barrington, Massachusetts
Photo: Courtesy of Fred Harwood and S.A. Morse

In 1902, they bought the Tuller Farm in the hills of Great Barrington.
They called their new adventure Edgewood Farms. Pearson addressed the
development of the estate with the same energy and thought as his great
engineering projects. On the old farm's cornfield, he built a large but unpre-
tentious 20-room house in the New England Shingle style. The house had
a view of Long Lake, as well as the surrounding hills. A local lawyer was
hired to buy adjoining land. Over the next 12 years, Edgewood expanded
to 13,000 acres. Pearson added a large carriage house of his design, and
numerous barns, cottages, water towers, and a 16-foot-wide gravel drive
lined with ginkgo trees. A tea house overlooked the lake. Extensive gardens
and orchards covered part of the grounds. In the pastures were pureblood
Shropshire sheep and Guernsey cattle shipped from England to breed as a
revenue source and to help rebuild the distressed local farming economy.
Between 45 and 70 employees worked on the property. Pearson imported
deer and javelinas from Mexico and grouse from Hindustan. In the forested hills, the workmen erected a seven-foot-high fence seven miles long
to keep these animals from wandering.[390]

Edgewood became Fred Pearson's permanent home address. Although away much of the time, he paid close attention to the details of the farm. The Pearsons still spent time in New York and Surrey, England, but Edgewood was their home.

While not known as a great philanthropist, Dr. Pearson was very generous. He helped many aspiring engineers and willingly gave technical advice without compensation.

He was particularly generous to his adopted town of Great Barrington. Officials sought his help to improve the local highways at a time when "macadam" paving was first used to cover dirt roads. Dr. Pearson also donated to the newly formed Boy Scouts of America, and to the Pearson Educational Loan Fund for students to attend the new local high school.[391]

The huckleberry patch story is another example of his generosity. On one of Edgewood's parcels, neighbors for years had picked the berries and sold them to augment their incomes. They were concerned about the new owner's attitude toward their trespassing. When Pearson found out, he made it clear they were welcome to the entire berry crop, even though it could have been a revenue source for Edgewood. For this act, the locals dubbed him "The Huckleberry King of the Berkshires."[392]

After the Pearsons' premature deaths, the complicated estate did not generate enough cash for the three children to maintain it. Various parcels were sold at auction.

In 1921, the Commonwealth of Massachusetts bought 5,000 of the woodland acres and created Beartown Mountain State Forest. There is no record as to what happened to the animals.

As the parcels sold one by one, the estate shrank to 500 acres. The house stood empty until October 1923, when the youngest son, Frederick Pearson, tried to salvage family ownership by founding the Edgewood Vacation Music School with a music educator from New York. The house had a substantial music room that still contained the large organ that his father had installed. Never profitable, the school lasted less than three years.

In 1925, a wealthy businessman from Chicago, Prentiss L. Coonley, and his wife Mary bought the property. Both were well-connected in political, social, and business worlds and Mr. Coonley later served as an economic advisor to President Franklin Roosevelt during the implementation of the

New Deal. The couple had grand ideas based on their time in England. They tore down the Pearson mansion except for the chimney and music room and replaced it with a Cotswold-style stone house. The Coonleys continued to use the house until 1944.

That year, the American Economic Research Institute (AERI) bought 133 of the remaining acres, the house, and surrounding buildings.[393] AERI, the oldest continuously operating economic institute in the country operates from Edgewood today. The tea house still overlooks Long Lake, and the gingkoes still line the roadway.

Dr. Fred Stark Pearson reigned there as the Huckleberry King of the Berkshires, but, attesting to his later obscurity, the Great Barrington Historical Society has no file on him.[394]

The Streetcar Era

Electrified street railways had a profound effect on communities worldwide. The easy transport of people without encumbering animals enabled towns to expand beyond their basic core. By 1895, over 900 lines existed in America alone. By 1900, Dr. Pearson had acted as engineer/designer or consulting engineer for the Brooklyn Heights Railroad, Toronto Street Railway, Montreal Street Railway, Winnipeg Street Railway, Halifax Electric Tramway, Consolidated Traction of New Jersey, Metropolitan Elevated of Chicago, Syracuse Transit, Staten Island Electric Railroad, Atlantic Coast Railway, City of Birmingham Tramways, Union Railroad of Providence, Rhode Island. In addition to his role with the Dominican Coal Company, he sat as a director for other companies related to the electrical industry including American Air Power, Electric Storage Battery (today Exide Technologies), and New York Gas and Electric Heat and Power.[395] This long list of companies illustrates the breadth of his activities.

As the 20th century progressed, electric streetcars gradually gave way to the internal combustion engine. Only a few lines still operated after World War II. Perhaps Dr. Pearson's name would be better known if the extensive transportation systems he helped create had not been superseded by automobiles. Also, his most dramatic projects—massive hydro-electric systems to illuminate large cities—were outside the United States.

Projects South of the Border

Two major accomplishments for Pearson and his engineering and financial associates were the massive integrated hydro-electric systems generating, transmitting and distributing power to the growing cities of Sao Paulo and Rio de Janeiro and the accompanying tramways. At the turn of the century, he had a staff of electrical-engineer "apostles," working under the Pearson Engineering Company name, on the twentieth story of the Broad Exchange Building, the largest office building in New York City.

Fred had been attracted to Brazil years before. He and Mabel had been married less than six months when he received an assignment to investigate a gold mine near Sao Paulo. The trip would take a few months, and Mabel was very pregnant. Fred read books on obstetrics and assured her that he could handle the delivery if necessary. What Mabel thought of this backup plan is not recorded, but they returned to Somerville in time for Ward Pearson's birth without needing to test Fred's obstetric skills.[396] He also returned with an appreciation for the business opportunities in Brazil.

They went back to Brazil on another mining exploration in 1886. With a guide, mules for himself and the indomitable Mabel, and three pack mules, they spent a month in the highlands above Sao Paulo. Brazil was in a revolutionary turmoil, struggling to free itself from Portugal's colonial rule. Ignoring the raging politics, Pearson studied the terrain and determined the rivers cascading from the high plateaus above Sao Paulo could produce a great deal of hydroelectric power—this in a country with limited power sources, largely because of the lack of coal. He did not return until 1899, ten years after Brazil became a republic. Mabel came again, this time with the children. In the still-disrupted country, he and his associates, utility-magnate William Mackenzie, E.R. Wood, and financer James Dunn, secured the concession to build dams and power plants on the highland rivers. Capital was an issue, but they were able to raise five million dollars, an enormous sum for the day. Pearson with his characteristic optimism and self-confidence pledged most of his own assets. His confidence paid off. Eleven thousand incandescent bulbs lighted the city, and the first annual report of the Sao Paulo Tramway, Light, and Power Company, Ltd. in 1902 showed a substantial profit. Bondholders were paid, and a dividend distributed to stockholders.

Pearson began the second Brazilian project in 1905 with the formation of the Rio de Janeiro Tramway, Light and Power Company. His team of engineers and financiers overcame physical and political obstacles, including Brazil's growing xenophobia. The resulting system so illuminated Rio's already beautiful setting that enthusiastic writers compared the city to Paris.[397] All of Pearson's Brazilian companies, including the developing telephone companies, consolidated as the Brazilian Traction, Light and Power Company. Pearson remained president of this conglomerate until his untimely death in 1915. Canadian railroad magnate William Mackenzie became chairman of the board. Pearson and Mackenzie had worked together on several Canadian streetcar and hydroelectric projects. Mackenzie had a growing reputation for unscrupulous methods, but he had considerable railroad and utility skills and was a shrewd investor. Dr. Pearson should have paid more attention to his associate's unscrupulous side. Mackenzie would haunt the Pearson family in just a few years.

Mabel accompanied Fred on an inspection trip to Sao Paulo in 1901. Back in the American Southwest, they toured mining properties and ended in El Paso. Mabel waited there while Fred crossed the border to meet the manager of Dos Cabezas, a silver mine he owned in the mountains of Sonora, about 60 miles west of Casas Grandes. They camped near the mine under the clear night sky. Pearson never forgot that night.[398]

He always had an interest in mines, and this visit was preliminary to a trip to Mexico City to make arrangements for additional development at Dos Cabezas. He had letters of introduction to the highest officials in the Porfirio Díaz government. After retrieving Mabel, they traveled on the rail line from El Paso through northern Chihuahua, then booming as the result of North American and European investment. He noted the potential of the region but for the time being filed his impressions in his mind for the future.

In Mexico City, he met President Porfirio Díaz and by the next year, 1902, Pearson had obtained concessions on the Río Necaxa in the state of Puebla, 150 kilometers from Mexico City. Financed by the Bank of Montreal, he and Canadian partners incorporated the Mexican Light and Power Company Limited (MLP) in September 1902. In Mexico the company was known as Tranvías Eléctricos de México. After Pearson's system of dams, power plants, tunnels, high-voltage transmission wires, and substations brought power to the capital, the syndicate created Mexico Tramways to build and operate a streetcar system. All of these companies were incorporated in Canada.

The MLP project on the Río Necaxa presented daunting, unprecedented engineering and logistic challenges. Hydro-electric projects at Victoria Falls on the Zambezi River in Africa and at Niagara Falls, where Pearson was involved, and those in Brazil were brilliant engineering feats but relatively simple compared to this. The terrain to be covered between Necaxa and Mexico City was vast, rugged, and mostly unmapped. The engineering challenges have been compared to those of the Panama Canal. Pearson had been approached by the Roosevelt administration about the position of Chief Engineer for the canal. Uncharacteristically, he decided he was over committed for such a large undertaking. Colonel George Washington Goethals, who did take the position, gained great fame as the result. Colonel Goethals later inspected the completed MLP project.

The dam on the Necaxa was the highest earth-filled dam in the world at the time. Mexico City was considered to be among the best illuminated cities in the world. The system consisted of the great dam, eight large reservoirs (one covering three square miles), and thirty-two tunnels. The generating station at Necaxa produced 80 percent of the power while other stations placed along the length of the system produced the remaining 20 percent.[399] Colonel Goethals said at the conclusion of his visit that the difficulties encountered were more intricate that those with the canal. He called Necaxa "the most complete, the best equipped, the most wonderful plant of its kind under private control in the world."[400]

President Díaz was also impressed. He paid a visit to the dam site and even agreed to ride with Pearson in a cage raised and lowered by cables to the bottom of the Necaxa gorge. The two men appeared to have established a warm relationship. Dr. Pearson and Mabel later were invited to Chapultepec Castle to accept Díaz's thank you.

The old president personally inaugurated the hydroelectric project on December 3, 1905. Switches were thrown and electricity flowed over 86 miles of transmission wire to the city.[401] The system has continued to operate in one organizational form or another ever since.[402]

The fortunes of the MLP and Mexican Tramways Company followed a path similar to many foreign companies during the political changes in Mexico in the first half of the 20th century. Dr. Pearson remained as corporate president until his death in 1915. The operation continued to expand through the benevolent regime of Díaz and well beyond despite disruptions caused by the Revolution. The Constitution of 1917 restricted the activities of foreign companies, but clever lawyers devised ways, such as creating subsidiary Mexican companies, to satisfy both government bureaucrats and foreign investors. In 1929, a large international holding company, Société Financiére de Transports et d'Entreprises Industrielles (SOFINA) acquired a majority ownership in the MLP and its related companies previously held by British and Canadians.[403] The liberal Mexican governments of the 1930s began to take more and more control, fixing lower rates and directing development to underserved, less profitable rural areas. President Lázaro Cárdenas created a state-run electrical company in 1937, *Comisión Federal de Electricidad* (CFE), as the agency to oversee the industry. MLP profits declined in the 1930s. As a sign of things to come, the government nationalized the Mexican Tramways Company in 1947. In 1960 during the administration of President Adolfo López Mateos, a constitutional amendment required all electricity production and transmission be nationalized. That year, the huge MLP with all of its subsidiaries was converted to a state-run company. The government paid SOFINA $52,000,000 and assumed $78,000,000 in debt. The investors saw the deal as fair, and the Mexican public hailed it as a major achievement comparable to the land reforms of the 1920s and the expropriation of the oil industry in the 1930s.[404] CFE now controlled most of the country's electrical industry.

Dr. Pearson also brought electricity to his namesake town of Pearson in the Casas Grandes Valley through the mill powerhouse but only until the early 1920s. Older residents remember the kerosene and Coleman lanterns used for over 50 years until 1975 when CFE installed poles and strung wire to the town. Today, power plants, thermal energy, and a large solar plant near Galeana supply the power grid in northern Chihuahua.

High Finance

The years 1903 to 1907 may have been the busiest of Pearson's career. He engineered the dams, power plants, transmission, and distribution for the Mexico City and Rio de Janeiro projects, plus the related streetcar lines. At the same time, he obtained the financing and organized the companies and personnel to manage the various components. While immersed in these Latin American projects, he consulted on a generating station in the Niagara River gorge for William Mackenzie's Toronto and Niagara Power Company and on the Manitoba to the Lac du Bonnet hydro-power station for Mackenzie's electric railway in Winnipeg.[405]

Pearson-style projects required a high level of engineering skill, enormous amounts of money, and stable governments. These attributes combined with unfailing self-confidence created his recipe for success, serving him and investors well. A few years into the new century, weaknesses began to appear in these requirements, weaknesses that Pearson tended to ignore or downplay.

The Panic of 1907, the Wall Street crash that contributed to the severe recession in northern Mexico that set back Luis Terrazas's empire and so badly damaged the rising Mexican middle class, also severely diminished Canadian and European cash sources. This caused a reshuffling among Pearson's companies. The Brazilian Light and Traction Company in Rio de Janeiro was particularly hard hit. That company and the others survived, but the scare left money markets nervous and contributed to the growing xenophobia, particularly in Brazil. The indomitable Pearson accepted the setbacks, regarding them as challenges. He did not hesitate to plunge into more and bigger projects.

James Dunn, who had been part of the corporate and financial team on the Sao Paulo project, became the key financier for Dr. Pearson. A Canadian lawyer from Nova Scotia, Dunn previously worked for B.F. Pearson, a lawyer/financier in Halifax, with whom Fred Stark Pearson had done business (this relationship adds more confusion to the Pearson name). Dunn established his own brokerage firm in Montreal in 1902. In 1906, he moved his office to London to be closer to the world's largest financial market. The economic crash occurred the following year, and from London, he worked to restructure the finances of Pearson's companies as well as prepare and sell bond issues for new projects. Dunn, while willing to take risks, was steadier and less impetuous than Pearson. They respected each other's strengths and made an effective team.[406]

Dr. Pearson was fortunate to have a friend and associate of Dunn's caliber. The convoluted early 20th century financial arena involved laws, politics, and the manipulations of shrewd, often unscrupulous money men from different countries. James Dunn became a master in this arena. His own story is amazing and adds to the list of characters contributing to the northern Chihuahua story. From humble circumstances in a small town in New Brunswick, he rose to be named a baronet by King George V. He advised prime ministers, became a major art collector, and gained fame in England and Canada for his philanthropy. What gained him prominence in both countries was his ability to salvage distressed companies during the Panic of 1907 and later during the Great Depression. He died a very wealthy man in 1956.

Dunn would need all of his skills because Dr. Pearson had a new idea. Memories of camping under the stars of northern Chihuahua and remembering the potential there drew Pearson back to Mexico in 1908. This venture would be about railroads, forests, and lumber mills rather than hydro-electricity or streetcars. It would involve assembling the pieces of a grand plan that other men had started and but could not finish.

The Sirens' Call, Kansas City to Topolobampo

The boom in railroading continued through the end of the 19th and into the 20th century in both countries. Entrepreneurs, scrupulous and unscrupulous, continued to promote schemes to create new rail lines and monopolies. In Mexico, the disparate governments of Maximilian, Juárez, and Lerdo de Tejada recognized the need for infrastructure but shared a common reservation about foreign investment, particularly for railroads and especially by North Americans. The only railroad line of any significance in the entire country linked the port of Veracruz with Mexico City. The origins of the line dated to 1837. Work began under the Emperor Maximilian. President Lerdo de Tejada dedicated the completed line on January 1, 1873.

Porfirio Díaz had a different view about foreign investment. After taking power 1877, he endorsed U.S. and European entrepreneurs, granting concession after concession and even financial subsidies. By 1899, his administration had granted 222 concessions, involving huge amounts of land, in addition to development rights, and railroad rights of way. These involved all kinds of schemes, sound and unsound. Most failed or barely started if they started at all. One hundred thirty forfeited and only about a dozen accomplished anything significant.[407] The net economic effect was uneven and depended on the individual situation. Failed companies left unpaid bills and wages, but the vast sums of foreign capital spent on profitable as well as unprofitable ventures stayed in Mexico as did the resulting infrastructure. In spite of the failures and setbacks, that infrastructure growth was spectacular. When Porfirio Díaz assumed office, Mexico had 416 miles of railroad in the entire country. By 1884, the total increased to 3682 miles. When he was deposed in 1910, the country was linked in all but the most rugged regions by 15,360 miles of track.[408] Small cross-road towns became commercial and industrial centers as the country's resources were opened to national and international markets.

Foreign companies and capital built most of the rail lines, something that concerned Díaz's *Científico* advisors, especially José Limantour, the Minister of Finance. They did not want Mexico to be economically dominated by others, particularly the Colossus of the North. Late in Díaz's regime, Limantour convinced him to create the National Railways of Mexico, a government-owned line. This laid the groundwork for complete railroad nationalization between 1927 and 1939.

In Chihuahua, Luis Terrazas, his family, and son-in-law Enrique Creel understood very well how foreign infrastructure investment added to the value of their holdings. They made sure that projects in their domain served their interests.

Díaz granted one his first and most important concessions to a subsidiary of the Atchison, Topeka, and Santa Fe in 1880. Incorporated in Massachusetts, the Mexican Central Railroad (with Enrique Creel on the board) completed a line between Ciudad Chihuahua and Ciudad Juárez and El Paso across the border. Service began in 1882. Branches ran to

Tampico on the gulf coast and throughout central Mexico, becoming Mexico's "greatest railroad."[409]

Great as it was, the Mexican Central's profitability never reached the expectations of its parent companies. Owners were happy to relinquish shares to the state-owned National Railways. By 1909, National owned all of Mexican Central.

In 1884, the U.S. transcontinental system for the first time reached across the Rio Grande to Chihuahua and all of Mexico, At Torreón, the line connected to the Mexico International Railroad, developed by Collis P. Huntington of the Southern Pacific. That line ran northeast from Torreón trough Eagle Pass on the Texas border to a connection with the transcontinental Southern Pacific in San Antonio.[410]

As important as the Mexican Central was with its expansive connections to the U.S. in two directions and to central Mexico, it did not serve the rich mining, timber, and cattle resources of the western part of the state including the Casas Grandes Valley or the mining and timber area farther south in Guerrero District. The transport techniques of pack mule and wagon had not changed since Spanish times.

A significant factor that affected how rails came to these western regions was a recurring dream of entrepreneurs on both sides of the border. They had studied maps and discovered that the shortest route from the industrial centers of the United States to the Pacific ran not to the California coast but southwest across the border, through Chihuahua to Topolobampo, a port in Sinaloa, a name that rolled off the tongues of future promoters. The thought of such a route leading to a Pacific port and the markets of the Far East excited freebooters and sober investors alike. That such a grandiose venture would require grading and laying track across northern Chihuahua and over the barrier of the Sierra Madre did not seem to be more than a technical detail. Knowledgeable engineers, when consulted, found the prospect daunting and expensive. Estimates varied widely, but the minimum exceeded $12,000 per mile in 1880s' dollars, using workers paid 25 cents per day.

For thirty years, throughout the Porfiriato, the siren call of Destination Topolobampo confused railroad development in the Casas Grandes Valley and beyond with a maze of concessions, overlapping corporations with similar names, and unrealistic promotions[411] All failed. It was not until 1961 that the famous Copper Canyon route fulfilled the elusive dream. That effort covered 418 miles and required 37 bridges and 87 tunnels.

Most of these entrepreneur/dreamers followed a similar road to failure. Promoters presented a plan and convinced wealthy businessmen (who often should have known better) to invest and become part of a company to build their version of the yellow brick road. Usually, they had the applicable government concessions. They hired surveyors, engineers, and construction companies. Exciting promotions led to grand inauguration celebrations. Sometimes work actually began at one or both ends of a proposed line. Invariably the money ran out. Whatever the budget for the plan might be, basic costs always were wildly underestimated. Convoluted reorganizations followed, dissolving corporations and founding others, stalling creditors, and seeking new investors.

The dream was old, but Chihuahua Governor Carlos Pacheco Villalba initiated the process in the Díaz era. Pacheco also served in the federal government as Díaz's Secretary of Public Works. It was Pacheco who helped straighten out the crisis, when the acting governor, General Fuero, tried to expel the LDS colonists from the Casas Grandes Valley.

Using his powerful position, Pacheco obtained concessions in November 1884 to build two railroads west to the coast from the just-completed Mexican Central. Pacheco's railroads never went beyond the talking stage, but they opened the door to other players, three of which should be mentioned.

Lewis or Luis Huller already had a reputation as one of the largest concessionaires in Mexico. He had been involved with LDS colonists in a failed property deal near what became Dublán. A naturalized Mexican citizen from Germany, he appears to have been a reasonably honest, marginally competent administrator, and a superb salesman. He, along with the other two promoters, who came later, had the ability to spin out visionary projects in which he believed himself and dazzled prospective clients, at least initially. Typically, Huller's projects combined his vision and their money.

Following the dream and Pacheco's lead, he proposed a line from the border, through the Casas Grandes Valley to the port of almost mythical Topolobampo. The general heading of his operation was the Sonora,

Sinaloa and Chihuahua Railroad (SSCR), even though it involved a bewildering number of corporations (often with similar names) over its six-year life.

In the early 1880s, he and his partner Major George H. Sisson, a successful New York businessman, held large concessions or owned multimillion-acre tracts of land in Chiapas, Sonora, and Baja California. Their Baja land, held in a Connecticut company called the International Company of Mexico, exceeded eighteen-million acres, almost all of what is now the state of Baja California (north). Ensenada already existed, but they laid out the town and developed the first lots. Sisson was the manager, but apparently not a very good one. They were not making any money. Desperate for cash by 1889, they sold to an English company interested in Baja's gold and silver mines.

The partners associated with Tomás MacManus, an influential Mexican businessman, banker, and politician from Ciudad Chihuahua. His connections in Mexico City helped obtain and extend the Pacheco concession. Most important, he had money.

Tomas' father, Francisco MacManus, an Irishman from Philadelphia, immigrated to Chihuahua in 1841. With his sons, he developed several businesses. He and Luis Terrazas's early land-holding partner, Enrique Müller, established the mint in Chihuahua. In 1875, the senior MacManus established the Bank of Santa Eulalia in which Tomás held a high position.[412]

The SSCR route involved three separate railroad companies. The Deming, Sierra Madre and Pacific Railroad would run due south from Deming, New Mexico to the border near the custom station at Palomas, about 37 miles. The Sonora, Sinaloa and Chihuahua Railroad would continue the line southwest through the Latter-day Saint colonies over an unspecified mountain route to connect to a portion of Pacheco's old right of way, now called the Sierra and Chihuahua railroad, the final leg to Topolobampo. All three companies were officially located in Deming, but it appears the real headquarters was Huller's fourteen-room mansion across the border in Palomas.

Government colonization incentives added more complexities to this maze of concessions, promotions, and development. Huller formed yet another company and obtained two million acres around Palomas. The government, eager to attract settlers to the remote region, offered $50 for each adult colonist on the land. Colonization had been part of the Baja project and Huller and Sisson were familiar with the concept. Build the railroad, the people will come, and the government will pay handsomely or so they believed.

Needless to say, the Deming residents were very excited. Just a few years before in 1881, the Southern Pacific building from the west and the Atchison, Topeka and Santa Fe building from the east met in southern New Mexico to form the second U.S. transcontinental railroad. The town that grew up around the junction was named after Mary Ann Deming Crocker, the wife of Charles Crocker, one of the "Big Four" of the Southern Pacific. Now another major line would intersect in their town. Huller relished and played on the excitement, giving tours of the route, entertaining potential investors, potential colonists, and journalists (including Frederick Schwatka, one of those to write observations of traveling in Chihuahua). With surveys almost complete he sent off grading and track-laying crews to Sinaloa and Sonora and other points along the proposed line. On April 16, an inaugural celebration was held in Guaymas. Carlos Pacheco spoke extolling the wonders to come as did George Sisson, now with title of "General." In Deming, thirty teams of horses, harnessed to Fresno scrapers, began grading. A short bit of track was laid for the inaugural celebration there. While the band played, dignitaries drove no less than five silver spikes through rail base plates into the new ties.

It is hoped that Huller and Sisson retrieved the silver spikes because by September only seventeen miles of track had been laid. They needed new investors with cash, and they found one. A conservative, teetotaling Methodist banker from Lima, Ohio, named Benjamin Faurot, bought into their dream. As part of the deal, he obtained the Palomas colonization concession. Optimism returned. Work restarted. Unfortunately, a government audit caught the abstemious Faurot "adjusting" the Lima bank's books. In less than a year, he was trying to unload his SSCR investment. He must have been shrewd, because he sold most of his shares, including the rights to the Palomas land, to a most unlikely buyer.

John Willard Young was the son, and some say the favorite son, of LDS President Brigham Young and his second wife Mary Ann Angel. His father designated John Willard as an Apostle at age 11, and at age 55 he was in line as the immediate successor to the Church presidency. This caused great consternation at the highest levels and led to a change in succession policy. Church officials knew, after long experience, that John Willard lacked any real interest in the Church affairs. He preferred New York to Utah. Far from being a religious man, he was a business wheeler-dealer in the classic late 19th century mold. Articulate, charismatic with a flair for public speaking, he turned out to be a likely candidate for a high-flying deal in Mexico.[413]

He had experience supplying and building railroads in Utah and Arizona. By 1890 he was working out of an elegant New York hotel suite, speculating in land and railroads, making and losing large sums of money. His agent in Mexico was a good friend, Bishop W. Derby Johnson, Jr. of Colonia Díaz, a highly respected businessman, educator, and Church leader.[414]

In a series of meetings in El Paso, Ciudad Chihuahua, and New York City, Huller, Sisson, and Faurot, negotiated a deal with Bishop Johnson and Young, with terms satisfactory to all present. Not everyone involved was present, however. Huller had omitted to mention one little detail. Tomás MacManus had not been invited to or made aware of the meetings.

As part of his deal with Huller and Sisson, MacManus followed through and arranged, and paid for Carlos Pacheco's concessions. These were inconveniently but officially recorded in MacManus' name.

When MacManus found out what was going on, he was not happy. To bring him into the new arrangement, Young had to pay more than he should have, although MacManus accepted notes for most of the amount due. The record is not clear, but it is doubtful if many or any of the notes were ever paid. MacManus did lose his fortune during the 1890s, whether because of this deal or something else is not known. In 1896, he accepted employment as Colonel William Greene's contact man in Mexico City.[415]

Young's new company needed MacManus because of his record of integrity, particularly with government officials. Luis Huller had lost his credibility with the government and almost everyone else.

The new agreement with Young was almost too convoluted to understand. Huller and the other players remained on the boards. Sisson appears to have wanted out and disappears from the action. Young was the driving force, with Huller fluttering in the background. The dream was reborn. The Saints in the colonies were particularly excited because of the job opportunities. Many did not plant that spring after accepting jobs on the railroad. Local sawmills began cutting railroad ties.

In less than six months, money ran out, and Young left for England. Bishop Johnson was stuck with creditors, unpaid workers, and the abuse. Young remained incommunicado. By summer, some of the Saints were hurting badly with no wages and no crops. Mexican workers, who had relocated to the various construction sites, lived in hovels without wages and no place to go.

It was always Young's intent to create a going concern to sell to other investors. In England, he tried and failed to sell or raise more money. All he did was create an English competitor intent on taking over the enterprise. A year of confused corporate maneuvering, lawsuits, and creation of competing companies, followed. Amazingly by 1892, Young and the English competitor emerged together as sole owners of a new company with control of the concession. Bishop Johnson was engaged again to help. The old optimism rose, but they barely began before the past overwhelmed them. The mountain of old debts claimed any funds raised. The government cancelled the concession in October 1893.[416]

Luis Huller, somewhat surprisingly, disappeared from the scene. John Willard Young lost everything. He spent his last years working as an elevator operator in the New York hotel where he once lived in grand style.[417]

The efforts of the next two entrepreneurs only affected the Casas Grandes indirectly. They are included here because they and their projects were so well known.

Albert Kimsey Owen was unique. Trained as an engineer and surveyor, he also was a utopian reformer. His plans always called for colonists living along the railroad to maintain the line and to enjoy its benefits while living in a communal society. Owen must have had a promoters' charm because he gained access to the highest political levels in both Mexico and the United States. It helped that his father, a prominent physician, was a personal friend of President Ulysses S. Grant.

In 1873, he was asked to join an eleven-month horseback expedition that explored the Sinaloa and Sonora coasts. He spent several days around

the double-bay at Topolobampo. He had the technical data from explorer/
surveyors who had come by sea. It was cold when he first arrived at the bay.
Wrapped in a blanket, he stood on the shore and envisioned a great port
serving all the ships at sea.[418]

On his return home, he devised a grand plan for a railroad that would
run from Norfolk, Virginia to Presidio, Texas, across the Rio Grande from
Ojinaga, Chihuahua. In Mexico, the proposed route appears to have followed more or less that of today's Copper Canyon line. The plan called
for the U.S. government to issue Treasury notes that would be redeemed
by railroad revenue. His first presentation was before a conference of state
governors in Washington. That went well, and he followed it with meetings with Senators and Congressmen and appearances before Senate committees. Legislation was actually introduced and progressed with approval
through Congressional committees. Things were going well. Owen even
asked a favor of the president.

After receiving a letter from Owen, President Grant ordered Commodore George W. Dewey, the future hero of the Battle of Manila Bay ("You
may fire when ready Gridly."), to steam to Topolobampo and prepare a
detailed survey. Dewey carried out the order and filed a very favorable
report as to the port's potential.[419]

Owen formed a company that included Grant's son and other dignitaries, notably famous former Civil War generals.

The Mexican government granted him a right-of-way concession, but
not a mile of track was laid in either country. There never was enough capital to even start.

Albert Kimsey Owen's grand coast-to-coast railroad dream dissolved
as did his efforts to establish and maintain the utopian community at
Topolobampo. The colony limped along finally losing all official sanction
in early 1899. Owen sold out his remaining rights and assets to the next
player to adopt the dream, Arthur E. Stillwell of Kansas City, Missouri.

The name of the next and most notable visionary project, the Kansas
City, Mexico, Orient Railway clearly expressed the promoter Arthur Stillwell's intent.

Stillwell may have bought into the dream, but he was no empty-
pocketed visionary. He came from a prosperous New York family with

many connections. What he shared with the previous dreamers was a glib tongue. He was a born promoter and had been since childhood. With little formal education in spite of his elite background, he learned the business world, starting a successful printing shop while still a teenager. Tall, athletic, with wavy blond hair, a mustache, and striking blue eyes, he exuded confidence in colleagues and clients.[420] After moving to Kansas City, he started several successful businesses including real estate. He made his name by promoting railroad projects that established the emerging rail center of Kansas City as the gateway to the Southwest and the Gulf Mexico.

Forced out of his own railroad company by brutal stock-holder maneuvering, characteristic of the era, he studied other projects in Texas and around the Gulf. At a grand banquet in his honor in February 1900, he astonished the distinguished crowd by announcing formation of a company to build a railroad south from Kansas City through Oklahoma, Texas, and Chihuahua to Topolobampo.[421]

Stilwell had done his research. Eight governors and the Assistant Secretary of State were asked to send letters to President Porfirio Díaz endorsing Stillwell.[422] A month later he traveled with associates down the Mexico Central to call on Enrique Creel in Ciudad Chihuahua. They got on well. Creel outlined previous projects and indicated that his Mexico Central had built an extension west from the main line to the mining town of Miñaca south in Guerrero District. The railroad had rights to continue the line west with government subsidies to Topolobampo. It has been suggested that Creel lacked the financial ability himself to take advantage of these rights.[423] This is doubtful considering the vast resources controlled by the Terrazas family. It is more likely he was content to let outsiders finance the projects that would benefit the family. Whatever the motive, Creel agreed to reassign the rights and join Stillwell's Kansas City, Mexico, and Topolobampo Railroad as vice president. During their meeting, Creel suggested another concept. Extending the line from Miñaca north over the mountains to the rich Casas Grandes Valley. It was a novel idea that foretold the future, but Stillwell was focused on Topolobampo and the dream. After the Chihuahua meetings, he went on to Mexico City, where he had an audience with President Díaz, who was well aware of previous failures and showed great interest in Stillwell's approach. The final negotiations included significant per-mile subsidies in the revised concessions.

From the capital he took a circuitous route by land and sea to Topolobampo. Creel had advised him see Albert Kimsey Owen. After a tour and long discussions, Stillwell obtained Owen's rights and property in the proposed destination harbor. Stillwell's line would start in Kansas City rather than Norfolk, Virginia and follow Owen's route more or less. Another similarity was the lack of a clear understanding of what lay ahead in the mountains of northern Mexico.

Arthur E. Stillwell's effort to build a shortcut to the Far East was by far the largest in terms of resources expended and time spent. It lasted over 13 years and touched directly or indirectly all railroading in the Southwest and northern Mexico.

Stillwell appears to have understood railroad-construction costs. He built a financial structure based on conventional investment from the U.S. and London; grants from local governments eager to have the route pass through their towns; bond payments to construction companies in lieu of cash; and Mexican government subsidies. Despite his experience, he did no better than his predecessors and did not come close to adequately forecasting the cost of crossing the Sierra Madre.

Stillwell's plan called first for building the line in sections across the numerous jurisdictions of Kansas, Oklahoma, Texas, and later in Sinaloa and Guerrero. As he progressed, he created a pyramid of companies representing all phases of railroad construction from producing ties to unrelated enterprises such as mining.

Stillwell's grandfather was a friend of George Pullman. The sleeping car magnate provided Stillwell with a fancy car in which he installed an organ and pulpit. While his potential investors enjoyed a dinner served on fine china as they traveled through the countryside, Stillwell played the organ or lectured from the pulpit on the wonders to come when the KCMOR made the connection to fabled Topolobampo.[424]

Arthur Stillwell's charisma and quirky problem-solving abilities carried the project. He completed 642 miles of track with accompanying infrastructure in the U.S. and 237 in Mexico, a portion deep into the

Sierra Madre. The unfinished mountainous gap still stretched for almost 400 miles of rough Sierra Madre terrain. By 1911, the Revolution began to disrupt operations. Corporate raiders and powerful railroad competitors, who had plagued him from the beginning, sabotaged his financial efforts. Finally, there was no more money. British investors forced receivership beginning in March 1912, and Stillwell stepped down as president. Even in receivership, he tried to keep the project alive, but he was forced to retire after being badly injured in an elevator accident. The property of the Kansas, Mexico, and Orient Railroad sold at a foreclosure sale in July 1914, for six million dollars. Arthur Stillwell, a semi-invalid, but always in demand as a public speaker, never attempted another project. He died on September 25, 1928. Two weeks later, his wife jumped out of a twelve-story window, leaving a note saying she could not live without him.[425]

All track laid by Stillwell in the U.S. became part of the Santa Fe system. Another dreamer from the Topolobampo area tried to resurrect the Mexican sections but failed. By 1940, these were all part of the National Railways of Mexico.

The dream never died, but other more practical objectives brought actual railroad track into the Casas Grandes Valley.

In March 1896, a New York syndicate, owners of the Hacienda Corralitos Cattle Company and the Candelaria Mining Company since 1880, obtained a right of way that extended southwest from Ciudad Juárez. The front man for the transaction was a speculator named A. Foster Higgins.[426] The organizers of the syndicate included Wall Street bankers Edwin D. Morgan (cousin of J.P. Morgan), Levi P. Morton (former vice president of the United States under Benjamin Harrison), and Texas developer Thomas Wentworth Peirce, Jr. The railroad right-of-way crossed 60 miles of Corralitos' property. The promoters wanted to ship cattle and ore by rail to El Paso and maybe (the old dream lived on) build a line in the other direction over the mountains to the Pacific Coast. After Higgins obtained the rights, the syndicate formed the Rio Grande, Sierra Madre, and Pacific Railroad in New York. They raised enough money to begin constructing a line from Ciudad Juárez past the Candelaria mines to a stop near Hacienda Corralitos.

The New York construction company hired for the work moved quickly. On June 25, 1897, trains began running as far as Corralitos. By

August, the tracks ran to a stop just south of Colonia Dublán called Nuevo Casas Grandes.[427] Three passenger trains a week soon ran, demonstrating the importance of rail service in that era.[428]

A ticket holder looking out the window on one of those trains leaving Ciudad Juárez would first see miles of sand dunes and dry, empty grazing land, much of it part of the Palomas Land and Cattle Company. After about 60 miles, past Corralitos and the mines, the view would change to farmland. The passenger would see to the west orchards belonging to LDS colonists. When the train reached the last stop in the emerging community of Nuevo Casas Grandes, the passenger would have traveled 150 miles.[429] The line had a long way to go before realizing its potential, but this first section made a significant impact of the Casas Grandes Valley economy.

Colonel Bill, the Copper King

The west was filled with many colorful characters both real and fictional. For those that were real, it is sometimes hard to separate truth from legend. William "Colonel Bill" Greene was one of those. What set him apart from other gun-toting gamblers was for a brief time, he became one of the richest men in the world.

Colonel Bill fit the role. A large man with curly hair and an impressive mustache accenting his florid face, he had an expansive if somewhat volatile personality, dominating any room he entered, and often challenging one and all to bet on the outcome of almost anything.[430]

According to the stories, he drifted west from his home state of New York, working on anything that came his way, laying track and in the mines. He worked in Tombstone mines during their heyday and then prospected on his own in other parts of Arizona and in Sonora. He gambled what he made or found, making a small fortune or going broke on the turn of a card. The Apaches were terrorizing the territory, and Greene had enough status among his peers to lead volunteers in pursuit of Indian raiders. They called him "Colonel Bill." Other versions of the title suggest he gave it to himself when he went to New York to sell his mining company shares, or that he earned it as a high-stakes poker player. Whatever the source, the unofficial title stayed with him the rest of his life.

By 1890, he was prosperous enough to marry and buy a ranch in Arizona just north of the border on the San Pedro River. He lived the relatively quiet life of a rancher and knew everyone in the region. His affability served him well when he was freed by the local sheriff and jury after murdering a neighbor, who Greene mistakenly thought had removed a dam that caused the drowning death of his daughter.

Mining intrigued him, and he was attracted to Cananea in Sonora about 30 miles south of his ranch. A wide belt of copper-yielding ridges stretched from southern Arizona across the border into the Cananea region of Sonora. Indians gave the place its name. Coronado noted the village site in 1540, and Padre Eusebio Kino included it on his 1696-97 map. Spanish soldiers in the mid-1700s dug for gold in shallow mines. For the next 100 years various Spanish and Mexican entrepreneurs tried their luck developing gold and silver mines with limited success. They failed because of Apache depredations or lack of resources. Rich copper ore was largely ignored until the last decades of the 19th century when demand (caused in large part by the booming electrical industry) turned the attention of the mining community on both sides of the border to copper. Greene's timing was perfect. In 1898 after the Apache threat was over and demand for electrical wire was high, he started leasing the old Cananea mines for a favorable price from the latest owner, the widow of a former Sonoran state governor. The Byzantine array of deals, purchases, leases, partnerships, interlocking corporations, which enabled Colonel Bill to control a large portion of the Cananea mining region, is too complex to describe. In fact, his tangled affairs never were completely straightened out in spite of strenuous efforts by lawyers, advisors, receivers, and heirs.

Basically, he started with a U.S. company to develop the mine, lost it though a hostile takeover and regained it through the trick of incorporating the company in Mexico. He then formed another company in West Virginia, Greene Consolidated Copper Company, and bought all of the shares of the Mexican company. He had little cash even though the mines were producing. On the strength of the production figures, he traveled east to Wall Street in New York City to raise money. With little more than his natural bravado, the uneducated Greene went to America's financial center and established himself as "Colonel Greene, the Copper Magnate."[431]

He sold stock to some of the country's most sophisticated investors. These were wily and often unscrupulous men, some of whom bought shares with the motive of wresting control of Greene's company. One investor with this in mind withheld his cash at a key time in a take-over attempt. Other investors (including one of Southern California's most prominent developers and citizens, Henry E. Huntington) provided the needed cash in time. The Colonel allegedly solved another problem by pointing his pistol at an unscrupulous investor and inviting him to return one million dollars in stock options.[432] True or not, the story added to Colonel Bill's reputation. As clever as he was, Greene continued to be plagued by lawsuits and Wall Street manipulators, a combination that eventually helped bring him down. However, his initial efforts in the world of finance paid off.

Old mines were expanded, and more acquired. Production and revenue rose to unprecedented levels. The growing town of Cananea boasted the largest smelter in Mexico. The expanding operation needed more and more miners and support personnel. By 1905, the workforce exceeded 5,000, including, interestingly, over 800 Chinese. Most Chinese did not work in the mines but served as cooks, houseboys, or operated laundries and other small businesses. The company town boasted electricity, telephone service with 150 connections, a fifty-bed hospital, a bank, office buildings, and housing for the employees.[433]

Cash flow from the Cananea mines enabled Greene to buy other mines and ranches on both sides of the border, but it was his grand timber project that made such an important impact on northern Chihuahua and the Casas Grandes Valley.

Expansion of the underground mines and the Cananea community required large amounts of expensive lumber, up to 10,000 board feet per day. Greene's managers had to buy and ship it from Puget Sound. To alleviate the high cost, Greene purchased timber land in Chihuahua in 1901. Small sawmills cut lumber that mule-drawn wagons hauled to Cananea.[434]

That purchase introduced the Colonel to northern Chihuahua, and he saw there a land of opportunity. An array of new prospects opened before him. In a short time, he connected with powerful people in the state. In 1904, his new friend, Acting Governor Enrique Creel, helped him obtain almost three million acres of timberland on the eastern slopes of the Sierra

Madre. This gigantic tract straddled the Sonora-Chihuahua border from above the Casas Grandes Valley south 150 miles into the Guerrero District above the future lumber-mill town of Madera.

The size and scope of the properties were unprecedented even for the Díaz era of pro-foreign investment. Greene now controlled rights to some of the richest timberland and mineral land in the country. In addition, he had rights to build water-driven sawmills on the Aros and Yaqui Rivers and to develop telegraph and railroad systems to service the region. Significantly, no taxes would be due for twelve years.[435] Colonel Greene could see he needed a railroad.

Others had dreamt of connecting to the Pacific Coast or of using rails to go in and out of the timberland and mines. Colonel Bill saw a much bigger picture. The valleys and timberlands east of the Sierra Madre must be joined at either end via a loop that would serve all forms of economic enterprise—lumbering, mining, ranching, and farming. This would provide access to northern markets across the border and southern markets in the heart of Mexico. It is clear that Enrique Creel knew this as well. He had recommended such a project to other entrepreneurs years before. Creel had watched and encouraged virtually every railroad entrepreneur in the region. All failed or gave up, but pieces of the railroad infrastructure were put in place. Colonel Greene, at the height of his meteoric career, took his turn.

He initially formed two companies, the Sierra Madre Land and Lumber Company as a Connecticut corporation and the Greene Gold and Silver Company as a West Virginia corporation. He followed with the purchase of the Rio Grande, Sierra Madre, and Pacific Railroad.

The original developers of the line, Foster Higgins and E.D. Morgan's Corralitos syndicate had not been able to extend the tracks beyond Nuevo Casas Grandes. The railroad stimulated the local economy but did not make a profit despite efforts to expand. Their engineers surveyed a route that continued southeast from Nuevo Casas Grandes several miles before turning west and crossing the mountains to the coast. Potential investors were not convinced, and the company ran out of money. In 1905, Greene purchased the existing right-of-way and all of the rolling stock.[436] He created the Sierra Madre and Pacific Railroad to extend the line.

His fortunes were at their zenith. Even though he was beginning to lose financial control of Cananea, he still was considered one of wealthiest men in the U.S. His plan to develop infrastructure to serve his lumbering and mining projects within Chihuahua was approved by all the political interests from Díaz to Terrazas and Creel. Greene proposed to connect Ciudad Juárez, and thus El Paso and the U.S., to Ciudad Chihuahua with a line that looped southwest through the Casas Grandes Valley via the San Diego Valley and south over the Sierra Madre into the Guerrero District, and northeast to Ciudad Chihuahua. On the map, the route looked roughly like a reverse D with Ciudad Juárez at the top and Ciudad Chihuahua at the bottom. The plan became a reality but in bits and pieces and not under Greene. It was Dr. Fred Stark Pearson who finally pulled all the pieces together.

The Mexican Central Railway, in place since 1884, had been absorbed into the National Railroad. It made the straight north-south line of the reverse D between Ciudad Juárez and Ciudad Chihuahua.

In the north, Greene's new Sierra Madre and Pacific Company added a few miles of track to the loop from the end of the old Rio Grande, Sierra Madre and Pacific line at Nuevo Casas Grandes to Terrazas, a stop built to serve Luis Terrazas's Hacienda San Diego. Greene had the concession rights to continue south over the mountains, into the Guerrero District but he went no farther than the Terrazas stop.

To the south in the Guerrero District, another Topolobampo Dreamer surfaced to build a segment of what became the loop. Prominent New Jersey financier, Grant B. Schley, with Enrique Creel very much involved, formed the Chihuahua and Pacific Railroad Company in 1905 (the name would resurface later on Chihuahua's nationalized rail system).

Schley believed in the dream. In 1899, his company completed track from a junction just south of Ciudad Chihuahua east to the mining center at Miñaca, and north from there to Temósachic.[437] Schley apparently became disenchanted with the project because in 1904, Colonel Greene bought his interest in the Chihuahua and Pacific. Another source identifies a financier named Alfred A. Spendlove as the Chihuahua and Pacific developer.[438] The dates and facts are generally the same. The important point is this railroad segment penetrated deep into a region rich with natural resources.

No one understood this better than Colonel Bill. With Enrique Creel hovering in the background as a vice president of the company, he extended his new railroad acquisition to a small town called San Pedro. He changed the town's name to Madera (wood or lumber) to recognize the mill he constructed there the following year.[439]

Greene poured money into the mill, and in 1907, output was 500,000 board feet per day. The Cananea Herald stated that Madera was the largest lumber mill in North America.[440] While this newspaper may not have been an unbiased source, it is clear that Greene had developed a system to tap into a huge natural resource. Unfortunately for the old gambler, his timing was bad. The Wall Street Panic of 1907 that so devastated northern Chihuahua, damaged Colonel Greene's companies beyond recovery.

Greene's fall has been portrayed as an overnight crash brought about by any number of factors, depending on the author, including poor management, personal excess, a workers' strike, fraudulence, manipulation by powerful Wall Street enemies, and the Panic of 1907. All of these played a part, but the actual fall was more gradual and less dramatic than an overnight crash. In the early years of the new century, a few of these factors were evident, but the Cananea operation paid huge dividends, particularly in 1905. This mollified suspicious investors but not for long.

The following year in June 1906, the mineworkers went on strike. The classic mixture of low wages, discriminatory pay between Mexicans and North Americans, and poor working conditions ignited unrest fueled by radical U.S. unionists, Mexican activists from the PLM party, and the revolutionary writings of Ricardo Flores Magón. The strike was widely publicized in both countries and became the most famous labor revolt in Mexican history. President Díaz immediately sent in a particularly ruthless detachment of local Rurales as well as regular federal troops. Greene invited vigilantes from Arizona Territory, who crossed the border illegally with arms eager for a fight of any kind. Intimidation led to confrontations in town and inevitably to violence and shooting. Bullets flew and struck strikers, bystanders, and a few North Americans. No one knows how many were killed or wounded. Later reports disagreed wildly. Regardless, it was enough to inflame public opinion. The overwhelming firepower of the Rurales, troops, and vigilantes put down the strike in only two days. Bitter memories lasted for decades. News of the strike helped bring down Porfirio Díaz and effectively finished Colonel Bill in Cananea.[441]

Greene carried on with his extensive ranching, railroad and lumber businesses, but these drained more funds than they generated. In 1907, he lost control of the Cananea mines and with that, loss of the lucrative contracts for his mills and railroads to provide lumber to the mines. In 1908, he declared bankruptcy.[442] The curtailment of operations or outright shutdown of his enterprises took paychecks from thousands of Chihuahua workers already suffering from the previous year's recession.

These hard times coupled with the bad feelings leftover from the strike, added to the discontent spreading through Chihuahua. Colonel Bill finally was forced out of all of his enterprises and his properties were taken over by mortgage holders. He retired with his wife to a ranch in northern Sonora. It was hard to believe he was really gone. Rumors circulated that he was attempting a comeback, investigating mines in this place or that. In reality, he lived quietly, too debt-ridden to try anything in spite of his reputation. One day while driving his buggy, the horses suddenly stampeded. He was thrown from the carriage and broke his collar bone and two ribs. Back home, he soon contracted pneumonia. While his wife frantically tried to reach doctors in El Paso by telegraph, the swashbuckling captain of industry died on August 8, 1911.

The Valley in 1909

A look back at the Casas Grandes Valley and surrounding area in 1909, when Dr. Pearson arrived, reveals a region dominated by large landowners both Mexican and foreign and an incomplete railway system. North along the New Mexico border stretched the 1,012,000 hectares (2.5-million acres) Palomas Land and Cattle Company, headed by Edwin J. Marshall, a California entrepreneur. South of that huge ranch at the head of the Casas Grandes Valley was Colonia Díaz—the LDS town, farm, and rangeland covering several thousand acres. On the east side of the valley was the 384,450 hectares (950,000 acres) Corralitos Cattle Company presided over by New York banker E. D. Morgan as president. Other LDS colonies lay to the southwest extending into the Sierra Madre. Luis Terrazas's Hacienda

San Diego covered 109,300 hectares (270,000 acres) in the San Diego Valley branch of the Casas Grandes Valley. Southeast of San Diego, his 348,960 hectares (862,270 acres) Hacienda San Miguel Babícora extended into the Santa María Valley. On the other side of the extension of the Sierra Madre that forms the south end of the San Diego Valley was the 1.5 million-acre San José Babícora (not to be confused with Terrazas's San Miguel Babícora), owned by William Randolph Hearst. Cattle production dominated these vast holdings. Dr. Pearson would add another large complex of properties devoted to timber and build a railroad that connected them all.

Putting the Pieces Together

With the collapse of Colonel Greene's empire, Dr. Pearson saw opportunity in northern Chihuahua. He remembered the night he camped near the Dos Cabezas Mine, and how he felt about the country's potential. Because of the Mexico City hydro-electric project, he retained many contacts at the highest levels in Mexico. President Díaz held him in high regard, always welcoming him to his office in Chapultepec Castle.

In 1908, Pearson took the train from Ciudad Juárez to the capital, riding in a private car leased from the Pullman Company. He later purchased Colonel Greene's elaborate car called *Verde* that Pullman had taken back and re-furbished.[443] Welcomed by Díaz, Pearson secured the necessary approvals for a new and grand project to build railroads to exploit Chihuahua's vast forests.

Back in London, James Dunn was busy straightening out the financial problems leftover from the 1907 recession. He was surprised and even shocked at Pearson's move into a massive new project so soon after surviving the financial panic. Dunn knew Pearson and respected his judgment. He listened, and once he understood the details of the Chihuahua plan, he became enthusiastic.

Dr. Pearson saw clearly what Greene had tried to do and also the defects in the Colonel's approach. Pearson would follow Greene's overall concept but with better organization, management, and above all, financing. Pearson planned to acquire the existing railroads and connect them to create the reversed-D loop from El Paso/Ciudad Juárez through the Casas Grandes

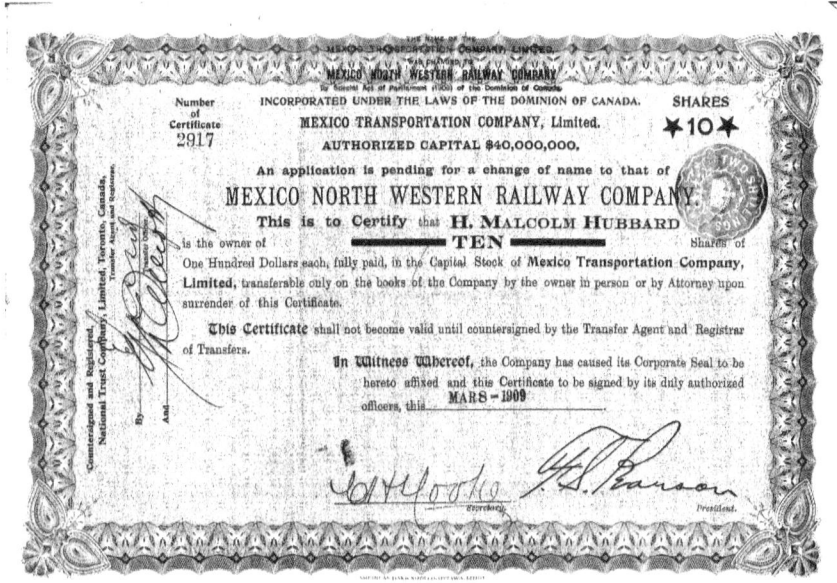

1909 Mexico North Western Railway Company stock certificate signed by Dr. F.S. Pearson. Note the name change from the Mexico Transportation Company, Ltd.

Valley, and over the mountains to Madera and Ciudad Chihuahua. He would obtain control of Sierra Madre timberlands and build lumber sawmills large enough to supply markets throughout the U.S. and Mexico.

Dr. Pearson had always been interested in mining, and his long list of projects show many mining consulting jobs and mine investments. The lands he had just purchased contained operating mines and good prospects, particularly south in the Guerrero District. Despite this interest, he would focus on lumber first and later on mines.

Raw material for the sawmills consisted of millions of acres of pine, fir, and other varieties. While locals had always cut trees and operated small mills driven by water wheels and primitive steam engines, surveyors for Murphy, Greene, and Pearson reported vast tracts of untouched, high-quality trees, some with trunks as thick as four feet. The pine trunks extended as high as 70 feet without limbs, meaning the cut lumber would be straight and free of knots. At lower elevations were commercially viable stands of oak, walnut, maple, ash, cedar, juniper, and sycamore that could be cut for specialty markets.[444] The problem for Greene, Creel, and everyone else who recognized the potential was access. Once in place, the difference in speed and cost of transporting tons of freight by rail compared to mule-drawn wagons was dramatic. Dr. Pearson would provide the access.

Stocks and Bonds

Dunn wasted no time. By February 1909, he completed the work necessary to incorporate the Mexican North Western Railway Company, Ltd (MNWR) in Canada. This became the parent company for the Chihuahua operation.

By February, he also had organized a stock and bond offering of 12 million dollars in the name of the new company. Pearson and Dunn subscribed for a portion of the stock and the rest was marketed through brokers. The stock initially did not sell well, probably because both the London *Times* and the *Economist* were less than enthusiastic. A quote in the Times went right to the point, "… bonds apparently secured largely on railways that are yet to be built can only be regarded as highly speculative investments." The *Economist* was also negative, but apparently the editors' moral stand on the "speculative" nature of the offering did not reach to their advertising department, which posted glowing advertisements for the stocks in the same issue.[445] Dunn was not deterred. In spite of the *Times* and *Economist,* he put together a syndicate of investors to generate enough funds for Pearson to get started, and he continued to raise more.

The company's Interim Report of the Board of Directors filed at the end of 1909 showed $25 million dollars (it is not clear whether U.S. or Canadian) in stock issued and £3 million pounds in bonds. These were enormous amounts. In 2019, the equivalent amount for the bonds would equal €344 million. Of course, the company did not receive all of the sales proceeds. Costs of the subscriptions were high. The syndicate members and the private brokers paid 90 percent of the bonds' face value. The syndicate members received a 40 percent stock bonus on the bonds purchased plus a half percent cash commission for bonds resold. Other brokers received a 20 percent stock bonus and a five percent stock commission for bonds resold.[446]

Power and Prestige

Despite skepticism in the newspapers, the financial skills of James Dunn and Dr. Pearson, combined with their standing in the financial world, are illustrated not only by the huge amounts of money they raised, but also by the prestigious men willing to serve on the Board of Directors. Pearson of course was president. A vice-president and general counsel was Walter Gow, a director of the Canadian Bank of Commerce. Based in New York, he also served as Chairman of the Board of Pearson's Rio de Janeiro Tramway and Light and Power. Another board member was the prominent financer E.R. Wood, also a Bank of Commerce board member. William Van Horne, an American from Illinois, had gone to Canada and became one of that country's most important railroad developers. He played a major part in the transcontinental Canadian Pacific Railway. Schools and streets are named for him in Canadian towns. Minor Keith, not a board member but a member of the original syndicate, was a pioneer/entrepreneur in the Central American banana industry and one of the founders of the United Fruit Company. Enrique Creel, the governor of Chihuahua and representative of the Terrazas family, was one of the vice-presidents. His inclusion demonstrated that Pearson had the support of Chihuahua's power structure. Another important name, Guillermo Landa y Escandón, governor of the Federal District of Mexico (Mexico City) and an advisor to President Porfirio Díaz, served the first year. Also on the list was the influential, well connected lawyer Luis Riba in Mexico City. Other board members represented various banking interests or the management of the company such as the Managing Director of the lumber operation, Hiram C. Smith. These powerful Canadians and Mexicans provided all the elements necessary to make the project a success under the benevolent conditions of the Porfiriato. At least this was Pearson's opinion. His hydroelectric projects in Mexico and Brazil had depended on Canadian capital. He is credited with opening Latin America to the major Canadian investment bankers in Montreal and Toronto.[447] Needing even more investors, Dunn soon moved his offices to London, the center of the world's financial markets that included Brussels and Paris.

The constant need for cash caused a rare riff between the two. Dr. Pearson had underestimated the cost of pulling this widespread project together, a familiar failure for Mexico's railroad entrepreneurs. In June 1910, he decided to raise money on his own. Without telling Dunn, he announced a plan on July 8 to sell $2 million in bonds in Canada. Apparently, he had gone back to Toronto from Mexico to make these arrangements. Dunn in London was outraged. Friend or no friend, he sent a telegram to Pearson telling him in no uncertain terms to back off. There absolutely would be no sale of Canadian bonds. He went on to express his opinion of the Canadian securities market and of the Canadian "figureheads" serving on the board that "are of no possible value to the company." Pearson realized he had gone too far and canceled his proposed bond sale. The confrontation created a new understanding between the two. They realized the Mexican project would require significantly more money. New and different investors would have to be involved. Arrangements were made secretly as to not panic the original syndicate and earlier investors. Another syndicate was quietly formed to purchase $3.75 million of a new issue of MNWR bonds.[448] Even though Pearson and Dunn participated with their own money, the secret maneuver stretched their financial ethics to the limit, even for that day. But it worked.

Acquiring the Land

Even with Díaz's overall approval, there was much legal and political work to be done to secure official approvals and concessions. Pearson was aided by several high-level contacts including Enrique Creel, who had helped Pearson acquire the Chihuahua al Pacífico Railroad, a key link in the loop-railroad plan. Creel pressured the Chihuahua courts to settle Greene's bankruptcy. Another important associate was Pearson's well-connected lawyer, Luis Riba. In this era of interlocking directorships, Riba served on many boards and represented several international companies, including the English lord Weetman Pearson's Mexican Eagle Oil Company.[449] He, along with the Federal District (Mexico City) Governor Guillermo Landa y Escadón (again, no apparent concerns about conflict of interest) dealt with the negotiations in the capital. Both became original members of the MNWR board of directors.

While these men worked through the political and bureaucratic maze in Mexico City, Pearson concentrated on obtaining Greene's bankrupt Chihuahua empire. The receiver wanted at least $3 million and rejected Pearson's initial offer. Pearson countered by hiring survey crews to lay out a new route from Ciudad Juárez to Terrazas station.[450] This ploy worked. On August 14, 1909, *The New York Times* reported that in Chihuahua the previous day, "Two and a half million acres of timber and mineral lands, with all the sawmills and machinery located thereon, the property of W.C. Greene ... were sold at public auction." The article noted that the property was appraised at $3 million and the "Pearson syndicate" paid $2 million.[451]

Sources vary as to the exact size of the purchase. Some are as high as 1,214,000 hectares (3,000,000 acres). These figures may be rounded up figures or may include other land purchases. Other sources refine the figure to 1,059,850 hectares (2,618,890 acres).[452]

The land purchased from Colonel Greene, sometimes referred to as the García tract, shows on the map as a long, irregular rectangle straddling the Sonora-Chihuahua border with protrusions extending to the east on

The New York Times, August 14, 1909

the Chihuahua side. The Sonoran town of Bavispe marks the top northeast corner. The property continues south past Madera into the Guerrero District. The southern boundary was near and roughly parallel to the east-west Chihuahua al Pacífico line.

This phase of Pearson's plan seemed to go well, and he turned his attention from acquisition to construction and left the remaining details to his lawyers. It probably was not Luis Riba, who was in Mexico City, but someone slipped up. All of the deeds were recorded in Toronto but not in Ciudad Chihuahua. This defect would lay dormant until long after Dr. Pearson was gone but it would surface.

The Murphy Tract

A significant second purchase of land by Pearson was the Murphy Tract. Frank Morrill Murphy was one of Arizona's prominent mining and railroad entrepreneurs. His company had purchased forest land southwest of the Pearson/Mata Ortiz site. Murphy had been a developer of the Congress Mine, the largest gold producer in the southern part of the Arizona Territory, a region of productive mines. In 1901, he and his partners folded the Congress and other mine operations into a new entity, the Development Company of America (DCA), based in Douglas, Arizona. This was a large corporation, a competitor of ASARCO, Phelps-Dodge and Colonel Greene's Cananea operation. All of these large entities exploited the rich mineral veins in southern Arizona and northern Mexico. Murphy also had experience with timber lands and sawmills.

Railroad construction and underground, hard-rock mining required a large, steady supply of lumber for ties, trestles, and supports. Small mill operators could keep up only with the local demand. Railroad and mining entrepreneurs knew the virgin forests of the Sierra Madre produced high quality lumber and saw an opportunity. However, there was no mill or lumber company large enough to produce and market the product.

The Terrazas family also saw the potential, but they wanted someone else to develop it. Murphy heard a glowing report of the timber potential from no less a person than Enrique Creel at an arranged dinner in New York City. Creel was well aware of Murphy's reputation and DCA's capacity for large projects, and he apparently painted a glowing picture of the millions of board feet of lumber ready to be taken. Murphy was intrigued. The facts are not known, but it appears he or his agents inspected enough of the forest to convince Murphy to invest. Roads, created by LDS colonists, led into a large tract of prime trees, called the García Tract because the surveyor/speculators Telésforo and Mariano García had held the land. Within the tract were the LDS colonies of García and Chuichupa, southwest of Casas Grandes, purchased in 1885. The surrounding forests were some of the finest in the Sierra Madre.

The exact location of the Murphy Tract is vague, but it extended east from the Greene boundary line and surrounded the García and Chuichupa properties.

The DCA purchased approximately 202,000 hectares (500,000 acres), completing the transaction on March 31, 1902. Murphy and his partners created a subsidiary, the American-Mexican Lumber Company. They intended to ship logs to Arizona to be cut into lumber for their railroads and mines. Enrique Creel was involved, and as part of the deal they did not expect to pay taxes. For this, Creel apparently expected DCA to add a line over the mountains that would connect the Rio Grande, Sierra Madre, and Pacific railroad to the Pacific Coast, another incarnation of the illusive dream.

Murphy miscalculated the distances involved. The cost of shipping the logs by wagon to the railhead at Nuevo Casas Grandes and then to Arizona by rail proved prohibitive. DCA did nothing with the land for six years. After Colonel Greene's collapse, DCA sold what had become known as the Murphy Tract to Dr. Pearson's MNWR for $3,000,000. In his 1909 year-end report to the DCA stockholders, Murphy explained the sale saying that the after the cost of infrastructure—railroads, lumber mills—commensurate returns could not be expected for several years.[453]

The Bank of London Tract

After the oil boom in Texas in the early 1900s, North Americans bought large amounts of property in Mexico. A group of Texas oil entrepreneurs (including Edwin Jessup Marshall, the owner of the Palomas Land and Cattle Company) had created the Texas Oil Company (Texaco). In the early

1900s, they expanded operations into Mexico, led by Richard E. Brooks. He acquired several large parcels, apparently financed by the Bank of London. He and a man named Harris Masterson bought 210,147 acres (85,042 hectares) of land west of the Pearson townsite. The land extended from the prairie into the hills to the base of the Sierra Madre. The land contained relatively poor timber and was best suited for grazing. Pearson purchased the acreage on July 1, 1909.[454]

The Booker Tract

During the same period of fast-paced land purchases, Lewis Booker bought 66,775 hectares (165,000 acres) twelve miles west of Pearson for $33,000. He constructed mills and outbuildings at Colonia Pacheco, the LDS mountain colony. He intended to build a railroad down the mountain to connect with the MNWR station at Pearson. Constant raiding by rebels shut down Booker's operation and he sold out to Dr. Pearson for $65,000. This gave Pearson a direct if rugged route into the timber lands due west of the Pearson/Mata Ortiz site.

Assembling the Railroad

Dr. Pearson's company, the MNWR, followed his plan and bought the existing sections of the loop railroad.[455] In what became the "Chihuahua" Administrative District of the railroad, one of the two lines acquired was the former Chihuahua al Pacífico line that connected with the National Railroad just south of Ciudad Chihuahua and ran 175 miles east and north to Temósachic. The other was Greene's former Sierra Madre and Pacific line that extended north from Temósachic 32 miles deep into the timberlands to the town of Madera and Greene's former sawmill.

In the north, in the "El Paso" Administrative District, Greene's Sierra Madre and Pacific (the former Rio Grande, Sierra Madre and Pacific) ran 160 miles from Ciudad Juárez to Terrazas Station.

The fourth purchase was the El Paso Southern, a former subsidiary of the Sierra Madre and Pacific that crossed the Rio Grande River on a private bridge between Ciudad Juárez and El Paso. This short but vital link connected the Mexican lines with major U.S. railroads such as the South-ern Pacific and Santa Fe.

The combined track totaled 367 miles and passed through 13 tunnels and over 446 bridges. A formidable 116-mile gap in the loop remained between Terrazas Station and Madera.

Railroad Right-of-Way

To fill the gap and operate the combined railroads, Pearson needed the right-of-way concessions from the federal government. This was Luis Riba's job.

On November 22, 1909, he signed a concession contract on behalf of MNWR. The Secretary of State, representing the Mexican Office of Com-munication and Public Works, signed for the government. The document summarized the entire past railroad concessions back to 1887 governing Baja California and Sonora as well as Chihuahua. These concessions repre-sented a long history of mostly failed projects. The document consolidated them all into the current contract.

The wording was very precise about the specifications of the track, the width of the right-of-way (60 meters), and the maximum rates that could be charged for different kinds of freight and for different classes of passen-ger service. Charges also were set for sending messages along the railroad telegraph lines. The telegraph was still working in the Mata Ortiz station as late as 1984. A deposit of $132,000 was required to guarantee performance within ten years.

The most significant clauses laid out the railroad-line construction responsibilities. Pearson was primarily interested in filling the gap, but there were other construction requirements. One was to finish a line in Sonora from Topolobampo to Madera. The old dream lived on. How much Pearson subscribed to the dream is unknown. He did send surveyors to examine routes. Their reports of the engineering obstacles and the financ-ing needed may have caused even Dr. Pearson to put that project on hold at least for the time being. The other required projects, mostly in Sonora, also seemed to have been ignored even thought there were deposit forfeitures in the contracts for lack of performance within ten years.[456]

Luis Terrazas's Concession

It should never be forgotten that no matter how powerful friends were in Mexico City, those wanting to do business in Chihuahua eventually had to deal directly or indirectly with Luis Terrazas. In this case, most of the 160-mile gap crossed his San Miguel de Babícora hacienda. He and his son-in-law Enrique Creel recognized the value of the loop line. Still there was a price.

On November 13, 1909, Don Luis met in an El Paso office with representatives of MNWR. One of these was R. Home Smith, a Toronto lawyer shown in the resulting legal documents as in charge of company lumber operations. The other was H.C. Ferris, also listed as a general manager of lumber operations. Ferris has been identified elsewhere as the general manager of the railroad. They appeared with Don Luis before a Mexican lawyer to sign the document that contained 23 clauses. A summary of these officious clauses is listed below. Much can be learned by a review of the list and reading between the lines about conditions in northern Chihuahua as they were in late 1909:

1. General Luis Terrazas, as the owner of the Hacienda San Miguel Babícora, granted to the MNWR exclusive rights to exploit the forest west of the San Miguel River (Palanganas River). The clause expressly prohibited cutting on the east side.
2. The concession was for 17 years.
3. MNWR would pay a total of 250,000 pesos in U.S. gold, 50,000 thousand at the signing and the remainder in six months.
4. The minimum tree size that could be cut was 15 centimeters in diameter measured at 45 centimeters in height.
5. Only pine trees cut be cut for export, no other varieties.
6. The property could only be cut once. After a part was cut, the concession for that part would revert to Terrazas. The company could not return to that specific site again.
7. Three hundred hectares (741 acres) would be granted for the specific purpose of building a mill and offices.
8. Absolutely no alcohol could be sold on the premises.

9. A 40-meter-wide railroad right-of-way was ceded to Madera from the connection at the border of Hacienda San Miguel Babícora to the railroad from Nuevo Casas Grandes.
10. All wildfires would be suppressed.
11. San Miguel Hacienda employees would be ordered to fight fires at the company's expense.
12. For each grazing animal killed, the company would pay 25 pesos for ordinary cows, 130 pesos for purebred bulls, and 50 pesos for horses.
13. The company would have the right to divert stream water on the Hacienda San Miguel to transport logs and to use wells and other water sources as needed.
14. The company could use these water sources to build a mill pond within the 300-hectare (741 acres) mill site. If these prove inadequate, flow could be diverted from the San Miguel River.
15. The company had the right to enter into other contracts for other concessions such as land east of the San Miguel River.
16. The company's right-of-way should avoid cultivated land. Where unavoidable, the company would pay indemnity of 100 dollars per year.
17. Two stations would be created for cattle shipments, the locations to be determined by Luis Terrazas.
18. Individual permits, issued by Luis Terrazas, would be required for hunting. Moreover, the company would maintain morality and order so that no damage to the interests of General Terrazas would occur in the administration of Hacienda San Miguel Babícora.
19. The company had the right to build temporary railroad lines to access timber areas.
20. General Terrazas maintained the right to graze animals throughout the concession area.
21. The expenses of preparing the concession document would be paid by the company.
22. Mr. Smith and Mr. Ferris would personally guarantee that the terms of the agreement would be fulfilled
23. The contract will be filed by the notary public and the deed issued.[457]

The clauses reveal that Luis Terrazas was primarily a cattleman in spite of the breadth of his family's activities. His requirements made it clear that he would continue to run cattle on the concession, but he made no demands on the timber business. "Stumpage" fees (payments for each tree cut) were not required. However, compensation for cattle killed was definitely required as were two stations to load cattle.

In the document, Terrazas was addressed as "General," suggesting his preference for military rank over his other titles.

The clauses restricting cutting to pine trees only, minimum tree sizes (small as they are), fire suppression, and the single-cut restriction hint at the conservation movement underway in Mexico at that time. Leading the rapidly growing effort was Miguel Ángel de Quevedo, a French-trained engineer from a wealthy Jalisco family who became known as the Apostle of the Tree. From his position as Mexico City's Director of Public Works, he cajoled President Díaz's government to create a national forest service in 1908.[458] This was only a year before the concession document was signed but the conservation movement had been growing. The document wording suggests professional foresters were involved. De Quevedo later gained enough influence to have forestry conservation rules codified in the Constitution of 1917, during the Carranza administration.

It is not recorded how the 741-acre mill site was selected. It was near water but several miles from quality timber in contrast to Madera that at 7,000 feet altitude was surrounded by forest. Perhaps Don Luis felt that giving up that piece of land at the northern extreme of San Miguel would least affect the hacienda operations. Also, Pearson may have planned to adopt Booker's idea and extend a branch line from the mill to the Pacheco area.

Other than a hint of concern for the greater good provided by the conservation clauses, this was a document between two powerful entities, who could do whatever they wanted as long as they agreed. The effect on Mexican people living in the area was not considered. What these people were vaguely beginning to realize and Terrazas and Pearson chose to ignore was that the time for this kind of thinking was running out.

Work Begins

With characteristic energy, Pearson immediately organized the resources and hired the people necessary to construct the line to Madera and upgrade the older lines. Survey crews followed the Palanganas River and its tributaries south into the Sierra Madre. They found a route along the Río Caballo (a tributary of Río Tres Treinta) with a maximum grade of three percent as it approached the Cumbre summit. A steam engine could manage a three-percent grade while pulling a train of heavy cars full of ore or logs.[459] On existing roadbeds, ballast was replaced and heavier 70-pound rails installed. Bridges and culverts were strengthened, all in antici-pation of heavy ore and lumber trains. At first the local Chihuahuans were excited by the flurry of construction. The area had been hit hard by the 1907 Recession, and jobs were scarce. Soon resentment began to build. It did not help when the William Jennings Engineering Company, purchas-ing agent for the railroad, announced that all materials would be purchased in El Paso—good for the budget but bad public relations. There may have been right-of-way or other property-use issues as several landowners pro-tested to Díaz. The president responded by sending a detachment of his Rurales to ensure no one interfered with the railroad construction.

Rurales in Pearson
Photo: Courtesy of Williwood Meador Collection,
West Texas Collection, Angelo State University.

A bigger issue was the growing reaction in general to foreign investment. This caused a strange dichotomy in northern Chihuahua between those enjoying Pearson's good wages and the stimulus to the economy and those hearing the dangerous appeal of rebellion.[460]

By September 4, 1910, the MNWR construction gangs had extended the line south to the mill site, where they built a train station.

This new rail segment ran southwest from the Terrazas Station along the east side of the Palanganas River not far from the Hacienda San Diego compound. It continued southeast, past Los Cables, the old Mimbres/Casas Grandes moctezuma site, into the mill property, still on the east side of the river. The Massillon Ohio Bridge Company constructed a steel bridge to carry the track to the west side. The exact date of the bridge's completion is not known. It must have been during the summer of 1910, because it is recorded that a teacher from the Colonia Juárez Academy with the unforgettable name of Erastus K. Fillerup fell off the bridge and died in July 1910.[461]

Juan Quezada sitting on the Mata Ortiz bridge constructed about 1910.
Photo: Bobby Furst, 1976, San Diego Museum of Us

Past the bridge, and the place of Fillerup's demise, the line curved south past the train station and continued toward the mountains and the Cumbre summit. A few hundred yards north of the track curve, Pearson prepared plans to build his second lumber mill, one even larger than Madera. The state of Chihuahua officially established the Pearson Pueblo in 1910.[462]

On October 5, one month after the line was extended to the Pearson mill site, Francisco Madero issued his *Plan de San Luis Potosí* declaring Díaz's recent election fraudulent and calling for revolt. He named a specific date, November 20, for a general uprising,

Pearson ignored the political warnings. He had other technical challenges to consider. Fifty miles south of the new town of Pearson lay the 7,195-foot crest of the Sierra Madre at Cumbre. Just to reach there required eleven tunnels, one 2,200 feet long. At the crest, the workers cut and blasted through 3,925 feet of rock, three quarters of a mile, to form the Cumbre Tunnel. It was hard, slow work. It would be February 1, 1912, before the track was open to Madera.

Late as it was, the completed loop lived up to expectations. Now the company could access the rich timber and mining region and ship lumber, ore and other products efficiently in two directions without the expensive backtracking through Ciudad Juárez or Ciudad Chihuahua. The pieces were in place.

Madera Lumber Company

Dr. Pearson took over the lumber mill at Madera as part of the transaction to acquire Colonel Greene's Chihuahua enterprises. Pearson formed the Madera Lumber Company Limited, a MNWR subsidiary, to operate that mill and all other logging and milling operations. Greene had built the Madera mill just three years before in 1906. Pearson added another sawing operation next to Greene's original, doubling the capacity. By early 1910, the mill employed 100 North Americans and 2,000 Mexicans. Madera was described as a "modern town with every convenience."[463]

Three young North Americans came from the Long Bell Lumber Company in east Texas. One became a sales manager, another the office manager, and the third, Roy Hoard, a "timber cruiser." This meant, he toured the forests and developed a survey plan for a specific section of the forest. Samples were taken from plots throughout the surveyed area. These were compiled into an overall estimate of variety, size, quality, and board-foot potential. Hoard was a small, energetic man, whose courage and capability made him the major player in the railroad and mill operations during the tumultuous years of the Revolution and afterwards.

Pearson had pushed hard on the elements of his plan. Log cutting and sawing began in late 1909, the same year as the mill purchase. Production for the following year, ending December 31, 1910, was 54.6 million board feet total and 27.1 million board feet sold and shipped. The remainder 27.4 million remained at Madera ready for shipment. Lumber prices stood at about $16 per thousand board feet according to Dr. Pearson's statement in the MNWR 1910 annual report. Multiplying the unit price times the board feet shipped yields gross revenue of $433,600. Pearson's report was vague about costs, suggesting them to be about half of the revenue. One half of the gross is $216,800, a figure consistent with "net earnings" of $205,920 as shown in the annual report for the lumber operation.

The annual report also shows net earnings from the railroads of $597,223 and "Miscellaneous Income from other sources" of $128,970 for a grand net earnings total of $932,115. Bond interest was $861,339, leaving a surplus of $74,776. This exercise in arithmetic indicates that Pearson and

*The Mexico North Western Railway with a view southeast
toward El Indio beyond the Pearson site.
Photo: 3635866_AZSW
Courtesy of the University of Arizona Libraries, Special Collections*

Dunn met all of their financial obligations in just one year of full operation. Dr. Pearson characteristically presented an optimistic picture in the report. The financial statements summarized data, leaving out detail. Full disclosure was not the standard for the day. Nevertheless, given the information available, Dr. Pearson, Dunn, and their associates in a very short length of time were able to assemble the funds, properties, and expertise to create an integrated organization that did better than break-even the first year. An amazing feat, but it took a great deal of money. The financial statements show 25 million in stock outstanding and 25 million in bonds. Presumably the bond total included the secret issue.

Dr. Pearson did note at the end of the report that "political disturbances" had occurred toward the end of the year and that railroad operations had been "interfered with" to prevent the movement of government troops. This interference consisted mostly of wrecked bridges and culverts. Pearson did not expect any serious loss in revenue for the succeeding year.[464]

They Called It Pearson

The Chihuahua project had begun well. In Dr. Pearson's parent company, the Mexican North Western Railway Ltd., (MNWR) owned almost 1,214,000 hectares (three million acres) of timberland, a large lumber mill, and four existing railroad lines. Luis Terrazas sold the company 132 hectares (326 acres) taken from the southern part of his Hacienda San Diego and 168 hectares (415 acres) from the northern edge of his Hacienda San Miguel Babícora. These two parcels joined just north of the new train station and became a town site and second mill site.[465] Experienced mill and railroad employees were hired from the U.S., supplemented by LDS colonists from nearby Colonia Juárez. Mexican workers with a variety of skill levels came from many places looking for jobs. Construction began immediately on the new mill, on the expansion of the Madera mill, and on the railroad line extensions.

At the new mill site, engineers designed a channel that laborers dug to divert water from the nearby Palanganas River to a mill pond. Beyond the mill, building sites were laid out in the area that became known as Barrio Americano. Company carpenters constructed houses, stores, and a hotel,

Director's house on the hill above Barrio Americano.
Photo: Courtesy of the El Paso Public Library, Special Collections,
Border Heritage Center

usually of wood with pitched roofs in a style closer to 19ᵗʰ century Middle America than to traditional Mexican adobe. Although, a small adobe building survives north of Barrio Americano that local residents say was a hospital during the Revolution. The mill power house, driven by coal, generated electricity for homes and commercial buildings and even for street lights. No complete description exists, but as the community evolved, it appears most of the North Americans lived in Barrio Americano. Mexican and Chinese merchants and Mexican technical employees lived in Barrio Centro or Barrio Adobe (Barrio López). Workmen and farmers lived south across the arroyo in Barrio Porvenir.[466] This description is probably an oversimplification. What is clear is what was an empty site became a thriving community in just a few months. They called it Pearson.

On the west side of Barrio Americano on a long low hill, three buildings faced toward the river. Dr. Pearson and perhaps other officials used the first (Amida Sáenz Flores lived in the house on the site in 2008). The large center building became the Casa Grande Hotel, the scene for several dramatic events during the Revolution. A label on an old photo calls it the "Director's house." Apparently, mill manager, C.H. Cooper, lived there (Luis Martínez lived in a house on the site in 2008).

Fong Poi, the Chinese patriarch, lived in the third house. Below the floor was a concrete chamber that served as a hiding place for Fong Poi and for children during rebel raids, according to local lore.[467] Only the foundation with the chamber exists today.

The mill at the new pueblo of Pearson was designed to produce a very large volume of lumber, 175 million board feet per year. As the mill was many miles from the timber to the west, Dr. Pearson planned to transport logs by rail to supplement logs hauled by wagon from the mountains. Madera had two sawing complexes, basically two separate mills, but the new mill would have three. The cut lumber would be transported to the El Paso mill for finishing into box wood, sashes, doors and other forms. From El Paso, the lumber would be shipped north and south to markets throughout the U.S. and Mexico.

C.H. Cooper, an employee in the Madera mill, was put in charge of building the huge Pearson facility. Cooper must have been an incredibly capable man. His son said that he only had a fifth-grade education.[468] Roy Hoard, who headed the MNWR for many years during and after the Revolution, called Cooper a brilliant engineer.[469]

Pearson mill under construction, 1910.
Photo: 3635866_AZSW
Courtesy of the University of Arizona Libraries, Special Collections

It is not clear how frequently Dr. Pearson communicated with Cooper, probably often via telegraph. Whether it was his own idea or Pearson's, Cooper followed Pearson's style and ordered the very best equipment.

Barrio Americano with mill behind. The mill pond is to the right of the mill buildings. The railroad track is beyond the pond and adjacent to the line of trees that mark the river. Barrio Centro is out of the picture to the right.
Photo: 3635866_AZSW
Courtesy of the University of Arizona Libraries, Special Collections

Cut lumber from the Pearson Mill.
Photo: Courtesy of the El Paso Public Library, Special Collections,
Border Heritage Center

One example was the state-of-the-art McGiffert Log Loader, designed to straddle the tracks and load the cars by crane as they passed under the loader. Another was a monorail designed to quickly move lumber around the mill.[470]

Pearson was in Spain with his family in May 1911, when he received the news that Porfirio Díaz had abdicated. He reacted with an extremely generous act, as he apparently understood the disruptions and hardships the months of fighting caused the local people. His managers were instructed to pay a bonus to all Mexican employees. In addition, provisions were to be offered at cost to everyone in the region.

He immediately sailed to New York and went directly to El Paso by train, postponing a family trip to Great Barrington. He arrived in El Paso in July as a hero. The El Paso papers reported that Dr. Pearson was the man that was making El Paso grow to 100,000 people. Also, he had helped relieve the terrible want in northern Chihuahua after what the reporters thought was the end of the Revolution.[471]

Always optimistic, Pearson apparently thought the same thing and chose to believe that Mexico would return to "normal" with Madero in charge. His objective for the trip was not only to assess the condition of the company but to study engineering surveys of routes to the Pacific Coast with an accompanying group of high-ranking railroad executives.

The surveys may not have been encouraging, and Dr. Pearson's attention turned elsewhere. The Revolution was far from over. The most brutal part lay ahead, and already MNWR operations suffered disruptions.

Projects on the Brink

Since his days at Tufts College, Dr. Pearson had the uncanny ability to meet and overcome technical, financial, and organizational challenges. People liked him and believed in him. Talented engineers and financiers wanted to be at his side as he designed and built great projects no one had attempted before. Entrepreneurs hired him to solve difficult technical problems, and he had literally moved mountains. Skilled as he was, he could not master the tide of world events. Recession, xenophobia, revolution, and war in the early 20th century ruined many powerful men and their carefully laid plans.

Pearson Mill power house
Photo: Courtesy of the El Paso Public Library, Special Collections,
Border Heritage Center

By 1911, all was not well. While the first year of operations had shown a profit, the year ended just one month after Francisco Madero's call for revolution. For the next six months, terrible battles raged in northern Chihuahua from Casas Grandes to Ciudad Juárez, disrupting rail operations. Even though the Madera mill delivered twice as much lumber as the first year, the workmen stacked a great deal more than could be delivered. Costs escalated, and the loss for the second year exceeded the first-year profit. Pearson, writing in the 1911 annual report, remained optimistic, assuming as did others that the country would return to normal with Francisco Madero as president.

There were other reasons for Pearson's optimism as 1912 opened. After Madero took control of the government, there was the period of calm that Pearson predicted. Workers finished the Cumbre Tunnel and the MNWR loop was a reality. Scheduled trains ran between Pearson and Madera. Construction continued on the Pearson mill, and on the El Paso Box and Milling Company.

In Pearson's Dos Cabezas mine, always an important revenue source, miners discovered a rich "off shoot." Wagons regularly carried quantities of high-grade ore to smelters from the expanded mine.[472]

In Mexico City, Pearson resolved the problem of a Necaxa hydroelectric project board that had become hostile by reorganizing Mexico Light and Power. The company continued to deliver services to the capital.

In Brazil, Pearson's companies had difficulty maintaining profit payouts because of the deteriorating currency exchange rates. The power companies in Rio de Janeiro and Sao Paulo were consolidated into one entity with Canadian railroad and utility mogul William Mackenzie as chairman of the board. This was represented to financiers as an organizational move, although critics called it a stock-watering scheme.[473] However, the company continued to provide service.

While these actions generated optimism with employees, customers, and investors, they turned out to be no more than temporary fixes. The ominous signs that began after the Panic of 1907 intensified. Pearson carried on as before, confident in his project organization, his development formula, and his abilities to overcome all obstacles. He attempted more and bigger projects until he became enmeshed in a terrible railroad-acquisition debacle. Later critics admitted it was a brilliant idea, but the result depleted his resources and damaged what had been an impeccable reputation.

The Rock Island Line and More Projects

Industry consolidation was a trend during the late 19th and early 20th centuries, whether it was steel, oil, automobiles, or railroads. The Chicago, Rock Island, and Pacific Railroad, made famous by the folk song, "Rock Island Line," had evolved into a major network extending through 12 states from Chicago to Denver and Galveston. In 1911, Pearson joined a syndicate that attempted to buy the Rock Island Line and other lines to merge into a megasystem, perhaps extending to the Pacific (although Pearson denied this later in a rare interview). Connection could be made to Pearson's Mexican railroad to facilitate cross-border commerce. This was not an engineering project, although Pearson had been hired to evaluate the condition of the rolling stock and roadbeds prior to joining the syndicate. It was a takeover and it failed spectacularly with widespread publicity highly critical of the speculators. Many factors contributed, including sabotage by insiders, but basically, as newspaper financial analysts wrote under blazing headlines, Pearson's syndicate did not have enough money in spite of the enormous sums they did raise. Another larger syndicate finally bought the depressed Rock Island shares. It is not known how much Pearson lost. It certainly diminished his reputation in the increasingly conservative European financial markets. A story circulated that the strain turned his hair white.[474]

Whatever the color of his hair, Pearson remained undeterred. Even before the Rock Island debacle was resolved, he was in Texas working on a new project. On July 12, 1911, he helped dedicate the construction of a dam on the Medina River that his cadre of engineers had designed. He was the featured speaker at the grand celebration.

Pearson had conceived a unique irrigation project using water from Lake Medina, a reservoir created by the dam. He intended to sell several hundred farms on 60,000 acres purchased by the Medina Valley Irrigation Company. This was a subsidiary of his San Antonio Land and Irrigation Company, a Canadian holding company formed for his various Texas projects. The Medina Valley Company began an elaborate sales campaign and planned a town called Pearson around a Southern Pacific Railway station. Pearson's engineers built the dam using state-of-the-art techniques and cement-mixing equipment. Later they shipped this equipment to Spain for use on Pearson's Barcelona project.

The July 16, 1911, headline of the *San Antonio Express* read, "Pearson opens the gates to riches."[475] It was a valid prediction, but unfortunately, it did not happen during the few remaining years of Pearson's life. World War I interrupted sales to potential small farmers and cut off the flow of European capital. Debt forced the company into receivership. The Texas town of Pearson died as well.

The irrigation system survived in the form of a public utility and still provides water to Medina Valley farms over 100 years later. The U.S. Secretary of Interior declared the Medina dam a National Historic Landmark in 1976.

Another town, named Natalia after Pearson's daughter Natalie also survived. The town founders misspelled the name, but they created a small but thriving agricultural center. A street called Pearson runs through it. [476]

Despite Dr. Pearson's optimism in Texas, the year 1912 did not end well.

Receivership

Dr. Pearson was wrong about stability under President Madero. Radical leaders, frustrated by Madero's moderate approach, began to fall away, spawning various factions and "armies" that fought each other as well as Madero's federal troops.

In February 1912, in Ciudad Juárez, factions loyal to General José Inés Salazar, who was one of the first to break with Madero, joined dissidents in the city and forced out the federal troops. The following March 6, a group of rebel generals and other officers that had revolted against Madero signed an agreement, *Plan de la Empacadora*, making Pascual Orozco their supreme leader.[477] This rare display of cooperation started the Orozco Rebellion and created a designation of rebels known as "Red Flaggers" that terrorized the countryside. The Revolution that began as a unified effort to oust a dictator now degenerated into civil war.

C.H. Cooper could not finish the Pearson plant. Only one of the three planned sawmills ever operated. Both rebel and federal troops regularly commandeered trains and then destroyed track and bridges to deny use to

Rebels in front of the wooden houses of Barrio Americano.
The lines from the mill power house supplied electricity to the homes.
Photo: PHO25-2-1-033 Courtesy of University of Texas at El Paso Library,
Special Collections Department

the other. Construction crews in one report listed 50 bridges burned.[478] The Madera Mill could not ship lumber to fill their orders nor could they ship logs to Pearson. The Madera Mill managers also were desperate for spare parts and finally suspended operations later in 1912.

Company construction gangs continued to work hard under dangerous conditions to reopen the lines. The mill opened and closed sporadically over the next three years when parts were received and deliveries could be made.

Hard work by employees at all levels was not enough. The final blow came in February 1914, when rebels caused a train wreck inside the Cumbre Tunnel. Not only were over 50 people killed, but the blocked tunnel cut the railroad loop. By late summer, 1914, cash flow was so low the Company could not make payments on accumulated bond interest, totaling $2,874,000. The Company went into receivership. On September 14, the court appointed Dr. Pearson and R. Home Smith as receivers. Pearson was in London at the time of the Cumbre disaster working the finances of his last project, the massive Barcelona hydroelectric system.

Barcelona and the Monument

Dr. Pearson did not linger in Texas after dedicating the Medina Valley Irrigation Project. Before July 1911 ended, he was on his way to Barcelona, Spain. The street railway system there had come to his attention. Following his basic development formula, he wanted to acquire the line and build a hydroelectric system from dams on the Ebro River in the Pyrenees to power an expanded streetcar railroad and provide cheap electricity to Barcelona. Spain's glory days had passed, and it moved slowly into the Industrial Revolution. Barcelona in the Catalonia Province was an exception. Based on a thriving textile industry, the city had grown to 800,000. The textile mills depended on steam plants, and coal was expensive. Dr. Pearson saw the solution and did a good job selling the project. He even had two meetings with King Alfonso XIII. The Spanish authorities, including the king, clearly understood the advantages of cheap power for the region and gave broad property and easement concessions to Pearson's new company, the Barcelona Traction and Power Company, Ltd. The government's

Pearson monument, Barcelona, Spain
Photo: Courtesy of Kevin O'Connor

enthusiasm was partly due to the irrigation component of Pearson's plan. The dams on the Ebro and its tributaries would provide water to irrigate vast areas of Catalonian wasteland, rejuvenating a poverty-stricken region.

Bonds were sold to raise cash in Great Britain, Belgium, France, and Canada. Work began in early 1913. The size and complexities of the project are difficult to describe. In steep rugged country cut by deep gorges, Europe's largest and the world's fourth largest dam would be built. On top of a mountain near the dam site, a cement plant was constructed that eventually produced ten million cubic feet of concrete. Steam traction trains and 1,000 mules supplied coal to the plant. A custom electric crushing and mixing machine, designed for the Medina project, was dismantled and the entire apparatus shipped to Spain. One work camp housed 2,000 men. Within two years in May 1914, electric power began to flow. Barcelona's powerhouse with their smoke-belching chimneys shut down, replaced by clean hydropower at half the cost.[479] It was an engineering marvel but the project was not complete. Serious problems remained.

One month after power began to flow to Barcelona, on June 28, a Serbian nationalist shot and killed Austria's Archduke Ferdinand and his wife Sophie, igniting Europe's volatile mix of alliances, mobilizations, border disputes, and age-old grievances.

Belgian and French subscribers had purchased large amounts of the Barcelona Traction and Power Company's bonds on the installment plan. That summer the cash flow needed to drive the project to completion slowed, then stopped completely when the German army marched into Belgium on August 4.

Fear and uncertainty swept through Europe. The company reacted by ordering all work shut down immediately. Before the end of the second week of August, before the borders closed, thousands of foreign workers were shipped home. Without experienced workers, the unfinished system deteriorated and service became unreliable. In November 1914, the Barcelona Traction and Power Company defaulted on interest payments and was in receivership by the end of December.

The problems were both political and financial, but powerful investors (and some historians) blamed Pearson for cost overruns and lack of strict control.[480] Pearson had assigned highly competent engineers to oversee the construction, but it was true that after the Panic of 1907, he had to spend much of his time in London, Brussels, and Montreal seeking financing and reassuring investors.

Despite these distractions and the problems in Mexico and South America, Pearson continued to implement new ideas. He led an effort to build a hospital for wounded soldiers in Yvetot, France and worked with the Canadian government to build a nickel-refining plant in the Sudbury mining district of Ontario.

In Spain, King Alfonso was displeased. His country was officially neutral, and economic development in Catalonia, his most prosperous province, had slowed. He appealed to Pearson to restart the project. Pearson had never lost interest. In January 1915, he appointed the highly respected electrical engineer, Dr. Horace Field Parshall to go to Spain and prepare a restructuring plan. It was a good choice and Parshall saw the project through to completion. Pearson brought the diverse bond holders together and in a rare act of unity they approved Parshall's recommendations including a refinancing plan. Pearson scheduled a bond-holder meeting in London for May 12, 1915, for formal approval.

On May 1, Dr. Pearson and Mabel boarded the Lusitania to attend the meeting. With his secretary, he continued to work, dictating and preparing reports. He dictated his annual report to the Brazilian Traction Company and placed the typed draft in his vest pocket. Fred and Mabel were last seen standing holding hands on the ship's listing promenade deck.

Both bodies were recovered and after a public memorial in England, the ashes were shipped to New York for another elaborate memorial and burial in Woodland Cemetery. The water-soaked draft was found in Pearson's pocket and was included in the company's annual report.[481]

Immediately after Pearson's death, there was an outpouring of eulogies and impressive memorial services in London and New York. Newspaper articles covered his demise only to be followed by a period of vicious attacks on his reputation by a few but very effective critics with their own agendas. In spite of a lifetime of accomplishments and the highly publicized attacks, his name fell into obscurity surprisingly soon, but not in Barcelona. There they continued to remember the great engineer that took their community to a new level of prosperity. In 1927, the Rotary Club of Barcelona passed a motion to honor Pearson with a monument. In a plaza in the suburb of Pedrales, near a street called Pearson, stands a Greek-style statue on a monument bearing Pearson's name. Time did not erase his memory there. In 1985, Barcelona and the regional government of Catalonia sponsored a large exposition on the history of Catalan industrial technology and the industrialization of the region, *Catalunya, la Fábrica d'Espanya*. Many industrialists and inventors were featured but only one professional engineer. Dr. Pearson's hydro-electrical accomplishments assumed almost "mythic dimensions" in the presentation.[482]

The Rotary Club of Barcelona restored the Pearson monument as part of an anniversary celebration in 1997. [483]

U-20 and the Aftermath

Dr. Pearson had been warned, and he did understand undersea warfare. In spite of an incredibly busy schedule, he had taken the time to work with a small radio company to design a device to detect submarines under water. The concept had been shown to U.S. Navy Department officials, and Pearson's first appointment in London was with the British Admiralty to discuss the theory and designs.[484] Devoted associates begged him not to leave New York for Liverpool on the Lusitania. Pearson was very familiar with the Lusitania and its capabilities. He and Mabel had made the inaugural cruise in 1907, when the great ship had broken all speed records for the Atlantic crossing. It may be Pearson believed the fast liner could outrun the slow German submarines. Many other prominent passengers felt that way. This was a routine voyage for them. The Lusitania had made 202 crossings since 1907. It was not as though they did not know of the danger. The German embassy had placed notices in the shipping newspapers stating clearly that Germany was at war with Great Britain. Waters around the British Isles had been declared a war zone. On the day the Lusitania left the New York docks, May 1, 1915, an advertisement inserted in *The New York Times* by the German embassy, clearly directed to Lusitania passengers, stated that "travelers sailing in the war zone on ships of Great Britain or her allies do so at their own risk." Those on board in the Grand Salon, reading the paper with their morning coffee, scoffed. They might have been more concerned had they known dock hands had loaded 5,468 rounds of small-arms ammunition and other military supplies in a forward hold.[485] They also might have been less complacent had they known the British Admiralty helped finance the ship in return for certain design features, including gun-mount bases, to enable a quick conversion to a merchant warship in time of war. Lusitania was officially listed as a "merchant cruiser." German Imperial Navy intelligence knew all of this.

As the ship approached the Irish headlands on the morning of May 6, there was nothing to suggest the scoffers were wrong. The voyage had been uneventful and the seas calm. The captain ordered routine precautions. The crew closed portholes and hatches, swung out the 18 lifeboats, and posted additional lookouts. Life boat drills were held but only for the crew. Passengers strolling on deck could see the Irish headlands as a smudge on the horizon.

Captain Walther Schwieger in U-boat U-20 had been on patrol in the Irish shipping lanes for just a few days and already had sunk three freighters. He had only one torpedo left. With the submarine moving slowly, just under the surface, he scanned the sea through the periscope.

That evening the Lusitania received a message from the Admiralty warning of submarine activity. Another message said avoid the headlands. The night passed quietly as did the morning of May 7. At 2:08 in the afternoon, a prominent London artist was strolling on the starboard side when a woman asked, "This isn't a torpedo is it?" At the same instant, a forecastle lookout shouted in is megaphone, "Torpedo coming on the starboard side."

Captain Schwieger's last torpedo ran true and struck the Lusitania's starboard bow. Seconds later a huge explosion, perhaps caused by coal dust in the forward boiler room, blew out the side of the starboard bow. The ship immediately began to list. The ensuing minutes saw a range of reactions to the sudden shock of the disaster: disbelief, heroism, cowardliness (but not a lot), denial, frantic searches for children, stoic acceptance, and instant action. Surprisingly, in the chaos as the ship listed farther to starboard and began to sink by the bow, there was little panic. In less than 20 minutes the ship was gone. Only the twin screws on the stern showed above the surface. In less than three minutes, they too were gone.

The total number aboard was 1,962, made up of 1,263 passengers, 696 crew, and three stowaways. Sixty-one percent (1,198) died, including 129 Americans. More bad luck made the numbers high. The blast destroyed the power system, making it completely dark below deck. The list made it difficult to lower and enter the lifeboats from the starboard side and impossible on the port side. Only six of the 18 boats were launched successfully. The worst luck was the Lusitania's location. Even though she sank within eleven miles of the Irish headland, no ships or fishing boats of any kind were closer than two hours. The telegraph operator stayed at his key tapping out the SOS on a weak battery backup system. One message was received by a shore station and relayed. Ships were immediately dispatched from several ports, but it took too long. Many floating in life jackets died of hypothermia and injuries before help arrived. The relief ships found scores of dead among those still alive floating in the wreckage.[486]

Immediately, from the U.S., Great Britain, and Germany, came recriminations, protests, and justifications. What Captain Schwieger knew or did not know and what his specific orders were continue to be debated to this day. The loss of its citizens became a major factor in turning isolationists in the U.S. towards entry into the war.

None of this was relevant to the families, friends, and associates who had lost someone in the disaster. For each death, a vacuum existed where a vital, functioning person once stood. In no situation was this more evident than that of Fred Stark Pearson. The master juggler suddenly disappeared and the objects he so easily kept in the air crashed around those who watched.

The Will

The press reported that Pearson left an estate worth 50 million, and Tufts and other institutions would receive large bequests.[487] It is unlikely that many if any beneficiaries, including family members, received much.

Ward Pearson took the brunt of the fallout from his parents' sudden absence. Ward was competent and a well-trained engineer. Dr. Pearson had provided him with an excellent education and broad experience in the Pearson enterprises including banking. In 1915, he was working for the

Pearson Engineering Company in New York. At 27 years old, he was no match for the trickery and machinations he was about to face. In spite of his interest in the education and careers of his two sons, Dr. Pearson apparently had not kept them up to date on the scope or detail of his operations.

The will named Ward as executor along with Henry Irving Miller, president of the Mexico North Western Railway Company and the Madera Lumber Company. As probate dragged on, James Dunn, Pearson's financial partner, replaced Miller.

Gilmore G. Cooke, author of *The Existential Joys of Fred Stark Pearson,* wrote his book to describe and display in print Fred Stark Pearson's engineering achievements. Cooke also wanted to clear Pearson's name and reputation. After his death, Dr. Pearson was eulogized as the greatest engineer in the world. Shortly thereafter he was slammed by a sustained effort to destroy his reputation and businesses. Cooke refers to this as the "Great Hoax." First, rumors began to circulate in the financial markets that Pearson was bankrupt. Next, he was accused of illegally obtaining loans to shore up his companies. Lenders and investors in London, New York, and Montreal became concerned.[488]

It is impossible to know how much Pearson was really worth in 1915. Assets like the Edgewood estate were in Mabel's name and were sold piecemeal by the family. In Chihuahua, the Mexico North Western Railway was in receivership and lumber-mill production erratic. It would have been difficult to determine what value this operation or other Pearson projects would add to his estate. Still, the portfolio did have stocks and bonds that could be actively traded.

Cooke identifies Canadian railroad-magnate William Mackenzie as the prime perpetrator of the Great Hoax. Mackenzie was powerful and intimidating. He was chairman of the board of the Brazilian Traction complex and familiar with Pearson's affairs. In 1915, at age 66, it is clear he intended to fill the leadership vacuum left by Dr. Pearson for his own benefit.

Barely two months had passed after the memorials and the burial before Mackenzie filed a lawsuit challenging the probate. This began eight years of litigation, smears, and struggle for control. Ward Pearson was not only no match for Mackenzie, correspondence uncovered by Cooke suggests that he began to doubt his father.

Mackenzie gained enough control that he was able to disband the Pearson Engineering Company and replace it with his own company, the Canadian Engineering Company. He purged the Pearson companies in Brazil, Mexico, Canada, Spain, and Texas of many of Pearson's loyal officers and employees, including Henry I. Miller, president of the Madera Lumber Company and vice-president of the MNWR, duties he had assumed in 1912. Miller was also president and an investor in the Texas Land and Development Company. [489] Another was John O. Crockett, vice president of the MNWR since 1911 and one of the men responsible for holding the railroad together during the worst of the Revolution. He opposed Mackenzie's move to issue receivers' notes to generate cash and was fired in August 1916.

Stock shares and bonds in Mexico Tramways and Mexico Light and Power made up a significant portion of Pearson's estate. Mackenzie generated a letter to investors in the board's name, stating that Pearson had lied about the companies and conditions were much worse than he had reported. Company bond prices dropped, and the stock plunged from $80 to $5, wiping out that portion of the estate.

Behind Mackenzie's actions, at least in part, was the fact that his North Canadian Railway was failing and would be nationalized shortly after his death in 1923. His financial back was against the wall, and he needed money desperately. Yet, this makes his maneuvers against Pearson's reputation and estate puzzling and seems counterproductive. How did it help his financial problem to fire key officers and employees of the productive companies or to drive down the value of companies in which he was invested? His actions seem more vindictive than practical. There is evidence that Pearson family members were spied on. Another extreme example involves the chemistry building at Tufts. Mackenzie had nothing to do with Tufts, but when the university administrators wanted to honor Dr. Pearson by naming the new chemistry building after him, Mackenzie intervened and was so intimidating they backed down.

Cooke suggests he might have tried to take control of the growing Pearson enterprises in the early days of the tramway boom but was unsuccessful.[490] Mackenzie appears to have held a grudge. Whatever his motives, he did not save his railroad empire, but he did destroy the Pearson estate and besmirched Dr. Pearson's reputation.

The Tufts' chemistry building eventually was called Pearson Hall, one of the few monuments with his name. Large, still-operating hydroelectric and irrigation projects on four continents are mute monuments to his memory. His street railway projects followed him into obscurity, but they remember him in Barcelona. The monument with his name still stands in the Pedrales Plaza.

10

—

Three Haciendas

Palomas Land and Cattle Company

Edwin J. Marshall was one of the transplanted entrepreneurs that developed Southern California in the late 19th and early 20th century. From a Quaker family in Maryland, he left home at age 15 in 1875, and in a few years owned a successful ranch in Texas. He moved to Beaumont, Texas at the beginning of the oil boom and used his administrative skills to help form the major oil company called Texaco.

Marcus, Edwin Marshall's only son, had health problems, and in 1904 the family decided to leave Texas for the more healthful California climate. Marshall joined a bank and began speculating with J.S. Torrance, the founder of Torrance, California. His new partner convinced him to buy a 36,166-acre coastal ranch in Santa Barbara County called Jesús María, a former Mexican land grant. Marshall was involved in many businesses over his lifetime, but ranching was his first love. The Jesús María became the family home. After his death in 1937, the government took over most of the ranch, and in 1958, it became Vandenberg Air Force Base.[491]

Marshall bought more ranches, including the Chino Ranch, a 46,000-acre spread east of Los Angeles that became the City of Chino.

In 1906, he acquired 1,012,000 hectares (2.5 million acres) in northern Chihuahua and formed the Palomas Land and Cattle Company. The property stretched from the Sonora border east across northern Chihuahua to the outskirts of Ciudad Juárez. He shipped 50,000 Hereford cows to the new ranch from his breeding operation at the Jesús María.

Ranch fences were always a part of Marshall's careful plans. According to a *Los Angeles Times* article, the Palomas fence started 15 miles west of El Paso and stretched 160 miles to the Arizona border, the "largest fenced ranch in the world."[492] Much of the land was desert, but Marshall's management enabled his employees to ship 4,000 head each year to the Jesús María for fattening and subsequent sale in the Los Angeles market.

Ranch operations continued through the Revolution, apparently without serious interruption. Edwin Marshal and Marcus (whose health recovered in California) made many trips to Palomas during the conflict. A family picture shows Marcus' wife holding a Lewis gun in front of a bullet-pocked adobe wall. The photo was obviously posed, but the pock marks were real.[493]

After the Revolution, the wave of resentment against foreign ownership pushed the somewhat reluctant Mexican government to expropriate large landholdings. The process accelerated during Lázaro Cárdenas' presidency, 1934-40. He nationalized the oil fields and created PEMEX. He also used Article 27 of 1917 Constitution to break up haciendas and create ejidos. The Marshall family still owned Palomas as late as March 1931, when Marcus became ill on an inspection trip there and died.[494]

Six years later in 1937, his father Edwin Marshall died. By that time others had taken over his interest in Palomas and President Cárdenas began breaking up the huge rancho. In 1940, the Palomas Land and Cattle Company ceased to exist.[495]

San José Babícora

George Hearst left Missouri at age 30 to join the California Gold Rush. He had some success buying and selling mining claims, but after investing in Comstock Lode silver mines, he became fabulously wealthy. With his new-found wealth, he bought several large ranches including Piedras Negras on the California coast, today's San Simeon State Park. He was part of the syndicate that bought the famous Gray Ranch in the bootheel of New Mexico. In 1886, just after Gerónimo left northern Chihuahua forever, he traded his interest in the Gray Ranch for a basin of rolling grassland, south of the Casas Grandes Valley, called San José Babícora. The ranch headquarters was almost equidistant from the 17th century mission town of Namiquipa to the east and the new mill town of Madera to the west.

After his death in 1891, the property passed to his widow, Phoebe, and then to their son William Randolph Hearst, after she died in 1919. The younger Hearst had built a powerful newspaper empire, and while the ranch interested him, it was just one of his diverse activities that ranged from politics to movie making.

The exact property size of the San José Babícora is not certain, but it exceeded 405,000 hectares (one million acres). The Hearsts eventually put 60,000 Herefords on the ranch plus other quality stock.

A year after George Hearst purchased the ranch in 1887, his vaqueros drove 4,000 head across the border into the U.S. at the Antelope Wells crossing, reputed to be the largest single herd driven into the U.S. as of that date.

Antelope Wells, *El Berrendo*, was considered and still may be the most remote official entry between Mexico and the U. S. President Ulysses S. Grant supposedly created the entry station in 1872 to accommodate his friend Luis Terrazas.[496]

In addition to the Hereford cattle, the Hearsts put other quality blooded stock on the ranch, including Morgan horses. The Morgan, the first horse breed developed in the United States, became a passion for both George and William Randolph Hearst. They shipped several back and forth from San Simeon to San José Babícora as they attempted to improve their quality.

A story circulated that during the Revolution Hearst's ranch manager moved some of the best Morgans to a hiding place in the Casas Grandes Valley. An old local LDS resident told historian Philip Stover that he knew the location of the hiding place. About three miles north of Mata Ortiz, old cottonwood trees along the Palanganas River formed a thick canopy. Underneath the foliage, wide cool areas provided ideal space for picnics, nocturnal assignations, and hiding horses. This was where Hearst's vaqueros hid the Morgans, according to the old man.[497] The horses could have grazed at night in the tall grass along the river and then moved under the trees during the day. No one really knows what happened to the Morgans, but Mata Ortiz has a reputation for breeding quality horses. While it seems unlikely any Mata Ortiz horses descend from Hearst's Morgans, the story adds to the local lore.

The San José Babícora Ranch survived the Revolution intact in spite of depredations on the herds by Pancho Villa and other rebels. Perhaps even more amazing, the ranch, a huge foreign-owned property, survived the volatile political decades after the Revolution ended. The government expropriated portions three different times. It appears even the liberal President Lázaro Cárdenas was unwilling to challenge the muckraking power of Hearst's newspapers. It was not until after Hearst died in 1951 that the government confiscated the last tract. Even then, the Hearst family was paid 2.5 million dollars in compensation. A *New York Times* headline, dated August 16, 1953, read, "Mexico Will Take Vast Hearst Ranch: One Million Acres in Chihuahua Area to Become Small Farms—Family to Receive Bonds."[498]

In 1954, government agronomists divided 123,000 acres (49, 776 hectares) into small farms.[499]

Hacienda Corralitos, Apaches to Revolution

No rancho in the Casas Grandes Valley ever played a larger or longer role than Corralitos. The Zuloaga family owned it for over 40 years. After Captain José Zuloaga died in 1868, his son Carlos took charge along with ranch manager Ramón Remigio Luján. By 1880, the family mining interests had shifted to other locations south of Ciudad Chihuahua, and they sold Hacienda Corralitos. Perhaps the heirs could not deal with the Apaches as well as Don José.

Two Texans bought the property, Major George B. Zimpelman, a Confederate veteran, rancher, and speculator from Austin, Texas and Josiah F. Crosby, a lawyer and pioneer developer of El Paso. He was part of a syndicate that purchased the Ponce de León property (originally owned by the family of Juan Azcárate, the founder of Corralitos), which became the core of El Paso.

An employee at that time was William A. Wallace, described as a sheepherder, butcher, and flour-mill operator. The Wallace family later would play a major role in Corralitos history, a role that continues today.

Zimpelman and Crosby wanted a quick turnover. Almost immediately after obtaining title, they brokered a deal to sell to a New York syndicate headed by Edwin D. Morgan, (not to be confused with J.P. Morgan, a sixth cousin).[500] Crosby and Zimpelman retained shares in the new company and Major Zimpelman stayed as manager.[501]

The powerful banker Edwin D. Morgan, a Civil War general, former governor of New York, and former U.S. Senator, saw that conditions were ideal for profitable cattle production in northern Chihuahua. He was in poor health and very shortly turned control of the Corralitos Company to his grandson and protégée of the same name. The young Edwin D. Morgan was not yet 30 when the Corralitos Cattle Company was formed. He was born into his grandfather's elite New York family and became an accomplished horseman and famous racing yachtsman. Substantial investors in the company included former U.S. vice president Levi P. Morton and Thomas Wentmore Peirce, Jr., the son of a Texas railroad magnate and landowner. Peirce, a board member, held a major position in the Corralitos Company stock as well as holding notes for loans. When George Zimpelman died, Peirce bought his shares from the estate.

Dr. C.E. Campbell in his book on Corralitos, *Mines, Cattle, and Rebellion*, reproduced hundreds of telegrams as well as business and personal letters sent among officers, board members, managers, lawyers, and government officials of both countries. A careful reading of these letters reveals not only historical facts, but the attitudes, dreams, and frustrations of the various players, from campesinos to Wall Street magnates. The correspondence tells an intimate story of 50 years of North American capitalism in the Casas Grandes Valley during the most difficult period in Mexico's history.

The syndicate's initial interest was the cattle operation. However, by 1889 Mexico's mining-tax laws had changed, making mining investment more attractive. Morgan reorganized the company into two separate entities with a common board: The Corralitos Cattle Company and the Candelaria Mining Company. Morgan was president of both companies between 1899 and 1917. It was a good business decision. The revamped mines around San Pedro Peak produced a stream of rich ore.

To comply with Mexican law prohibiting foreign ownership within the "Protective Zone" of approximately 100 kilometers from the border, two Mexican subsidiaries to the cattle and mining companies were created, Compañía Ramos S.A. and Compañía San Pedro S.A.[502]

To process the ore, the company built a smelter in El Paso and a concentrator to separate the minerals. To bring the ore (and cattle) from Corralitos to El Paso, a third company was incorporated to build a railroad, the Rio Grande, Sierra Madre and Pacific Railroad. Whatever dreams Morgan and his associates held to justify the "Pacific" part of the title, the practical effect was to create the first railroad in the Casas Grandes Valley. The inaugural train ran to Corralitos on June 25, 1897. By August, the track passed through Dublán to end at a new location called Nuevo Casas Grandes.

In none of the Corralitos transactions do the names Luis Terrazas or Enrique Creel appear, in contrast to other developments by foreign entrepreneurs. Terrazas was governor in 1880 at the time of the hacienda purchase. Perhaps he felt this was Zuloaga territory and did not interfere.

Lt. Britton Davis replaced Zimpelman as Corralitos manager in 1886. The son of a former Texas governor, he had distinguished himself as a junior officer during General Crook's campaign against the Apaches and Gerónimo. How this honorable service qualified him to manage a large cattle and mining operation is a question. However, he served as general manager for almost 20 years and appears to have accomplished a great deal. Under Davis, company ranch lands expanded significantly through acquisitions of ranchos Ramos, Las Varas, Tres Alamos, and Arroyo Seco.

Corralitos cattle were a mix of ordinary range stock. In 1900, the entire northern border of the ranch was fenced with barbed wire. This enabled Davis and his foremen to upgrade the quality of the animals by keeping them separate from neighboring range cattle. Over 6,000 employees, mostly Mexicans, worked for the two companies. This helped the relationship between company officials and the local people.

Offsetting this feeling of tolerance for their North American employers was company use of Governor Creel's Municipal Land Act of 1905 that allowed people of means to "denounce" and take over properties of owners unable to pay new fees or provide clear titles. The record is not clear, but it appears Britton Davis used the law to denounce Casas Grandes communal land. These acquisitions angered local people and sowed more seeds of rebellion.

Davis became increasingly diverted by his own projects and resigned in 1906, perhaps under pressure. His replacement was an assistant, Edward C. Houghton.

Houghton proved to be a devoted and capable manager. Both his sons worked for him and served him well. He had a good relationship with Morgan and often rode with him in a private railroad car to and from ranch headquarters and company offices in El Paso. Houghton lived at Corralitos but was able to maintain his own farm he purchased in 1912 near Mesilla Park, New Mexico. His wife lived for a time at Hacienda Ramos and became an amateur archaeologist, amassing over 200 Casas Grandes pots. Most of this collection, originally acquired by the Gila Pueblo Archaeological Foundation, was transferred to the Arizona State Museum in Tucson in 1950.

The railroad opened the Casas Grandes Valley but lost money for Morgan's investors. In 1904, the line was sold to Colonel Greene. The cattle and mining companies continued operations on a large scale until the Revolution.

The year 1911 may have been a high point for the two companies. In a November report to the Corralitos Board of Directors, Morgan described the many improvements that had been made to support the cattle, now numbering over 60,000. The market price for their premium animals was high. Corn, alfalfa, and vegetables grew well at several locations, and experimental farms had been set up to test other potential crops. Forty thousand five hundred hectares (100,000 acres) had been cleared of prairie dogs. The infrastructure—fences, corrals, loading chutes, barns, windmills, irrigation pumps, watering tanks—was in excellent condition. The only downside was the deteriorating relationship with H.C. Ferris, head of the newly named Mexico North Western Railroad. The line had been resold by Col. Greene to a syndicate headed by Dr. Fred Stark Pearson. Issues remained over easements and parcel ownership that affected the rail service.

Morgan also noted in his report that the "late insurrection" had caused some labor problems, but he expected everything to be normal by January 1, 1912.[503]

The Candelaria mines at San Pedro were also doing well. In 1898, Britton Davis had hired Morris B. Parker, a young but experienced mining engineer. Parker would play a major role in the mines of Chihuahua and Sonora over the next three decades.

After his initial assessment of Candelaria, Parker could see that the mines were inefficient and losing money. The mining operation was actually being supported by the cattle company. Board members in New York reviewing the financial statements could see this as well. They objected to "throwing cattle down the mine shaft." Parker was given six months to turn the mines around.

Seeping water always had been a problem. In Spanish times, lines of workers carried cow-hide bags of water up the ladders to dump outside. Parker had tunnels hacked and blasted through the rock to drain water. By broadening the productive rock faces or "stopes" and finding new stopes, ore shipping increased significantly. Losses turned to profits, and the Candelaria Mining Company became one of the richest in northern Chihuahua as well as a significant asset for the board.[504]

During his first inspection, Parker found underground chapels in each mine. Experienced employees told him to ignore them and not to interfere with his workers' religion or politics. It proved to be good advice.

Parker left in 1903, but successors continued to add bigger, more powerful pumps and expand operations with the latest equipment. A town grew up with business offices, machine shop, carpenter shop, maintenance facilities, storage buildings, hotel, employee's quarters, general store, and assay office. By 1910, almost one half million dollars had been invested to significantly increase ore production and profits.[505]

In January 1912, Dr. Pearson made an inspection trip to Mexico with one of the railroad vice presidents, H.I. Miller. In Ciudad Juárez, he heard about the problems between his railroad manager, H.C. Ferris, and Corralitos' Edward C. Houghton. Pearson invited Houghton and the Candelaria mine manager, George A. Laird (since 1908 one of Parker's successors), to meet with him and Miller. Ferris was not present. With characteristic charm, Pearson said the mistreatment of Corralitos had been a "deplorable mistake," and after two meetings resolved the issues that had been at the core of the animosity. There is no record, but he apparently contacted H.C. Ferris and gently or firmly explained the importance of Corralitos as a customer. He told Houghton and Laird that the railroad was there to serve them, even offering a private car and engine for Morgan to use whenever he wished.[506]

After Pearson's tour, political stability in Chihuahua deteriorated rapidly. Within three months, Pascual Orozco and José Salazar revolted against President Madero and occupied Ciudad Juárez. Their loosely controlled rebel troops terrorized the countryside, killing cattle and looting towns and ranchos. General Salazar forced the LDS colonists into the Exodus that began in July 1912. Houghton and Morgan pleaded their case in vain with the American Consulate, politicians in Washington, and representatives of President Madero's government. One high Madero official denied there were any rebels left in Chihuahua.[507]

At the San Pedro mines, the looting of company stores and the disruptions of coal delivery, caused by confiscation and railway-line destruction, forced Laird to close the mines. This caused great hardship for the Mexican employees. General Salazar sent a warning to the North Americans at San Pedro that they were not safe. Most left for the U.S.

Ambrosio Castañeda "Bill" Hernández was a small child when the raiders began to attack Corralitos. His father worked there, and the family lived in a compound of attached houses on three sides of a small plaza. A horse corral stood at the open north side. In an interview in 1997, he proudly recalled that he was assigned as a lookout. He sat on top of a large boulder. When he saw a cloud of dust, which signaled approaching horsemen, he ran to warn the neighbors.[508]

Corralitos suffered so much stock loss and damage that Houghton developed a contingency plan. On behalf of the cattle company, he began buying ranch land in New Mexico's Las Cruces-Mesilla Park area and even sold his own ranch to the company. Eventually, he accumulated 400,000 acres into a ranch called the C.S. Ranch. It is not clear what the initials stand for. People in New Mexico always called it the "Corralitos" Ranch.

The property stretched past Lordsburg to the Southern Pacific rail line near Deming. The plan was to move the remaining cattle and horse herds across the border to the new property.[509]

Houghton obtained government permits, paid the fees, and began shipping cattle to the C.S. and continued for the next three years. For the permits, there always was the question of who the "government" was at any given time.

On July 19, 1912, as the LDS colonists were about to send the first trains from Pearson, Houghton was arrested and brought before the rebel General Salazar at his headquarters in Casas Grandes. The charge was exporting horses without a permit. In his letter to Morgan, he did not repeat what the bombastic Salazar said, but when he was temporarily released the next day, he was convinced Salazar would demand a heavy fine.[510] There was no further correspondence with Morgan on the subject, suggesting that in spite of the threats, there were no more consequences other than a bad experience for Houghton.

Ten months later in late May 1913, he shipped 32 car loads of cattle to the border. John O. Crockett, a vice president of the Mexico North Western Railroad, telegraphed him that the train had been stopped by troops under Máximo Castillo. The rogue general demanded $1.25 per head, which presumably was paid.[511]

In another letter to E. D. Morgan, dated October 10, 1915, Houghton wrote about his two meetings with Pancho Villa at Villa's headquarters in Ciudad Juárez, when Villa was preparing his campaign into Sonora to attack Agua Prieta. Houghton wanted written permission to transport 4,000 head of cattle and horses across the border. In the first meeting in Villa's personal railroad car, the general demanded eight dollars U.S. per head. He insisted on a decision by the next day, warning that he planned to lay waste to northern Chihuahua to deny resources to Carranza's forces. This was a great deal of money for a businessman like Houghton. Prior to Villa taking control of Chihuahua, he had paid Huerta's federal government officials one and a half pesos per head. The dollar and twenty-five cents paid to General Castillo may have been the highest price previously paid.

The following day, Houghton tried to negotiate, but Villa was adamant. Houghton contacted a Carranza representative and was assured that Villa would soon be driven from northern Chihuahua. As far as the Carranza representative was concerned, Villa's permission to move stock was irrelevant.[512]

Prior to Villa's departure, Morgan reluctantly approved the eight dollar permit price. In his letter to board member Thomas Wentmore Peirce on

November 29, he enthusiastically reported that after paying for 4,000, they had shipped 5,000. The best animals had been sent to the New Mexico ranch and the remainder sold for a good price. All bills were paid.[513]

He doesn't mention it, but shipping arrangements must have been made with Roy Hoard of Pearson's Mexico North Western Railway. Hoard played a major role in the struggle to keep the railroad running during the Revolution.

By the time of that shipment, the company ranch holdings, particularly the main Corralitos ranch and the Casas Grandes ranch (the communal land "denounced" and taken over while Britton Davis was manager) had suffered serious damage and loss of stock. Houghton's contingency plan had worked and a large herd of transferred animals were grazing on the C. S. Ranch.

Many of the Mexican employees had gone to the New Mexico ranch as well. A.C. Hernández said in his interview that his father left with a group of men, and three months later the company sent for the families. By this time, Villa's roving patrols searched for men and boys to recruit, willing or not. Those caught trying to run were killed. The group that included Hernández and his mother and an escort of six men left as quietly as they could by wagon for the train station at Ascensión. A patrol caught up with Hernández's group and as the women and children watched, hung the six men. One was Hernández's uncle. The patrol had done its job and allowed the rest to proceed to the station at El Paso and eventually to Mesilla Park and the ranch. Hernández grew up, became a citizen, and spent the rest of his life in the U.S.[514]

Only a small loyal group of Mexican employees remained as Corralitos' caretakers. Gregorio Polanco, the foreman, was born and worked all of his life on the Corralitos. He would pay for his loyalty with his life.

A few months after his defeat at Agua Prieta, on March 9, 1916, Pancho Villa crossed the border with several hundred men and sacked and burned the small town of Columbus, New Mexico. Two days after the Columbus attack, a detachment of Villa's raiders rode into the Corralitos compound on exhausted horses, trailed by eight wagons carrying 26 wounded. During the retreat, their comrades had strapped the wounded men to their horses until they reached Ascensión. There, the raiders confiscated the townspeople's wagons, teams, forage, and food.

After a strenuous eight-hour march from Ascensión toward Casas Grandes, Villa stopped at Vuelta de Alamos about ten miles northwest of Corralitos. He sent 20 men with the wounded to the rancho.[515] They found a large supply of bandages and medical supplies at the ranch compound and turned the Casa de Amo building into a makeshift hospital.

A very angry Villa arrived the next day with more Columbus survivors. He demanded Polanco tell him where the gringos and horses were located. When the foreman replied that the gringos had gone to the U.S. with the horses, wagons, and other equipment, Villa's men beat him, his brother, and his sons. They were hoisted by ropes around their necks on the chapel bell rack (that still stands), tortured, and all shot. Villa spared one son, Gregorio, Jr. Villa shouted to Polanco's wife, the grieving witness to the massacre of her family, that her son had been spared to warn others of their fate if they continued to aid the gringos.[516]

A few frightened workers from Corralitos ran all the way to Dublán to warn friends that Villa was coming to kill gringos and Mexicans who worked for them. Many Mexicans left for Casas Grandes where there was a small garrison of Carranza's soldiers. Villa had sent a message to the garrison commander to join him in killing gringos and any Mexican supporters. If received, the message was ignored. The LDS colonists in Dublán also received word of Villa's intent. Bishop Anson Bowen called a meeting to discuss options that included running to the mountains, escaping by train, trying to hide the women and children, or standing and fighting—all with fatal flaws. Bishop Bowen and two other men drove sixteen miles in an automobile to Colonia Juárez to ask Stake President Joseph C. Bentley what to do. Sick with worry, those waiting behind felt increasing fear as each hour dragged by. Some packed wagons, preparing to run. Late in the evening, the men returned. President Bentley had no solution. The townspeople crowded around Bishop Bowen in the street near Gaskell Romney's house. After a shouted discussion of all the futile options they had already discussed over and over, he looked at them and finally told them to go home, pray, and go to bed. After a few protests, everyone turned and walked home.

They were sleeping when Villa and his troops approached the town at 3:00 a.m., March 13. At the edge of town, the troop paused. Villa gazed at the rows of darkened houses, then gave the order to turn southeast toward Chocolate Pass and out of the Casas Grandes Valley. Villa later said the town had been reinforced by Carranza's army. No one saw the reinforcements. For the LDS residents, there was no question as to what happened. Bishop Call wrote, "We feel that no greater miracle has been wrought in the history of the Mormon Church than this."[517]

Without even a caretaker crew at Corralitos, Carranza's government forces as well as Villa's rebels looted and destroyed what was left of the ranch's infrastructure.

Sometime after the murders, Houghton's son, E.C. Houghton, Jr., returned to Corralitos. General John Pershing's troops, on their campaign to hunt down Villa, camped nearby at Dublán. Houghton felt secure enough to make the trip. With what workers he could find, he cleaned out Casa de Amo and the surrounding buildings and grounds. His father and Morgan visited in May 1916 and were impressed by the cleanup. There was little else going on at Corralitos.

The dedication shown to the business at Corralitos by both Edward C. Houghton and Edwin D. Morgan was impressive. Morgan, as a blue-blood yachtsman with plenty of money, could have diverted himself in other ways. Houghton was capable and well known in New Mexico and already managing the C.S. Ranch. He could have found another ranch management position or gone on his own. Neither needed the problems in Mexico, but they believed in what they had created there and wanted to continue.

In spite of Pershing's presence, it took considerable courage for North Americans to return to the ranch and ride out on inspection tours. On the May trip, they covered all of their extended ranches and properties on horseback. The cattle operations had been destroyed as expected, but surprisingly, they found 3,000 head untouched. They optimistically developed a plan to sell some of the cattle and keep the best for breeding.

Another surprise was the prosperous farms. Raiding parties had ignored the fields of alfalfa, corn, and vegetables. Tres Alamos, southwest of Janos, was particularly impressive with one tract of alfalfa exceeding

1,000 acres (404 hectares). Houghton's and Morgan's restoration plan would center on this farm production.

Each of the farms had workers, and Houghton was particularly concerned that they continue to be paid, quite aware families would suffer if wages stopped. He also knew loyal workers would do their best to protect the properties. He asked permission from Morgan to help the destitute Polanco family now living in a small house in Casas Grandes. Morgan agreed, and they created a small pension for each survivor.

As practical as Morgan and Houghton were, their expectation for a future in Mexico was a dream. They believed Pershing would remain for an extended length of time, but they were wrong. By January 1917, the American Expeditionary Force was gone. The U.S. had shifted its attention to war in France.

A new round of looting and destruction throughout Chihuahua, primarily by Carranza's federal troops, made any recovery plan at Corralitos hopeless. In December 1917, federal soldiers systematically ransacked the Candelaria mines ruining the pumps and all other machinery, tearing down all the buildings—shops, houses, hotel, stores—and hauling off everything that could be carried in wagons. A few months later on June 18, 1917, in a New Jersey court, the Candelaria Mining Company declared bankruptcy. The company lost all of its mineral rights in the San Pedro mining district. Other than some minor surface work, it would be eleven years before other corporations obtained the rights and attempted to reopen the big mines.[518]

The company focus now was on the C.S. Ranch in New Mexico. Work on the Mexico holdings consisted primarily of filing futile claims against the U.S. and Mexican governments.

The tireless Houghton did what he could to keep track of the Chihuahua properties. One source was E.D. Bluth from an old Dublán LDS family. Members of the family had worked at Corralitos in calmer days. Houghton hired him to go periodically to Corralitos to help the remaining caretakers.[519] Bluth would later cause problems for the company.

By this time, Morgan and the board members had decided not to attempt to return to Mexico, at least for the time being. He retired as president after 30 years but remained active on the board, concerned with both business matters and the plight of the loyal Mexican employees. Edward

Shearson, a New York broker, investment banker, and Corralitos stock-holder, became president. He was a poor choice. His financial investment and personal interest in the company were not enough to claim his full attention. He was not even in the U.S. for two years while in France working on war-relief projects. Another investor and a vice president, Richard Trimble, assumed his duties. After his return, Shearson wrote a letter to Thomas Wentmore Peirce in 1919 complaining bitterly about his lack of time and interest to be president.[520] Yet, he still held the title until 1923.

It was a bad time for New York bankers and for the Corralitos investors. Shearson's letter was written as the country was slipping into a world-wide post-World War I recession. Wholesale prices plummeted and bank interest rates rose. Prolonged drought in southern New Mexico turned C.S. Ranch profits into losses. The board was frustrated as their other invest-ments were probably in trouble as well.

On July 21, 1920, the major stockholder, Thomas Wentmore Peirce, wrote an insulting letter to Houghton, implying mismanagement and that he, Peirce, take over direct control of day-to-day operations. Peirce was particularly angry about reports he had received about E. D. Bluth publicly stating that the Corralitos Company was deliberately letting the rancho deteriorate in order to obtain higher reparations. True or not, Peirce knew such rumors would damage relationships with both governments and potential buyers. Obregón was about to supersede Carranza as president of Mexico, and Peirce was convinced that the new president would establish control and allow foreigners to reclaim their properties.[521]

The letter appears not to have offended Houghton. Little was happening at Corralitos. Despite his efforts, most of the ranch land contained no cattle and except for squatters, most farms lay fallow. Houghton could do nothing about it. Peirce was right about one thing. Obregón's ascendency to the president's office ended the Revolution and most of the fighting.

However, the weary end of ten chaotic years did not mean the country would be run for the benefit of foreigners. Squatters already were a serious problem. As early as the summer of 1918, Houghton was receiving reports from his contacts of a channel cut across Corralitos property and of cotton-woods cut down along the river.

A law passed on June, 22, 1920, just before Obregón took power, called *Ley de Tierras Ociosas*, Law of Unused Lands, allowed anyone to "denounce" unused lands and move on to the property for a stipulated length of time, usually three years. The obvious question was the definition of "unused lands." Local people moved on to someone else's property, filed a denouncement, and began farming. Once there, the local government officials were reluctant to remove them, regardless of the protests by the legal owners.

In December 1920, it was safe enough for Houghton to once more travel across the properties to make an inspection trip. For the first time, he drove an automobile. Most large ranchers around Casas Grandes, both Mexican and foreign-owned, had large numbers of squatters, particularly around water sources in order to divert water to fields for spring planting. The dams and diversions cut water off from the remaining Mexican farmers either working for Corralitos as employees or under a tenant arrangement. Even Luis Terrazas could not stop the flood of squatters on Hacienda San Diego. Houghton tried to set up long-term leases with what he called "denouncers" at Casas Grandes and Corralitos, but they refused. Government officials had led them to believe their contracts would be renewed after the initial three years had expired.[522]

They believed for good reasons. For most campesinos, land reform was what the Revolution was about. Bloody battles were not fought to allow the old hacendados and foreign syndicates to again dominate the land.

Faced with these obstacles, Houghton persevered. The focus of the Corralitos Cattle Company had reverted to an exclusively Mexican operation. The C.S. Ranch portion of the New Mexico holdings had been sold, but the company received only partial cash and notes for the balance. The cash did not pay all the debts. Somehow, 6,000 head of cattle had not been included in the sale, and Houghton managed to move them across the border. His vaqueros placed them in an obscure tract of land northeast of Corralitos headquarters.

They salvaged parts from wrecked windmills to rebuild functioning mills that pumped water to troughs. Barbed wire also was salvaged and 155 square miles fenced in an amazingly short length of time.

While Shearson, Peirce, and the other board members fumed, Edwin Morgan made a three-week trip in February 1921 to see for himself. The itinerary included Mexico City. He had prepared well and had letters of introduction to the highest officials. He met with the U.S. Consul and the Mexican Secretary of Agriculture. This led to a cordial meeting with President Obregón in Chapultepec Castle. All tried to reassure Morgan, including Obregón, who made a curious statement, "… it was not at all the intention to pauperize the well-to-do holders to further pauperize the poor."[523]

This may have reflected the government's dilemma as it tried to rejuvenate a stagnant economy in a radicalized atmosphere throughout the country. Whatever it meant, nothing happened at the local level to stop the denuncios at Corralitos, Palomas, San Diego, San José Babícora, and other large holdings.

Morgan found no cordiality at Corralitos. At least 100 squatters claimed land along a six-mile stretch of the Casas Grandes River. Many were hostile and tried to occupy the headquarters compound. At Casa de Amo, Houghton had the doorways filled with adobe bricks to keep intruders out. Pilfering was persistent, and Houghton and his key workers carried guns and never went out at night. It is unclear where Houghton lived at this time, but he may have commuted from Dublán in his automobile.

Morgan wrote a lengthy report to the board with alternative recommendations. Shearson dismissed them all. This appears to be Edwin Morgan's last serious effort to aid Corralitos.

Not so Houghton, who continued to pester officials from the Casas Grandes municipio to Mexico City. A very influential contact, Judge Elbert Gary, president of U.S. Steel, arranged for Houghton to meet with President Obregón. The President was cordial, other officials indifferent. Nothing happened, and the denuncios at Corralitos alone increased to 159.

The problems for landowners were compounded by the arrival in the Casas Grandes Valley of the socialist and communist ideas that had spread through Europe and the U.S. after the Russian Revolution. Radical newspapers and public speakers advocated resisting any form of authority. Extremists began attacking Mexican public figures and North Americans, creating a murderous crime wave. Gunmen fired several shots at George Houghton while he drove through Dublán with several local officials in his father's car. A bullet, perhaps intended for Edward Houghton, who usually sat in the right-hand seat, killed Guadalupe Ponce, the brother-in-law of General Rodrigo M. Quevedo, commander of the local federal troops. George was wounded in the leg and another passenger in the hand.

That same night, the Casas Grandes Municipio president's car was stoned as he drove through Dublán. One stone hit his wife. Enraged, the president pulled out a pistol and emptied it in the direction of the now not-so-brazen attackers, who scattered. The extent of his wife's injuries is unknown. Houghton reported three other murders in an October, 1921 letter to Shearson.[524]

To add to Houghton's problems, he read in the newspaper on March 31 that the governor by executive order had turned over 250,000 acres (101,171 hectares) of company land to the Casas Grandes Ejido. While he protested vehemently to all levels of government, he had to admit that much of the property had been confiscated by Porfirio Díaz in 1886 and sold to the Corralitos Company. The ejidatarios claim dated to the grant made by Teodoro de Croix in 1778.

Also in Janos, the municipio arbitrarily quadrupled its size by expanding borders to include 450,000 acres (182,108 hectares) of improved Corralitos land along the San Pedro River.[525] Houghton's logical legal arguments fell on deaf ears.

In New York, Shearson was doing all he could to find a buyer for any part of the company properties. It is doubtful that he, the board members, or the potential buyers had a realistic understanding of the situation in the Casas Grandes Valley. Some board members and note holders had died and their interests were represented by estate attorneys. On November 22, 1923, Thomas Wentworth Peirce, Jr. died suddenly of a heart attack while hunting on his estate in Massachusetts. He was 46. Other than Morgan, he was the last remaining board member close to the Corralitos operation.

During this entire period, the unstable Mexican federal and state governments led to inconsistent guidance and law enforcement at the local level. The fractious Mexican society of the 1920s and 1930s formed a backdrop for what was happening at Corralitos and the rest of the Casas Grandes Valley. Prerevolutionary hacendados and business magnates were pitted against post-revolutionary elites. Both struggled against campesino organizations, worker unions, and radical reformists. Federal, state, and municipio governments competed for control. The strengths among the factions were relatively equal, prolonging the conflict and delaying true reform. What emerged to stabilize the country was a single political party, *Partido Nacional Revolucionario,* PNR.

Plutarco Elías Calles, starting in 1929, and Lázaro Cárdenas, during his presidency from 1934 to 1940, used their political skills to gradually bring the diverse factions under one wide political tent. Everyone got something, but everyone gave up power to the central federal government. The PNR transitioned into the *Partido Revolución Mexicana,* PRM, and in 1946, to the *Partido Revolucionario Institucional,* PRI. The party, under its various names, tightly controlled politics for the rest of the 20th century.[526]

Obregón's choice to run for president in 1924 (then a four-year term) was Plutarco Elías Calles, Obregón's subordinate commander at the Battle of Agua Prieta in 1915. Adolfo de la Huerta, the finance minister and a former supporter, challenged Obregón and had to be put down forcibly. Calles was elected for the four-year term, beginning 1924, but his political machinations made him the power behind the throne for the next ten years. His strong anti-church views and crackdown on the Catholic Church led to the First Cristero War. This bloody episode indirectly led to Obregón's assassination.

Pressured by Calles, the Congress in Mexico City passed a law eliminating presidential term limits and permitting the non-consecutive reelection of a past president. This opened the way for Obregón to run in 1928. Before he assumed office a Cristero supporter shot him in a restaurant.

Calles, initially a reformer, became a strongman politician. After Obregón's death, he held the government together in an increasingly conservative grip, until Lázaro Cárdenas was elected in 1934. Calles tried to control Cárdenas, who eventually had him arrested and exiled to the United States.

During this volatile period, large land-owner problems in remote Chihuahua were ignored, except for ineffective directives that made no impression on local officials.

In Ciudad Chihuahua, the governor's office almost literally needed a revolving door. In 1923, the governorship changed eight times. Ignacio C.

Enríquez, with whom Houghton and Mexico North Western Railway President Roy Hoard, often dealt, went in and out three times. This unstable pattern continued until the election of General Rodrigo M. Quevedo in 1932. Consistent direction was missing, which gave municipio and other local officials the power to interpret laws and policies as they saw fit. José Quevedo, brother of General Rodrigo M. Quevedo, became president of the Casas Grandes municipio. He was totally unsympathetic to Houghton's claims, even though he was shown directives from Ciudad Chihuahua and Mexico City to enforce certain restrictions on the squatters.

In New York, the Corralitos board struggled in vain to find a buyer or some other solution. To Shearson's and Trimble's credit as major note holders, they were able to secure enough additional funds from the note-holder group to stave off bankruptcy. This plus the sale of the last properties in New Mexico enabled them to pay all current debt and leave the company diminished but financially stable.

Edward Houghton retired to El Paso in 1923. What his thoughts were about his years riding the Corralitos and cajoling politicians and investors will never be known. He died five years later at 66. His son George, with the bullet scar on his leg, became manager.

There was not much to manage. The ranch operation was essentially defunct. What happened to Houghton's hidden herd and how long the employee payroll and pensions continued is unknown. Most of the employees, farmers and vaqueros, gradually left to work elsewhere. The government continued to take land for ejidos, and some undoubtedly stayed to work communal land.

Nothing significant happened for 10 to 12 more years, until Richard Trimble and George Houghton sold the remaining Corralitos property to General Rodrigo M. Quevedo and William Wallace, sometime between 1938 and 1941.[527]

11

Another Culture, the Chinese

Siete Culturas

D rivers passing through the city of Nuevo Casas Grandes on their way to Mata Ortiz cannot miss the political signs and painted walls promoting various candidates. They are sometimes startled to see a name like Wong showing up among the office seekers. Such a name on an otherwise forgettable sign hints that in some past time Chinese joined the complex ethnic mix that became the people of Northern Chihuahua.

The U.S. Chinese Exclusion Act of 1882

The expansion of ranches, farms, mines, and later railroads in the 19th century required hands. There simply were not enough European immigrants, mestizos, or indigenous people to perform the necessary labor. While most Chinese workers did not come to Mexico until after 1880, there was a labor demand that dated back at least as far as the 1860s. Emperor Maximilian in 1865 granted a concession to a contractor to recruit Chinese and Egyptians to work in Mexico. Five hundred Egyptians came along with an unknown number of Chinese. How the Egyptians fared is not reported, but the Chinese did well.

The California Gold Rush brought the first Chinese to North America. This began a contradictory sequence of demand for their services versus overt racism and demand for their exclusion. Thousands of Chinese laborers were used by the Central Pacific to build the first transcontinental railroad across the Sierra Nevada Mountains. Completion of the railroad in 1869 was followed by thirteen years of legal and social rejection, culminating in the Chinese Exclusion Act of 1882. Variations of this law persisted in the U.S. until 1952. All Chinese were denied immigration or even entry with a few exceptions such as diplomats, students, businessmen, and other categories that varied as the law evolved over 70 years.

Mexico was different. Overt discrimination of Chinese did not begin for the most part until the Revolution and accelerated during the post-revolution years. The U.S. and Mexican policies toward the Chinese diverged sharply. The Porfirio Díaz regime wanted to build infrastructure. This caused a spike in Chinese immigration to Mexico. The contrasting laws also had the contrary side effect of stimulating a vigorous human smuggling business from Mexico into the U.S.

In 1926, the total number of Chinese living throughout Mexico was estimated to be 26,000.[528] The number probably never exceeded 40,000. At the beginning of the Revolution in 1910 about 1,325 had found their way to Chihuahua, many of those to Ciudad Chihuahua.[529] A few came as early as the 1890s to the Casas Grandes Valley. According to one source, about 100 worked in the Candelaria mines. Some became houseboys or cooks for the mine managers.[530] The flamboyant Colonel William Greene loved Chinese food. When he began the extension of the railroad line from Nuevo Casas Grandes, he hired several Chinese, who had worked their way across Baja California and Sonora into Chihuahua. These workers settled around the Nuevo Casas Grandes station. Soon they had two hotels, a laundry, and three restaurants, presumably frequented by Colonel Bill.[531]

The New York Times, November 20, 1900, reported that large mine owners in Chihuahua and other northern states were so short of mine workers that they negotiated contracts with agents to bring 10,000 Chinese laborers to Mexico.[532] Numbers of this size never materialized, but the article reflects a process that had begun the previous year. Qing Dynasty officials resisted efforts to recruit workers in their country for at least fifteen years. Under pressure from the Mexican government, China and Mexico formally agreed with the Treaty of Amity and Commerce to allow citizens of both countries to travel back and forth without restrictions. This led to a system that allowed businessmen in Mexico to contract with tong (Chinese immigrant societies or brotherhoods) representatives in San Francisco, California for delivery of workers.

Chinese immigrant laborers brought a work ethic and business sense that enabled many of the first generation to become owners rather than renters and lenders rather than borrowers. While they scattered across all of Mexico, their numbers were never large, and they tended to concentrate in the northwestern states—Baja California, Sinaloa, Sonora, Coahuila, and Chihuahua. They were very visible, having found a profitable niche in the small capitalist world of retail trade and services. North Americans and Europeans for the most part invested in large capital projects, and the ordinary Mexican knew them only as remote employers. In contrast, the people, particularly the poorer classes, dealt with the neighborhood Chinese shopkeeper every day on a very personal level, haggling over credit to secure basic necessities and often behind on payments. While this caused resentment, it did not surface until the Revolution unleashed a poisonous mixture of nationalism, envy, and racism, particularly in Sonora. For the next 25 years the Chinese endured official and unofficial persecution, causing them to lose property and even their lives. Some gave up and returned to China, but others picked up whatever they had left and moved on. Today, Mexicali, on the northern Baja California border, has a high concentration of the descendants of Chinese who escaped persecution elsewhere.

Agustín Chinolla of Casas Grandes

On a barren hill north of Casas Grandes stands the moldering walls of the 17th century Spanish mission called El Convento. Archeologists say the shallow depressions, overgrown with mesquite in front, are the remains of pit houses of an ancient people from the thousand-year-old Viejo Period. Down the slope from El Convento lies a cemetery that is new compared to the old Spanish walls or pit houses, but still shows wind-worn inscriptions dating back almost 100 years.

Most names etched into the stones are in Spanish, reflecting the classic mestizo culture—the mating of the conquering Spanish and the native

Remains of El Convento, the Franciscan mission church of San Antonio
de Padua de Casas Grandes, abandoned in the late 1680's.
Photo: Courtesy of John Wingate, 2005

peoples so dramatically represented in Mexican history and art by *conquis-*
tador Hernán Cortés and his Indian mistress Malinche and more subtly by
the Spanish walls of the *Convento* and the nearby pit houses. However, a
few headstones show evidence of another bloodline injected into the basic
mestizo mix. At least seven have names etched with Chinese characters.

Each week an elderly Chinese man, past ninety, came to the cemetery
to water the trees and clean around the graves. He brought water in his
pickup to fill a small cement pond built by him. From the pond, he carried
a bucket of water to each eucalyptus and cypress tree lining the cemetery.
He planted every tree himself as a memorial to a lost son, a lost brother,
and to a vanishing Chinese culture in Mexico.

Agustín Chinolla was the patriarch of the Chinese/Mexicans of northern Chihuahua.[533] A plaque on the wall of a restaurant once owned by his
daughter in Casas Grandes honored his work to preserve the heritage of the
local Chinese/Mexican community. His family story provides a window

into the lives of the Chinese people who immigrated to northern Chihua-hua and assimilated into its culture.

Agustín's father, Chew Gee Hing, known as José Chinolla in Mexico, came to Sonora about 1878 when he was 12 years old.[534] He worked on the railroad in the Agua Prieta-Douglas area. By age 18 he had accumulated enough money to return to China to seek a wife. The bride selected was Chou Lee See, whose Mexican name became Elisa Lee (or Li). A misunder-standing during an interview in the immigration office changed his family name forever to "Chinolla."

Chew, now Chinolla, brought Elisa Lee back to Fronteras (a town that played an important role in the last days of Gerónimo and the Apache Wars) in northeastern Sonora, began a family, and went into business. He eventually established a significant commercial enterprise consisting of stores and farms.

José Chinolla built and lost three small fortunes, similar to the experi-ences of many other Sonoran Chinese. These indefatigable small-time cap-italists persevered and despite adversity, acquired many farms and most of

Agustín Chinolla Lee and Spencer MacCallum. Chinolla's mother's maiden name "Lee" follows his surname in typical Spanish fashion. Photo: 2008

the laundries, barbershops, and stores in the state. They paid off whomever necessary to be allowed to do business. Chinolla was shrewd enough to gain the friendship and protection of one of the powerful local leaders, General Plutarco Elías Calles. This stood him in good stead, at least for a while.

Agustín Chinolla was born on January 18, 1915, in the midst of the Revolution. He grew up as warring factions across the nation gradually absorbed or annihilated each other. General Plutarco Elías Calles, one of the commanders at the Battle of Agua Prieta, became governor of Sonora the year Agustín was born. Calles moved on to the presidency of all of Mexico in 1924.

The Sonoran Chinese were internally divided as well. They separated into two "tongs" that competed for control and fought each other for an edge. Bribes to government officials played a big part in this ongoing struggle.

In 1926, the state government demanded money from Chinese businessmen, perhaps thinking the political infighting between the tongs was a sign of weakness. All refused to pay, and in fact grew stronger over the next few years. By 1928, Chinese controlled 80 percent of the retail grocery business. Anti-Chinese feelings remained and grew during the early years of the Depression. By 1931, Governor Francisco Elías felt in a position to begin a campaign of persecution. This became part of nationwide anti-foreigner sentiment that swept Mexico. Jews, particularly in Mexico City, also suffered during this time. In Sonora, the unofficial goal became eradication of the Chinese. The goal became official with the election in 1931 of Rodolfo Elías Calles, General Calles' son.

Property was vandalized and confiscated. Chinese were attacked and murdered. Many were rounded up and shipped across the border to the U.S., where immigration officials promptly deported them to China. Some fled to other parts of Mexico, particularly Baja California and Chihuahua. Over the next four to five years, 300 crossed the rugged Sierra Madre mountains east through Púlpito Pass from Sonora to Chihuahua. The rendezvous point was Casas Grandes, the first major town over the mountains. Some stayed in the valley and others moved on.

For José Chinolla, the old friendship with General Plutarco Elías Calles paid off. In 1931, his son Governor Rodolfo Elías Calles, announced triumphantly the conclusion of the anti-Chinese campaign. However, apparently

at the insistence of his father, the governor sent troops to Fronteras to protect the Chinolla family and their property. They were the only Chinese
left. They held out until 1936, when General Calles fell into disfavor and
was exiled from Mexico. The Chinollas lost their protector and the family
including Agustín's brother Salvador, finally fled across the pass to Casas
Grandes. Agustín was twenty-one. With him was his bride from China.

Although Agustín had never been to China before, he followed the
tradition of his father. He traveled by ship to China in 1933 to find a wife
and returned with Mac Choi Chin (her Spanish name became María Mac).
Their first child, Antonio, was born in 1936, the year they reached Casas
Grandes. Three children followed a daughter who now lives in Nuevo
Casas Grandes, another daughter who lives in Hawaii, and a son who died
at the age of eight.

Times were not easy anywhere during the Depression era, let alone in
a remote corner of poverty-stricken northern Mexico. But in many ways,
it was a land of opportunity. The land itself was plentiful, productive, and
water was available. The Chinolla family stayed.

They started by renting land on Jacobo Anchondo's Hacienda El Refugio. They experimented with onions and potatoes, which turned out to be a
great success. They expanded, acquired land, and became the first growers
in Chihuahua to produce these products on a large scale.

The arrival of the Chinolla family and other Chinese added their special skills to those of the eclectic mix of Mexicans, LDS settlers, Mennonites, Japanese, and Indians, who (except for the Indians) also had found
this place during the late 19th and early 20th centuries.

Agustín Chinolla, Mac Choi Chin (María Mac) and children

Even in remote Chihuahua the Chinese still had to contend with persecution and corruption. José Chinolla farmed, raised cattle, and opened stores,
rebuilding his fortune, only to lose it a fourth time. Frustrated he began
sending money to China to protect his assets. The investments there grew
to the point that he sent his wife back to look after them. Unfortunately, he
picked the wrong time. Elisa Lee returned to China in 1948, the year Mao
Tse-tung's Communists gained control. Not only did the Chinolla family

lose their assets, but Elisa Lee ended up in the communal fields working with a hoe. Her husband and children never saw her again.

José died the following year on December 3, 1949. Following the old tradition, his family sent his remains to China for burial. Elisa Lee died in Hong Kong in 1961.

Agustín's marriage to María Mac did not last. They separated, divorced, and Agustín remarried in 1943. María Mac moved to Nuevo Casas Grandes while Agustín remained in Casas Grandes. His new wife was also named María—María Ruiz Morales. The new couple had five children, three sons and two daughters: Humberto, Blanca, Oscar, Hortensia, and René.

Agustín's daughter Blanca owned a popular restaurant in Casas Grandes and was active in local affairs. Following her father's family tradition, she made a pilgrimage to China to visit the tombs of her grandparents—Chew Gee Hing/José Chinolla and Chou Li See/Elisa Lee.

Blanca's older brother, Humberto, also well known locally, died tragically in an automobile accident in 1990. He joined his Uncle Salvador and a little half-brother in the small cemetery below *El Convento*. Agustín felt something should be done to preserve Humberto's memory. Even though he was 75 at the time, he obtained permission from the Casas Grandes authorities to work on the old cemetery where his son rested along with six others of Chinese ancestry. He cleaned around the old graves, planted eucalyptus and cypress trees, and constructed the pond. For more than 20 years, he maintained the gravesites, watered, and watched the trees grow. He died in November 2010.

With his passing another immigrant, Russian thistle, tumbleweed, threatens to undo Agustín's efforts, encroaching on the cemetery and obscuring the writing on the gravestones.[535]

Fong Poi of Pearson

Dr. Pearson's timing for his grand dream in northern Chihuahua could not have been worse. However, despite the chaos that soon crippled his projects, the new town of Pearson experienced a brief boom. The company constructed stores, offices, homes, a hospital, and a hotel in the area northwest of the center of town that became known as Barrio Americano. The

Fong Poi, José Flores, lived over 30 years in Mata Ortiz. Many of his
descendants became potters.
Photo: Courtesy of the Gallegos family

Mata Ortiz elementary school, Adobe Inn, and private homes occupy the
location today. Workers came from all over seeking employment. Some
were Chinese. One of the best remembered is Fong Poi.

Five prominent potting families in Mata Ortiz trace their ancestry
back to the Chinese cook and hotel manager, Fong Poi. The first name
in the potters' genealogy is actually Flores not Fong. In Cantonese, Fong
roughly translates to "pleasant fragrance" or "flower."[536] When Fong Poi
came to Mexico, he changed his name to the Spanish version, Flores, and
became José Flores.

As did so many others, Fong/Flores came to the new town of Pearson
to work for the North American managers of the mill. He lived only a few

miles from the Chinolla family in Casas Grandes. He was almost the same age as José Chinolla, but whether they ever met is unknown. Agustín Chinolla, José's son, had never heard of Fong Poi or José Flores.

Born in Guangdong Province near Canton in 1868, the young Fong Poi made the long voyage to the U.S. with others from his province and entered through San Francisco. Unable to make enough money there, he moved on to Los Angeles and then to Ciudad Juárez, Chihuahua. It is not known what he did initially, but at some point, he met the two owners of the Cooper Hotel. They may have been executives with Pearson's Madera Lumber Company. They hired him to manage the hotel. About this time, he Hispanicized his name to José Flores.

The owners had adopted an eight-year-old orphan girl named Gregoria Ibarra. She grew up working in the hotel. When Fong Poi arrived, they became acquainted and eventually married. They did not live happily in Ciudad Juárez because the same sort of envy and xenophobia that later forced the Chinese exodus from Sonora burst into violence in northern Chihuahua. The hotel may have been attacked by arsonists. They moved on to the large Chinese enclave in Torreón in the southwest corner of the state of Coahuila. Fong Poi opened a dry goods store. That store was burned, probably during the sack of the city by Madero's rebel forces and an anti-Chinese mob in May 1911. More than 300 Chinese were killed and Fong Poi and Gregoria lost everything, but they escaped and moved to Pearson.

Details of the move are not clear. Apparently the two Madera Lumber Company executives remembered the young couple and hired them to operate the company hotel, *La Casa Grande* in Pearson. This impressive structure was located on a hill above Barrio Americano. A rooming house addition was under construction.[537] Three houses sat in a row on the hill. To the left or south was the "Big House" or *Casa Grande,* built for Dr. Pearson and other visiting company officials. It was single story with high ceilings. The rooms opened onto an interior central courtyard. The mill manager, Clarence C. Cooper, occupied the center house, and the third house to the right belonged to Fong Poi.

Amelia Martínez Flores, a granddaughter of Fong Poi and Gregoria, remembers the hotel as a grand place when she was a little girl. She and her cousin Luz Elena Rodríguez would sneak in to look excitedly at the mounted trophy deer heads with their glass eyes staring down at them. The large wooden building had a central courtyard. Rooms with verandas faced the courtyard. Each room had a bath with a porcelain tub. One room was a library with floor-to-ceiling bookshelves. An elderly LDS saint from Colonia Juárez remembered Casa Grande as a "big fancy" hotel. When guests arrived, often in private railroad cars, Fong Poi would meet them at the station in a Ford Model T car.[538]

During his years in the hotel business, Fong Poi became an excellent cook. He served meals to guests and to company managers in their nearby homes. Gregoria provided him with produce from her garden in the courtyard. When most U.S. employees left during the Revolution, the hotel apparently closed, Fong Poi continued to serve meals and provide beds for the occasional company official.[539]

Many reports, official and unofficial, exist concerning the treatment of the Chinese. One most assuredly refers to Fong Poi/José Flores. A longtime lumberman, Mr. Duncan Jones, worked for the Madera Company at the Pearson mill. He lived with two other Americans in a house in Barrio Americano. A Chinese cook named Joe prepared their meals. The brief boom in Pearson was over, and times were chaotic. Following Pancho Villa's example, raiding rebels particularly brutalized Chinese wherever they found them. Villa called North Americans he wished to insult *chinos blancos*.

In March 1919, Villa's second in command (and one of his favorites), General Martín López, rode into Pearson with four hundred men and 75 extra horses to carry off loot. They plundered the town, particularly Chinese stores. Horsemen roped and dragged two Chinese men around town and ultimately killed as many as seven. After dark about 7:30 p.m., two of the Villistas rode up to Jones's unlighted porch, dismounted, and pounded on the door. When he opened it, they made a point about the lights being off. Jones turned them on and asked what they wanted. They pushed a gun in his stomach and demanded to know if any Chinese were inside. Jones said no, assuming Joe had already fled. With the gun still in his stomach, they pawed through his pockets, took some silver dollars, and demanded his watch. Jones had earlier fastened it to his underclothes, but it ticked loudly. He still stoutly denied having one, and the rebels, perhaps not recognizing what Jones could clearly hear, turned away and began searching the house.

In Jones's room, they poked under the bed and hit something. Jones tried to convince them that it was just a blanket, but they insisted it was *un hombre,* and they dragged out Joe. They put a gun to his head but did not shoot. Instead, they robbed him of seventeen dollars and a watch. They turned their attention to Jones, asking why he had lied to them. Jones convinced them he thought Joe had gone. He showed them the lunch that had been packed for Joe to take with him. This turned the Villistas attention to food. They ordered Joe to prepare a meal to be ready when they returned later with their colonel. When they came back, Jones was cooking. He explained that Joe had had run out into the night as soon as they left. The colonel did not seem overly concerned, and he even offered to pay for his supper. He came back in the morning, and Jones cooked him breakfast. More soldiers came, and Jones continued to cook until he ran out of food. Fortunately, López ordered his men out of Pearson before Jones faced a food-shortage crisis.[540]

Joe/José/Fong Poi survived that episode and others during the Revolution, but Martín López did not. Shortly after the raid on Pearson, in the waning years of the Revolution, López received a fatal wound to the stomach while leading a senseless attack on a railroad station in the state of Durango.[541]

The U.S. Consul in Ciudad Juárez collected statistics on the Chinese victims' losses and deaths in Pearson for a two-month period later that year. He sent this information in a letter to Roy Hoard dated May 23, 1919. The raw data hints at the number and importance of the Chinese in the town's commercial life. How many Chinese lived in Pearson no one knows, but clearly their number was significant.[542]

During the first five months of 1919, Martin López and Rodrigo Vega were responsible for most of the atrocities. The consul's letter, covering just two months, identified 31 individuals and their occupations. These were the owners or employees of four stores, one shoe shop, a lunchroom and bakery, and a ranch between Pearson and San Diego. Four others were peddlers. López's men robbed and killed one on his way to San Diego to make a delivery. The consul included in his report the earlier murders of two other peddlers and wounding of a third when General José Salazar entered Colonia Juárez to threaten the LDS residents on February 17, 1917.

Fong Poi and Gregoria survived these turbulent times but the Pearson Lumber Mill did not. The mill operated at reduced capacity in the last years of the Revolution but closed permanently in 1921. Fong Poi and his family remained in Mata Ortiz. Graciela Martínez de Gallegos remembers her grandfather living as a cattleman supporting the family with about 50 cows grazing on the plains.[543]

The couple's house on the hill above Barrio Americano was near the current home of one of their descendants, Luis Rodríguez. According to family lore, they added an underground hiding space beneath this house. José Martínez, Graciela's father, said his mother-in-law, Gregoria, told him Fong Poi used the underground hideout when the rebels rode into

Potter Jorge Quintana Rodríguez, great grandson of Fong Poi,
stands next to the remains of the hiding place under Fong Poi's home.

Pearson.[544] The house is gone now, but the little hiding place is clearly visible in the concrete foundation.

Gregoria gave birth to their first child, Aurora, on June, 17, 1919, just two months after the Martín López massacre. Eight children followed: Antonia, Amalia, Guadalupe, Ramón, Miguel, Manuel, José, and Gustavo.

Fong Poi died in 1944, lying in state in an open coffin in his home before burial in the Mata Ortiz cemetery north of the village. A cross without a name or other inscription marks the gravesite.

Gregoria lived to be 105, dying in 1976. In contrast to Fong Poi, her gravesite is well marked. Several in the village, including Graciela and the other Martínez sisters, remember their little grandmother, *sus abuelita,* well.

One can muse on the twists of fate that brought a young Chinese man half way around the world to a foreign place where he survived prejudice, persecution, and revolution to end his life as a respected citizen of a little village on the high plains of northern Chihuahua. However, time has passed.

Gregoria Flores 1871-1976
Photo: Courtesy of the Gallegos family

Recently, even his great-grandson, Jorge Quintana, had trouble finding his grave. After another generation, his existence might have been forgotten altogether if not for the attention given to his well-known descendants—the skilled potters of the families Flores, Martínez, Rodríguez, Quintana, and Gallegos. Interest in these artists and their background has stimulated the artists themselves to delve into their own heritage—to seek out old photos, find abandoned graves, and to remember old stories. Fong Poi's story takes its place in the unique mix that makes up the northern Chihuahua heritage. There were others.

Reynaldo Jión Enríquez Marries Elisa Sujo Morales

Sometime around the turn of the century, two Cantonese men, unknown to each other, made the long journey to Mexico. José Jesús Jion settled in San Buenaventura, where he met and married María Enríquez Flores. Their oldest son was Reynaldo Jion Enríquez.

Luis Sujo Wong came to Cumpas, in northwestern Sonora, where he married Pacífica Morales Gutiérrez. She gave birth to a daughter, Elisa Sujo Morales in 1926, at a time when anti-Chinese sentiment was particularly vicious. The Jion and Sujo families both elected to migrate east over the mountains to Nuevo Casas Grandes. Reynaldo and Elisa met and were married in Mata Ortiz, November 14, 1945.

Reynaldo Jion became a successful businessman. He and Elisa owned a house and property in Barrio Americano just north of today's school that included the current Gallegos home and the Adobe Inn. They built another larger house in Nuevo Casas Grandes as Reynaldo prospered. He opened a movie theater, an ice cream parlor, and grew vegetables in the sandy soil of the barrio. Reynaldo also was a carpenter, and Jorge Quintana, growing up, knew him well and worked on his house in Nuevo Casas Grandes.[545] Later Reynaldo joined with another prominent local businessman, Luis Orozco, to open a restaurant where the central plaza is now located.

Reynaldo Jion was a great friend of Fong Poi in spite of the age difference. Each month they met in Fong Poi's house on the hill to socialize and discuss business matters.

*Elisa Sujo Morales and Reynaldo Jion Enríquez
on their wedding day in Mata Ortiz, November 14, 1945.*

Forgotten Stories

Other than these few, there are no records for most of the Chinese that lived in Mata Ortiz. There are passing references to them particularly in Revolution histories usually describing abuses and murders. No one knows who they were or even their burial sites. There used to be gravestones in the Mata Ortiz cemetery engraved with Chinese characters. Jorge Quintana

417

said that most of these were looted and sold for garden decorations. One remained in 2008 because it had fallen over, hiding the writing. When the stone was turned, it revealed an inscription marking the passing of a Mr. Hui Yao Yee, a native of Canton, who used the Mexican name Arturo. His name survives in two languages but not his story.[546]

Gravestone of Mr. Hui Yao Yee, Mata Ortiz cemetery.
Translation courtesy of Cornell Naihong Fung.

12

The Dream Interrupted

Pearson's People

The timing of Dr. Pearson's grand dream could not have been worse. By 1909, he had assembled an extremely capable team to build and operate his railroad and lumber operation. They not only had experience but also the ability to adapt and keep pace with his visionary, rapid-fire concepts. Unfortunately, within months after his crews began in Chihuahua, Francisco Madero's call to arms turned the MNWR system into a battleground. The line became a vehicle for rapid movement by federal and rebel troops as well as civilians trying to escape the battle zones. The line suffered confiscation, track destruction, and train wreckage. Pearson's managers worked hard to keep the system running, but none had any experience with the dangerous uncertainties of revolution. The challenges added to the already massive task of creating a huge lumber and transportation complex.

Many terrified U.S. employees immediately left for the border, only to return, then leave again, as the conflict ebbed and flowed. Mexican workers found themselves trapped in the middle between the popular revolutionary cause and their well-paid steady jobs. Rebel leaders, as well as family members and friends, caught up in the fervor, pressured the employees to verbally and physically attack the employer who paid their wages.

Even though managers and employees changed as the revolutionary years dragged on, the company maintained a dedicated core group that carried on the daily struggle to keep trains running and lumber cut and shipped.

Dr. Pearson's ability to place people with particular skills or influence in key positions had always enabled him to develop and maintain his widespread enterprises. The MNWR Annual Report demonstrated this. The cover page for the first full year of operation, ending December 31, 1910, displayed Pearson's upper-management structure for the company and its subsidiaries. The Report listed several Toronto and Montreal financiers as vice presidents. These well-known names lent prestige to the enterprise and helped in the financial markets. The remaining names were company officers holding high positions in the chain of command. Hiram C. Smith was a vice president and managing director of the Madera Lumber Company.

The second-year Annual Report for 1911 showed that Henry Irving Miller replaced Smith as director of the Madera Lumber Company. Smith remained on the board.[547]

Miller, who had both railroad and lumber mill experience, already oversaw other Pearson enterprises working from the company offices in New York City. Apparently, Pearson and Miller shared an interest in the new science of reforestation, a subject Miller had researched extensively.

A few months after the appointment, Pearson introduced him to key personnel during an inspection trip to Mexico in January, 1912. The orientation included a trip to Mexico City, where Pearson held a press conference and described Miller's qualifications to reporters.[548]

Both Annual Reports listed Harry C. Ferris as the General Manager and highest on-site officer. How Pearson selected him is unknown. He had been a division superintendent for Union Pacific and had worked as superintendent and construction engineer for a new railroad in Pennsylvania. He had the technical experience, but at least one instance suggests he might have lacked people skills. Ferris let some minor issues regarding rights-of-way and ownership of a small parcel of land grow into outright antagonism toward the Corralitos Cattle Company, a major customer. Ferris obstructed shipments of ore and cattle, particularly ore from Corralitos' San Pedro mines, according to long time Corralitos manager E. C. Houghton. For the fledgling MNWR in need of revenue, this attitude made no sense. The standoff lasted for much of 1911, until Dr. Pearson personally intervened to resolve the dispute during the inspection trip with Miller.

Despite his personal enmity toward a major customer, Ferris seemed to recognize the importance of advertising and promotion. Very soon after he took over in 1909, and before the Revolution broke out, the company published a well-written sixteen-page illustrated brochure extolling the virtues of the railroad and the country it opened for every kind of traveler. Madera was pictured as a modern town with wonderful weather and a spacious hundred-room hotel catering to vacationers, hunters, and invalids.

Mexico North Western Railway promotional brochure, 1909, showing the Hacienda Bustillos, owned by the powerful Zuloaga family. — Photo: University of California, San Diego, Geisel Library, Special Collections and Archives

One paragraph admonished big-game hunters not to go to Africa, but instead to book expeditions into the Sierra Madre for jaguar, bear, mountain lion, and deer. A similar pitch was made to fishermen. The brochure offered tours to local sights such as the Cave of the Olla, where artifacts could be seen from an ancient culture, described as a race of pygmies. The brochure also made a unique appeal to Midwest farmers to leave the U.S. and resettle on the rich lands along the Mexican railway.[549] Land development had been part of earlier failed railroad promotions. However, the company produced the brochure before November 20, 1910, and the idea died after that.

The company traffic manager, T.R. Ryan, and Ferris authored the brochure. Ryan, age 40, had worked for railroads in Texas and more importantly in Mexico as a freight agent, clerk, and traffic manager.[550] Just prior to the job at MNWR, he had worked for the Mexican Central Railway, soon to be part of the National Railroad. Promotion may have been one of his responsibilities. However the brochure was prepared, the result was a compelling promotional piece even by today's standards. It described Dr. Pearson's dream and made it seem real.

Whoever hired the Chief Engineer B.H. Bryant, either Pearson or Ferris, made an excellent choice. Bryant was well respected in the field and responsible for laying thousands of miles of track in Central America. His experience included building a short railroad line through the high peaks of the Rocky Mountains, where he designed a roadbed that pushed the grade to the edge of the three percent maximum limit. Bryant's finished roadbed allowed steam-driven trains to creep over a 9,000-foot pass, the highest standard-gauge line in the country.[551] He would need all of the skills learned in Colorado to build the last 25 miles of MNWR track to the 7,195-foot Cumbre summit. As it was, it took almost two years to cut eleven tunnels, grade, and lay the track necessary to close the final gap in the loop. Bryant had steam-driven shovels and horse-drawn Fresno scrapers, but dozens of laborers with picks, shovels, and blasting powder did much of the work.

Pearson's other key employees included: E. Dimmick, Superintendent of the railroad's Chihuahua Division based in Madera; George Rutledge, Superintendent of the El Paso Division, based in Ciudad Juárez; C.T.

Carson, the company auditor; and E.M. Warren, manager of the Pearson plant. When Dr. Pearson took over from Colonel Greene, C.H. Cooper already worked for the Madera mill. Dr. Pearson put him in charge of building the Pearson mill. Roy Hoard and F.J. Clark fit Pearson's mold, but they came to the company as young employees in lower positions and rose later to run the company.

War Along The Railroad

Rapid deployment always has been a tenet of warfare, but the railroad introduced a new modern dimension in the last half of the 19th century. Throughout history the speed of a horse determined strategy and tactics. Railroads changed that. Generals, who understood and mastered this change, won battles as shown by wars in Crimea, Italy, and in the U.S. Civil War. Those conflicts became proving grounds for rail transport of troops, equipment, artillery pieces, and supplies.

As a military man with extensive experience, President Porfirio Díaz understood the importance of modern weapons, training, and transportation. He had distinguished himself in many battles, and when he assumed power, he used his practical experience to reorganize and modernize the Mexican army to meet both external invasion and internal rebellion. He encouraged development of railroads for economic reasons but saw clearly their military value. He pushed for a widespread rail network available to transport troops quickly to meet challenges anywhere in the country.

While the rebels started the Revolution as guerilla fighters, early combat taught them the tactical advantages of deployment by trains. Pancho Villa became especially adept at using the railway system. Classic examples of the positive and negative impact of rail transportation on the battlefield occurred in 1915. The fragile rebel alliance had fallen apart after the defeat of usurper General Huerta. Pancho Villa now confronted Venustiano Carranza for control of Mexico. Villa decided to attack Carranza's forces at Agua Prieta, Sonora, in the country's extreme northwest corner, in order to expand his control in the north and convince U.S. President Wilson that he, Villa, should be recognized as head of Mexico, not Carranza. He commandeered nineteen trains to transport his army from his temporary headquarters in central Mexico. Long lines of engines and cars of every description transported 10,000 soldiers and camp followers and 8,000 horses, along with supplies, artillery, small arms, machine guns, and hospital cars. The trains went north to the LDS town of Colonia Dublán in the Casas Grandes Valley.

It was a logistical tour de force, showing what the rebels had learned, but it was the easy part of the campaign. Agua Prieta was many miles to the west on the other side of the Sierra Madre. No trains ran east and west across northern Chihuahua into Sonora. When Villa's army moved out from Dublán toward the passes, some rode, but most marched on foot in long straggling lines. Wagons pulled by horses or mules carried equipment and supplies at a pace no faster than the Roman legions. Villa understood the hardship this march placed on his men. He also knew, or thought he knew, Carranza's garrison at Agua Prieta was small.

What Villa did not know was U.S. President Woodrow Wilson had given Carranza's General Obregón permission to transfer federal reinforcements across the southwest of the United States on rail lines owned by U.S. companies. Four thousand five hundred experienced soldiers rode Mexican trains on U.S. rails from Piedras Negras, Coahuila, across from Eagle Pass, Texas, to Douglas, Arizona, about 750 miles. They disembarked, marched across the border, and dug in. Villa's attacking troops were massacred. While the politics and ethics might be suspect, the tactical maneuver, using the railroad, was brilliant.

The rebels understood from the beginning days of the Revolution that obstructing federal train transport would be a key to success. Dr. Pearson reported the reduced lumber shipments because of wrecked track and bridges in his 1911 Second Annual Report to the board. His managers doggedly worked to repair or bypass the destruction to keep their lines open and maintain some kind of schedule. This struggle became the story of the Revolution in the Casas Grandes Valley and along the entire MNWR reverse D loop. The next ten years featured confiscations, troop movements, track destruction, raids, battles large and small, exodus, and bankruptcy, only offset by tough company managers determined to keep the trains running and the mill saws cutting.

Francisco Madero with the famous diaper bandage after the Battle of
Casas Grandes. Photo: Courtesy of the Library of Congress: cph 3c00794

Independence Day, November 20

Francisco Madero's writings opposing the concept of presidential re-election caught the attention of the nation at the right moment. His book, *The Presidential Succession of 1910*, published in 1908, propelled this small, unassuming idealist into the leadership of the Anti-reelectionist party. He was nominated to run for president in April 1910. His campaign gained so much traction across the country that Díaz had him arrested and sent to San Luis Potosí on June 6, two weeks before the polls opened. The election was so grossly rigged that no one believed the results, but Porfirio Díaz remained in Chapultepec Castle.

Though the irony may have been lost on him, Díaz incarcerated Madero in the town where the Mexican Liberal Party, the PLM, held the organizing convention in February 1901. Whether Madero felt that inspiration or not, he wrote his seminal *Plan de San Luis Potosí* just before he escaped to the

U.S. In this proclamation, he abandoned his previously moderate, peaceful approach to change and called for armed rebellion. He even named a date, November 20, 1910.

Based in San Antonio Texas, he, his brother Raúl, and their cadre of supporters, including Abraham González, began to buy Winchester rifles and whatever other arms they could find to ship across the border. The Taft administration did not restrict arms' shipments to Mexico, and there was no shortage of merchants willing to sell.

The Winchester Repeating Arms Company's famous lever-action 30-30 had evolved into the Winchester 95 with a distinctive box magazine. While not used by the U.S. Army, Winchester sold large quantities to civilians and to foreign governments. Madero's future rebels needed thousands of these as well or any other make or model they could find. The Anti-reelectionists, particularly Abraham González, worked hard with the funds available, but it was not enough. On the day of the uprising, arms were woefully short in most rebel centers.

The hodgepodge of arms created another problem that plagued rebels for the entire Revolution. Most of their various rifles and pistols used different ammunition. Even the Winchester 95 had different caliber configurations. Rebel soldiers often went into battle short of bullets. Scavenging for weapons and ammunition became a way of life and the need for ammunition provided the motive for many raids on towns and private citizens.

Francisco Madero, with no military experience, called for a revolt against President/Dictator Porfirio Díaz, who spent his life as a soldier with an outstanding record. During his 31-year regime, he sent his quartermasters to Europe to buy weaponry, particularly the German Mauser 7mm rifle, then considered the best available military rifle in the world. This five-shot, bolt-action repeater led virtually all competitors in range, accuracy, velocity, and other firepower characteristics.[552] Díaz's quartermasters also bought modern cannon and machine guns. Deficiencies within the army such as over-aged generals, corruption, and low morale among conscripts would cause problems, but rarely did federal forces enter battle short of arms or ammunition as did the rebels.

Abraham González was Madero's anti-reelectionist leader in Chihuahua. From the Guerrero District in southwestern Chihuahua, he, like

Rebel with homemade machine gun.
Photo: Courtesy of the University of California, Riverside,
Special Collections & University Archives

Madero, was well educated (Notre Dame University) and from a very wealthy family. His was one of the Guerrero families that lost out to Luis Terrazas in the late 19th century political struggles.

González began recruiting leaders in Chihuahua for the November 20 uprising. He probably already knew Pascual Orozco, who also came from the Guerrero District. Orozco is often referred to as a mule driver, which is misleading. He did have mules, but they were part of his successful transportation business. His family also owned stores and other small businesses. They were examples of capable people rising into the fledgling middle class during the prosperous years before the financial crash of 1907.

González persuaded Orozco to join the upcoming rebellion and put him in command of the Revolutionary forces (then non-existent) in Chihuahua. Orozco was tall, strong, a superb rider and shot, who always inspired a cadre of loyal followers. He had led a very tough group of *arrieros*, muleteers, over mountain trails with long trains of mules loaded with valuable ore from the numerous mines. It was profitable but very dangerous. As a side benefit, he learned the trails and hiding places in remote areas of the Sierra Madre. His arrieros became his first recruits, soon joined by disaffected men, some idealists and some with simply nothing to lose. Orozco became the most important commander in the Madero phase of the Revolution. Unfortunately for the future of that phase, his motives would turn out to be more personal than idealistic.

In addition to González and Orozco, the Guerrero District produced several other important revolutionaries including the strong-minded Protestant minister and school teacher, Braulio Hernández. Historian Philip Stover attributes the widespread challenge to oppression in Guerrero in part to the Protestant movement that had taken root with anti-establishment and anti-Church liberals. Orozco's family was Methodist, and Stover writes that González himself subscribed to a Calvinist-style ethic. When he became Chihuahua's provisional governor during the Revolution, González selected Hernández as his Secretary General, the second-in-command in the state's structure.[553]

Doroteo Arango, another of González's recruits, did not come from the disenfranchised middle class. He was a wanted renegade. By the time

González sought him out, he had adopted the name Francisco "Pancho" Villa after one of his former outlaw leaders.

Pancho Villa made a reputation for himself as a bandit in the Guerrero District and farther south in the state of Durango. What has been attributed to him and what he actually did will never be known. His story has been documented and dramatized repeatedly. Legend and fact have long since intertwined. Villa's relationship with the well-off, well-educated Abraham González adds to the mystique.

Coronel Francisco Villa
Photo: Courtesy of the University of California, Riverside,
Special Collections & University Archives

Friedrich Katz opens his epic tome, *The Life and Times of Pancho Villa*, with a detailed description of the extremes in the versions of Villa's history. Villa has been cast as everything from murderous brute to Robin Hood to the legendary face of the Revolution. Katz divides the versions into three categories: the White Legend, the Black Legend, and the Epic Legend.[554] According to the White Legend, Villa was born the son of a share cropper on a large hacienda in Durango. Strong and stocky, he stood about five feet ten inches tall. Not a particularly impressive figure in the numerous photographs of him, in person he inspired fear or devotion from those around him. Like Orozco, he was a crack shot and superb rider, good enough to win prize money in local rodeos. He combined his physical skills with an intelligence and energy that made him a quick learner with a willingness to listen to those with expertise beyond his own. He could be very generous, had few personal vices, and did not drink. The White Legend goes on to depict him as a genius on the battlefield.

According to the Black Legend he had serious flaws. Seen as a womanizer, he "married" several women without benefit of previous divorce and fathered 20 children. He could fly into terrible rages and kill anyone in front of him. Even when calm, he could kill any man he thought betrayed him or any man who happened to be Chinese. In battle, he had only one tactic, a hard frontal attack.

Many revolutionary leaders shared these white and black characteristics, real or imagined. What set Villa apart and made him bigger than life, was the Epic Legend. It is easy to recognize charisma but hard to describe. Even before the Revolution, his exploits had gained him a reputation. Campfire musicians picked out on their guitars long story songs, *corridos*, about how Pancho Villa became a bandit to punish the hacendados who had violated his sister, oppressed peons like them and stolen their land. Rebel soldiers on the march, workers in the field, and loungers in the village cantinas soon picked up and repeated the corridos. After the initial skirmishes, the musicians added words that told of Pancho's invincibility in battle. This aspect of his reputation solidified his troops' loyalty and confidence as they attacked and terrified the defenders. The stories, embellished over and over, spread throughout the country and to the United States. Soon Villa was not only a legend but the face of the Revolution to the world.

Katz notes that the actual verifiable facts about Villa's early life are sparse and contradictory. This applies to Villa's relationship with the patrician revolutionary Abraham González. Katz suggests a plausible version, based on information González later passed on to friends.

González knew about Villa, and though he did not ask any other bandit leader to join the Revolution, he did invite Villa to a late-night meeting in the Anti-reelectionist office in Ciudad Chihuahua. There he briefed Villa on the history and purpose of Madero's call to revolution. By the end of the meeting, Villa agreed to go at once into the mountains to recruit men.[555] González may have offered immunity to Villa, once Madero became president. For whatever reason, Villa remained loyal to González (and Madero) in spite of later differences. Such loyalty became the exception rather than the rule as the Revolution progressed. Many prominent revolutionaries changed sides, some several times, but not Villa.

As the November 20 deadline approached, González and his supporters stepped up the purchase of arms and ammunition and organized the distribution to leaders throughout Chihuahua. From his base in San Antonio, Madero sent funds provided by sympathizers to a bank in El Paso to which González had access. González and his team also distributed hundreds of copies of Madero's Plan de San Luis Potosí throughout the state.[556] Unfortunately, they had more leaflets than Winchesters.

Madero expected a massive uprising, but it did not happen. Several days prior to November 20, informers gave Díaz a reasonably clear idea of the uprising plan. In preemptive strikes around the country, he ordered the roundup of hundreds of suspected insurrectionists. In several states that did try to rebel, the leaders did not have adequate plans or firearms. Federal troops crushed these uprisings almost before they started.

Not in Chihuahua. González had prepared much better than most. Word spread quickly that federal troops were on the move. Rebel leaders realized they had to start before the November 20 deadline.

Toribio Ortega Ramírez is credited with the first act of the Madero Revolution in Chihuahua. As head of the Cuchillo Parado Anti-reelectionist party in the Ojinaga Municipio area on Chihuahua's eastern border with Texas, Ortega wanted to make some kind of rebellious act on November 20. Díaz's crackdown preempted this schedule. When word came to Ortega that he was about to be arrested, he reacted quickly. On November 14, six days ahead of appointed date, he led a poorly armed but highly motivated group of 60 men to the municipal office. The despised mayor ran for his life.[557] Without the means to hold the town, Ortega established a base in the nearby mountains and continued to harass the local Díaz officials until the dictator was deposed. The first to heed Madero's call, Ortega remained an effective revolutionary. Three years later, he became a trusted commander in Pancho Villa's army.

Villa engaged in the first actual combat of the Revolution in western Chihuahua. By the bloody standards to come, it was a minor action, but it was the beginning.

On November 17, Villa and another rebel leader named Cástulo Herrera with 20 to 40 mounted men followed the MNWR tracks though the San Andrés area east of Ciudad Guerrero and south of Madera. Riding with Herrera was Máximo Castillo, who later as a rogue rebel leader would have significant impact on Pearson and the Casas Grandes Valley.[558] Villa and Herrera intended to clear this part of the Guerrero District of government officials and Rurales. They turned off on a road to a ranch they knew, Rancho de Chavarría, to get provisions and information on the local Rurales. The ranch foreman and his workers had little interest in revolution and plenty of experience with bandits. They began to shoot at the approaching horsemen. Villa's men fired back, killing the foreman and one worker, but not before losing one of their own. Three unknown men on this remote ranch would be among the first, if not the very first, of millions of dead and wounded men, women, and children over the next decade.

With more caution, Villa and Herrera continued up the line to the town of San Andrés, where intimidated officials and a small detachment of Rurales quickly fled.

Pascual Orozco and his Guerrero District recruits had started a sweep of railroad towns on November 18, meeting little resistance. He now threatened the important town of Ciudad Guerrero. Frantic telegraph messages warned the federal authorities in Ciudad Chihuahua, 140 miles away, of the attacks and asked for help. Federal commanding General, Juan Hernández, immediately put 170 soldiers on a train and sent them to reinforce the contested towns. On November 21, the day after Madero's declared uprising, word came to Villa in San Andrés that a trainload of federal soldiers would soon arrive. It is not clear how many men Villa had. Máximo Castillo later said only 20. Whatever the number, Villa deployed them near the train station and waited.

When the train stopped at San Andrés, the soldiers disembarked, Mauser rifles at the ready, apparently intending to retake the town. Villa's hidden rebels rose up and opened fire. The fight lasted 20 minutes. The federal colonel in charge and twelve men fell. The second-in-command, Captain Sánchez Pazos, ordered a retreat. The soldiers did not attempt to get on the train but walked toward Bustillos, a town 20 miles up the track in the direction of Ciudad Guerrero.

Captain Pazos maintained control of his men as they retreated in good order. It is not known how many Villa lost, but he chose not to pursue. It did not matter. The anti-reelectionist rebels had defeated government army regulars in their first firefight. Word quickly spread, and more men enthusiastically joined Villa and also Pascual Orozco, now outside Ciudad Guerrero.

On the same day, November 21, Orozco attacked. With just a few troops, the garrison captain in the city had prepared the defenses well. After three days Orozco had made little progress. Word came to him that Captain Pazos' troops were marching toward him. Orozco left off the siege and took a large rebel contingent to confront the advancing federal force. In the ensuing fight, Captain Pazos rallied his men but fell, shot dead. Another officer took command, apparently effectively, as his remaining federals fought their way out. A week later, 28 ragged, bloody men led by their third officer made it to Ciudad Chihuahua. That same day, December 3, the out-manned Ciudad Guerrero garrison surrendered to Orozco.[559]

The El Paso newspapers reported that several comrades of the 28 federal survivors had deserted or joined Villa and Orozco. This is probably true as the papers cited eyewitnesses. It is also true that many others fought well before being killed or captured. These initial skirmishes provide evidence of the condition of Porfirio Díaz's federal army and the relative strengths of the two adversaries. In battle, federal troops with superior arms and questionable morale faced motivated rebels with inferior arms. Díaz's senior officers for years had filled out their ranks with petty criminals as a form of punishment and others with no motivation other than to desert. Corruption and favoritism existed among the officer corps. However, many, like Captain Pazos, were not only brave in battle, but competent, and maintained tight military discipline. Nevertheless, the first two weeks of fighting showed the all-powerful Porfirio Díaz could be defeated. This had enormous impact on the course of the Revolution, well beyond the military significance of those first few days.

News spread that a real revolution was happening in Mexico and the "cradle" of that Revolution was Chihuahua. This infuriated Díaz as he had put down the insurgency everywhere else. Not only was his reputation at risk, Mexican bond prices were falling on the international market. Some Chihuahua land owners negotiated with rebel leaders and suggested a truce. Díaz would have none of it. He ordered General Juan Hernández to take command of all of Chihuahua. Two more detachments of troops, one headed by General Juan Navarro, were sent by train from Mexico City. The number of federals in Chihuahua soon reached 5,000, a substantial number in those early days when compared to the rebel bands that numbered in the hundreds or less.

December, The First Month

Although anti-reelectionists, like Práxedis Guerrero in the north and Toribio Ortega in Cuchillo Parado, led uprisings in other parts of the state, the most important first actions occurred along the MNWR line between Ciudad Chihuahua and Ciudad Guerrero. General Hernández sent General Navarro and his troops down the line. Using trains, Navarro quickly retook the towns, only to be thwarted by another kind of rapid military movement—irregular cavalry on familiar ground—guerilla warfare. Orozco and Villa employed hit and run tactics across a land they knew, populated by supportive people—the classic mix for such warfare.

The key was the tacit or active support of the people. Díaz and Terrazas made a serious miscalculation. They believed their hacienda workers, the peons, would remain loyal and even fight for their patrons. This might have been true in the days of the Apache or the French invasion, but not now. The Revolution threw open the haciendas, not only to pillage, but as a source of recruits for the roving guerillas.

The federals initially experienced some success, re-taking some towns, even Ciudad Guerrero, but the rebels kept moving and harassing, rarely committing to large-scale battle. The situation rapidly changed from day to day, but in a few weeks, rebels controlled the countryside and key towns along the rail route, at least most of the time.

The MNWR mill and railroad managers had little interest in social revolution. They had a business to run. Practical men, they desired stability to conduct their now-profitable operations. Everyone, from the company president, Dr. Pearson, to the on-site managers, thought Díaz, the strongman in Mexico City, would prevail as he always had. Dr. Pearson sent a reassuring telegram on November 24 that the U.S. press quoted the following day.[560] "Everything was "absolutely normal," he said. That was four days after Madero's call to arms.

It quickly became clear that things were not normal along the MNWR. The rebels were the strongmen. Federal troops could force their way into a town or commandeer company trains, but overall, rebels controlled the line.

E. Dimmick managed the line south of the Cumbre gap in the Guerrero District and George Rutledge managed the northern section in the El Paso District, which included the Casas Grandes Valley to Ciudad Juárez. These company managers found themselves caught trying to satisfy both sides in a fluid situation that changed almost daily. General Hernández had enough strength under his command to force the use of trains. He put soldiers on the repair trains to protect work crews and even ordered the troops themselves to help repair track. However, as quickly as the federals re-occupied a town, the rebels shifted their operations elsewhere.

By the second week of December, rebels occupied Madera.[561] Probably based on instructions from Abraham González, rebels initially minimized harassment of the local employees and the North Americans. However, as the company managers attempted to re-establish schedules, rebels repeatedly stopped trains looking for federals. The rebel leaders were playing by unfamiliar rules as well. Unless they were outright renegades, they showed some respect for the equipment and property of the company, at least at the beginning. Rarely did they fire on the trains for fear of hitting civilians.

One early rebel action did suddenly and completely cut off the town of Pearson and create the first martyr of the Revolution. In late December 1910, shortly after Madero's call to arms, Práxedis Guerrero, the army officer turned radical journalist and PLM party founder, with about 50 men commandeered a train engine with several cars. They headed southwest toward Casas Grandes, attacking towns in the name of the Revolution. They stopped to set fire to each bridge they crossed and cut telegraph lines. The federal garrison at Casas Grandes proved too strong for their small force, and they left the train, marched north to Janos and captured it. The idealistic young Práxedis Guerrero stood up toward the end of the battle and was shot dead, becoming the first martyr of the Revolution.

The damage to the track and telegraph line severed all communication links to Pearson. On December 29, E.M. Warren, the Pearson mill manager, wrote to Hiram C. Smith, the director of the Madera Lumber Company in the El Paso company office. Warren considered the letter so important and the route so dangerous that he sent two copies via different couriers. At least one copy got through. In it, Warren reported that several employees had been stranded in El Paso, including George Rutledge and a Dr. West. They could not return to Pearson. When the company tried to transport them on a special train, they rode for about 62 miles from Ciudad Juárez, until a burned-out bridge blocked the way. With a handcart, they somehow bypassed the burned bridges and rode all the way to Pearson, arriving late that night. Dr. West counted 14 wrecked bridges.[562]

After Rutledge's crews reopened the line, some of the employees that had been stranded in El Paso at Christmas returned, but many did not. This began a sequence of employee evacuations and returns. The back and forth lasted for years as the violence ebbed and flowed along the line.

At the end of 1910, more than 1,000 U.S. citizens worked for the lumber company and railroad at Madera and Pearson. For the railroad, these included engineers, mechanics, and conductors. The mill jobs had titles such as planers, filers, loader men, hoist men, and skidders. Clerks and accountants staffed the offices.[563] Part of Dr. Pearson's plan was to make both towns attractive for families as described in the brochure. However, fewer and fewer employee families returned after evacuating. Company managers began to rely more on Mexican workers, eventually employing over 3000.[564] As most lacked mechanical experience, it took time and training to move them into skilled positions.

Also, the Mexican employees were conflicted. Many, if not most, supported the rebel cause but relied on their good jobs to feed their families. More opportunities had opened. If they joined the rebels, they would lose their wages and further destabilize company business.

Dr. Pearson understood this dilemma. Regular wages meant stability for the employees and therefore for the company. He ordered his managers to provide jobs for Mexican workers even if it meant taking on more men than they could use economically.[565]

As rebellion accelerated in Chihuahua, it quickly became evident that accommodations had to be made with the rebels to keep the railroad open on some semblance of a schedule. Cooperation with the government and Díaz's personal blessing had been fundamental to Dr. Pearson's grand plan, but the government could not protect his operation. The managers began negotiating with Orozco, Villa, and others, and denying use to the federals.[566] An angry Díaz complained to the company managers and sent more troops.

MNWR General Manager H.C. Ferris received veiled threats in back-to-back letters from Luis Riba. The influential Mexico City lawyer had paved the way for Dr. Pearson's Chihuahua concessions the year before, and he had served on the MNWR board. In the second letter, he complained about "… assistance given the disturbers by employees of the company …" He said he had "proof" the telegraph operators gave access to the disturbers and malcontents. If these employees were not found and fired, "… the company might be considered to be working against the best interests of the government."[567] While the threats appeared to be serious, they were not backed by any real action. Díaz could fume, but he had already done about all he could do.

In spite of its vulnerability, the telegraph remained the vital form of communication throughout the Revolution. It was easy, and all factions used it. Rebels with a portable telegraph key and batteries could tap into the line to send or intercept messages. MNWR personnel developed at least two codes to conceal their message contents.[568] Rebels did cut wires to gain a tactical advantage, but usually it was more advantageous for them to keep the lines open. The MNWR also had a telephone line along the tracks that station masters and work crews used.

The new year, 1911, began with most of the railroad restored to operating condition. Construction projects continued along the line and at the mills. The company managers had quietly adopted a policy to tacitly support whoever held the balance of power in their territory.[569]The impotence of the government and the general if erratic cooperation of the rebels allowed business to continue.

No such rapport existed on the National Railroad (the former Mexican Central) between Ciudad Chihuahua and Ciudad Juárez. The rebels did not hold back, wrecking bridges and track of the government-owned line. Service became so disrupted that the Madera mill could not make deliveries. The Company shipped lumber from the Madera mills and ore from mining customers south and east on their MNWR line to a junction with the National Railroad just south of Ciudad Chihuahua. Lumber stacked up in the yard of the undamaged mill, which had doubled production.[570]

Dr. Pearson pushed Chief Engineer B.H. Bryant hard to complete the direct route north over the Cumbre summit, but it would be another year before workers could finish the tunnels and roadbed to close the last 25-mile gap. Progress slowed further when the rebels discovered and regularly confiscated company shipments of dynamite and blasting powder. After a few mishaps, they learned to use the lethal material to blow bridges and track. They also made hand-thrown bombs that proved highly effective at close quarters.

The Madero Revolution

After the New Year, January 1911, the center of action briefly shifted north from the Guerrero District. Rebel bands, sticking to guerilla tactics, raided from Janos to El Rucio, a small railroad town a few miles south of Pearson. Pascual Orozco brought more rebels under his command, and on January 16, he marched them north along the National Railroad tracks. No one knew his intent or location much of the time. He bypassed Ciudad Chihuahua, an obvious target, probably knowing from sympathizers that the defenses were too strong for his kind of warfare.

Orozco attempted to attack Galeana in the Santa Maria Valley and withdrew. Several miles north on a hillside called La Mojina, he deployed his men, dug in, and essentially invited the federals to attack. They did, on January 27, and lost 31 killed to Orozco's five.

On the same day, Luis García, a local rebel leader, attacked San Buenaventura, south of Galeana. After two days of fighting, the federal garrison commander surrendered. The rebels recovered a bounty of guns and ammunition. While García lost his next encounter, his actions caused the federals to expend troops and resources chasing from place to place.[571]

Pascual Orozco became the dominate leader during December and January, but not all rebel bands accepted his authority. Even Villa operated more or less independently, collaborating with Orozco as the situation dictated. Villa's original chief, Cástulo Herrera, during the first uprisings, refused to join Orozco. He convinced Máximo Castillo to go with him to see to see Abraham González in El Paso. Don Abraham seemed to have full confidence in Orozco and was far more interested in smuggling ammunition to him than his squabble with Herrera. This ended Herrera's not-so-glorious military career.

Máximo Castillo, on the other hand, took the dangerous assignment from González to transport 16,000 cartridges across the border and through the federal lines. With about a dozen men, Castillo made the trek and arrived at Orozco's encampment near Galeana on January 28, the day after the fight at La Mojina.

With the cartridges, Castillo carried a message from González to Orozco to concentrate all rebel forces on taking Ciudad Juárez. This was the strategic objective. With control of this major port of entry, the Maderista rebels would control all shipments from the U.S., collect import taxes, and readily receive arms.

Madero and his cabinet had made a crucial decision. They recognized the Revolution was going nowhere. President Díaz's government controlled virtually all of the country except Chihuahua and areas in the state of Morelos under Emiliano Zapata. Madero did not have the resources to escalate the campaign in Chihuahua beyond the guerilla level. With Ciudad Juárez, he could gain enough economic control to expand the Revolution throughout the country. That did happen but not exactly as planned.

Orozco moved his band, still numbering just a few hundred, back from the Galeana area to the National railroad. At Moctezuma Station, about halfway between Ciudad Chihuahua and Ciudad Juárez, he commandeered four trains as they came into the station, two passenger and two freight. He put his men, camp followers, horses, and supplies aboard and all four headed north. What the passengers thought, mixed in with the armed rebels is not known, but they were not harmed.[572]

At Samalayuca Station, the rebels disembarked and Orozco sent the passenger trains safely on to Ciudad Juárez, followed by an engine and a few of his rebels to tear up track. Orozco took his main body on the fourth train and continued on the National Railroad to the MNWR junction just south of Ciudad Juárez. Changing to the MNWR track, they continued southwest to a station called Bauche, where they disembarked and set up camp nearby. A detachment began to tear up track beyond the station.

Orozco had selected a good position from which to prepare his siege and eventual attack on the city. He was between the two railroad lines and could block and harass all federal traffic. This was born out shortly after his arrival at Bauche Station.

Colonel Antonio Rábago had been sent earlier with a full regiment of 500 federal soldiers to garrison Casas Grandes, considered an important town. Rábago received orders to return his regiment immediately to Ciudad Juárez. He commandeered a MNWR train, boarded the soldiers, and left quickly. At four in the morning, February 3, the train's engine hit a gap or warped track and derailed, just before the Bauche Station. The waiting rebels opened fire. The soldiers returned fire, and shooting lasted all day. In spite of their bad position, the federal contingent was large and well-armed. Orozco, with a smaller force, would ambush but not risk a frontal attack. That night Colonel Rábago organized a successful retreat from the train around the rebel position. After a two-day march, he arrived in Ciudad Juárez with his regiment intact, minus the dead and wounded lying along the track at Bauche Station.

Overall, the rebel guerilla strategy proved successful. Díaz's generals had been forced to abandon their strategy of controlling the state by controlling the railroad. Instead, they concentrated on protecting the major cities, specifically Ciudad Chihuahua and Ciudad Juárez. General Navarro even abandoned Ciudad Guerrero and moved his large garrison to Ciudad Juárez. Orozco's movements and the concentration of rebels increasingly pointed to that border city as the rebel objective. Navarro's move north essentially turned over to Madero's supporter all of towns along the MNWR line on both sides of the remaining Cumbre-summit gap.

On February 4, rebel Antonio Rojas occupied Pearson with 80 men.[573] Rojas, a hard man, came from Sonora. Very early, he had formed a band and rebelled against Porfirio Díaz. After skirmishing on his own in Sonora and Chihuahua, he joined Madero, who promoted him to the rank of Colonel. Later in the Revolution, he would terrorize towns in the Casas Grandes Valley.

During the winter months until March, Pancho Villa independently raided towns and haciendas in the Camargo and other districts south of Guerrero. He and Orozco may have had some sort of falling out.[574] Other than providing an additional distraction to the already harassed federal army, Villa had few meaningful successes and even a few embarrassing defeats. This did not diminish his growing reputation. His men knew no one braver in battle, and that he would take care of them, making certain they were fed and paid. The legend grew and more recruits joined him.

North at the border, rumors flew about Orozco' impending attack on Ciudad Juárez. Everyone on both sides of the border was convinced it would happen soon. General Navarro and his subordinate commanders including Colonel Samuel García Cuellar and now Colonel Rábago continued to reinforce the city in spite of the transport difficulties. By the middle of February, they had 1,400 men, plus cannon and even a few machine guns. The soldiers labored to set up sandbag barricades on the main streets

All of this created another problem for the MNWR managers. In order to prevent federal re-enforcements using the line to reach Ciudad Juárez, Orozco refused to let Superintendent George Rutledge remove the wrecked engine that blocked the track at Bauche Station. This not only cut off regular service to El Paso but prevented the company from receiving supplies and construction materials for the Pearson mill and for the final gap in the railroad loop. Rutledge's entreaties could not move Orozco. On February 4, Rutledge sent a telegram from El Paso to E.D. Kenna, a company vice president in the New York Office, advising him about the blocked track, the downed telegraph lines, and the paralyzed rail traffic. According to Rutledge, Orozco had about 650 men, all mounted. Orozco, himself, added to the confusion. He told Rutledge he would attack Ciudad Juárez the next day, February 5.[575] Everything pointed to an imminent attack that did not happen, at least not then.

The Battle of Casas Grandes

A paradoxical sequence of events, only partially understood, led to a different battle and an outcome quite the opposite of what was expected.

February began with Francisco Madero and Abraham González still in the U.S. Different rebel leaders operated in various locations following the guerilla strategy, but most, including Madero and González, recognized Orozco as the main force preparing to attack Ciudad Juárez. In just days, everything changed.

Madero held a council of war in El Paso, which Orozco, supposedly the overall commander, did not attend. In fact, he had left his position outside Ciudad Juárez and returned with most of his men to the Guerrero District, his home. He claimed federals had re-occupied towns along the MNWR there in his absence, but there was more to the story.

On February 8, before he left, about a dozen representatives from Madero's "General Staff," including his brother Raúl, crossed the border to Orozco's encampment. They stood around the campfire with Orozco's officers drinking coffee while their spokesman, Eduardo Hay, Chief of the General Staff, explained their mission.[576] Hay, an educated man from a prominent Mexico City family and later foreign minister under Lázaro Cárdenas, laid out the General Staff's new organizational plan for conducting military operations. Madero would take overall command and Orozco would report to an intermediate commander, José de la Luz Soto, an older career army officer.

Orozco had been in the field independently for two and a half months. His ambush and raid tactics were the main reasons Madero's Revolution remained alive at all. However, in spite of all of the rhetoric, he apparently understood he did not have enough men nor enough arms to overrun the

From left, revolutionary leader Pascual Orozco, industrialist and landowner Oscar Braniff, Francisco "Pancho" Villa, and Italian soldier Giuseppe Garibaldi II . Photo probably taken during peace negotiations with the Porfirio Díaz government (May 16-21, 1911). — Photo: ggbain 09417 //hdl.loc.gov/loc.pnp/ggbain.09417 Courtesy of the U.S. Library of Congress

defenses at Ciudad Juárez. That did not mean he had any intention of taking orders from city-bred intellectuals, their designees, or even Madero himself. He would continue to fight Díaz but on his own terms. Turning to face his officers, he told them he would have nothing to do with this delegation. His officers grunted their approval, mounted and rode off into the night to organize their troops for departure.

The representatives were suddenly very alone, very angry and unprotected in the cold Chihuahua night. Máximo Castillo wrote in his autobiography that he heard about the group's plight as he was preparing to follow Orozco. He found them unarmed and on foot. He convinced Mariano Hernández, another leader with a small detachment of rebels, to help him guide the representatives back to safety and Madero's headquarters.[577]

Regardless of the accuracy of Castillo's self-serving memories or the lack of a complete understanding of Orozco's motives, the Revolution had come to a defining moment. Madero and his close advisors had changed direction. Madero would take direct military command, cross the border, and meet an army of supporters he was sure would congregate in response to his advance orders. This army would march on Casas Grandes to demonstrate to the rest of the country and the world that his revolution was viable. This all happened in just a few days.

At least some of Castillo's story must have been accurate because the episode of rescuing the General Staff gave him a reputation of reliability that brought him to Madero's attention. The political and now military leader of the Revolution asked Castillo to head his security detail, essentially his body guard, a good choice as it turned out.

On February 14, six days after the meeting at Orozco's camp, Madero crossed the border accompanied by González, his general staff, other supporters, and about 80 (estimates vary) North Americans and Europeans. The latter group was called the *Falange de los Extranjeros*, the Foreign Phalanx. The leader of this rather exotic mix was Giuseppe Garibaldi II, the grandson of Italy's most famous general. The grandson had considerable experience of his own as a soldier fighting for revolutionary causes in Greece, Venezuela, and South Africa. At first Madero was suspicious of foreigners, but Garibaldi understood guerilla warfare from his experience in the Boer War. Soon Madero accepted him as a close advisor. The Falange represented a mixed crew of idealists, soldiers of fortune, and adventure seekers, who joined Madero in El Paso. Several had been soldiers in various armies and brought a needed element of military professionalism. They all carried Winchester 95 repeating rifles.

General Navarro soon heard that that Orozco had left, and the immediate threat to Ciudad Juárez was over. He dispatched Colonel Cuéllar with a large force of infantry, cavalry, and artillery pieces to search for rebels in the Ascensión area between Ciudad Juárez and Casas Grandes. Ascensión was not on the railroad, but with Orozco gone, Cuéllar was able to open the track and go part way on MNWR trains.

Madero's crossing into Mexico almost was a non-event. Only a few of those he expected came to meet him, and the leaders of those could not

Many of the important rebel leaders at the beginning of the Madero Revolution. Photo: photographic print (postcard) Southern Methodist University, DeGolyer Library. Other variations of this photo can be found at the Library of Congress.

agree among themselves whether to follow him or not. Then the unimaginable happened. Word got out in the countryside that Francisco Madero had returned to Mexico. His presence somehow inspired local campesinos to join him and his cause. Several who initially had met him at the border caught the spirit and decided to abandon their indecisive leaders and stay with him.

Madero ordered the march. His tiny but growing army did not use the trains. They straggled in a long column through the Chihuahua desert and over high plains, often at night. At the head of the column rode Francisco Madero. People in small towns greeted them as conquering heroes. More men left their homes and joined the column. They arrived at San Buenaventura without discovery on March 1, where another contingent waited, ready to join. Three days later, they were in Galeana and on March 5 at Rancho Anchondo just south of the Paquimé ruins, less than two miles from the sandbag walls of Casas Grandes. Madero now had about 500 men.

Before dawn on March 6, they moved out and launched the attack at 5:00 a.m. Madero divided his force, ignoring Garibaldi's advice to hold the army together. Castillo stayed close to Madero's side and, later wrote (after he repudiated Madero) that Madero had little idea about what was happening.[578] Details of the battle vary, but the overall facts are simple. The rebels attacked the town from the southeast and north. Although inexperienced and poorly armed, they did well. After hours of hard fighting, the federal garrison gave way and surrendered. Before the exhausted rebels could celebrate, they heard bugles, and Mauser rifle fire. Federal cavalry and infantry reinforcements charged into them. Many ran for their lives. Some tried to fight back. Garibaldi's Falange, caught at the point of the federal attack, kept up a punishing fire with their Winchester 95s until they were overwhelmed. Several were killed and about sixteen captured.[579] The federals mounted a machine gun in the church tower, and soon it was a rout. The reinforcements were Colonel Cuéllar's troops, who had moved to an encampment about four miles from Casas Grandes, unbeknownst to Madero's officers. Colonel Cuéllar appears to have been aware of the attack and one version says he was on the telephone directing the defense from the beginning.[580]

A bullet hit Madero in the arm or wrist, and although the battle was lost, he refused to leave the field. Castillo half-cajoled, half-forced him out of danger and to Rancho Anchondo and then to Hacienda San Diego, thereby saving his life.

Nightfall let the remaining rebels get away. The federals did not pursue. If they had, the Revolution might have ended right there, near the ancient fallen city of Paquimé. As it was, Colonel Cuéllar's troops fought hard after a forced march and had little left. Colonel Cuéllar had also suffered a terrible wound. His arm had been shattered, and he could not command a night pursuit. Some of Madero's fleeing men had the presence of mind to burn two bridges south of Casas Grandes to delay pursuit by train.[581]

Many of Madero's General Staff had been in the battle. Eduardo Hay received a wound in the eye and was captured. He managed to escape prison in Mexico City, dressed as a woman.[582] Despite the handicap of one eye, he went on to a notable career as a revolutionary and politician.

At San Diego, excited men crowded into the grand salon around Madero, as the nurse Kingo Nonaka tended his arm and bandaged the wound with a diaper. The survivors at San Diego reacted as though they had won rather than suffer a crushing defeat. The spirit that accompanied

Madero after he crossed the border seemed to swell. His supporters had seen their leader stand bravely in the midst of battle, and even wounded, be the last to leave. They declared him their president, cheered, and posed for photographs. For a very short period of time, Hacienda San Diego became the first presidential palace of the Revolution.

The Photo

One often-published photograph from the El Paso Public Library archive shows thirteen men on the steps of the Hacienda San Diego. One features the giant sombrero, high boots, and crossed bandoliers of a true revolutionary. The others in their hats, coats, and ties look like middle-class businessmen. Each had a hat band in the three colors of the Mexican flag, which proudly denoted them as a Madero staff member. Arizona historian Rondal R. Bridgemon has done an extensive study of Hacienda San Diego

Francisco I. Madero and supporters at Hacienda San Diego
after the Battle of Casas Grandes.
Photo: Courtesy of the El Paso Public Library, Special Collections,
Border Heritage Center. Individuals identified by Rondal Bridgemon

and of the men in the photograph. He has identified ten.[583] Most played significant roles in the various phases of the Revolution and its aftermath. Their personal stories, except for Máximo Castillo, do not directly involve the Casas Grandes Valley history, but they represent a cross-section of the beliefs, values, ambitions, and animosities that influenced the course of Mexican history for the next thirty years.

Francisco I. Madero—Little can be added here to the man, who ignited the Revolution against the president/dictator Porfirio Díaz. He succeeded in his major objective but failed to control events afterwards.

Abraham González—During the Madero phase of the Revolution, he oversaw the political administration of Chihuahua as the rebel provisional governor. Very capable, he combined the qualities of an intellectual with practical management skills. He chose many of the leaders that made the overthrow of Díaz successful including Pascual Orozco and Pancho Villa. Without his preliminary organization in Chihuahua, there would have been no revolution in 1910. A few months after Díaz fell, Chihuahua held regular elections, and the voters elected González governor. His later assassination in 1913 was a serious blow to Chihuahua's stability.

José de la Luz Soto—As a trained military officer with long experience, de la Luz Soto had Madero's confidence. He had served in most of the major campaigns in Mexico's turbulent history, starting with the fight against Maximilian. A supporter of Díaz's rise to power, he became disillusioned, resigned his commission and joined the radical PLM party. Madero chose him to command rebel forces in Chihuahua, a move Orozco completely rejected. However, the following year, de la Luz Soto became disillusioned with Madero and joined the Orozco Rebellion. Later as military commander of Parral, Chihuahua, he lost a major battle to Villa and was taken prisoner. Villa had no mercy on those he viewed as traitors. De la Luz Soto was taken to Mexico City and executed. (José de la Luz Soto should not be confused with José de la Luz Blanco, an officer that fought for Madero from the initial uprising to the assassination, never wavering in his loyalty).

Giuseppe Garibaldi II—Grandson of the famous soldier who helped unify Italy, Garibaldi made his own reputation fighting for idealistic causes as a soldier of fortune. He joined Madero in San Antonio and became a close advisor. His presence brought an element of romantic adventure to the obscure rebellion that caught the attention of the world press. He headed the other foreigners, the Falange, who came to fight for Madero. After the Battles of Casas Grandes and Ciudad Juárez, bitter conflict with Villa forced him to leave the country.

Raúl Madero—The brother of Francisco is usually described as a more capable administrator. His long career as an officer with Villa and as an elected official through the tumultuous decades of the 1920s and 1930s bears this out. He became governor of Nuevo León in 1914.

Máximo Castillo—A small farmer from a Chihuahuan village now called Gran Morelos, Castillo was one of the few *campesinos* in northern Chihuahua to become a ranking revolutionary military leader. Unique among others from Chihuahua, he appears to have lacked political ambition. Also, in contrast to many of the Chihuahuan leaders, he genuinely believed in land reform and was a great admirer of Emiliano Zapata and his land distribution policies. His career began as Madero's body guard. Later, he joined the Orozco Rebellion, then repudiated Orozco and tried to start his own rebellion, based on land redistribution. He never acquired the men and resources to be successful, but his raiding and harassment had great impact on Casas Grandes and Pearson. He is most famous for an act he probably did not commit, the Cumbre Tunnel Massacre.

Manuel García Vigil—From a well-to-do family in Oaxaca, García attended Mexico's main military college, known as the Heroes Military College, in Mexico City. Caught up in the revolutionary fervor at a young age, he traveled to El Paso to join Madero in 1910 at age 22. He eventually joined Carranza's Constitutionalist movement, served in congress, and was governor of Oaxaca. He split with Carranza and did not survive the murderous post-revolution politics. He was executed after a failed anti-government uprising in 1924.

Mariano Hernández—Also trained at the Heroes Military College, he led a small band of rebels associated with Orozco. An older man, little is known about him after he fought with Madero at Casas Grandes.

Eleuterio Hermosillo—Not a great deal is known about him other than he served on Villa's staff.

Juan Sánchez Azcona—Madero met Sánchez at the Sorbonne in Paris where they both studied political and social science. Sánchez's father had represented the Benito Juárez and Porfirio Díaz governments in several countries. Sánchez received degrees in Germany and France. He returned to Mexico for a career as a liberal journalist. Madero asked him to be his private secretary. He helped draft the Plan de San Luis Potosí. Sánchez remained as private secretary until 1913, when Madero was arrested and assassinated. He narrowly escaped to Cuba, later returning to serve in the Carranza and Obregón administrations.

These short biographies illustrate that many of the early revolutionaries were middle class men of substance, often well-educated professionals. They represented the liberal side of Mexico's perpetual liberal-conservative conflict.

After their contradictory celebration, Madero's people realized that San Diego was too close to the federal army that had just defeated them. Gathering what troops they could, they retreated to Bustillos in the Guerrero District where Orozco was waiting.

Mound of the Heroes

After the battle, residents of Casas Grandes emerged from their houses to assess the damage. Most of the fighting took place on the south side of town, and many dead men and horses lay sprawled where they fell. Local officials organized crews to collect the bodies and take them to a pit within the Paquimé ruins.

About 26 or 27 years before the battle, a man named Miguel Bastidas became obsessed with the idea that ancient people had buried a gold statue, Buey de Oro, or Golden Ox, in a tunnel deep in a large mound in Paquimé. The mound was probably a ceremonial platform, not a ruined building.

The pioneering anthropologist Adolph F. Bandelier explored Paquimé in 1884 and met Bastidas. Bandelier spoke with him and described him in his journal as a "monomaniac and a lunatic."

The obsessed Bastidas started from the top of the mound and dug a wide, slanting shaft 90 feet long. He cut a road up the side of the mound to facilitate the work and remove the dirt. After this enormous effort and spending all his money, he found only water—no golden ox or even a tunnel.

The huge hole at the top of the mound remained. The Casas Grandes crews hauled the dead bodies, men and animals, up the access road to the pit and buried them. It is reported that 85 of Madero's rebel soldiers lie there along with an unknown number of federals and horses. The crew marked the site with "1911" laid out in stones. Called the *Montículo de Héroes*, or Mound of Heroes, the site immediately became a place of honor. So many visitors came that Bastidas' road had to be reinforced with cement steps. When Charles Di Peso began the excavation in 1959, German Galaz, president of the Casas Grandes Municipio, and Teófilo Borunda, governor of Chihuahua, asked him to leave the graves in the mound undisturbed.[584]

The Battle of Ciudad Juárez

Madero wanted to make a grand statement at Casas Grandes, and he did. Even in defeat, the idealistic and unrealistic idea had worked. Strategically, the attack made no sense. Casas Grandes was an important town, but not critical to the defense of Ciudad Juárez. The spirit that pervaded San Diego after the defeat somehow spread. Men individually and in small bands walked or rode to the rebel camp at Bustillos.

After Madero arrived, he and Orozco reconciled, at least for the time being. Orozco assumed overall military command. Madero never led in battle again. Working together, they began the task of organizing their mix of guerilla fighters, federal deserters, soldiers of fortune, and untrained campesinos into some form of fighting unit.

Late in March, Villa rode in at the head of 700 men. He maintained tight discipline, and this large contingent of loyal men set the tone for Madero's entire army. Alcohol was forbidden and the ban enforced by military police. Madero placed Villa, Garibaldi, and José de la Luz Blanco directly under Orozco in the command structure. José de la Luz Blanco was another anti-reelectionist leader from the Guerrero District, who had led a successful band of guerillas before joining Madero. In a matter of days, their combined efforts converted a rabble into a semblance of a disciplined army. One of de la Luz Blanco's officers was José Inés Salazar. In little over a year, he would terrorize the Casas Grandes Valley.

451

The supply of small arms seems to have been adequate enough to provide a rifle for each man. The problem lay with the lack of heavier weapons. Everyone to the lowest rifleman knew they would face cannon and machine gun fire they could not match when they tried to storm the barricades. Giuseppe Garibaldi came up with an idea that if nothing else boosted morale. He decided to make two cannons in the MNWR machine shop in Madera. Among his Falange and Mexican volunteers, he found four skilled machinists. Benjamín Aranda built the cannons, assisted by Rafael Rembao.[585] They took two eight-inch railroad-car axles and bored them lengthwise, creating three-inch tubes, the cannon barrels. They would be smoothbores since rifling was beyond their capabilities. At one end of each tube, they made and installed a breech block with a spring-loaded, pistol-cartridge igniter connected to a firing pin and trigger. They wrapped the breech blocks with metal straps to help withstand the pressure of the exploding powder. Instead of cannon balls, I.R. Pimentel, a machinist, devised projectiles from short pieces of three-inch pipe. One end was filled with lead and the other left hollow with wide slits in the side to create a howling sound as the projectile flew through the air. Using heavy wagon wheels and other wagon parts, they constructed carriages with a tongue and harness for a four-mule team. The men worked quickly and their home-made artillery pieces were ready in time for the battle.[586]

Orozco and Villa were already on the move. On April 7, each led a column of 500 mounted men out of camp. Madero followed with 1,500 men. They met little opposition as most federals had withdrawn to Ciudad Chihuahua or Ciudad Juárez, not sure which city would be attacked.

While preparing, Madero moved his headquarters to San Andrés (the site of Villa's first fight with federal troops), just 30 miles from Ciudad Chihuahua. Federal troops could not leave the city to attempt a pincers movement on the rebel's rear as they moved north for fear the real objective might be the capital.

By early April, the rebels allowed the MNWR managers to reopen and run freight and even passenger service as long as no federal soldiers rode. George Rutledge's crews had repaired the tracks and bridges sufficiently to allow trains to run even into beleaguered Ciudad Juárez and Ciudad Chihuahua. The Madera mill reopened and shipped some of its accumulated inventory. The MNWR still had to contend with rebel orders to provide engines and cars whenever needed. Preliminary to the upcoming battle, four engines and 100 flat and box cars stood by on sidings in Pearson.[587]

In Madera, the cannons were put on flat cars along with some rebel troops. Most of the rebels marched cross country to Pearson. Learning that the federals had left Casas Grandes, Madero moved his headquarters there. A month after his great defeat, he walked into town.[588]

At Casas Grandes, he consolidated his units. He assigned officers to buy clothing in town for the men, suggesting that the rebels by now were a ragged crew. He put Salazar in charge of obtaining wagons and mules and delivering the clothing. The two cannon arrived, but one had to be sent on by train to the Pearson mill machine shop for final assembly.

Midmonth, Madero began the move to Ciudad Juárez. On April 14, he was at Guzmán Station. He sent a train full of rebels up the line to Bauche Station. The federals, now on the defense, had their own tricks, including placing mines on the rebel-controlled tracks. As a countermeasure, the rebels learned to put two empty boxcars in front of the train engine. Just before Bauche, the train did hit a mine, but the boxcars prevented derailment or worse. As the rebel troops scrambled out of the train cars, hidden federals opened fire. A major firefight ensued. The embattled rebels sent the train back three times for more troops. The federal General Navarro, back in the city, did not want to risk weakening his defenses and did not send reinforcements. The federals at Bauche finally retreated. The road lay open to entrenched Ciudad Juárez.

General Navarro, with his back to the river, had blocked the streets in a semi-circle sequence of barricades and 400 trenches. Orozco moved up and positioned Madero's troops around the perimeter. He placed the two cannons in the center. Navarro refused Madero's surrender demands. He had a strong position and he thought Madero would be reluctant to attack because the trajectory of the rebel bullets could fly into El Paso, injuring or killing civilians. Already, El Paso residents had seats on top of the hotels to watch the action. Rumors had flown about for weeks that the U.S. would intervene against the rebels. The possibility of U.S. intervention, while probably remote in reality, was a serious issue for both sides. Everyone knew President Taft had 10,000 U.S. Army troops along the border. The fact that this was more of a protective measure to make a point, rather than prelude to aggressive intervention did not reassure either rebel or federal leaders.

U.S. business interests in Chihuahua, including the MNWR, did not want intervention. MNWR had just moved its general offices from Ciudad Chihuahua to Ciudad Juárez and was in a precarious position The company already had suffered severe losses, and managers tried to move as much equipment as possible across the border to El Paso.

In spite of the danger, Dr. Pearson did not believe U.S. intervention was the answer. He wrote that intervention would set off a brutal war on hostile foreign soil that would rival the English experience in the Boer War.[589] He and his managers now hoped for a new government and stability.

General Navarro's gamble not to surrender almost worked. On the eve of battle, politics intervened. After rebel successes in Chihuahua, uprisings began to occur throughout the country. Facing these and the potential loss of their important port of entry, hacendados, bankers, and others of the economic and political hierarchy began to panic. They reasoned that if limiting the presidential re-election was the big issue, then let it happen. There was too much else to lose and they urged Díaz to negotiate a settlement. Most of the army commanders disagreed, including the high-ranking Victoriano Huerta. The old president disagreed as well but was willing to deviate from his hard line and take a subtler approach. He had made mistakes and underestimated the situation in Chihuahua but remained a wily politician. He understood the arrogance and paranoia of the military class and knew it was time to choose the *pan* option of his long-time *pan o palo*, bread or stick, policy. *Palo* had not worked. Through Madero's elite family he applied pressure to hold back at Ciudad Juárez and negotiate. This did work.

At the culminating moment of his Revolution, at the moment he was being compared to Benito Juárez, Madero hesitated. He agreed to an armistice.

On the surface, the concept of an armistice seemed reasonable. Negotiations might save lives on both sides. The rebels strengthened their positions every day and could still attack. They could and they finally did, but the fragility of the Madero Revolution had been exposed, revealing disunity and distrust among the factions.

Competing ideologies and revolutionary objectives promoted by the Flores Magón brothers, Práxedis Guerrero, the PLM, the Anti-reelectionists, Emiliano Zapata, and Madero himself had unleashed social forces that could not be controlled by moderate reasoning. For a moment, Madero held it all together in his hands. The moment called for decisive action. Hesitation knocked him from his pedestal and even though he won the battle and was elected president, he never recaptured that moment.

Offers by Díaz's negotiators created fractious discussions. Díaz's resignation remained the core issue, but Madero dithered. Family pressure mounted. Finally, and unbelievably to his followers, he decided not to attack at all. Díaz's skillful use of pan seemed to have paid off, but the old man had miscalculated again. Orozco and Villa refused to obey Madero's order. The two met and decided to attack the next morning without telling Madero. Early on the eighth of May, the rebel troops on the perimeter opened fire. Federal troops in the outer trenches fired back. It took the MNWR managers and office staff, who were still unpacking from the move, a half an hour to catch the last streetcar across the bridge to El Paso.[590] Madero received the news midmorning and tried to order a ceasefire. The most important battle of the Revolution to date was underway and unstoppable. It lasted two days.

The machinists-turned-artillerymen loaded the two cannon and aimed at the federal barracks. It is not clear what the pipe projectiles hit, but they made an incredible howl over the federal entrenchments. Smoke from the black powder charge rose in clouds. They loaded and fired again. This time the breech block blew out of one cannon, but one of the howling shots pierced the town water tank. The defenders' water supply soon drained on the ground. The intact cannon kept firing.

Under the smoke and din, the rebels fought their way into the city. Orozco ordered the initial attack to follow a line parallel to the border to avoid firing into El Paso. They met withering fire down the barricaded streets. Stymied, Villa directed his men to enter the houses and proceed block by block by knocking holes through the interior walls. When they encountered federals at close quarters, they threw their homemade dynamite bombs. Orozco and Villa had enough men to rotate the fighters, bringing in fresh troops to relieve those on the line. This kept the pressure on the federals day and night. By the beginning of the third day, they reached the center of the city. The exhausted federals had run out of options as well as water. At 2:00 in the afternoon, General Navarro surrendered. He refused to submit his sword to Orozco or Villa and Garibaldi accepted the formal surrender.

By the second day, Madero realized he had no choice. He authorized the attack. Orozco and Villa in turn acknowledged him as the overall commander. After the surrender, he immediately declared Ciudad Juárez the provisional capital of Mexico and appointed cabinet officers. Madero had survived the outright disobedience of his principal commanders, but he continued to make mistakes. The next was treating General Navarro as a respected adversary.

The rebel soldiers of all ranks hated General Navarro. A story that he had ordered rebel prisoners bayoneted had become an article of faith, and they charged into battle shouting "Death to Navarro." After his surrender, Madero ordered Castillo, whose detachment still protected him, to guard Navarro, treat him well, and let no harm come to him. Again, it was logical reasoning but bad timing. Orozco was already fuming because Madero had selected Venustiano Carranza as Secretary of War in the cabinet. The man, who arguably, had done more than anyone to keep Madero's Revolution alive, had been superseded by a civilian politician, who saw no fighting in Chihuahua. Further, after initially taking good care of his troops, Madero seemed to have forgotten them and neglected the payroll. As far as Orozco was concerned, Madero was coddling the enemy. All of this led to an ugly confrontation between the two. Villa may have been present for part of it. Castillo said he physically intervened to protect Madero. In the end, Madero prevailed. Of all the issues, he only agreed to draw funds in El Paso to pay the troops. He retained Carranza and personally drove Navarro in a car to the border and refuge in the U.S.[591] Madero did Juan Navarro a great favor, but his generosity may have helped bring on his own demise, at least indirectly.

Pardoning Navarro was another step in loosening his grip on his most powerful supporters. Madero would be assassinated in two years on February 22, 1913. That same year, General Navarro returned to Mexico to serve President Huerta, Madero's successor (and murderer). Navarro later held several political positions and lived to age 93.

Madero's Revolution Ends

Nine days after Navarro's surrender, Emiliano Zapata, the great land reformer in the state of Morelos, soundly defeated the federal army sent to eliminate him. The Battle of Cuautla, a terribly bloody eight-day fight, finally ended on May 19, 1911.

In spite of these major military victories, Madero was willing to negotiate with Díaz's governmental establishment. Díaz had to go, but beyond that, it would be business as usual. This became clear in the Treaty of Ciudad Juárez.

The May 21, 1911 agreement between the Díaz government and Madero as head of the successful revolutionary movement accomplished only a few things on the rebel agenda: Díaz's resignation; a presidential election in October; and a general amnesty for all rebels. A career foreign affairs officer and the current ambassador to the U.S., Francisco León de la Barra became interim president. Díaz, his family, Vice President Ramón Corral Verdugo, and a few top advisors left for exile in France on May 25. The remainder of the Díaz government remained in place—congress, courts, army, and most state governments. For five months, Madero and his supporters were excluded from the decision-making process. Nothing in the treaty spoke to the long-awaited and frequently promised social reforms.

Surprisingly, most of Madero's close supporters did not object to the Treaty, except for Pancho Villa, who could see the Revolution slipping from those who fought and made it happen into the hands of *los perfumados,* the perfumed elite.[592] Emiliano Zapata in Morelos was not even consulted.

León de la Barra's five-month administration enabled Díaz-era politicians and army generals to maneuver to regain positions of influence and power. This set the stage for renewed conflict between the conservative elite and various squabbling liberal factions, such as the radical followers of the Flores Magón brothers and land reformers aligned with Zapata.

Madero still enjoyed wide popularity with the Mexican people. Huge crowds greeted him when entered Mexico City on June 7. León de la Barra oversaw the October elections without serious incident, and Madero assumed office on November 9, 1912, a few days before the second anniversary of his call to revolution.

What the country needed now was a president like Benito Juárez, a man with an iron will to keep the diverse social forces unleashed by the Revolution in check and channeled to establish a democratic society. Instead, with the reelection issue settled, the country got a man, who seemed content to retain the old establishment. He failed to understand that the Revolution he had unleashed, aroused profoundly different expectations among the Mexican people.

Post-Revolutionary Politics in Chihuahua

As part of his revolutionary organization, Madero had appointed Abraham González as provisional governor of Chihuahua with Braulio Hernández as his second-in-command, with the title Secretary General. The pair did a good job, recruiting leaders, obtaining arms and supplies, and setting up the administrative structure in rebel-held areas.

Immediately after the surrender at Ciudad Juárez, González took charge of the city. Guards were stationed to prevent looting and closed saloons and gambling halls. Dr. Ira J. Bush set up hospitals for the wounded and organized work gangs of federal prisoners to bury the dead and clean the city. These sanitary measures were particularly important as a few cases of typhoid already been diagnosed. Fortunately for the city, Dr. Bush had training in public health and knew what measures to take.[593]

Dr. Bush represents another unique character in the northern Chihuahua story. He could be labeled a "noncombatant soldier of fortune." Prior to the Revolution, he had set up hospitals and medical programs in El Paso and Temósachic, Chihuahua. González knew him well. After seeking his help with the wounded the previous winter, during Orozco's march north, González recruited him as Chief Surgeon to oversee the revolutionary army's medical facilities. Dr. Bush and Pancho Villa became friends, and he later helped set up Villa's famous hospital train.

With a firm hand, González took other steps to normalize conditions and restore the economy. He contacted the MNWR managers and authorized them to proceed rapidly to resume normal service. He sent Garibaldi to El Paso to restore relations with U.S. border officials and reopen the international bridge, particularly for commercial traffic.

González accomplished a great deal in less than two weeks. Suddenly, after the signing of the Treaty of Ciudad Juárez on May 21, he no longer had legal status as provisional governor. Under existing law, the state legislature in Ciudad Chihuahua needed to ratify his appointment, pending a general election. That body, still packed with Díaz sympathizers, was in no hurry. In fact, they met in special session and attempted to keep the former governor in office and ignore González.

Order had been restored in Ciudad Juárez, but serious problems remained in the state. Except for the surrender at Ciudad Juárez, no one had given orders to other federal units. Six days after the surrender, a still-intact federal army unit attacked Cuchillo Parado, Toribio Ortega's rebel stronghold on the east side of the state. At the other extreme, a few rebel bands did not accept the authority of either Madero or González and continued to roam and raid. The situation cried out for strong leadership.

Madero had not yet left Ciudad Juárez for Mexico City and still controlled rebel troops under arms. When he heard about the Chihuahua legislature's action, he realized something had to be done. He ordered troops under Pascual Orozco to move down the National Railroad to El Sauz, a Terrazas hacienda 30 miles north of the city. The legislature understood the message. On June 2, the previous governor resigned, and Abraham González became the official provisional governor with only one dissenting vote.[594]

The almost-unanimous vote and the members' public statements hid their real intentions for the August gubernatorial election. They planned to use Madero's own anti-reelectionist rhetoric to make the case that González could not serve a second term or even run for the office. After all, González himself was the head of Chihuahua's Anti-reelectionist Party that stood for one term. The legislature, the Terrazas family, and other powerful interests, who sought the status quo, would bide their time.

On the surface, it appeared to be a period of reconciliation. Governor González's arrival in Ciudad Chihuahua on June 9 set off a series of exuberant celebrations, banquets, rallies, a baseball game, and bull fight. He and former antagonists gave speeches and publicly embraced each other. Some of the rebel army had been disbanded, but Pascual Orozco still had the large unit camped at El Sauz. He enjoyed widespread popularity as the military hero of the Revolution, but he made it clear he was under González's command.

At the same time, a federal army contingent remained in Ciudad Chihuahua, also under González, who as governor commanded the local federal military district. González ordered Orozco into the city in late June. The governor arranged for the federal and rebel soldiers to march together into the city plaza to the beat of a federal military band in a grand show of reconciliation. When the people lining the plaza saw Orozco, they cheered him as their hero. González addressed the crowd from the palace balcony with rebel and federal commanders on both sides. He used a metaphor, describing the "alliance of the (Winchester) 30-30 and the Mauser" that reunited Mexico.[595]

This was the political highpoint for the Madero/González phase of the Revolution. Many professing loyalty had their own agendas, particularly Pascual Orozco. While a great guerilla leader in the fight against Díaz, his motives appear to have been more about political ambition than social idealism. Enrique Creel shrewdly saw that Orozco appeared dazzled by the trappings of wealth and lavishly entertained him to gain influence.

González believed in and wanted reconciliation as a path to a democratic society, but he was a realist and no fool. He also was a particularly good administrator, doing whatever he could to ease out of office bureau chiefs, officials, and judges he deemed unfit because of lack of loyalty or competence. He made strenuous efforts to appoint veterans to a variety of government jobs and widows and daughters of those killed to office jobs. This was not mere patronage but a genuine effort to restore a middle class society. He combined this with indemnification programs and pensions. At the same time, he mustered out rebel soldiers. Casas Grandes was one of the centers where each man was paid and received a railroad voucher to the stop closest to his village. By August, the Casas Grandes garrison had been reduced to 80 men. Those soldiers that left had been promised 50 pesos and 25 more if they turned in their rifles. Some received the full amount, but some did not because of lack of funds. Even the full fifty pesos was not enough to start a new life, and the mustering-out process unfortunately added to an underlying but growing disillusionment.

Several former rebel fighters were able to stay in the service without joining the federal army. When Madero had selected Carranza as the Minister of War over Pascual Orozco, he appointed Orozco to the lesser position as commander of the "first rural zone," which covered the state Chihuahua. Orozco enlisted troops for this rural constabulary from former rebel soldiers loyal to him, He stationed garrisons at Chihuahua's major cities and towns. Two other former rebel officers had been promoted to the rank of general. José de la Luz Blanco commanded 350 men at Ciudad Juárez and José de la Luz Soto had the same number at Parral.[596]

González took action in other fields. He successfully dealt with several strikes and pressured large companies to increase wages and eliminate company stores. He clamped down on the rogue rebel action along the border. The U.S. government inadvertently helped this effort by arresting Ricardo Flores Magón, who had been agitating against Madero from Los Angeles, California. Remnant groups of his followers, *Magonistas*, caused problems after his arrest but Orozco's rural force suppressed them.

To help the lower and middle classes and stabilize government revenues, González began to revise the tax system with considerable success. He eliminated many tax privileges, which added to his opposition, as might be expected. Even with the new revenue, Chihuahua's treasury was burdened by high interest payments on an accumulation of outstanding bonds. Luis Terrazas owned many of these. González and his advisors devised a plan to issue new bonds at lower rates to generate cash to pay off the old bonds. For once, Terrazas's interests meshed with those of the new government. Don Luis personally pushed the sale of the new securities to El Paso bankers that eventually meant millions to him in the payout of the old bonds.[597]

Another change González pushed through was political. Since the days of Captain José Zuloaga, the political chiefs, the jefes políticos, of the cantons or districts, such as Galeana that covered the Casas Grandes Valley, had exercised enormous local power. Often corrupt and overbearing, these state-appointed positions were a specific line item on the rebel agenda. When the newly elected Chihuahua legislature took office in September, González convinced the members to alter the state constitution to eliminate the position. Today, the Districts still provide judicial and other services, but political power shifted to the presidents of municipios like Casas Grandes.

González made progress on many fronts but still had his hands full. The August election was approaching, and Pascual Orozco had shown his true intentions and become a potential gubernatorial candidate. Powerful people supported him, but in the end, he decided not to run. During the weeks leading to the election, no one was ever sure what he would do. González, playing the political game, made a serious mistake. Forces against him pushed the anti-reelectionist issue. This could be technically remedied by resigning as provisional governor before election day. This move had political dangers and González after agreeing to resign, changed his mind. This did not affect his election, but it had a major effect on his future.

With Orozco not running, the issue submerged temporarily, and González received 48,474 votes on election day, August 20, while all other opponents less than a thousand. The figures turned out to be a misleading show of support. The anti-reelectionist issue soon resurfaced along with other serious opposition issues. Not resigning had been a political mistake. Now he made another.

The national presidential election still lay ahead in October. Francisco Madero, in a political maneuver, decided to change his vice-presidential running mate. Dr. Francisco Vázquez Gómez had been the original candidate with Madero in the 1910 presidential election challenging Díaz, and the presumed candidate ever since. A wealthy doctor with broad support, he had been President Díaz's personal physician before joining the Anti-reelectionists. Madero did not trust him and wanted to substitute a loyal friend from the early founding days of the movement, José María Pino Suárez. This move met resistance from the liberal base, and Madero urged González to convince Chihuahua political parties to support Pino over Vázquez Gómez. Out of loyalty, González reluctantly agreed. His effort for Pino split the strong Anti-reelectionist party in Chihuahua, alienated the previously favorable press, lost him some of his most loyal friends, including his closest confidant, Hernández, and worse, cost him the popular support. Adoration turned to resentment.

Madero and Pino would be elected on October 11, 1911, but control of the Revolution had slipped out of their hands. The mix of reactionary power on the right and the splintered liberals on the left soon would boil over into a decade of civil war.

The Orozco Rebellion

Madero governed as president for thirteen months. Some historians say it was remarkable he lasted that long. He made many mistakes, alienating friends, clamping down when he should have shown leniency or the reverse. Even the new social freedoms, such as freedom of speech and the press, worked against him. Porfirio Díaz had forcefully muzzled the press at the very beginning of his long reign. His gag rule or *ley mordaza* made it dangerous for independent editors. After he was deposed, decades of repression were suddenly gone. The press went into a frenzy of investigative reporting. Every aspect of Madero's government and personal life was examined and ridiculed. It became so bad that advisors suggested he re-institute the ley mordaza. He would not do that and the damage was done.[598] To add to the forces tearing at the Madero government, U.S. President Taft's administration became disillusioned with Madero, prompted by the pro-Díaz ambassador, Henry Lane Wilson. Ambassador Wilson did all he could to undermine Madero, thinking this would protect North American business interests. He schemed with General Huerta and Díaz's nephew Félix Díaz. After Madero's assassination, Wilson urged the U.S. government to immediately recognize Huerta as president. Taft's successor, President Woodrow Wilson, would have nothing to do with Huerta and recalled Ambassador Wilson, but it was too late for Francisco Madero and the Mexican people. A new dictator had usurped the Revolution.

Discontent stirred among the Mexican people in many places, especially in Chihuahua, the "Cradle of the Revolution." However, the next revolutionary phase began in the state of Morelos.

Emiliano Zapata never accepted Madero as the duly elected president, in spite of personal visits in June and August 1911. The last straw was

Madero's appointment of a Morelos governor sympathetic to hacendado interests. Just three weeks after Madero officially took office on November 9, Zapata stood on a table in a mountain cave, surrounded by his peasant fighters, and proclaimed the Plan of Ayala, another in an era of "plans." Madero's Plan de San Luis Potosí that had guided the first phase of the Revolution was essentially an anti-Díaz plan, weak on land and social reform. The Plan of Ayala clearly laid out procedures to return confiscated land to villages and to take one third of private large holdings for re-distribution. These and other features caused historian Friedrich Katz to call the plan the most explicit agrarian document the Revolution produced.[599]

The Plan also demanded the removal of Madero as president and recognized Pascual Orozco as the "Chief of the Revolution." Madero responded by sending federal armies into Morelos. They did considerable damage, but the people solidified behind Zapata even more and drove out Madero's federals.

In Chihuahua, José Inés Salazar and Máximo Castillo were among the first to repudiate their allegiance to Madero. Neither ever had a strong relationship with the man they had acknowledged as their revolutionary leader. Madero seemed to distrust Salazar, the former PLM member, as too liberal. Castillo may have been the strongest believer in land reform of any of the Chihuahua revolutionaries. He idolized Emiliano Zapata, whom he had met when he accompanied Madero on the trip to Morelos in June 1911. He saw firsthand how Zapata had broken up large holdings and re-distributed parcels to campesinos. The lack of action or even interest in land reform by Madero was an excuse many used to turn on the new president. For Castillo, the issue was very real. Further, Madero personally offended his former bodyguard Castillo, who only a few months earlier had saved his life. Callously, as Castillo related it, Madero said he did not need his services anymore and refused to see him.[600]

In January 1912, Salazar and Antonio Rojas along with what men they could muster joined Emilio Vázquez Gómez and occupied Ciudad Juárez. They soon controlled Nuevo Casas Grandes, Casas Grandes, and Pearson. Emilio Vázquez Gómez, the brother of the deposed vice-presidential candidate, had emerged as an anti-Madero revolutionary with staunch supporters such as Braulio Hernández, the protestant minister and alienated former Secretary General under Abraham González.

The news shocked Madero. Ciudad Juárez was not only an important city, it was the scene of his greatest military triumph. Madero ordered Pascual Orozco, still the most popular man in Chihuahua, to take military command of Chihuahua and roust the Vázquez Gómez rebels from Ciudad Juárez. The order forced Orozco to decide whether or not to fight his recent comrades in arms. The rebels in Juárez did not want to fight against their hero Orozco either. Instead, Orozco met with them, talked of unity, and they actually agreed to lay down their arms peacefully. The grace period lasted only a few days. Orozco reconsidered, resigned, and repudiated Madero on March 3, 1912. Not long after, Orozco met with most of Chihuahua's rebel chiefs in an old meat packing plant in Ciudad Chihuahua where they signed the *Plan de la Empacadora,* also known as the *Plan Orozquista.* Inspired by Zapata's Plan of Ayala, this called for a comprehensive program of political and land reform. The signatories included many important rebel veterans, such as Orozco, Salazar, Castillo, Hernández, and Rodrigo M. Quevedo, the Casas Grandes-born future governor.[601] Notably absent was Pancho Villa. Orozco took command from Vázquez Gómez and the *Colorado* or red-flagger rebellion against Madero's government began.

Ironically, Enrique Creel and the Terrazas family supported Orozco. Creel felt he could exploit Orozco's weakness for the good life and influence him to the family's benefit. In May, the family paid a large "export" duty to Orozco, who allowed them to ship 40,000 head of cattle across the border.[602]

Orozco's rebels also shipped rustled cattle across the border on MNWR trains to augment the custom fees collected in Ciudad Juárez that financed their cause.

It started well for Orozco. He quickly organized a large army from his rural force, men commanded by the rebel signatories to his plan, and other volunteers, including a contingent from Galeana. In a few days his army, reported to be almost 8,000, marched and rode trains toward Mexico City. After skirmishes in route, he met the federal forces at Rellano near the Chihuahua/Durango border. Madero's ranking general, General José González

Salas commanded the federal forces. Orozco prevailed, although the actual battle was indecisive. Humiliated, Salas committed suicide. Madero panicked and turned to Victoriano Huerta.[603] This was the high point of the Orozco Rebellion, but the federal army remained largely intact. General Huerta had extensive experience suppressing uprisings for Porfirio Díaz. He took the field in May and by coincidence met Orozco again at Rellano. Huerta defeated the rebels and drove them north. President Taft's strict border controls on arms and ammunition shipments contributed to the rebel defeat. Lack of ammunition became a severe problem for Orozco and forced him to make strategic decisions that often put his campaign on the defensive. However, he remained powerful and popular in his Chihuahua stronghold.

The beleaguered Madero now relied on Huerta. Although Madero did not trust him, with good reason, he lacked an effective alternative. During 1912, he ordered Huerta to put down the three insurgencies: Pascual Orozco in the north; Emiliano Zapata in Morelos; and Bernardo Reyes and Félix Díaz in Mexico City. Huerta ultimately defeated Orozco, failed against Zapata, and came to an arrangement with Reyes and Díaz. These two perpetual conspirators became Huerta supporters. Changing sides and allegiances was not usual during the Revolution but became almost chronic during 1912 and 1913.

Orozco's offer to Pancho Villa to join him came in a letter from Braulio Hernández. Villa's response was clear, "Unmask and bid Pascual unmask, you pair of traitors. I will join neither you nor anyone so degraded."[604]

Villa's loyalty to Madero and particularly to González made little difference in how they treated him. Everyone was wary or even afraid of him. Madero had somewhat summarily dismissed him from the rebel army with a cash payoff. Villa continued to hold a small force together, nominally under the command of González. This small contingent of loyal *Villistas* would prove to be important.

Before his defeat at the Second Battle of Rellano, Orozco controlled almost all of Chihuahua except for Parral, where the people remained steadfastly loyal to Madero. The federal military commander, José de la Luz Soto, another veteran of the Madero Revolution, wavered and wanted to defect to Orozco. When he finally announced his intentions, many of his garrison refused to follow him. Villa found out about this split and saw an opportunity. With about 60 men, he infiltrated Parral and captured de la Luz Soto and his garrison without firing a shot.

Villa now controlled this key town in Madero's name. This set up an attack by José Inés Salazar acting under Orozco's orders. Salazar's overwhelming numbers finally drove Villa's small force out. Salazar's men then sacked the town, completely out of control. It was bad. When the details of rape, pillage, and murder became known, the storm of adverse publicity soured Chihuahuans on Orozco, so recently their hero. Creel and the Terrazas family quietly withdrew their support.

Orozco retreated to his northwest Chihuahua bastion, based in Ciudad Juárez and included the region serviced by the MNWR.

Villa's stout defense at Parral had blunted Orozco's drive south. The grateful Madero realized he could use this so-called bandit commander. He asked Villa to bring his troops and become part of the federal army under the command of General Huerta. In another strange Chihuahuan twist, the quintessential revolutionary, now fought as a *federale*. He led an estimated 400 troops in two successful battles against Orozco. Villa hated his commander, General Huerta, and Huerta in turn hated and perhaps feared his unpredictable subordinate.

It was not long before Huerta ordered Villa arrested and executed for alleged insubordination. Madero, his brother Raúl, as well as local soldiers intervened, and Villa was imprisoned rather than shot. He escaped on December 25, 1912 and crossed the U.S. border to El Paso. He would return but too late to save Madero.

Less than two months later, Huerta staged a coup. Madero and Vice President Pino Suarez were murdered on February 22, followed by Abraham González in March.

Confrontation in the Valley

During the Madero phase of the Revolution, action along the MNWR line caused damage and serious disruption but few employee casualties.[605] Most rebels showed a degree of respect to the railroad management, mill workers, track repair crews, and train engineers, despite their often-onerous demands. Any respect or restraint ended with the Orozco Rebellion.

Orozco's Plan de Empacadora contained specific language calling for nationalization of railroads and exclusive operation by Mexicans.[606] This guiding policy gave the rebels an excuse to take what they wanted from the railroad facilities and to threaten North American managers.

There had been a brief period of relative calm after the Battle of Juárez and Díaz's exile. Dr. Pearson wrote to the company shareholders with characteristic optimism in the second Annual Report for the year ending on December 31, 1911. He referred to the "political disturbances" of the past year but said there was little "physical damage." This stretched the point considerably. Nevertheless, new and ongoing construction projects had continued through the previous year but behind schedule. These included construction of the mill at Pearson, extension of a railroad spur off the main line to Chuichupa, and completion of the tunnel at the Cumbre summit.

A separate specialty mill in Madera designed to cut door, sash, and box lumber had completely burned in late December. By the time Dr. Pearson wrote the 1911 year-end report, probably in February, insurance had covered the loss, and the mill had been rebuilt. The output was designed for the Mexican market. Dr. Pearson went on to write that many civic improvements had been made at both Madera and Pearson to make the towns more attractive to employees and their families.[607]

Dr. Pearson presented the best possible picture. His shareholder report stretched the facts and he knew it. The El Paso and San Antonio newspaper editors knew it as well or thought they did. Both the El Paso newspapers had been deeply involved with the Revolution from the beginning. The Times was now pro-revolutionary and the Herald pro-Madero.[608] Lurid stories of disaster and destruction of the railroad and mills circulated widely and reached as far as the financial markets in Canada and London. As usual, Dr. Pearson provided a solution. He hired a public relations man, New York journalist P.S. Krecker. The term was not yet in use yet, but Krecker understood his assignment. He went to Mexico to monitor the political and business situation and file "correct" reports to a central news bureau in New York City. This helped put a good face on the situation, but the company still faced diminishing returns.

One positive event occurred at the Cumbre Summit. Work gangs finally hacked and blasted through the summit ridge to finish the

Cumbre Tunnel entrance completed Feb. 1912. Photo: 2009

three-quarter-mile long tunnel that now connected Pearson to Madera and beyond. The tunnel fulfilled the dream of creating a loop through the Casas Grandes Valley from Ciudad Juárez to Ciudad Chihuahua. The celebration was short-lived. Once again Dr. Pearson suffered from bad timing. Within weeks Orozco's rebels occupied all of Chihuahua served by the loop.

The company ran the first train from El Paso to Ciudad Chihuahua on February 1, 1912.[609] In a few days, José Inés Salazar, acting in Orozco's name and the Plan de Empacadora, occupied Casas Grandes and made it his headquarters. Antonio Rojas took over Madera.

The Orozco Rebellion set off a year of chaos along the loop. At first, the federal army did much of the damage, burning bridges to hinder movement of Orozco's large force. As the Orozco Rebellion started to fall apart, rebels began a rampage of destruction. MNWR reported 712 bridges burned by the end of the Orozco phase of the Revolution.[610] The restoration progress, made by Governor Abraham González during the summer of 1911, disintegrated during the summer and fall of 1912.

Orozco's red-flagger troops and semi-independent bands commanded by Salazar, Máximo Castillo, Antonio Rojas, and others destroyed equipment, harassed North Americans, and confiscated supplies, horses, and arms in Pearson, Madera, and the Latter-day Saint communities. Many skilled North American mill and railroad workers left for home. Although in April 1912 there were still 500 North Americans in Pearson, a figure that gives a clue as to the size of the town and the fledgling mill operation. However, many more panicked in July when Salazar made a speech in Pearson declaring his intent to destroy all industry in the state in order to raise recruits for the Revolution.[611] In the days that followed, his men broke into the Pearson commissary and Director's house. They continued to threaten North Americans and LDS colonists in their nearby communities.

At this time, Junius Romney, President of the LDS Colonia Juárez Stake, ordered all of the colonists to abandon their homes, farms, and businesses and leave for the U.S.—the famous "Exodus."

Dr. Pearson and Henry I. Miller, president of the Madera Lumber Company, had come to El Paso in May after visiting the Medina Irrigation project in Texas. In spite of the chaos, Pearson still believed in his project. He and Miller negotiated a deal with the Terrazas family to buy thirteen miles of track between the rich Santa Eulalia mining district and the junction in Ciudad Chihuahua. This was at a crucial time when others might have considered consolidation to cut losses. They also visited the almost-finished El Paso Milling Company facility that sat on twelve acres near the company railroad bridge across the Rio Grande. It was the largest of its type, perhaps in the world, and featured state-of-the-art equipment. Dr. Pearson left for Barcelona before the grand opening the following month. Demand was high for the finished product, but the company could only occasionally ship raw lumber from Pearson and Madera. Before Dr. Pearson left, he selected Malcolm Masteller to replace George Rutledge as manager of the railroad's El Paso Division. The tireless Rutledge had finally worn down and resigned for health reasons.[612] It was another good choice. Masteller had experience, and he turned out to particularly adept at negotiating with the erratic rebel chieftains.

That spring, it became evident that top management had lost confidence in Harold Ferris, the company general manager. There had been

El Paso Milling Company
Photo: 022-1983-012 Courtesy of the El Paso County Historical Society

personality conflicts the year before, but now Henry I. Miller seemed particularly critical. More and more key correspondence was sent to Ferris'
second-in-command John Crockett. Ferris resigned on August 1 to conduct his own business affairs, and Crockett succeeded him.

Chaos still reigned in northern Chihuahua. General Huerta was gradually but relentlessly moving north. Orozco evacuated the capital, Ciudad Chihuahua, on July 5. Two days later, Governor Abraham González
entered the city with Huerta's army from the temporary state government
location he had established in Ojinaga. He worked quickly to restore the
government in Ciudad Chihuahua.[613]

Orozco's red-flagger forces still controlled much of northern Chihuahua. In July, Pearson was full of Salazar's men and their camp followers, families, and animals. The general occupied the Director's house, and his officers took over the hotel. The troops and camp followers went wherever they wanted, occupying houses and spaces in the mills. They stole lumber for cooking fires and uncoiled fire hoses to provide water. When a passenger train did run, those that needed to go somewhere loaded children, dogs, chickens, and animals as large as sheep into the passenger compartments. Fare payments were out of the question.[614]

Orozco and his commanders remained seriously short of resources. In their frantic attempts to secure arms, ammunition, and cash to pay smugglers and clothe their men, they made many mistakes. Driven by desperation and lack of understanding of the consequences, they often took counterproductive actions that spring. Antonio Rojas robbed a Banco Minero, owned by the Terrazas family. The press had a field day, and the Terrazas family found another reason to withdraw their support. Orozco was angry and had Rojas jailed but later released him because of the need for experienced officers. However, Rojas and others continued to take shortsighted action. He ordered all houses in Madera and Pearson searched for arms and ammunition, including those of the Mexican workers. Arms were one thing, but Rojas's rebels took anything they wanted including all the horses and saddles. They loaded everything in railcars for transport to Ciudad Juárez. They stole not only from the remaining North Americans but also from the Mexican workers, the people for whom the rebels were supposed to be fighting. Local disillusionment became another factor that hastened Orozco's fall.

In Ciudad Juárez, Orozco sent men to the MNWR office to kidnap Harold Ferris and Thomas Ryan. Orozco said he would hold them hostage until ASARCO, an unrelated smelting company, paid a $9,000 "custom duty." ASARCO managers made clear they had no intention of making such a payment. MNWR eventually paid $5,000 after intervention by the American consul. That bit of extortion succeeded, and Orozco tried it again just three days later. He invited Ferris to a meeting at his headquarters. Ferris knew better than to attend, but he could not ignore the request. He sent the railroad's Mexican attorney. Orozco demanded $25,000 in one day. As an incentive, he telegraphed an order to Salazar and Rojas to destroy the entire line from Madera to Pearson. The two subordinate generals knew this was a bad idea. Masteller, the Division manager, convinced them to respectfully decline the order and explain how loss of the transportation of supplies would hurt their cause. The American consul intervened again and Orozco backed off, which saved the company property, but did not help his desperate situation.

Finally, a bizarre extortion attempt by General Salazar acted as a catalyst to end the Orozco Rebellion as a serious threat to Mexico City and Madero's government. Salazar contacted Porter C. Thede, the Madera Lumber Company manager, and demanded $100,000 US in one hour. Otherwise, he would begin destroying the Pearson mill complex. Thede knew Salazar had the manpower to carry out the threat, and he also knew that over four million dollars had been invested in the unfinished mill. He immediately sent a telegram to Henry I. Miller in New York City. Miller ordered Thede to stall, give Salazar anything he wanted from the store, but stall. He then sent a telegram to Dr. Pearson in Barcelona asking for instructions. Pearson replied emphatically that no payment should be made. He sent a message to President Madero via Luis Riba, the powerful attorney who still represented company interests in Mexico City.

Riba explained to the president that this was an extremely serious matter. He convinced Madero that significant company share holdings and debt held by English and other foreign banks could turn Salazar's demand into an international incident not unlike the French invasion of the 1860s. Madero guaranteed the MNWR he would drive the rebels out of Pearson. Ferris and the other managers were skeptical, but they used the argument with Salazar that approvals were needed from England to transfer funds. Salazar extended the deadline by one day.

It made no difference. He had gone too far. By August 5, 4,000 federal troops were in five MNWR trains moving north through the Cumbre Tunnel toward Pearson. One of the federal commanders was Antonio Rábago, now a general, who as a Díaz officer, had fought Orozco at the Bauche Station over a year before. He now pressured his old adversary.

Thede and Masteller rode on the lead train to make arrangements for track repairs. Hearing of the approach of the federal army, Salazar put his men and their horses on trains at Pearson and retreated to Nuevo Casas Grandes. He could go no farther because other rebel troops under Orozco's orders had burned bridges between Nuevo Casas Grandes and San Pedro. There was nothing he could do but break the army into small bands and scatter on horseback. While not an army anymore, these mobile guerilla bands remained dangerous. They immediately burned more bridges. Thede and Masteller had them reopened, and by August 15, the federals were on the outskirts of Ciudad Juárez.

With no other option, Orozco agreed to surrender the city and in return was allowed to move with 500 men by the National railroad to Ahumada south of Ciudad Juárez.[615]

The MNWR had survived the Orozco Rebellion. The mills were intact, the railroad loop was complete, and the damaged line could be repaired. The workforce, though diminished, remained loyal and could be expanded now that calm had returned to the valley. Even families of North American employees began to filter back. The market for lumber of all grades remained strong, and company mangers negotiated with the government to reopen trade across the border. Everyone in the company from

Derailed Noroeste de México engine. — Photo: Courtesy of the El Paso Public Library, Special Collections, Border Heritage Center

Dr. Pearson to the site managers badly wanted to transport their inventory and generate revenue.

Unfortunately, roving bands of former Orozco red-flagger rebels remained active. Loosely led by Salazar in the Casas Grandes Valley, raiding and bridge burning became endemic.

In the Madero and Orozco phases of the Revolution destruction along the railroad usually had a purpose. The new phase became one of wanton destruction, a reign of terror focused on the railroad. Rebels, who formally had a cause, degenerated into bandits. The commissary, storerooms, and houses at Pearson and Madera were looted repeatedly. Remote stations between Madera and Pearson were attacked, forcing closures.[616] Repair parties were harassed and threatened. Not only did the renegades cut telegraph wires, they also chopped down the poles. Others, looking for a little sport, would stop a train at gunpoint, force the crew to disconnect the cars, and start the empty engine down the track at a high speed to watch it crash, explode, and roll down the embankment. If the stalled cars contained lumber, the perpetrators set them on fire.

Salazar directly commanded a force of about 500 fighters, a large number by guerilla warfare standards. He openly threatened to kidnap Thede or Crockett. That did not happen, but an El Paso cattleman was pulled off a train and held until company officials negotiated his release. Antonio Rojas's men also kidnapped a North American contractor working on the Chuichupa spur line. This incident caused more U.S. citizens to flee Mexico.

As late as January 30, 1913, Salazar continued his wave of destruction. On that date, he and Generals Antonio Rojas and Marcelo Caraveo led their band of red-flagger Orozquistas along the track north of Bauche Station. They encountered a MNWR work crew of six drilling a well next to a water tank set up to refill train-engine boilers. Salazar raged at the foreman, a North American named A.H. Dunderstadt, for working on the line. When Dunderstadt explained that his crew was not repairing track or bridges, just digging a well. The furious general shouted back that he forbad work of any of any kind on the line. He threatened to shoot any Mexican, Chinese, Japanese, "Negro," or gringo who did any kind of work along the line. His wild threat inadvertently made an interesting statement regarding the ethnic mix of the work force in the northern Chihuahua valleys.

The red flaggers searched the three Mexicans and three North Americans and took their watches and the few pesos in their pockets. Salazar then ordered his men to gather all of the tools and equipment and stack them next to the well derrick and water tank. They soaked the stacks with engine oil, lit them, and the resulting fire destroyed everything. At the workers campsite a few kilometers away, Salazar again ordered a detail of his men to take everything—food, possessions, clothing, bedrolls, tents—and pass them out to the troops. Anything left, they threw into a huge pyre nearby of burning railway equipment. After more threats, they departed, leaving Dunderstadt and his crew unhurt but without food, water, and on foot. They walked to the empty Bauche Station, where they found food, water and an undamaged hand cart. They rode the cart to Ciudad Juárez and crossed the bridge to El Paso. Dunderstadt sent a two-page letter to his supervisor J.J. Pruitt explaining what happened and noting that he had counted 26 damaged bridges. This detail and the matter-of-fact tone of the remainder of the letter is impressive for a man, who must have just experienced the most terrifying event of his life.

Dunderstadt also wrote that, while Salazar's men were destroying his camp, General Caraveo took him aside and apologized, saying they were not bandits but fighting for a cause. Dunderstadt's tone in the letter clearly indicates he found Caraveo's comments feeble. Further, the entire band did not look like it could hold out against serious opposition.[617]

Like Caraveo, other Orozquista rebels continued to maintain the façade that they fought for Orozco and Revolution. Some leaders even established a "government" in Ojinaga, out of reach of the federals—the same location as González's earlier state government in exile. Orozco himself had been wounded. With his father and a secretary, he crossed into the United States to recover and avoid capture.[618]

The beleaguered MNWR management could not keep up with the damage. Fewer and fewer trains of any sort ran. Mexican work crews were afraid to go out on the track. Managers had difficulty manning the trains and keeping the mills open. Too often, trains ran with inexperienced crews, which compounded the problems on the line.

Dr. Pearson and Miller pushed Crockett to increase production to cover costs, but it was impossible. In September and October 1912, the mills cut and sold 31,000,000 feet of lumber. The railroad could only ship 4,500,000, less than 15 percent. After the first of the year, London bankers refused any more loans to the Madera Lumber Company, having already lent five million dollars.[619]

Federal garrisons manned towns such as Pearson and Casas Grandes, but local commanders were reluctant to chase the guerillas, to the frustration of company managers. From their employees, they often had useful information about rebel locations that they passed to the garrison commanders. These officers, including Captain Telepeña at Pearson, usually did nothing. They lacked motivation and commanded troops with low morale. In one instance, a Pearson manager found out that Salazar was hiding in Chuichupa after he had torn up track in the Guzmán area. Telepeña refused to move in a timely manner. When he did, Salazar was long gone into the Sierra Madre.

By early 1913, several LDS colonists had moved to Pearson to work on the mill construction. Some had returned after the Exodus, a few had never left. Apparently, there were enough to establish a Relief Society building. Captain Telepeña confiscated it to house his troops.[620]

One exception to the weak garrison commanders was General José de la Luz Blanco at Casas Grandes. De la Luz Blanco had been one of the few to meet Madero with fighting men after he crossed into Chihuahua and marched toward Casas Grandes. He had remained loyal to Madero and protected Casas Grandes well. Several times he sortied and caught up with rebel bands, killing and capturing several.

For the most part, the federal effort under General Huerta's overall command remained lethargic. Critics claimed Huerta stalled to weaken Madero's government and hasten its fall. Governor González certainly believed this. He suspected the general's intentions, and the two bickered over jurisdiction and lack of military action. As noted, González was a very competent administrator. To meet this situation, he organized a state militia, independent of the federals. He arranged to buy arms in the U.S. and transport them legally across the border (a smart move that later backfired).

Madero finally realized the command structure in Chihuahua would not work. In December, he relieved Huerta and installed General Antonio Rábago. Huerta went back to Mexico City and waited for one month.

MNWR management at all levels bombarded Madero's government with demands for protection. In spite of explicit descriptions in the company communications, Madero received mixed reports from his advisors, which confused him about the real situation. His foreign minister in El Paso even claimed the company had destroyed its own bridges. While some additional troops were sent, the federal response was too slow. The north remained chaotic until the Ten Tragic Days of February 1913, Huerta's coup d'état.

Huerta arrested Madero and Vice President Pino Suárez on February 18. Four days later General Rábago's men surrounded the government office on Ciudad Chihuahua's plaza, arrested Abraham González and forced him to resign. A hastily assembled tribunal charged him with several crimes and corruption. He was convicted among other things of illegal arms shipments. Several U.S. officials were concerned and made strenuous efforts to protect González, in spite of a flow of misinformation to Washington from Ambassador Henry Lane Wilson. Madero already had been murdered on February 28. General Rábago and others of Huerta's people reassured the U.S. Consul about González, but on the night of March 7-8, they murdered him.

After Huerta gained control of the government in Mexico City, he sent agents to meet with representatives of Pascual Orozco. The hero of the Madero Revolution agreed to take command of the new dictator's federal forces in Chihuahua. He and at least ten of his loyal officers met with Huerta on March 13. Orozco and Huerta embraced, and Huerta agreed to seven demands to give lip service to the Revolutionary cause. These covered land reform, the ability of former rebels to join Orozco, and aid to rebel widows. Salazar hesitated and did not attend the meeting. In spite of his recent ruthlessness in the Casas Grandes Valley, he may have remembered some of his reformist ideas as an early PLM member and companion of Práxedis Guerrero. Any such idealistic ideas were short-lived. The offer of the position of jefe político (reinstated by Huerta) of Galeana District brought him into Huerta's camp. Máximo Castillo did not join. He contacted Emiliano Zapata and tried to start a Zapatista land-reform movement on his own.[621]

In the evening of the day Orozco and Huerta embraced and five days later after Abraham González was murdered, Pancho Villa and eight men swam their horses across the Rio Grande to Chihuahua.[622]

13

Pancho Villa's Revolution
Along the Railroad

An Exchange of Dictators

After two years of a bitter, bloody revolution to oust one tyrannical regime, General Victoriano Huerta emerged as the new dictator of another. He skillfully manipulated the conservative anti-reform, pro-Díaz factions to support his coup. Thus began what has been called "… one of the most grotesque tyrannies in Mexican history." The struggle against this absolute power constituted the next phase of the Revolution. As in the earlier phases, much of the action took take place in the northern states and in Morelos.

Madero did not have an immediate successor to pick up the banner and resume the Revolution against the new oppressor. Abraham González would have been an obvious candidate, but Huerta knew that and had him murdered. Orozco had switched sides; Zapata in Morelos could not capture national support; and Villa was hiding in the U.S.

The major players of the next phase of the resistance emerged from separate regions. In northern Mexico, they would be Venustiano Carranza of Coahuila, Álvaro Obregón of Sonora, and Pancho Villa of Chihuahua and Durango. Emiliano Zapata continued his independent struggle in Morelos. The three northern leaders, wary of each other, generally agreed on an overall strategy to advance on Mexico City: from Sonora down the west coast, from Coahuila and Nuevo León down the east coast, and from Chihuahua and Durango down the center. This strategy originated with General Felipe Ángeles, a well-trained professional army officer who had joined Villa and became an important advisor. As sound as the strategy was, arrangements among the regions featured mutual distrust and lack of coordination. Most initially accepted Carranza as the nominal leader, except Zapata.

Dozens of books and articles have been written about every aspect of Villa's history during this phase of the Revolution. Little can be added other than a summary supplemented by the tumultuous events along the Mexico North Western Railway.

Immediately after the coup in February 1913, Venustiano Carranza, the governor of Coahuila, repudiated Huerta. Carranza had no legal authority, but he stepped into the national leadership vacuum and proclaimed himself the First Chief of the Constitutionalist Army. "Constitutionalist" in his title referred to the Constitution of 1857, adopted in the Benito Juárez era. Like Madero, Carranza came from a wealthy Coahuila family. He opposed Huerta but remained class conscious and much more conservative than his contemporary revolutionaries. Tall and imposing, he wore small, tinted glasses and had a long white beard that made him look older. Clever politically, he had no military background. General Álvaro Obregón, who did, became his military commander.

Huerta reacted quickly to Carranza, and his federal troops overran Carranza's ill-prepared insurgents in Coahuila. This forced Carranza to move his base of operations to Sonora, where strong opposition to Huerta existed, not only among the people, but at the highest echelons of state government. The Sonora legislature had even passed a formal motion to resist Huerta.

Álvaro Obregón, the tall, handsome Sonoran military commander, accepted Carranza's leadership and began a campaign against Huerta's federals. In contrast to Carranza, Obregón had grown up in poverty among the Mayo Indians of Sonora. He spoke their language and had sympathy for their needs. These sympathies would surface in the political years of his career. For the time being, he took a wait-and-see attitude politically and concentrated on leading his Sonoran army. Many Mayo and Yaqui Indians served in his ranks.

He initially had considerable success taking border towns and the port of Guaymas. Moving farther south toward Sinaloa proved difficult because of the lack of a railroad system.

Huerta had murdered Chihuahua Governor González, and federal forces controlled the state. The new dictator appointed General Antonio Rábago as governor. Rábago, just days before had been Chihuahua's military commander under González and President Madero. Huerta now reasoned that with no effective rebel leadership in Chihuahua, he could use the state as a central base of operations to combat his opponents on either side—in Coahuila and particularly in Sonora. His strategic assessment overlooked a forgotten exile. Huerta should have executed Pancho Villa when he had the chance.

Villa and eight men crossed the Rio Grande on March 13, 1913. They continued south for seven days, following more or less the National Railroad but avoiding major garrison towns. As they rode, old comrades managed to find them. Their number increased to 25 by the time they reached San Andrés, west of Ciudad Chihuahua, the site of Villa's first fight to begin the Revolution in November 1910.

Eager to fight, Villa and his 25 men attacked San Andrés but had to withdraw. However, this was familiar territory. More men joined him and he overwhelmed San Andrés and made it his temporary headquarters. He soon controlled most of the towns along the MNWR Chihuahua-Division line from San Andrés to Madera. Ciudad Chihuahua remained too large and too well defended.

The romanticized versions of this part of Villa's story suggest that thousands of men, shouting "Viva Villa," flocked to their hero as soon as he crossed the border. He did raise an army in an amazing short length of time. In reality, it took a several months for word to spread to his former officers and followers and for some to give up their own independent raiding. For the first weeks after crossing the border, he had only a few hundred men. By June, he had 1,000. Three months later in September, he had assembled an armed force of 8,000—strong enough to overpower the fixed entrenchments of the major rail center of Torreón in southwestern Coahuila. It was a feat worthy of the legend, and more men joined him.[623]

The Revolution had never ended for most of the veteran rebels from Chihuahua. Each had fought for some vague or specific dream of a better life, and each felt betrayed in one way or another by Madero, Orozco, or even Abraham González. Their lives and prospects were no better and perhaps worse than before. With Villa, they found a new cause, a new banner to follow carried by a great leader. They knew Pancho cared for them, and with him they were invincible. For a while, it proved to be true.

The Battle of Pearson

President Huerta put José Inés Salazar back in charge of federal forces in the Casas Grandes region. Salazar had commanded this same area the previous year as an Orozco rebel. This was his home territory, and he established his headquarters in Casas Grandes. General Rábago, Huerta's appointee as Chihuahua's governor and military commander, ordered Salazar to establish or reinforce federal garrisons in Madera and in the larger towns from Pearson to Ciudad Juárez. A Colonel Rojas commanded at Pearson.[624] It was a terrible time for the Casas Grandes Valley. Salazar's federals had little control of the outlying country, particularly the mountains. Remnant bands of former Orozco red flaggers roamed freely, attacking and pillaging. As vicious as the previous conflict had been for the people, this was worse. Civilian murders had been rare (other than Chinese), in spite of dire threats. Now, no one was safe on the roads or in the mountains. LDS men had been killed when they ventured west into the mountains to inspect their properties. In addition to the renegade bands, Máximo Castillo with his small army emerged as major terrorists along the MNWR and National Railroads.

"General" Castillo had refused to join Huerta after fighting for Orozco. According to his autobiography, he met with Salazar, his former comrade in arms, at the mining town of San Pedro. Salazar tried to convince him to join Huerta, but he remained adamant to carry on alone.[625] Idealistically, Castillo wanted to be a Zapatista land reformer. Practically, he became an indiscriminate raider, using his ideals as an excuse to carry out a reign of terror along the railroad. Castillo claimed he and Salazar had a deal not to engage each other's forces, which freed him to rampage.[626] In spite of his notorious reputation, Castillo apparently genuinely believed in land reform. He was the only Chihuahuan leader during the Revolution to actually expropriate hacienda land and assign it to landless peasants. That did not stop him from raiding and pillaging.

In the dark early morning of June 9, 1913, Castillo led his troops in an attack against the federal garrison at Pearson. No one knows Castillo's motive for this apparently carefully planned operation. Perhaps he wanted to strike another blow at Huerta's government forces. More likely he simply needed supplies, arms, and horses. This was borne out by the systematic looting of the entire town after the battle. In his autobiography, Castillo only admitted to taking 100 rifles and 15,000 rounds of ammunition, but witnesses claim the looting was indiscriminate.

Also, no one knows the exact size of either force. Earlier, Castillo had 600 men encamped at nearby Hacienda San Diego. In their report to senior management, MNWR officials stated that Castillo used 200 to attack the federal garrison of only 91 defenders.[627] This must have been close because Castillo estimated his opposition to be 100 federals.[628] David Brown, an LDS member staying in the Casa Grande Hotel, stated later that he was surprised at the rebel attack because the federals had a "pretty fair-sized garrison" in town.[629]

Brown and James L. "Bert" Whetten had just arrived in Pearson with a herd of 40 horses they had driven from their former ranches in the bandit-infested mountains near the Chuichupa and García Colonies. Brown and Whetton and their extended families had gone north during the Exodus the previous year. They eventually settled in central New Mexico, where they had a logging contract. They could not obtain enough horses for their log-hauling teams and decided to make the dangerous journey back to their mountain ranches to find any of the stock they left behind. They planned to drive the horses to Pearson and ship them by train to El Paso. The two friends probably did not realize how dangerous the Casas Grandes Valley area had become in their absence, particularly the mountains. The fact that their MNWR train from Pearson to El Paso delivered them without incident might have lulled them even more. In spite of numerous warnings from friends in Pearson, they borrowed horses and rode into the Sierra Madre.

Their luck held. They encountered Tec Villa, an old friend who had ranch near Chuichupa. He and his vaquero helped Whetten and Brown find their scattered horses. Despite heavy demand for horses during this time of conflict, they rounded up a significant herd and began the drive to Pearson.

Another old friend, a rancher named Juan Martínez, from Hop Valley, helped them avoid trouble until a band of outlaw red flaggers spotted them driving the herd toward the road that descends from Pacheco to the valley. After a harrowing break-neck chase, they drove the horses down the steep route to the safety of the valley and Pearson. Tec Villa and his vaquero hid the herd in a meadow across the river.

Brown took a room at the hotel, and Whetten stayed with Morley Black, an LDS friend living in Pearson's Barrio Americano.

A few LDS mill employees, like Black, had not joined the Exodus the previous year. Others, like Heaton Lunt (from the Lunt family that had settled Pacheco) and his wife, Chloe Laws Lunt, had returned to try to pick up the pieces of their former life. They did not have a proper place to stay in Pearson, and a couple named Wormer asked them to move into their house temporarily and care for their two children. The Wormers needed to go El Paso for several days to buy supplies and conduct other business. After settling his family, Lunt borrowed Morley Black's horse and saddle and rode into the mountains to Pacheco to see if he could find any of his cattle.

After David Brown moved his gear into a hotel room, he went out to pick up other belongings he had left behind before going into the mountains. He met Tec Villa on the street, who said he had heard a rumor in the local saloon about Villistas attacking the next day. Neither considered the source reliable and went on their way. Brown found what he was looking for and returned to the hotel and went to bed.

Whetton and the Black family slept a few houses away. Farther up the street, Chloe and the children slept alone in the Wormer house. The federal soldiers slept in the nearby barracks. No sentries were posted.

In the predawn darkness of June 9, 1913, General Castillo quietly placed half of his men behind the embankment of the dry mill pond on the east side of town below the huge unfinished mill. He positioned the remaining men on the opposite side of town on the long hill above Barrio Americano. A deep drainage ditch ran near the base of the hill. The federals had dug trenches nearby. The ditch still exists just west of the Adobe Inn to divert floodwater from Barrio Americano. At 3:00 a.m. the rebels opened fire. Their massed fire cut down the federals as they stumbled out of the barracks toward the trenches. Caught in the crossfire, Colonel Rojas tried to rally his troops and return fire. A bullet caught him in the stomach. More bullets ripped into the nearby houses and hotel.

David Brown awoke in his hotel room to a crackling sound like burning juniper wood.[630] He jumped up, looked out and heard shouting. Then bullets smashed through the walls of his room. This was no campfire. He ran to the lobby as other panicked residents appeared in their night clothes. As he ran out the front door to find shelter, he remembered Chloe Lunt alone with children at the upper end of town. He hurried toward her house, prodded on by whistling bullets overhead. Nearing the house, he could see her standing on the porch with the children watching the battle. He shouted that she must go inside, but she calmly indicated that the wooden walls provided no more protection than the open air. She was just as safe on the porch where she could see all the action—men ducking and firing from the left and right, their shots making winking lights in the gathering

Castillo divided his command, placing men in the dry pond below the mill and the others on the hill in the foreground. The federal troops slept in one of the large buildings. — Photo: 033-2001-014 Courtesy of the El Paso County Historical Society

dawn. Brown finally convinced her they must leave and find a safer hiding place. Inside, she decided to telephone her husband, Heaton. The company had extended a line from its railroad telephone system across the prairie into the mountains to the mill at Pacheco.[631] She left a message for Heaton and began collecting her valuables as Brown prepared food for the children. Who knew when they would eat again?

Morley Black, his wife, two children, and Bert Whetten ran from the house when they heard the shooting and jumped into the drainage ditch. They huddled there as bullets smacked into the earthen bank above. Federal soldiers dropped in near them. The family scrambled around a curve as the rebels came off the hill and began firing up the ditch. They hid in a side arroyo listening to the shots and yells for what seemed a very long time. Finally, the gun fire began to diminish. They started off when a large group of rebels—it seemed like a hundred—walked right past them, heading for the center of town. The captain of the band noticed them and politely assured them that the battle was over. They could still hear an occasional shot and they waited a bit before hurrying back to the house.

At the Wormer house, just as David Brown and Chloe Lunt were about to leave for safety, a large group of women and children came streaming by shouting "*Viva Villa! Viva Villa!*" They said they were going to the center of town because the Villistas had taken the town and they were very glad. Right or wrong, they gave the credit for liberating their town to their hero, Pancho Villa.

The battle did seem to be over. Brown decided Mrs. Lunt and the children were safe enough for him to go back and see what had happened. He saw men dragging the bullet-riddled bodies of federal soldiers and placing them in rows along both sides of the road. One federal lieutenant and thirteen soldiers had been killed and fifteen to twenty wounded. Colonel Rojas lay among the wounded. He died two days later. The surviving federals stood bareheaded in lines under rebel guard. They had been ordered to throw their offensive federal caps away. Other rebels dug a long trench across the road from the hotel and began burying bodies.

Castillo claimed none of his men were killed, but he probably lost at least two killed and seven or eight wounded. He more than made up for his losses with federal prisoners who defected to him. Bullets had struck many houses but no townspeople were injured.[632]

More Mexican residents gathered and cheered for Villa, but quickly returned to their homes when Castillo's men began to systematically loot each house. Several of the men entered the store owned by Luis Orozco and C. H. Cooper and began to grab merchandise. Luis Orozco (not to be confused with a distant cousin, Pascual Orozco) worked for Cooper at the mill, and together they owned a large store. Orozco complained to Castillo's Colonel Manuel Gutiérrez, who posted guards to prevent entrance without a signed commissary order from Castillo. This provided temporary relief from wanton looting, but by midday, goods worth 20,000 pesos had been "purchased" from the store with Castillo's paper.

Castillo set up temporary headquarters in the hotel to deal with prisoners, accept new recruits, and oversee the search for arms, horses, and supplies. He did not execute any federals but rather chose to free those who did not join him. To prevent the arrival of federal reinforcements, he sent crews north and south of Pearson to tear up track.

MNWR officials first heard of the attack from the Spilsbury brothers who ran a tourist and hunting business in Pearson.[633] When the shooting started, they immediately left and made their way to Casas Grandes. The telegraph operator there notified Crockett in Ciudad Juárez. The operator said he could see smoke over the hills to the southwest, probably from a burning bridge. Crockett forwarded the news to Miller in New York City. More details came a few days later in a three-page letter, dated June 13, from M.J. Gilmartin, an assistant to Cooper.

Gilmartin had waited out the shooting in the Director's house on the hill not far from the rebel position. About 11:00 in the morning, six rebels came to the house and escorted him to Castillo's room in the hotel. With Castillo sat Professor Braulio Hernández, the Protestant firebrand who had been an important player in Governor Abraham González's administration during the Madero Revolution. He later repudiated González and Madero and joined his old friend Pascual Orozco in the Orozco Rebellion.[634] He resurfaced as a tough-minded advisor to Castillo. Hernández demanded $1,000 or Castillo's men would burn the town and the mill. Gilmartin tried to explain that the company did not have that amount of cash in Pearson,

Pearson store operated by Clarence Cooper and Luis Orozco.
Photo: 3635866_AZSW
Courtesy of the University of Arizona Libraries, Special Collections

and he could not contact company office in El Paso because the telegraph line had been cut. Hernández forced him to go to the mill and railroad offices with the company cashier to search for money. They turned up only a few pesos. Very disappointed, Hernández made more threats and returned to the hotel. That evening Castillo and his staff left for Hacienda San Diego.

The next day Castillo ordered Gilmartin brought to San Diego. Castillo and Hernández made it clear that he would remain in custody until the company sent the money. A few hours later, Gilmartin spoke with Colonel Gutiérrez, who appeared to be sympathetic. Gutiérrez interceded with Castillo, who granted Gilmartin permission to return to Pearson under Gutiérrez's supervision. They arrived about 8:00 in the evening and met with Luis Orozco in the store. A message had come for Gilmartin (how is unclear as the telegraph lines were cut) reporting that his child was very sick in Ciudad Juárez. Luis Orozco convinced Gutiérrez to allow Gilmartin to go to his child, even though Gutiérrez appeared to fear Castillo and Hernández.

The news that Gilmartin had left infuriated Castillo. His extortion plan had failed and he threatened to execute Gilmartin when he caught him. Gilmartin made it to his child's bedside and Castillo never caught him. However, eight months later, Gilmartin tragically died in the Cumbre Tunnel Massacre.[635]

Brown and Whetton had another serious concern now that the shooting had stopped. They clearly could not ship their horses by train as originally intended. They could drive them to the border, but they knew they had been lucky to get out of the mountains with the herd, let alone drive it to the border without trouble. Brown decided to meet the problem head on and request safe-passage, a *salvo conducto,* directly from Castillo.

Brown waited several hours outside the hotel, but a heavily armed guard finally admitted him to present his case. Castillo must have been in an expansive mood because he readily consented and instructed his secretary to write out a document ordering anyone Brown encountered to respect his rights and let him pass with the horses.

The Battle of Pearson was over. One report states that the fighting lasted into the afternoon,[636] but the experience of the LDS families suggests it barely lasted through breakfast. Castillo stayed only one night in Pearson before returning to San Diego. He left three men in charge.

As a battle, Pearson was a petty affair. The size and sweep of coming events make it seem insignificant. However, it marked the beginning of the end for bandit control of northern Chihuahua, whether the red flaggers or Castillo understood it or not. A new star was rising.

Viva Villa

Pancho Villa was coming. The women and children streaming to the center of Pearson chanting *"Viva Villa"* already knew it. They were just a bit premature. Villa had nothing to do with the Battle of Pearson, but he did arrive by train from Madera with his new army few days later, June 19.

The MNWR El Paso Division had experienced heavy damage during and after the Orozco Rebellion. The Chihuahua Division, along the southern portion of the MNWR loop, suffered as well. There in the Guerrero District, Huerta's federals, not the rebels, did most of the damage, burning bridges and smashing telegraph offices in a frantic attempt to block pursuit by Villa's advancing troops. At Madera, rather than confront Villa, the federal garrison decided to abandon the town and make a run for Ciudad Chihuahua in a confiscated train.

Isolated bands of red flaggers still raided from hideouts in the Sierra Madre, but Pascual Orozco himself had changed sides and joined Huerta. The famed military leader of the Madero Revolution was now a *Huarista* federal. Many from his former rebel army remained loyal to him. Orozco consolidated these loyal followers with the forces of the federal commander in Chihuahua, General Salvador Mercado.

This gave the federals a strong position in the capital city, and the commander of the Madera garrison felt reaching there was his best option. He was too late. Villa caught him at Bustillos and killed 180 of his men.[637]

F.J. Clark, the company's traveling auditor, had replaced Masteller as manager of the Chihuahua Division in Madera.[638] On June 14, after the federal garrison pulled out, Clark tried to supervise a work train to repair the wire and track. Rebels, coming up the line from the successful battle at Bustillos, grabbed him and took him to Villa's headquarters at San Antonio station just west of Bustillos and San Andrés. Villa had just burned two bridges to prevent the surviving Madera federals from taking a train east to Ciudad Chihuahua.

Clark must have been a good negotiator. He had met Villa before and knew what to expect. Villa raged at him, threatening to destroy the line if MNWR did not stop transporting federals. He demanded trains to transport his men to Madera. Clark in this and subsequent meetings over the next several days calmed Villa and convinced him the MNWR could not prevent the federals from forcefully commandeering trains. After arguing for hours, they came to an agreement.

Clark wanted the company to remain neutral, but he could see that Huerta's government could not protect the railroad or mills. Company survival depended on cooperation with Villa.

For his part, Villa recognized that destroying property owned by foreign investors would antagonize the United States and perhaps bring intervention. Also, he needed the trains.

He understood that the next phase of the Revolution would involve conventional armies transported to battlefields by rail. Protection of the rail infrastructure was in his best interest. Therefore, Villa and Clark came to an understanding that served them both. Clark even asked Villa to put someone in charge of Madera to establish and maintain order so that the mill operation could continue. Villa agreed and installed a man named Macario as jefe for the town.[639] Villa now controlled the Chihuahua Division.

In June, his ranks still numbered just 1,000 men. On June 17, five trains brought his men, their equipment and horses into Madera from San Antonio. The *caballerangos* or wranglers, cared for their large herd of horses in cattle cars.

They left the next morning, leaving a small garrison to assist Jefe Macario. Company employees attached fourteen cars to one of the trains loaded with ties to repair track and add cribbing to support damaged bridges.[640] They arrived in Pearson on June 19. The soldiers probably made camp on the west side of town while caballerangos walked the horses down the cattle-car ramps out to grazing areas.

When Villa saw the situation in Pearson, he made his views known in the strongest terms. He did not like Castillo or Hernández, nor did he like Castillo's anti-Americanism and impractical land reform ideas. He particularly did not like free-roaming "generals" raiding in what he considered his domain. As for Hernández, Villa had already branded him a traitor.

Villa ordered Castillo's three men shot and vowed to shoot Castillo himself if he caught him. He reassured MNWR officials that his forces would respect the company's mill and railroad property. He stayed somewhere in town overnight and left early in the morning leading his mounted army for Casas Grandes. They left the trains behind.

Villa's stopover in Pearson remains an unnoticed detail in Mexico's history. The proof that it happened at all is a single telegram sent to Henry I. Miller in New York City on June 23, 1913. The telegram read: "Villa arrive Pearson Thursday evening left Pearson Friday morning overland. While in Pearson executed three Mexicans who had been making trouble there and stated he would execute anybody creating disturbances, that he represented law abiding government, forbade burning of any more bridges under pain of ..." [641]

Villa likely passed through Pearson other times. Residents retell old stories of him playing pool in the pool hall on the main plaza. The Eduardo

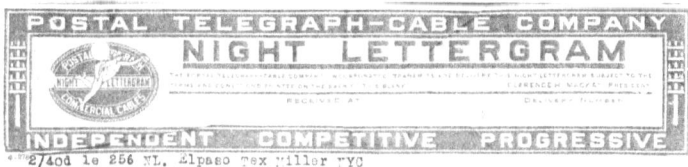

Telegram confirming Pancho Villa's presence in Pearson.
Courtesy of the University of Texas at Austin,
Benson Latin American Collection

Martínez family owns property in the northeast corner of town that has a cement slab, said to be the floor of Pancho Villa's stable. José "Pino" Molino, who worked for the railroad for 40 years beginning in 1943, told the "shoe" story. Luis Orozco, the father of Pino's friend, Miguel Orozco, was tending the store he owned with C.H. Cooper. Pancho Villa came in and demanded 300 pairs of shoes for his troops. Orozco said it was not his store, and anyway he could not supply that many shoes. Villa hotly responded that the store belonged to the Revolution, and he expected to see 300 pairs by the next day or Orozco would be executed. The next morning, Villa's men arrived and hauled away boots, work shoes, dress shoes, children's shoes, baby shoes, and women's high heels, 300 pairs.[642]

As a child, Mata Ortiz potter Ana Trillo, heard stories from her family about the Revolution. Ana is descended from one of Villa's secretaries and occasional chauffeur, Colonel Miguel Trillo. He died with Villa in the Parral ambush, July 20, 1923. A younger brother of Miguel was a seventeen-year-old soldier escort for General Felipe Ángeles. Venustiano Carranza had him convicted of treason and executed along with General Ángeles.[643] Ana collected a bowl-full of cartridges, dated 1903, along with pieces of clips and fragments of leather bandoliers, from under her mother's house. Her mother said that when Villa came through Pearson, the neighbors hid their guns and ammunition.[644] The remains in the bowl of the hidden stash and the story behind them may be another example of blame or credit given Villa, whether he was involved or not.

An exact line between truth and legend cannot be found when it comes to Villa, but the telegram proves he definitely was in Pearson the night of June 19, 1913.

The telegram also describes Villa's attack on Casas Grandes the next day, June 20, the Second Battle of Casas Grandes, an event not nearly as well known as the first battle. Villa deployed his dismounted men around the town and ordered them to crawl forward silently. When they got close, they stood and opened fire at close range. General Salazar's federals were completely surprised. Trapped, they fought back all day until 9:30 that night, but it was almost a massacre. Only a few escaped and 60 were captured. Villa ordered the survivors put in a formation in groups of three facing front to back. Each group of three was executed with one shot to "save ammunition."[645] This episode added another chapter to the Villa legend.

It is not clear what happened to Salazar or whether he even was present during the battle. He surfaced later in Ciudad Chihuahua as one of Pascual Orozco's commanders.

Castillo Survives

Despite his threats, Villa never caught Castillo. For the rest of 1913, country people in the Casas Grandes and Santa María Valleys continued to support Castillo and to recognize his authority. Unlike Villa, he never attracted many fighting men. Even with small numbers, he maintained control of the valleys for at least a few months, while the much larger Villa and Huerta forces were distracted elsewhere. The situation created the strange anomaly of a third independent force operating within the larger conflict between government and rebels. Some historians have characterized Castillo as a murderous brute, primarily because he was widely blamed for the Cumbre Tunnel Massacre.[646] He may or may not have perpetrated that highly published crime, but brute or reformer, he treated towns in the Casas Grandes Valley very harshly, particularly Pearson.

After his attack on Pearson, Castillo returned to San Diego where he began distributing parcels of hacienda land to local campesinos and inviting them to harvest the crops already in the ground. Probably to deter units of Villa's army from chasing him, he sent a contingent to destroy Moctezuma Station on the National Railroad south of Ciudad Juárez. He and his staff moved on to other Terrazas haciendas in the Santa María Valley, where he gathered local people together and passed out parcel deeds. People accepted the deeds with some skepticism. Castillo felt the cynicism of the people, who had heard so many promises and seen so much devastation. They gladly took the deeds and crops but most refused his entreaties to join his army. The skeptics proved to be right when the Terrazas family later reclaimed much of their original hacienda land, rendering Castillo's deeds worthless.

Castillo continued to operate independently until February 1914. His influence remained wide enough to validate his salvo conductos and ensure safe passage to the border for David Brown and Bert Whetten with their precious herd.[647]

Castillo occupied Pearson and raided the stores there several times. He was less fortunate with extortion attempts against U.S. companies. They refused or delayed tribute payments. According to *The New York Times*, January 27, 1914, this so frustrated him that he ordered all U.S. citizens to stay out of Chihuahua or be shot.[648] Time ran out on Máximo Castillo before he could carry out his threat.

Cumbre Tunnel Massacre

Exactly 50 miles, 80 kilometers, south of the Pearson/Mata Ortiz train station is the Cumbre summit and the Cumbre Tunnel. There occurred one of the most shocking and highly publicized events of the ten-year Revolution. On February 4, 1914, a small group of armed men captured a freight train with two engines that had passed through the three-quarter-mile long tunnel going south towards Madera. The train's cars were loaded with empty boxes designed to transport cattle. The renegades forced the four crew members to back the train into the front of the tunnel. They uncoupled the engines and with no one aboard, opened the throttle of the first. The engine lurched forward until it hit it a torn track, then tipped and rolled down a steep canyon. The renegades opened the throttle of the second and sent it crashing into the canyon. The train crew protested because they knew that a southbound passenger train from Ciudad Juárez and Pearson was on the track behind them. The conductor pleaded to go back through the tunnel to flag down the train. The renegades ignored him and sent the four crew members south on foot through the snow. They then entered the tunnel and set the freight train on fire. The supporting timbers began to burn. One version says they saved one engine and used it to escape south. Regardless, the perpetrators disappeared, never to be positively identified.

The previous day, February 3, 1914, M.J. Gilmartin, the assistant manager based in El Paso, scheduled passenger train Number One to run from Ciudad Juárez to Madera. Number One had been idle since January 26, when Máximo Castillo and his band robbed the train and threatened to burn it at the San Pedro Station near the Candelaria mining district. Number One's single engine pulled a first-class car, a second-class car, a baggage car, one freight car and possibly a caboose. The passengers included about 50 Mexican citizens, M.J. Gilmartin, six other railway officials, and the wife and five children of a train engineer in Madera. Some of the officials were new and on an orientation trip with Gilmartin. An engineer, conductor, and two brakemen operated the train.

Number One left Colonia Juárez at 9:30. After a delay caused by downed telegraph lines, the train arrived at Pearson in the afternoon. Two railroad employees came down to the station to greet Mr. Gilmartin. He asked them to join him for the trip to Madera. Mr. Morris, a roadmaster, had business in Madera and accepted even though he was not feeling well. A roadmaster was responsible for a designated length of track. Morris took with him the time book for a payroll to be prepared in Madera. Mr. McClanahan, the railway Assistant Superintendent for Pearson, begged off, saying his shoes were completely worn out. His next trip had to be to Ciudad Juárez as none were to be had in Pearson. A pair of worn-out shoes saved his life.

The train left Pearson at 4:15 and arrived at the Cumbre Station at 6:30. A Mexican watchman from a nearby lumber camp waited there to meet his father, a passenger. The two saw no smoke or anything else unusual before they left for the camp. They did see Mr. Gilmartin get off the train with another man for a few minutes, apparently to describe the local area. Gilmartin looked around but showed no indication that he saw anything out of the ordinary and reboarded. The train started up, and the watchman and his father went on their way.[649]

The train entered the dark tunnel, rolled toward the other end, and smashed into the burning freight train. The cars piled up on one another and caught fire. The engine boiler may have exploded. The crash, explosion, fire, and gases immediately engulfed all passengers and crew—except for one. Brakeman Juan Hernández apparently had been standing near an open door at the end of the train at the moment of impact. He flew out and hit the ground as smoke, gas, and intense heat filled the tunnel. When he got to his feet, he started toward the entrance 2,000 feet away. At some point he tried to cover his face with a bandana before he fell and began to crawl.

The initial MNWR reports and ensuing publicity blamed Máximo Castillo for the horrific crime. In a letter written to friends, Superintendent H.C. McMaster, implies the freight-train crew talked with Castillo himself before they started to hike down the tracks.[650] Historians are not sure. Some suggest it might have been Castillo's subordinate Manuel Gutiérrez.

Gutiérrez led his own band, nominally under Castillo's command. While Gutiérrez raided and destroyed property, nothing in his sketchy history suggests he was a brutal murderer. After the Battle of Pearson, he had actually protected M.J. Gilmartin (a victim of the Cumbre wreck), when Castillo held him for ransom. Others blamed Pancho Villa himself. It is conceivable that some of his men patrolling Chihuahua, but remote from his direct control, carried out the massacre on their own. However, Villa himself became enraged when he heard the news and made a quick train trip back to Ciudad Juárez to organize a massive hunt for Castillo. He also assigned a detachment of his own troops to protect and guarantee the safety of MNWR employees working at the disaster site.

Over a century of research has not provided definitive answers as to the motive, responsibility, or even the exact details for what happened. However, someone gave the order and Castillo was blamed. His career as a land-reforming renegade ended abruptly after arrest and incarceration in a Fort Bliss, Texas jail.

On February 4, F.C. Clark sat in the Madera Station office as evening approached. MNWR Vice-President Pruitt had just put him in charge of repairing the track and bridges in the Chihuahua Division. The dispatcher informed him the regularly scheduled passenger train had not arrived. In these times, anything could have happened and it worried him. Early the next morning with still no word, he and another employee took a train engine and headed north. Before reaching the summit, they saw the freight-train crew trudging down through the snow. They had walked all night. Clark gave the engine to the exhausted crew members and walked the rest of the way to the tunnel. They saw the wreckage at the entrance and realized something terrible had happened. They tried to work their way into the tunnel, but the heat drove them back. They could see the number on the engine, 41, and knew it was the passenger train. They hiked back to

Madera and returned the next day with a searchlight. The heat remained intense and they could do little.

John O. Crockett and the other company officials initially were confused. Crockett contacted Luis Orozco in Pearson and asked him to investigate what Clarke and everyone in Madera already knew. They soon clarified the situation and in spite of rumors that Castillo still lurked in

C.H. Cooper ready to enter the burning Cumbre Tunnel
in an early-day hazmat suit.
Photo: MS039 Courtesy of the El Paso Public Library,
Special Collections, Border Heritage Center

the area, sent a well-equipped rescue train with a doctor the following day. C.H. Cooper, wearing a protective helmet with an oxygen supply that looked like an old-fashioned deep-sea diver's helmet, and others with lights entered the tunnel. They went far enough to determine no one could have survived. Brakeman Juan Hernández's body lay 200 feet from the entrance. A message was sent to the office in El Paso via a portable telegraph key spliced into the nearby wire. Officials immediately dispatched another train with coffins, undertakers, and experienced mine-rescue workers. It arrived the next day February 7, 1914.[651] Most of the bodies were burned beyond recognition. Personal belongings like jackknives served as identifiers. The unburned time books in a back pocket identified Mr. Morris.[652]

The rescue crews intended to take most of the dead to Ciudad Juárez and El Paso for burial. However, on February 25 and 26 , 200 federals led by General Rodrigo M. Quevedo and his cousin Silvestre Quevedo avoided Villa's troops and burned 39 bridges south of Ciudad Juárez. They also burned stacks of repair lumber.

The railroad crew built a vault in Pearson to hold the bodies until the track could be reopened. Because of the heat and smoldering timbers, it took weeks before all the bodies could be cleared. Some like Mr. Gilmartin were never found.[653]

A few days before the train wreck, a troop of Villa's men had ambushed Castillo's main band at El Valle near San Buenaventura and killed or executed most of them. Regardless of whether Castillo was at El Valle, Cumbre, or somewhere else at the time of the massacre, he now was now a fugitive on the run. With only six men, he decided to cross the border to find supporters he thought might be in El Paso. The small band crossed near El Berrendo, the remote border crossing about 45 miles south of Hachita, New Mexico.

The fugitives walked right into a patrol of U.S. 9th Cavalry, the famed Buffalo Soldiers, looking for border jumpers like them. The soldiers took the prisoners to Fort Bliss, near El Paso. The commanding officer put Castillo in a cell near another inmate, José Inés Salazar, his old comrade in arms. Salazar had fled across the border after Villa's victory over Huerta's forces at the Battle of Ojinaga the previous January. Salazar sat in the

Máximo Castillo, a prisoner at Fort Bliss.
Photo: Courtesy of the El Paso Public Library, Special Collections,
Border Heritage Center.

Fort Bliss cell, charged with gun running and violation of neutrality laws. The U.S. Army held at Fort Bliss at that time almost 8,000 men and 250 women—battle survivors, refugees, bandits, and deserters that had tried to escape across the border.

From his cell, Castillo vehemently denied any involvement or any knowledge of the massacre. He became something of an attraction as people came to see the famous bandit/rebel. To one crowd, he gave a long passionate speech accounting for his whereabouts during the sabotage, blaming Villa's men for the carnage, and proclaiming that he himself only wanted to help the people.

The U. S. Army did not know what to do with him since the crime had been committed on Mexican soil. Officials knew if they sent him back, Villa's men would not hesitate to execute him. After several months in various military prisons, the Army relented and released him. He ended in Havana, Cuba, and never returned. The Casas Grandes Valley would continue to suffer depredation, but at least one scourge was gone.

The massacre came close to being an international incident. Secretary of State William Jennings Bryan demanded security for those working to clear the tunnel damage. Ironically, Pancho Villa's troops already had security in place. Huerta's government in Mexico City protested what they perceived as U.S. intervention. Before the disaster escalated into a serious international situation, incidents at Tampico and Veracruz diverted national attention away from Cumbre in both countries. The MNWR was left to mourn the loss of their people and clean up the mess.

The gap that had delayed the completion of the loop for so long now lay obstructed again. For the railroad managers, the highest priority was to somehow reconnect the line and resume service.

The Detour

Phelps-Dodge mining engineers from Bisbee, Arizona, inspected the damage and found that part of the center of the tunnel roof had collapsed when the supporting timbers burned, leaving tons of rocks and debris. They concluded that it would take many months to clear and rebuild the tunnel at the prohibitive cost of $150,000. MNWR did not have that much cash available. In fact, mill managers were desperate to ship lumber to generate cash. During the relative calm as Villa gained control of Chihuahua, the company had reopened the Madera mill. The demand for lumber was high in both the U.S. and Mexico. Also, the calm period had created a demand for shipping potatoes, corn, and other farm products.[654] However, the mill managers could not ship beyond Ciudad Chihuahua. Villa's rebels controlled the National Railroad and could not or would not make track time available for MNWR trains. Madera managers needed to get lumber over the Cumbre mountain ridge as quickly as possible. They opted for a detour.[655] With remarkable ingenuity, they managed to construct a long winding roadbed along and over the ridge to the steep south side, where a series of switchbacks connected with the original track.

Switchbacks were not generally used in railroad design. They were awkward arrangements, requiring long extensions at the end of each zigzag turn. Trains had to drive into the extensions and stop while brakemen left the train to switch the track. The train engineer then reversed the engine and backed into the next zigzag leg. Repeating the process, the engine alternately pulled and pushed the train of cars forward and backward up or down the side of the ridge. For steam engines, it was very slow and difficult, which is why railroad companies used tunnels wherever possible. As far as it is known, the Cumbre switchbacks were the only such installations ever constructed in Mexico.

Nevertheless, the 20-mile bypass was an engineering marvel worthy of the people who worked for Dr. Pearson. Within two months trains loaded with lumber and agricultural products followed the route north to market. The detour continued in use for three years.[656]

In modern times, little was known of this old bypass until David Nelson, a retired electrical engineer from Santa Fe, began to explore the area in the early 2000s. Fluent in Spanish, he had made many trips into various parts of the Chihuahua backcountry and had become intrigued with the Cumbre switchback story. A new road allowed relatively easy access to the area, and he began two years of research.

In the meantime, in 2008, ten years after the Chihuahua al Pacífico trains stopped running on the old MNWR line, frustrated residents of villages south of Mata Ortiz gathered to complain to the Casas Grandes Municipio about a long-standing problem. Their farms and ranches lay along the Palanganas River that paralleled the tracks south of Mata Ortiz. The dirt roads had always been bad along the river, and they had depended on the railroad for access. Forced for a decade to use terrible, often flooded roads, they now wanted something done.

Municipio officials responded by removing all the rails on the 50-mile stretch between Mata Ortiz and the tunnel. The ties not needed to reinforce the roadbed also were removed. Municipio contractors graded the roadbed and covered it with gravel, producing an acceptable road all the way to the summit.

A subsidiary story suggests that the rails were stolen and the culpable municipio officials driven out of Casas Grandes. Regardless, a road now existed, and Nelson could access the rugged area for his research.

He made several trips with friends including local historian Miguel Méndez García from Nuevo Casas Grandes, Señor Godina, an old-time railroader, and Dr. Clarence Cooper, a physics professor and son of C.H.

Cooper who had played a major role in MNWR history. Dr. Cooper had written a book about his father. The book cover shows a picture of the senior Cooper in front of the tunnel entrance wearing the oxygen helmet. Clarence, the son, had never been to the site and was quite moved to stand at the spot where the old photograph had been taken.

Nelson made one another good friend who helped him. On one trip, he saw a couple trying to pull some old rails out of a deep ditch along the road, using their car and a tow rope. Nelson could see the small woman was not able to manage the rope. He stopped to help and they pulled up the rails. The couple thanked him but seemed suspicious of the stranger, even after Nelson told them of his research project. They became very friendly when he mentioned other friends in the mountains, who turned out to be the couple's relatives. Nelson was standing on ranch property owned by the couple, Ramón Chávez and his wife Nely. Nelson visited the Chávezes at their ranch several times after that. They became good friends, enjoying evenings of Ramón's guitar music and a bottle of local sotol.

Chávez ran cattle and knew the area well. He gave Nelson permission to pass through his gates to explore, and he showed Nelson where the old bypass began.

The Cumbre Station still stands on the east side or left as the track approaches the north tunnel entrance. Just before the station, the bypass roadbed split left and went behind the station, then curved right or west and passed over the tunnel entrance. An old photograph shows the entrance with a locomotive several yards above. Across from the station, Chávez showed Nelson a dirt road that followed the old roadbed. Marking GPS waypoints, Nelson traced the curves and turns of the old detour west and then over the ridge to where the dirt road turned away from the railroad bed. Rusty iron spikes, rotted pieces of railroad ties, and two short tunnels helped him verify the rail route to the ridge top, but he could go no farther in his vehicle.

The switchbacks began on the south side of the ridge beyond where the dirt road separated from the rail bed. That slope was a mass of overgrown brush and trees. He and Miguel Méndez García had no other option but to hike up the slope through the brush. After considerable time, they found remnants of the elongated switchbacks. They noted GPS waypoints as they traced the obscure route down to the place where it had connected with the track on the south side of the tunnel.

Nelson had found the unusual switchbacks and satisfied his curiosity, but then confirmation came from an unexpected source. He received a box full of documents that had been copied from files in the Mexico City National Archive. Among them was a letter with a federal department logo that been sent to MNWR management complaining that the bypass had been constructed without a permit.[657] The department, in Huerta's administration, considered the violation serious enough to have the entire 20 miles surveyed. The letter contained the survey points. When Nelson read the document, he found the survey points almost exactly matched his GPS waypoints. It is not known if the issue was resolved. Huerta's federal government had other serious distractions as it was about to fall. However, not only did Nelson have the satisfaction of discovering the old bypass with its unique switchbacks, he had also plotted the exact route.

Dr. Pearson's Chihuahua enterprises saw terrible times over the next two years. His parent company, MNWR, had to declare bankruptcy, and Pearson and his wife lost their lives in the Lusitania tragedy on May 7, 1915. The company struggled to operate in receivership. Roy Hoard, who had worked in the U.S. for a year, returned and soon became MNWR president. Back in El Paso in April, 1917, he discovered that the company's large El Paso finished-lumber mill had a backlog of orders it could not fill because of an acute shortage of rough lumber. The delivery bottleneck from Madera was the convoluted Cumbre bypass with its switchbacks.[658] The loaded trains moved very slowly and sometimes derailed causing long delays. Hoard and one of his roadmasters, Hilario Aguilar, decided to take another look at the ruined tunnel.

Hoard and Aguilar entered the tunnel and climbed through the rocks, dirt, and crushed cars. In spite of the terrible destruction and the Phelps Dodge engineers' pessimism, they thought something could be done. Aguilar selected a crew and went to work. They removed all the debris, dug out the rock and dirt, and reinforced that part of the ceiling that had collapsed. Soon, trains rolled on new track with lumber for El Paso.[659]

The new Cumbre Tunnel, built about 1963, accommodated the larger diesel engines. The old tunnel is on the far right. The detour roadbed, later restored by Bosques de Chihuahua, shows above the tunnels. Photo: Courtesy of David Nelson

The switchbacks were abandoned and forgotten. However, Bosques de Chihuahua, a successor company to MNWR, continued to use sections of the well-engineered old bypass tracks well into the 1950s to connect the Cumbre station with lumbering operations in the western mountains.

The story makes another point. In the company correspondence and references, more and more Mexican names like H.C. Aguilar appear indicating that capable workers were moving up through the company ranks. In 1914, Roy Hoard reopened the Madera mill, and appointed G. U. Armendáriz as manager.[660]

Booker's Dream, the Caracol

Dr. Pearson's dream of a lumber and railroad empire would not survive the destruction brought by the Revolution. His capable, creative managers met each seemingly insurmountable challenge with amazing ingenuity. It was not enough. Erratic lumber sales and shipping revenues could not cover the relentless costs of infrastructure reconstruction and expensive train-engine replacement. On September 14, 1914, the MNWR declared bankruptcy in Toronto.

During virtually the same timeframe another capable but restless entrepreneur had a similar if not quite as grand a dream. Lewis Erasmus Booker moved to El Paso from North Dakota in 1897, where he had been a successful businessman and politician. He started businesses and bought cattle ranches in Texas and by 1900 had expanded into Mexico. There his interests encompassed cattle, lumber and mining, including the Central Mine at Sabinal east of Corralitos.

Like Dr. Pearson, Booker saw the potential profit in the vast timberlands of the Sierra Madre. He purchased 66,775 hectares (165,000 acres) in the mountains, twelve miles west of Pearson. He paid twenty cents per acre. In Colonia Pacheco, the LDS mountain community, he built a lumber mill that produced 20,000 board feet per day by 1910 and employed twenty to thirty lumberjacks, mill workers, and mule drivers. The market price for lumber delivered to El Paso stood at about fifteen cents per thousand or $3,000 per day in sales. Labor and other costs were under $1,000 per day. Booker's company could generate an enormous gross profit—if the lumber could be shipped.[661]

Booker was well aware of Dr. Pearson's project. It is not known whether they ever met, although Pearson and his first vice president were in El Paso in January 1912 on their tour of the MNWR railroad and mill facilities. Shortly thereafter, the Booker Lumber Company entered into an agreement with the Madera Lumber Company to deliver 100,000 linear feet of logs to the Pearson mill per day, the equivalent of 300,000 board feet of cut lumber, an enormous amount. By 1912, the Booker Lumber Company had grown to four mills and Pacheco featured sixteen framed buildings with a general store, mess hall, and bunkhouse.

Mule-drawn wagons provided the only means to transport the logs and lumber down the mountain. Drivers had to maneuver the heavily loaded wagons down the steep, rutted road to the Pearson station and mill, creating a bottleneck as the slow wagon transport could not keep up with the logging and mill production at Pacheco.

Also, hauling required 25 work horses, 102 mules, and the requisite barns, sheds, silos, and corrals—an expensive operation for such slow service.

To solve the problem, the irrepressible Booker decided to build a railroad from Pacheco, down the mountain and across the plains to Pearson, about 35 miles. He took in as a partner Bishop Orson Pratt Brown, the influential LDS leader, who spoke fluent Spanish and had many contacts within government and the local Mexican community. Bishop Pratt invested in the land, but title remained in Booker's name.

In late 1911, Booker hired a well-known civil engineer, Levi P. Atwood, to design and construct the railway. Atwood was Booker's former son-in-law. Atwood and Booker's daughter were no longer married, which did not seem to influence the business relationship.[662] Atwood had a great deal of experience including work in the Casas Grandes Valley. A graduate of the University of Illinois, he worked on midwest railroads before taking a job with the syndicate that owned the Corralitos Cattle Company and the Candelaria Mining Company. The syndicate had created the Rio Grande, Sierra Madre and Pacific Railroad to transport ore and cattle to El Paso. When the famed copper-mining magnate Colonel William Greene bought the railroad in 1905, he hired Atwood to engineer an extension to the Terrazas Station near Hacienda San Diego.[663] Atwood lived in El Paso but moved to Dublán for the project.

Booker and Atwood contracted with Henry Eyring Bowman and Niels Larson for the grading. Bowman had been the driving force behind the construction of the just-finished canal that carried water from the Casas Grandes River to a reservoir east of Dublán, now known as Laguna Rodolfo Fierro (named after one of Pancho Villa's most notorious generals, who drowned there). Bowman was president of the Laguna Water Company that in a few months would begin delivering irrigation water to expanded fields around Dublán. Bowman also managed the LDS Union Mercantile Cooperative that had stores in Casas Grandes and Dublán. When Colonel William Greene's railroad and mining empire collapsed, his companies owed Union Mercantile a great deal of money. In payment, Bowman took Greene's construction equipment, work animals, and tools. He used this equipment to construct the canal and then to grade the Pacheco to Pearson short line. The project became known as *El Caracol*, the snail.

It is entirely possible that a rail connection into the mountain timberlands had been part of Dr. Pearson's plan from the beginning. The large state-of-the-art lumber mill was too far from the timber sources to be served by mule and wagon. It is unlikely Dr. Pearson would have overlooked this in his planning.

Work began in October 1911, and by July 1912, Bowman and Larsen had completed about 75 percent of the grading. However, by this time, the Orozco Rebellion was in full swing against President Francisco Madero's federal government. General José Inés Salazar, now with Orozco, controlled the Casas Grandes Valley and began to terrorize all foreigners, particularly North Americans, with his Orozquista red-flagger rebels.

In El Paso, Booker chose to ignore the rapidly deteriorating situation, perhaps because Salazar initially had assured the LDS colonists and other foreigners they would not be molested. He soon withdrew any pretense of protection.

Manuel Gutiérrez (now with Salazar, later one of Máximo Castillo's officers) raided the construction work camp, fifteen miles west of Pearson, and demanded horses and supplies from the commissary. More raids followed in the valley, and Salazar's demands and threats forced the LDS Exodus that began July 27, 1912.

Several of Booker's stolen horses turned up in the hands of the federals and were seen in garrison towns along the railroad. President Madero's officials refused to honor Booker's claims to recover the animals. Also, the garrison commanders made little effort to confront Salazar. Once, Salazar himself rode to Booker's Central Mine near Sabinal (Salazar's hometown) and tried to extort cash from the superintendent.[664]

Salazar and his subordinates spread the word that since President Taft supported the Madero government, the United States was the enemy. Therefore, all property of North Americans, real and personal, belonged to the Mexican people revolting against Madero. Anything could be confiscated. In one instance that meant Niels Larson's Stetson hat off his head.

This rhetoric caused several Mexican employees to turn ugly and antagonistic—employees that a few months before had been clamoring for the good-paying jobs. By late July 1912, rebels came into the camp almost daily, taking what they wanted. Larson was forcefully seized and robbed of $100. Fearing for their lives, Atwood and Larson and eight other North American employees abandoned the railroad camp and ran for the border. Riding night and day through the mountains and desert for five days— once riding 36 hours with only brief stops for rest and water. They covered 175 miles, finally crossing the border undetected to end their ordeal in Hachita, New Mexico. They left behind all of the mill and unfinished railroad infrastructure including the remainder of the tools, wagons, supplies, dynamite, stock and feed.[665] That finished the Pacheco to Pearson railroad and the Booker Lumber Company. All that remained of Booker's dream was the name, El Caracol, on the route.

Booker sold the 66,775 hectares (165,000 acres) to Dr. Pearson's company for $65,000. Orson Pratt Brown was supposed to receive ten percent but received nothing. The energetic dreamer L.E. Booker died five years later on April 15, 1918, in Isleta, Texas.[666]

For the next 92 years, the same rock-strewn, rutted road served mountain ranchers and lumber trucks. In 2004, a new highway was graded and paved through the San Diego Valley to Mata Ortiz. A branch extended into the mountains. Part of the new paved mountain route followed Booker's Caracol railroad bed.

Historian Rondal Bridgemon has made a careful study of the route, using GPS maps and on-the-ground observation. He has hiked onto ridges above the cuts in the mountainsides to obtain and photograph a panoramic view of the roadbed. He also found the graded area where the proposed tracks would have joined the MNWR track in Pearson just north of Arroyo Sección, the arroyo that bisects the town.

Bridgemon's research confirms that Atwood's design allowed for the sweeping curves necessary to keep the grade below three percent—the maximum for the steam engines of the era.[667]

The project would have worked. However, like Dr. Pearson, Lewis Booker's dream collided with the region's tumultuous history.

The Legend Grows

Two years later, Orozco's forces were scattered, President Madero was murdered, and General Huerta ruled in Mexico City while Pancho Villa continued to consolidate his forces. After the Second Battle of Casas Grandes, Villa moved his army to an encampment near Ascensión. He did not have enough men, arms, or ammunition to attack Ciudad Juárez, although the June 23 telegram quoted him as saying he would attack in a few days, and everyone should leave. This was pure bravado. Instead, he continued to recruit and train more men and purchase arms from the proceeds of rustled cattle, forced loans, and, at least once, from the theft of 122 silver bars from a train.[668] Toribio Ortega from Cuchillo Parado near Ojinaga on the Texas border brought in 500 men, a significant number in those early days. Ortega is credited with the first act of rebellion in November 1910. He remained a loyal peasant revolutionary without political aspirations. Villa used him as a battle commander until he died of typhus in 1914.

Several other chieftains, even some of his old lieutenants like the ruthless Tomás Urbina and the politically ambitious Manuel Chao, still did not recognize his authority. They did not want to give up the little fiefdoms they had established in the southern regions of Chihuahua and in Durango. A series of defeats inflicted on these independent commands by Huerta's federals convinced most of them that they must consolidate with Villa or be destroyed piecemeal. Also, Villa enjoyed widespread popularity and they did not. As a result, Villa's troop count jumped during the summer of 1913.

On September 16, 1913, most remaining independent chieftains met with Villa and those that had already joined him, in the railroad town of Jiménez, 146 miles south of Ciudad Chihuahua on the National Railroad. They actually took a formal vote to accept Villa, as voting to establish officers was common among the revolutionary bands and armies. This vote was the formal beginning of Villa's famed *División del Norte.*

The vote also ignored Carranza, who had come to Chihuahua the previous month to advocate for Manuel Chao as the overall leader in Chihuahua. Carranza wanted a man closer to his own social class, which provides a clue as to his real motives regarding the Revolution.

Villa now had 8,000 men, enough to make a major thrust south. Carranza, Obregón, and Villa had agreed on a three-pronged strategy to push south toward Mexico City from Coahuila in the east, Sonora in the west and Chihuahua in the center. The offensives bogged down in the east and west, and only Villa in the center made significant moves. His immediate objective was the major rail center of Torreón in southwestern Coahuila. Villa commandeered trains and moved his hodge-podge army south in just a few days, a major exercise of administrative skill. The División del Norte still lacked artillery and ammunition for such an ambitious invasion, but it had something else—*Las Soldaderas.*

Most armies had camp followers, particularly in Mexico, but the División del Norte carried it to an extreme. The use of trains permitted large numbers of the soldier's wives, women, and sometimes children to travel with the army. Photographs of soldiers and women in wide sombreros riding on the tops of train cars created one of the classic images of the Revolution. The women set up the camps, scrounged for food, cooked, and cared for the wounded. Many carried a rifle into battle alongside their men.

The Battle of Torreón lasted three days between September 29 and October 1, 1913. Villa's crude tactic consisted of repeated frontal attacks by mounted cavalry until the demoralized defenders gave up.

This was by far Villa's largest and most important battle to date. Not only was capture of the city important strategically, but the spoils were enormous. His jubilant troopers took away heavy artillery, a half-a-million rounds of ammunition, and armored rail cars. Villa also extracted "loans" from Torreón's bankers.

Villa had one of the captured trains converted into a modern hospital train, with Dr. Andrés Villarreal, a noted surgeon, in charge of what may have been the most advanced mobile hospital in the world at that time.[669] Flush with his victory at Torreón, Villa moved his army north to confront Ciudad Chihuahua in early November. Against the advice of several of his officers, he hurled his troops in frontal assaults against the entrenched federals, this time with a different and disastrous result. In General Salvador Mercado, Ciudad Chihuahua had a better commanding officer than at Torreón. He had more motivated troops, backed up by Orozco's veterans. Murderous machine-gun and cannon fire cut down the charging Villistas.

After using most of his hard-won ammunition and arms, Villa had to call off the attack and retreat up the National Railroad about 30 miles to El Sauz, one of Luis Terrazas's haciendas.

The news of the federal victory convinced a jubilant Huerta that he had broken the rebellion in Chihuahua. He sent more troops north to retake the lost towns and cities. While Villa still controlled much of the state except for its two major cities, he had lost men, prestige, and strained the confidence of

La Soldadera
Photo: 034-1983-070 Courtesey of the
El Paso County Historical Society

the people. His army lay in a perilous position between federal strongholds at Ciudad Chihuahua and Ciudad Juárez. It had happened before and it would happen again. Everyone, Huerta, the local people, and even those in his own army, underestimated Pancho Villa. He was about to pull off one of the most audacious military operations in the history of warfare.

The Trojan Iron Horse

To most observers, Villa's main army was trapped with no place to go. Immediately to the south, the army that had just defeated him stood ready to move out with overwhelming numbers and firepower. Ciudad Juárez to the north not only was heavily fortified, but it backed up against El Paso across the river. Stray shots by attackers could incite the U.S. to intervene. Villa seemed to have no alternative but to break up his army into guerilla bands and escape to the mountains.

While at the Sauz Station, Villa's men captured a long train of coal cars on its way south to Ciudad Chihuahua from Ciudad Juárez. Villa ordered the cars emptied. Two thousand of his troops with their weapons and what ammunition they had left boarded the cars. A Villista telegraph operator took over the key in the station and sent a message to the railroad headquarters in Ciudad Juárez stating that the track had been torn up by rebels and requested instructions. The immediate response directed the conductor and his crew to return the train to Ciudad Juárez. Further, a telegram should be sent from each station to inform headquarters of the train's progress.

The train moved north, stopping at each station for Villa's operator to send the reassuring message, after securing cooperation from the station master with a pointed pistol.

The train rolled through the entrenchments on the outskirts of Ciudad Juárez into the city center at 2:00 in the morning, Saturday, November 15. The surprise was complete. Villa's army occupied the center of the city and, not a shot had been fired yet. The expectant station master was greeted by 2,000 battle-ready Villistas climbing out of the coal cars. They moved to the barracks and opened fire. Some federal soldiers held out there for an hour before surrendering. A federal militia group established a good position in a baseball stadium and fought until they ran out of ammunition. By 5:00

in the morning, it was over. The federal commander, General Francisco Castro, surrendered the city.

At least the shooting part was over. The reaction to Villa's sleight of hand, making a train disappear and reappear loaded with soldiers in the middle of the enemy's fortress, swept through Mexico, the U.S. and much of the world. The Mexican and foreign press had a field day, and Pancho Villa, already well known, became a household word.

Some like Tomás Urbina wanted to loot after the battle, but Villa maintained strict discipline as he took over administration of the city. His treasurer and paymaster went immediately to the custom house to assume the duties of custom officer and collect fees, one of the lucrative features of this major port of entry. Businessmen on both sides of the border wanted no delays in the flow of goods. Other officers turned their attention to collecting arms and, above all, ammunition. Still others supervised executions. This sullied Villa's image somewhat in the U.S. press, but it added to his opponents fear of him and brought in recruits.

Villa gave strict orders that General Francisco Castro, the city's commanding officer not be molested in any way. Castro had interceded with Huerta to spare Villa, after the latter's arrest the previous year. Villa remembered and sent Castro with an escort to cross the bridge to safety.

The remainder of his army from El Sauz arrived and within a few days he had about 5,500 men in the city. He needed them because a serious problem remained.

When General Mercado in Chihuahua heard the news of the fall of Ciudad Juárez, he detached a 6,000-7,000-man army made up of his toughest units, commanded by Pascual Orozco and José Salazar, supported by a large number of cannon and machine guns. He sent this formidable force north in trains to retake Ciudad Juárez. Villa knew what he faced. He did not have enough men or heavy weapons to withstand a siege within the former federal fortifications around the city. U.S. authorities in El Paso expressed deep concern to Villa about a major battle so close to them. This in spite of the number of El Paso residents claiming seats on roof tops to watch the action they were sure was coming.

On November 21, General Villa reviewed his assembled troops and ordered them to prepare to move out. The destination, which Villa revealed to only a few officers, was a series of hills south of the city, separated from the Tierra Blanca Station by sand dunes. The height of the hills and the heavy sand would slow charges up the slopes as well as the movement of federal artillery. Leaving only a small garrison, Villa led out of the city on foot and horseback about 5,500 men and some women.

University of Chicago historian Friedrich Katz described these straggling troops as they crossed the desert to their positions above Tierra Blanca, about 35 miles away. It was truly a peasant army, made up of Indians and mestizos, mostly from the mountains and valleys of northern Chihuahua.[670] They trusted their Villa but otherwise approached the lethal dangers of combat with a stoicism bred from a life of hardship. The officers ordered the camp followers to stay behind, but any woman with a gun and a horse could go as a soldadera. Young boys, many who had lost fathers, carried a heavy rifle with bandoliers over their skinny shoulders.

When they reached the hills, Villa and his commanders placed their troops in defensive positions, right, left and center. What artillery they had, they put in the center under the command of Martiniano Servín, an experienced soldier, who served Villa well in several battles until he was killed in action.

Trains from the south came into the Tierra Blanca Station loaded with cannon and federal soldiers. The federals moved the artillery pieces and unlimbered them in spite of the sand. They pounded the rebel positions for two days, but each charge up the slopes was repulsed. Each of these charges took its toll on the defenders and their ammunition. Orozco and Salazar could continue the siege much longer.

On the third day, with ammunition almost gone, Villa resorted to desperate tactics. A few of his men took a train engine from somewhere north of Tierra Vista, filled it with dynamite and ran it to the station and right into a parked federal train. The explosion panicked many of the federal soldiers. Villa then ordered an infantry charge directly into the center of the federal position. Enough of the federal soldiers recovered from their shock to lay down a murderous fire on the rebels advancing in front of them through the sand. Suddenly Villa's mounted rebels charged into the federal flanks from both sides. In the chaos that followed, some of the federals including the generals got away on a train, but the battle was over. Villa's tactics and the brave peasants not only finished off the federal effort to retake Ciudad Juárez, but the victory also finished the federal occupation of Ciudad Chihuahua.

General Salvador Mercado realized his position in the capital was untenable now that he had lost a significant part of his army. The city's Huarista elite begged him in vain to stay, fearing chaos and reprisals when Villa arrived. However, on November 28, three days after the battle at Tierra Blanca, General Mercado abandoned Ciudad Chihuahua and fled with the remainder of his army to Ojinaga on the Texas border in eastern Chihuahua. Many of those fearful, well-off Huerta supporters, with much to lose, accompanied him in a long dreary column. Two in the column with their entourage were Luis Terrazas and Enrique Creel,[671]

Villa rode with his army from Ciudad Juárez to Ciudad Chihuahua, arriving December 5, 2013. The representatives of General Mercado that he left behind met Villa and submitted to his authority. In spite of fears and rumors, the transition of power was quiet and orderly. Villa assumed the governorship of the state of Chihuahua.

Governor Villa

Villa's official governorship lasted four weeks and against all odds, produced positive results.

The state had endured three years of fighting. The economy was in chaos and food in short supply. The people mistrusted the revolving-door leadership, making the state almost ungovernable.

In addition to domestic problems, Mercado and Orozco had regrouped their army in Ojinaga. Of greater concern was Huerta's renewed offensive. He had sent a large army north and retaken Torreón in Coahuila and towns in Durango and southern Chihuahua.

Those, members of the middle class and sophisticated elite remaining in the capital were suspicious of the uneducated "bandit" now in charge of their lives. The lower classes adored Villa but expected change, particularly land distribution. As inexperienced as he was, Villa understood he needed the skills of the middle class. Widespread breakup of haciendas would be economic disaster for the state in the short run. Also, U.S. companies still held large tracts of land. Confiscation would alienate the U.S., something Villa was anxious to avoid. He needed to maintain the flow of arms, supplies, custom fees, and the market for cattle.

Villa usually, but not always, selected competent advisors and listened to them. At this critical time, he made an excellent choice. Silvestre Terrazas (a distant part of the Luis Terrazas family), a well-educated newspaperman, had edited the highly regarded newspaper, *El Correo de Chihuahua,* since before the Revolution. Not a radical, Silvestre Terrazas and the paper would be labeled "moderate" in today's vocabulary. As such, it appealed to the middle class. Terrazas had been a friend and confidant of Governor Abraham González before they split over the controversial issue of Francisco Madera's vice president. After Huerta's coup, Silvestre began to support Villa. Huerta responded by shutting down the newspaper. Terrazas met Villa for the first time after the Battle of Juárez. He impressed Villa and they became friends.

After Villa took control of Ciudad Juárez, he wanted Terrazas to be governor. Villa knew he needed the support of the middle class, particularly the department heads, accountants, lawyers, teachers, and other administrators that made the state and city run. Terrazas would help gain this important faction's confidence. However, Terrazas refused, citing lack of administrative experience. Villa insisted, and he finally accepted the position of General Secretary, second-in-command to the governor, in charge of civilian administration.[672] The two made a good team.

Within days they developed a plan that surprisingly began to stabilize the immediate chaotic situation. Silvestre Terrazas drafted a decree whereby Villa's government took control of the large haciendas, including those of Luis Terrazas and Enrique Creel, and forced the owners to leave the state. Foreign-owned lands were excluded to avoid issues with the United States. Villa encouraged the MNWR and other foreign enterprises to resume mine, ranch, and timber operations.

The confiscated hacienda ranches and farm lands continued to operate, but all proceeds went to the state treasury. This enabled Villa to pay his soldiers, now about 10,000, and pay pensions to widows and orphans of men killed fighting for Villa.

Another decree set up a food program. Soldiers delivered beef and other food products regularly to the capital and to areas of high unemployment such as the Casas Grandes Valley. The program administrators set up commissaries to distribute food in Pearson and Casas Grandes.

In their plan, Villa and Terrazas made a series of promises to the people regarding land reform. After the Revolution, the hacienda estates would be divided into three parts: Revolutionary veterans would receive parcels; ejido, and private lands confiscated by the hacendados would be returned; the remainder would be held by the government to generate revenue for the widow-and-orphan fund.

No provision was made for hacienda workers or other landless peons, but they could qualify by joining Villa's army. The Chihuahuans understood the concept of land for army service.[673] Enlistments rose and desertions decreased.

The war-weary and generally suspicious Chihuahuans accepted the package that had been conceived and executed in such a short time. Villa had fed the hungry, provided for widows and orphans, deflected the land distribution issue, and encouraged employment. At the beginning of 1914, he stood at the height of his popularity.

Resources to support an army are always an ongoing problem. Villa solved it in a number of ways, often by just taking what he needed. In one famous story, he opened a butcher shop to sell beef at bargain prices—from rustled cattle. As governor, he printed money and insisted everyone use it just like gold. Even the El Paso merchants accepted it for a while. The LDS colonists had no option but to take it in exchange for supplies even though predictably it soon devalued.

The conflicting forces that the Revolution had unleashed would disrupt Villa's actions and promises, but the concepts that he and Silvestre Terrazas promulgated in those four weeks would survive and be incorporated into future policies that ultimately benefited the people of Chihuahua.

Huerta's End

The military situation had not improved for Villa. Huerta now sent his best officers and best-trained troops into Chihuahua. General Mercado with Generals Orozco, Salazar, Quevedo, Rojas, and Caraveo remained in Ojinaga with a force. Villa wanted to prepare his army and strike back at Huerta's offensive. Specifically, he wanted to retake Torreón and move toward Mexico City, but first he had to clear Ojinaga at his back.

Hampered with administrative duties, he sent 2,200 men commanded by several subordinates to clear Ojinaga. The commanders quarreled and did not coordinate. Mercado and Orozco ordered a preemptive attack and the federals inflicted heavy losses. The rebels had to retreat. Half-hearted attempts to launch attacks the next day led only to more casualties. Martiniano Servín's artillery fire kept the battle from becoming a complete rout. Villa heard the news on January 6, 1914 and immediately led a detachment of reinforcements to Ojinaga. Arriving four days later, Villa reorganized his force and overwhelmed the federal defenses. Mercado and Orozco escaped over the border. Villa entered the city to the cheers of his men. He forbade looting and reassured the townspeople of their safety.

Across the border, Brigadier General John J. Pershing with part of his Eighth Brigade from Fort Bliss had been standing by to protect U.S. interests while the battle raged. He wanted to meet Villa and made arrangements to cross the bridge for a visit. The two conferred amicably. Pershing congratulated Villa on the victory and offered help with the wounded. Villa declined but thanked him for taking care of the federal wounded that had escaped into U.S. Army custody.[674] General José Salazar was also in U.S. custody.

With the threat to his rear eliminated, Villa returned quickly to the capital to plan for Torreón.

The battle at Ojinaga effectively ended Orozco's career. As an exile in the United States, he continued to scheme and conspire to foment futile rebellions. Arrested for violating U.S. neutrality laws, he escaped into the west Texas hills, where a Texas posse trapped and gunned him down on August 30, 1915. In spite of his fame and accomplishments, Orozco was just 31 when he died. He remained a hero and martyr to many in northern

Chihuahua. Several thousand crossed the bridge to El Paso to attend his funeral, conducted by a Methodist preacher.

Villa could not organize a major offensive and administer the state's complex domestic affairs. He selected one of his officers, Manuel Chao, an educated middle class man, to be governor. This solved a few political problems as well as freeing Villa from daily administration. Villa did not trust Chao, but he knew him and understood his political ambitions. Also, Carranza in an effort to weaken Villa, had been pushing him to name Chao. Villa had been giving lip service to the "First Chief" but largely ignoring him. This appointment mollified Carranza for the time being. However, Villa did not cede control. Silvestre Terrazas remained in position as a watchdog over Chao. Also, Villa then decreed that military commanders at all government levels, from the state to the municipio, had final authority. This meant that the officer in charge of the garrison in a municipio like Casas Grandes had the final word over the municipio president on any local issue. A General Ochoa was in charge at Casas Grandes for Villa as of July 1915.[675] The commander in the capital had the same authority.

Free of domestic duties, Villa prepared his army. The scale of the proposed offensive dwarfed previous operations. In January 1914, his purchasing agents placed an order for 10,000 Mauser rifles and one million rounds of ammunition. He wanted to standardize the basic weapon used by his troops. With the threat of war in Europe, it is unlikely the order was filled, but it demonstrates the magnitude of Villa's planning.

By March, he was ready. The connecting link between Ciudad Chihuahua and Mexico City was the National Railroad that stretched 800 miles through towns guarded by federal garrisons. Villa's troops and soldaderas boarded ten long trains that started south to Torreón. They cleared the garrison towns and fought battles to take cities. The División del Norte arrived at Torreón on March 26, 1914 and began a bloody battle that did not end until April 2.

With Zapata scoring victory after victory in Morelos and Obregón finally moving rapidly from Sonora, through Sinaloa to Guadalajara in Jalisco, the race was on to Mexico City.

Just after Torreón fell, an incident occurred that had the effect of strengthening Carranza and weakening Villa. The previous year on March 3,

Villa with a shipment of rifles.
Photo: Courtesy of the University of California, Riverside,
Special Collections & University Archives

1913, President Woodrow Wilson had assumed the U. S. presidency. He disliked Huerta intensely and allowed for a much more open border for arms shipments than did his predecessor Taft. Unfortunately, President Wilson became embroiled in a minor incident in the oil port of Tampico that escalated into armed conflict between the two countries.

The Tampico Affair began April 9 as an innocent act of trespass by a detail of U.S. sailors that had come ashore from their ship to pick up fuel. Huerta's federal troops controlled the port city, where anti-U.S. sentiment ran high because of the U.S. Navy ships anchored in the harbor without permission from Huerta's government. The ships had been ordered there to standby to protect U.S. interests in the oil fields during the Revolution. A federal patrol arrested the sailors but later released them with an apology. That was not good enough for the U.S. Naval commander, who demanded a 21-gun salute from Mexican soldiers as an additional apology. From there, misunderstandings, pompous egos, and misdirected nationalism allowed the incident to escalate into confrontation between the two countries. Huerta made empty, bombastic threats against the U.S. government that received wide publicity. Then word came to Washington that Huerta's troops were trying to unload a shipment of arms from a German ship. Now furious, President Wilson ordered the occupation of the port of Veracruz.[676] This led to armed clashes and casualties on both sides. Wilson stated adamantly that he would not pull the occupying troops out of Veracruz until Huerta was deposed. That happened two months later in July, but the U.S. troops did not leave until November.

The invasion of their country angered all factions in Mexico, rebel to conservative. Carranza protested with little effect. The wave of anti-U.S. sentiment, already festering in the port cities, swept across Mexico. U.S. newspaper headlines screamed of the danger to North Americans in Mexico, and many left. Wilson clamped down on arms shipments across the border. In the end, Wilson's action hurt Villa more than any of the other contending factions.

The Tampico and Veracruz incidents were blown out of proportion and strained Mexican-U.S. relations for years. Tensions eased somewhat when Carranza marched into Mexico City with General Obregón's army and became the face of the federal government. He had his hands full and did not want the United States as an enemy. Relations were repaired later in the year to the extent that arms shipments resumed to Carranza's government but not to Villa. However, despite pressure from the U.S., Mexico remained neutral during World War I and refused to curb German business activity in Mexico.

As a consequence, Villa lost the good relationship and tacit support of the U.S., and he did not fully understand why. However, he would not feel the fallout of the port incidents for several months. He still faced Huerta, a desperate enemy.

The División del Norte had overcome many obstacles in a short time as it fought its way toward the prize, Mexico City. Another, the town of Zacatecas, with its vital railroad junction, stood in the way. For years, the rail connections there had provided easy access for Zacatecans to immigrate to the Casas Grandes Valley looking for jobs. Villa's trains needed to pass through the junction there, and it was well defended. The surrounding hills provided a natural defensive position. Huerta knew this and poured in more reinforcements.

Carranza ordered Villa not to attack Zacatecas, but Villa proceeded anyway. General Felipe Ángeles had left Carranza's staff and now planned Villa's assault. It began on June 23 and ended as another bloody battle with thousands of federal soldiers killed. Villa, knowing that Orozco veterans were among the prisoners, ordered the execution of all officers and enlisted men over the rank of corporal. When Ángeles found out, he convinced Villa to stop what some of the other Villa commanders carried out with gusto. Politically, Ángeles may have been too late.

Zacatecas finished Huerta. On July 15, he resigned and fled the country. He was helped in his escape by the German cruiser *Dresden*. Huerta later managed to enter the United States and with Pascual Orozco engaged in conspiracies with German agents. Arrested for sedition, he died in a Fort Bliss jail cell on January 31, 1916.

Villa now seemed to be at the height of his power. He controlled Chihuahua and the road to Mexico City lay open. During Huerta's last days, Villa and Carranza's relationship went through complex phases. Villa appeared still willing to accept Carranza as First Chief as long as he did not get in his way. Carranza, more devious, still needed Villa. Attempts to use other generals north of Mexico City had failed. Yet he needed to sow enough confusion and even sabotage Villa to allow Obregón to get to Mexico City first. After Zacatecas, Carranza made his move. He was able to delay shipments of coal that Villa needed for his trains, allowing Obregón to win the race to Mexico City and march into the capital on August 15. Carranza triumphantly followed a few days later.

Villa Versus Carranza

The rebels had won and Huerta, the cruel dictator, was gone. Unfortunately, instead of nation building, a new phase of battle and killing broke out among the victors.

Villa and Zapata had never liked or trusted Carranza. He was basically a conservative with little genuine interest in social reform. They had grudgingly accepted his pretention as First Chief because it worked strategically to unify against Huerta. Now because of the coal-train sabotage, Villa openly broke with him. Zapata had repeatedly made it clear he would not support anyone who did not accept the reforms in his Plan de Ayala, particularly the land-distribution program. Attempts by Obregón and others to mediate and find common ground failed and only made matters worse.

After the fall of Huerta, Obregón took charge and held a convention at Aguascalientes to organize the government and the presidency. Leading intellectuals and lawyers attended. Three of Mexico's four most powerful men came in person, Obregón, Zapata, and Villa. Carranza would not attend nor would he accept any of the convention's recommendations. The weeks-long sessions ended with the factions polarized. Obregón had to make a choice, and he remained as Carranza's commander. Mexico degenerated into yet another phase of civil war.

The Constitutionalists, Carranza and Obregón, faced the "Conventionists," Villa and Zapata. The latter name referred to the failed Aguascalientes Convention that had proposed, among other things, limiting the powers of the president and specifically blocking Carranza from ever becoming president.

Villa and Zapata both had large forces near Mexico City, large enough to compel Obregón to pull his army out of Mexico City and retreat to Veracruz. By late fall, Villa and Zapata occupied the city, leading to the famous photograph of Villa sitting in the president's chair with Zapata nearby. Zapata's army stood between Veracruz and Mexico City. Villa's army had cleared out Carrancistas north and west of the City, including Guadalajara.

This appeared on the surface to be a Conventionists victory, but the two powerful rebel generals had been out maneuvered. In Veracruz, Carranza and Obregón had Mexico's most important port. They could bring in arms and other war supplies still denied Villa. Obregón took time to rebuild his army and to pick the most advantageous area to fight Villa. Carranza continued to claim that he was the legitimate head of government. During 1915, the Conventionists made feeble attempts to govern. It did not help that Villa in the field could not suppress the excesses and corruption of some of his subordinate generals lounging in the capital like minor potentates.

In January, Obregón went on the offensive. He broke through Zapata and by the end of January had reoccupied Mexico City. Zapata withdrew to Morelos instead of remaining at Obregón's back, which Villa needed. Now the rebuilt Constitutionalists faced only Villa. Obregón wheeled his army north and marched into the Bajío, the region he had selected for his planned defensive warfare. The Bajío was an agricultural region, northwest

General, later President, Álvaro Obregón,
lost an arm in the Battle of Torreón against Pancho Villa.
Photo: hec 09853
//hdl.loc.gov/loc.pnp/hec.09853 U.S. Library of Congress

of Mexico City, crisscrossed with rivers and canals, making it difficult for offensive operations.

Much has been written about Pancho Villa's prowess as a field commander, some going to extremes with praise. There is no doubt that Villa had extraordinary leadership and organizational skills as well as a natural charisma that inspired his men. General Felipe Ángeles helped with some of Villa's successful battles. However, it turned out Obregón was a better tactician. He studied the new warfare unfolding in the Great War in Europe and built defensive positions based on what he learned. Succeeding battles would feature Villa's hard-charging, sharp-shooting cavalry against Obregón's carefully prepared defensive positions.

In the Bajío, Obregón moved his army to Celaya, not far from León in northwestern Guanajuato state. His men dug trenches, installed multiple tangles of barbwire, and set up protected machine gun nests with intersecting fields of fire. He had set the trap and waited for Villa to take the bait.

Villa, after his string of victories, now commanded an army approaching 50,000. He arrived in the Bajío ready for battle in April 1915. General Ángeles appraised the situation at Celaya and warned Villa not to attack or to at least modify his tactics. Over-confident, with a two-to-one advantage, he ordered a massed mounted charge into Obregón's trenches and barbed wire. It was a huge, vicious, bloody affair. Thousands of men and horses went down. With moves and countermoves, the first part of the battle lasted two days. An explosion blew off Obregón's forearm and nearly killed him. After battlefield surgery, he remained in command. Villa withdrew for a week, regrouped, and attacked again. In the end it was a slaughter and the first of three battles Villa would lose in the Bajío.

These stunning defeats did not finish Villa. He remained a presence and a threat until the Revolution wound down five years later. However, Celaya proved to be the beginning of the end for him as a serious contender for control of the country or even the state of Chihuahua.

The complex national politics of the next several months consisted of shifting alliances, power plays, and some fighting. Many still opposed Carranza and his basic conservatism. Nevertheless, he assumed executive control of Mexico on May 15, 1915. President Wilson recognized him as provisional president on October 19. Carranza would not be formally elected president until 1917.

The Last Fight of the División del Norte

It had been a bad year for Pancho Villa, but he was not finished. Although he no longer controlled regions like Guadalajara and Monterrey, he still commanded a large army of 12,000 men. He always had reasonably good relations with the United States and thought highly of President Wilson and the U.S. Army generals he had met. He particularly liked General Hugh L. Scott, who had commanded U. S. Army units at Fort Bliss, patrolling the border. After Scott became U.S. Army Chief of Staff in 1914, he remained involved in border issues. There are pictures of Scott and Villa smiling together, and also the famous photograph of Villa with General John Pershing standing on the international bridge to Ojinaga. Those days were over.

On October 19, 1915, President Wilson's government recognized Carranza as the chief of the de facto government in Mexico. The reasons for President Wilson's recognition of Carranza have been debated, but it is clear Wilson was looking for stability at the border as he faced the prospect of entering the European war. Villa's losses suggested Carranza would eventually dominate. The executions of prisoners after Villa's victories over Huerta had not played well in the United States and sullied his image. Also, in spite of his tolerance for North Americans, Villa had begun to expropriate money and other assets from U.S. companies including the MNWR. Various company owners sent strong complaints to Washington. Carranza still bitterly resented the occupation of Veracruz but recognized he needed the United States. He now claimed to support U.S. interests in Mexico and promised to protect their assets and citizens.[677] Historian Philip Stover notes that Carranza placed Protestants in key positions in his government, something that pleased Wilson.[678] Regardless of Wilson's motivation, Villa now was a renegade in the eyes of the U.S. government.

Recognition of Carranza was a setback, but Villa convinced himself that if he could defeat Carranza's federal forces on the border and establish a presence, Wilson would change his mind. He decided to invade Sonora and attack Agua Prieta, which he believed would fall easily. At

Aguascalientes where he had retreated, Villa commandeered nineteen trains from the National Railroad and sent 10,000 troops and camp followers, 8,000 horses plus cannon, supplies, and the other paraphernalia of war north into the Casas Grandes Valley.

Villa established his camp at Dublán, the largely abandoned LDS colony on the MNWR.

Villa and his staff spent three weeks organizing the march to Agua Prieta, just across the border from Douglas, Arizona. Since no trains ran east and west across the Sierra Madre, this would be a slog, dragging cannons, ammunition, and supply wagons down deep canyons and high passes. Winter was coming and the march began in a cold rain.

In an amazing feat of organization, logistics, and endurance, General Villa led his infantry, cavalry, cannon, supply wagons, and ambulances across the Llanos de Carretas, then up the rugged Púlpito pass and across the mountains into the desert of Sonora. The exhausted men and horses paused outside Agua Prieta. Villa let them rest for a full day. In front of him lay the low adobe buildings of Agua Prieta with a garrison he estimated to be between 1,200 and 2,000 federal soldiers. In command was General Plutarco Elías Calles, a crafty politician and later president, but not known for his military skills. Regardless of his military reputation, he had prepared a good defensive position with trenches and barbed wire. Still, one assault by Villa's hard-charging cavalry should overwhelm him.

What Villa did not know was President Wilson's government had acceded to an unprecedented request. General Obregón prepared a telegram, and U.S. Army officers he knew in El Paso forwarded it to the president in Washington. Wilson's reply allowed Obregón to transport Mexican troops by train across United States territory. While Villa's troops dragged cannon across high passes, General Obregón sent 4,500 federal soldiers across the southwest on U.S. tracks to Douglas. These were experienced troops, veterans of the Battle of Celaya. Detraining in Douglas, they marched across the border to Agua Prieta and set to work digging more trenches, stringing barbwire, and laying mines, techniques Obregón had learned worked so well against Villa's charges. These veteran troops had something else—they knew Villa could be beaten, legend or not.[679]

Villa, unaware of what he faced, planned a night attack on November 2, a grand blow that would overwhelm the garrison. With a preliminary bombardment and feints to disguise the point of attack, he gave the order. His tired, discouraged men of the División del Norte rose to the occasion and charged hard—right into blinding searchlights. In the instant after the lights went on cannon, rifle, and machine gun fire cut down the attackers as they struggled in a tangle of barb wire and exploding mines.

It was another slaughter and this time Villa would never fully recover. The proud División del Norte effectively ceased to exist. Not only did he lose Sonora and much of his army that day, but he lost his absolute hold on Chihuahua, his base.

Pancho Villa would roam the state for the next three and a half years, striking fear in the countryside. His abilities and influence would allow him even to rebuild a small army, fight battles, reclaim and lose cities, but essentially President Wilson and the Mexican politicians, who bet on Carranza, were right, Villa would lose in the end.

It is unclear whether the two searchlights that lit the battlefield and blinded the attackers were plugged in on the U.S. or Mexican side. The actual facts are immaterial. Villa believed the searchlight wires were connected in Douglas. Also, three regiments of U.S. troops had been assigned to Douglas in anticipation of the battle to protect U.S. citizens against any kind of incursion. Villa could see them across the border in formation and was convinced they participated in the battle.

Villa's attitude toward all North Americans changed dramatically. As far as he was concerned his loss was due to their treachery, starting with President Wilson. He made widely publicized threats that added to the fears of North Americans and the many Mexicans who associated or worked with them in Pearson, Corralitos, and the LDS colonies.

The "Black Legend" side of Villa's larger-than-life story now surfaced. With a large guerilla troop, he began to carry out his threats, viciously plundering throughout northern Mexico. Plundering meant not only stealing and burning, but kidnapping and murder. His depredations ranged from deep in Coahuila to Madera and the MNWR Chihuahua District. Twice, he raided Hearst's San José de Babícora killing cattle and kidnapping managers.[680] Carranza had promised Wilson that he would keep order, but he could not, despite sending more troops to Chihuahua. The railroad, mines, towns and the ordinary local people in the Casas Grandes Valley now had to deal with *Carrancistas* and *Villistas* as well as roving bandit bands.

Villa's rampages led to a bizarre incident that most North Americans and many Mexicans remember best about the Revolution—Villa's attack on Columbus, New Mexico, March 9, 1916.

The Columbus Raid

In spite of all the research and countless articles, no consensus has been reached on Villa's motives or even the details of the attack. In the succeeding years, many told of riding with Villa at Columbus. Others claimed with absolute certainty that he was not there. The *El Paso Herald-Post* in 1960 published a story about the attack that quoted a Frank T. Padilla. He had worked for years on a road project between Palomas, across from Columbus, and Casas Grandes. He had seen Villa many times. He claimed to have witnessed the attack, and said Villa was not there. According to Padilla, the leader was one of Villa's officers, Martín López with his brother Pablo López. Others in similar articles over the years agreed.[681] Despite those "eye witnesses," others confirmed Villa's presence. Part of the confusion stems from Villa's role in the attack. Likely, he observed on a hill with a rear guard and horse holders and was not in the center of the action. Most historians now agree he was there in person. But why be there at all?

Arguments for various motives include blind hatred for North Americans, the need for supplies, the need for arms, particularly machine guns, known to be in the 13th Cavalry's nearby camp, and subversive influence from the German secret service. The old Juan Quezada family friend, Don Chuy López, told the story after dinner one warm September night in Juan Quezada's kitchen. The adults sat around the large wooden table with children tucked into all corners behind. A single light bulb hanging from a cord lighted the faces. Don Chuy came from Zacatecas as did several other of the older generation in Mata Ortiz. He had witnessed the great battle there between the forces of Villa and Huerta in 1914. The old gentleman told many other stories and voiced strong opinions about young people. When he turned to the Columbus raid, he said a storekeeper, Sam Ravel, had sold Villa bad ammunition. When fired it only went "phtt." Villa vowed he would catch that store keeper and "kill him at his pleasure."[682]

Villa biographer Friedrich Katz never heard Don Chuy's story, but he heard versions of all the arguments and points out flaws in each. He suggests that Villa planned the attack carefully well in advance. Loot, arms, and even revenge may have been side benefits, but his primary objective was to demonstrate the weakness of the Carranza government and its inability to protect U.S. citizens and their interests.[683]

It should be noted that the famous Columbus attack was not the only incursion into U.S. territory. This chaotic Revolutionary era featured a number of raids and pursuits across the border both ways. Collectively these are known as the Border War. They became particularly vicious leading up to Columbus.

Villa's force was formidable but a pale reflection of the División del Norte. Most of his former officers were dead. Some troops remained intensely loyal, but volunteers no longer flocked to him as before. He had to stoop to forcibly calling up veterans of the old División. Most of the forced recruitment occurred in Namiquipa, while the Casas Grandes Valley men were spared for the most part.[684]

In 1916, Columbus, New Mexico was a growing town of 300 U.S. citizens, located directly across from Palomas, Chihuahua. A few hundred Mexican refugees from the Revolution also lived in the town. The border crossing, the U.S. Army camp, and surrounding ranches had generated significant commercial activity along Broadway, the principle east-west street. The town boasted the Hoover Hotel, a bank, and several stores, one owned by the Ravel brothers, who did a good trade with Mexicans, including selling arms and ammunition. Trains of the El Paso and Southwestern railway made regular stops at the large station near Broadway. South of the railroad tracks, the U.S. Army had established Camp Furlong as the headquarters for the U.S. Army 13th Cavalry. The regiment was charged with protecting a 65-mile segment of the border. The permanent garrison numbered about 375 of which 120 were in camp, sleeping in the barracks that night.[685]

In the predawn of March 9, approximately 500 Villistas (sources vary) crossed the border south of the regular Palomas border station. They divided into two columns and advanced on the army camp and town from two sides. Screaming *Viva Villa* and *muerte a los gringos*, they charged, firing wildly. Spreading out, they broke into homes, and businesses, and set fire to buildings. The surprise was complete. For several chaotic minutes, people ran in all directions. In the camp, soldiers stumbled out of the barracks half-dressed into the hail of bullets. The tight discipline of a few officers and men saved the attack from being a complete massacre. Lieutenant James P. Castleman, the Officer of the Day, ran from the guard tent to the barracks and found his sergeant already formed up with thirty men with rifles. He ordered the men forward and then to the ground as they came under fire. Prone in the darkness, the well-trained soldiers fired back at the muzzle flashes and the shouts in Spanish. Suffering casualties, the raiders began to scatter. On their feet and formed up again, Lt. Castleman led the riflemen north across the tracks, through two brief firefights, into the east side of town. He positioned them near the bank, looking west down Broadway.

In the meantime, Lieutenant John P. Lucas, commanding officer of the regimental machine gun troop, ran from his quarters barefoot and under fire. With two of his men, he retrieved a machine gun from its locked space in the guard tent, only to jam it in their haste. They quickly retrieved another. A few minutes later, an officer joined him with about thirty men. With Lucas in command, they moved across the tracks toward town and took up a position on the south side. With Castleman on the east and Lucas south, the Villistas found themselves in a crossfire illuminated by burning buildings. They retreated in reasonably good order to the railroad station and tried to regroup and make a stand but soon were in full flight to their horses.

Major Frank Tompkins had remained in his house to protect his wife and daughters when the shooting started. Now he ran to the camp commander, who had arrived on the scene, and received permission to pursue the retreating invaders. His mounted troopers rode hard, caught up, and fought a running battle that extended five miles across the border into Mexico. Villa's rearguard fought fiercely, and Tompkins broke off the action and returned to Columbus. Approaching daylight revealed seventeen North Americans dead, mostly civilians.

Like other aspects of the incursion, it is not clear whether the Villistas carried off much loot or arms, likely not. They never found and killed Sam

Ravel, the storekeeper, because he was at the dentist in El Paso. Also, Villa lost over a hundred men with many more wounded or captured.

On the surface, the attack was a disaster. However, the incursion was a success if Villa's primary motive was to further question Carranza's control of the country and to encourage U.S. intervention that would provoke the Mexican people and discredit Carranza. The raid, perversely, opened a way for Villa to restore at least some of his power and continue the fight. What he probably did not expect was the overwhelming reaction of the U.S. aimed directly at him.

A particularly bizarre story emerged from the already bizarre raid. The report of the kidnapping of Maude Wright first broke in *The New York Times*, March 10, 1916. Maude and Edward Wright came from New Mexico to the Casas Grandes Valley in 1910 as a newly married couple ready to start their life together. Ed worked hard and saved enough to purchase a few head of cattle and a small ranch in Hop Valley (Jovale), the tiny LDS settlement about three miles from Colonia Pacheco, and 30 miles from Pearson. Rebel thievery and harassment forced them to leave with the Exodus in 1912. They returned in February 1916 and after more hard work, rebuilt and restocked their ranch. With them was Johnny, their two-year old son. A few weeks later, Ed and Frank Hayden, a young associate, rode to Pearson for supplies with two pack mules. Unknown to them, Villa and his small army was camped in nearby Cave Valley to prepare for their raid on Columbus.

Just before the two men returned, a group of Villa's men rode into the Wright's yard and demanded food from Maude. She had dealt with Orozco's Red Flaggers and other rebels before the Exodus, but this was somehow different. She did the best she could, but more men rode in, and soon 60 rebels ransacked the house and the store room. They lit fires with anything that would burn and began butchering cattle. When Ed and Frank returned, the Villistas took the supplies from the mules and tied the two men on their horses. The leader told Maude to give Johnny to Mrs. Augustine Morales, a neighbor, and then made her mount a horse. She had a chance to say a few last words with Ed, who told her to come back for Johnny and take him to the U.S.

The Villistas forced her to ride with them through the freezing night to Cave Valley. Villa saw her and made no comment other than to assign two men to her with orders that she not be molested.

When Villa gave the order to the troopers to move out, Maude again was told to mount. She rode with the army for five days and nights with an old, dirty serape for warmth. She and the troops ate only hastily cooked meat, seared on the outside and virtually raw inside, with no salt. She saw a man riding Ed's horse and knew her husband and his friend were dead. Devastated by thoughts of Ed and worried about Johnny, she rode on day after day in the cold. Villa took a convoluted route to avoid detection. She saw him often, riding with his men, encouraging, cajoling, and giving orders. They talked a few times. Once he said he would free her after the raid if she was still alive. Clearly, he thought she would not make it. His motive for taking her never was clear. She could hear him rail against the treacherous North Americans, but he showed no particular animosity toward her.

She did make it to Columbus. In the dark before the attack, her captors brought her to the edge of town and told her to hold several horses. These would be reserves for anyone whose horse was shot. She thought of escape, but there were other rebel vaqueros around her watching the reserve herd.

The attack began, and she could hear the screaming charge and see the burning buildings. Villa rode a big paint stallion that was shot from under him. As the retreat began, Maude saw him ride out of the battle on a grey horse.

She stopped him and asked if he would free her as promised. He pointed toward the border and rode off. She struggled through the battlefield on foot and ultimately was taken in by Colonel Herbert J. Slocum, the commanding officer, and his wife. Slocum sent word of Maude's plight to the highest levels in both countries. A special train ran from El Paso to Pearson to pick up Johnny. Mrs. Moreno and her husband had brought the baby there from Hop Valley, and Mrs. Moreno refused to give him up without specific word from Maude. Fortunately, the telegraph wires were up and the requisite reassuring telegram sent. Carranza soldiers escorted them and took pictures of the mother and child reunion to prove Johnny had been delivered safely.

Maude honored Ed's last request and raised Johnny in the U.S. They both lived long productive lives in Safford, New Mexico. Maude married another cowboy, and they had seven children and lived happily for 41 years.

In 1960, close friends toured Columbus with Maude and Johnny. Maude recalled vividly the details of her traumatic kidnapping, which her friends put in writing. The story of Maude's ordeal survives because of their documentation and *The New York Times* article.[686]

Maude Wright's eye-witness account adds intriguing detail about the Columbus raid, especially the harsh life of the rebel trooper. However, like so many other accounts, it adds to the contradictions. She verifies that Villa was there, but did he lead the raiders into battle on a big paint horse?

Columbus today has a population of about 2000. In 1961, the New Mexico legislature created the Pancho Villa State Park. The old depot became a museum. The town including the Camp Furlong site was declared a National Historic Landmark in 1975. Starting in 1999, civic representatives from both sides of the border started *la Fiesta de Amistad*, using the history of the old battle to promote friendship between the two countries. The high point each year is the arrival of the *Cabalgata*, a group of U.S. and Mexican horsemen that ride across the border together, many in Revolution-era costumes.

The Punitive Expedition

The attack sparked outrage and a sense of violation in the U.S. A war-mongering press led by the Hearst papers and powerful senators had already put pressure on President Wilson to intervene in Mexico. Now they cried out that not since the British stormed Washington D.C. in 1812 had the U.S. borders been violated. The fact that these statements ignored years of violent border history made no difference. Wilson faced an election and had no choice politically, even though personally he had showed sympathy for the plight of the Mexican people, battered by years of fighting among factions.

The day of the attack, the U.S. State Department sent a protest message to Carranza, asking that he capture Villa. Carranza replied vaguely that the situation was in hand and complained about Apache attacks into Mexico from Arizona twenty years before.

The next day, March 10, Wilson issued orders to the War Department, to U.S. Army Chief of Staff General Hugh L. Scott, and to General John Pershing to mobilize forces to cross the international border and chase down and capture Villa and disperse his bands. The orders made clear to Pershing, the press, and to Carranza's government that there was no other objective or motive. Wilson definitely did not want a war with Mexico. He had enough concerns dealing with the up-coming election and the potential U.S. entry into the European war. He and his military advisors knew that entering Mexico created the possibility of matters spinning out of control into all-out war. They planned accordingly and alerted Army and Navy forces, cautioning Pershing to cooperate and avoid confrontation with Carrancista forces. Fortunately, the contingency mobilization plans were not necessary. Carranza, as anti-American and as opposed as he was to the violation of Mexican sovereignty, knew that he could not withstand a foreign war. The two countries came close as they danced around each other while both pursued Villa.

The U.S. Army established the 2nd Provisional Cavalry Brigade, commonly known as the Mexican Punitive Expedition. "Provisional" referred to a temporary organization created from various regular Army units for a special purpose. This concept was used extensively during the Punitive Expedition. Also, the cavalry often used the term "squadron" to denote a company of mounted troopers. This usage should not be confused with aviation squadrons.

The commander, General Pershing, had been assigned to the U.S. Army Southern District under General Frederick Funston. Pershing had considerable combat experience. Just three years before he commanded the U.S. troops during the Moro Rebellion in the Philippines.

Orders went out to Army units throughout the Southern District—cavalry, infantry, artillery, machine-gun troops, wagon companies, and other support—to mobilize at two locations in New Mexico, Hachita and Columbus. According to Pershing's plan, two columns would enter Chihuahua one from each of the two mobilization locations. The columns and following support units would rendezvous at Casas Grandes.

At the same time Carranza ordered General Luis Gutiérrez to Palomas with a substantial force. General Gutiérrez had orders to hunt down Villa, but the general made it very clear that he would oppose any incursion by U.S. troops into Mexico.

The east column left Columbus under the command of Colonel Herbert J. Slocum, on March 15, 1916, just seven days after Villa's attack. The 13th Cavalry Regiment took the honored lead position in recognition of the gallant response to the assault. Major Frank Tompkins, who had led the pursuit that day, commanded the advance guard. Each trooper carried a Springfield 1903, 30-6 caliber rifle and the Colt M1911 45 caliber pistol, the pistol that had proved so effective in the Philippines.[687]

At midday, March 15, they crossed the border into Palomas expecting resistance, but General Gutiérrez's Mexican troops and all residents had abandoned the town. Slocum's column halted beyond Palomas and camped their first night on Mexican soil. Lieutenant Edgar S. Gorrell of the First Aero Squadron led a two-truck convoy loaded with bread and several regular Army officers, who had not made it back to Columbus by departure time the previous day.

The Punitive Expedition would record several "firsts" for the U.S. Army, particularly in the use of mechanical equipment. The inauspicious arrival of the two trucks at Palomas appears to be the first use of trucks by the Army in a combat situation. The vehicles belonged to the First Aero Squadron that had arrived at Columbus March 15 to provide reconnaissance.[688] As the Carranza government denied Pershing the use of the MNWR or the National Railroad, supply trucks proved vital. However, the War Department's procurement office had delayed sending trucks to Columbus. Desperate, Pershing turned to the First Aero Squadron. For the first days of the expedition the squadron's trucks, pilots, and mechanics functioned as Pershing's motor-transport corps, making runs between Columbus and the encampments with men, supplies and equipment.

Horse-drawn wagons still provided much of the supply at the beginning of the Expedition. By the end, trucks had taken over. The location of fuel depots took priority over grazing fields for supply convoys.

In the succeeding days, the cavalry column from Columbus rode ahead making 20 to 25 miles per day, passing rough the ruined LDS town of Colonia Díaz and through Ascensión. The retreating Villa troops had stripped the town of horses and wagons to haul their wounded. The war-weary people watched with a mixture of curiosity and apathy as yet another army marched through their town. The night of March 18, three more motor trucks from Columbus drove into camp full of supplies.

The next day, the column stopped at the Casas Grandes River crossing at Vuelta de Alamos, southeast of Janos, to bathe and wash clothes. Villa had camped there the previous week with his wounded raiders before going to Corralitos, where he murdered the ranch foreman. Tompkins posted a heavy guard, not knowing if any of Villa's men still lurked nearby. In the morning, March 20, they continued through Corralitos to the designated encampment one mile north of Dublán. General Pershing had arrived three days earlier in the evening of March 17.

The general personally had led the west column that crossed the border at Culbertson's Ranch, south of Hachita, just past midnight on March 16. He sent the supply wagons and artillery units by more accessible routes and with the 7th and 10th cavalry, forced march south through mountains

General Pershing's truck convoys assemble at Columbus, New Mexico
Photo: cph 3c32203
//hdl.loc.gov/loc.pnp/cph.3c32203 Courtesy of the U.S. Library of Congress

and plains to Dublán. The two regiments covered 125 miles in 44 hours, including stops to rest men and animals.[689] Neither column encountered opposition.

When local people informed Pershing that Villa was not in Casas Grandes but in the Santa María Valley near Hacienda San Miguel de Babícora, he immediately ordered three provisional columns south. The 7th Cavalry troopers of the First Column remounted after less than seven hours rest and moved out at 3:00 a.m. for the Santa María Valley. Colonel George A. Dodd commanded.

The hard-riding 7th Cavalry experienced only frustration in the Santa María Valley as they repeatedly found Villa gone from his reported positions. Whether fighting or not, the Expedition troopers found themselves in hostile country with freezing temperatures and long supply lines.

Colonel Dodd did establish communication with Carrancista generals, also hunting Villa. Through this contact, word came that Villa had been wounded in the leg in a fire fight with the Carrancistas near Namiquipa. This proved to be true.

Although, as the campaign progressed, it became evident that much of the information from Carrancista sources was either misleading or outright false. Most locals still regarded Villa as their hero and provided little help. Sifting through dubious information, Colonel Dodd determined that the wounded Villa might be heading for Ciudad Guerrero. Exhausted troopers on exhausted horses pushed on through the cold. Guides deliberately took them by an extra-long route, until they reached the rugged arroyo-filled outskirts of the city. Pascual Orozco found this same terrain difficult for an attacker six years before in the opening days of the Revolution.

Dodd ordered the troopers forward, and they advanced as quickly as possible over rugged ground. Shooting broke out in isolated arroyos, and it became evident that the U.S. troopers had caught the Villistas leaving the city. Several of them stood their ground and returned fire but soon scattered into small groups and ran for the mountains. The U.S. troopers' worn-out horses could go no farther, and they did not pursue.

Colonel Dodd's 7th Cavalry did well, but this battle turned out to be the only significant direct action against Villa's band. As for Villa himself, he was not at Ciudad Guerrero. He had left just a few hours before the troopers arrived—fateful hours they had spent on the long, indirect route to the city.

Believing Villa to be in the Guerrero District, Pershing wanted to use rail to transport the second and third provisional columns south. Both columns contained units of the 10th Cavalry, the Buffalo Soldiers that had just arrived in Dublán from Fort Huachuca.

Carranza had denied use of Mexican trains to the Expedition, but this did not seem to apply to North American trains. Pershing telegraphed the manager of the El Paso and Southern Railroad (by 1924, part of the Southern Pacific), who immediately sent a train with an engine and 28 freight and flat cars. Unfortunately, the cars the manager so quickly assembled and sent were in miserable condition. Carpenters had to repair large holes in the floors and cut ventilation windows before the cars could be used by men and horses.

The two columns of troops and horses finally loaded at Dublán on March 19. Fuel problems forced the engineer to stop the train twice before reaching Pearson to break up stock-corral posts and railings for wood for the engine fire box.

No one in Pershing's headquarters had bothered to telegraph the MNWR district superintendent in Pearson that a foreign train would be on his tracks.[690] When he saw the large, overloaded train, he did not want it to continue. The nervous El Paso engineer agreed. Colonel W.C. Brown, the commanding officer, finally convinced both to let the train pass. It turned out the railroad men were right. The straining engine, belching black smoke, could not pull the long heavily loaded train as the grade began to increase. The crew detached the cars with the troops of Column Three and delivered Column Two to El Rucio.

There, Colonel Brown's troopers unloaded the horses and he led the column to the conjunction of the Palanganas and San Miguel Rivers. They followed the San Miguel east up a steep, rocky trail to the Hacienda San Miguel. The foreman said Villa had never been there. The column marched on chasing dead-end leads in the numbing cold for a month, until they were recalled.

The train with just the third column aboard now had fewer cars but remained heavy for the long grade through the tunnels and over the Cumbre summit. Colonel Brown's orders were to take the train and disembark near Madera and operate in the area of Hearst's San José Babícora ranch. The train proceeded slowly and made the bypass turn before the burned-out Cumbre Tunnel. The engineer turned the train into the bypass that led to the switchbacks. Without warning on one switchback leg, two cars overturned, spilling men, horses, and equipment down the embankment. It is not recorded how many men plunged down the slope, but eleven suffered injuries and one died, the first fatal casualty of the Punitive Expedition.

Major E.W. Evans, commanding the Third Column, organized the retrieval of the men and horses that survived. A sergeant of the Hospital Corp cared for the wounded in the caboose, in spite of the deep cuts on his own face. Major Evans ordered the uninjured troopers to mount and complete the trip on horseback. The train crew somehow cleared the track and reconnected the wrecked cars and completed the switchback descent. After stopping for repairs, the crippled train made it to Madera. A foreman from the Hearst Ranch took some of the wounded back to Dublán on a handcart, a very cold two-day trip.

In the next few days, the two columns joined together under Colonel Brown and operated in the southern Santa María Valley. Supply became a problem.

Trucks, and wagons from the main base at Dublán needed to cross the Río Santa María to the east side as they followed the main road south of Galeana. It was winter, but the command staff learned the spring flood could make fords impassable. Pershing's engineering companies solved the problem by grading a new road, navigable for trucks, which ran straight south, starting in the Chocolate pass above Galeana. They laid it out along the east slope of the Sierra America (part of the range separating Pearson in the San Diego Valley from the Santa María Valley). In San Joaquín Canyon, Company K of the 17th Infantry set up a camp near a large spring. This served as a guard post for the road and a place to park and service trucks.

The Punitive Expedition is known for being the last major U.S. Army campaign to use mounted cavalry and the first to use gasoline-powered vehicles. Over 100 trucks eventually were shipped to Pershing's forces. This inadvertently provided valuable training for the Army's upcoming participation in the war in Europe. Issues such as standardized parts, fuel depots, maintenance facilities, and mechanic training presented new challenges to the Army's horse-oriented mentality. The lessons learned served the American Expeditionary Force well in France, beginning in April 1917. Pershing used a 1915 Dodge touring car to follow and inspect his advancing columns. His command had three convertible, four-door Dodge cars as well as several Ford Model T cars.

Meanwhile, Company K had little to do after finishing the basic camp routine each day. Finding shards and stone implements littering the canyon floor, some of the officers began digging into mounds. To keep the men busy, they eventually found and excavated twenty mounds. While they knew nothing of local archaeology, the young officers had enough education to appreciate what they uncovered. They kept careful records and contacted the Smithsonian Institute for information regarding the Casas Grandes culture. The Smithsonian staff expressed serious interest in the artifacts, and before the Punitive Expedition left Mexico, Lieutenant J. Warren Weissheimer wrote a detailed report for the Smithsonian, and the collection bears his name.

Chihuahua historian Rondal R. Bridgemon and Sylvia Brenner, former educator at the Pancho Villa State Park, researched the origins of the Weissheimer Collection, aided by original material provided by Dr. David Phillips of the Maxwell Museum. This led Bridgemon to visit San Joaquín several times to search for remnants of Company K's camp. On his first trip in 2008, he talked with a local farmer living near empty houses and a schoolroom. A small community had existed there from sometime in the 1930s until the mid-1990s when the spring dried up. The farmer had searched the canyon with a metal detector and found U.S. coins, uniform buttons, and a bayonet. Careful GPS map study, an old hand-drawn map from Dr. Phillips, and a row of aligned rocks enabled Bridgemon to find the campsite. There he found empty 30-06 cartridges with head-stamp dates from 1907 to 1913, ammunition for the 1903 Springfield rifle.[691]

The camp remained in operation throughout the campaign even though the main action moved farther and farther south through the Santa María Valley, Namiquipa, Ciudad Chihuahua, into the Guerrero District and beyond to Parral, almost 400 miles from the U.S.

U.S. troops passed through Casas Grandes several times, but Pershing ordered only one actual deployment in the San Diego Valley branch of the Casas Grandes Valley. A 275-man provisional squadron of the 13th Cavalry left Dublán March 20, with the objective of taking Chuichupa to cut off Villa if he tried to move west from the Santa María Valley. Pershing's staff was denied a MNWR train, so the provisional squadron rode through the cold to Casas Grandes and across the plains to San Diego Canyon at the foot of the Sierra Madre, west of Pearson. The troopers saw abandoned tracks from entrepreneur Lewis Booker's failed attempt in 1909 to build a short line to connect Pearson with lumber mills in Pacheco.

That night the troopers made a cold camp in San Diego Canyon. The next day, after emerging from that steep canyon, they saw ancient cave dwellings in the high cliffs before passing through Colonia Pacheco. The town was empty of people as were all ranches along the 100-mile route.

Approaching Chuichupa, advance scouts reported the old LDS town too was abandoned. The LDS colonists had left Chuichupa during the Exodus four years before, and their crumbling brick houses and overgrown gardens showed the years of neglect.

It became apparent that any action, or at least the rumors of action, regarding Villa was elsewhere. A garrison at Chuichupa was unnecessary, and the provisional squadron left to join the many other units chasing leads in the Santa María Valley, the Namiquipa area, and the Guerrero District.

After Colonel Dodd's fight at Ciudad Guerrero, Pershing organized four "flying columns." With one at the point, two on either flank, and a fourth behind as a reserve and rear guard. They searched the Guerrero District for several days before, moving south toward Parral. Credible intelligence suggested that just ahead some of Villa's men carried their badly wounded leader by wagon and litter toward Parral, a city of 20,000. Major Frank Tompkins led the center flying column of just 100 men.

Tompkins later wrote of this experience and the confused relationships the U.S. Army had with the local people and the Carrancista federal army units operating around them. Villagers expressed a combination of hostility, fear, indifference, and friendliness toward the North Americans troops. After all, the U.S. had invaded their country. On the other hand, they had watched helplessly as rebel and federal armies swept back and forth, taking what they wanted from farms, stores, and their private homes, leaving at best worthless receipts or dubious paper money. Pershing's troops paid with silver pesos wherever possible which delighted the villagers and opened hidden stashes for sale. Whenever the Carrancista federals found out about the sales, they threatened the villagers, ordering them not to cooperate with the gringo soldiers.

By the second week of April, Tompkins knew Villa was not in Parral and probably had gone farther south toward the passes leading to Durango. Instead, a large Carrancista garrison occupied Parral. Tompkins arranged with the Carrancistas to enter the city peacefully and be provided with a camping space, food, and fodder before continuing after Villa. The column rode into the Parral's center plaza on April 12. Instead of the promised welcome, it was a trap. Shots killed one trooper and in a three-hour running fight, Tompkins' troopers retreated back north to the small community of Santa Cruz Villegas. A courier galloped on to Colonel Brown's flying column waiting in reserve. The Carrancistas caught up but stayed their distance, having suffered the accurate, coordinated fire from the Springfield rifles. Brown's column arrived to the sound of bugles, and the Carrancistas withdrew back to Parral.

The fight was over, but Tompkins lost three men killed and five wounded including himself. It was a serious incident but nothing came of it except denials and protests from the Carranza government.[692]

The Punitive Expedition went no farther than Parral. Through the remainder of April and May the four flying columns operated north of Santa Cruz de Villegas into the Guerrero District. They caught up with a few small Villista bands and engaged in minor fire fights. Mostly the troopers rode for long hours in the cold on short rations and with little rest.

The situation for Pershing's forces deteriorated rapidly through the spring as open and often aggressive hostility of the local people and the Carrancistas hampered operations.

General Scott and General Funston met many times with General Obregón and other Carrancista representatives in frustrating sessions that led nowhere. Carranza's position had evolved from vague cooperation to leave-or-else. Veiled threats in messages to Pershing and a buildup of Carrancista troops, indicated preparation for an outright attack. The

Carrancista garrison commander at Casas Grandes actually received orders to standby to support such an attack. Then Carrancista troops boldly raided across the border into Glen Springs, Texas, killing U.S. soldiers and civilians, a deliberate provocation. Still, President Wilson's no-war-with-Mexico policy remained unchanged, and Pershing could take no direct action against Carranza's federals. His orders permitted him only to pursue Villa, and the increasing numbers of Carrancista troops to his south, east, and west, and along his lines of communication prevented any significant movement. The net effect was a gradual withdrawal north. By June, most of Pershing's command was back, encamped on the windy plains near Dublán.

In the first few weeks of the campaign, the First Aero Squadron's eight JN3 "Jenny" aircraft had flown reconnaissance missions. They provided good intelligence for Pershing and his commanders, but the fragile, underpowered aircraft proved inadequate. One by one they crashed until the last two were sent back to Columbus to be scrapped. Pershing had to depend on mounted patrols in hostile country for information. In mid-June, after hearing rumors of Villa's whereabouts, Pershing ordered two troops of the 10th Cavalry Buffalo Soldiers to ride east to reconnoiter. The senior officer was Captain Charles T. Boyd. About 70 miles east of Dublán, near the National railroad, they approached the ancient 18th century village of Carrizal in the Ahumada District. They were deep in federal-occupied country, and the town of Villa Ahumada had been a major staging area for Carrancista federals.

Eight members of the LDS colonies had been acting as guides for Pershing's units in the northern regions of Chihuahua. One of the most prominent of these was Lemuel H. Spilsbury of Colonia Juárez. He spoke fluent Spanish and had many friends among the Mexican people. General Pershing had specifically requested that he accompany Captain Boyd that day.

Local ranchers told Boyd and Spilsbury that Carrizal had a garrison of 400-500 Carrancista federals. Near the town, they conferred with the garrison commander under a white flag but were refused entry. Spilsbury saw the situation as extremely precarious and advised Boyd to withdraw. Instead, the Captain ordered his sixty Buffalo Soldiers to dismount, send their horses to the rear with handlers. The impetuous captain then ordered the dismounted troopers to charge. Fire from federal machine guns and 400 Mauser rifles sent them to the ground on their bellies as they tried to shoot back.

In the first minutes, both Captain Boyd and the Mexican garrison commander went down. Accurate fire from small groups of troopers brought down many federals, but it was not enough, and the devastating fire quickly overwhelmed them. Some scattered into the desert and were later found by rescue patrols. Others had no choice but to surrender. The battle lasted only a few minutes, but the toll was terrible on both sides. In addition to Captain Boyd, two other officers, and 10 troopers were killed, and 26 taken prisoner, including Lem Spilsbury.[693]

The Carrancistas lost their commanding general and many men. The enraged officer, who assumed command, ordered the prisoners immediately lined up and shot. Facing the officer, Spilsbury talked as fast as he could, pointing out to the officer the retribution the U.S. Army would exact for such a deed. The officer decided not to give the execution command but let that decision be made at a higher level. The shackled prisoners boarded a train for Ciudad Chihuahua. There, Spilsbury continued to talk and again the prisoners stayed alive for ten more days. After a flurry of diplomatic communications, all twenty-six were taken to El Paso and released. In spite of the rhetoric and his threatening actions, Carranza really did not want all-out war. He knew, if the prisoners had been executed at Carrizal, even President Wilson could not have withstood the pressure to declare war. Lem Spilsbury's fast talking prevented that fatal step.[694]

General Pershing certainly was angry enough to go to war, but Carrizal proved to be the last fighting against anyone, Villista or Carrancista. President Wilson called up the newly reorganized National Guard and thousands of guardsmen crowded into U.S. Army camps along the entire border. Carranza lowered his aggressive stance and the Punitive Expedition units remained in the Dublán encampment for seven more miserable months.

There, dust storms blew away tents and covered everything with dirt. Heavy summer rains turned it all to mud. Pershing kept the men busy from dawn until dark with a strenuous training schedule. However, the weather prevented normal camp-life recreation. Remarkably, morale remained high. The men respected their general, maintained discipline, and unpleasant incidents with local people were few.

In fact, the local people in the Casas Grandes Valley, Mexicans, LDS colonists, and Chinese enjoyed an interim time of peace. In spite of the terrible weather, farmers and ranchers with produce, hay, leather, and meat to sell prospered. They received payment in silver pesos, which went a long way to restore the devastated local economy. The Pax Pershing was all too brief.

Finally, orders came to return to the U.S. Pershing broke camp on January 30, 1917. Soldiers, motor vehicles, and wagons of the Punitive Expedition stretched in a long column, augmented by at least 500 wagons and cars with Chinese, LDS colonists, U.S. company employees, and Mexican citizens, all seeking refuge in the U.S. from reprisals they feared would come from both Carrancistas and Villistas. The last of the column passed into Columbus on February 5, 1917. Officers and men returned to their regular units and the 2nd Provisional Cavalry Brigade, the Punitive Expedition, disbanded. In June, the first units of the American Expeditionary Force, commanded by General John Pershing, would be in France.

The Chinese had provided a significant service to the dirty, dusty troopers stuck on the Dublán plain. They braved dangerous roads to bring and sell products such as soap, otherwise unattainable to the troops. They laundered the soldier's filthy uniforms, and even cooked. Pershing recognized the services these men provided in making his troops more comfortable in a bad situation. In spite of the Chinese exclusion laws that had essentially shut down legal Chinese immigration, Pershing obtained amnesty for 427 men, enabling them to stay in the U.S. and probably saving their lives.

The Punitive Expedition had not met its objective. In fact, ten and a half months of hard riding had the opposite effect. Pancho Villa emerged much stronger than before the incursion. His popularity among the common people soared. Their hero had not only evaded the powerful gringos but also the unpopular Carrancista soldiers.

As with most Villa stories, his actual location during the incursion remains a mixture of fact and legend. Very early, he suffered a bad bullet wound in the leg in a skirmish with Carrancistas. His horse went down and he was pinned underneath. Some accounts say he suffered for months with perhaps a broken leg bone or infection. Likely, his men took him to a cave in the mountains above Ciudad Guerrero, and he remained there for months, in spite of the rumors of his presence from Namiquipa to Parral. According to one story, a detachment of troopers came close enough for Villa and his guards to hear them talking in English. Another prevalent story suggested he moved deeper into the Sierra Madre to a cave called Coscomate, in the San Francisco de Borja municipio, not far from Ciudad Cuauhtémoc. At some point, a doctor treated his wound, and he began to recover.[695]

Regardless of Villa's exact location, it seems clear he lay in a cave somewhere during for the first several weeks of the Punitive Expedition's chase and did not personally participate in any of the skirmishes. As the months passed and he recovered, he began to reassemble his guerilla army.

He would never lead a División del Norte of 50,000 again, nor would he rule all of Chihuahua, but he would remain a factor in the fight against Carranza and Obregón until the Revolution wound down three years later.

The First Aero Squadron

The Punitive Expedition never captured Villa. Nevertheless, the effort generated several "firsts" for the U.S. Army—the most dramatic being the first use of airplanes on a military combat mission. This first effort could not be sustained beyond a month. In that brief time, eleven brave pilots in unreliable airplanes demonstrated the immense value of air reconnaissance and communication to an Army hierarchy still wedded to the horse.

The Theodore Roosevelt administration created the Aeronautical Division of the U.S. Army Signal Corps in 1907. The Chief Signal Officer issued a memorandum stating in part that, "This division will have charge of all matters pertaining to military ballooning, air machines, and all kindred subjects." The name changed to "Aviation Section" in 1914. The unit received its first airplane, a Wright Flyer, in 1909. Orville and Wilbur Wright helped train the first Army pilots. A young officer named Benjamin D. Foulois, who had flown Dirigible 1, the Army's first flying machine, flew with Orville Wright as navigator on the Wright Military Flyer's test flight.

Lieutenant Foulois was an infantry and Signal Corps officer and veteran of both the Spanish-American War and Philippine War. He became a major player as the U.S. Army took fledgling steps to understand and develop the potential of military flight. Although his name is not well known beyond the realm of military-air historians, he could rightly be called the "Father" of U.S. military aviation.

In January, 1910, the Signal Corps shipped the Flyer to a new air station at Fort Sam Houston in San Antonio, Texas. Foulois was assigned as the only air officer. The commanding officer pointed to the newly arrived Wright Flyer and ordered Foulois to teach himself to fly it.

Foulois did, corresponding with the Wrights, and trying to learn how to keep the primitive craft in the air. He crashed often, which inspired him to invent the seat belt from a cavalry-saddle strap. He made many other technical improvements and recommendations, one of which led to the elimination by the Army of Wright (and other manufacturers') pusher-type aircraft, and adoption of the "tractor" configuration with the propeller in the front. Tractors were considered to be much safer in that early era when crashes and pilot fatalities were all too common.

The efforts of Foulois and others led to the establishment of an Army flying school on North Island in the harbor at San Diego, California. In August 1912, the Signal Corps purchased its first tractor-type airplane, a Burgess Model H (The Burgess Company later merged with the Curtiss Aeroplane Company). The Corps purchased five more (the company only made seven). On March 5, 1913, the Signal Corps created the First Aero Squadron with the newly trained pilots. The Squadron transferred to Texas City, Texas, as part of the U.S. Army expansion along the border. There the pilots flew the Burgess aircraft on cross-country training missions. The following year, after promotion to captain, Foulois took command of the Squadron.

When the Squadron returned to the training facility in San Diego, Foulois reorganized its structure and began ordering the support vehicles and tools necessary for an active military air campaign. Foulois struggled to get the equipment he needed, but his dogged persistence gradually paid off as he dealt with an Army bureaucracy that did not understand the requirements of air operations. One of these requirements was effective ground support.

In January 1915, the Squadron received ten truck chassis from the Thomas B. Jeffrey Company in Wisconsin (later Nash Motors). Foulois and his men made custom bodies designed to hold the Squadron's personnel, equipment, and supplies. They converted one chassis into a mobile machine shop. These 37 horsepower, four-wheel drive vehicles were called Jeffrey Quads.

By late 1914, the Squadron had eleven pilots, eight airplanes, 82 crewmen, ten trucks, six motorcycles, and a car. The car would serve to deliver parts and fuel to downed airplanes.

The expertise of Foulois's personnel with truck mechanics played an unintended but vital role in the first days of the Punitive Expedition. Pershing's Quartermaster Corps had little experience with motor transport, and the First Aero Squadron filled in. Foulois took temporary command of the Expedition motor transport. Part of Foulois' crew stayed in Columbus to assemble the chassis and truck beds of Pershing's first 27 Jeffrey trucks, delivered late to Columbus on March 18.[696]

In the years immediately before the Punitive Expedition, several aircraft companies worked on different airplane designs for military use. The Curtiss Aeroplane Company developed the JN series of training planes, based on English designs and data sent by Foulois from San Diego. After reviewing several proposed airplanes, the Signal Corps bought eight JN2 models, and First Aero Squadron received the tractor-style biplanes in San Diego in July 1915.

Foulois had learned from the temporary transfer to Texas City that the Squadron could be sent on short notice to locations beyond the range of the aircraft. Therefore, the original Army specifications called for the Curtis Company to design an aircraft that could be disassembled by four crewmen in two hours and reassembled in one and a half hours. Packed in crates, they could be shipped by rail.

Later that same July the Squadron transferred by train to its new base at Fort Sill, Oklahoma with the JN2s in crates and the trucks on flatcars. Pilots and crewmembers unpacked the crates on the Fort Sill parade ground and reassembled the airplanes. Using the Jeffrey trucks, they towed them to the polo field and prepared the planes for takeoff.

The later model of the Jenny series, the 1918 JN4, became one of the best-known airplanes in the post-World War I era, but not the JN2. Grossly underpowered with critical design defects, only the most skilled pilots could keep it in the air. After two crashed resulting in serious injuries and one death, Foulois grounded the rest. The Curtiss Company replaced the two wrecked planes with upgraded JN3s. Foulois, his pilots, and crew used them as models to convert the grounded planes to JN3s. They disassembled the six JN2s, altered the wing size, aileron placement, and control mechanism to convert them to JN3s. The new model retained the Curtiss OX5 90 hp engine. They also were equipped with the state-of-the-art Paragon Propeller, provided by the American Propeller Company of Baltimore.

Spencer MacCallum played a major role in the early days of the Mata Ortiz ceramic art movement. His grandfather Spencer Heath, a patent attorney, engineer, and inventor, had developed several innovative propellers and owned the American Propeller Company, the largest such company in the country. One of Heath's inventions was the laminated Paragon Propeller, which had been enormously successful with the emerging aircraft industry. They now were installed on the JN3.

The First Aero Squadron consisted of eight aircraft, eleven pilots, and 82 crewmen when Foulois received orders to move to a new base at Fort Sam Houston in San Antonio, Texas. The years of fighting in Mexico already had caused the U.S. government to station most of the U.S. Army along the long border. After attacks on North Americans, even more units were sent, including the First Aero Squadron. On March 12 more orders came, sending the Squadron to Columbus to join General Pershing's Punitive Expedition.

The crew disassembled the airplanes and put them on train flatcars with the equipment by midnight, a tribute to Foulois's organizational skills. They traveled 400 miles and arrived at Columbus on March 15 and began reassembling the planes.

The next day, Captain Townsend Dodd, with Foulois as observer, flew a reconnaissance mission around Pershing's east column on the other side of the border, the first use of U.S. Army aircraft in an actual military combat operation. Dodd and Foulois reported no trace of Carrancistas or Villistas within a day's march of the column.[697]

Curtiss JN-3s with Spencer Heath's Paragon propeller.
Photo: Courtesy of Sylvia Brenner, Pancho Villa State Museum,
Columbus, New Mexico

In addition to Foulois and Captain Dodd, the pilot roster included Lieutenants Joseph E. Carberry, Thomas S. Bowen, Carleton G. Chapman, Herbert A. Dargue, Edgar S. Gorrell, Walter G. Kilner, Ira A. Rader, Arthur R. Christie, and Robert H. Willis.

The next air operation did not go as well. On March 19, Foulois received orders to report to Pershing's encampment at Casas Grandes "without delay." Foulois took the orders literally and had the Squadron airborne at 5:25 late that afternoon.[698] Foulois planned to fly in single file to the destination 125 miles away. Sources differ, but it appears he intended to fly to Casas Grandes that night. Fires would mark the field. As a backup, the Army detachment at Ascensión had been instructed to mark a landing area near there with fires at the corners. Each plane had four hours of fuel (32 gallons). However, the planes were heavily loaded. The pilots had to carry all of their personal gear, clothing, mess kit, emergency rations, a sleeping bag, and blankets as well as field glasses, tool kit, extra battery, propeller and engine covers, tie-down bands, pistol, and ammunition. Foulois flew with Dodd, loading their plane even more. All eight of the underpowered, overloaded aircraft struggled into the air with no crashes. The elevation at

Columbus is 4,000 feet. None of the pilots, except Dodd had experienced the loss of lift in the higher, thinner air. Walter Kilner barely cleared the barbed-wire fence at the end of the strip. His sputtering engine forced him to circle back and land.

None of the pilots except for Dodd had ever flown at night. All of their training had been during the day, navigating by visual landmarks. For this trip, they had only a compass, an inadequate map, and a vague idea of where they were going. They formed up in a column behind Dodd and Foulois. The first four airplanes did stay together and landed in the dark without incident at the Ascensión backup strip. Herbert Dargue fell behind right away but continued flying until after dark. He missed the Ascensión fires and finally landed in an open space south of Janos. In the morning, he took off, and may have seen the MNWR track, because he somehow found his way to Dublán and landed safely on the so-called airfield.

Mechanics back in Columbus changed out the engine in Kilner's plane that night, and he also took off in the morning and, perhaps following the tracks, found Dublán as well.

Dodd and Foulois and the four planes took off from Ascensión and flew to Casas Grandes as ordered. Flying around the town, they saw no evidence of the Expedition encampment or any kind of landing area. Dodd put the plane down on a level space and Foulois made inquiries. He finally determined their destination was Dublán, just north of Nuevo Casas Grandes, sixteen miles away. Flying over the huge encampment, they discovered another serious problem.

It turned out regular army personnel had no idea how to prepare a landing field. The pilots could see from their cockpits a dry marsh covered by high clumps of grass. Large cottonwood trees surrounded the site on three sides. The signal fires the previous night had been small cooking fires lighted under the trees. How Dargue and Kilner landed safely is not recorded.

Thomas Bowen, one of the three other pilots with Dodd and Foulois, tried to land and completely wrecked his plane. He survived with only bruises and a broken nose. Dodd and the other two pilots managed to land without serious damage. Foulois could see a night landing would have been disastrous. He wrote in his memoir, "If we all had made that night flight and attempted landings on their field, the entire combat air force of the United States would have been wiped out in a few minutes." [699]

Five of the eight airplanes had landed safely, but Willis and Gorrell were missing. Search-party patrols from the 11th Cavalry rode out in all directions.

Foulois requested work crews, and a large detail of soldiers began clearing and leveling the field, following Foulois's instructions. Shortly, he had a serviceable airstrip, and he ordered the first reconnaissance flight.

Robert Willis, alone and lost, also missed Ascensión the previous night. At some point, he turned south and flew into the San Diego Valley until he ran out of gas and crash landed in the dark. Crawling out unhurt, he had no idea where he was, except he knew he was deep in dangerous country. Below the mesa, where the plane crashed, he could see railroad tracks. He began to walk north. The crash site was less than a mile north of El Rucio and six miles south of Pearson. Out of fear, he apparently circled Pearson, somehow crossed the river and kept going. When morning came, he hid, waiting until nightfall. Finally, during the following day, March 21, he encountered U.S. Army soldiers near Casas Grandes and was taken to Dublán. The next day, Foulois sent him with two men in a truck to salvage what they could. Someone fired on them and they turned around and returned to Dublán. A large, heavily armed detail later found the remnants of the aircraft stripped of anything useful except the engine.

Tenth Cavalry troopers on the train going south to intercept Pancho Villa, could see the crash site through the train windows at kilometer marker 282. A friend showed long-time Mata Ortiz resident, José 'Pino' Molino the crash site (or what he thought was the site) above the 282 marker. His friend had found a U.S. Indian head penny there, dated 1909.

The last missing pilot came in several days later. Lieutenant Gorrell had put down south of Ascensión at Ojo Caliente. Sources vary, but Gorrell was quoted as saying he had followed Willis, seen him crash land, and turned back north until he ran out of gas. He said they mistook a forest fire for the signal fire. An old Mexican, living on a small ranch, had guided him to the 6th Infantry detachment guarding the supply route, just south of Ascensión.[700]

Dangerous landing strips, missing pilots, and organizational logistics all concerned Foulois, but he had a mission—specifically observation and communication. As soon as the field was ready, he and Dodd took off with Foulois in the observer's foreword cockpit and Dodd behind at the controls. They intended to fly south following the MNWR tracks through the San Diego Valley toward the Cumbre summit. All of the shortcomings of the JN3s suddenly came into focus. Dublán was at 5,000 feet and the passes between valleys and surrounding hills one to two thousand feet higher. These were all before reaching the highest mountains of the Sierra Madre. Flying in the thin, high-altitude air reduced lift and made control difficult. All of the Curtiss JN series were difficult to fly by today's standards, even the later model JN4 with a more powerful engine.[701] Despite Dodd's skills, the altitude and gusting wind forced him to turn around before they had gone 25 miles. Foulois had to report a failed mission to General Pershing.

Foulois also sent a message to General Frederick Funston at Fort Sam Houston in San Antonio stating that the JN3s were totally inadequate and the Army needed to purchase better, more powerful aircraft. Funston, commander of the Southern District, and considered one of the Army's most capable generals, reflected the times by replying in no uncertain terms that he did not understand the difficulties of flying the "aeroplanes" in view of the fact that the "machines were flying daily at great altitudes" around San Antonio (elevation 663 feet) before deployment to Mexico.[702] Foulois was stuck with the JN3s.

The next mission was more successful. Communication had been lost with part of the 7th Cavalry squadron, commanded by Colonel Erwin. Pershing ordered Foulois to find Erwin and report on his status. Dodd and Foulois flew into Santa María Valley and located Erwin near Galeana. They landed and delivered dispatches and deployment instructions. Erwin needed supplies badly, and after returning to Dublán, Foulois sent seven loaded First Aero Squadron Jeffrey Quads back to the 7th Cavalry encampment.

Kilner with Rader as observer and Joseph Carberry alone made successful communication flights to the 7th Cavalry the next day.

Dodd with Arthur Christie and Carlton Chapman tried the San Diego Valley again, looking for the 13th Cavalry Provisional Squadron that was supposed to be crossing the mountains toward Namiquipa after leaving Chuichupa. With their throttles wide open, struggling with the wind, they flew just over the tree tops and managed to reach the Cumbre Tunnel. They could see U.S. soldiers, but conditions made contact or positive identification impossible.

A combination of dust storms and blizzard grounded the planes for a few days. Christie had flown to Galeana. Before soldiers at the landing strip could tie down the aircraft, driving wind wrecked the frame. Christie had to abandon the plane and hitch a ride back to Dublán.

After the weather cleared, three of the serviceable planes carried dispatches along Pershing's line of communications between Columbus and Dublán, in the Santa María Valley, and as far south as Namiquipa. By the end of the month, most of the planes had been refitted, giving Foulois six serviceable airplanes. The pilots and mechanics made modifications that made them more flyable in the adverse conditions, and the pilots gained experience with each flight.

After a meeting with Foulois, General Pershing altered the First Aero Squadron's mission from communications flights to more reconnaissance for the combat units. All aircraft would move to Namiquipa and maintain contact with the forward columns as they advanced south.

In spite of the bad weather, the pilots flew several missions, pushing beyond Namiquipa to another base at San Gerónimo and one at Satevó. Major Tompkins became aware of them as his small flying column of troopers advanced. Once he saw an aircraft, caught in a dust storm, suddenly flip over and plunge to the ground. Tompkins rushed to the crash site, thinking he would see a horrible scene. He saw the airplane sitting upright, undamaged, with a dapper Lieutenant Christie climbing out. After a brief discussion about the whims of the Almighty, Christie handed Tompkins a packet of orders directing him to move to El Valle and took off.[703]

Other flights were not so lucky. On April 6, Captain Dodd hit a hidden ditch at San Gerónimo, wrecking the plane. He and his observer, Walter Kilner, salvaged some parts and burned the rest of the wreck. Foulois now had five aircraft.

As the lines of communication lengthened, the distances for the trucks became longer and longer and supply became critical. Pershing ordered

Foulois to fly to Ciudad Chihuahua and confer with the U.S. Consul to see if he could buy supplies for the advancing U.S. troops. A large contingent of Carrancista federals garrisoned the capital city. On April 7, Dargue and Foulois in one plane and Dodd and Carberry in another took off from San Gerónimo. Foulois's plan was for each plane to carry a duplicate message. One plane would land at the north side and the other on the south side of town. After landing, one pilot would stay with the plane and the other walk into town and find the consulate. Dodd and Carberry on the north side had no problem. Dodd met with the consul and made arrangements for the purchase and shipping of the goods by train. The consul took him to visit the governor, who turned out to be a classmate of Dodd at the University of Illinois.

While Dodd and the governor exchanged reminiscences, Foulois was in jail. Angry soldiers with pointed rifles had greeted him when he climbed out of the plane on the south side of town. He told Dargue to take off immediately and find Dodd's plane. Foulois would join them as soon as he got this straightened out. An angry mob soon escorted the federal soldiers and their prisoner. The soldiers threw him into a cell and shut the barred door. As Foulois noted later in his memoirs, "I became the first United States aviator to become a prisoner of war."[704]

After negotiation, the warden marched him under guard to the military commander. The commander agreed to allow Foulois to return to his men and the airplanes, accompanied by several soldiers. Meanwhile, the mob had found Dargue and Carberry on the north side of town. Angry townspeople began burning cigarro holes in the fabric-covered wings, slashing it with knives, and climbing on the planes, loosening fittings. Dargue and Carberry jumped in the cockpits and started the engines. Carberry made it into the air, but a loosened section of Dargue's fuselage flew off and he had to land. When Foulois and the guards arrived, Dargue was fighting the mob with his fists. The soldiers calmed the mob, and Carberry returned and landed. With many apologies, the Carrancista military commander posted a guard detail on the airplanes, and all four pilots spent the night as guests of the governor. After making emergency repairs in the morning, they took off for San Gerónimo.

In spite of close calls with mob violence and his time in jail, Foulois could report a successful mission. However, the mission also exposed the deep resentment felt by many Mexicans at all levels against the Punitive Expedition.

Pershing ordered the First Aero Squadron to San Antonio de los Arenales. All five landed on April 9. They now were almost 300 miles from Columbus.

Pershing moved his mobile headquarters south of Ciudad Chihuahua and directed Foulois' pilots to fly long-distance reconnaissance. Chapman flew almost to Parral on the day Carrancistas attacked Major Tompkins's troopers entering Parral. Chapman flew over the area but did not see the running fight that followed.

Even though Chapman missed Tompkins' plight, the pilots provided valuable service for General Pershing over the next few days. They all remained relatively unscathed, but their overworked, fragile airplanes did not.

On April 15, Lieutenant Ira Rader flew from Satevó on a mission to locate the 11th Cavalry somewhere southwest of Parral. He found the troop at Ojito but wrecked the plane trying to land on rough ground. Too far away for any salvage operation, he took what he could and left the area with the cavalry. Rader's unfortunate flight appears to be the deepest penetration for any of the JN3s aircraft during the campaign.

After the missions, when the pilots reunited, Captain Dodd called them together as a formal board, and they voted to take one virtually unflyable plane out of service. The parts were salvaged and the lower wing put on the aircraft damaged when Herbert Dargue escaped the mob in Ciudad Chihuahua. Now Foulois had three planes, two at Satevó, south of Ciudad Chihuahua, and one at Columbus. He would soon have two.

Dargue was about to have an even more harrowing experience than he did when he escaped the mob at Ciudad Chihuahua. On April 19, he and Robert Willis flew one of the first photo missions with a new, especially designed Brock camera that took sequential pictures. They were to photograph the roads and approaches to Ciudad Chihuahua, which they did successfully. Dargue turned the aircraft toward San Andrés just west of the city. Over rugged hills the engine suddenly quit. There was no place to put down and they crashed on a 45-degree hillside. Dargue climbed out, but Willis lay trapped inside with a head gash and his legs pinned under the engine. Dargue worked to lift the debris and dragged Willis out. Even though his legs and feet were badly bruised, they started to walk. They walked for two days and nights 60 miles to San Antonio de los Arenales, arriving on April 21. The Squadron medical corpsmen treated them, and they rested until the 23rd. A car took them back to Namiquipa, where Pershing had temporary headquarters as he withdrew north. Unbeknownst to them at the time, their accident sparked a very large forest fire.

By the time Dargue and Willis reached Dublán, most of the First Aero Squadron had left Mexico. On April 19, the day they crashed, General Pershing ordered Foulois back to Columbus with his two airplanes, trucks, equipment, and most of his personnel. New airplanes would be waiting there. Foulois expected to reorganize the Squadron with the new airplanes and return to Pershing's command. Events did not work out as he planned.

At Columbus, Foulois found twelve aircraft of a different Curtis model that was supposed to be an upgrade from the JN3s. After an inspection, Foulois immediately rejected them as unfit for Mexican service. Other models came, which proved to be made of such shoddy material and with such poor workmanship that they could not be flight tested without extensive repair and modification. Within weeks, the primitive Columbus airfield evolved by default into an airplane rebuilding and testing site, run by Foulois and his pilots (Dargue and Willis had made it back). They built an engine test stand but lacked tools and large machine-shop equipment for the job. They struggled, but their frustrated efforts began to draw attention.

One ongoing problem was the Paragon propellers. Spencer Heath had designed and produced a laminated propeller he sold all over the world. He did not realize that hot, arid climates dried the wooden blades and caused them to warp and delaminate.

The numerous reports and dispatches from Pershing and Foulois concerning the propellers and other chronic inadequacies of the First Aero Squadron and the Aviation Section of the Signal Corps caught the attention of the War Department and more importantly Congress. Journalists interviewed the pilots, read the reports, and wrote scathing articles that not only alerted Congress but embarrassed the Curtis Company executives. They sent their experts to Columbus. Clearly their factory-production quality control and the Signal Corps inspection procedures had failed badly. Congress passed the Urgent Deficiency Act and appropriated $500,000 for more airplanes and equipment. More model types came to Columbus from several different companies. By April 6, 1917, almost a year after departing Mexico, the First Aero Squadron had tested 51 different aircraft.[705] By this time, the Punitive Expedition had left Chihuahua, and the United States now focused on entry into the European War.

The First Aero Squadron had been in Mexico only one month. The lessons learned there and in the much longer testing phase at Columbus caused the War Department to totally reorganize the Signal Corps' flying function. New policies demanded quality control, standardization of parts, and production of specialized tools. Benjamin Foulois led this effort, and his recommendations filtered into all phases of U.S. military aircraft design, production, and operation. By November 1917, Brigadier General Foulois was in France as Chief of the Air Service, American Expeditionary Force.[706]

One month of flying in the Casas Grandes Valley and adjacent regions had changed the direction of the entire military aviation and industrial complex in the United States.

The memory of the Squadron's historic airport as the "birthplace of American military aviation," is kept alive by the First Aero Squadron Foundation, based in Columbus, New Mexico.

Roy Hoard, a Story of Persistence

Roy Hoard missed most of the Punitive Expedition. He had left Mexico for a job in North Carolina and returned to El Paso in April 1917 as Pershing withdrew.

A small, energetic, even-tempered man, Hoard had risen from "timber cruiser" to manager of the Madera Mill. He and his friend F.J. Clark joined the company in 1910. Clark started as a traveling auditor and had been promoted to manager of the MNWR's Chihuahua Division at the time of the Cumbre Tunnel massacre.

Hoard spoke Spanish fluently and his fair-minded, positive personality made him many friends in the Mexican community. These included employees, community leaders, and politicians like General Ignacio Enríquez, a Chihuahua governor, Luis León, Minister of Agriculture, and General Rodrigo M. Quevedo, a prominent Casas Grandes citizen. At the time, Quevedo was a Villista but he had fought for and against many factions during the Revolution.

Partly because of his contacts and partly because of his personality, Hoard turned out to be much better at handling delicate high-level business in Mexico City than his company Vice President John O. Crockett or other managers in the El Paso headquarters.

In March 1916, Crockett asked him to go again to Mexico City. The damage to the railroad had been so extensive that company management wanted him to seek financial help from the federal government. The timing could not have been worse. The Mexican newspapers had just announced with screaming headlines that General Pershing had invaded Mexico. The resulting animosity toward all North Americans seriously impeded Hoard's trip. No one would cooperate with him from the train-ticket agent to General Obregón in the capital. It took him three weeks to complete the trip and Obregón flatly turned him down. Totally frustrated, Hoard thought of quitting. So many bridges were ruined that the railroad barely operated and the Madera Mill was closed. He definitely did not want to have anything more to do with government negotiations. Instead, he put the railroad on standby status with minimum staff, and he took a year's leave of absence.[707]

Something else was going on as well that probably influenced Hoard to leave. Now that Dr. Pearson was dead, R. Home Smith had complete control of the MNWR and its subsidiaries. He believed he had to answer only to the Ontario Supreme Court in Canada. When Dr. Pearson and Smith acted as co-receivers, they retained Pearson's people and operated the mills and railroads for the benefit of the bond holders in London. After Pearson was gone, Smith made it clear he had only an obligation to the court. He appeared to have little interest in salvaging the business and rebuilding it for the investors. He initially proposed stripping the mills of Pearson's state-of-the art equipment and selling it for whatever it would bring. He also proposed selling off train engines. Some equipment that had not been installed at Pearson may have been shipped back to the U.S. and sold on the second-hand market.

In early 1916, he, a lawyer, and an accountant arrived in El Paso and spent five weeks examining the books and all aspects of the railroad and mill operations and assets. As a result, he and his team revamped the operating, accounting, and reporting procedures. He made it clear the new rules would be followed.[708] Smith received court approval to issue "receivers certificates," a form of short-term loan allowed under the bankruptcy laws. The cash paid off $500,000 of immediate operating debt but none of the unpaid bond interest. This approach put him in conflict with John O. Crockett, the company vice president, who for years managed the company from El Paso. He reported to Henry I. Miller at the Pearson company office in New York. Both were long-standing loyal Pearson employees, who had seen the company through the difficult early years of the Revolution. Crockett objected to Smith's micro-managing and saddling the company with the receiver certificate debt. Smith's radical changes in policy also may have been too much for Hoard as well and a reason for him to take his leave.

R. Home Smith was highly regarded in Toronto financial circles. Trained as an attorney, he worked as a trust officer and bankruptcy specialist for the National Trust Company. As the fiduciary for the MNWR, National Trust had filed the bankruptcy petition in the Ontario court, after the company defaulted on bond interest payments. It is not clear why Smith made all of the changes after Pearson's death that seemed to lead to the short-term dissolution of MNWR, particularly the lumber mill business. He might have been influenced by the Machiavellian hand of Canadian railroad magnate William Mackenzie, who spent years trying to destroy Pearson's reputation and take over his business interests.[709] As it turned out, selling receiver certificates was a good move. The revenue eliminated short-term debt and provided enough cash to keep the company operating.

During the year in North Carolina, Hoard restored a large ailing lumber mill company to solid profitability. He could have stayed or taken other lucrative offers, but he chose to return to Chihuahua.

Hoard liked Mexico and his numerous Mexican friends. Also, he did not marry until 1920 and had no family.[710] Most North American employees with families had already left or at least had sent their families back to the U.S. Hoard was young, described as fearless, and did not have to worry about protecting loved ones. Based on subsequent events, R. Home Smith may have encouraged him to rejoin the company. For whatever reason, he returned in April 1917.

During Hoard's absence, Smith had modified his approach to managing the assets of the MNWR. Dr. Pearson had not wanted the receivers to interfere with the operation of the company. Such a restriction had been included in the court order. Smith had sufficient influence to have the restriction removed, which allowed him to assume the presidency of the company in June 1916 as well as remain as receiver.[711] Henry Miller was asked to retire. The following August, Smith also fired John O. Crockett as managing vice president and purged other Pearson-era employees. However, he left the railroad and mill infrastructure in place, apparently laying the groundwork for restarting operations under new management. When Hoard came back and reopened the Madera mill and cleared the Cumbre Tunnel in order to provide rough-cut lumber to the El Paso finishing mill, all seemed to be in accordance with Smith's new approach.

Just after Hoard returned, Smith came to El Paso from Toronto with lawyers to address a serious company problem. Carranza's government had informed Smith that the land purchases made by Dr. Pearson had never been properly recorded in Mexico. The government planned to declare the vast acreage in question to be public lands, or *baldíos*, that would be turned over to the Mexican people. This would be a disaster and Smith made the trip to meet with an assemblage of Canadian and Mexican company lawyers and representatives of the government. The meeting went on for days without any resolution. Smith vented his frustration in a conversation with Hoard, who asked that he be allowed to try. Smith quizzed him, and Hoard indicated in his low-key manner that he knew some people that might put in a good word for the company. Smith had no other option, and Hoard left for Mexico City. Who Hoard contacted and details of his negotiations are not known. It took three months, but finally, the government issued the necessary approvals. The stamped documents were sent to the Mexican ambassador in Washington D.C. Both Smith and Hoard traveled there to accept their copies.

While in Washington, Smith offered to put Hoard in charge as vice president and general manager of the MNWR and its subsidiaries. By now it is clear Smith wanted to develop a plan to make the company profitable. He offered Hoard the job and asked him to develop the plan.

After analyzing possible company configurations Hoard determined that the railroad company could not survive without the lumber business. Mining, agriculture, cattle, and passengers all provided revenue, but the projected potential from those sources would not sustain the railroad. Hoard already had started production at the Madera mill. The plan he submitted to Smith involved a number of cost-cutting measures but maintained the flow of rough lumber to El Paso. The volume of production at Madera could be varied. The company contracted to harvest timber at Hearst's San José Babícora ranch and cut it in a small mill there. Even one of the three saw mills in Pearson was restarted. To balance these sources and keep a steady flow of lumber to El Paso, Hoard contracted with C.H. Cooper, a well-known former employee. Cooper had been in charge of building the Pearson mill until construction was halted by Smith. Cooper understood the lumber business and he and Hoard worked well together. He stayed with the company, under contract, until 1924, when he took a job in New Mexico.[712]

Part of Hoard's plan required releasing many of the remaining North American employees. He retained his good friend F.J. Clark as vice president in charge of both divisions of the railroad. O.W. Borrett, the certified public accountant R. Home Smith had brought to El Paso to inspect the company books, stayed on as financial vice president, and became Hoard's trusted friend. This trio ran the MNWR for the next twenty years. As resources permitted, Mexican employees replaced North Americans.

R. Home Smith maintained tight control, requiring Hoard to make numerous tedious trips to Toronto. Earlier, when Smith offered Hoard the job as president, Smith told him that he did not speak English properly and wrote the worst letters Smith had ever seen. He gave him books to read to improve his vocabulary, speaking and writing. Hoard took this in stride, became a reader, and particularly enjoyed Dickens.[713]

Regardless of his criticism, Smith liked and trusted Hoard. More importantly, he realized that Hoard knew how to deal with the social and political complexities of the time. The Revolution dragged on in Chihuahua with the resurgent Pancho Villa on one side and the demanding, destructive Carrancista federal soldiers on the other. Hoard struggled to keep the railroad on some sort of normal schedule. Beyond the constant threat of violence, foreign companies faced confiscation by the government, strikes orchestrated by hostile unions, and defiant squatters moving on to company land.

To meet these challenges, the company needed support from influential Mexicans at the local, state, and federal levels. To develop and maintain this support, Hoard's plan recommended selling selected company properties to certain important individuals. Hoard had proved he understood the value of contacts, and Smith approved the sales.

Arrangements were made to sell a small timber tract to General Ignacio Enríquez, Chihuahua's governor at the time. Enríquez occupied the governor's chair ten times between 1915 and 1924, and Hoard maintained a good relationship with him in and out of office. General Rodrigo M. Quevedo received another tract.

Hoard kept the company alive for the next 28 years. For the first three, he had to deal with Pancho Villa and the ongoing war with the Carrancistas. Hoard, Clark, and Cooper all had dealt with Villa and generally got along with him. Villa called Hoard "the kid." However, as Villa's fortunes varied so did his attitude toward the MNWR, ranging from amiable conversation, to demands for rail transportation or money, to murderous threats.

Hoard, Clark, and Cooper found themselves in the middle as had MNWR managers since 1910. If they appeared to support the government, Villa might carry out his threats to them personally or to the railroad infrastructure. If they appeared to support Villa, the government might revoke their concessions or nationalize the railroad, putting them out of business.

Villa himself seemed conflicted. Even though Carranza and Obregón made serious mistakes in Chihuahua, Villa may have realized he could never completely drive them out and reclaim dominion there. The number of Carrancista troops in the state always outnumbered him as much as eight to one.[714] Certain actions suggest that he may have quietly introduced the amnesty concept as a backup position, which in fact happened in 1920. In the meantime, he took advantage of the new situation in Chihuahua in the spring of 1917.

Pershing had left, and the state was invaded again, at least as far as the Chihuahuans were concerned. Carranza and Minister of War Obregón sent in an army to essentially occupy the state. All of the soldiers including the commanding officers came from other regions. Few if any had any affinity with the local people. They acted as an occupying force ravaging towns, ranches, and farms, taking whatever they wanted, and shooting those who protested.

The fiercely independent Chihuahuans bitterly resented this invasion and turned to their old hero, Pancho Villa.[715] Country people opened their hidden meager stores for Pancho, and old comrades picked up their Winchesters and joined him.

The Constitution of 1917

By 1916, Carranza and Obregón had established control over most of the country except for Chihuahua and Morelos. Carranza wanted to update the Constitution of 1857 to give his government legitimacy. Also, in spite of his own conservative views, he felt pressure from many quarters, including some of his own supporters, perhaps even Obregón, for a new constitution that reflected the ideals of the Revolution. Therefore, in November 1916, while fighting still raged in Chihuahua and Morelos (Pershing was still in Chihuahua), Carranza called for a constitutional convention in Ciudad Querétaro. That city was picked because it was the site of the defeat and execution of Emperor Maximiliano fifty years before.

Carranza did not attend in person, but he made every effort to control the outcome. He made absolutely sure no Villistas or Zapatistas were invited. All delegates received in writing a draft of what he wanted in the new constitution. He believed he could influence the delegates to produce a document that concentrated power in the federal executive branch (his hands), emphasized nationalism, and remained nonspecific regarding land and social reform. He miscalculated on the reforms.

The 220 delegates did not uniformly represent the country. Only one came from Chihuahua. Few could be considered peasants or workers and even fewer from the powerful military officer class. Most were young, middle-class, educated professionals. Only a few had actually fought in a battle. Carranza did not realize that so many held high expectations for a new social order as a result of the Revolution. Like the framers of the U.S. Constitution, the delegates showed foresight that went far beyond their immediate experience. After eight weeks of deliberation, they produced a document that did create a strong executive branch. This showed an understanding of their own history. The new document also included a nationalistic/anti-foreign emphasis, reflecting Carranza's views. However, land, labor, education, and other reforms went far beyond what Carranza and other conservatives envisioned. The Constitution of 1917, adopted February 5, 1917, and still in effect, became a model for other countries.

Fear of dictatorship had caused the framers of the 1857 constitution to create a relatively weak central authority. The 1917 delegates understood that social reform needed to be combined with strong central authority in order to offset powerful conservative opposition forces.

But what made the new constitution unique was 137 articles that established very specific guarantees for all the people, managed by a centralized government. Three articles stand out. Article 123 established labor minimum wages, an eight-hour work day and a six-day work week, equal pay for equal work, plus the right to organize and to strike. The article also banned the "company store," the notorious *Tienda de Raya*. As beneficial as these labor reforms were to the workers, they had enormous impact on the MNWR as it struggled to stay solvent in the post-revolution era.

Article 27 concerned land reform. Containing many of the features of Zapata's Plan de Ayala, this famous article essentially turned control of all land over to the central government and provided procedures for land expropriation and distribution. Land used "inappropriately" could be repossessed for the public good. Ownership of all subsoil resources would revert to the federal government. President Lázaro Cárdenas used Article 27 in March 1938 to expropriate the Tampico and other oil fields and create the national oil company, Petróleos Mexicana or PEMEX. The potential expropriation of property and cancellation of concessions hung over Roy Hoard's head throughout the remaining history of the MNWR.

Language in Article 27 provided the mechanisms for restoring confiscated communal lands and creating new ejido organizations under specific rules for administration and operation.

Landless campesinos without any claims to communal land could band together and petition for land to form an ejido. Hundreds of thousands did just that, and over the next 70 years, 29,500 ejidos were eventually created, covering half of Mexico's land surface.

The delegates to the constitutional convention wanted land reform, and Article 27 provided the authority for this massive redistribution to communal ejidos. However, they clearly understood that private ownership could not be abolished. Specific language in the article permitted owners to hold up to 50 hectares, later 100 hectares (247 acres), of irrigated land. Range land could be held up to the amount necessary to support 500 cows. Governors would determine the maximum for each state. For Chihuahua 44,000 hectares (108,726 acres) was the limit. Ranch land over that limit was subject to expropriation.[716]

Article 27 also stated the government was responsible for ecology and conservation. This authorization led to forestry regulations and to the Forestry Law of 1926. The law established a Forest Service to regulate all forests whether on public, private, or ejido lands. Further, all log transportation had to be documented with forms and permits.[717]

Article 3 established free, obligatory, and secular public education for all children of all classes, no matter how remote their region. President Obregón and President Calles in the 1920s created hundreds of new schools throughout the country. The Constitution forced the Catholic Church out of its long-standing role as the primary provider of Mexico's education.

New teaching colleges educated thousands of teachers. These graduates accepted assignments at new schools throughout the country. However, by the 1940s only about fifty percent of the people could read, which illustrates the enormity of the literacy problem. Also, a powerful teachers union arose, *Sindicato Nacional de Trabajadores de la Educación (SNTE)*. The union may have improved wages and working conditions, but in a few years, it gained a reputation for repeated strikes and a stranglehold on public education in many regions of the country.

Other articles covered matters as diverse as public health and cultural activities. The framers of the constitution not only wanted political and economic reforms, they envisaged a healthy society uplifted by art and culture, particularly of Mexican origin.

Cultural agencies created to promote art, history, anthropology, and archaeology followed this pattern. The ruins and museum at Paquimé are part of the Instituto Nacional, Antropología y Historia (INAH), a federal bureau created in 1939 to manage Mexico's vast prehistoric heritage. A later agency, dating to 1974, is FONART, Fondo Nacional para el Fomento las Artesanías. FONART promotes traditional arts and crafts. Representatives buy work from village artists all over Mexico for sale in upscale FONART stores in Mexico City. Juried exhibitions, *concursos,* provide large prizes that encourage the artists to do their best work. Since 1994, FONART concursos have played an important role encouraging Mata Ortiz potters.

Obviously, the Constitution's lofty objectives would take decades to accomplish, if ever. Large land owners, the Church, foreign companies, and independent local chieftains, *caudillos,* resisted. Corruption, bigotry, bureaucracy, and paternalism all stood in the way. Carranza certainly had no intention of carrying out significant reform. However, his immediate successors, Adolfo de la Huerta (1920), Álvaro Obregón (1920-1924), and Plutarco Elías Calles (1924-1928) all made progress, emphasizing or deemphasizing reforms in accordance with political pressure and their own biases. De la Huerta was distracted by the need to meet the ravages of the Spanish flu. Obregón instituted many reforms but was reluctant to break up the large land holdings that he thought more efficient than small farmers or ranchers. Nevertheless, he created new ejidos, including Pearson. Efficient or not, the Revolution called for land reform and small parcels for individual campesinos. Calles strongly opposed the Church. He laid down heavy restrictions on Church activity and expropriated Church property. Calles also centralized power into one political party that evolved into the Institutional Revolutionary Party (PRI) that maintained a political monopoly for decades until the election of Vicente Fox of the conservative National Action Party (PAN) in 2000.

Overall, with important exceptions, reforms moved slowly until Lázaro Cárdenas was elected president in 1934 to begin the first six-year presidential term. Cárdenas overcame conservative opposition and consolidated power in the PRI party, which enabled him to turn his attention to genuine reform.

The Revolution brought unprecedented change. The old politics, economics, and social structure were gone. Everyone had their own version of what the new order should be. Disagreements led to either compromise or rebellion, such as the Cristero Wars and the Escobar Rebellion. While Mexico had a long way to go to achieve the ideals of the Revolution, the Constitution of 1917, created while battles still raged, provided and still provides the road map toward those ideals.

The Return of Felipe Ángeles

The adoption of the Constitution of 1917 provided a glimpse into the future, but the Revolution would go on for three more years. Venustiano Carranza in Mexico City faced many problems. His increasingly conservative stance on social issues and dictatorial approach began to alienate his subordinates. Álvaro Obregón, Carranza's best general, finally had enough and retired to his estate in Sonora. Emiliano Zapata still plagued Carranza, who launched a scorched-earth campaign in Morelos. Lack of resources forced the Zapatistas to give ground. Then in 1918, Spanish flu swept through Morelos killing thousands and severely weakening Zapata's forces. He still hung on, fighting fiercely for many months. Frustrated, Carranza ordered him assassinated. A Carrancista officer, claiming he wanted to defect, lured him into a meeting and shot the great reformist leader multiple times.

Villa fared better, at least for a while. By a stroke of good fortune, General Felipe Ángeles left a self-imposed exile in the U.S. to rejoin him. This was the catalyst that changed Villa's resurgence from guerilla action to a full-fledge army campaign. The incorruptible, intelligent Ángeles provided not only military expertise, but a restraint on Villa's excesses. While they did not always agree, Ángeles' presence gave legitimacy to Villa's movement on both sides of the border and attracted even more recruits.

Ángeles believed the Revolution to be a noble cause. As Villa's campaign progressed, Ángeles missed no opportunity to speak to village crowds or talk to the press about restoring the ideals of Benito Juárez and Francisco Madero. He also convinced Villa that it would be in his best interest to be less harsh on North American companies, in spite of Villa's hatred for President Wilson.[718] Ángeles' public voice added to the disillusionment with the Carranza regime, both in Mexico and with the Wilson administration.

Hoard and Clark, of course, knew nothing of Villa's plans nor of the changing politics. They could only prepare for an uncertain future. Whatever happened, they faced the practical problem of rebuilding the railroad. Traveling in a handcart one day, Hoard counted 87 badly damaged or destroyed bridges. The task was daunting, but during the past seven years of warfare, they had developed techniques to keep traffic moving. A damaged bridge with the rails intact could be "cribbed" by stacking railroad ties beneath it for support. If the terrain of the canyon to be crossed permitted, crews laid temporary track in a long decline on both sides to create a detour, called a "shoo-fly." Sometimes repairmen wired rails together and extended them across a canyon. Handcarts or other light vehicles could

This blurry photo show the desperate measures taken to keep the railroad line open.
Photo: Courtesy of Clarence Cooper

cross suspended in midair by sagging, unsupported rails—operated by very brave drivers.[719] The railroad had several gasoline-driven vehicles adapted to run smoothly on the rails to avoid the almost nonexistent dirt roads along the line. Some of these vehicles resembled the jitney used on the line near Mata Ortiz after trains stopped running in 1998. Hoard had a Model T Ford adapted to drive on the rails. Whether he ever drove across an arroyo on a wired track is not recorded.

As most of the fighting during this phase of the Revolution occurred in the Santa María Valley and south to Parral, demands on Hoard for troop trains were minimal. He kept the business in reasonable order and the trains running.

Conflicts occurred when Villa demanded money. Villa always needed men, money, and ammunition. For this campaign he depended on extortion from foreign companies. In March 1919, he demanded $300,000 from the MNWR or he would sack Pearson. Hoard stalled and contacted federal officials in Ciudad Juárez, who sent a train loaded with troops. The Villistas, probably commanded by a Villa favorite, the brutal Martín López, tore up track and destroyed bridges north of Pearson, trapping the train. López ambushed the federals, and then turned his men loose on Pearson. They directed their rampage particularly on the Chinese, looting their homes and stores, torturing several and killing at least two.[720] Afterwards, Villa contacted Hoard and told him this was the way it was going to be unless the company paid up. This time, it turned out to be an empty threat. No one knew it, but the railroad would never be severely damaged again by contending forces. Bandits would posture and demand protection money, but the serious threats were over.

In the meantime, another type of calamity struck just after the Martín López attack. The Madera mill burned in spite of state-of-the art fire alarms and sprinkler systems. The El Paso Times reported on April 8, 1919, that damages were estimated at $500,000, the amount of the insurance policy. The headline stated some equipment was saved. The fire raises questions. It seems remarkable that the company could maintain such a large insurance policy for an obscure struggling mill in war-torn Mexico. The answer may merely reflect Dr. Pearson's negotiating skills ten years before. However, the fact that the company had a large policy combined with a modern fire suppression system that apparently did not work raises questions. Was the system turned off? Historian Gilmore G. Cooke, a Fred Stark Pearson biographer, has a conspiracy theory linking William Mackenzie to the fire. Mackenzie, the powerful Canadian railroad magnate, who worked so hard to sully Dr. Pearson's reputation, had no known business in Mexico. Yet Cooke found evidence that Mackenzie had made a clandestine trip to Mexico in March 1919. Cooke could not find who he contacted, but a few days later the mill burned and the fire system did not function.[721] It seemed a mysterious coincidence.

As far as Hoard was concerned, it worked out very well. The insurance company paid, and Hoard used the funds to pay off the receiver certificates. This elimination of debt improved the cash-flow and enabled the company to continue over the next three years.

The Last Campaign

April 1919 proved to be a significant month in Mexican history. Zapata was murdered on April 10, and Villa, with Ángeles' help, launched his final campaign a few days later. Loaded in trains, his troops moved south down the National Railroad, intending to sweep through the federal garrisons along the line. They fought the first battle, a minor affair, near the Moctezuma station, then moved into the Chihuahua District. Most of the federal garrison towns fell easily, or the defenders surrendered without a fight once they heard they would not be executed. The Villista trains reached Parral. There, Villa launched his classic smashing attack, which became particularly bloody, because of the fierce fighting by a local defense force. Maintaining his promise to Ángeles, no prisoners were shot, except José de la Luz Herrera and his two sons Maclovio and Luis, all of whom had been officers in the División del Norte and had defected to Carranza. Villa never forgave disloyalty. After taking Parral, Villa turned his attention back north to Ciudad Chihuahua. Finding that most of the federals there had withdrawn to Ciudad Juárez, Villa rushed his troops north in pursuit. Ángeles knew the U.S. Army had a large detachment across the Rio Grande River in El Paso. He warned against the attack, fearing that stray bullets causing damage in El Paso could antagonize the U.S. enough to intervene. Ignoring this advice,

Villa ordered his troops forward on June 15. He directed the attack be made from the east and west to avoid fire to the north across the river. Villa's men quickly overran the defenses, breaking the defenders into isolated pockets. The day was almost won, when a confused melee broke out, caused partly when Martin López's men begin looting and partly by a pocket of defenders that suddenly counterattacked. Bullets flew in all directions, wounding several civilians in El Paso and perhaps two soldiers. The U.S. War Department, embarrassed by the Punitive Expedition's withdrawal, had given orders to General James B. Erwin, the El Paso commander, to cross the border in force if any U.S. citizens were harmed. Erwin, a veteran of the Expedition and perhaps feeling his own embarrassment, did not hesitant. He sent a regiment of Buffalo soldiers across the river. Unwilling to confront the strong force and provoke further U.S. intervention, Villa withdrew. The city remained in Carrancista hands. Villa's campaign was over. Except for a failed skirmish at Parral (where Martín López was killed) and an excursion into Coahuila, he never again would he lead an army into battle. With a small band of guerillas, he retreated into the mountains.

Once again Villa blamed the North Americans for his loss. As he did after the Columbus raid, he vowed to hunt down and kill all North Americans and all Mexicans that worked or associated with them. The threats reached Roy Hoard and he expressed his concern to R. Home Smith in a telegram sent July 3, 1919, shortly after the battle.[722] This time Villa did not murder anyone as he did the unfortunate Corralitos foreman after the Columbus raid. He seemed to calm down and appreciate Ángeles' earlier counsel that inciting the U.S. into another intervention in force would be a disaster for the country and for Villa personally.

As for General Felipe Ángeles, the loss devastated him. He thought if Villa could have maintained control of Ciudad Juárez, Ciudad Chihuahua, and Parral, the Revolution could have been snatched from corruption and restarted following the ideals of Benito Juárez and Francisco Madero. That dream ended in the bloody streets of Ciudad Juárez.

Ángeles' speeches, and his very presence as a symbol to the people, represented a political threat to Carranza. Villa was very concerned for Ángeles' safety and insisted he go into hiding. Villa was right. In November, Carranza's men tracked Ángeles to where he was camped near a remote mountain cave and captured him and two of his bodyguards. One of the guards was Antonio Trillo, brother of Miguel Trillo, Villa's secretary and chauffer, and a relative of Ana Trillo, a well-known Mata Ortiz potter. The captives were taken to Ciudad Chihuahua, where Carranza chose to court martial Ángeles in a show trial. The court made up of Carranza generals charged Ángeles with insubordination and rebellion against the government. Carranza wanted to publicly discredit Ángeles in a show trail in order to regain some of his own waning prestige. His plan backfired.

The trial was held in Ciudad Juárez's grand Teatro de Héroes that seated 3,000 people. Thousands more gathered outside. The fact that the theater had been dedicated in 1901 to the great heroes of the Mexican people such as Hidalgo, Morales, and Juárez was not lost on many in the crowd.

Instead of humiliating Ángeles, the trial provided a pulpit for him to expound on the noble aspects of the Revolution. He spoke of the need for peace and reconciliation without directly criticizing Carranza. He also praised Villa, saying he was basically a good man, who unselfishly fought bloody battles for the benefit of the people. Those in the theater burst into applause several times in spite of the presiding general's pounding gavel. The Chihuahuans listening and clapping, felt renewed justification for supporting Villa and for the years of fighting and suffering.

Ángeles knew Carranza and he knew what his fate would be. The court found him guilty and condemned him to be executed. In spite of practical advice from advisors and humanitarian entreaties, Carranza would not commute the sentence. On November 26, 1919, General Felipe Ángeles stood before a firing squad and was shot. Five thousand mourners walked with the burial detail to his grave. The backlash of bad publicity caused Carranza to free the guard Antonio Trillo and his companion.

Carranza had made a serious mistake. Supporters turned against him, most notably General Álvaro Obregón. Carranza knew he could not run again because of the strong anti-reelectionist feelings dating to the Díaz regime and the 1917 constitution's one-term limitation. However, he wanted to stay in control. For a year he dueled politically with Obregón over succession. Finally, in April 1920, a powerful combine in Sonora of Plutarco Elías Calles, Adolfo de la Huerta, and Obregón fomented a rebellion and marched on Mexico City. Carranza fled on horseback for Veracruz but was caught and assassinated on May 21, 1920. De la Huerta served as provisional president until Obregón could be formally elected in December 1920. De la Huerta inherited the Pancho Villa problem.

Villa had rejected inquiries that he might join the Sonoran revolt. He still harbored dreams of another comeback. The rapid fall of Carranza cooled that dream, and he began to seek an accommodation. Many in power now were old enemies, especially Obregón, who wanted Villa dead. Others knew all too well that his spirit, *villismo*, still lingered in Chihuahua. Any misstep, such as making him a martyr like Zapata, could rekindle rebellion.

Negotiations proved difficult as both sides feared treachery with good reason. Villa had a past relationship with de la Huerta and an element of trust remained. De la Huerta's representatives met with Villa, and after much sparing, they reached a tentative agreement. Obregón would have nothing to do with it.

Villa made his point in his own way. With a small force of loyal guerillas, he made a forced march across the desert into a prosperous, but defenseless region of Coahuila and occupied the important town of Sabinas. This clever move put de la Huerta's government in a bad position by raising the possibility of a split in the ruling coalition, or even renewed civil war and, U.S. intervention. The furious Obregón had to agree to a peaceful accommodation with his hated adversary, who, in the end, had outmaneuvered him.

In July 1920, the fabled leader and the remnants of his once proud División del Norte laid down their arms and disbanded, except for a personal bodyguard of 50 men. The agreement between the government and Villa did not give him everything he wanted, but he did receive a large rancho, a general's pay, mustering-out pay for his men, and land for his men. Villa retired to Hacienda de la Limpia Concepción de Canutillo, just south of Parral in Durango. To the surprise of many skeptics, he kept his word and refrained from any action against the government.

His enemies had long memories, and many still feared him. In July 1923, he decided to go to Parral to take care of business. Also, he had been asked to be the godfather for the child of a friend. Bodyguards and his secretary/chauffeur, Miguel Trillo, accompanied him. Driving through Parral on the return trip, a man shouted "Viva Villa," the old battle cry, but now it

*Pancho Villa and a new Indian motorcycle. Villa loved motorized equipment
and he acquired modern farm machinery for his rancho.
Photo: Courtesy of the University of California, Riverside,
Special Collections & University Archives*

was a death sentence. Multiple rifle shots rang out, hitting the car 40 times.
One bodyguard got off a shot and killed one assassin, but it was too late for
Villa. He was hit nine times.

Like many Pancho Villa stories, his assassination, facts and myth have
become entangled. Conspiracy theories abound. Obregón, with only one
arm as a result of a battle with Villa, has always been a likely suspect. No
one knows who gave the order, but Pancho Villa was dead.

Spanish Flu 1918-19

Estimated deaths from all causes during the Revolution exceed one million.
No one knows with certainty. What is known is that between 300,000 and
600,000 died of the Spanish Flu—more than the number killed in combat.

Little has been written about the flu in the Casas Grandes Valley or even in Chihuahua. It is known that Ciudad Juárez (and probably other border towns) was an entry point into Mexico for the disease from the U.S.

The influenza pandemic of 1918-1919 killed an estimated 500 million worldwide. Its origins are not clear. The name resulted from the wide publicity after Spain's King Alfonso XIII contracted the flu, but the first known cases originated with soldiers in Kansas and Massachusetts. When the U.S. Army deployed to France, the flu rapidly spread throughout Europe and soon the world.

Spanish flu entered Mexico in 1918 through the northern border and via ships docking in Veracruz harbor. It hit states west and south of Chihuahua especially hard, such as Coahuila and Nuevo León as well as the central and southern states. Twenty-two thousand died in Oaxaca. Zapata's resistance to Carranza suffered a serious setback when the flu ravaged Morelos.

Flu reached Pearson, and Cooper had to shut down the Pearson mill for three months. He, his store partner Luis Orozco, and a company doctor worked hard to care for the sick, provide provisions from the store for the affected families, and bury the dead.[723]

Overall in Chihuahua, the number of cases apparently did not significantly hinder Villa's efforts to reestablish his army in 1918.

Carranza reacted quickly to the pandemic in Mexico, despite his typically slow movement on social issues. He turned to an agency that had its origins among progressive elements of Porfirio Díaz's regime, called the Superior Council of Public Health. A noted surgeon and Carranza's personal physician, Dr. José María Rodríguez, headed the agency. This was not a patronage job. Dr. Rodríguez's passionate approach, termed the "Sanitary Dictatorship," affected public health in Mexico for the next several decades.

The "dictatorship" label referred to the centralized control of decision making and the apparatus of public health that Rodríguez established throughout the country.

Rodríguez had been an envoy to the 1917 Constitutional Convention that established the reform principles for the post-revolutionary era. He made sure public health was a national priority, and the Superior Council of Public Health was completely independent of any other political agency. In spite of his close relationship with the conservative Carranza, Rodríguez was a revolutionary. While he harbored some class and racial biases, he genuinely wanted to provide public health to all levels of society. This set the Superior Council apart, even though Rodríguez employed an autocratic approach as the most efficient way to achieve that end.

The Superior Council had the benefit of experience. During President/ Dictator Huerta's last days under siege in Mexico City, a typhus outbreak killed 22,000 people. The Superior Council moved in to care for the sick and install measures to curtail the spread.

When the flu arrived, Carranza was desperate to show the world that his fragile government could deal with crisis. He gave his friend a completely free hand. Rodríguez established "Sanitary Brigades," made up of doctors, nurses, and medical students. They set up offices in every state and sent teams into every community to carry out the dictates from the central Superior Council. They dispensed medicine, conducted education programs, and coordinated relief provided by local charitable organizations. Few if anyone in the world at the time understood that the Spanish Flu was a virus. The Sanitary Brigades can be excused if many of their techniques, like burning sulfur to purify rooms, were ineffective. However, other efforts such as educating rich and poor alike on basic hygiene and sanitation, and the isolation of the sick, did help curtail the flu and improve public health. The crisis peaked in October-November 1918, and then tapered off rapidly.

The country's excursion into a massive social program to meet the flu pandemic turned out to be a prophetic preamble for reforms, based on the Constitution of 1917 that followed in the 1920s and 1930s. Land reform, labor reform, petroleum expropriation, and public education reform all followed a top-down autocratic approach from central agencies in Mexico City. However, the intent for the most part was to benefit all levels of society, not just a political agenda.

Dr. Rodríguez and the Superior Council for Public Health received criticism for making class and even racial distinctions as it carried out its work. Some of the criticism might be justified. However, tearing down these distinctions was a revolutionary objective, and for the most part, the Sanitary Brigades sought to help everyone—the poorest Indians in their primitive hovels as well as the rich in their elegant mansions. As terrible as it was the Spanish flu and Mexico's response to it became a practical demonstration of the egalitarian ideals of the Revolution and a blueprint for future reforms.

Aftermath to Chaos

The final scenes of the decade-long revolutionary conflict shifted away from Chihuahua to other venues. The people of the Casas Grandes Valley were left with a local economy in shambles. The hacienda system had been broken up and great herds of cattle no longer grazed on the plains. The former hacienda workers were free and had no debt, but many were illiterate and had no sustainable work.

The MNWR still operated after ten years of discouraging disruption and destruction. Now in the sudden calm of the post-revolutionary era, the MNWR provided employment opportunities in the mills, lumber camps, and on the railroad.

The company never finished the Pearson mill. However, by 1917, C.H. Cooper had completed enough of the huge complex to permit Roy Hoard to start lumber production.[724] In 1920, volume peaked at 25 million board feet.[725] In addition to rough lumber for the El Paso mill, much of the end product included railroad ties for sale in both the U.S. and Mexico. The mill and lumber camps employed over 3,500 people. The town grew. One source said Pearson boasted a market, supermarket, post office, ice plant, hotel, hospital, school, 72 houses for salaried employees, and 85 for workers.[726] This may be an exaggeration and some of the facilities confused with those at Madera. However, there is no question Pearson prospered, if only briefly.

Despite the high cost of the ongoing railroad repairs, the combined revenue from all operations covered expenditures for the year 1920.[727]

Before the year's end, Hoard and R. Home Smith could see market weakness. Commodity prices began to show the effects of the global recession that followed World War I. Several silver mines closed in the Guerrero District that provided significant freight revenue. Lumber prices fell, which not only worried Hoard and Smith because of lost revenue but because of concern for their employees. Like Dr. Pearson ten years before, they understood that a regularly paid workforce helped the relationship with local and state governments and maintained stability.

After a year, another problem developed. Most of the trees convenient to Pearson had been cut. The magnificent Pearson mill was too far from the timberlands. Hoard badly needed Booker's connecting railroad, the Caracol, that never could be finished because of bandit harassment. This created a logistical oddity. Logs had to be carried by primitive wagon many miles to one of the most modern mills in the world. Hoard and Cooper determined that it would be more economical to locate small portable mills in the timberlands and haul out the cut lumber. On December 31, 1921, they closed the Pearson Mill. The following September 1922, they also had to shut down part of the El Paso mill because of depressed box-shook prices in the U.S. coupled with additional Mexican export fees on rough lumber.

In Mexico, however, the fruit-box market remained strong. That same year, Hoard, Cooper, and mill manager G.U. Armendáriz organized crews to rebuild the burned-out Madera mill. Using salvaged machinery, they built a finishing mill and box factory. They created a new subsidiary, per-haps for political purposes, called the Employees Lumber Syndicate, which soon shipped the boxes and boards throughout Mexico.[728] The crew also set up saws that could cut logs into rough lumber to supply the box mill.

It is not clear, but the new company may have been a Mexican subsidi-ary created to avoid new taxes and other pressures on foreign corporations. Roy Hoard does not clarify this point in his detailed report to the receiver R. Home Smith and the Board of Directors in Toronto in December 1928. However, he made it very clear that after six years, he thought it would be advantageous to fold the Employees Lumber Syndicate back into the Madera Lumber Company.[729] This suggests that the syndicate organization had served its political purpose and was no longer necessary. Hoard rein-forced this later in the report, when he states that relations with the gov-ernment at all levels were "friendly" and "… at the present time, no foreign corporation has a better standing with various authorities than the Mexico North Western Railway."

The reorganized lumber operation was smaller than before the fire, but it remained a critical component of Madera Lumber and the parent, MNWR. The mill employed 580 full-time workers and 640 more in the timberlands.

Local woodcutters from the newly established ejidos dragged logs to stops along the railroad.[730] Such employment was critical to the depressed economy, and log and timber transport provided significant revenue to the railroad. On the parent MNWR consolidated books, such transport showed as revenue to the railroad and an expense to the subsidiary Madera Lumber Mill.[731] Lumber-product sales supported the entire company.

Expenditures exceeded revenue in 1921, but overall, for the 1917 to 1921 period, the company broke even. Without the receiver-certificate debt, cash flow remained strong for the succeeding years. Nevertheless, those years would be difficult.

By 1922, it was evident that the recovery in Chihuahua would be slow. Little ranching and farming existed beyond the subsistence level. More mines closed. Foreign investors, facing anti-foreign restrictions and recession in their own countries, hesitated to put more money into Mexican projects.

Hoard was a tough businessman, but he made friends easily, and his friends trusted him. He used his network of contacts to keep the MNWR functioning as he faced a new set of issues.

Roy Hoard's Friends

During the confused political situation in the late 1920s, Hoard found himself again in the middle with friends on both sides of serious conflicts and in at least one instance, a bloody battle.

Álvaro Obregón's presidential term expired in 1924. The constitution forbade immediate reelection but did not rule out running again after another president has served in the interim. Obregón did just that and was reelected after Plutarco Calles's term ended in 1928. Before he could assume office, a Roman Catholic supporter, who blamed Obregón for Church persecution, shot him during an election celebration. Calles, now known as *Jefe Máximo*, the Big Chief, had become a kind of strongman during his term and beyond. He caused Congress to elect a sycophant, Emilio Portes Gil, as provisional president until 1930, when national elections would be held. Calles had himself appointed as Secretary of War, which led to the Escobar Rebellion.

General José Gonzalo Escobar, the highest-ranking officer in the army, had presidential ambitions and wanted the Secretary of War position. He represented a large number of army officers and enlisted men unhappy with the Calles regime. Many wanted more army officers in government, and others opposed his heavy-handed suppression of the Church. On March 3, 1929 (the day before Herbert Hoover's inauguration), Escobar declared himself head of a new Revolution. He attacked and occupied several northern cities with a force of about one third of the army's officers and men. Chihuahua Governor General Marcelo Caraveo joined him. Caraveo, like José Inés Salazar, was a long-time revolutionary, who had changed sides several times. Unlike Salazar, he had survived.

Hoard was close to both Escobar and Caraveo and had a good relationship with Calles. Also, his good friend General Rodrigo M. Quevedo stood by Calles.

Calles threatened to expropriate the railroad and confiscate company lands if Hoard did not remain completely loyal to the central government. Again, Hoard was in the middle of a conflict he could not control.

Within a few days, Escobar's forces captured Ciudad Juárez, as U.S. Army units and citizens of El Paso watched a battle from rooftops for the fourth time.

The tide quickly turned. General Escobar did not receive the hoped-for support from the new Hoover administration, and Calles rallied the demoralized federal army. After losses, Escobar moved his main force south and the decisive battle took place at Jiménez, near the National Railroad line.

In the bloodiest fight of the rebellion, Calles and Quevedo routed Escobar and Caraveo, but Escobar saved his army by retreating north toward Ciudad Juárez in fifteen National Railroad trains. Calles did not want Escobar's main army to reunite with the rebel garrison in the border city. A large rebel army there could cause serious trouble with the United States. He called Roy Hoard on the telephone at the Mexican Consulate in El Paso to make an unusual request. Hoard did not want to take the call. He wanted to keep a low profile, and rebel sympathizers might see him go to the Consulate. Finally, an official hand delivered the message. Calles wanted Hoard to intercept the fifteen trains at Arena Station, the junction of the National and MNWR lines in Ciudad Juárez, and divert them onto the MNWR track during the night. Hoard reluctantly agreed. The trains came into Arena Station in the middle of the night. Hoard's crews quickly changed engines and the trains left the station, one by one for Casas Grandes, not Ciudad Juárez. By dawn, the station was empty. In Casas Grandes, the rebels could do nothing but disperse. Calles' trick had worked, and he was very pleased. Hoard had secured the favor of the most powerful man in Mexico. Later, when Hoard made a claim for the costs of providing the engines, Calles saw that MNWR was paid.[732]

Cornered in Nogales, Escobar surrendered and sought asylum in the U.S. after making a deal with Calles that none of the rebels would be executed. That act of mercy was a fitting end to armed rebellion in Mexico.

The 20-Year Report

Annual MNWR reports had been prepared for the Board of Directors in Toronto, starting at the end of 1909, and the receiver R. Home Smith had insisted on regular management reports. However, at the end of 1928, Roy Hoard, assisted by Controller O.W. Borrett prepared a long, comprehensive document that appears unique. The first page had no addressee, although the recommendations at the end were clearly meant for the receiver and Board of Directors. The title on the embossed cover reads "Memo. Re Mexico Northwestern Railway," nothing more.

Hoard's descriptions of the countryside, the towns of Madera and Pearson, and of company facilities provide a picture of conditions in the Casas Grandes Valley as the end of the decade approached. This word picture came from a company executive concerned with practical business and lacks any romantic or human flourishes. Company employees or other local people might have looked at things differently, but their views can only be inferred from the facts Hoard presents.

Hoard's description of the MNWR line began in Ciudad Juárez where major railroad facilities were located. These included a passenger station, a freight station in the same building as the Customs Office, a car shed, a round house, a paint shop, and machine shops. The track crossed the desert 125 kilometers to Guzmán, southeast of Laguna Guzmán, where the Casas Grandes River ends. The land for the next 112 kilometers to

Dublán supported cattle but little agriculture. Mines were located at San Pedro. Farm lands covered the next 33 kilometers from Dublán to Pearson. According to Hoard, little development existed for the next 78 kilometers to the Cumbre Tunnel.

At Pearson, the company railroad buildings included the station, a 150-ton coal hoist and section houses for track-repair workers. Some of these houses remain today along the old right-of-way near the arroyo bridge in an area referred to as *La Sección*. At the time of Hoard's report, the huge mill sat abandoned and decaying adjacent to the river. The sawmill and powerhouse machinery were intact, but much of the structure had been removed because of dry rot and the danger of fire. Presumably, the power house generators were shut down and the town was without electricity. That would not be restored until 1975. Several conspiracy theories exist about the final removal of the mill. José Martínez, the village mechanic for many years, said in 2008 that the "Russians" dismantled and took away all of the salvageable machinery. No one knows the basis for this old recollection. However, Don José was very clear about important dates, and he had

Pearson mill foundation blocks. Photo: October, 2003.

carefully written them down. He said the mill came down in 1956.[733] All that is left today are large cement foundation blocks.

Hoard said in his report that the company's wooden houses, hotel, and other structures also had deteriorated by 1918. Sometime prior to 1928, the big store burned down, probably the one owned by Luis Orozco and C. H. Cooper. The local people gradually tore down the buildings to reuse the lumber. Graciela Martínez, Don Jose's daughter, was born in a wooden house in 1957, showing it took years to totally dismantle the old Barrio Americano.

Beyond he Cumbre Tunnel, the MNWR line passed through 30 kilometers of forest land on Luis Terrazas's old San Miguel Babícora hacienda to the Drake Station on the hacienda property line. In 1909, a contract between the company and Don Luis permitted loggers from the Madera mill to cut pine trees in specified areas. The contract was renewed in 1918. Past the Drake Station, the track crossed forested areas of the Hearst Babícora Ranch and continued 68 kilometers to Madera. Loggers on the Babícora also cut trees for the Madera mill under a contractual arrangement. In spite of land expropriation, William Randolph Hearst had managed to hold on to more than 161,900 hectares (400,063 acres) of the original 526,100 hectares (1,300,021 acres).[734] Since the Revolution roughly half had been expropriated in three major tracts. Fear of the power of the Hearst newspapers restrained even President Cárdenas from taking all of it until after Hearst's death in 1953.[735]

At Madera, railroad buildings consisted of a passenger station, freight station, and round house. The four major stations all had shops, but the largest was at Madera. The town also had a company hospital.

The Employees Lumber Syndicate still operated the mill and box factory, which seemed to allay conflicts with unions. However, representatives from five different unions pushed Hoard hard to let them represent the railroad workers. Meetings lasting five weeks were held in 1925. Finally, they agreed on contracts between the Company and two unions, *Sociedades Ferrocarrileros de la República Mexicana* and *Unión de Conductores, Maquinistas, Garroteros, Fogoneros.*

The labor contracts based on the articles in the Constitution of 1917 called for an eight-hour day and seven-hour night shift, a six-day week, double time for overtime, and sick benefits—very progressive for 1925. For the company, labor cost almost doubled.

To manage the Company's labor relations, Hoard hired José Murguia, a railroad mechanic who had risen to the high ranks of the union movement. It turned out to be a good choice. Murguia later became general manager of the railroad.

Labor relations was not an easy job. At a meeting in Madera, during a heated discussion, an employee pulled out a pistol and shot Murguia. The hospital in Madera must have been closed or lacked a doctor, because he was taken to Ciudad Chihuahua for treatment. He survived and afterwards always carried his own pistol.[736]

In late 1928, new forestry laws required treating ties and railroad timbers with creosote. Madera Lumber Company workmen constructed a modern plant, capable of treating 300,000 ties per year. Hoard thought this would add 50 cents per tie to the replacement cost, a large amount even if he could sell the surplus. The plant must have been a success because it did not close until the mid-1980s.

Mexican officials added more cost. During the 1920s the company had to pay export fees on all lumber shipped to the U.S. However, by the date of the report, Hoard had been able to negotiate elimination of this fee. The government officials making the decision apparently reasoned that protecting local producers, even if foreign owned, was more beneficial for the country than the fee revenue. Hoard's many friends in high places undoubtedly helped.

The company maintained a fire insurance policy on the Madera mill facilities of $200,000. This seems unusual given the high fire danger in sawmills and the fact the Madera mill had already burned once, and the company had collected on the full value of the policy. Hoard's acceptance of the added cost demonstrates the importance of Madera's mills to the MNWR's financial survival.

After Madera, the line descended out of the mountains through the Guerrero District 345 kilometers to the junction of the National Railroad, south of Ciudad Chihuahua. On this stretch between Ciudad Guerrero and Ciudad Chihuahua, Pancho Villa and Pascual Orozco fought some of the opening battles of the Revolution.

Hoard described much of this country as good farm and ranch land, just starting to recuperate. He saw agricultural products as a potential source of traffic for the railroad.

In the report, he discusses the tonnage hauled by source that year. Lumber and lumber products constituted 30 percent and were the most profitable. Ore and refined metal were 50 percent and the least profitable. The MNWR had entered into a contract to haul ore from the Calera mine in the Guerrero District, owned by El Potosí Company of Canada. The unit rate was low, but the volume of business caused the company to buy 60 new steel ore cars—the only new equipment purchased in twenty years. El Potosí Company had just closed the Calera mine because of a recent drop in commodity prices, and Hoard projected a significant decrease in mineral traffic the following year. Agriculture provided only four percent and cattle three percent of the traffic. However, the traffic from these sectors had been steadily increasing each year.

The company still faced many operational problems. All of the rolling stock was old, and at least 245 freight cars needed replacement. There was a chronic need for passenger cars as only 21 remained in the entire system and five of these were in poor condition. Nevertheless, Hoard looked ahead with cautious optimism. Despite the loss in business from closed mines, he projected that an increase in lumber sales combined with decreased costs, would lead to a small income surplus in 1929.[737]

Revenues did receive an added boost the following year when Hoard made a deal with a competitor. His old friend C. H. Cooper had left the company and worked in the U.S. for about six years. In 1929, Hoard received a long-distance call from the president of a large lumber mill competitor in El Salto, Durango. He wanted a recommendation for an experienced, Spanish-speaking lumberman. Hoard recommended Cooper who needed a job. In El Salto, Cooper discovered what Hoard already knew. The cut-throat competition between the two companies, in addition to increased costs, hurt both. They agreed to set prices, a practice illegal in the U.S., but not in Mexico at that time. The arrangement worked well, and the financial statements improved substantially for both companies.

As the decade of the 1930s began, the railroad continued to operate under Hoard's direction, and Pearson remained an important terminal in spite of the deteriorating buildings. Sometime after 1928, Hoard established a repair facility, an engine round house, *La Redonda*, with a large machine shop.[738] It was located to the north of the station across the road as it enters the village.

The MNWR fell into a routine, based on the requirements of the company, its customers and employees. The constant need to react to confrontation and violence had largely passed. The next fifteen years would present many challenges but would play out in a relatively quiet time.

Mexican North Western Railway engine 571 sits beside La Redonda (roundhouse) and workshop, one of only two known pictures of this facility. The water tank to fill the steam engine boilers is at right.
Photo: Courtesy of Miguel Méndez García

They Came from Somewhere Else

Inmigrantes

Mata Ortiz is a 20th century town. Everyone's grandparents or great grandparents came from somewhere else. Casas Grandes is a very old town, but even there only a handful of family names go back more than a few generations. Spanish pioneers first settled the Casas Grandes Valley, and the Apaches, hacendados, and LDS colonists all played a role in the succeeding centuries. It was not until after the turn of the 20th century that the Mexico North Western Railway and its predecessors opened the valley to more widespread development, in spite of the Revolution.

Railroad, mill, and timber-cutting operations attracted thousands of Mexican job seekers from other parts of the country. They added their local customs, crafts, and cuisine to the northern Chihuahua cultural mix. During the tormented decade of the Revolution, that culture was in a state of flux. People came, and left, returned, and left again. A significant number of the grandparents and great grandparents of those living in Mata Ortiz today came in the decades of the 1920s and 1930s after the Revolution.

Each family has a story. All cannot be told here. However, relating a few helps illustrate how Mata Ortiz evolved and developed from a former mill and railroad town to a famous ceramic art center.

Gallegos and Martínez

One couple that can date the arrival of their grandparents to Pearson's earliest days is the well-known pottery team of Héctor Gallegos and Graciela Martínez de Gallegos. Graciela has told the story many times, sitting in her Barrio Americano home, not far from the house site of her grandparents, Fong Poi (José Flores) and Gregoria Ibarra.

Fong Poi, a Chinese cook and hotel manager, brought his wife Gregoria to Pearson from Ciudad Juárez via Torreón at the beginning of railroad operations.[739] Their oldest daughter, Aurora Flores Ibarra, Graciela's mother, was born June 17, 1919.

At age seventeen, Aurora married José Martínez Trujillo, who became the village auto mechanic. Martínez's parents also had come to Pearson shortly after the town began. His father, Eduardo Martínez, brought a herd of cattle but lost them all during the Revolution. He got a job with the railroad, working as a mechanic. José was born in a boxcar parked at Corralitos, but his birth was registered in Pearson.

Young José Martínez struggled to make a living doing odd jobs, working as a train fireman, and operating a *molina de nixtamal*, a small mill to mix corn and the other ingredients to make *masa* for tortillas. Packaged tortillas forced the closure of that business. He decided to open an auto-repair business under a large tree in his yard and became the village mechanic for the rest of his working life.[740]

José and Aurora had three daughters, Amelia Martínez de Tena, Martha Martínez de Dominguez, and Graciela Martínez de Gallegos, all of whom became potters.

Héctor Gallegos's story is a wonderful example of how the swirl of events over generations cause families to drift apart, change, and go on to different destinies in different countries.

Two brothers, Héctor's grandfather Severiano Luévano Gallegos and great uncle, Higinio Luévano Gallegos (surname Luévano, mother's name Gallegos), came to Pearson shortly after the lumber mill began operating. Severiano brought his wife, Leopolda Sánchez. His brother, Higinio, met and married María Eribes Caño in Pearson, who bore him three children: Higinio Jr, 1915, Emeterio, 1916, and Eva, 1918.

The brothers appear to have come to Pearson amicably, but a rift set up a curious situation regarding their names. In one family story they quarreled over a piece of farm machinery. For whatever reason, Severiano began signing his name, Severiano L. Gallegos, apparently to distance himself from his brother. Eventually he dropped the middle initial and his new surname of Gallegos was born.

Whatever the fraternal differences, Higinio did well. He opened a store called La Batalla in a building that still exists near the entrance to the town on the street opposite the train station. Arriving travelers saw and still see the building as they top the rise and descend across the tracks into the village. Twenty-five years later the store was called "Pearson." And still later it stood empty.

The store was successful enough to earn Higinio the reputation of being rich. His reputation may have caused his tragic death and disappearance. On a trip to Ciudad Chihuahua to buy supplies, assailants ambushed and murdered him. Evidence at the scene apparently verified an ambush had occurred, but his body was never found.

María, his wife, could not manage the store with three small children and few business skills. She turned it over to her sister Tula and moved to Arizona. Another sister Matilde and her husband had moved there to start a dairy. María joined them in 1922. A murder altered history and brought this branch of the Luévano family to the United States. María eventually remarried, had another family, and lived out her life in Pasadena, California.

Her son, Emeterio, was six when they came to the U.S. He became a citizen at 22 in 1937. He married and had five children including the eldest Higinio (Gene), named after his grandfather, and a younger sister Patricia Jobin, her married name.

Maria's sister, Tula, remained in Pearson and with her husband, Miguel Castrejón, ran the store for many years. They are still remembered in Mata Ortiz.

In 1962, Emeterio decided to revisit the birthplace he had not seen in 40 years. That summer he drove with his children from their home in Norwalk, California to Mata Ortiz. Gene was seventeen and Patricia eleven.

Emeterio reunited with his Tia Tula after 40 years, and their children met their great aunt and visited her store.

Gene described the trip 55 years later.[741] He drove much of the way and remembered the endless desert as they traveled through the hot Southwest to El Paso and the crossing to Mexico at Ciudad Juárez. No paved road reached the Casas Grandes Valley from Sonora in those days. U.S. Interstate 10, which follows the route of the old stage coaches and the Southern Pacific Sunset Limited line, was only partially completed. Long stretches remained of slow two-lane highways that added miles to the trip.[742]

From Ciudad Juárez, they drove across northern Chihuahua through Nuevo Casas Grandes to where the pavement abruptly ended. Three dirt tracks led off into the mesquite. There were no signs. As they sat wondering what to do, a pickup raced by with men in the truck bed clinging to the rail. The truck took one of the dirt tracks, raising an enormous cloud of dust. With no other option, they chased the truck through the brush, trying to keep the dust cloud in sight. After about 25 miles of rough bouncing, they topped a rise and the village lay in front of them. They immediately recognized the store and went there. Gene, with his over-active, teen-age imagination, saw the buildings as fortresses with their thick adobe walls, slits in the heavy shutters, and broken glass embedded on top of courtyard walls. He thought they must have been built to repel Apaches, federales, or Pancho Villa's desperados.

Tia Tula welcomed them warmly and they stayed a few days becoming reacquainted. The trip home went without incident, but Gene said it seemed much longer. Apparently, no mention was made of Severiano, who was still alive living nearby, or any others in the Gallegos family.

Severiano with his new surname became a prominent citizen in his own right. In 1921, he was a founding member of Ejido Pearson. He was unique in that he served at one time as the Comisario de Policía and as President of the Ejido. The only other person to hold both positions was Héctor, his grandson. Severiano died in 1963 at age 89 and is buried in the Mata Ortiz cemetery.

He and Leopolda had three daughters and five sons. The youngest, Guadalupe, was Héctor Gallegos' father.

When Guadalupe was only 38, a man nicknamed Choforo, shot him in the back while he played dominos at a Barrio Centro cantina. His older brother Manuel had also been killed in an earlier shoot-out. For unknown reasons, Manuel had been attacked and shot, but before he collapsed, he managed to pull his pistol and mortally wound his assailant. Apparently, Guadalupe's murder was revenge for the death of Manuel's killer. Choforo fled Mata Ortiz and was never heard from again.

Héctor's maternal grandfather, Tomás Esparza lived in Los Angeles with his fiancé. Tomás caught her in bed with another man and shot them both. Mexico suddenly seemed a good option for Tomás. He arrived in Pearson about the same time as Severiano and Higinio, just after the mill began operation. He met and married Concepción Rueda. Their daughter Josefina Esparza Rueda was Héctor's mother.[743]

Héctor was born in Mata Ortiz May 11, 1954. He said that all of his own children were born in hospitals, but Magdalena Franco, a midwife delivered him. Señora Franco was very skilled and delivered most of the babies of that generation. She lived in a wooden house in Barrio Americano just beyond and on the other side of the street from today's elementary school. The house, like the other wooden houses, is long gone, but a tree from her yard still grows there.

After the tragic death of her husband Guadalupe, Héctor's mother, Josefina, had no means of support other than a few cows left by her husband and a mule and cart. She took a train from Mata Ortiz to Ciudad Juárez and walked across the bridge to El Paso. There she bought various household items and dry goods including used clothing. She packed her purchases on the train and returned to the village. A passport and visa apparently were not needed in the late 1950s. With her mule and cart, Josefina walked through the village selling her goods. Héctor was just a little boy, but he helped with the mule.

After about seven years, Josefina married a man named José Dominguez. They had two children, but Dominguez abandoned the family soon after. Josefina never used his name and the two children bore her maiden name, José Esparza Rueda and Elizabeth Esparza Rueda.[744] Josefina later moved to Nuevo Casas Grandes. Héctor and his brother built a house for her there, hauling adobe bricks made in Mata Ortiz over 25 miles in a mule-drawn wagon to the building site. In her last years, she lived with Héctor and Graciela in Mata Ortiz.

Héctor and Graciela knew each other growing up, although he lived on the other side of the village in Barrio Iglesia, beyond the church, near the river. Héctor received training at the Instituto Commercial in Nuevo Casas Grandes and returned to the village to teach school. At the elementary school he taught fourth grade and middle school mathematics, typing, and accounting.

Graciela worked awhile in a factory in Ciudad Juárez, where she also learned to style and cut hair, a skill she still uses as a side occupation. After about a year, she returned and one night saw Héctor at a dance. The large building directly across from the train station on the corner was a dance hall in those days. In spite of close chaperoning, the romance bloomed. Graciela's mother, Aurora, apparently aware of the scandals in Héctor's family history, objected to the relationship. They solved the problem by eloping on October 26, 1975.

Héctor taught school only one year. He could not make enough as a teacher, so they moved to Ciudad Chihuahua, where he worked for a mining company for five years. The young couple accumulated enough to return to Mata Ortiz and build a house near her parents' home and auto repair shop. Héctor bought ejido rights, *derechos,* for two separate parcels, one from Máximo Guillén and the other from Chemino Ponce.

Like his grandfather Severiano, Héctor became a respected member of the community and the ejido. He farmed and ran cattle, while Graciela cared for their four children and styled hair for local clients. By 1987, pottery sales were having a significant effect on the local economy. Héctor and Graciela learned to make and paint pots. Before the end of the decade, they were prominent figures in the emerging Mata Ortiz ceramic-art movement.

The marriage of their son Héctor Jr. to Laura Bugarini Cota joined Gallegos to another old Mata Ortiz family. Laura, a well-known potter since she was a teenager, learned from her mother Guadalupe (Lupita) Cota Delgado, one of Juan Quezada's first non-family students. Laura's father, Pablo Bugarini Silva, and grandfather, Primitivo Bugarini, both were born in Mata Ortiz. Her great grandfather, Pablo Bugarini came from Italy, probably through the United States, and eventually found his way to Mata Ortiz to work in the mill. He became one of the original ejidatarios in 1923. On the maternal side, Laura's grandfather Miguel Cota Delgado also was born in Mata Ortiz.

Ortiz and Ortiz

Many among those migrating to Pearson looking for work came from the north central state of Zacatecas. An early influx arrived in the Casas Grandes Valley even before the Pearson project began. Northern Chihuahua needed miners, and the railroad provided easy access after the completion of rail connections between Zacatecas City, Ciudad Chihuahua, and Ciudad Juárez by the Mexican Central Railroad (later the National Railroad). When Morris Parker took over management of the Corralitos Cattle Company's Candelaria mines at San Pedro in 1898, he faced a serious labor shortage. Zacatecas was a major mining district and the largest producer of silver in the world. Parker hired an agent to bring train-car loads of experienced miners and their families to San Pedro.[745] Family members and friends followed in the succeeding decades. The turmoil of the Revolution caused many to leave or go back and forth. Some stayed, although it appears that many ancestors of those living in Mata Ortiz today arrived after the Revolution. Whenever they came, they all had a story. This includes the grandparents of the well-known Ortiz brothers, all potters: Salbador "Chava," Santos Jr., Eduardo "Chevo," Osbaldo, Nicolás and Macario. They were well known because they were potters, musicians, and all very tall. (Salbador Ortiz Estrada and his brother Osbaldo spelled their names with B because that is how it was written in their birth certificates. In a similar fashion, Rojelio Silveira and Jerardo Tena wrote their names with J.)

At 14, their grandfather, Salvador Ortiz followed an older brother, Manuel, to San Pedro about 1917. His wife-to-be, Tomasa Cárdenas, already lived there. She probably was born in Corralitos. Her father had come from Zacatecas to work in the mines.[746] Salvador may have worked in the mines briefly, but if his arrival date of 1917 is correct, he could not have worked for long because the Candelaria mines were ransacked, and all equipment destroyed in December 1917.

By 1921, the young couple had married and lived in Barrio Porvenir, Mata Ortiz. Salvador had a small farm and occasionally worked on the railroad, while Tomasa bore eight children. Only their second son Santos and the youngest Aureliano stayed in the village after they were grown.

Not long after Salvador's move to Mata Ortiz, his older brother Manuel joined him. Both seem to have been more interested in farming than working in the mill or on the railroad. All of Manuel's family eventually left except for one son, Rubén. His family formed another branch of the Ortiz family in the village.[747]

Salvador's and Tomasa's son, Santos, married Julia Estrada and they had the six tall sons and one daughter, Amalia. All six sons were exceptionally talented. Eduardo, Macario, and Nicolás became famous for their museum-quality pottery and pioneering pottery techniques. The brothers' talent extended to music. They formed a band and had considerable success in the 1970s and 1980s, playing in venues as far away as Baja California.

Santo's wife, Julia, was born in 1921 in Bavispe, west of Casas Grandes in the state of Sonora. Her father, Florencio Estrada, left the family when she was born to seek work in the Pearson lumber mill. Her mother moved with her to Mata Ortiz in 1930 when she was ten. Her father Florencio still worked there, and Julia met him for the first time.

In 2015, when Julia was 94, she still remembered the big mill. In a conversation in her home, she recalled her father-in-law, Salvador. She said when he worked on the railroad, he was a fireman or *fogonero* on the run from Mata Ortiz to Madera. She also said there were many fewer houses in Porvenir in those days and the chapel had not been built. In the corner of her house was an old wood stove she said belonged to Salvador.[748] Several Mata Ortiz houses retain the old stoves as a reminder of family and heritage.

By coincidence, another important early family named Ortiz, with origins in Zacatecas, lived and worked in Barrio Porvenir. The most prominent member was Félix Ortiz, who not only made pots but taught many other neighbors and friends to become successful potters. Félix's grandfather, Jesús Ortiz, as a young unmarried man, left his home in Salitral de Carrera in the state of San Luis Potosí and moved to Guadalupe, a large town adjacent to the city of Zacatecas. Two brothers, Gregorio and Cirildo, may have already lived there. The following year, 1911, he married Rumalda Aguilar, who had grown up in the nearby community of Bañuelos. After the birth of their first child, Hesiquio in late 1912, the three brothers and their families decided to move to Pearson to work on the railroad. They had heard about jobs on a spur line to be built in the mountains to haul lumber. They picked a bad time to move. President Madero in Mexico City was losing control of the Revolution, and the country was slipping into chaos. The spur line was never built. In spite of the times, Jesús was able to turn to farming. He and Rumalda built a home in Porvenir and had five more children. Their arrival sometime during the 1912-13 time period makes this Ortiz family one of the oldest in the village.

Hesiquio, their eldest, married Jesusita Rodríguez, presumably from the village. Three of their five children— Emeterio, born 1938, Félix, born 1942, and daughter Teodora born 1945—became potters and lived out their lives in Mata Ortiz. Hesiquio died tragically in 1947 at age 36.

When Emeterio was in his early 20s, he served as the postman. He lost that job when the post office closed, after La Redonda, the big round house and repair shop facility, moved to Nuevo Casas Grandes. He also worked as a village barber.

Emeterio and Félix worked together in the 1970s to learn to make pots. They were part of an early group that learned the basic techniques with Juan Quezada, other Quezada family members, Salbador Ortiz (the oldest of the six famous brothers from the other Ortiz family), Taurina Baca (a teenager and Juan's first non-family student), Lupita Cota Delgado (the mother of Laura Bugarini), and Luci López.

As Félix and Emeterio became proficient, they developed their own style and techniques. Félix particularly became known for his innovative work. Perhaps his greatest contribution to the village was his willingness to teach others. Many potters in Porvenir learned from Félix and Emeterio, which led to a distinct style, easily recognizable in the early years as from Barrio Porvenir.

The two Ortiz clans joined on the maternal side at least twice. Jesusita, Hesiquio's widow, married again and had a daughter, Eduvigas. Salbador from the other Ortiz family was a good friend of Félix and worked on pottery with him. Salbador married Félix's half-sister Eduvigas, which joined the two Ortiz clans.

Salbador's (and the other Ortiz brothers') only sister Amalia, who lived in Casas Grandes, had a son César, known as Chester. He stayed with his Uncle Macario Ortiz for a period of time until he was proficient enough as a potter to go out on his own. He signed his pots César Ortiz and otherwise used his mother's maiden name. Félix Ortiz lived nearby, and his daughter Raquel and Chester became acquainted and married. This united the two families for the second time.[749]

Silveira

Hesiquio Ortiz's older brother Gregorio and his wife Manuela Pérez had a daughter Soledad who married an itinerant worker named Juan Silveira. Juan's father had been a miner from Zacatecas. He obtained a plot of ground in Mata Ortiz and became a farmer.[750]

Juan Silveira and Soledad eventually had six children as they moved from place to place. In 1958, he was killed working on a well. Soledad moved back to Mata Ortiz, her parents' village, with her family, and in a few years remarried. Four of Soledad's sons with Juan Silveira became potters: Rojelio, Nicolás, José, and Gregorio nicknamed "Goyo."[751] The extended Silveira families joined the Ortiz clans to become the major producers of Porvenir-style pottery.

Quezada

José Quezada, Juan's father, was born in Santa Bárbara de Tutuaca (just Tutuaca on modern maps), a small mountain town in the Belisario municipio, south of the MNWR's Chihuahua District line. José had been raised by his uncle and aunt, Don Savino Hernández and Doña Lupe. José worked his uncle's cattle and raised horses, performing the work of a Chihuahua cowboy. When he was twenty-eight, he met Paulita, who had come from nearby San Lorenzo to work in a kitchen in Tutuaca. When she returned to San Lorenzo, José rode over to court her and they soon married. Juan Quezada often talked of his parents and the mestizo mix of his family. He said his mother was more Indian and his father more Spanish. Apparently, as a young man growing up, José had contact with Tarahumara Indians because Juan said he understood some of the language.

José and Paulita had ten children. The first six, Consolación, Reynalda, Genoveva, Jesús, Hilario, and Juan were born in Santa Bárbara Tutuaca. Four more, Nicolás, Rosa, Lydia, and Reynaldo were born in Mata Ortiz. Juan's birth date is May 6, 1940, one year before the entire family, including Don Savino and Doña Lupe, moved north to Mata Ortiz.

Long before the move, their future new home had a special significance for the Quezada family. Don Savino told and retold the story about his long trek there during the Revolution. Desperate to save the family's possessions from marauding soldiers, he loaded everything on six burros and escaped north. He walked through the mountains to the railroad line and followed the track as it curved north.

No one in the family knows the exact year Savino plodded along the tracks in that dangerous rebel-infested country. The MNWR completed the line through the Cumbre Tunnel in February 1912, which suggests he went after that date. He passed through many tunnels. The old man described his fear as he drove his burros into the dark entrances, never knowing if a bright headlight might suddenly appear before he reached the end.

After descending from the mountains onto the high plains near Pearson/Mata Ortiz, he found extraordinarily tall grass, tall enough to conceal his loaded burros lying down. Moving his burros into this grass, he hid from renegade soldiers passing by. Eventually, he felt comfortable enough to return to Lupe in Tutuaca with their possessions and animals intact. It was an extraordinary journey, and he never forgot that tall grass.

One day, years later, Don Savino decided to go back to Mata Ortiz. When he was ready to make the move, there was no question but that José would leave his birthplace with Paulita and six children and accompany his aunt and uncle to the new community. Their youngest child was year-old Juan. This innocuous move was to have an impact on the community equal to Dr. Pearson's first visit in 1908.

When they moved in 1941, northern Chihuahua was a remote and rugged place still showing ravages of the Revolution. Communication remained primitive and travel by horse and wagon commonplace. The

MNWR provided the most important communication link and, for many in the village, the only employment. However, Savino and José chose to ignore the railroad and stayed with the land, raising cotton and later cattle.

Even with five new children, José and Paulita faithfully cared for aging Don Savino and Doña Lupe until the old couple died. As time passed, José and Paulita witnessed many changes as the trappings of the twentieth century—trucks, electricity, television—found their way to them. But nothing seemed so remarkable as the development of their home into a major ceramic center, led by their third son Juan, and involving all of their sons, daughters, grandchildren, and neighbors.

Corona

Corona is the name of a street near the elementary school. While there is no sign on any of the Mata Ortiz streets, the intent was to recognize one of the pioneering families.

Before the Revolution, José Corona had worked for Luis Terrazas at Hacienda San Diego. He became close enough to Don Luis to be an *hombre de confianza*, a special relationship of trust.

Sometime after the fighting of the Revolution wound down, he moved to Mata Ortiz and ran cattle.[752] He became the patriarch of the extended Corona family. His grandson Mónico is the brother of Guadalupe Corona, Consolación Quezada's second husband and the father of potters Mauro Corona Quezada and Hilario Corona Quezada.

The Mennonites

Another group was added to the cultural mixture of Chihuahua in 1921, right after the Revolution ended. Mennonites living in Canada faced mandated military service if they remained in that country. These committed pacifists had experienced this particular persecution twice before and again sought a place where they could practice their religion and lifestyle unmolested.

The Mennonite religion began in 16th century Switzerland as an offshoot of Martin Luther's Reformation. The movement would take many paths, but the conservatives did not believe in violence, military activity, taking oaths, or participation in civil government. In modern times, the most conservative, such as the Amish and Old Colony Mennonites, practiced a pre-20th century lifestyle, without electricity or other powered equipment.

The Catholic Church, other Reformation-inspired sects, and local governments harassed the Mennonites and many scattered afar. One Old Colony group went to Ukraine. After farming successfully for a few years, the Russian-controlled government insisted that only Russian be spoken in their schools and that all males be subject to military service. Several thousand left for Saskatchewan and Manitoba, Canada, where the government welcomed them with promises of religious freedom. Governments change, and by the turn of the century, Old Colony leaders began to explore other countries, particularly in Central and South America.

An advance team of six Mennonites came into Mexico in 1921. President Álvaro Obregón led Mexico's fledgling post-Revolution government, which under the new constitution discouraged foreign land ownership. However, Obregón viewed the Mennonites as an industrious people, capable of converting unused semi-arid land into productive farms. He not only encouraged them, he also personally met with representatives and issued them an amazing document, given the times. It listed five guarantees: no military service; no requirement to take an oath; no restriction on religious freedom; the right to operate their own schools in their own language without restrictions or outside requirements; and the right to operate their properties without outside regulation. The Mennonites put great value in this document they called *Privilegium*, or an irregular right.

At the same time, President Obregón's government continued to break up the haciendas and large foreign holdings. Obregón was not a radical land reformer, but such reform was a basic tenet of the Revolution. Foreign companies like MNWR and other large landowners definitely felt the pressure. Roy Hoard wrote in his 1928 report to the receiver that Mennonites purchased 200,000 acres (80,937 hectares) near the Chihuahua District station of San Antonio de los Arenales, about 60 miles west of Ciudad Chihuahua.[753] Hoard saw this as an opportunity for business. The once-powerful Zuloaga family (former owners of Hacienda Corralitos) owned the Hacienda Bustillos. Either voluntarily or under pressure they sold part to the Mennonites. As experienced farmers, the new arrivals saw the open prairie as excellent land for growing wheat. The government approved and the transaction was completed the following year.

The MNWR line passed through the Hacienda Bustillos, and Hoard anticipated hauling agriculture products for the new owners.

The Constitution of 1917 limited individual land holdings to 50 hectares (123 acres). While the Mennonite groups typically bought their land in much larger blocks, it was understood that the blocks would be divided into parcels of 50 hectares or less and assigned to individuals. This met the government's legal requirements.

In 1922, about 2,000 Old Colony men, women, and children left Canada in seven trains loaded with household goods, farm equipment, and farm animals. They established colonies around San Antonio de los Arenales, built houses, and ploughed fields. The men wore overalls and straw hats, and the women wore old-fashioned dresses and bonnets. They spoke and taught school in a Low German dialect, *Plautdietsch* that had survived from Switzerland. The Mennonites knew how to farm, and they brought much of the necessary equipment and animals with them. This minimized the need for ready start-up capital. In a few years, they produced significant quantities of wheat and other agricultural products.

By 1928, the population had increased to 7,500. Roy Hoard's prediction proved correct as rail traffic in agricultural products increased roughly ten percent per year. At some point, the name San Antonio de los Arenales was changed to Cuauhtémoc, which grew to be the third largest city in Chihuahua, after Ciudad Chihuahua and Ciudad Juárez.

In 1935, the strongly anti-church Chihuahua governor, Rodrigo M. Quevedo, forced the closure of 41 Mennonite schools in accordance with the anti-sectarian provisions in the Constitution of 1917. After formal protests, President Cárdenas in Mexico City overrode the governor. Former President Obregón's Privilegium held up, at least this time.

Old Colony Mennonites may have had friends in high places, but they could not push back progress. For forty years bad dirt roads preserved their isolation. By the late 1950s, the colonies found their isolated way of life threatened by a combination of factors that brought outsiders, including the construction and opening of the railroad line through the Copper

Canyon to the coast. As had their ancestors, they began to look for other remote places. In 1958, one group from Cuauhtémoc found the Buenos Aires ranch in the Janos Municipio in the northwest corner of the state. The owner appeared anxious to sell to avoid government expropriation.

Over the next 20 years other Mennonites followed, establishing more colonies including, Las Virginias, Colonia Cuervo, Buena Vista, and Capulín, southeast of Janos.

One of the best known is Capulín (sometimes Campo Siete), located in the Nuevo Casas Grandes municipio, north of the city, six miles east of Highway 10. The colony's local fame comes from its cheese. At the turn off from the highway, handmade signs on little cabañas advertise *queso menonita*.

The Capulín settlers acquired this property in 1962 from the Wallace family that owned what was left of the Hacienda Corralitos. The Revolution had been over for 40 years, but land-reform pressure still existed on large land holdings. William "Bilo" Wallace was good friends with the governor, who warned him of a proposed government plan to expropriate "unused land." A deal was worked out whereby a large Corralitos parcel was sold to the Mennonites. The newcomers quickly developed farms and dairies, which pleased the government and took the pressure off of Bilo Wallace.[754]

Old Colony settlers from Capulín can be seen among the mix of people on the streets of Nuevo Casas Grandes. Stores there cater to their needs. In a concession to modernity, they drive pickup trucks.

The Old Colony population in Mexico approaches 100,000 with a high percentage still living in Cuauhtémoc Municipio. An unknown number of other Mennonites practice the religion but do not follow the Old Colony lifestyle.

The Mennonite numbers are relatively small in Janos Municipio, (which has a total population less than 11,000), but their impact on the area has been enormous and is growing.

Three events occurred almost at the same time in the early 1990s that stimulated this growth. Overnight, Janos Municipio changed from a remote grazing land to a major producer and exporter of crops grown in vast irrigated fields.

The first occurred in 1992, when the Mexican government, under President Carlos Salinas Gortari, entered into the North American Free Trade Agreement, NAFTA. This opened the borders of Mexico, Canada, and the U.S. to tariff-free trade. Government planners in Mexico City felt that to make this work, the restrictive clauses in Article 27 of the 1917 Constitution regarding privatization and sale of land would have to be changed. The new laws in 1992 constituted the second event that changed the Janos Municipio.

Article 27 guided policy for more than 70 years. Much of the land in the entire country had been converted to a communal status with strict rules that prohibited land sales or land mortgages. The system had worked to break up the large haciendas and to provide land for millions of Mexicans. However, government investment had never been enough to provide the agricultural infrastructure to reach potential production levels. In 1992, the planners felt that private ownership of individual land parcels would free the owners to use their parcels as collateral to buy modern farm machinery, better quality cattle, irrigation systems, and whatever else they needed to improve production. Also, the new laws would allow the owners to sell their parcels if they desired. This opened the way for a new set of entrepreneurs to accumulate large tracts by buying individual private parcels.

A third event provided the catalyst that, when combined with the new laws, caused the agricultural boom in Janos. Electricity came to the remote Mennonite communities in 1992. Like the pickup truck, use of electric power represented a   major concession to modern technology. A number of Old Colony Mennonites viewed this as contrary to their values, and they moved on, as they had so often in their past. About half of those living in the five Janos Mennonite towns left for even more remote areas such as Bolivia.

Others saw opportunity and took a more modern view. Electrical power meant wells could be dug and water pumped to irrigate large fields.

Deep beneath the surface of this arid corner of Chihuahua lies a huge aquifer, virtually untapped, until the application of modern-day well-digging techniques and electric pumps.

Prior to the advent of electricity, occasional surface water and shallow windmill pumpers provided water for stock tanks and small farm plots. As far back as the 17th century, Captain Francisco Ramírez, a Spanish officer and *alcalde* of Casas Grandes, found a major spring, called *Ojo de Ramos,* He obtained a *merced de real,* official authorization, from the Crown, to establish a rancho. The surface water created lush grass that fattened cows for the next four centuries. However, overall, there was not enough water for large-scale agriculture until the advent of electricity.

Groups of well-financed Mennonites began to acquire more parcels around Janos and combine them into large farms. They dug more and deeper wells and planted lucrative crops. In a very short time, thousands of acres of range land had been plowed and planted to chilies, onions, and cotton, all with a ready market in the U.S., and all needing a great deal of water.

Mexicans working newly privatized ejido parcels and even some small Mennonite farmers could not compete. They sold out and left the area.

Those Mexican ejido members, *ejidatarios,* who attempted large-scale farming, had limited success. It was a question of culture. Mexican agriculture since the Revolution had been dependent of government credit and support. Private financing now was limited or completely unavailable. The closed society of the Mennonites had always rejected outside aid. Their internal system of long-term no-interest loans generated the capital for expensive farm equipment, seed, fertilizer, as well as land purchases. The Mennonite church provided an organizational structure for purchases, loans, and land distribution.[755]

Agricultural production soared and the region prospered—at least statistically. However, the gap between rich and poor widened. Critics claimed the Mennonites employed low-wage Central American laborers. Rising electricity rates affected the struggling ejidatarios more than the large-scale Mennonite producers.

The on-going conversion of range land to field crops meant more wells, which began to drain the aquifers as far away as the Ramos Rancho. Years of drought have compounded the problem, leading to serious hostility in the region.

In spite of their closed society or perhaps because of it, the Mennonites have been generally accepted by the Mexican people. Some resented the special concessions granted by the government, but generally Mennonites found a welcoming place in Chihuahua. They responded by making a significant economic contribution. Whether they can overcome the rising hostility, caused by the growing water conflict, remains to be seen.[756]

Matachines

The very old ritual of Matachines dancing came to Mata Ortiz from different places. The origins of the ceremonial dance have been lost, and scholars debate whether the ritual originated in Mexico with Aztecs or other Indians and evolved into a Christian ritual or came from Spain and became appended to Indian/mestizo Christianity. The old Spanish town of Bernalillo, New Mexico can trace its Matachines tradition back 300 years—not quite far enough to truly understand its origins but enough to show it is very old. The most likely story is that over time many European ceremonies and rituals evolved into a Spanish ceremonial dance celebrating the defeat of the Moors by the Christians. Many scholars believe the dance represents a Christian and Moor battle. The verb *matar*, to kill, appears to be the base for the word Matachines, which suggests battle. Whatever the origin or specific meaning, the performance represents a triumph of good over evil. In Mexico, the actions of Hernán Cortez, his Indian consort, Malinche, and the Aztec Emperor Montezuma have been woven in to the dance story.

Groups from ten to thirty in red costumes dance in unison, weaving in and out, following proscribed steps. Men and women both participate, sometimes separately and sometimes together. The costumes often are elaborate, reflecting long hours of work by the dancers or their seamstresses. Many wear a conical headdress decorated with turkey features. Bells and other noisemakers are sewn into the costumes. They carry noisemakers that make a clacking sound and sometimes tridents that represent the Holy Trinity.

The dancers view their performance as a religious ceremony, honoring a particular saint. That is why virtually all of the dances are on saint feast days. The most common is December 12, the day of the Virgin of Guadalupe, the patron saint of Mexico. Another important date is May 15, the day of San Isidro, the patron saint of farmers. Churches often invite Matachines to dance on the saint's day for which the church is named.

In Mata Ortiz and surrounding towns, there are distinct groups that perform occasionally or often. One of the most active is based in Barrio Porvenir.

There the well-known potter Jerardo Tena has taken over his family's Matachines responsibilities and become *El Monarca* or leader. His great-grandfather on his mother's side, Genovevo Sandoval Due, brought the dance to Santa Rosa, the village just south of Mata Ortiz. He came from the old colonial town of Zacatecas, where Matachines had a long history. Jerardo Sandoval eventually had 24 children with two wives. This accounts for the considerable number of Sandoval families in the area. After his death, one of his sons, Antonio Sandoval, continued to organize dancers and lead them in Santa Rosa. Antonio's daughter, Sofía Sandoval (Jerardo Tena's mother), married Roberto "Beto" Tena from the mountain community of Jovales (Hop Valley), a former LDS colony that became an ejido. Her sister, Otila Sandoval de Ortiz, married Félix Ortiz, the important early Mata Ortiz potter.

Jerardo's paternal great-grandfather, Francisco Tena came from Namiquipa to find work. He eventually settled with his wife and son, Manuel Tena Delgado (Jerardo's grandfather) in Jovales where Jerardo's, father (Beto), and Jerardo himself were born.

In 1980, when Jerardo was seven, the Tena family moved to Mata Ortiz. The incentive to leave Jovales came from Félix Ortiz. He told his sister-in-law Sofía to come to Mata Ortiz and he would teach her to make pots. Beto drove his cattle to Mata Ortiz from the mountain valley, where four generations of Tenas had lived. The family took up residence in Barrio Porvenir.

Sofía learned to make pottery while Beto tended cattle and worked in the LDS apple orchards. He later learned pottery as well. According to Jerardo, his mother Sofía remembered well anthropologist Spencer MacCallum, who did so much to publicize Mata Ortiz pottery between 1976 and 1984.

As Jerardo grew up, he learned to make pots from his mother and Félix Ortiz. Despite the difference in age, he and Félix became good friends and collaborated on pieces that Félix shaped, and Jerardo painted.[757]

In Porvenir, Jerardo's uncle, Eusebio "Chevo" Sandoval assumed the role of El Monarca of the Matachines group. He kept the tradition alive even though other groups may have run into trouble with a local priest, who considered the dancing a pagan rite. Also, for a while, Sandoval had trouble attracting younger people outside his family.[758]

More recently, Jerardo succeeded his uncle, and the group has flourished. They perform often at La Virgen de Guadalupe, the church in Porvenir, and at San José, the church in Barrio Iglesia, as well as churches in surrounding communities.

In Barrio López at the north and opposite end of Mata Ortiz from Barrio Porvenir, Fabián Hernández is El Monarca for another group. They are oriented to honoring San Isidro, the patron saint of farmers. On his day, May 15, the dancers in full costume gather in the country on a dirt road near a large field. A small shrine to San Isidro stands at the side of the

Matachines, Barrio Porvenir, Mata Ortiz,
feast day of the Virgin of Guadalupe. Photo: 2019

road. These dancers execute particularly intricate steps, sometimes slowly, sometimes vigorously, all the while snapping a noise maker. This device looks like a small bow and arrow and is called a *naguilla*. While the dancers move through their steps, a little girl with no mask or costume wanders in and out among them. She represents Malinche.

The tradition had come down through both of their families, but neither know many of the details. They clearly enjoy the dancing. For them it combines a social occasion with a celebration of life as they honor San Isidro at the beginning of the growing season.

Two miles farther north and not far from the old Hacienda San Diego compound, another group dances out in the country on the feast day of San Isidro. Down a road behind San Diego's stone corral, El Monarca José Gallardo has selected a location under large cottonwood trees near his broad wheat field. The ruined walls of his grandfather's house stand nearby. José Gallardo's dances feature a jug of the local version of the ancient corn beer *tesgüino*. His group of about fourteen dancers performs on the day of Our Lady of Guadalupe as well as San Isidro's day and occasionally on other saint's days.

Other groups have come and gone over the years, but Matachines survive in Mata Ortiz and the Casas Grandes Valley, in spite of modern inroads into old traditions.

The Weavers

Before the pottery movement began in Mata Ortiz, crafts centered around the cattle industry. Vaqueros needed saddles, bridles, saddle blankets, and lariats or *sogas*. Guillermo Loya from San Diego specialized in rawhide lariats. He cut long strips from cattle hides, hooked the strips into a tree, trimmed the edges of the strips with a sharp pocket knife, and braided them into lariats or *sogas*.[759] He had a market in Mata Ortiz as many there ran cattle. Several were known for their skill with horse and soga, and local ranchers hired them regularly during roundup and branding times.

José Camacho had learned weaving in his hometown of Saltillo, Coahuila, famous for its serapes. In the 1980s, he lived and worked in a box car on a siding on the north or left side of the road where it crossed the tracks entering Mata Ortiz. He made a primitive spinning wheel with spokes leading from a spindle hub to a rim held together by a band of thin sheet metal. A large loom, made of salvaged lumber, stood nearby.

Watching Señor Camacho work was a step back into another century. He took a handful of raw wool from a pile, carded it with a big comb, and held it to the spindle as he rotated the wheel with his other hand. The spindle grabbed the wool and twisted it into yarn. He attached the strands of yarn vertically to the loom. Then he wove horizontal strands in and out of the vertical strands. He created stripes by varying the color of the wool, white, grey, or black. After several hours, the result was a saddle blanket or bed blanket, a *cobija*. Another weaver named Valbueno did similar work. He lived and worked in a solitary house on the bank of Arroyo Mimbres, one of the tributary drainages to the Palanganas River north of town.

The Casas Grandes Valley contains a mix of European and Indian cultures that stretch back into prehistoric time. However, with a few exceptions, the families of the people living there today brought their skills and traditions from somewhere else a relatively short time ago.

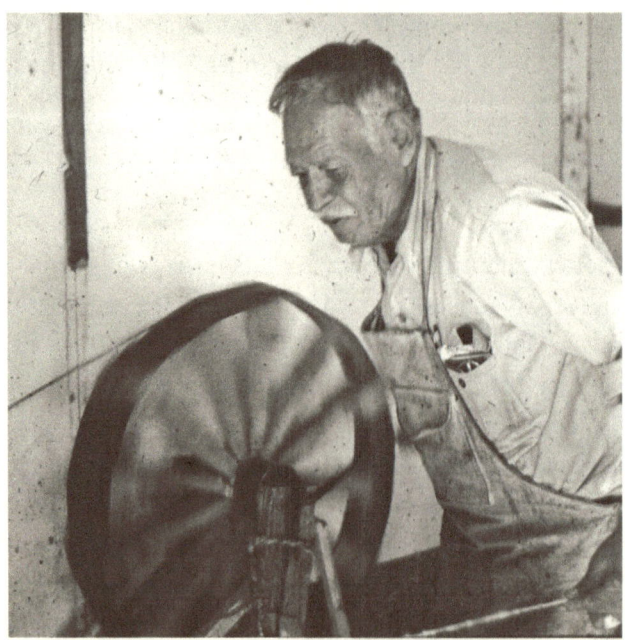

José Camacho, weaver of saddle blankets. Photo: 1985

15

Quieter Years

Daily Rhythm

With the drama and violence of the Revolution over, the daily railroad schedule set a rhythm for the Casas Grandes Valley as the people rebuilt their lives. A combination of railroading, *labors*, or small farms, and cattle raising sustained the families as these quiet years rolled by. Some of the LDS families returned to claim their property in Colonia Juárez and Dublán. Their rejuvenated apple orchards and packing houses provided additional employment. The decade of the Depression in the 1930s caused hard times everywhere, but Pearson/Mata Ortiz escaped the terrible suffering of other regions and continued to draw job seekers.

La Redonda

Sometime after 1928 Roy Hoard established a large roundhouse and engine-repair machine shop facility, *La Redonda*, in Pearson.[760] It was located just to the left or north of where the current road crosses the tracks entering Mata Ortiz. Houses and a market occupy the site today. Many residents worked for the railroad, repairing track, on the trains, or in *La Redonda*. Every other day, a regularly scheduled train pulled by a steam engine would arrive in Pearson from Ciudad Juárez. The engine would be serviced and take on water. A second crew would take over and drive the train over the mountains to Madera. The original crew would stay overnight enjoying the local amenities—saloons, pool, gambling halls, and two movie theaters. The next day, the second crew would return with the northbound train, and the original crew would take it back to Ciudad Juárez. Steam-powered trains traveled slowly in that era, pulling long rows of heavily laden cars up the steep grades.

Today behind the houses on the Redonda site is a vacant area that extends to the old railroad right-of-way. A close inspection of the ground there by the authors and Jorge Quintana in January 2013 revealed fragments of brick, rusted iron, and the remains of a well that evidently provided water for the engine's boilers. Cast in the bricks was the name "Howard St. Louis," It appears the brick used in the building was shipped all the way from St. Louis, Missouri. The MNWR now connected Pearson with the U.S. through El Paso, but why would such a heavy but easily manufactured product be shipped so far? An investigation of the Evens and Howard Brick Company revealed that the company specialized in fire or refractory brick used in furnaces, incinerators, and fire boxes. This brick is typically much lighter than conventional construction brick. In the early 20th century, the

Remnants of the bricks used to build La Redonda made by the Evens & Howard Fire Brick Company of St. Louis, Missouri.

company shipped their special brick all over the United States and even to a rubber plantation in the interior of Africa.[761]

The Redonda was torn down in 1956 when the faster, more powerful diesels made the interim stopover in Pearson unnecessary.

Pearson Becomes Juan Mata Ortiz

After the Pearson mill closed, Hoard terminated most of the remaining North American employees to cut costs. The center of town for Pearson shifted from Barrio Americano to El Centro across from the train station. The wooden houses and stores built by the company deteriorated and several burned.[762] Others were torn down to be replaced by conventional adobe buildings. In Barrio Centro, hotels, stores, and places of entertainment grew up to serve transient railroad employees as well as the local community. The transients brought a rough element to the otherwise tranquil town. Men on the streets and in the saloons at night often carried pistols.[763]

Efraín Rodríguez Flores in front of the closed mill, 1950s.
Photo: Courtesy of Manuel Rodríguez Guillén

The Hotel Colón, conveniently located across from the railroad station, later became the home of Juan Quezada.

Kerosene or Coleman lanterns provided light as electricity no longer flowed from the defunct mill power plant. Laborers across the arroyo in Barrio Porvenir converted their tents and shanties into more substantial adobe homes. Longtime residents say that the age of the buildings can be determined by the size of the adobe bricks—the older the home the larger the bricks. Mail was delivered regularly from the post office in Barrio Centro. Emeterio Ortiz, one of the first potters in Barrio Porvenir, was the postman in the early 1950s.[764]

On May 4, 1925, the Congress of the State of Chihuahua approved a change of name for the town from Pearson to Juan Mata Ortiz in honor of the old Apache fighter and hero of the Battle of Tres Castillos.[765] Dr. Fred Stark Pearson's dream of grand enterprise in Mexico did not last. It is poignant that not even his name survived on his town as a memorial to his endeavors.

Ejidos

The roots of communal versus private land ownership extend deep into Mexico's Spanish and Indian heritage. The fundamental issue of who controls the land has shaped the country's history. It came to a head during the 1910-1920 Revolution when agrarian reform reached an almost mystical level of aspiration for the common people.

For most of the major players of the Revolution (except Emiliano Zapata) such reforms were not their highest priority, but none could ignore the issue. Article 27 of the Constitution of 1917 made it very clear that the government controlled all of the land surface as well as the minerals below. The article spelled out in detail how land could be expropriated and granted to communally operated ejidos. The definition of an ejido is property granted by the government to a group of landless campesinos or to those who held old Spanish titles to land that was taken from them during the Porfirio Díaz era. The transfer of land from haciendas and other large holdings to ejidos became the core of Mexican agrarian reform.

At the same time, Article 27 recognized private property rights. Language in the article's sections permitted private land owners to retain at least part of their holdings up to certain sizes and to be compensated for land taken beyond the proscribed limits. Owners could also sell their land. This permitted them to sell off parcels in anticipation of expropriation.

When the idealistic delegates convened in Querétaro in 1917 to create a constitution, they could not have foreseen how their efforts would shape northern Chihuahua's culture and agricultural economy for the next seven decades. Three very different entities emerged: private ranches and farms, ejidos, and Mennonite farms.

Cattle raising has always been and remains a major economic activity. The difference in the post-revolution era was the size of the ranches and the ownership. The great multi-million acre haciendas were gradually broken into parcels to be sold or expropriated. Millions of acres were converted to ejidos, even though private ranching continued within the limitations set by Article 27. Cattle raising dominated, although some private landowners, including LDS colonists, had farms and orchards. Mennonites represented a radically different cultural group that took advantage of the situation created by the breakup of the haciendas to acquire large parcels for farmland. A large percentage of the land eventually ended in ejidos, but it was a slow process.

Article 27 laid out the authority and framework for restoring communal land that had been taken. Both Casas Grandes and Janos qualified and *La Caja*, the government land agency, recreated Ejido Janos on February 22, 1927, and Ejido Casas Grandes on May 12, 1927 during the Calles administration.

The framers of the Constitution also intended to create new ejidos to benefit the large population of landless campesinos. Article 27 specified that groups of 20 or more could petition the government for land. The concept worked extremely well, although slowly. Over the next seven decades, 29,500 ejidos were formed covering one half of the land surface of the entire country.[766]

President Lázaro Cárdenas, a strong believer in land reform, was particularly aggressive. During his administration between 1934 and 1940, his government granted approval for 20 million hectares (49.4 million acres),

In the background is La Redonda (roundhouse) and workshop, the only known picture of this facility. The water tank to fill the steam engine boilers is at right. The car was the 1936 Chevrolet owned by the first doctor in Mata Ortiz, Dr. Jesús Bautista Fregoso. — Photo: Courtesy of J. Arnoldo Bautista Corral

reducing the number of landless peasants by over fifty percent. Different sections in the article caused the return of 16,500,000 hectares (40.8 million acres) to indigenous groups. These communally held Indian lands were called *communidades*.[767]

Starting with President Obregón's term in 1920, the federal agency responsible for ejido administration was *La Caja de Préstamos para Obras de Irrigación y Fomento de la Agricultura S.A*, known as *La Caja*.

Article 27 contained specific restrictions on the transferability of ejido rights and the use of ejido land. Basically, the land could not be bought, sold, leased, or mortgaged, only inherited. The land had to be worked. If La Caja determined a parcel had not been used for two years, the agency could declare the parcel vacant, and it would revert to the ejido.[768]

Presidents, who came after Obregón, strengthened or weakened the ejido system in accordance with their own biases and the pressures of the times. Regardless of politics, Article 27 remained the guide for Mexico's communal land-use for 75 years.

On the other side of the equation, the once powerful hacendados lost most of their enormous estates. The breakup followed an erratic course, beginning before the fighting stopped. Pancho Villa confiscated hacienda cattle operations to generate revenue for his cause, but Carranza enabled the aggrieved hacendados to recover much of their land before the Revolution ended.

Before and during the Revolution, Luis Terrazas stood as a symbol of tyranny to the people of Chihuahua, second only to Porfirio Díaz. Yet shortly after, in 1921, his family was able to enter into negotiations with Arthur J. McQuatters, a U.S. banker, to sell 2.3 million hectares (5.7 million acres) (sources very on the size) for a massive irrigation and farm development. Chihuahua Governor Enríquez expedited the deal as a way of refilling the empty state treasury. Whether the plan made good economic sense or not proved irrelevant. The outcry from those who felt such a transaction violated everything the Revolution stood for forced President Obregón to cancel the sale. However, to make up for Terrazas's loss, he agreed to pay the family seven million dollars for the property, only a million less than McQuatters' offer.[769]

La Caja now had an enormous amount of land that could be reallocated. Similar if less dramatic transactions allowed other large landowners to survive on a smaller scale, while large tracts of their former land became ejidos.

Provisions in Article 27 recognized that the maximum of 50 hectares, (124 acres) was too small for a cattle ranch. The article allowed for larger private ranches based on a formula, called the "500-cow" limit. In Chihuahua, the formula permitted 44,000 hectares (108,726 acres). Even these limits were not permanent and subject to expropriation.

Article 27 called for three ejido land-use classifications: individual parcels of arable land held and worked by specific members, called *ejidatarios*; common land, (generally forest, mountain, and grazing lands or waste land), monitored and managed by the ejido officers and land for houses.[770] Ejidatarios had a "right," or *derecho*, to use individual parcels under the first classification, and communal land under the second. Also, each house-holder received a derecho from the ejido, allowing him to occupy his house.

The head of family held the ejido *derechos.* Each ejido governing body, *comisariado,* established its own internal policies and rules for land man-agement, subject to forest environmental regulations. Forest use was an important issue in the Casas Grandes region. Tree cutting for firewood was widespread and felling trees to sell to lumber mills a source of revenue for many.

In spite of local management, all ejido properties were considered national lands. The federal agency, La Caja controlled the land for fifty years. Complaints, claims, counterclaims, conflicting legal interpretations, and bureaucratic inertia slowed an already complicated process. By 1930, only 20 percent of the Terrazas holdings had been distributed to old and new ejidos.

The Palomas Land and Cattle Company lost land in 1923 but did not lose more for the next 23 years. In 1947, President Alemán expropriated the remainder of the huge ranch and subdivided it into 40,000-hectare (98,842 acre) ranches. The government sold these at auction to Mexican buyers, often former generals or other elites.[771]

All land holdings over the proscribed limit were still subject to expro-priation. The Terrazas family represented an extreme example, but all ranchers faced the same problems. They could buy and sell their land, but La Caja could step in at any time and take all or part of a private ranch for a new or existing ejido. Ranches near ejidos were particularly vulnerable as ejidatarios often petitioned for more land as their population grew.

Of all the presidents that followed Obregón, Lázaro Cárdenas was the most ardent in implementing land distribution. Committed as he was, he realized he had a problem when he took office in 1934. After 14 years of relative peace, the country's beef industry still had never recovered, espe-cially in the ravished battleground state of Chihuahua. A beef shortage had existed for several years. Also export fee revenue for shipping to the lucrative U.S. market had fallen far below pre-Revolutionary levels. The ongoing threat of expropriation discouraged ranchers from taking on loan obligations for investment. They held back from sinking cash into rebuild-ing fences, wells, and barns, or purchasing the necessary bulls and cows to rebuild their herds. Even some ranches within the constitutional size limits had been taken by La Caja. This meant that virtually all ranchers felt threatened, regardless of ranch size.

Cárdenas did not act on this problem until 1937. That year, he issued a *reglamento,* a decree, designed to protect the ranching industry. Ranchers could now apply for *certificados de inafectabilidad,* literally certificates of inaccessibility or sometimes certificates of immunity.[772]

These provided a layer of protection for ranchers and many in Chihuahua applied. Between 1937 and 1958, 197 certificates were issued covering 3.9 million hectares (9.6 million acres). Additional changes were made in the 1960s, after the certificados expired, which maintained protection until the radical changes were made to the constitution in 1992.

Ejidatarios had become dissatisfied with La Caja. In the early 1970s, pressure from around the country forced President Luis Echeverría to make significant administrative changes. La Caja ceased to function. Beginning in 1974 and continuing until 1992, the *Secretaría de la Reforma Agraria* received petitions and distributed land to ejidos. The *Registro Agrario Nacional* recorded the ejidatarios' derechos, or rights, for each land classification and issued the appropriate certificates.[773]

For the ejidos at the local level, most of the old rules still applied. The ejidatario members of each ejido made up an assembly that was required to meet monthly. The assembly elected the *comisariado,* consisting of a president, secretary, and treasurer. Officers serve three years and could not be reelected. A vigilance council is also elected to oversee the actions of the comisariado.

In the early 1990s, the administration of Carlos Salinas de Gortari took the radical step of modifying the Constitution of 1917 and its historic Article 27. This opened the door to privatizing communal lands. Advocates for privatization believed the old rules to be too restrictive for economic efficiency, which led to overuse and abuse of the land. Opponents worried about a return to large landholdings held by a few at the expense of the campesinos. A new Agrarian Law superseded parts of Article 27. The new provisions did not sweep away the communal system, but rather provided a path for ejidatarios to privatize.

After 1992, the *Secretaría de la Reforma Agraria* stayed in place and continued to regulate the national lands by enforcing land laws, identifying unused empty lands, and expropriating property for public use.

While Carlos Salinas de Gortari opened the door to ejido privatization, most ejidatarios across the nation approached the opportunity with caution. Land reform had been the fundamental promise of the Revolution. Nevertheless, the old ejido system was over. The government no longer provided subsidies and support and significant adjustments had to be made. Most ejidos in the Casas Grandes Valley survived. They maintained their administration and rules, while allowing private titles that can be bought, sold, or mortgaged.

Pearson/Mata Ortiz followed the entire arc of ejido history from 1921 to the present day.

Ejido Pearson

Very soon after the fighting finally ended, the Mexican residents of Pearson organized and prepared a petition for land in accordance with Article 27. Pearson was unique. Most of the early petitioners from other communities wanted communal land returned to them that had been confiscated by Porfirio Díaz's 1884 Law of Vacant Lands and Chihuahua Governor Enrique Creel's Land Act of 1905. The claims of communities like Casas Grandes dated back to 18th century Spanish grants. Not so for Pearson. The residents there had all come from somewhere else and lived on company land. Perhaps employment on the railroad and/or the union organization made them more sophisticated and politically aware. Whatever the stimulus, on May 1, 1921, they submitted a petition or *dotación* for land and ejido status. Álvaro Obregón was still president, and the process moved slowly. A year and a half passed before notification came from the governor that 14,300 hectares (35,336 acres) had been approved for the new Pearson ejido as of October 28, 1923. The parcel came from the Terrazas's Haciendas San Diego and San Miguel Babícora.[774] The new ejidatarios drew lots for their assigned parcels or *labors*.[775]

In 1925, Pedro Acosta Chávez, an activist, proposed that the pueblo and ejido name be changed from Pearson to Juan Mata Ortiz, a hero of the Apache Wars. The Cárdenas administration officially made the change.[776]

The ejidatarios petitioned La Caja for an *amplicación,* allocation of additional land, on September 7, 1934 It took almost four years, but finally the governor forwarded approval for 23,544 hectares (58,178 acres), effective July 31, 1938. The amplicación was in a U shape, surrounding the original ejido property on the west, south, and east. On the north, the Ejido Pearson/Mata Ortiz bordered Ejido Casas Grandes.

Twenty-seven years later, on January 27, 1966, the ejidatarios submitted a second amplicación request. Again, there was a delay, but finally, on September 17, 1970, they received approval for 6,000 more hectares (14,826 acres).

Private land sales occurred within Mata Ortiz as well as ejido allocations. This is confusing, and the record is unclear as to what exactly happened. Dr. Fred Stark Pearson's parent company, the Mexico North Western Railway, MNWR, originally purchased land to form the town and mill site from Luis Terrazas's Hacienda San Diego and Hacienda San Miguel de Babícora. The MNWR held title to the property. The west boundary ran about where the road is today after it curves north from Mata Ortiz. That west boundary continued north to the cemetery. The north boundary ran from the cemetery to the river. The south boundary ran from the road (the west boundary) east toward the river to the tank and well on the hill. Past the well it made a sharp turn north for some distance and then turned east again to the river. The Catholic Church area, Barrio Iglesia, and Barrio Centro are all south of that southern dog-leg boundary line and not part of Pearson's original purchase.

In 1945, Roy Hoard, president of the MNWR, signed the final sales documents to convey all of the MNWR assets to a Mexican syndicate, El Grupo Industrial Bosques de Chihuahua, headed by a Mexico City banker, Eloy Vallina.[777]

Sometime later, Bosques de Chihuahua sold the mill site, on the hill north of town, 132 hectares (326 acres) to a man named Hilario Aguilar.

Aguilar did not use the 132 hectares and in the late 1970s sold it to J. Guadalupe Duran Renteria. An astute businessman, Duran had a reputation for unscrupulous dealings. Nevertheless, he dug a well, planted an orchard, and built a substantial brick building on the hill above the old Pearson mill foundation, to house a molding mill operation.

Beyond the mill, on a flat area on the hill, he cleared an area for a short airstrip. He commuted to the site in a surplus World War II Fairchild PT 19 trainer, the only such commute ever made into Mata Ortiz.

The eastern border between Duran's private property and the surrounding ejido was the ejido-controlled acequia that ran and still runs roughly north and south.

Inside that border Duran's property extended northeast to include Barrio López. People had built homes there, and now they were squatting on Duran's private property. The ejido officials intervened and reached an agreement with Duran. The ejido traded ejido land on the northwest side of his mill-site land for the Barrio López property.

It is not clear how much molding Duran's mill produced. What is known is that he secured a sizeable bank loan against the property, then abandoned the mill and left town, leaving the bank with a bad debt.[778]

Guadalupe Duran's airplane landing on a Mata Ortiz airstrip.
Photo: Courtesy of Lila Orozco

Mickey Vanderwagen, from New Mexico, who had spent his entire life working with Zuni Indian jewelers, bought the property in 1999. He knew the jewelry business and planned to train young, talented artists in Mata Ortiz, as he had in Zuni, to create a second craft industry. Some of Vanderwagen's trainees did good work, particularly Ariel Renteria. However, they did not continue with jewelry after the Renteria family took over the property and Vanderwagen left Mata Ortiz.

Bosques de Chihuahua made a second sale in the early 1980s. Guadalupe Duran's son, Carlos Mario Duran, bought Barrios Americano, Iglesia, and a part of Barrio Centro, the center of the village, including the main plaza. The ejido later acquired this area at an unknown date. A building on the east side of the plaza might be the oldest building in Mata Ortiz. It once featured a food kiosk called El Faro and later a billiard parlor.

Mata Ortiz Ejido members, 1961. Severiano Gallegos, Héctor Gallegos's paternal grandfather, is seated in the center with hat in hand. Tomás Esparza, Héctor's maternal grandfather, and his uncle, Jesús Luévano Gallegos, are seated to his right. Pablo Bugarini, the great-grandfather of Laura Bugarini, is in overalls behind Jesús. The photograph was taken in front of the ejido building that was later converted into the town's first library.

The ejidatarios made another deal to trade Duran for land on the west side of the hill, parallel to the road for 300 hectares (741 acres) of ejido land in the northwest corner.

Before 1992, the Mata Ortiz ejido paid property taxes to the Casas Grandes Municipio. Then, the ejido issued a document giving each householder a right or *derecho* to their home. The derecho could be sold only with permission of the ejido assembly.

After privatization in 1992, the residential area became a *Comunidad Urbana*, and the federal government issued a private title to each householder that had the earlier ejido derecho. Now the householder's property

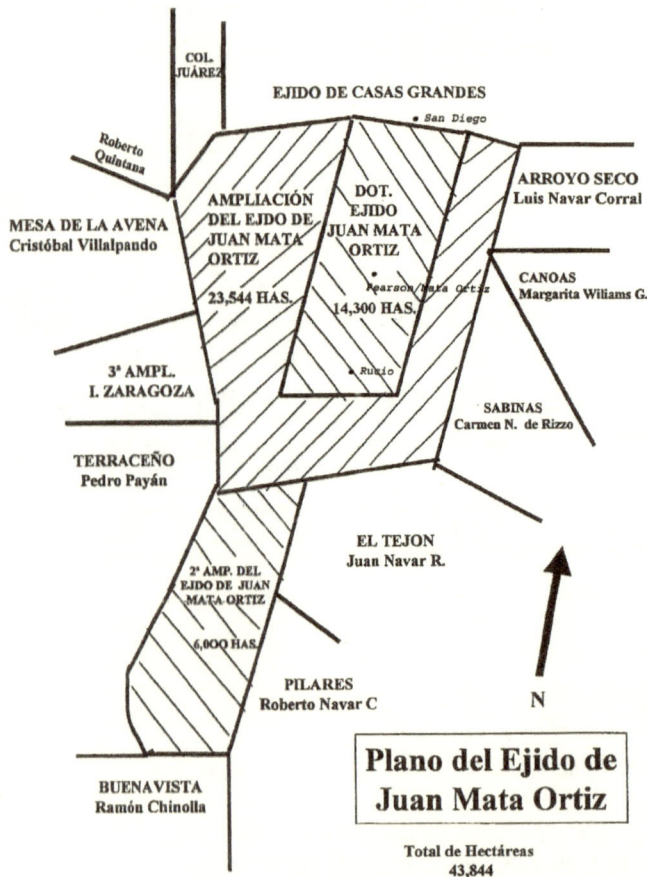

Mata Ortiz Ejido boundaries

can be mortgaged or sold without permission from the ejido assembly, although approval is often requested out of respect for neighbors and the ejido tradition. Householders now pay the property tax directly to the municipio.

The local residents with derechos to agricultural parcels, labors, also received federal titles.

Some communal land, usually range land, is still held by the ejido and assigned in parcels to ejidatarios by issuing derechos. One or more ejidatarios can hold a single parcel or an individual ejidatario can hold derechos to one or more parcels. These parcels can be fenced and used exclusively by those holding the derechos. If the land is misused in some way or abandoned, the ejido can rescind the derechos. The ejido organization still exists as a legal entity.

Because Mata Ortiz is a "pueblo," it has no government organization or officials. This is in contrast to a "colonia" that has a council and officials. Therefore, the ejido officers represent the community when dealing with the municipio or other outside agencies. The ejido retains authority over rangeland and issues are resolved by vote of the ejidatario assembly at *La Junta*, the monthly meeting.[779]

Ejidos in Municipio Casas Grandes

The charismatic Spanish chevalier, Teodoro de Croix, established five communal entities when he came to the sparsely populated northwest frontier in the 18th century. The Viceroy of New Spain had assigned him to command Nueva Vizcaya. His mission was to reorganize the administration of the region, encourage more settlers, and protect the communities from Apaches. He gave titles, known as *bandos*, dated November 15, 1778, to Casas Grandes, Janos, Galeana, Las Cruces, and Namiquipa (their modern names). In return, the settlers would organize into militias to counter the Apache as well as develop the land.

Chevalier de Croix specified that each grant should include the property that stretched four leagues in all four directions from a center point in the community. For Casas Grandes, the center point was the original San Antonio de Padua church, now the *Convento* ruin on the north side of town. This large square parcel contained 112,339 hectares (277,596 acres), a figure that became imbedded in the minds of generations of local inhabitants as the ejido entitlement.

The language of the bandos expressly stated that part of the land would be commonly used.[780] The succeeding generations interpreted this to mean de Croix had established the five entities as "ejidos," as they understood the term. Copies of the bandos were found in the Janos ejido offices and are jealously protected there as the ultimate verification of the inhabitant's claim to ejido ownership.

In spite of the authenticity of these documents and subsequent governmental verification, the confiscatory laws of Porfirio Díaz and Governor Enrique Creel allowed private land owners, large and small, foreign, and Mexican, to take parcels from Casas Grandes communal lands.

The land-reform process moved slowly. For Casas Grandes, it took six years to establish the ejido. Even then official verification remained so vague that conflicts persist to the present day.

Casas Grandes residents started the process early enough. They organized and prepared their petition, and their leaders traveled by train to Ciudad Chihuahua. They presented their case in person to the governor in his palace on May 18, 1921. The residents included a copy of Chevalier de Croix's bando with their petition.

Efrén Valdez happened to be the governor on that date, but that quickly changed. During 1920-21, eight individuals turned over the office 16 times, often after only a few days. Ignacio C. Enríquez (Roy Hoard's friend) returned to the chair more often than any other and dominated until his last term ended in 1924.

It was common for official transactions with the federal government to be transmitted back and forth through the governor's office. Governor Enríquez supported the petition, but for reasons having nothing directly to do with Casas Grandes, he decided to challenge La Caja, the federal agency responsible for land management.

After the McQuatters affair was resolved, La Caja held 2,679,954 hectares (6,622,311 acres) of former Terrazas land. Enríquez, who had resisted land reform and had promoted the sale to McQuatters, now supported land distribution but on his terms. He wanted land expropriated from

Terrazas and others sold to relatively small owners. In 1922, he drew up his own plan, a division of the large estates into farms and ranches similar to McQuatter's proposal, but without foreign involvement. The state legislature adopted the plan as Chihuahua's Agrarian Law. These political moves reflected the power struggle between Chihuahua (and other states) and Mexico City in the chaotic years following the Revolution. Enríquez gave La Caja six months to implement his plan. The federal agency officials made excuses, but they obviously had no intention of acting on the state's impudent plan. Enríquez' deadline expired on December 31, 1922, but he continued to pressure La Caja until his term of office ended in 1924.[781] After years of activism, he did not see his efforts implemented but he did leave a legacy of ongoing dissatisfaction with La Caja in northern Chihuahua. His Chihuahua Agrarian Law survived at least as a political rallying cry for action.

Regardless of his motives, pressure applied on La Caja by Enríquez was justified. Agency officials seemed more concerned about appeasing large land owners and the United States than distributing land. They even negotiated a deal with Texas ranchers to move cattle across the border to graze on former Terrazas pastures.[782]

Very early, La Caja acquired a large amount of territory in the Casas Grandes Valley. In January 1923, while Obregón was president, the agency expropriated parcels from the Palomas Land and Cattle Company, the Corralitos Cattle Company, the LDS land-holding company in Dublán, and the Terrazas haciendas—all properties that had been within the boundaries of de Croix's bandos. The petitioning communities thought the government had acted in anticipation of creating ejidos. Yet by 1930, only seven percent had been assigned to ejidos. La Caja still held 61 percent. Landowners like the Terrazas family had reclaimed 20 percent and 12 percent had been transferred to towns with the "colonia" designation.[783]

The governor's interference and La Caja's procrastination impeded the Casas Grandes petition, but other factors contributed to what turned out to be a vague final approval. The residents may have asked for too much.

All of the relevant documents, decrees, and proclamations referred to Chevalier Teodoro's bandos. He had allocated 112,339 hectares to each of the five communal entities he created. Galeana and Namiquipa applied to

La Caja and received that amount, apparently without issue.[784] The Casas Grandes petitioners applied for the same amount but ran into resistance from other entities. The old bando's four-leagues-on-a-side configuration now included most of Municipio Casas Grandes with its numerous private homes and businesses, part of Municipio Nuevo Casas Grandes, newly formed in April, 1923, and significant parts of the LDS colonies of Dublán and Colonia Juárez.

After years of delay, President Plutarco Elías Calles finally issued a proclamation on January 6, 1927 that led to official acknowledgement of Ejido Casas Grandes. The proclamation hinted at the underlying problem and attempted to resolve the political issues. Calles expressed approval of former Governor Enríquez's Chihuahua Agrarian Law, even though Enríquez's law was based on a different concept and did not specify communal land.

While some of the language was vague, the proclamation specifically dictated the sources of the land for the ejido and the number of hectares from each source: Corralitos Cattle Company, 20,427 (50,476 acres); Hacienda San Diego, 11,363 hectares (28,078 acres); Hacienda Tapiecitas, 17,470 hectares (43,169 acres); Rancho Arroyo Seco (part of Corralitos), 6,623 hectares (16,365 acres); Hacienda San Luis, 5,272 hectares (13,027 acres); and others, 7,237 hectares (17,883 acres).[785] The total of 68,392 hectares (169,000 acres) fell well short of the 112,339 hectares requested.

Nevertheless, at 10:00 in the morning on February 13, 1927, a group of dignitaries assembled in front of the Casas Grandes municipio building. A government engineer represented the Comisión Nacional Agraria. By this time the leadership of the petitioners had formally organized into the Comité Particular Administrativo to lobby for their cause. Present for their final act as committee members were Santiago Chávez, Guadalupe Villanueva and Ricardo Varela the committee president and spokesman. These were old family names in Casas Grandes. Also present were Lorenzo E. Quevedo, president of Nuevo Casas Grandes municipio and Julián Aguilar, president of Casas Grandes municipio. They were surrounded by residents who held endowment rights, or thought they did, and wanted to hear the public reading of the president's proclamation. It was a grand moment, and the ejido became official with publication in the *Diario Oficial de la Federación* on May 12, 1927.[786] Decades of conflict would follow.

Some of the men crowding the steps of the Municipal Building traced their lineage back to de Croix's bando, but many others had only political promises. Eligibility to be an ejidatario had to be determined. The overriding problem was that all felt they were entitled to more than had been allocated. They clung to the full 112,339 hectares concept, based on the ancient bando. Other entities challenged even the lesser amount and went on to challenge the legality of the Casas Grandes ejido formation itself.[787] The remainder of the 20th century saw lawsuits, confrontations, and even violence. Ongoing land disputes became a political issue as outside activists tried to aid the ejidatarios' cause. Nevertheless, Ejido Casas Grandes was reborn.

Members of the first governing body, El Comisariado, included Santiago Chávez, Pantaleón Ontiveros, and the brothers Isidoro and Leonardo Chávez.[788] Land was divided into individual field-crop parcels, urban lots, work plots, and common-use land, primarily range land. The list of ejidatarios has exceeded 550, and the ejido still functions in the post-1992 privatization era.

The ejidatarios worked their land successfully for the rest of the century and into the next, but their resentment never waned against those who occupied the remainder of de Croix's bando. Their bitterness and their efforts to reclaim land focused on their LDS neighbors. Vicious accusations on both sides, claims and counter claims would not move the government to act until 1959. That year, the government granted *Certificados de Inafectabilidad,* to six prominent LDS landowners. These certificates, first used by President Cárdenas, guaranteed the designated land would not be expropriated. This "victory" for the LDS Casas Grandes community did nothing to calm the situation.

The ejidatario's lawyer summarized their position in a letter, written in 1980, to the landholding agency in Mexico City, the successor to La Caja. He argued that the LDS colonist's original land purchase in 1886 was invalid in spite of confirmation by the federal government in 1893. No matter what had happened in the interim, the ejido had prior claim based on all of the land designated in Teodoro de Croix's bando. Mexican law respected contracts made in the Spanish Colonial era, which made this a reasonable argument.

During the 1960s, the government, probably feeling some pressure, authorized studies by engineers and other land "experts." Their final reports often contradicted each other. One stated clearly that the LDS colonist's titles were valid, and that the ejido's blanket request for more land, based on de Croix's four-league square, included a careless hodge-podge of properties owned by legal title holders, public entities, and even other ejidos. Mention was made of the LDS colonists' agricultural and business skills that had improved the economy.

The pro-ejido reports usually characterized the LDS owners as North American foreign "invaders," even though most had been born in Mexico by the 1960s. One report suggested the bureaucrat who issued the certificados must have been bribed. The studies were put on the shelf.

The barrage of petitions and letters to officials continued into the 1970s. They focused on the LDS lands but included any ownership within their four-league square. Local committees were formed, backed by national activist organizations. In 1972, one group as 35 "heads-of-households" petitioned for 100 hectares (247 acres) within the Nuevo Casas Grandes municipio.[789] As with the previous petitions, correspondence, and appeals, the government took no action.

The scenario remained the same for the next 40 years with the local and national activists pushing for reform and many, particularly in high places, believing the LDS colonists and other private ranchers and farmers had made a major contribution to the economy. The decision makers in Ciudad Chihuahua and Mexico City opted for the economy. No more land was expropriated from LDS or other private owners for Ejido Casas Grandes.

In addition to Casas Grandes and Pearson/Mata Ortiz, Municipio Casas Grandes has eight other ejidos within its borders. Several received authorization years before Casas Grandes. Most have very small populations. Ejido Heroínas was founded in 1933 primarily as a cattle operation in the remote Sierra Madre south of the San Diego Valley, along the railroad right-of-way and close to the Madera municipio border. Only three people live there today.

Vicente Guerrero was founded by ten families in 1923 in the Valle Seco region. Seventy-two people live there today.

High in the Sierra Madre, 29 miles northeast of the town of Casas Grandes is Hop Valley, not far from Colonia Pacheco. LDS families first settled there in the 1890s, although Church officials never designated it a Colonia. Spanish speakers gradually converted the name into "Jovales," which became the common name. The official ejido name is completely different, Ejido Hernández.

Names can evolve in strange ways, particularly when two cultures with different languages meet. Many assumed the name Hop Valley came from wild hops that were supposed to have grown there. Another story says that the valley name came from a Colonel Hope, a former confederate officer, who lived there in a small community called Pinal, between García and Jovales. He helped bring families to the valley from Alabama, including Maude Wright, who, later as a captive, witnessed Pancho Villa's raid on Columbus, New Mexico.[790]

Jovales/Hernández has one hundred forty-seven residents that raise crops and operate a small lumber mill. In cliffs a few miles away above the Jovales River are five relatively unknown prehistoric cave dwellings, known as the Cave of the Eagles. As of 2011, INAH had not officially classified the site.[791]

Colonia Pacheco was a large LDS mountain colony until the Exodus in 1912, and even today LDS members retain some ranches and other property. However, after the fighting stopped, the area became a confused mix of ownerships and rentals, involving Anglo LDS members, Mexican LDS members, and non-LDS owners. Some lived on and worked their land. Others, like Alma (sometimes Julian) Lunt of Colonia Juárez, lived elsewhere and hired local men to do the work. The family of Dayer LeBaron, the excommunicated proponent of polygamy, lived south of Galeana in the community of Colonia LeBaron. They rented their Pacheco land, probably to Lunt. Some Mexican owners rented their land and took jobs working for others, often more prosperous Anglo-LDS neighbors.

Into this potentially volatile mix stepped an activist group that called itself the *Comité Executivo Agrario*. The members' avowed intent was to aid the landless, but they had a clear bias against landowners, particularly foreigners. This included Anglo-LDS members, whether they were Mexican citizens or not.

The committee prepared the petition in the name of local Pacheco residents with little or no land. The petition included lists of 20 to 22 owners (committee lists vary) of property that could be expropriated to form the ejido. The lists identified nine LDS owners, one or two Mexican LDS members, and at least one campesino who owned no property. The wording of the petition, filed in 1953, implied that the Anglo-LDS owners had acquired their properties in some underhanded, perhaps even illegal, manner. The Mexican LDS members were also suspect.

The request at first did not receive approval. In fact, the petition was denied at the state level. Undoubtedly, the threatened owners contacted their political representatives to strongly object. Those efforts only delayed action. In 1959, the federal government overrode the state's decision and created the ejido.[792]

It is not clear exactly which parcels the government appropriated or whether the owners were compensated. A significant amount certainly came from LDS owners. It is known the LeBaron family struggled financially for years after losing their Pacheco rent income.

The ejido applied for *amplificaciones* and received additional land in 1959 and 1965.[793] Another grant of 636 hectares (1,572 acres) was made in 1998. The entry was made in the Diario Oficial de la Federación on March 10, 1999.[794] The ejido land is located between Ignacio Zaragoza (El Willy) on the east and the Sonora border on the west. Ranching and farming continue in Colonia Pacheco, but the community continues only in the cemetery. LDS families from the valley gather to bury loved ones next to the old family headstones of their pioneer ancestors.

Most locals know the area because Cave Valley with its famous Cave of the Olla is just a little over a mile beyond the village. About 101 people live there.

The extremely remote Ejido Las Playas (Bajío de la Sal) has only six people. Their houses have no electricity or running water. Most work in the forests. The home sites are 43 miles northeast of Casas Grandes.

To the southeast, deep in the forest near the Sonoran border, is the tiny community of El Oro, part of the Ejido Ignacio Zaragoza.

Ejido Llano de los Cristianos, dating to 1967, can be reached by a rough road through the hills east of Mata Ortiz. Several of the ejidatarios own cattle but live at the base of the hill in valley towns like Mata Ortiz and Madero.[795] On the east side the property drops down into the Arroyo Seco area of Municipio Nuevo Casas Grandes.

The largest and most important ejido after Casas Grandes and Pearson/Mata Ortiz is Ejido Guadalupe Victoria, named for Mexico's first president after independence from Spain. Initially formed in 1924, it was reestablished in 1930, when Governor Rodrigo M. Quevedo caused 10,132 hectares (25,037 acres) to be added and a new comisariado established. The intent was to bring in campesinos to grow cotton, corn, alfalfa, sorghum and beans. The site stretches along the Casas Grandes River, 25 kilometers north of Nuevo Casas Grandes and three kilometers east of Highway 10. Two ejidos, Hidalgo and Sección, within Municipio Nuevo Casas Grandes, adjoin to the southeast.

At Guadalupe Victoria, José Varela and other members of the Varela family joined the founding ejidatarios. The ejido did well. A small town grew up with a chapel dedicated to the Virgin of Guadalupe. The residents experienced a terrible flood in July, 1941. Rapidly rising water from the river covered the plains and farmland. Everyone evacuated, carrying the image of the Virgin from their church and whatever else to the Ramos Rancho and the Pajarito hills. All except José Varela, who stayed behind to guard the town as was his duty as Comisario. José and the town survived and prospered. In 1946, they used a gasoline-driven tractor for the first time, and in 1950 they dug a well with a pump powered by a diesel motor. About 447 people of all ages live there. Guadalupe Victoria stands as an example of a successful ejido that enabled residents to live at a "dignified level of life," as one historian put it.[796]

Janos Municipio Ejidos

At least three types of groups petitioned for ejido status in the Casas Grandes Valley. For old communities like Casas Grandes, ejido formation under Article 27 became the mechanism for restoring communal grants that dated back to Spanish times. In similar fashion, Ejido Janos, within the Janos Municipio, was created from old communal lands that had been taken during the Porfirio Díaz era.

In newer communities like Pearson, friends and neighbors came together under their local leaders to petition for land. A third type of group formed the remainder of the ejidos in the Janos Municipio. In contrast to the first two, these groups did not already live on the land but came from all over Mexico seeking a new life on land distributed to the common people as promised by the Revolution.

Tucked against the Sierra Madre Mountains in the northwest corner of the state, the area covered by Janos Municipio had been cattle country for 300 years. Farming, other than subsistence plots, occupied only a fraction of the land. A few farmers worked fields along the San Pedro/Janos River that flowed eastward erratically from the Sierra Carcay region of the Sierra Madre across the Llano Carretas through the town of Janos. As the Apache threat diminished in the latter part of the 19th century, most of the grazing land fell under the control of very large land owners such as Luis Terrazas, and foreign companies such as the Corralitos Land Company and the Palomas Land and Cattle Company.

Janos Municipio, created after independence from Spain in 1820, eventually contained fourteen ejidos. These were created at different times from 1924 to 1992. All but three, Ejido Janos. Ejido Pancho Villa, and Ejido Casa de Janos, were formed by landless people from around the country who had petitioned individually, seeking the promise of the Revolution. After the government assigned them to an ejido, they found their version of the promise had placed them on communal land with strangers without commonly accepted leadership.

Most had little or no farming experience and lacked capital for machinery, tools, or seed. After arriving, they looked out at land that had never seen a plow.

Turnover was high. Those who stayed fell back on cattle grazing to eke out a living. The government provided some financing, price supports and other incentives, but these were not adequate or consistent enough to help the Janos ejidatarios convert much of the dry grassland to field crops.[797]

In six of the ejidos, virtually none of the land was converted. The other eight did cultivate parcels with varying degrees of success. None could ever put their full allotment of land into crop production.

Three of the fourteen ejidos were formed differently. Radicalized squatters had occupied the future Ejido Pancho Villa property since the early 1960s. They took over developed farm parcels and clashed with the land owner's ranch hands who tried to drive them off. In 1967, the government settled the issue by declaring 11,546 hectares (28,530 acres) of the disputed land an ejido. In 1978, the ejidatarios petitioned for an additional 6,652 hectares (16,437 acres).[798]

Ejido Janos had been one of the five Spanish presidios, established by Chevalier Teodoro de Croix, where the government restored all five of the presidio communal lands. It was the largest of the five, with over 112,000 hectares (276,758 acres) and included the town of Janos with its existing infrastructure.

The third ejido with a different origin was more successful than most of the other fourteen in the Janos municipio. Ejido Casa de Janos had been an outpost of Corralitos Cattle Company. A dam had been built on the San Pedro/Janos River, which irrigated several thousand acres of crops, using a seasonal canal. The local workers petitioned and received 19,625 hectares (48,494 acres).[799]

Chihuahua had never been connected to Sonora by a highway. In 1982, a long-awaited project finally connected Janos with Agua Prieta in Sonora on the U.S. border (the site of Pancho Villa's definitive defeat in 1915).[800] This opened a shortcut to significant markets and placed the remote town of Janos at the crossroads of major truck routes.

Ten years later, in 1992, President Carlos Salinas de Gortari's administration changed the Constitution to allow privatization of ejido land. Most ejidatarios approached the changes with caution—not so in Janos Municipio.

The new law opened the door for mass sales to Mennonites and other large land owners by Janos ejidatarios and an exodus of these former Mexican owners ensued. All fourteen ejidos survived, but all decreased in population except for Ejido Janos, which includes commercial areas of the town of Janos.[801]

Most of the remaining ejidatarios depend on grazing cattle and most are relatively poor. Ranching remains the number one economic activity in Janos Municipio, but large farmers continue to expand their crop lands and dig more wells.

Corralitos and the Wallace Family

By the end of the 1930s, only a small portion remained of the Corralitos Cattle Company lands. Ninety percent of the once vast hacienda had been sold or expropriated. Even though the remaining ten percent still represented a large holding, the infrastructure was wrecked. Buildings at the old hacienda headquarters compound lay in ruins. Most of the ancient cottonwoods had been cut down. The roof had collapsed in Casa de Amo, the great house once used as a temporary hospital by Pancho Villa after the Columbus raid.

George W. Houghton, son of long-time manager, Edward C. Houghton, struggled to maintain an essentially inactive operation through the 1930s. The board of trustees managed to pay off some debt and to keep the company from bankruptcy. The objective was to sell the company. In 1941, Houghton and Richard Trimble, a trustee with a sizeable investment, negotiated to sell 500,000 acres of Corralitos land for $100,000. The purchasers were General Rodrigo M. Quevedo and William W. Wallace.[802]

Rodrigo M. Quevedo grew up on a ranch near Casas Grandes as part of a very old and well-known middle-class family. He survived the Revolution and emerged as part of the post-revolution elite, who contended for economic and political power with pre-revolutionary landowners, campesino organizations, labor unions, and moderate and radical reformers.

Quevedo fought as a young officer in the Madero Revolution and with various factions until the end. Most in the region consider him a hero, and his image appears in the mural in the portico of the Casas Grandes Salon de Actos.

In the 1930s, Quevedo used his positions to accumulate large properties. Other generals did the same thing, but Quevedo was enormously

successful, becoming one of the major producers in the resurging Chihuahua cattle business.

William W. "Bilo" Wallace was born on Hacienda Corralitos in 1904.
His grandmother and his father, William A. Wallace had emigrated from
Scotland to Ohio. As a teenager, William A. left home after a conflict with
his stepfather and eventually joined a community of Scot emigrants in El
Paso. When some of the more adventurous decided to go to Mexico in the
early 1880s to seek opportunity, he accompanied them. He took a job as a
sheepherder with Corralitos Cattle Company and stayed the rest of his life.
He worked as a butcher and baker among other jobs as he ascended in the
company, assuming more and more responsibilities under the supervision
of Edward Houghton.

He married Gregoria Chávez, who had lived her entire life at Corralitos. They had three daughters and one son, William Walter Wallace, nicknamed "Bilo." The son really never knew his father who died in 1905.

After her husband's death, Gregoria and her family left the ranch and
went to El Paso, where young William, (Bilo), grew up, went into business.[803] He became a cattle broker in El Paso and dealt often with General
Quevedo. They became friends and worked on other projects including a
racetrack in Ciudad Juárez.

After the purchase of Corralitos, General Quevedo divided the 500,000
acres into five parcels of approximately 100,000 acres each. His motives for
dividing Corralitos are unclear. Likely, he wanted to circumvent the acreage limitations in Article 27. He sold two parcels, kept two, and the third
went to Wallace for only $1,500. Friendship and appreciation for Wallace's
services appear to have been part of Quevedo's reasoning.

Bilo Wallace's property included the old headquarters compound with
Casa de Amo and the chapel, all badly damaged. Edward C. Houghton, the
former manager had tried to rebuild, but squatters had ruined that effort.
Now most of those campesinos lived on ejido land.

For Wallace, rebuilding Corralitos was more than a business project but also a labor of love. Soon after the purchase, his workmen began
restoring Casa de Amo, the 18th century home of Juan Azcárate and José
Zuloaga. Carpenters salvaged timbers from wrecked railroad trestles for
ceiling joints. After they put on the roof and completed the walls, windows,

and floors, Wallace hired a skilled woodworker from Mexico City to build furniture. Using hand tools, he made large beds with carved head boards supported by four posters with carved rosettes at the top. Other elaborate pieces included tables, cabinets and counters.[804] The family gradually covered the cabinets and walls with photos, paintings, and memorabilia found on the ranch such as French and U.S. military uniform buttons, coins, arrowheads, prehistoric pots, and stone tools.

Wallace reintroduced quality cattle to the range and rebuilt the ranch operation. Laws covering sizeable land holdings prohibited him from large-scale farming, but he leased the parcels suitable for farming to others, such as the Frito-Lay Company, to grow potatoes.

Bilo Wallace knew many people at all levels, and it served him well. In 1992, the governor of the state, suggested it would be a good idea to sell part of the farmland west of the ranch headquarters to Mennonites. Wallace understood and sold land that became the cheese-producing community of Capulín. When the Mennonites arranged to bring electricity to Capulín, they enabled Wallace to bring a line to Corralitos. Prior to the connection, he and the family relied on generators.

Wallace rebuilt Casa de Amo and a thriving cattle operation as he lived out his life at Corralitos. He and his wife Emerida had four children: Wanda, Wilna, Carmela, and William II. He died in 1972, and was buried next to the family chapel, *Nuestra Señora de Refugio*, Our Lady of Refuge.[805] This little ancient building with its two towers serves as place of worship for the family. Three very old bells hang on a bell rack outside.

William Wallace Jr., a graduate of New Mexico State University in Los Cruces, took over the ranch. Also involved are his sons William W. Wallace III and John Wesley Wallace. The latter, Wes, is the day-to-day ranch manager. Other family members, such as Carmela Wallace, own ranches nearby. Carmela lives in Casas Grandes in a 19th century house she restored near the plaza.

The grand Hacienda Corralitos has shrunk to 64,000 acres (25,900 hectares). The Wallace family manages a modern cattle operation with about 1,200 breeding cows plus calves, bulls, and stock ready for market, for a total of about 2,000 head.[806] No one knows exact dates, but the story of Corralitos started at least 245 years ago and has touched virtually every phase of Casas Grandes Valley history.

Hacienda Tapiecitas

Another revolutionary general, named Ortega, took advantage of his position and acquired Luis Terrazas's Hacienda Tapiecitas. The property is located between the towns of Casas Grandes and Colonia Juárez, north of today's highway. Terrazas had acquired the 194,000 hectares (479,384 acres) in 1898. Ejido Casas Grandes had taken 17,400 hectares (42,996 acres), in 1927 and perhaps more. It is not known how much land Ortega purchased or whether he did anything with the property. Sometime during 1940-41, he sold it to George Martin Jeffers, the grandfather of the present owner Jacquie Jeffers, a niece of Carmela Wallace. Jacquie Jeffers continues to operate Tapiecitas as a cattle ranch.

Bosques de Chihuahua and Chepe

The Mexican North Western Railway Company continued to provide services and substantial employment in the Casas Grandes Valley through the 1930s. However, revenue simply was not adequate to cover each payroll let alone provide a return to investors. Profitable years for the Madera Lumber subsidiary did not consistently offset the railroad losses.

Roy Hoard outlined the problem in a speech to the British bond-holders at Winchester House in London in April 1936. His audience included well-known London financiers. Hoard told them Dr. Pearson and his associates had designed the railroad to service a very large timber and milling industry. The industry never developed fully because of the Revolution. The railroad struggled to survive just by servicing the local economy in the Casas Grandes Valley. The MNWR line looped 800 kilometers from Ciudad Juárez to Ciudad Chihuahua and found it difficult to compete for the lucrative Ciudad Juárez to Ciudad Chihuahua business that could run straight south only 400 kilometers on the state-owned National Railroad.

Hoard tried three-day work weeks and other drastic cost-cutting measures, but legislation benefiting workers negated these cuts and added even more expense. Hoard proposed selling the railroad either to private investors or the government, and the London bond holders agreed.[807]

In 1936, the same year as Hoard's trip to London, the crumbling Pearson mill was torn down. Various, somewhat conflicting stories circulate as to what exactly happened to the mill, but it is clear that the abandoned machinery was hauled away for scrap, and the buildings demolished. The local residents gradually tore down most of the remaining company houses in Barrio Americano to use the materials for other building projects. Some of the plumbing fixtures ended up in homes in Colonia Juárez.

Hoard worked hard to find a buyer, but it took several years of negotiations before an actual sale could be made. He used his connections in Mexico City in an attempt to convince the government to add MNWR to the national system but was rejected after prolonged discussions.

He then opened negotiations with Eloy Santiago Vallina García, the Spanish-born founder of Banco de Comercio Mexicano, the largest bank in Chihuahua. Vallina had connections with investors in Mexico and bankers in New York City. World War II had begun and the demand for lumber and prices increased. This made the uncut timber on the MNWR holdings valuable enough for investors with the capital to exploit. Hoard and the London bond holders thought five million dollars to be a fair price. Vallina agreed, and the lands and railroad sold in 1945.[808] The sale ended Roy Hoard's 35 years with the company and the last vestige of Dr. Pearson's dream. Hoard lived out his life in El Paso as a prominent businessman, philanthropist, and local politician. He died in 1973 at age 87.

Vallina and his syndicate of powerful investors formed an *empresa* or corporation, with headquarters in Madera, *Bosques de Chihuahua Sociedad de Responsabilidad Limitada de Capital Variable*. The president of Mexico, Miguel Alemán Valdéz, was said to have been a silent partner. True or not, the business oriented Alemán issued to Bosques de Chihuahua the all-important forestry permit, *Unidades Industriales de Explotación Forestal*.[809] These permits and their requirements for ecological logging techniques dated back to provisions in the Constitution of 1917.

Bosques de Chihuahua now controlled 315,000 hectares (778,382 acres), an area about a third as big as Dr. Pearson's original purchases. The company expanded rapidly as loggers pushed south and west deep into untouched forests. The Madera mill continued to operate, but the center of the company's sawmill operations shifted to Mesa del Huracán west of the Cumbre Tunnel. The company restored part of the old railroad road-bed that had been constructed in 1915 to bypass the wrecked tunnel. The restored tracks went west to the main line at Cumbre Station and connected the mills on Mesa del Huracán.

The move to Mesa del Huracán placed most of Bosques de Chihuahua's lumbering southeast of Casas Grandes Valley. The company continued to exploit the forests in that direction, leasing lands from ejidos and from the Tarahumara Indians. The company did buy logs and rough-cut lumber from mountain ejidos in Municipio Casas Grandes. The ejidatarios cut trees and hauled the logs by wagon to the railroad at Mata Ortiz and to the Chico station near Chuichupa for transport to the mills.

The rapidly expanding, well-capitalized company formed several subsidiaries to build factories to process forest products like *Celulosa de Chihuahua* near Cuauhtémoc, the Mennonite town. One subsidiary built what became the largest plywood company in Mexico, *Plywood Ponderosa de Mexico*.[810]

When Bosques de Chihuahua took over full operation of the MNWR assets, it became evident the railroad could not make money. Perhaps it was President Alemán's influence, but the government had a change of heart and agreed to take the railroad into the national system. In 1952, Dr. Pearson's old MNWR line became part of the national *Chihuahua al Pacífico*, nicknamed "Chepe," from the logo initials CHP so familiar in northern Chihuahua for the next forty years. Bosques de Chihuahua, as a separate railroad, retained the short 33-kilometer branch line from Cumbre Station to Mesa del Huracán, running the little railroad with three engines.

In November 1954, the Southern Pacific railroad acquired Bosques de Chihuahua's other short line, the El Paso Southern that ran four tenths of a mile over a private bridge from Ciudad Juárez to the El Paso station, where it connected to major U.S. lines.

The huge Bosques de Chihuahua conglomerate rode the 20-year wave of Mexico's economic growth, called the "Mexico Miracle." By the 1960s, payrolls exceeded 25,000 employees. With its financial success, the company also gained a reputation in the forest regions for exploitation and ruthless treatment of small landholders. A variety of protest organizations rose up, representing a wide range of middle-class intellectuals, students, factory workers, and landless campesinos, a familiar pattern in northern Chihuahua. In a broad alliance, they focused on large corporations and the federal government, which they claimed fostered corporate oppression. Their protests took many forms. Workers struck factories. They filed endless complaints and petitions. Sympathetic newspapers published vitriolic accounts of public and private wrongdoing. One extreme radical group carried out an armed attack on the military barracks in Madera. The attack failed, but the fact that the government felt compelled to station soldiers there is indicative of the volatile situation.

Most of the intense conflict took place over the mountains in Madero and Cuauhtémoc municipios and farther south, away from the Casas Grandes Valley. Even there, squatters invaded ranch land, encouraged by radical rhetoric in Janos Municipio. Also, at least one protest organization publicly accused the Jeffers family at Hacienda Tapiecitas of violating land laws.

Bosques de Chihuahua fought back hard, but by the 1970s, the economy had slowed. A terrible setback for the company occurred when the Ciudad Chihuahua chief of police shot and killed Eloy Vallina as he entered his bank one morning in May 1960. The chief claimed Vallina was having an affair with his daughter. Vallina's sons took over the company, but much of the Vallina's political backing had disappeared.

President Luis Echeverría Álvarez, elected in 1970, was not fond of the Vallina family or what it stood for. In April 1971, President Echeverría stepped down from a helicopter in Madera and walked to a podium. There he made a speech, punctuated by the stunning announcement that 250,000 hectares (617,763 acres) of Bosques de Chihuahua's prime timberland would be expropriated and added to a small ejido founded in 1950 called El Largo. This presidential stroke created the largest ejido by area in Mexico.

Government forestry experts deployed to El Largo to help the ejidatarios organize a company to exploit their newly acquired timberlands. Ironically, the ejido contracted with Bosques de Chihuahua to process the cut timber. Nevertheless, the deteriorating economy, strikes, and political disfavor took their toll.

In 1988, Bosques de Chihuahua closed down most of the mill complex at Mesa del Huracán and abandoned the short railroad. From then on, trucks carried whatever lumber was produced.[811] Bosques de Chihuahua's far-flung empire shrank until the remaining assets sold in the 1990s.

The Chihuahua al Pacífico, Chepe, continued to operate on Dr. Pearson's loop from Ciudad Juárez through Madera to La Junta, where it connected to the line that went east to Ciudad Chihuahua and west through Copper Canyon to the coast.

In the late 1950s, Chepe began to convert from steam to diesel engines and in 1956, La Redonda, the Mata Ortiz steam engine round house and repair facility, closed. The powerful diesels could make the run faster and more efficiently, making the intermediate change at Mata Ortiz unnecessary. At the Cumbre summit, workmen blasted a second, larger tunnel through the rock to accommodate the big diesel engines.

As highways improved, demand for train service diminished. The last train from Nuevo Casas Grandes to Ciudad Juárez ran May 15, 1992. When the engineer brought the train to a full stop in front of the station, he was surprised to see a crowd led by prominent citizens and a band playing the railroad corridas, *Maquinista 501* and *La Rielera*. The mood was festive but also bittersweet. The assembled crowd knew they were witnessing the last run between the two cities of a train system that had created their town of Nuevo Casas Grandes and caused it to grow and prosper.[812] Trains continued to operate on reduced schedules south of Nuevo Casas Grandes.

Without fanfare the last train with passenger cars ran from Nuevo Casas Grandes through Mata Ortiz and Madera to La Junta in October of 1996. Freight trains continued to run for a year and one half. The cars carried various products including feed for a large turkey ranch. On February 14, 1998, a train ran from La Junta to Nuevo Casas Grandes and returned with 18 empty cars the next day for the last time.

That month, February 1998, President Ernesto Zedillo Ponce de León privatized Mexican railroads. Ferromax, part of a conglomerate that controlled most of the railroads in Mexico, took over the Chihuahua railroads. Ferromax retained the Chihuahua al Pacífico and Chepe names on the Copper Canyon route. Apparently, the company had no interest, and the government did not issue a concession for the line through the Casas Grandes Valley, finally shutting down the loop line completed by Dr. Pearson 76 years before.

Pino

By the 1990s, it was evident that the loop line's time had passed. The dispatchers ran fewer trains and those mixed passenger and freight cars. In January 1996, José "Pino" Molina, a former railroad employee from Mata Ortiz, took three North American friends on an overnight tour from the Mata Ortiz station to Madera. The brakeman and engineer knew Pino so well that there was never an issue about fares. They and the other railroad workers referred to the three North Americans as *gente de Pino*, Pino's people.

Pino's father and mother moved from Zacatecas to Madera sometime during the Revolution. In those difficult times, Pino's father worked as the Madera dispatcher for the MNWR, controlling movement of the trains by telephone and telegraph. Pino was born in 1928, and he went to work for the railroad in 1943. On his first job, he got up at 4:00 in the morning to make up the trains leaving the Madera terminal. He directed the switch engines as they moved freight and passenger cars around the yard to connect to engines to create trains destined for specific locations.

Pino's mother did not like the cold weather in Madera and the family moved to Mata Ortiz with the younger children, daughters Gregoria "Goya" and Taide and son Amado. Pino followed in 1946 when he became the Mata Ortiz assistant station manager. The company, now owned by Bosques de Chihuahua, promoted him to station chief in 1950. For the next 30 years, he worked in several positions, eventually becoming an inspector, travelling regularly over the entire line. An enthusiastic, outgoing personality, Pino knew everyone on the railroad, and everyone knew him. He was a close friend of Miguel Orozco Franco, the son of Luis Orozco, the Pearson mill employee and partner in the Pearson store with mill-manager C.H. Cooper.

Pino started his own family and had at least one son, who became an accountant. He acquired a property in Barrio Americano that had been built for a station chief named Humberto García. However, his marriage failed, and Pino chose to live in back of his sister Goya's little store near the center of town for many years. He moved back into the house during the last years of his life.

Pino escorted his three guests onto a train that consisted of an engine, one passenger car, one freight car, and a caboose. The logo on the engine had been changed from Chihuahua al Pacífico to Ferromax, suggesting the transfer from national to private control took a few years. The train stopped at desolate stations like El Rucio and Santa Rosa, where a few families boarded while other passengers returning from a shopping trip to Nuevo Casas Grandes disembarked. The train passed through the half-mile long, 33-year-old "new" tunnel at the Cumbre summit. The entrance to the old tunnel, site of the Cumbre Massacre, could be clearly seen from the caboose window.

The jitney on the old MNWR line in Mata Ortiz. Photo: 2006

At Madera, the large, dilapidated station had only one employee. Pino said that when he worked there, the railroad employed sixty. It was a memorable ride but less than two years later, trains on that route were also just a memory.[813]

An immediate problem arose. Despite its diminished condition, the railroad provided a valuable service to those families in the tiny communities and remote ranches along the line. The dirt roads were terrible at best and impossible during rain and floods. To relieve their isolation, a gasoline-powered jitney car provided passenger service. This helped the families, and tour groups even used the car for excursions.

Unfortunately, sometime after 2008, the Casas Grandes municipio removed all of the track from the border of the Nuevo Casas Grandes municipio to the border of the Madera municipio. To compensate, the municipio officials had the right-of-way graded to provide an all-weather road to serve the isolated areas.

Municipio Nuevo Casas Grandes

In 1898, Porfirio Díaz's government built an army barracks near the end of the track that had been laid from Ciudad Juárez the previous year. In 1911, Dr. Pearson's Mexico North Western Railway bought the building and converted it into the Nuevo Casas Grandes station, the beginning of what became a major commercial center. The building served the developing community for the next 87 years, until the last train ran in 1998.

As evidenced by the crowd that gathered to honor the last run to Ciudad Juárez, the community remained conscious of its railroad heritage. Municipio representatives, local citizens, and former railroad men banded together and obtained diesel engine 525, (*Máquina 525*). The Fairbanks Morse 16-44 was built in Canada between 1960 and 1963. A Mexican movie company used it in a movie called *El Último Túnel*. Part of the movie was filmed at the Cumbre Tunnel. The movie had great success, receiving two nominations for the *Premio Ariel*, the Mexican Academy of Motion Pictures' annual award for cinema excellence.[814]

Volunteers and railroad employees installed the engine in front of the station in the refurbished Plaza Mayor. The plaque reads *Nuevo Casas*

Grandes fundó por el paso de una locomotor, "Nuevo Casas Grandes founded by the passage of a locomotive."

By the time Máquina 525 made its last run, highways connected Nuevo Casas Grandes to the major cities of Mexico and to the United States. The city had absorbed Dublán, San José, San Isidro and other surrounding communities to become northwest Chihuahua's economic center.

On April 21, 1923, the Chihuahua state legislature acted to separate Nuevo Casas Grandes from Casas Grandes and create a new municipio. The communities in the municipio included Nuevo Casas Grandes, Dublán, Colonia Madero, Buena Fe, Guadalupe, Corralitos, and Hidalgo. The first president was Tomas Fierro.[815]

Today, Nuevo Casas Grandes serves as the commercial, industrial, educational, health, and agricultural center for the vast northwestern region. The growing population exceeds 65,000 and the city features automobile agencies, a technical school, a university, hospitals, auto-parts factories, food-processing plants, fruit packing houses, grain mills, and a baseball stadium. Máquina 525 stands as a symbol of the community's evolution from an empty plain to a thriving city.

Mata Ortiz Doctor

Dr. Jesús Bautista Fregoso arrived by train in Mata Ortiz in October 1949. He had graduated from medical school in Mexico city, and the Secretary of Health had assigned him to this remote area to perform his social service before receiving his final degree. The obligation was designed to help overcome Mexico's chronic imbalance between medical service in urban centers and the rest of Mexico's small towns and rural countryside. While the young doctor had been educated in Mexico City, he came from a family of fourteen that lived in the country town of Villa Corona in the state of Jalisco. His father worked as the local property distribution agent, carrying out the land reform policies of President Lázaro Cárdenas. This put him in conflict with large landowners, who frequently accosted and threatened him in front of his family. Young Jesús, born in 1923, also witnessed, as a little boy, the terrible brutality in his neighborhood during the Cristero War, 1927-29. Fortunately, his parents sent him to Mexico City to live with an aunt and pursue his education, which eventually included medical school. He understood the social service obligation and accepted his assignment with enthusiasm. A handsome young man with a good sense of humor, he made many friends during his time in the village. After his social service, he established a practice in Nuevo Casas Grandes, becoming one of the medical leaders in the region over the next 50 years. Later in life, he wrote down his memories of those years. These writings provide a glimpse of life in Mata Ortiz at the midcentury mark of the 20th century.

The economic boom that started in Mexico during World War II and continued for 20 years in the postwar period affected Mata Ortiz, even though the huge Pearson mill was closed. Lumber prices remained high, and small mills in the Casas Grandes Valley and mountains above produced significant amount of wood products that freighters brought to a large lumber yard in Mata Ortiz for shipment. Several local men took out loans to buy trucks and become freighters. The introduction of trucks was part of the transition from mule-drawn wagons to gas-powered vehicles in the valley. This appeared to be a profitable business, but Dr. Bautista observed that the rough roads took a terrible toll on the trucks, and the would-be freighter often ended with a broken-down vehicle, no spare parts, and an unpaid loan.

Most of the residents were relatively poor but had enough disposable income to support several stores. Chinese men had small businesses, including an ice cream parlor, but Dr. Bautista makes no mention of them.

Many in town worked on the railroad or in the large repair facility, La Redonda. Others worked the small farms or ran cattle on the ejido land. No one had electricity or running water in their homes.

When Dr. Bautista arrived, Nuevo Casas Grandes, the largest town in the region had about 20,000 inhabitants. It featured a small eight-bed hospital, the Brohez Clinic, and five doctors.[816] Madera, over the mountains to the south, had a small hospital headed by an older doctor, nominally Bautista's supervisor. The new doctor, as a sole practitioner, was expected to cover everything in between, from Santa Rosa and El Rucio south of Mata Ortiz, San Diego, Anchondo, Madero, and Buena Fe to the north, and Pacheco and Jovales in the mountains to the west. There had been little or no medical service in these areas for over 25 years. One exception had been Dr. E. LeRoy Hatch, the Anglo-LDS physician, who had completed his social service in the remote mountainous region of Chuichupa in December 1945 and affiliated with the Brohez Clinic.[817] Later with his long-time partner Dr. Cruz Salas Caraveo, he founded the Cinco de Mayo Clinic in Nuevo Casas Grandes, the most important medical facility in the region for 30 years through the 1970s. Dr. Bautista joined this clinic later.

Like Dr. Hatch before him, Dr Bautista found himself delivering babies and performing life-saving surgeries on kitchen tables under lantern light in dirt-floored houses, sometimes after driving hours on rough dirt roads in his 1936 Chevrolet. The car also served as an ambulance to transport patients over dirt roads to the Brohez Clinic in Nuevo Casas Grandes.

At least one untrained "dentist," who owned a set of forceps, pulled teeth for the desperate in the area. Dr. Bautista obtained his own forceps and took over this role. Other untrained practitioners faded into the background with the doctor's arrival, except for the midwives, who provided a significant service

Dr. Bautista set up his first office and consulting room in two small rooms in the house of Carlos Fierro. He took his meals at Lencha's Comedor, a restaurant and gathering place for lumber and railroad workers and other locals, both men and women. Bautista's lively sense of humor attracted the restaurant regulars in spite of his city clothes and Mexico City accent. Clearly, they were delighted to have a doctor in the community if for only a year.

A particular friend was Miguel Castrejón, a gregarious local businessman and regular at Lencha's. After two weeks Castrejón and his wife, Lupe, proposed that the doctor move into rooms in their much larger house. This worked out well. Dr. Bautista had a patient receiving and waiting room, an examination room, and his own bedroom, all much larger than his previous space. Lupe took over management of Dr. Bautista's pharmaceuticals, a task that relieved Bautista of the embarrassment of prescribing a medicine then charging the patient for it.

He made another good friend at Lencha's, with an unusual heritage. Antonio (Toño) Villa was the son of Pancho Villa and Austreberta Rentería, one of Villa's many mistresses. Toño had a truck and came to Mata Ortiz to work as a lumber freighter. He lived in the village with his wife

Ruth and a son, who Bautista thought looked like his grandfather. His success as a freighter is unknown, but he later worked for the judicial police. After Bautista moved his practice to Nuevo Casas Grandes, he heard Toño had been killed in Ciudad Chihuahua, circumstances unknown.

Part of his required duties involved teaching a nursing assistant class. For six months, he taught medical basics to a group of local women, emphasizing obstetrics, as the services of midwives remained important in the region. His best student was Magdalena Orozco, the wife of Luis Orozco. She must have been considerably younger than Don Luis, who had long since retired from the railroad and Pearson mill. Other stores replaced the one he had run with C. H. Cooper, the manager of the mill 30 years before.

While Mata Ortiz appeared relatively prosperous to Dr. Bautista, the health of the people was poor. For years, the Mexico North Western Railway Company had contracted with doctors from the U.S. to administer to the thousands of employees working in the company mills, forests, and railroad. These departed as the company operations wound down. For more than 25 years, midwives and untrained "doctors" provided most medical services. While some of these women, like Magdalena Orozco, became well known for their skills, the general health of the people of Mata Ortiz and the region had deteriorated.

A chronic problem was typhoid fever. Drinking water from wells, contaminated by bacteria from nearby outhouses, caused the spread of the disease with its debilitating symptoms of fever, diarrhea, weakness, and rash, leading often to death. Another endemic problem was lack of fruit and vegetables in the diet that caused night blindness and scurvy. Dr. Bautista became a kind of public health doctor as he tried to overcome long-held customs to prevent the spread of these and other diseases as well as find cures.

He did have one spectacular success. While he was in medical school, chloramphenicol (Chloromycetin) had been developed. It was so effective against typhoid that he was given a stock of this antibiotic when he left school, along with other basic supplies and instruments necessary for his social service.

Thus, Mata Ortiz became one of the earliest communities in Mexico with access to this miracle drug. Instead of four to six weeks of illness, often with complications, patients now recovered in two to four days. Dr.

Bautista wrote his required thesis at the end of his social-service year on the topic "Epidemiology of Typhoid Fever in Juan Mata Ortiz." It was well received by his review panel in Mexico City, and he received his degree and title, on April 10, 1951.

He decided not to return to Mexico City to pursue his career. After his social service in Mata Ortiz, he saw his opportunity in the Casas Grandes Valley. He established his practice in Nuevo Casas Grandes near the Brohez Clinic. He married a girl from Ciudad Chihuahua he met at a dance and spent almost 50 years as a major figure in Casas Grandes medicine.[818]

Obsolescence and Hard Times

The nationalization of the railroad in 1952 did not affect life in Mata Ortiz much, but the conversion from steam to diesel in 1956 had a profound effect. *La Redonda,* the roundhouse and repair shop, became instantly obsolete and closed.[819] The job loss was significant and had a disastrous economic multiplier effect as stores, hotels, and places of entertainment lost business. The Chinese businessmen, who had survived the vicious persecution of the Revolution, shut down their restaurants and the ice cream parlor and moved. Nuevo Casas Grandes had become the central city in the region, even overshadowing Casas Grandes. Mata Ortiz stagnated.

Families did whatever they could to survive. The railroad still provided some jobs. Juan Quezada worked as a laborer, occasionally using his talents to repaint railroad signs. Sometimes he joined the *bracero* contract labor program in the U.S., as had his father before him. When he was not selected by the labor contractors, and after the program ended in 1964, he crossed illegally on his own. Juan and his brother Nicolás once walked 170 miles to the border to find work. Others worked seasonally in the LDS apple orchards for a few pesos a day. The *ejidatarios,* those with rights to communal rangeland, added more and more cattle. The overgrazed tall grass gradually disappeared to be replaced by thousands of acres of mesquite bushes. Cooperative ownership may be good social policy but can be hard on the range. Farming small plots, *labores,* had always been an important occupation and it became even more important in these hard times. A few women operated small stores from their front rooms selling sodas, toilet paper, dry goods and other nonperishable items. Business was reasonably good, because trains still ran and allowed customers from remote ranches and farms to access the village stores. Craftsmen wove saddle blankets, braided lassos from rawhide, or made wooden furniture to sell.

In spite of *la lucha*, the struggle, the villagers continued their lives following the rhythms of the northern culture. The basic style was Texas cowboy or *tejano* that had evolved on both sides of the border since Spanish times. On Sunday, men and boys looked like cowboys whether they owned cattle or not. Several were experts with stock. Local ranchers came to the village to hire these men, skilled with horses and rope, during round up and branding times. On holidays, the townspeople crowded into the baseball stadium to watch the young men ride bucking horses and small bulls to the enthusiastic accompaniment of a small brass band.

The first walls of the stadium were built in 1963. It was rebuilt with seating in 1989. It was named after Carmelo Ledesma, the father of potter Carmen Veloz, who had great success in the Mexican baseball leagues. Boxing was another local sport. The building that had been a theater and later became the Posada de las Ollas, served for a while as the boxing gym. José "Pino" Molina coached several of the boys there including Juan Quezada. Juan actually had three bouts before retiring undefeated after his mother Paulita intervened.

One teacher taught all six grades in a small building. In 1974, the villagers tore it down and began constructing a new school. It took two years to complete. In the meantime, classes were held in a box car. Several families also lived in box cars that stretched along a remnant of the railroad track at the former La Redonda site.

For twenty years, kerosene lanterns, Coleman lanterns, and candles, provided light. The school teacher, José Murguia López, campaigned for six years to bring electricity to Mata Ortiz. Finally in 1976 power lines were extended to the village. The new school opened with electric lights, the first since the lumber mill powerhouse closed.

Celebrations for weddings, births, birthdays, *quinceañeras* (the coming of age of 15-year-old girls), and deaths followed with their own special traditions. Each Sunday, the priest said mass in the main church, San José, then walked across the arroyo and presided again at the little Porvenir chapel dedicated to the Virgin of Guadalupe. School children with banners and flags marched in parades on Independence Day and Revolution Day. A queen in an elaborate long dress and her attendants rode on horses among the marching children. A community dance at the Salon de Actos followed.

Few came to Mata Ortiz seeking work anymore, but life went on.

The Big Change

This book attempts to pull together in one place the diverse parts of the Pearson, Mata Ortiz, and Casas Grandes Valley history. A picture emerges of a region formed by five centuries of turmoil since the Spanish entrada. Prior to the Spanish, prehistoric people from the north and south converged on the valley to form the Casas Grandes culture. That culture collapsed just before the Spanish arrived, but the ancient people left behind thousands of pieces of ceramic art buried in their ruined great houses. This finely executed ware would remain a curiosity for most and the subject of study by a few until the last quarter of the 20th century.

The Spanish brought European animals and crops to the valley grasslands and a new religion to the various indigenous tribes, who occupied the valley after the demise of the Casas Grandes culture. Few of these tribes survived as separate entities over the next few centuries. At virtually the same time as the Spanish, the Apaches arrived. The contest for dominance between these two vastly different interloper cultures swung back and forth like a pendulum for the next 300 years.

When this conflict finally wound down, Mexico had freed itself from Spanish rule, overcome a French invasion, and seen a liberal democratic government dissolve into dictatorship. By then, a few shrewd entrepreneurs controlled vast areas of northern Chihuahua. These *hacendados* had fought the Apaches, bought property at low prices and accumulated millions of acres they stocked with cattle. In doing so, they created a major economic enterprise as well as a hacienda culture that exploited their workers and kept them in poverty.

During the same period, the authoritative federal and state governments encouraged foreign companies to develop the country's resources

and infrastructure, particularly the railroads. While this provided employment and helped bring northern Chihuahua and the Casas Grandes Valley
into the modern era, resentment against foreign intervention smoldered.

The people of Chihuahua had a deep sense of independence honed by
centuries of combating the Apaches while settling in the rough Chihuahua
environment with limited government assistance. A fledgling middle class
resisted the conservative pressures of the Catholic Church, government,
hacendados, and foreign companies. It is not surprising that the initial
fighting of the 1910 Revolution broke out in Chihuahua and many of the
key battles were fought there along the railroad lines.

The Revolution shattered the Casas Grandes Valley's economy and social
structure. For decades after, those representing the fragmented pieces of the
old establishment struggled and competed with a new, diverse, power elite
to restructure a new society and economy. A revised constitution provided
guidelines, but the remnants of entrenched interests resisted and stalled
the implementation of its articles. Nevertheless, the new land program, the
ejidos, gradually caused a high percentage of the land to be transferred to
communal ownership. This system proved less efficient economically but
met an iconic goal of the Revolution, land redistribution. The government
eventually created over 26 ejidos in the Casas Grandes Valley.

Remnants of the old hacendado class plus new powerful politicians,
often former Revolutionary generals, managed to bypass restrictive constitutional provisions and create large ranches. None approached the size of
the enormous pre-revolution haciendas, but they had a positive effect by
reestablishing the cattle industry in the Valley.

Several of the Anglo LDS colonies did not survive, but enough settlers returned after the Exodus to reclaim their property and rebuild a large
fruit-growing, packing, and marketing industry.

Foreign enterprises, like the Mexican North Western Railway, struggled with new laws, hostile labor conditions, and the constant threat of
expropriation, until the company sold out and was eventually nationalized.

The path of history through the Casas Grandes Valley led to the founding of Pearson/Mata Ortiz just before the Revolution. The town grew,
despite the tumultuous times, until railroad shops closed 56 years later.
Little employment was left for the residents of this former industrial and

railroad town except agriculture through membership in the ejido and working for others.

The people were ready for something else and that came in the form of artistic inspiration from the very earliest era of their valley history. Juan Quezada and others, including Félix Ortiz and Emeterio Ortiz, took the prehistoric Casas Grandes pots they found and tried to make similar objects. With the depressed economy and only sporadic work, they had time to experiment over and over to teach themselves how to create a ceramic piece from finding and processing suitable clay through forming, painting, and firing.

The joint U.S. and Mexican excavation of the prehistoric city of Paquimé brought attention to Casas Grandes ceramics and fueled an illegal market in these finely made pieces. The first sales of Mata Ortiz pottery probably were to unscrupulous traders, who distressed them to look old and sold them as genuine prehistoric pots. Soon, however, others discovered the work and recognized it as a new pottery art form. Juan Quezada, his family members, Félix Ortiz, Emeterio Ortiz, and an expanding group of their neighbors began supplying a fledgling market. When the anthropologist and art historian Spencer MacCallum discovered three of Juan Quezada's pots in a Deming, New Mexico junk store, he made his now well documented odyssey into northern Chihuahua to discover the source.

After meeting Juan, MacCallum spent most of the next eight years working to expose the art world to the ceramic art produced in this obscure Chihuahuan village. His training and experience in art history and anthropology helped him make the right contacts that led to museum exhibitions and extensive publicity. He had a great story and he told it well. Soon a small stream of curious traders, collectors, and academicians braved the potholes and rocks of the road into the village to see for themselves what was happening there. These visits, and the resulting spread of gallery sales and museum exhibitions, had a huge economic impact as more and more pots sold. There was a great incentive. A Mata Ortiz laborer, who learned to make pots by watching Juan or Félix Ortiz, could sell a small pot for an amount equivalent to three full days of hard work in the apple orchards.

Juan Quezada, wearing the white cowboy hat, receives the prestigious Premio Nacional de Ciencias y Artes from the hand of President Ernesto Zedillo, December 1999.

Pottery sales stimulated the entire Casas Grandes Valley economy. This in turn led to an increased standard of living, paved roads, and opportunity for advanced education.

The 20th century ended on an optimistic note. A symbol of the new era was the *Premio* presented to Juan Quezada by the hand of President Ernesto Zedillo in December 1999. The Premio is Mexico's version of the Nobel Prize. Juan Quezada received the award for the category Popular Arts and Culture.

After a long, stormy history, the people of Mata Ortiz and the Casas Grandes Valley stood ready to meet the modern challenges of the 21st century.

Endnotes

Chapter 1

1   Charles H. Lange and Carroll L, Riley (eds), *Southwestern Journals of Adolph Bandelier, 1883-84,* (University of New Mexico Press, Albuquerque, NM, 1966), p. 313.

Chapter 2

2   David A. Yetman, *The Ópatas: In Search of a Sonoran People,* (Arizona Press, Tucson, AZ, 2010), p. 50.

3   Oakah L. Jones Jr., *Nueva Vizcaya: Heartland of the Spanish Frontier*, (University of New Mexico Press, Albuquerque, NM, 1988), pp. 21-23.

4   J. Lloyd Mecham, *Francisco de Ibarra and Nueva Vizcaya,* (Greenwood Press, NY, 1968), pp. 159, 162; Rebecca Carte, *Capturing the Landscape of New Spain, Baltasar Obregón, and the 1564 Expedition*, (University of Arizona Press, Tucson, AZ, 2015). Mecham states clearly that Obregón's and other written records describing the route are unreliable. In her much newer study, Carte makes the same point. The actual details of the expedition, the route, and even the dates may never be known. The account here is based on Mecham.

5   Charles C. Di Peso (au) and Gloria J. Fenner (ed), *Casas Grandes, a Fallen Trading Center of the Gran Chichimeca,* Volumes 1-3, (Northland Press, The Amerind Foundation, Inc./Dragoon, Northland Press/Flagstaff, 1974), p. 820.

6   George P. Hammond and Agapito Rey, *Obregon's History of 16th Century Explorations in Western America,* (Wetzel Publishing Co., Los Angeles, 1928), p. 205.

7   Mecham, p. 76.

Chapter 3

8   Jack Jackson and William O. Foster, *Imaginary Kingdom: Texas as seen by the Rivera and Rubí Expeditions, 1727 and 1767*, (Texas State Historical Association, Austin, 1995). Lafora kept a diary, which was published early and widely used by historians. It was not known until 1989 that Rubí also kept

a diary. It was discovered in an obscure collection of an old Texas family's personal papers.

9   José Agustín de Escudero, *Noticias Estadísticas del Estado de Chihuahua*, (México, 1834).

10 R.W.H. Hardy, Lieut., R.N., *Travels in the Interior of Mexico, in 1825, 1826, 1827 & 1828,* (Rio Grande Press, Inc., Glorieta, NM, 1977). p. 465. First published by Colburn and Bentley, London, 1829. Google digitally scanned the original and the illustrations and page number structure are the same as the 1977 reprint. The pot illustration is on page 465 of both printings.

11 Luz Fernanda Azuela, "Towards a Nationwide Geological Survey in Nineteenth Century Mexico," in *History of Geoscience: Celebrating 50 Years of INHIGEO,* (Geological Society Special Publication 442, 2017), p. 295.

12 Wirt Tassin, "The Casas Grandes Meteorite," *Proceedings of the U.S. National Museum,* 25, no. 1277, (1902), p. 69. This source written in 1902 cites an 1867 reference that describes Muller's involvement.

13 Tassin, p. 69; Oscar E. Monnig, "How the Casas Grandes, Chihuahua Mexico Meteorite Got to Washington D.C.," *Society for Research on Meteorites,* 2, Issue 5, (January 1939), p. 89. In Tassin, Pierson is quoted on the same page as the story about Muller, footnote 4. The 1873 date comes from Monnig.

14 O.C. Farrington, "Catalogue of the Meteorites of North America," *Memoirs of the National Academy of Science,* XIII, (Washington, D.C., 1915), pp. 111-12.

15 Donald Thornberry, personal communication, email July 13, 2015.

16 George P. Merrill and William F. Foshag, "Minerals from Earth and Sky: Part I, The Story of Meteorites," *Smithsonian Scientific Series,* 3, (1929), p. 38.

17 Monnig, "How the Casas Grandes Meteorite Got to Washington," pp. 88-91.

18 August Santleben, *A Texas Pioneer: Early Staging and Overland Freighting Days on the Frontiers of Texas and Mexico,* (The Neale Publishing Co., NY and Washington, 1910), pp. 180-83.

19 Lange and Riley, *Southwestern Journals of Adolph F. Bandelier.*

20 Henry E. Hooper, *Adolph F.A. Bandelier, 1840-1914,* https://henryehooper.blog/witness-post-adolph-bandelier/.

21 Lange and Riley, *Southwestern Journals of Adolph F. Bandelier,* p. 4.

22 Lange and Riley, pp. 236-39, 263, 276.

23 Lange and Riley, p. 287.

24 David E. Doyel, "Interpreting Prehistoric Cultural Diversity," in *Culture and Contact, Charles C. Di Peso's Gran Chichimeca,* Anne I. Woosley and John C. Ravesloot, eds., (Amerind Foundation Publication, University of New Mexico Press, Albuquerque, 1993), pp. 39-64.

25 Ralph L. Beals, "The Comparative Ethnology of Northern Mexico Before 1750," *Ibero Americano,* 2 (1932), p. 93; Di Peso, *Casas Grandes, a Fallen Trading Center,* p. 1.

26   Carl Lumholtz, *Unknown Mexico, Explorations in the Northern Sierra Madre and Other Regions, 1890-1898,* (Dover Publications, 1987). This is the main source for this section.

27   Lumholtz, plates I-IV, between pp. 95-98.

28   Lumholtz, p. 34.

29   Lumholtz, p. 22.

30   Andrew Alfred Jensen, "In Mexico," *Deseret Weekly,* 48, (1894), p. 812.

31   Jensen, p. 812; Lumholtz, *Unknown Mexico,* p. 69.

32   John Hatch, personal communication, March 28, 2018.

33   Lumholtz, *Unknown Mexico,* pp. 88 and 94.

34   David A. Phillips, Jr., Christine Van Pool and Todd Van Pool, *Archaeology and Prehistory of Northwest Mexico, Bibliography,* (2011); https://www.unm.edu/~dap/nwm/nwm-english.html

35   Paul F. Walter, "Edgar Lee Hewitt, Americanist, 1865-1946," *American Anthropologist,* 49 (2) (April-June, 1947), p. 260. https://anthrosource.onlinelibrary.wiley.com/doi/abs/10.1525/aa.1947.49.2.02a00050

36   Alfred V. Kidder, "The Pottery of the Casas Grandes District, Chihuahua," In *The Holmes Anniversary Volume: Anthropological Essays,* (Washington D.C., 1916), pp. 253–68. The publication honored Holmes, artist, cartographer, archaeologist, geologist, and director of the Smithsonian American Archaeology Museum, on his 70th birthday.

37   Donald D. Brand, "The Chihuahua Culture Area," *New Mexico Anthropologist,* 6, Issue 3, (September 1943), p. 116.

38   Di Peso, *Casas Grandes, a Fallen Trading Center of the Gran Chichimeca,* (Amerind Foundation, Dragoon, AZ and Northland Press, Flagstaff, AZ, 1974), First three volumes Viejo, Medio, and Tardio.

39   Centro INAH Chihuahua, *http://inahchihuahua.gob.mx/sections.pl?id=43*

40   Paul Minnis, "Casas Grandes," *Expeditions, The University Museum Magazine of Archaeology and Anthropology,* University of Pennsylvania 35, no. 1, (1993), pp 34-43.

41   Spencer MacCallum to Gloria Fenner, (December 12, 1982). Copy in Walter Parks Collection.

42   Phillips, Van Pool and Van Pool, *Archaeology and Prehistory of Northwest Mexico,* p.2.

43   Stephen Lekson, *Chaco Meridian, One Thousand Years of Political Power*, 2nd ed. (Rowman and Littlefield Publishers, Lanham, MD, 2015); David A. Phillips Jr., "Chaco Meridian, a Skeptical Analysis," revision of a presentation to the Society for American Archaeology in 2000. https://www.unm.edu/~dap/meridian/meridian-text.html Dr. Phillips of the University of New Mexico critically analyzes Lekson's theory.

44   David A. Phillips, Jr., "The End of Casas Grandes: The Legacy of Charles C. Di Peso Fifty Years After the Joint Casas Grandes Project," 73rd annual meeting of the Society for American Archaeology, Vancouver, Canada, (March 27, 2008), p. 6.

45   R. B. Brown, personal communication, notes from his lecture, Idyllwild Arts, Idyllwild, CA, (July 1, 1990).

46   Barbara Moulard, *Within the Underworld Sky, Mimbres Ceramic Art in Context,* (Twelvetrees Press, Pasadena, CA, 1984), p. xvi; Albert Schroeder, "Southwestern Ceramics, a Comparative Review," *The Arizona Archaeologist,* Arizona Archaeology Society, no. 15, (August, 1982), pp. 212-16.

47   Joe D. Stewart, Jane Kelley, A.C. MacWilliams and Paula J. Reimer, "The Viejo Period of Chihuahua Culture in Northwestern Mexico," *Latin American Antiquity,* 16, no. 2 (June, 2005).

48   Charles C. Di Peso, John B. Rinaldo and Gloria J. Fenner, *Casas Grandes, a Fallen Trading Center of the Gran Chichimeca,* vol. 6, (1974), p. 77. In Volume 6 of the Joint Expedition report, Di Peso and his colleagues present an extremely detailed analysis of the pottery from the Viejo and Medio Periods. This includes dozens of pictures of pots, dimensions, and design elements.

49   Cornelia G. Harcum, "Indian Pottery from the Casas Grandes Region, Chihuahua, Mexico," *Bulletin of the Royal Ontario Museum of Archeology* (December, 1923), pp. 4-11; M. J. Hendrickson, "Design Analysis of Chihuahuan Polychrome Jars from North American Museum Collections," (MA thesis, University of Calgary, AB, 2001), p. 64.

50   David Phillips, "Archaeology and Prehistory of Northwest Mexico: A Rough Essay," https://unm.edu/~dap/nwm/introduction.html

51   Donald D. Brand, "The Distribution of Pottery Types in Northwest Mexico," *American Anthropologist,* 37, (April-June, 1935), pp. 287-305.

52   Roy L. Carlson, "The Polychrome Complexes," in *Southwestern Ceramics: A Comparative Review, Arizona Archaeologist,* Albert H. Schroeder (ed), no. 15, (1982), p. 213.

53   Harold S. and Winifred Gladwin, "A Method for Designation of Cultures and Their Variations," *Medallion Papers,* no. XV, (1934), Gila Pueblo, Globe, AZ.

54   Gladwin and Gladwin, pp. 11-13.

55   A. V. Sayles, Forward to "Some Southwestern Pottery Types," *Medallion Papers* XXI, (1936), Gila Pueblo, Globe, AZ.

56   W. Rodney Long, *Railways of Mexico,* Trade Promotion Series no. 16, Department of Commerce, (Washington D.C., 1925), pp. 161-63.

57   Jane Kelley, David A. Phillips Jr., A. C. McWilliams and Rafael Cruz Antillón, "Chihuahua, Mexico: A Speculative History," *Journal of the Southwest,* 53, no. 2 (Summer 2011), p. 203.

58   Kelley, et al "Land Use, Looting, and Archaeology," p. 200.

59   Harcum, "Indian Pottery from the Casas Grandes Region," p. 4; Kelley et al., "Land Use, Looting, and Archaeology," pp. 201-02.

Chapter 4

60   Di Peso, *Casas Grandes, a Fallen Trading Center*, p. 827.

61   "Records of the Presidio de San Felipe y Santiago de Janos, 1706-1858," Nettie Lee Benson Latin American Collection, General Libraries, University of Texas at Austin. This appears to be the best source for the date. However, other sources have the founding date for Janos as late as 1640. See Ortega Urquidi, p. 29 and Di Peso, p. 998, note 20; Forbes, pp. 49-54. These passages describe an expedition north into New Mexico by the three padres and soldiers, led by Padre Rodríguez. Forbes says they were killed in New Mexico.

62   Javier Ortega Urquidi, *Casas Grandes, Tierra de Siete Culturas*, (Socia Creativa, Mexico, 2008), p. 29.

63   Di Peso, *Casas Grandes, a Fallen Trading Center*, p. 864; Anne E. Hughes, *The Beginnings of Spanish Settlement in the El Paso District*, University of California Publications in History, 1, no. 3, (University of California Press, Berkeley, 1914), pp. 311-12.

64   Dan Scurlock, *High Desert Land and Its Peoples: A Guidebook to the Eco-Cultural History and Archeology of the Casas Grandes Area, Chihuahua, Mexico*, (El Valle del Norte, Albuquerque, NM, 1992), p. 16.

65   France V. Scholes, Marc Simmons, and José Antonio Esquibel, eds., Eleanor B. Adams, trans., *Juan Domínguez de Mendoza: Soldier and Frontiersman of the Spanish Southwest, 1637-1693*, (University of New Mexico Press, Albuquerque, 2012).

66   Di Peso, *Casas Grandes, a Fallen Trading Center*, p. 900.

67   Lance R. Blyth, *Chiricahua and Janos, Communities of Violence in the Southwestern Borderlands, 1680-1880*, (University of Nebraska Press, Lincoln, NE, 2012), p. 25.

68   Di Peso, *Casas Grandes, a Fallen Trading Center*, p. 345; Elías Guerrero Ramos, personal communication, email, September 23, 2017.

69   Di Peso, *Casas Grandes, a Fallen Trading Center*, p. 900. Sources differ as to the spelling of de Gracia's name. Variations include Gracia, Gracía and García.

70   Di Peso, p. 867; Sonja Sonnenburg de Chávez, "After the Pueblo Revolt, Part 2," *Linealist* (December 18, 2015); Blyth, *Chiricahua and Janos*, p. 139. Di Peso says that the distance between Ramos and Casas Grandes was 15.5 miles. Map study indicates the distance by road or trail to be a minimum of 20 miles. Blyth's map on p. 139 shows Ramos in relation to Janos and Casas

Grandes. Sonnenburg de Chávez's research of original documents indicates that Ramírez was officially granted land in "Casas Grandes" in 1678.

71   Donald D. Brand, "The Chihuahua Cultural Area," *New Mexico Anthropologist*, 6, no. 3, (1943), pp. 115-58. This was based on his PhD dissertation, "The Historical Geography of Northwestern Chihuahua," University of California, (1933).

72   Victor "Cacho" Barrio, personal communication, March, 2018, Rancho Ramos, Chih.

73   Sonnenburg de Chávez, "After the Pueblo Revolt."

74   Jack D. Forbes, *Apache, Navaho, and Spaniard*, (Univ. of Oklahoma Press, Norman, OK, 1994), p. xiii.

75   Blyth, *Chiricahua and Janos*, p. 31.

76   Grenville and Neil Goodwin, *Apache Diaries: A Father-Son Journey*, (University of Nebraska Press, Lincoln, NE, 2000), p. 3.

77   Di Peso, *Casas Grandes, a Fallen Trading Center*, p. 867.

78   Forbes, *Apache, Navaho, and Spaniard*, pp. 35, 191; Blyth, *Chiricahua and Janos*, p. 33.

79   Di Peso, *Casas Grandes, a Fallen Trading Center*, p. 999, note 26.

80   Roberto César Baca Miranda, *Recopilación de datos históricos de Casas Grandes, La Antigüa Paquimé*, (Artedigital, Nuevo Casas Grandes, Chih., 2007), pp. 17, 20. A single copy of this rare book was found in the Library of Congress.

81   Baca Miranda, pp. 20-21. This source also uses Cañón del Diablo for the battle site. Blyth, p. 26, calls the site Sierra del Diablo and locates it 30 leagues from Casas Grandes. This is unlikely given the long distance to cover to and from in one day. Di Peso, p. 869 calls it Peñol del Diablo. By any name, the authors have not located the site.

82   Peter Krenn, Paul Kalus and Bert Hall, "Material Culture and Military History: Test Firing Early Modern Small Arms," *Material Culture Review*, 42, no. 1 (Fall 1995). https://journals.lib.unb.ca/index.php/MCR/article/view/17669

83   Hughes, *The Beginnings of Spanish Settlement in the El Paso District*, p. 364.

84   Forbes, *Apache, Navaho, and Spaniard*, p. 244.

85   Blyth, *Chiricahua and Janos*, p. 28.

86   Di Peso, *Casas Grandes, a Fallen Trading Center*, pp. 864-75, (smelter, note 26), and 1002 (bodies, note 76); Forbes, *Apache, Navaho, and Spaniard*, pp. 159, 182-83, 190, 200-201, 203, 208; Blyth, *Chiricahua and Janos*, 34-35; Hughes, *Beginnings of Spanish Settlement*, pp. 343-45; Baca Miranda, *Casas Grandes*, pp. 17-23. The narrative of San Antonio de Padua de Casas Grandes and the Battle of Penón del Diablo was compiled from these secondary sources. They do not always agree on the interpretation of the primary source letters and

reports. The compilation here attempts to follow the most logical sequence of events.

87   William B. Griffen, *Indian Assimilation in the Franciscan Area of Nueva Vizcaya*, Anthropology papers of the University of Arizona, no. 33, (University of Arizona Press, Tucson AZ, 1979), p. 88.

88   C. E. Campbell, *Mines, Cattle, and Rebellion, the History of the Corralitos Ranch*, (Green Street Publications, Sunset Beach, CA, 2014), pp. 23-24 and Notes 6, 9, and 10, pp. 373-74.

Chapter 5

89   Florence C. and Robert Lister, *Chihuahua, Storehouse of Storms*, (University of New Mexico Press, Albuquerque, NM, 1966), p. 65.

90   Jones, *Nueva Vizcaya*, p. 119.

91   Lister and Lister, *Storehouse of Storms*, p. 58.

92   Lister and Lister, p. 310.

93   Jones, *Nueva Vizcaya*, p. 121.

94   Thomas Naylor and Charles Polzer, *Pedro de Rivera and the Military Regulations for Northern New Spain, 1724-1729*, (University of Arizona Press, Tucson, AZ, 1988), p. 80.

95   Jones, *Nueva Vizcaya*, p. 131.

96   Jones, p. 105; Jackson and Foster, *Imaginary Kingdom*, p. 9.

97   Jackson and Foster, pp. 62-63.

98   Jones, *Nueva Vizcaya*, p. 139.

99   Lister and Lister, *Storehouse of Storms*, p. 67.

100   Jones, *Nueva Vizcaya*, p. 152.

101   Blyth, *Chiricahua and Janos*, p. 67. Jones, p. 153.

102   Jones, pp. 158-59.

103   Naylor and Polzer, *Pedro de Rivera and the Military Regulations*, pp. 71-72.

104   Lawrence Kinnaird, *The Frontiers of New Spain, Nicolás De Lafora's Description, 1766-1768*, (The Quivira Society, Berkeley, 1958, Arno Press Inc., New York, 1967), p. 99.

105   Griffen, *Indian Assimilation in the Franciscan Area of Nueva Vizcaya*, p. 88; Kinnaird, *The Frontiers of New Spain.* p. 99.

106   Jackson and Foster, *Imaginary Kingdom*, pp. 191, 198.

107   Jackson and Foster, pp. 211-21. These and subsequent pages discuss the reactions to Rubí's plan, his character and motives. After his Mexican assignment, he returned to Madrid.

108   Mark Santiago, "The Red Captain, The Life of Hugo O'Conor," *The Arizona Historical Society Museum Monograph*, no. 9 (1994), p. 5.

109   Santiago, p. 23.

110   Blyth, *Chiricahua and Janos*, p. 65.

111 Blyth, p. 67.

112 Jones, *Nueva Vizcaya*, p. 164.

113 Jackson and Foster, *Imaginary Kingdom*, pp. 214-15.

114 Lister and Lister, *Storehouse of Storms*, p. 68; *Historia de Ejido Casas Grandes: Resumen Ejido Casas Grandes, Chihuahua, Mexico*; https://sites.google.com /site/ejidocasasgrandes/historia-del-ejido

115 Jane-Dale Lloyd, *El distrito Galeana en los albores de la revolución*, (Secretaría de Educación, Cultura y Deporte, Gobierno del Estado de Chihuahua, 2011), pp. 255-56.

116 Blyth, *Chiricahua and Janos*, p. 56. Griffen, *Apaches at War and Peace*, p. 24. Griffen does not use the term "abandoned."

117 Griffen, *Assimilation in the Franciscan Area of Nueva Vizcaya*, p. 89.

118 Griffen, *Apaches at War and Peace*, p. 139.

119 Griffen, p. 175.

120 Edwin R. Sweeney, *Mangas Coloradas; Chief of the Chiricahua Apaches*, (University of Oklahoma Press, Norman, OK, 1998), p. 75.

121 Sweeney, p. 95.

122 Jones, *Nueva Vizcaya*, p. 198.

123 Blyth, *Chiricahua and Janos*, p. 89.

124 Blyth, p. 118.

125 Lister and Lister, *Storehouse of Storms*, pp. 84-86; Henry Bamford Parkes, *A History of Mexico*, (The University Press, Cambridge, Houghton Mifflin, Boston, 1938), pp. 144-54.

126 Lister and Lister, *Storehouse of Storms*, p. 81; Jones, Nueva Vizcaya, pp. 218, 223.

127 Parkes, *History of Mexico*, p. 157.

128 Joan Haslip, *The Crown of Mexico: Maximilian and his Empress Carlotta*, (Holt, Rinehart, and Winston, NY, 1976), p. 142; Robert McCaa, "The Peopling of Mexico from Origins to Revolution" in *The Population History of North America*, eds. Michael R. Haines and Richard Steckel (Cambridge University Press, 1997).

129 Jones, *Nueva Vizcaya*, pp. 222-23; Lister and Lister, *Storehouse of Storms*, pp. 87-88; Fernando Jordán Juárez *Crónica de un País Bárbaro*, (Centro Librero, La Prensa, Chihuahua, Chih., 1981), pp. 219-20.

130 CNN Wire Staff and AP Archive, https://www.youtube.com/watch?v =CDSLb3SRzTAhttps://www.youtube.com/watch?v=CDSLb3SRzTA,

131 Lister and Lister, *Storehouse of Storms*, p. 88.

132 La SEDATU, Boletín 316, *Resuelve el Gobierno de la República conflicto agrario del Ejido Casas Grandes, Chihuahua* (2016).

133 Griffen, *Apaches at War and Peace*, p. 142.

134 Griffen, pp. 30, 46.

135 Lieutenant R.W.H. Hardy, *Travels in the Interior of Mexico in 1825, 1826, 1827 & 1828*, (Rio Grande Press, Inc., Glorieta, NM, 1977), pp. 457-68. Hardy travelled throughout Mexico 1825-1828 and his experiences were originally published by Colburn and Bentley, London, 1829.

136 Lister and Lister, *Storehouse of Storms*, p. 98.

137 Blyth, *Chiricahua and Janos*, p. 133.

138 Sweeney, *Mangas Coloradas*, p. 64.

139 Sweeney, p. 84.

140 Lister and Lister, *Storehouse of Storms*, p. 118.

141 Michael Wasserman, *Capitalists, Caciques, and Revolution*, (University of North Carolina Press, Chapel Hill, NC, 1984), p. 49.

142 Jordán Juárez, *Crónica de un País Bárbaro*, p. 250.

143 Edwin R. Sweeney, *Cochise, Chiricahua Apache Chief*, (University of Oklahoma Press, Norman, OK, 1991), p. 6.

144 Blyth, *Chiricahua and Janos*, p. 145.

145 Parkes, *History of Mexico*, p. 200.

146 Parkes, p. 215.

147 John S. D. Eisenhower, *So Far from God, the U.S. War with Mexico 1846-1848*, (Random House, NY, 1989), pp. 246-47.

148 W. H. Timmons, "The El Paso Area in the Mexican Period, 1821-1848," *The Southwestern Historical Quarterly*, 84, no. 1 (July 1980), Texas State Historical Association, p. 24.

149 Paul Andrew Hutton, *The Apache Wars*, (Broadway Books, NY, 2016), p. 4.

150 Blyth, *Chiricahua and Janos*, p. 145.

151 Campbell, *History of the Corralitos Ranch*, p. 25. The exact sale date is unclear. Campbell uses a different date on page 24. The Zuloaga family controlled the hacienda by 1840.

152 Campbell, pp. 23-25, notes 9,10,11, p. 374. Dr. Campbell made an extensive six-year study of the archives, containing records and correspondence relating to Corralitos. He interviewed William Wallace II, other members of the Wallace family, and the descendants of other important figures in the Corralitos story. He also interviewed historian Dr. William Griffith, an expert in the region. Unless otherwise noted, much of the section is based on this reference.

153 Sweeney, *Mangas Coloradas*, p. 473, note 14; Campbell, *History of the Corralitos Ranch*, p. 30.

154 John Russell Bartlett, *Personal Narrative of Explorations and Incidents in Texas, New Mexico, California, Sonora, and Chihuahua*, (Appleton and Company, New York, 1854).

155 Miguel Méndez García and Leopoldo Horacio Chávez, personal communication with Adalberto Pérez Meillón, email February 17, 2019.

156 Campbell, *History of the Corralitos Ranch*, p. 28.

157 Griffen, *Apaches at War and Peace*, p. 244.

158 Campbell, *History of the Corralitos Ranch*, pp. 39-40 and Griffen, pp. 242-43.

159 Bartlett, *Personal Narrative of Explorations*, p. 346.

160 Bartlett, pp. 364-5.

161 Griffen, *Apaches at War and Peace*, pp. 227-28. Many of the reports and correspondence from the Janos presidio survived and are part of the Benson Collection at the University of Texas, Austin. See Bibliography, "Janos Reports." The authors of this narrative examined other parts of the Benson Collection but depended on Campbell, Blyth, and Griffen for interpreting the Janos material.

162 Hutton, Apache Wars, p. 11.

163 Blyth, *Chiricahua and Janos*, pp. 141-45; Ralph Adam Smith, *Borderlander, The Life of James Kirker, 1793-1852,* (University of Oklahoma Press, Norman, OK, 1999), pp. 152-66; Jason Betzinez, *I Fought with Geronimo,* (University of Nebraska Press, Lincoln, NB, 1987), pp. 3-8. Smith summarizes various versions of this double massacre.

164 Blyth, *Chiricahua and Janos*, p. 165.

165 John Carey Cremony, *Life Among the Apaches,* (University of Nebraska Press, Lincoln, NB, 1983), p. 177; Sweeney, Mangas Coloradas, p. 201.

Chapter 6

166 Blyth, *Chiricahua and Janos*, p. 171.

167 Parkes, *History of Mexico*, pp. 224-29.

168 Parkes, pp. 242-43.

169 Parkes, p. 243.

170 Parkes, p. 238.

171 Haslip, *Maximilian and his Empress*, p. 180.

172 Parkes, *History of Mexico*, p. 256.

173 Lister and Lister, *Storehouse of Storms*, p. 147.

174 Blyth, *Chiricahua and Janos*, pp. 178-79.

175 Michael Hogan, *Abraham Lincoln and Mexico*, (Egret Books, San Diego, 2016), p. 143.

176 Blyth, *Chiricahua and Janos*, p. 181.

177 Sweeney, *Cochise, Chiricahua Apache Chief*, p. 344.

178 Lister and Lister, *Storehouse of Storms*, p. 149.

179 Blyth, *Chiricahua and Janos*, p.189.

180 John Mason Hart, *Empire and Revolution, The Americans in Mexico Since the Civil War,* (University of California Press, Berkeley, CA, 2001), pp. 6, 26.

181 Hart, pp. 26-67. Hart provides an in-depth discussion of the complex financial issues and their effect on the rise of Porfirio Díaz to power.

182 Eve Ball, *In the Days of Victorio, Recollections of a Warm Springs Apache,* (University of Arizona Press, Tucson, AZ, 1970), p. 22.

183 Dan L. Thrapp, *Victorio and the Mimbres Apaches,* (Univ. of Oklahoma Press, Norman, OK, 1974), p. 8.

184 Thrapp, *Victorio and the Mimbres Apaches,* p. 205.

185 Ball, *In the Days of Victorio,* pp. 66-67. The author, telling Apache James Kaywaykla's story, provides a revealing description of a hideout and Apache life on the trail.

186 Blyth, *Chiricahua and Janos,* p. 192; Thrapp, *Victorio and the Mimbres Apaches,* p. 190. Thrapp provides a detailed description of Victorio's movements and the movements of the various Army units to intercept him.

187 Thrapp, p. 290.

188 Thrapp, pp. 255, 291, 366, Note 9.

189 Blyth, *Chiricahua and Janos,* p. 192; Thrapp, *Victorio and the Mimbres Apaches,* p. 294. The references use reales. Mexico converted to a decimal system of pesos and centavos in 1863 but retained the 8 reales coin, which equaled one peso. The U.S. Morgan silver dollar contained almost the same amount of silver as the peso in 1880.

190 Blyth, *Chiricahua and Janos,* pp. 192-96; Thrapp, *Victorio and the Mimbres Apaches,* pp. 293-311; Dan L. Thrapp, *Conquest of Apacheria,* (University of Oklahoma Press, Norman, OK, 1975), pp. 208-9; Lister and Lister, *Storehouse of Storms,* p. 64; Betzinez, *I Fought with Gerónimo,* pp. 52-53. Most of our summary of the battle was compiled from these sources.

191 Blyth, *Chiricahua and Janos,* p. 196.

192 Dan L. Thrapp, *Juh: An Incredible Indian,* (Texas Western Press, Univ. of Texas, Austin, TX, 1973), p. 21.

193 Thrapp, *Juh: An Incredible Indian,* pp. 25-28.

194 Ball, *In the Days of Victorio,* pp. 136-45; Betzinez, *I Fought with Gerónimo,* p. 56. Betzinez is said to have been born in 1860, dying at 100 in 1960. However, he describes himself in this account as a child below warrior age.

195 Betzinez, *I Fought with Gerónimo,* pp. 70-75; Ball, *In the Days of Victorio,* pp. 136-45; Britton Davis, *The Truth About Gerónimo,* (University of Nebraska Press, Lincoln, NB, 1976), pp. 144-50; Thrapp, *Juh: An Incredible Indian,* pp. 29-35; Thrapp, *The Conquest of Apacheria,* p. 292; Blyth, *Chiricahua and Janos,* pp. 197-98; Donald E. Worcester, *The Beginnings of the Apache Menace of the Southwest,* (University Press, Albuquerque, NM, 1941), pp. 252-54; Lister & Lister, *Storehouse of Storms,* p. 165. All of these respected sources have somewhat different versions of the exodus of Chief Loco's people from

San Carlos. Betzinez and Davis were eyewitnesses. This account attempts to summarize the core story from these sources. Thrapp says in *The Conquest* that the Janos attack was on Aliso Creek near its junction with the Janos (San Pedro) River.

196 Thrapp, *Juh: An Incredible Indian*, p. 29.

197 Blyth, *Chiricahua and Janos*, p. 198.

198 Betzinez, *I Fought with Gerónimo*, pp. 71, 77.

199 Lister & Lister, *Storehouse of Storms*, p. 165.

200 Philip Stover, *Traición a La Boquilla*, PowerPoint presentation, Chihuahua State Archive, Ciudad Chihuahua, Chihuahua, MX, October 16, 2021. Personal communication, email, November 2, 2021. Stover has made an extensive study of the massacre event. The exact location is not known, but he has determined the most logical place. Betzinez says the Apache camped outside the walls of Casas Grandes. Stover has discounted this for a variety of reasons, particularly safety. Apaches would not have picked such a vulnerable position. As it was, many were able to defend themselves and escape in spite of their drinking.

201 Betzinez, *I Fought with Gerónimo*, pp. 93-96; Blyth, *Chiricahua and Janos*, p. 199; Lister & Lister, *Storehouse of Storms*, p. 166; Thrapp, *Juh: An Incredible Indian*, p. 38.

202 Lister and Lister, *Storehouse of Storms*, p. 164.

203 Ball, *In the Days of Victorio*, p. 148; Betzinez, *I Fought with Gerónimo*, p. 122; Davis, *Truth About Gerónimo*, p. 71; Thrapp, *Juh: An Incredible Indian*, p. 39. There are several versions of Juh's death, some suggest he was not drunk or that he fell in the Casas Grandes River not a mountain river. This account is based on these three sources.

204 Worcester, *Beginnings of the Apache Menace*, p. 258.

205 Davis, *Truth About Gerónimo*, pp. 198-212.

206 Worcester, *Beginnings of the Apache Menace*, pp. 75, 269-70. Worcester provides a good description of the qualities and value of the Apache scouts.

207 Betzinez, *I Fought with Gerónimo*, pp. 112-14; Blyth, *Chiricahua and Janos*, p. 201.

208 Lange and Riley, *Southwestern Journals of Adolph F. Bandelier*, pp. 290-91.

209 Davis, *Truth About Gerónimo*, pp. 122-23.

210 Worcester, *Beginnings of the Apache Menace*, p. 163.

211 Davis, *Truth About Gerónimo*, pp. 144-46; Worcester, p. 289.

212 Davis, p. 153.

213 Davis, p. 144, map, pp. 183-84.

214 Worcester, *Beginnings of the Apache Menace*, p. 294; Davis pp. 188-89.

215 Arlington Cemetery Website, Emmet Crawford. https://ancexplorer.army. mil/publicwmv/index.html#/search-all/

216 Davis, *Truth About Gerónimo*, pp. 198-201; Jerry Eagan, *Desert Exposure* website, May, 2007, p. B14.

217 Eagan, *Desert Exposure* website, August, 2007, pp. B14-B16.

218 Arlington Cemetery Website, Emmet Crawford; Eagan, *Desert Exposure,* August, 2007, pp. B14-B16; Betzinez, *I Fought with Gerónimo,* pp. 131-33; Blyth, *Chiricahua and Janos,* pp. 203-05; Worcester, *Beginnings of the Apache Menace,* pp. 288-99.

219 Davis, *Truth About Gerónimo*, pp. 223-27. Davis was not present, but he had access to Gatewood's memoirs.

220 Worcester, *Beginnings of the Apache Menace,* p. 306.

221 Betzinez, *I Fought with Gerónimo,* pp. 197-98.

222 Douglas V. Meed, *They Never Surrendered, Bronco Apaches of the Sierra Madres, 1890-1935*, (Westernlore Press, Tucson, AZ, 1993), pp. 226-27; Worcester, *Beginnings of the Apache Menace,* p. 313.

223 Meed, p. 148.

Chapter 7

224 Héctor Chávez Barrón, *Luis Terrazas,* (Editorial Clío, Mexico City, 2004), p.198.

225 Francisco R. Almada and Guillermo Porras, *Luis Terrazas, Una Polémica Histórica*, (Ediciones del Azar A.C., Chihuahua, 1999), p. 6.

226 María Eloísa Solís Terrazas, "Vascos en Chihuahua: relato de migración histórico," *El Universal,* (26 November, 2005).

227 Almada and Porras, *Una Polémica Histórica,* p. 77.

228 Jane-Dale Lloyd, *El distrito Galeana en los Albores de la Revolución*, (Gobierno del Estado de Chihuahua, Chih., 2011), p. 45; Chávez Barrón, *Luis Terrazas,* p. 217.

229 Chávez Barrón, p. 49.

230 Diana Acosta Ramírez, *Ex Hacienda de San Diego, Patrimonio Histórico de Casas Grandes,* Agave Lindo Tours, (2010), p. 3; Zacarías Márquez Terrazas, *"Terrazas y su siglo,"* (Editorial Camino, Chih. México,1991), p. 292.

231 Alina Argüelles González, coord., *Inventario del Archivo Municipal de Cuauhtémoc,* (Apoyo al Desarrollo de Archivos y Bibliotecas de México, A.C., 2008), p. 11.

232 Almada and Porras, *Una Polémica Histórica,* p. 14.

233 Mark Wasserman, *Capitalists, Caciques, and Revolution,* (*University of North Carolina Press, Chapel Hill, NC, 1984),* p. 49; Chávez Barrón, *Luis Terrazas,* p. 217. Sources vary as to the purchase dates and size of Terrazas's haciendas.

This account relies on Wasserman's chart p. 49 and Chávez Barrón's chart, p. 217.

234 Chávez Barrón, *Luis Terrazas*, p. 134.

235 Lister and Lister, *Storehouse of Storms*, p. 153; Chávez Barrón, *Luis Terrazas*, p. 135.

236 Lister and Lister, pp. 151-52; Wasserman, *Capitalists*, p. 50; David Walker, *Kinship, Business and Politics, The Martínez del Río Family in Mexico 1823-1867*, (University of Texas Press, Austin, TX, 2021), pp. 222-26.

237 Walker, *Martínez del Río Family*, p. 224.

238 Lister and Lister, *Storehouse of Storms*, pp. 151-52.

239 Ortega Urquidi, *Tierra de Siete Culturas*, pp. 73-74.

240 Diana Acosta Ramírez, personal communication, San Diego, Chih., April 15, 2015.

241 Lister and Lister, *Storehouse of Storms*, p. 205.

242 Acosta Ramírez, *Patrimonio Histórico*, p. 5. Much of the description of the San Diego buildings comes from this source or personal observation by the authors.

243 Guillermo Porras Muñoz, *Haciendas de Chihuahua*, (Gobierno del Estado de Chihuahua, Coordinación de Comunicación Social, Chih., MX, 1993), p.79.

244 William B. Griffen, *Apaches at War and Peace, the Janos Presidio, 1750-1856*, (University of Oklahoma Press, Norman, OK, 1988), pp. 108, 196.

245 Sweeney, *Mangas Coloradas*, p. 46.

246 Lange and Riley, *Southwestern Journals of Adolph F. Bandelier 1883-1884*, p. 313.

247 Ejido Casas Grandes, Chih., México; https://sites.google.com/site/ejidocasas grandes/acerca-del-ejido

248 Lister and Lister, *Storehouse of Storms*, p. 145.

249 Ortega Urquidi, *Siete Culturas*, p. 77.

250 Internet Archives Open Library, Alfonso Lancaster Jones; https://open library.org/authors/OL4278177A/Alfonso_Lancaster-Jones?sort=old

251 Philip R. Stover, personal communication, August 15, 2018.

252 Chávez Barrón, *Luis Terrazas*, p. 217.

253 Wasserman, *Capitalists*, p. 49; Baca Miranda, *Casas Grandes*, p. 42. Sources differ on the San Diego acreage. Baca Miranda uses 91,098 acres.

254 Lloyd, *El distrito Galeana*, p. 252.

255 Miguel Méndez García, *Ejido Casas Grandes, 1778-2013, 235 Años de Historia*, self-published, pp. 111-15. In 2007, the president of the Janos ejido gave Méndez permission to copy the original document held by the Janos ejido archive. R. Nava interpreted the handwritten document and Méndez reproduced it along with other relevant documents.

256 Alonso Domínguez, "La Desintegración del Latifundio Terrazas, Historia de la Propiedad," en *Chihuahua Hoy*, (2011), p. 116. https://elibros.uacj.mx/omp/index.php/publicaciones/catalog/download/63/58/518-1?inline=1

257 Porras Muñoz, *Haciendas de Chihuahua*, Section about San Diego.

258 Wasserman, *Capitalists*, pp. 52-53.

259 Wasserman, p. 41.

260 Wasserman, pp. 77, 80, 81.

261 Jane-Dale Lloyd, "Rancheros and Rebellion: The Case of Northwestern Chihuahua, 1905-1909," in *Rural Revolt in Mexico: U.S Intervention and the Domain of Subaltern Politics*, Daniel Nugent (ed.), (Duke University Press, Durham and London, 1998), pp. 107-33.

262 Lloyd, *El distrito Galeana*, p. 231; Wasserman, *Capitalists*, p. 105.

263 Lloyd, *El distrito Galeana*, pp. 231, 233, 252.

264 Baca Miranda, *Casas Grandes*, p. 41.

265 Miguel Méndez García, personal communication, Nuevo Casas Grandes, March 25, 2018.

266 Lloyd, *El distrito Galeana*, pp. 252-64; Baca Miranda, *Casas Grandes*, p. 41.

267 John Mason Hart, *Empire and Revolution, The Americans in Mexico Since the Civil War*, (University of California Press, Berkeley, CA, 2001), p. 209.

268 Germán Galaz Levario, telephone interview with Señor Galaz by Adalberto Pérez Meillón, September 28, 2018.

269 Nellie Spilsbury Hatch and B. Carmon Hardy, *Stalwarts South of the Border*, (self-published, 1985), p. 319.

270 Lloyd, *distrito Galeana*, p. 260.

271 Lloyd, pp. 302-11.

272 Interpretative material in Tomochi Museum, Tomochi, Chihuahua, (March 2017).

273 Wasserman, *Capitalists*, p. 40.

274 Stover, *Religion and Revolution in Mexico's North*, (Río Vista Press, Deming, NM and Mata Ortiz, Chih., 2014), p. 117.

275 Lister and Lister, *Storehouse of Storms*, p. 207. The Lister's source is Emilio Portes Gil, *México: Cincuenta Años de Revolución*, vol. III, (Fondo De Cultura Económica, MX, 1961), p. 492.

276 Méndez García, personal communication, Nuevo Casas Grandes, (March 25, 2018).

277 Stover, *Religion and Revolution in Mexico's North*, pp. 327-28. Stover says references to Quevedo's attendance are uncertain.

278 Arturo Quevedo Rivero, "Rodrigo M. Quevedo Moreno, Una semblanza biográfica," (*Rancho Las Voces, Revista de Arte y Cultura*, Ciudad Juárez, Chih.,

2004). https://rancholasvoces.blogspot.com/2005/10/rodrigo-m-quevedo-moreno.html

279 Lister and Lister, *Storehouse of Storms*, pp. 207, 492.

280 *Monumentos Históricas Muebles Chihuahua, Catalogo Nacional*. (Secretaria de Educación Público, INAH, Mexico City, 1986), Cat. # 08013001 0006. This is a survey of historic buildings and this Cat. # refers to the building on the west side of the plaza used in the past as a school. The name "Secundaria Federales 58" is seen above the windows. The federal army used the building as a hospital, which may have led to the story about Madero being treated there.

281 Leopoldo Horacio Chávez, Cronista Oficial del municipio de Casas Grandes, personal communication, Casas Grandes, March 25, 2018.

282 Friedrich Katz, *The Life and Times of Pancho Villa*, (Stanford Univ. Press, Stanford, CA, 1998), pp. 93-94.

283 Jerry García, *Looking like the Enemy, Japanese-Mexicans, The Mexican State and US Hegemony 1897-1945*, (University of Arizona Press, Tucson, AZ, 2014); Sergio Galindo Hernández "Japanese Immigrants Who Joined the Mexican Revolution," *Discover Nikkei*, (Nov. 2016), http://discovernikkei.org/en/journal/2016/11/7/revolucion-mexicana/; Katz, *Pancho Villa*, p. 292.

284 Jesús Vargas Valdés, personal communication, Ciudad Chihuahua, May 25, 2017.

285 Manuel Plana, *Pancho Villa and the Mexican Revolution*, (Interlink Publishing Group, Inc., Northampton, MA, 2002), p. 104; Katz, *Pancho Villa*, p. 731; Miguel Méndez García, personal communication, Nuevo Casas Grandes, March 25, 2018.

286 Domínguez, "Desintegración del Latifundio Terrazas," p. 116; Katz, *Pancho Villa*, pp. 751-55.

287 Chávez Barrón, *Luis Terrazas*, p. 202.

Chapter 8

288 Hatch and Hardy, *Stalwarts*, p. 170. The statement was made by Maude Cluff Farnsworth, wife of Bryon Nephi Farnsworth.

289 Thomas Cottam Romney, *Mormon Colonies in Mexico*, (University of Utah Press, Salt Lake City, UT, 2005), p. 51.

290 Marion R. Lunt, *Heaton Lunt of Colonia Pacheco*, (CreateSpace Independent Publishing Platform, North Charleston, SC, 2013), p. 41.

291 Mark Wasserman, *Oligarchs, Elites and Politics in Chihuahua, Mexico, 1910-1940*, (Duke University Press, Durham, NC, 2012), p. 138.

292 LaVon Brown Whetten, *Colonia Juárez, Commemorating 125 Years of the Mormon Colonies in Mexico*, (Author House, Bloomington, IN, 2010), p. 9.

293 Philip R. Stover, "The Exodus of 1912: a Huddle of Pros and Cons—Mormons Twice Dispossessed," *Journal of Mormon History,* 44, no. 3 (2018), p. 19.

294 Whetten, *Colonia Juárez,* p. 15.

295 Philip R. Stover, personal communication, July 6, 2019.

296 Romney, *Mormon Colonies,* p. 62.

297 Rebecca Janzen, *Liminal Sovereignty: Mennonites and Mormons in Mexican Culture,* (State University of New York Press, Albany, NY, 2018), p. 43.

298 Romney, *Mormon Colonies,* pp. 55-63; Whetten, *Colonia Juárez,* pp. 9-15; Hatch and Hardy, *Stalwarts,* pp. 2, 3, 5, 345, 442, 443, and 627; Karl E. Young, *Ordeal in Mexico,* (Deseret Book Company, Salt Lake City, UT, 1968), pp. 1-3. This story has been told frequently by the families involved. Details vary. Unless otherwise noted, this overview of the immigration was compiled from these sources.

299 Mark P. Leone, "Mormon Town Plans," *Archaeology Southwest* 19, no. 2, (Spring 2005), p. 14.

300 Romney, *Mormon Colonies,* p. 85; Whetten, *Colonia Juárez,* p. 21.

301 Andrew Karl Larson, *Erastus Snow, The Life of a Missionary and Pioneer for the Early Mormon Church,* Volume five of publications on the American West, Center for Studies of the American West, (The University of Utah Press, Salt Lake City, Utah, 1971), p. 679. Larson has collected Erastus Snow's letters and reprinted significant excerpts, which provide observations of the transactions in his own words.

302 Larson, p. 688.

303 Romney, *Mormon Colonies,* p. 91.

304 Larson, *Erastus Snow,* p. 686.

305 Francisco R. Almada, *Diccionario Historia Geografía y Biografía Chihuahuenses,* (Ediciones del Gobierno del Estado de Chihuahua, Chih., MX, 1987), 2 ed., p. 307.

306 Robert L. Kovach, *Early Earthquakes of the Americas,* (Cambridge Univ. Press, Cambridge, UK, 2012), pp. 160-62.

307 Hatch and Hardy, *Stalwarts,* p. 345.

308 Romney, *Mormon Colonies,* p. 94.

309 Hatch and Hardy, *Stalwarts,* p. 608.

310 Elizabeth N. Mills, "The Mormon Colonies in Chihuahua After the 1912 Exodus," (MA thesis, University of Arizona, Tucson, AZ, 1950), p. 56.

311 Hatch and Hardy, *Stalwarts,* pp. 311-14; Romney, *Mormon Colonies,* pp. 130, 134.

312 Philip R. Stover, "Isolation and Integration: Apostles in the Mexican Colonies 1875-1912," (June 8, 2019), Presented to the Mormon Historical Society Annual Conference.

313 Romney, *Mormon Colonies,* pp. 128-29; Whetten, *Colonia Juárez,* p. 29.

314 Philip R. Stover, *Isolation and Integration.*

315 Hatch and Hardy, *Stalwarts,* p. 314; Whetten, *Colonia Juárez,* pp. 30-31; Romney, *Mormon Colonies,* p. 142.

316 Hatch and Hardy, *Stalwarts,* p. 487.

317 E. LeRoy Hatch, *Médico, My Life as a Country Doctor in Mexico,* (J. J. Hatch, Mesa, AZ, 1999), p. 20.

318 Lister and Lister, *Storehouse of Storms,* p. 195.

319 Romney, *Mormon Colonies,* pp. 74-76; Lister and Lister, *Storehouse of Storms,* p. 195.

320 Romney, *Mormon Colonies,* p. 65.

321 Jay Sutherland Grant, "Revolution and Rebellion, Mormon Colonies of Northwest Chihuahua, 1912-1917," (MA thesis, New Mexico State University, 1991), p. 42.

322 Romney, *Mormon Colonies,* p. 91.

323 Alan Ferg, "Mormon History and Archaeology in Northern Arizona," *Archaeology Southwest,* 19, no. 2, (Spring, 2005), p. 1; "Frick Company's Workshops," *Vintage Machinery,* http://vintagemachinery.org/mfgindex/detail.aspx?id=327; Jim Philp, "Brief History of Portable Sawmills," *Woodweb,* (September 10, 2001): https://woodweb.com/knowledge_base/A_Brief_History_of_Portable_Sawmills.html; Pat Stein, "The Mormon Lake, Dairy, Sawmill, and Tannery," *Archaeology Southwest,* 19, no. 2, (Spring, 2005), p. 10.

324 Romney, *Mormon Colonies,* p. 91; John Hatch, personal communication, Colonia Juárez, April 27, 2019. Romney says the first mill was in the Corrales Basin in 1887. Hatch thinks the first mill was in Colonia Juárez.

325 Hatch and Hardy, *Stalwarts,* pp. 321, 381; John Hatch, personal communication, April 27, 2019. Hatch told the flume story to a group of "Empty Nesters" on their monthly outing to which the authors were invited. From the mountain highway, he showed them the steep, narrow canyon where the flume was built.

326 Hatch and Hardy, *Stalwarts,* pp. 162, 165, 416-17.

327 Lunt, *Colonia Pacheco,* pp. 53-54, 63-64; Hatch and Hardy, *Stalwarts,* p. 419.

328 Hatch and Hardy, *Stalwarts,* pp. 708-09.

329 Romney, *Mormon Colonies,* p. 112.

330 Rondal Bridgemon, email communication, April 23, 2019.

331 Hatch and Hardy, *Stalwarts,* p. 719.

332 Adalberto Pérez Meillón, personal communication, April 24, 2019.

333 Hatch and Hardy, *Stalwarts,* pp. 394-98.

334 Hatch and Hardy, pp. 55-56.

335 Hatch and Hardy, p. 77.

336 Romney, *Mormon Colonies,* p. 115.

337 Stover, *Religion and Revolution in Mexico's North*, p. 324.

338 Stover, "Huddle of Pros and Cons," p. 51.

339 Stover, personal communication, July 6, 2019.

340 Stover, *Religion and Revolution in Mexico's North*, p. 326; personal communication, May 27, 2019.

341 Stover, p. 327; personal communication May 27, 2017. Stover, a historian living in Mata Ortiz, has studied in depth Salazar and other local individuals connected with the LDS immigration, and the Revolution.

342 Michael N. Landon, "We Navigated by Pure Understanding, Bishop George T. Sevey's Account of the 1912 Exodus from Mexico," *Brigham Young University Studies,* 43, no. 2, (2004), p. 79; *Investigation of Mexican Affairs Preliminary Report and Hearings of the Subcommittee on Foreign Relations of the United States Senate,* 66th Congress, Second Session, vol. 2, (Government Printing Office, Washington D.C. 1920), L. P. Atwood, affidavit, pp. 2599-2602. Senator Albert B. Fall of New Mexico conducted the hearings in 1912 and 1920 and included the minutes in the official report of the 1920 hearings. This report includes Atwood's affidavit to the committee in 1912.

343 This brief summary of the Exodus is a compilation of sources, primarily Romney, *Mormon Colonies,* Chapters 13-18; Whetten, *Colonia Juárez,* Chapters 8-10; Hatch and Hardy, *Stalwarts,* pp. 56, 57, 73, 316; Young, *Ordeal in Mexico,* Chapters 6-8; Landon, *We Navigated by Pure Understanding,* pp. 77-98.

344 Fred E. Woods, "Finding Refuge in El Paso: the 1912 Exodus from Mexico," *Meridian Magazine* (October 14, 2012): https://latterdaysaintmag.com /article-1-11596/

345 *Investigation of Mexican Affairs,* H. E. Bowman testimony, (August 10, 1912), p. 2559.

346 Landon, "We Navigated by Pure Understanding," p. 71; Rondal Bridgemon, "Return to the Stairs," (unpublished manuscript written for the Mata Ortiz Historical Society website describing the 2009-2010 search for the Stairs site by Bridgemon and David Nelson, December 22, 2010); Bridgemon, personal communication, July 2015, exchange of emails. Bridgemon described a discussion about the discovery of the lost Colonia Juárez Stake records that included Taylor MacDonald and Jess Martineau (Archivist for the Church of Latter-day Saints), and Bridgemon in July, 2015.

347 Romney, *Mormon Colonies,* p. 204. This source refers to Chávez as "presidente" of Colonia Juárez.

348 Romney, *Mormon Colonies,* pp. 204-5.

349 LaMond Tullis, *Mormons in Mexico,* (Utah State University Press, Logan, UT, 1987), p. 95.

350 Romney, *Mormon Colonies,* p. 235; Hatch, *Médico,* p. 12; Hatch and Hardy, *Stalwarts,* pp. 34-35, 663.

351 Hatch, *Médico,* pp. 16-17.

352 Katz, *Pancho Villa,* p. 336.

353 Whetten, *Colonia Juárez,* pp. 57-58; Hatch and Hardy, *Stalwarts,* pp. 83-84.

354 Mills, "Mormon Colonies in Chihuahua," p. 17.

355 Hatch and Hardy, *Stalwarts,* pp. 85-86.

356 American Consular Service report, Juárez, Mexico, May 23, 1919; Records of the Ferrocarril Noroeste de México, Benson Collection, Box 5, File 16.

357 Whetten, *Colonia Juárez,* pp. 66-67; Young, *Ordeal in Mexico,* pp. 229-33.

358 Philip R. Stover, "The General in the Plum Thicket," (unpublished manuscript, 2017).

359 Stover, personal communication, July 6, 2019.

360 Romney, *Mormon Colonies,* p. 247.

361 Mills, "The Mormon Colonies in Chihuahua After the 1912 Exodus," p. 32.

362 Hatch and Hardy, *Stalwarts,* p. 245.

363 Whetten, *Colonia Juárez,* pp. 73-75 and 110-11.

364 Mills, "Mormon Colonies in Chihuahua," p. 32.

365 E. LeRoy Hatch, "Mormon Colonies: Beacon Light in Mexico," https://churchofjesuschrist.org/study/ensign/1972/09/mormon-colonies-beacon-light-in-mexico?lang=eng

366 Stover, *Religion and Revolution in Mexico's North,* p. 331-32.

367 Mills, "The Mormon Colonies," p. 62.

368 Romney, *Mormon Colonies,* p. 257.

369 Mills, "Mormon Colonies in Chihuahua," p. 34.

370 Whetten, *Colonia Juárez,* pp. 245-47.

371 Virginia Romney, *The Colonia Juárez Temple,* Presented at the Gathering of Friends of Mata Ortiz, October 10, 2015.

372 Stover, *Religion and Revolution in Mexico's North,* p. 323.

Chapter 9

373 Desmond Young, *Member for Mexico,* (Cassell and Company, London, 1966).

374 Ben Brown, personal communications late 1980s through early 1990s. It is not known exactly when Dr. Brown corrected the Pearson name error. Discussions with Brown and a review of his unpublished research papers suggest the earliest date to be in the late 1980s.

375 Stearns Morse, "The Yankee Spirit: Fred Stark Pearson," (Part III, an unpublished manuscript, 1993, edited 2008). This is a biography of Fred Stark Pearson by Morse, a nephew by marriage of Pearson. Tufts Univ. Library has a copy.

376 Duncan McDowall, "Dictionary of Canadian Biography Online," (Library and Archives, CA, Univ. of Toronto, 2005), p. 1; Stearns Morse, "Slots in the Streets," *The New England Quarterly*, 24, no. 1, (March, 1951), p. 5.

377 Gilmore G. Cooke, *The Existential Joys of Fred Stark Pearson, 1861-1915*, (Gilmore G. Cooke, San Bernardino, CA, 2019), p. 15; Morse, *Slots in the Street*, p. 6; Morse, "Yankee Spirit," pp. 161-62.

378 P. Plummer, "Frederick Stark Pearson, Consulting Engineer of the Metropolitan Street Railway Co," *Cassier's Magazine*, XVIII, (May-October, 1900), pp. 446-47. Cassier's Magazine was a well-known engineering monthly at the turn of the century.

379 Russell E. Miller, *Light on the Hill*, (Beacon Press, Boston, 2000), pp. 547-49.

380 Cooke, *Existential Joys*, p. 30.

381 Morse, "Yankee Spirit," p. 163.

382 McDowall, "Dictionary of Canadian Biography," p. 1.

383 McDowall, p. 27.

384 Erin Dower, "Somerville's First High-Tech Startup," *Somerville Journal*, (June 30, 2005), p.1.

385 Gilmore Cooke, "Somerville Electric Light Company 1880-1903: The Design and Evolution of a Successful Enterprise," *Society for Industrial Archaeology*, (New England Chapters), 26, no. 1, (2005), p. 4.

386 Morse, "Slots in the Street," p. 11.

387 Morse, "Yankee Spirit," p. 206.

388 Morse, p. 187.

389 Cooke, *Existential Joys*, p. 27; Morse, "Yankee Spirit," p. 188.

390 Morse, pp. 213-15; Cooke, *Existential Joys*, p. 28; Carole Owens, "Connection: The Huckleberry King of the Berkshires," *The Berkshire Edge*, (September 3, 2019); https://theberkshireedge.com/connections-51

391 Fred Harwood, personal communication, email, December 16, 2008. Harwood sent an excerpt from an article titled "Country Estates," from *History of Great Barrington (Berkshire) Massachusetts, 1676—1882 & Extension, 1882—1922*, by Charles J. Taylor, Ralph Wainwright Pope and George Edwin MacLean (Town of Great Barrington, 1928).

392 Owens, "King of the Berkshires."

393 Carole Owens, "Connection: Cottage Industry," *The Berkshire Edge*, (September 10, 2019); https://theberkshireedge.com/connections-52/

394 Bernard Drew, personal communication, the Great Barrington Historical Society, email, December 10, 2008; Robert Kroll, personal communication, Great Barrington Historical Society, by telephone, February 14, 2022.

395 Plummer, "Consulting Engineer," p. 448.

396 Morse, "Yankee Spirit," pp. 166-67.

397 Morse, p. 210.

398 Morse, p. 199; Adalberto Pérez Meillón, personal communication, February 7, 2019. Pérez Meillón confirms that, according to the local people in Mata Ortiz, the Dos Cabezas Mine is located in Sonora. Morse states the mine was in Chihuahua. Either he is mistaken or there was another mine with the same name.

399 R. J. MacHugh, *Modern Mexico*, (Dodd, Mead, and Co., NY, 1914), pp. 192, 197.

400 Morse, "Yankee Spirit," p. 206.

401 "The Mexican Light and Power Co., Limited," in *The Manual of Statistics*, (1915), p. 644.

402 F. S. Pearson and P. O. Blackwell, "The Necaxa Plant of the Mexican Light and Power Company," *Transactions of the American Society of Civil Engineers*, LVIII, (June, 1907), pp. 37-50.

403 Reinhard Liehr and Mariano Torres, "From Free-Standing Company to Public Enterprise: Mexican Light and Power Company and the Mexican Tramways Company, 1902-1965," XIII Conference, *Doing Business in Latin America*, Buenos Aires, (2002). p. 13.

404 Miguel S. Wionczek, "The State and the Electric-Power Industry in Mexico, 1895-1965," *Business History Review*, (Cambridge University Press, 24 July 1965), pp. 550-51.

405 McDowall, "Pearson, *Dictionary of Canadian Biography*, http://biographi.ca /en/bio/pearson_frederick_stark_14E.html

406 Russel E. Chace, "The Mexico Northwestern Company, LTD, 1908-1914, Working Paper #4," CERLAC, Centre for Research on Latin America and the Caribbean, (York University, Ontario, Canada, 1982), pp 3-4.

407 B. Carmon Hardy, "Sonora, Sinaloa, and Chihuahua Railroad," *Jahrbuch für Geschichte Lateinamerikas—Anuario de Historia de América Latina*, 12, Issue 1, (1975), pp. 253–83.

408 Fred Wilbur Powell, *The Railroads of Mexico*, (The Stratford Co., Boston, MA, 1921), p. 1.

409 Powell, p. 130.

410 Powell, p. 137.

411 John Leeds Kerr, *Destination Topolobampo, the Kansas City, Mexico and Orient Railway*, (Golden West Books, San Marino, CA, 1968). This reference tells the story of two of the dreamer/entrepreneurs, Albert Kimsey Owen and Arthur Edward Stilwell, both seekers of a rail route to Topolobampo.

412 *Paper Money of Chihuahua*, https://papermoneyofmexico.com/index .php/history/chihuahua/banco-santa-eulalia

413 Todd Compton, "John Willard Young, Brigham Young and the Development of Presidential Succession in the LDS Church," https://dialoguejournal.com /wp-content/uploads/sbi/articles/Dialogue_V35N04_125.pdf; p.11.

414 Hatch and Hardy, *Stalwarts,* p. 362.

415 C. L. Sonnichsen, *Colonel Greene and the Copper Skyrocket,* (University of Arizona Press, Tucson, AZ, 1974), p. 11.

416 Hardy, "The Sonora, Sinaloa and Chihuahua Railroad." This article by the noted California State University, Fullerton professor and historian, B. Carmon Hardy, appeared in English in the German publication *Anuario de Historia de América Latina,* which can be accessed online. Unless otherwise noted, this was the source for most of the information regarding the Sonora, Sinaloa and Chihuahua Railroad.

417 Compton, "John Willard Young," p. 129.

418 David M. Pletcher, *Rails, Mines, and Progress: Seven American Promoters in Mexico, 1867-1911,* (Port Washington Kennikat Press, London and NY, 1971), pp. 107-108.

419 Kerr, *Destination Topolobampo,* pp. 34-35.

420 Kerr, p. 56.

421 Kerr, pp. 47-48.

422 Pletcher, *Rails, Mines, and Progress* p. 269, footnote.

423 Kerr, *Destination Topolobampo,* p. 50.

424 Kerr, p. 73.

425 Kerr, p. 105.

426 Powell, *Railroads of Mexico,* p. 157; Kerr, *Destination Topolobampo,* p. 107.

427 *The New York Times,* June 25, 1897.

428 Powell, *Railroads of Mexico,* p. 157; *Poor's Manual of Railroads,* (44 Broad St., NY, 1900), p. 844; Campbell, *Mines Cattle, and Rebellion,* pp. 32-33; Mark Edward Gemoets, "The Mexico-Northwest Railroad and the Maderista Phase of the Mexican Revolution, 1910-1911," MA thesis, (New Mexico State University, 2007), p. 16. Unless otherwise noted, these references provided the material for this section.

429 Chace, "The Mexico Northwestern Company," p. 4.

430 Pletcher, *Rails, Mines, and Progress,* p. 221.

431 Pletcher, p. 225.

432 Pletcher, p. 226.

433 Evelyn Hu-DeHart, "Immigrants to a Developing Society: The Chinese in Northern Mexico, 1875-1932," *Journal of Arizona History,* 31, (Autumn 1980), p. 52; Leo Michael Dambourges Jacques, "The Anti-Chinese Campaigns in Sonora, Mexico, 1900-1921," PhD. diss., University of Arizona, (1974), p. 64; Pletcher, *Rails, Mines, and Progress,* p. 230.

434 Sonnichsen, *Colonel Green*, pp. 98 and 115.

435 Sonnichsen, p. 154.

436 Kerr, *Destination Topolobampo*, pp. 107-09; Powell, *The Railroads of Mexico*, pp. 157-59.

437 Powell, *The Railroads of Mexico*, p. 57. Michael N. Mundt, "Revolution and Reaction: The Mexico North Western Railway Company During the 1912 Pascual Orozco Rebellion," MA thesis, (New Mexico State University, 1991), p. 6. Mundt suggests that the Scheley group built the entire railroad line from Chihuahua to Madero, which is probably incorrect.

438 Gemoets, "Maderista Phase," p. 19.

439 Sonnichsen, *Colonel Green*, p. 154.

440 Clarence Cooper, *Sawdust and Revolutions II, The Mexican Experience of C.H. Cooper,1911-1950*, (CreateSpace Independent Publishing, 2014), p. 3.

441 Pletcher, *Rails, Mines, and Progress*, pp. 248-49.

442 Hart, *Empire and Revolution*, p. 148.

443 Records of the Ferrocarril Noroeste de México, Benson Latin American Collection, Letter, November 15, 1916, J.O. Crockett, senior VP to receiver R. Home Smith, University of Texas at Austin.

444 Christopher R. Boyer, *Political Landscapes, Forests, Conservation and Community in Mexico*, (Duke University Press, Durham N.C, 2015), p. 43.

445 Chace, "The Mexico Northwestern Company," Notes, p. 6; *The Manual of Statistics, Stock Exchange Handbook, 1910*, "Mexico North Western Railroad," (Manual of Statistics Company, NY), pp. 194-95; *The Economist*, March 6, 1909, p. 557. The total amount of bonds authorized was $15,000,000.

446 Chace, "The Mexico Northwestern Company," p. 7.

447 Christopher Armstrong and V. Nelles, "A Curious Capital Flow: Canadian Investment in Mexico 1902-1910," *The Business History Review*, 58, no. 2 (Summer 1984), pp. 178-203.

448 Chace, "The Mexico Northwestern Company," pp. 10-11. This is based on letters from and to Dunn. See references 44-45 on p. 7 of notes.

449 Chace, "The Mexico Northwestern Company," pp. 6-7, Notes p. 5. This source identifies Guillermo Landa y Escandón as the Mexico City Federal District governor, which he was 1903-1915. The first Interim Report, 1909, and subsequent Annual Reports, identify him as a senator in the Federal Congress. Apparently as governor he also represented the District in the Senate.

450 Chace, "The Mexico Northwestern Company," p. 7.

451 *The New York Times*, August 14, 1909.

452 Mundt, "1912 Pascual Orozco Rebellion," p. 9.

453 Development Company of America, *Annual Report for 1909*. Boyer, *Political Landscapes,* p. 43. Boyer says much of DCA's land was first transferred to Colonel William A Greene.

454 L. Roy Hoard, "Memo: RE North Western Railway Company," December 31, 1928, Box 949, Special Collections, El Paso Public Library, El Paso, TX, p. 8; Hart, *Empire and Revolution,* pp. 157-61.

455 Chace, "The Mexico Northwestern Company," p. 8. Chace states that all of the acquisitions of Greene's property were made in August, 1909, citing *The New York Times*, August 14, 1909; Sonnichsen, *Colonel Green*, p. 230.

456 "Contrato, Despacho de Comunicaciones y Obras Públicas," (November 22, 1909), Archivo General de la Nación, Archivo Histórico.

457 Deed and contract conditions between the MNWR and Luis Terrazas, November 13, 1909, recorded as a notarized renewal contract, August 12, 1918, property transaction records, Office of Registration, District of Galeana, Nuevo Casas Grandes, Chihuahua, Book 7, pp. 131-48. The document was found during a search of the records in May 2017. Subsequent searches in the registration offices in í, Ciudad Juárez and El Paso have not revealed the original 1909 document.

458 Boyer, *Political Landscapes,* p. 56.

459 Hoard, "RE North Western Railway," p. 9; Cooper, *Sawdust and Revolutions,* pp. 24-25.

460 J. E. Hulse, *Railroads & Revolutions, the Story of Roy Hoard,* (Mangan Books, El Paso, TX, 1986), p. 9; Mundt, "1912 Pascual Orozco Rebellion," pp. 9-10.

461 Philip R. Stover, personal communication, October 6, 2012. This was part of his presentation to the 2012 Gathering of Friends of Mata Ortiz.

462 Juan Mata Ortiz Ejido papers in the custody of ejido officials. Interview with *Presidente* Héctor Gallegos, May 17, 2008.

463 Hulse, *Railroads & Revolutions,* p. 25.

464 Mexico North Western Railway Company, *Director's Report & Accounts, 1910.*

465 Juan Mata Ortiz Ejido papers; Deed and contract conditions between MNWR and Luis Terrazas, November 13, 1909, notarized August 12, 1918.

466 Scott Ryerson, "The Potters of Porvenir: The Lesser Known Artisans of Mata Ortiz," *Kiva, The Journal of Southwestern Anthropology and History,* The Arizona Archaeological and Historical Society, 60, no. 1, (Fall 1994), p. 98.

467 Jorge Quintana Rodríguez, Personal communication, March 5, 2008. Jorge, John Wingate and the authors visited the site on this date.

468 Cooper, *Sawdust and Revolutions,* p. 7.

469 Hulse, *Railroads & Revolutions,* p. 91.

470 Cooper, *Sawdust and Revolutions,* p. 7.

471 Morse, "Yankee Spirit," p. 235.

472 *Mining and Scientific Press,* December 25, 1909 and January 6, 1912.

473 McDowall, *Dictionary of Canadian Biography.*

474 Morse, "Yankee Spirit." pp. 223-27; McDowall, *Dictionary of Canadian Biography.*

475 Cooke, *Existential Joys,* p. 224.

476 Yancy L. *Russell, Frederick Stark Pearson, Handbook of Texas Online,* Texas State Historical Association, http://tshaonline.org/handbook/online/articles /fpe06; Morse, "Yankee Spirit," p. 227; Cooke, *Existential Joys,* pp. 224, 231; B. R. Brunson, *The Texas Land And Development Company, A Panhandle Promotion, 1912-1956,* (University of Texas Press, Austin and London, 1970), pp. 22, 47-48. There is confusion about the dates. Some sources have Pearson on his way to Spain on July 11, 1911. It is more likely he was at Medina on that date and left for Spain shortly after the dam dedication.

477 Katz, *Pancho Villa,* p. 140 and Campbell, *Mines, Cattle, and Rebellion,* p. 232.

478 Cooper, *Sawdust and Revolutions,* p. 20.

479 Morse, *Yankee Spirit,* p. 229.

480 McDowall: *Dictionary of Canadian Biography;* Cooke, *Existential Joys,* pp. 264 and 266. Cooke on page 266 presents an excellent timeline, detailing Pearson's last two years.

481 Morse, *Yankee Spirit,* p. 253, and Cooke, *Existential Joys,* p. 280. Morse says that the "bodies" were brought back to Woodland Cemetery.

482 Thomas F. Glick, "Catalonia, Factory of Spain, an Exhibition in Barcelona," *Society for the History of Technology,* 27, no. 3, (July 1986), p. 600.

483 Cooke, *Existential Joys,* p. 292.

484 Cooke, pp. 280-81; Morse, *Yankee Spirit,* p. 252.

485 Hanson Baldwin, *Sea Fights and Shipwrecks,* (Hanover House, Garden City, NY, 1955), pp. 223-24.

486 Baldwin, pp. 328-34.

487 *Boston Daily Globe,* July 13, 1915.

488 Cooke, *Existential Joys,* pp. 292-95.

489 Cooke, *Existential Joys,* p. 281.

490 Cooke, p. 6.

Chapter 10

491 Lois J. Roberts, "Appendix II, Historical Overview, Archaeological Investigations on the San Antonio Terrace, Vandenberg Air Force Base," in *Connection Facilities Construction* (Chambers Consultants and Planners, Stanton CA, 1984), p. 41.

492 Thomas F. Collison, "Just as of Yore, Cattle Still Graze on Ancient Rancho," *Los Angeles Times, Farm and Garden Magazine,* p. 5. March 13, 1932; John

Mason Hart, "Foreign Proprietors and the Mexican Constitution, Archeological Investigations," (Biblioteca Jurídica Virtual Instituto de Investigaciones Jurídicas de la UNAM, 1993), p. 138.

493 Roberts, "Appendix II, Historical Overview," p. 41.

494 Roberts, p. 57.

495 Morris B. Parker (au) and James M. Day (ed), *Mules, Mines, and Me in Mexico*, (University of Arizona Press, Tucson, AZ, 1979), p. 161; Lister and Lister, *Storehouse of Storms*, p. 280.

496 Kelley et al, "Land Use, Looting, and Archaeology," p. 16.

497 Brenda L. Tippin, "The California Morgans of William Randolph Hearst," https://www.morganhorse.com/upload/photos/904TMH_July2013 _HearstMorgans.pdf, July 2013.

498 Philip R. Stover, personal communication, Juan Mata Ortiz, Chihuahua, May 27, 2017.

499 Lister and Lister, *Storehouse of Storms*, p. 279.

500 Campbell, *Mines, Cattle, and Rebellion*, p. 376.

501 Campbell, pp. 30-31; Parker, p. 158, note 2; Thomas Wentworth Peirce, Jr. Papers, Benson Latin American Collection.

502 George E. Paulsen, "Reaping the Whirlwind in Chihuahua: Destruction of the Minas de Corralitos, 1911-1917," *Mexican Historical Review*, 58. no. 3, (1983), p. 255.

503 *Mexico North Western Railway Company, Second Annual Report*, December 31, 1911; Campbell, *Mines, Cattle, and Rebellion*, pp. 226-31.

504 Parker and Day, *Mules, Mines, and Me*, pp. 29-30.

505 Paulsen, "Reaping the Whirlwind in Chihuahua," p. 258.

506 Campbell, *Mines, Cattle, and Rebellion*, p. 231.

507 Campbell, p. 247.

508 A. C. Hernández, "Yes You Can," *Southern New Mexico Historical Review*, IV, no. 1, (January 1997).

509 Campbell, p. 34.

510 Campbell, p. 239.

511 Campbell, p. 257.

512 Campbell, pp. 269-70.

513 Campbell, p. 272.

514 Hernández, "Yes You Can," pp. 1-2.

515 John J. Pershing, Major General, *Punitive Expedition*, (U.S. Army Military History Institute, Carlisle, PA, 1916), p. 100.

516 Campbell, *Mines, Cattle, and Rebellion*, pp. 34-36, 275-76; Lorna Call Adler, William G. Hartley and Lane Johnson, *Anson Bowman Call: Bishop of Dublan*, (Lorna Call Adler, Provo, Utah, 2007), p 407. Adler, Hartley and Johnson

present a different version, indicating that more than just Gregorio Jr. were spared to spread the word that anyone found on property owned by North Americans would suffer the same fate.

517 Adler, Hartley, and Johnson, pp. 407-411.

518 Wendell E. Wilson, "Famous Mineral Localities, San Pedro, Corralitos, Chihuahua, Mexico," *The Mineralogical Record*, 35, no. 6; Wilson suggests operations had slowed or shut down by 1913, but the company was still paying taxes as of the spring of 1916; Campbell, *Mines, Cattle, and Rebellion*, pp. 35, 275, 290.

519 Campbell, *Mines, Cattle, and Rebellion*, p. 297, 307; Hatch, and Hardy, *Stalwarts*, p. 52.

520 Campbell, p. 304; Paulsen, "Reaping the Whirlwind in Chihuahua," p. 26.

521 Campbell, pp. 306-08.

522 Campbell, pp. 313-17.

523 Campbell, p. 322. Information taken from a letter, printed in its entirety, to the Corralitos Company board, March 2, 1921.

524 Campbell, p. 336.

525 Campbell, pp. 335 and 347.

526 Wasserman, *Persistent Oligarchs, Elites and Politics*, pp. 7, 51-52. Wasserman has written several books about Chihuahua. In this reference, he has provided a detailed guide through the convoluted maze of idealism, practicality, and corruption that made up the politics of post-Revolution Chihuahua and Mexico.

527 Campbell, *Mines, Cattle, and Rebellion*, p. 358.

Chapter 11

528 Robert Chao Romero, *The Chinese in Mexico, 1882-1940*, (The University of Arizona Press, Tucson AZ, 2011), pp. 3-4, 21, 26-29.

529 Romero, p. 58.

530 Parker and Day, *Mules, Mines, and Me in Mexico*, p. 32, 37.

531 Ortega Urquidi, *Casas Grandes, tierra de siete culturas*, pp. 232-233.

532 *The New York Times*, November 20, 1900, "Chinese Miners For Mexico," p. 3.

533 Ortega Urquidi, *tierra de siete culturas*, pp. 236-39.

534 Ortega Urquidi, pp. 236-37.

535 Personal communications. Unless otherwise noted, the Chew/Chinolla section is the compilation of interviews with Agustín Chinolla January 8, 2007 with Spencer MacCallum, Antonio Chinolla, January 7, 2007, and Blanca Chinolla, March 3, 2005 in Casas Grandes, Chih.

536 Cornell Naihong Fung, of San Diego, provided the translations.

537 Kiara Maureen Hughes, "The Women Potters of Mata Ortiz: Growing Empowerment Through Artistic Work," (PhD diss., University of New

Mexico, 2009), pp. 124-25. Dr. Hughes became good friends with Amelia Martínez Flores de Tena, Fong Poi's oldest granddaughter, during Hughes' years in Mata Ortiz doing research. Hughes lived with Amelia and her husband José Tena Durán for several months in 1997 and 1998. Unless otherwise noted, Fong Poi's story is a compilation of Dr. Hughes' conversations with Amelia, augmented by the authors' interviews with Amelia's sister Graciela Martínez Flores de Gallegos, their father, José Martínez, and one of Fong Poi's great grandsons, Jorge Quintana Rodríguez.

538　Ana Livingston Paddock, *Mata Ortiz: The Art of Survival, The Survival of Art, Graciela and Héctor Gallegos,* (Casa Aurora Publications, Santa Fe, NM and Juan Mata Ortiz, Chih., 2011), p. 14. Paddock resides in Mata Ortiz, speaks Spanish fluently, and talked many times with Martínez family members including Luz Elena Rodríguez; Hughes, "Women Potters of Mata Ortiz," p. 125.

539　José Martínez, personal communication, March 5, 2008, in the home of Héctor Gallegos and Graciela Martínez, Juan Mata Ortiz, Chih.

540　Haldeen Braddy, *Cock of the Walk, the Legend of Pancho Villa,* (University of New Mexico Press, Albuquerque, NM, 1955), pp. 79-80. The year 1915 given in the reference for López's raid should be 1919; Cooper, *Sawdust and Revolutions,* p. 37. A review of the Haldeen Braddy papers, MS 154, in January 2008, did not reveal additional information to support the stories in this book.

541　William Weber Johnson, *Heroic Mexico, The Violent Emergence of a Modern Nation,* (Doubleday and Co., Garden City, NY, 1968), p. 359.

542　American Consular Service report, Cd. Juárez, Chih., Mexico, May 23, 1919, Box 5, File 16, Records of the Ferrocarril Noroeste de México, Benson Latin American Collection, University of Texas, Austin, TX.

543　Graciela Martínez, personal communication, January, 2007. She provided much of the family genealogy, family history and lore. Additional family history was provided by Graciela's father José Martínez, and Jorge Quintana Rodríguez.

544　José Martínez, personal communication, March 5, 2008, Juan Mata Ortiz, Chih.

545　Jorge Quintana Rodríguez, personal communication, March 5, 2008 and April 25, 2019, Juan Mata Ortiz, Chih.

546　Cornell Naihong Fung, San Diego, CA provided the translations of the gravestone with the assistance of his son, Dr. Fred Fung.

Chapter 12

547　Mexico North Western Railway Company, *Director's First Annual Report & Accounts,* December, 31, 1910; Mexico North Western Railway Company, *Second Annual Report,* December 31, 1911.

548 Cooke, *The Existential Joys*, p. 333; *Mexico North Western Railway Annual Reports*, cover pages.

549 *The Road to Wealth*, Promotional Brochure by the Mexico North Western Railway Co., 1909.

550 Cooke, *The Existential Joys*, p. 341.

551 B. H. Bryant, "Letters on Regional Railroads," (Colorado College, Colorado Springs, CO, July, 1901), Tutt Library, Special Collections and Archives, Colorado Springs Century Chest Collection, Ms 0349, (63).

552 Lou Taub, Simi Valley, CA, personal communication, July11, 2022. Mr. Taub buys, sells, and collects historic weapons. He is an expert on historic rifles and pistols.

553 Philip R. Stover, *The Search for the Soul of Mexico, Religion and Revolution*, vol. 1, p. 266; Philip R. Stover, *The Search for the Soul of Mexico, The Anglo Quest for Naboth's Vineyard*, vol. 2 (Río Vista Press, Deming, NM), p. 162.

554 Katz, *Pancho Villa*, pp. 2-7.

555 Katz, p. 73.

556 Gemoets, "Maderista Phase of the Mexican Revolution," pp. 50-51.

557 Katz, *Pancho Villa*, p. 60; Gemoets, p. 52.

558 Máximo Castillo, "The Simple History of My Life," in Jesús Vargas Valdés, *Máximo Castillo and the Mexican Revolution*, (Louisiana State University Press, Baton Rouge, LA, 2016), pp. 94-95. Castillo's description of events often differs in detail from other sources.

559 Katz, *Pancho Villa*, pp. 76-77; Gemoets, "Maderista Phase of the Mexican Revolution," pp. 54-60.

560 Gemoets, p. 65.

561 Gemoets, p. 78.

562 Records of the Ferrocarril Noroeste de México, Box 1, File 1, Benson Collection.

563 William E. French, "Business as Usual: Mexico North Western Railway Managers Confront the Mexican Revolution," (*Mexican Studies*, 5, no. 2, University of California Press, 1989), p. 228.

564 Mundt, "1912 Pascual Orozco Rebellion," p. 154.

565 French, "Business as Usual," p. 229.

566 R. Home Smith to E.D. Kenna, telegram, March 11, 1911, Records of the Ferrocarril Noroeste de México, Box 1, File 4, Benson Collection.

567 EMV, Manager of the Pearson Plant, to H. C. Smith, letter, December 29, 1910, Records of the Ferrocarril Noroeste de México, Box 1, File 1, Benson Collection.

568 J. C. Crockett to H. I. Miller, telegram, July 12, 1912, Records of the Ferrocarril Noroeste de México, Box 1, File 21, Benson Collection.

569 Mundt, "1912 Pascual Orozco Rebellion," p. 27.

570 Mexico North Western Railway Company, *Second Annual Report*, December 31, 1911, p. 6; French, "Business as Usual," p. 227; Gemoets, "Maderista Phase of the Mexican Revolution," pp. 76-79; Chace, "The Mexico Northwestern Company," pp. 15-16.

571 Gemoets, "Maderista Phase of the Mexican Revolution," pp. 146-47.

572 Castillo, "The Simple History of My Life," p. 98; Gemoets, "Maderista Phase of the Mexican Revolution," pp. 148-49. The sources differ on details, but the important point is that Orozco controlled the railroad lines leading to Ciudad Juárez.

573 Gemoets, p. 158.

574 Katz, *Pancho Villa,* p. 97.

575 George Rutledge to E.D. Kenna, telegram, February 4, 1911, records of the Ferrocarril Noroeste de México, Box 1, File 13, Benson Collection.

576 Lawrence D. Taylor, "The Great Adventure, Mercenaries in the Mexican Revolution, 1910-1915," *The Americas,* 43, no. 1, (July, 1986), p. 33.

577 Katz, *Pancho Villa,* pp. 92-93; Castillo, "The Simple History of My Life," pp. 100-101.

578 Castillo, pp. 104-05.

579 Dr. I. J. Bush, *Gringo Doctor,* (Caxton Printers, Ltd., Caldwell, Idaho, 1939), p. 190.

580 Dr. I. J. Bush, "The Battle of Casas Grandes," *Sports Afield,* (August, 1912), pp. 116-20.

581 E. D. Kenna to F. S. Pearson, telegram, March 9, 1911, records of the Ferrocarril Noroeste de México, Box 2, Benson Collection. It appears that when Dr. Pearson was abroad, Kenna transmitted updated reports to him.

582 Bush, *Gringo Doctor*, p. 190.

583 Rondal R. Bridgemon, "Madero at Hacienda de San Diego," (unpublished, January 2011), pp. 1-2.

584 Eduardo Pío Gamboa Carrera, "La arquitectura de la Paquimé, Unidades IX y X, Los Montículos de los Héroes y Pájaro," GacetINAH (1 November 2021), pp. 5-6; Charles C. Di Peso, *Casas Grandes, a Fallen Trading Center of the Gran Chichimeca,* vol. 4, (Amerind Foundation, Inc., Dragoon, AZ and Northland Press, Flagstaff, AZ, 1974), pp. 465, 467; Lange and Riley, *Southwestern Journals of Adolph F. Bandelier,* pp. 324-25.

585 Cooper, *Sawdust and Revolutions,* p. 13.

586 Giuseppe Garibaldi, *A Toast to Rebellion,*(Garden City Publishing Co., Garden City, NY, 1937), pp. 270-72; Gemoets, "Maderista Phase of the Mexican Revolution," p. 191, 197-98. Garibaldi says the machine shop was at Pearson. Sources disagree on other details of the cannon's construction.

587 Gemoets, p. 206.

588 Gemoets, p. 201.

589 F.S. Pearson probably to E.D. Kenna, letter, May 6, 1910, Records of The Ferrocarril Noroeste de México, Box 1, File 11, Benson Collection.

590 Hulse, *Railroads & Revolutions*, p. 37.

591 Katz, *Pancho Villa*, pp. 111-12; Castillo, "The Simple History of My Life," pp. 109-11.

592 Katz, pp. 116-17.

593 William Beezley, *Insurgent Governor, Abraham González and the Mexican Revolution in Chihuahua*, (University of Nebraska Press, Lincoln, NE, 1973), pp. 51-52, 67; Taylor, "The Great Adventure," p. 29. Note 15.

594 Beezley, *Insurgent Governor*, p. 73.

595 Beezley, p. 75.

596 Beezley, pp. 92-95.

597 Beezley, pp. 107-08.

598 Enrique Krauze (au) and Hank Heifetz (trans), *Mexico: Biography of Power, History of Modern Mexico, 1810-1996*, (Harper Collins, NY, 1997), p. 364.

599 Katz, *Pancho Villa*, p. 392.

600 Castillo, "The Simple History of My Life," p. 46.

601 Castillo, p. 52.

602 Mundt, "1912 Pascual Orozco Rebellion," pp. 55, 149; Beezley, *Insurgent Governor*, p. 135.

603 Michael C. Meyer, William L. Sherman and Susan M. Deeds, *The Course of Mexican History*, (Oxford University Press, NY, 1999), p. 498.

604 Martín Guzmán, *Memoirs of Pancho Villa*, (University of Texas Press, Austin, TX, 1965), p. 57.

605 Gemoets, "Maderista Phase of the Mexican Revolution," pp. 227-28.

606 Meyer, Sherman and Deeds, *"The Course of Mexican History,"* p. 498.

607 Mexico North Western Railway Company, *Director's First Annual Report & Accounts*, December 31, 1910.

608 Mundt, "1912 Pascual Orozco Rebellion," p. 47.

609 Mexico North Western Railway Company, *Second Annual Report*, December 31, 1911, p. 6.

610 Mundt, "1912 Pascual Orozco Rebellion," pp. 147-48.

611 French, "Business as Usual," p. 232.

612 Mundt, "1912 Pascual Orozco Rebellion," p. 59.

613 Beezley, *Insurgent Governor*, pp. 139-40.

614 Mundt, "1912 Pascual Orozco Rebellion," p. 108.

615 Mundt, pp. 86-88, 90.

616 Mundt, p. 101.

617 A. Dunderstadt to J. J. Pruett, February 1, 1913, Box 2, file 14, documents 918-950, Benson Collection.

618 Beezley, Insurgent Governor, pp. 144-47.

619 Mundt, "1912 Pascual Orozco Rebellion," p. 127.

620 Grant, *Revolution and Rebellion,* p. 42.

621 Beezley, *Insurgent Governor,* p. 158 and Castillo, "The Simple History of My Life," pp. 55-57, 144-45.

622 Parkes, *A History of Mexico,* p. 338.

Chapter 13

623 Guzmán, *Memoirs of Pancho Villa,* p. 96.

624 Cooper, *Sawdust and Revolutions,* pp. 158-59.

625 Castillo, "The Simple History of My Life," p. 148.

626 Castillo, p. 148.

627 J. O. Crockett to I. Miller, telegram, June 9, 1913, Box 3, file 20, documents 1610-1632, Benson Collection. This is the first of several communications to top management about the attack; A. L. Lathrop to J. O. Crockett, telegram, June 13, 1913, Box 3, file 21, documents 1633-1667, Benson Collection; M. J. Gilmartin to J. J. Pruett, letter, June 13, 1913, Box 3, file 21, document 1644, Benson Collection.

628 Castillo, "The Simple History of My Life," p. 148.

629 Young, *Ordeal in Mexico*, p. 152.

630 Young, p. 152.

631 Lunt, *Heaton Lunt, of Colonia Pacheco*, p. 160.

632 Young, *Ordeal in Mexico*, pp. 151-61; Lunt, *Heaton Lunt, of Colonia Pacheco,* pp. 163-67; Castillo, "The Simple History of My Life ," pp. 148-49; Cooper, *Sawdust and Revolutions,* p. 159; J. O. Crockett to I. Miller, telegram, June 9, Box 3, file 20, documents 1610-1632, Benson Collection; J. O. Crockett to I. Miller, telegram, June 10, 1913, Box 3, file 20, documents 1610-1632, Benson Collection; M. J. Gilmartin to J. J. Pruett, letter, June 13, 1913, Box 3, file 21, document 1644, Benson Collection. The Battle of Pearson section is a compilation based on the referenced sources. These sources disagree on some details.

633 Hatch and Hardy, *Stalwarts,* pp. 129, 144.

634 Stover, *The Search for the Soul of Mexico*, vol. 2, p. 162.

635 M. J. Gilmartin to J. J. Pruett, letter, June 13, 1913, Box 3, file 21, document 1644, Benson Collection; Cooper, *Sawdust and Revolutions,* p. 159.

636 J. O. Crockett to I. Miller, telegram, June 10, 1913, Box 3, file 20, documents 1610-1632, Benson Collection.

637 J. O. Crockett to I. Miller, telegram, June 20, 1913, Box 4, file 1, documents 1658-1690, Benson Collection.

638 Hulse, *Railroads and Revolution*, p. 38.

639 Hulse, p. 42.

640 A. L. Lathrop to I. Miller, and J.O. Crockett, telegram June 20, 1913, Box 4, file 1, documents 1658-1690, Benson Collection.

641 A. L. Lathrop to I. Miller, telegram, June 23, 1913, Box 4, file 1, document 1683, Benson Collection. Lathrop was an assistant manager with the Madera Lumber Company based in El Paso. Cooper refers to Villa in Pearson on page 160 but uses the same telegram source.

642 Adalberto Pérez Meillón, personal communication, email, December 7, 2020.

643 Katz, *Pancho Villa*, pp. 713-15.

644 Rondal R. Bridgemon, "Pancho Villa and the Raid on Columbus," unpublished, July 1, 2005, updated 2007, pp. 31-32; Katz, *Pancho Villa*, p. 713.

645 Guzmán, *Memoirs of Pancho Villa*, p. 97. Guzmán quotes Villa as saying the battle started at night and only lasted two hours.

646 Lister and Lister, *Storehouse of Storms*, pp. 236-37.

647 Castillo, "The Simple History of My Life," p. 149; Young, *Ordeal in Mexico*, p. 167; and Crockett to Miller, telegram, June 10, 1913 Box 3, file 20, documents 1610-1632, Benson Collection.

648 Donald Charles Hatcher, "Impact of the Mexican Revolution on Foreign Investment in Chihuahua and Coahuila, 1910-1920," MA thesis, (University of Montana, 1975), p. 36.

649 H.C. McMaster, MNWR Superintendent, Chihuahua Division, to Messrs. Bowen, Metsdorf, and Gallagher, letter, March 18, 1914, copy in the authors' collection. McMaster's grandson, Robert Bedwell of Pinole, California, had the letter and sent a copy to Edmond Von Nordeck of Riverside, CA. Von Nordeck conducted railroad tours in the Southwest during the 1970s. He made a copy for the authors in 1991.

650 McMaster, letter, March 18, 1914.

651 *The New York Times*, February 8, 9, and 19, 1914; *San Francisco Chronicle*, March 15, 1914; Hulse, *Railroads and Revolution*, pp. 49, 51; Hatcher, "Impact of the Mexican Revolution," p. 64; Castillo, "The Simple History of My Life," pp. 63-64; Cooper, *Sawdust and Revolutions,* pp. 163-167, McMaster, letter, March 18, 1914. Sources vary on the details. Unless otherwise noted, this summary is a result of crosschecking the references listed with others to find the most likely story.

652 McMaster, letter, March 18, 1914.

653 McMaster, letter.

654 McMaster, letter.

655 R. Home Smith, telegram. February, 1915, Box 5, file 1, document 2151, Benson Collection.

656 David Nelson, "The Cumbre Bypass: On the Trail of the Rails," lecture to the Gathering of Friends of Mata Ortiz on October 7, 2017; Nelson; personal communications, January 22 and 23, 2021.

657 Mexican government letter, Archivo General de Nación. Michael Torrington of Cancun copied several documents from the archive and sent them to Miguel Méndez in Nuevo Casas Grandes. Méndez gave the copies to David Nelson, who shared them with the authors.

658 Telegram, November, 1915, Box 5, file 3, documents 2241-2302, Benson Collection.

659 Hulse, *Railroads and Revolutions,* p. 87.

660 Hulse, p. 49.

661 Hart, *Empire and Revolution,* pp. 209-10.

662 Rondal R. Bridgemon, "The Pearson and Pacheco Railroad," unpublished article, July 17, 2018, p. 5.

663 *Railway Officials in America. The Biographical Directory of the Railway Officials of America,* (1906).

664 *Investigation of Mexican Affairs,* "Preliminary Report and Hearings of the Subcommittee on Foreign Relations of the United States Senate," 66th Congress, Second Session, vol. 2, (Government Printing Office, Washington D.C. 1920), Lewis E. Booker testimony, pp. 2614-15. This report includes the testimony Booker made to the subcommittee. Senator Albert B. Fall of New Mexico conducted the hearings in 1912 and included the minutes in the official report of the 1920 hearings.

665 *Investigation of Mexican Affairs,* L. P. Atwood, affidavit, pp. 2599-2602; Niels Larson affidavit, August 10, 1912, pp. 2594-2596.

666 Bridgemon, "The Pearson and Pacheco Railroad," p. 3.

667 Bridgemon, pp. 4, 7-8; Bridgemon, personal communication, March 27, 2021.

668 Hulse, *Railroads and Revolutions,* p. 38.

669 Louis Stevens, *Here Comes Pancho Villa,* (Frederick A. Stokes Co., New York, NY, 1930), p. 103.

670 Katz, *Pancho Villa,* p. 226.

671 Katz, p. 228.

672 Katz, p. 233.

673 Katz, pp. 237-38.

674 Guzmán, *Memoirs of Pancho Villa,* p. 132.

675 Telegram, July, 1915, Box 5, file 4, documents 1745-1777, Benson Collection.

676 Katz, *Pancho Villa,* p. 336.

677 Hatcher, "Impact of the Mexican Revolution on Foreign Investment," p. 43.

678 Stover, personal communication, July 6, 2019, Juan Mata Ortiz, Chih., MX.

679 Katz, *Pancho Villa*, pp. 524-25; Edgcumb Pinchon, *Viva Villa! A Recovery of the Real Pancho Villa*, (Harcourt, Brace and Company, New York, 1933), pp. 326-33; Whetten, *Colonia Juárez*, p. 59. There are numerous versions of Pancho Villa's history and details vary, sometimes widely. This ambiguity applies to the events surrounding the Battle of Agua Prieta. Our version relies on these sources.

680 Hatcher, "Impact of the Mexican Revolution on Foreign Investment," p. 44.

681 *El Paso Herald-Post*, September 7, 1960, Haldeen Braddy Collection, MS 154, University of Texas, El Paso Special Collections Library, MS 154. This collection includes many El Paso newspaper clippings primarily about Villa as well as Braddy and his writings. Most clippings are from the 1960s and 70s. Also, the *El Paso Times* ran a "Forty Years Ago" column, which often featured Villa items.

682 Walter Parks, personal journal, September, 1984.

683 Katz, *Pancho Villa*, pp. 547-48.

684 Katz, p. 562

685 Haldeen Braddy, *Pancho Villa at Columbus, the Raid of 1916*, (Texas Western College Press, El Paso, TX, 1965), pp. 15, 17, 24-25; Frank Tompkins, *The Last Campaign of the U.S. Cavalry*, (Military Service Publishing Co, Harrisburg, PA, 1934, High-Lonesome Books, Silver City, NM, 1996), pp. 48-49.

686 Rondal R. Bridgemon, "Maude Wright's Experience as a Captive of Pancho Villa," unpublished document, March 11, 2011. Wallace and Verna Crawford were the friends that took Maude Wright back to Columbus in 1960. A few historians apparently had access to the Crawford's written account of what Wright told them. Bridgemon was able to obtain a copy of the original Crawford version.

687 In the cavalry, a "troop" was the equivalent to an infantry company, and a "trooper" to a private. "Troops" is a general term, referring to soldiers of any kind.

688 Roger G. Miller, *A Preliminary to War, The 1st Aero Squadron and the Mexican Punitive Expedition 1916*, (Air Force History and Museums Program, Washington, D.C., 2003), p. 18.

689 Tompkins, *The Last Campaign*, pp. 76-77.

690 Cooper, *Sawdust and Revolutions*, p. 17; Tompkins, *The Last Campaign*, p. 91.

691 Rondal R. Bridgemon and Sylvia Brenner, "San Joaquín Canyon and the 1916 Punitive Expedition," *Journal of the Southwest*, 54, no. 1, (Spring, 2012), pp. 48-56; Tompkins, *The Last Campaign*, p. 208.

692 Tompkins, pp. 137-44; Lister and Lister, *Storehouse of Storms*, p. 259.

693 Tompkins, p. 209; Young, *Ordeal in Mexico*, pp. 217-24; Lister and Lister, *Storehouse of Storms*, p. 262.

694 Bridgemon, *Pancho Villa and the Raid on Columbus,* pp. 31-32.

695 Enrique Krauze, *Francisco Villa, entre el ángel y el fierro,* (Fondo de Cultura Económica, S.A. de C.V., México, D.F., 1997), pp. 95-97.

696 Roger G. Miller, "Wings and Wheels," *Air Power History,* (Winter, 1995), First Aero Squadron Foundation, Columbus, New Mexico, p. 20.

697 Townsend F. Dodd, "The First United States Aero Squadron, Mexican Adventures of Foulois, Carberry, Kilner, and Gorrell," *U.S. Air Service Magazine,* (September, 1919), Army and Navy Air Service Association, Washington D.C., p. 17.

698 Dodd, p. 17.

699 Benjamin D. Foulois, *From the Wright Brothers to the Astronauts, Memoirs of Major General Benjamin D. Foulois,* (McGraw-Hill Book Company, 1968), p. 28.

700 Karen M. Keehr, "Air Power in Mexico During the Punitive Expedition of 1916," *Southern New Mexico Historical Review,* VII, no. 1, (January, 2000), p. 42.

701 Jon Goldenbaum, personal communication, February 27, 2021. Colonel Goldenbaum is a retired combat Air Force officer, who has flown a wide variety of aircraft from antique planes to commercial jetliners. He flew a JN4 Jenney. Even with the more powerful Hispano Suiza engine, he found the aircraft difficult to fly by today's standards.

702 Miller, *A Preliminary to War,* p. 23.

703 Tompkins, *The Last Campaign,* pp. 108, 112.

704 Foulois, *Wright Brothers to the Astronauts,* p. 131.

705 Miller, "Wings and Wheels," p. 46.

706 The authors relied on a number of references regarding the First Aero Squadron, many of which were cited. These references did not always agree. This narrative is an attempt to tell what most likely occurred.

707 Hulse, *Railroads & Revolutions,* p. 76.

708 Hulse, p. 87; Cooke, *The Existential Joys of Fred Stark Pearson,* p. 117.

709 Cooke, pp. 216, 294-95.

710 *Who's Who in Railroading,* vol. 10, (1940, Simmons-Boardman Publishing, New York), p. 30.

711 L. Roy Hoard, *Memo. RE North Western Railway Company,* December 31, 1928, Box 949, Special Collections, El Paso Public Library, El Paso TX. This lengthy document is a report to the receiver and Board of Directors of MNWR by Vice President and General Manager L. Roy Hoard assisted by Controller O. Borst. Hulse, *Railroads & Revolutions,* pp. 86, 91.

712 Cooper, *Sawdust and Revolutions,* p. 49.

713 Hulse, *Railroads & Revolutions*, p. 88. This source says Smith offered Hoard the "presidency" of the Company. All other references, letterheads, etc. call him vice president and general manager.

714 Katz, *Pancho Villa*, p. 704.

715 Katz, pp. 580-81.

716 Tracy V. Hruska, "Agrarian Dreams, Agricultural Realities: Agricultural Land Conversion in Mexico's Chihuahuan Desert," PhD diss. (University of California, Berkeley, 2020), p. 37.

717 Boyer, *Political Landscapes*, pp. 79-81.

718 Katz, *Pancho Villa*, p. 705.

719 Cooper, *Sawdust and Revolutions*, p. 20.

720 American Consular Service report, Juárez, Mexico, May 23, 1919, Box 5, File 16, Benson Collection.

721 Cooke, *The Existential Joys of Fred Stark Pearson*, p. 218.

722 Katz, *Pancho Villa*, pp. 708, 900.

723 Cooper, *Sawdust and Revolutions*, p. 49.

724 Hoard, *Memo. RE Mexico North Western Railway Company*, p. 38.

725 Mexico North Western Railway Company, *Third Report of R. Home Smith, Receiver, June 22, 1921*, p. 3.

726 Boyer, *Political Landscapes*, p. 73.

727 Mexico North Western Railway Co., *Third Report*, p. 4.

728 Boyer, *Political Landscapes*, p. 116; Mexico North Western Railway Company, *Fourth Report of R. Home Smith, Receiver, November 14 , 1922*, p. 5.

729 Hoard, *Memo. RE Mexico North Western Railway Company*, Recommendations of the Management, #2, p. 57.

730 Boyer, *Political Landscapes*, p. 116.

731 Hoard, *Memo. RE Mexico North Western Railway Company*, p. 47.

732 Hulse, *Railroads & Revolutions*, pp. 109-110.

733 José Martínez, personal communication, March 5, 2008, interviewed in the home of Héctor Gallegos and Graciela Martínez.

734 Wasserman, *Capitalists, Caciques, and Revolution*, p. 75.

735 Lister and Lister, *Storehouse of Storms*, pp. 278-79.

736 Hulse, *Railroads & Revolutions*, pp. 102-103.

737 Hoard, *Memo. RE North Western Railway Company*. Unless otherwise noted, Roy Hoard's report of December 31, 1928 is the primary source for this section.

738 Ryerson, "The Potters of Porvenir," p. 96.

Chapter 14

739 See Chapter 11 for more of Fong Poi's story.

740 José Martínez, personal communication, March 5, 2008, in the home of Héctor Gallegos and Graciela Martínez, Juan Mata Ortiz, Chih; Livingston Paddock, *The Art of Survival, The Survival of Art,* p. 16.

741 Higinio (Gene) Luévano, personal communication, Norwalk, CA, February 9, 2016.

742 Higinio Luévano, "La Familia Luévano de Norwalk," Unpublished memoir, pp. 102-8.

743 Livingston Paddock, *The Art of Survival, The Survival of Art,* p. 16.

744 Livingston Paddock, p. 18; Héctor Gallegos and Graciela Martínez, personal communication, Juan Mata Ortiz, Chih., April 17, 2015.

745 Parker and Day, *Mules, Mines, and Me,* p. 33.

746 Ryerson, "The Potters of Porvenir," pp. 109-10.

747 Ryerson, p. 111.

748 Julia Estrada Ortiz, personal communication, Juan Mata Ortiz, Chih., with the aid of granddaughter Paty Ortiz and Adalberto Pérez Meillón, April 4, 2015.

749 Ryerson, "The Potters of Porvenir," pp. 104-6, 109-12; Walter Parks, *The Miracle of Mata Ortiz,* (Rio Nuevo Publishers, Tucson, AZ, 2011), pp. 25, 184-85. This section drew largely from these sources. The references in the "Miracle of Mata Ortiz" were gathered through a series of personal interviews over several years.

750 Gregorio Silveira, personal communication, Juan Mata Ortiz, Chih., July 26, 2021.

751 Ryerson, "The Potters of Porvenir," p. 107.

752 Mónico Corona, personal communication, home of Alfredo Rodríguez Corona, Juan Mata Ortiz, Chih., April 18, 2015.

753 Hoard, *Memo. RE North Western Railway Company,* p. 21.

754 Wes Wallace, personal communication, Corralitos, Chih., April 13, 2013.

755 Hruska, *Agrarian Dreams, Agricultural Realities,* p. 6.

756 Hruska, pp. 128-29.

757 Jerardo Sandoval Tena, personal communication, Juan Mata Ortiz, Chih., June 26, 2021 and May 24, 2022.

758 Eusebio Sandoval, personal communication, Juan Mata Ortiz, Chih., May 12, 2008.

759 Héctor Gallegos, personal communication, Juan Mata Ortiz, Chih., July 10, 2022. Another lariat maker named Antonio Herrera also lived in San Diego, Chih.

Chapter 15

760 Ryerson, "The Potters of Porvenir," p. 96.

761 "Evens and Howard Brick Company," *Brick, Special Issue on St. Louis,* XX, no. 5, (May, 1904), pp. 232-33.

762 Hoard, *Memo. RE Mexico North West Railway Company*, December 31, 1928.

763 Livingston Paddock, *The Art of Survival, The Survival of Art*, p. 16.

764 Ryerson, "The Potters of Porvenir," p. 105.

765 R. B. Brown, "Boceto de la Historia Regional: Datos sobre la Introduccción e impacto del Ferrocarril en el Noroeste de Chihuahua," Unpublished manuscript,(early 1990s), p. 10.

766 Hruska, "Agrarian Dreams, Agricultural Realities," p. 39.

767 Jennifer Brown, *Ejidos and Communidades in Oaxaca, Mexico: Impact of the 1992 Reforms*, Rural Development Institute Reports on Foreign Aid and Development #120, (February, 2004), p. 3.

768 Brown, *"Ejidos and Communidades,"* p. 5.

769 Domínguez, "Desintegración del Latifundio Terrazas," p. 116.

770 Brown, *"Ejidos and Communidades,"* p. 8.

771 Hruska, "Agrarian Dreams, Agricultural Realities," p. 44.

772 Hruska, p. 37.

773 Brown, *"Ejidos and Communidades,"* p. 7.

774 Domínguez, "Desintegración del Latifundio Terrazas," p. 132.

775 Héctor Gallegos, personal communication, Juan Mata Ortiz, Chih., January 22, 2022.

776 Jesús Bautista Fregoso, *50 Años, La historia médica personal,* (Ediciones del Azar A. C., Chih., 2004), p. 74.

777 Hulse, *Railroads & Revolutions*, p. 116.

778 Efraín Rodríguez Flores and Jorge Quintana Rodríguez, personal communications, Juan Mata Ortiz, Chih., May 16, 2008; Héctor Gallegos, personal communication, May 24 and 25, 2022, Juan Mata Ortiz, Chih; Jorge Quintana Rodríguez, personal communication, May 26, 2022, Juan Mata Ortiz, Chih.

779 Héctor Gallegos, personal communication, June 27, 2021, Juan Mata Ortiz, Chih.

780 Méndez García, "Ejido Casas Grandes, 1778-2013; 235 Años de Historia," pp. 111-115.

781 Domínguez, "Desintegración del Latifundio Terrazas," p. 119.

782 Domínguez, p. 120.

783 Domínguez, p. 121.

784 Méndez García, "235 Años de Historia," pp. 42-46. Reprint of the Periódico Oficial de La Federación. November 22, 1926.

785 Comisión de Reforma Agraria, Legislatura 61, Estado de Chihuahua.

786 Méndez García, "Ejido Casas Grandes," p. 45.

787 Comisión de Reforma Agraria, Legislatura 61.

788 Ortega Urquidi, *Casas Grandes, Tierra de Siete Culturas*, p. 223.

789 Janzen, *Liminal Sovereignty*, p. 52.

790 Philip Stover, personal communication, email September 1, 2022. Historian Stover has interviewed several older residents, who related various versions of this story. He has found no tangible evidence (deeds, etc.) to confirm the anecdotal accounts.

791 Froilán Meza Rivera, "Dan a Conocer Ruinas Similares a Las Cuarenta Casas," *Crónica de Chihuahua,* (April 2011), http://cronicadechihuahua.com /Dan-a-conocer-ruinas-similares-a.html

792 Janzen, *Liminal Sovereignty,* pp. 42-55.

793 Rebecca Janzen, "Conflict and Change in the LeBaron Community in Mexico," *Journal of Mormon History,* 47, no. 3, (July 2021), p. 78.

794 Diario Oficial de la Federación, March 10, 1999.

795 Diario Oficial de la Federación, February 2, 2017.

796 Ortega Urquidi, *Casas Grandes, Tierra de Siete Culturas,* pp. 222-31. Unless otherwise noted, much of the text, especially about Ejidos Casas Grandes, Heroínas, and Guadalupe Victoria was based on this source. Ortega Urquidi provides lists of the original ejidatarios and other details.

797 Hruska, "Agrarian Dreams, Agricultural Realities," p. 2.

798 Hruska, pp. 28, 65; Elizabeth Hansen, "Madera 1965, Obsessive Simplicity, the Agrarian Dream and Che," PhD diss., (University of Arizona, Tucson, AZ, 2015), p. 115.

799 Hruska, p. 41.

800 Spencer MacCallum, Newsletter no. 6, December 1, 1981.

801 Hruska, "Agrarian Dreams, Agricultural Realities," p. 10.

802 Campbell, *Mines, Cattle, and Rebellion,* p. 359.

803 Campbell, pp. 360-61. Wallace's daughters were Elisa, Herlinda and Adela Magdalena.

804 John Wesley Wallace, personal communication, Casa de Amo, Corralitos, Chih. April 13, 2013.

805 Campbell, *Mines, Cattle, and Rebellion,* p. 362.

806 Wallace, personal communication, April 13, 2013.

807 L. Roy Hoard, "Summary of a Speech Made by Mr. L.R. Hoard, President of Mexico Northwestern Railway Company," at an Informal Meeting of Shareholders of Mexico North West Holding Company Ltd. 7 1/2% Cumulative First Income Debenture Stock, Held at Winchester House, London, E.C. on Wednesday, 15th April, 1936, Roy Hoard Collection, El Paso Public Library.

808 Hulse, *Railroads & Revolutions,* pp. 114-16.

809 Boyer, *Political Landscapes,* pp. 131 and 145-46.

810 Thomas Weaver, "Mapping the Policy Terrain: Political Economy, Policy, Environment and Forestry Production in Northern Mexico," *Journal of Political Ecology,* 3, (1996), pp. 45-46.

811 Chris Guenzler, "Bosques de Chihuahua," unpublished account of a railroad tour by Let's Travel railroad tour company of Riverside, California, May, 1988.

812 Miguel Méndez García, "Máquina 525, El Simbolo de Nuevo Casas Grandes," unpublished manuscript provided by Sr. Méndez, a historian from Nuevo Casas Grandes, pp. 1-3.

813 José "Pino" Molina, personal communication, May 15, 2008, Juan Mata Ortiz, Chih. Molina took Arthur Miller, John Wingate, and author Walter Parks on the train in January, 1996.

814 Méndez García, "Máquina 525, El Simbolo de Nuevo Casas Grandes," pp. 1-3.

815 Miguel Méndez García, "La Fundación de Nuevo Casas, 96 Aniversario."

816 Hatch, *Médico, My Life as a Country Doctor in Mexico,* p. 87-88.

817 Hatch, p.56.

818 Bautista Fregoso, *50 Años*; Jesús Bautista Fregoso, *Historia de la Medicina en la Región Noroeste de Chihuahua,* (Editoriales Bauco, Nuevo Casas Grandes, Chih., Primera Edición, undated). Unless otherwise noted, the material for this section came from these two sources.

819 Interview with the late José Martínez, long time resident of Juan Mata Ortiz, Chih., March 5, 2008.

Bibliography

Archival Sources:

Archivo General de la Nación, Mexico City

Angelo State University, San Angelo, TX, Porter Henderson Library

Arizona State Museum, Library and Archives

Brigham Young University Library, L. Tom Perry Special Collections

California State, Fullerton, Pollak Library, University Archives & Special
    Collections

El Paso County Clerk, Historic Index Books

El Paso County Historical Society, Archival Collections

El Paso Public Library, Special Collections, Border Heritage Center

The Huntington Library

New Mexico History Museum, Fray Angélico Chávez History Library, Santa Fe

New Mexico State University, Library Archives and Special Collections

New York Public Library, Special Collections

Registro Público de la Propiedad de la ciudad de Chihuahua

Registro Público de la Propiedad de Ciudad Juárez

Registro Público de la Propiedad de la ciudad de Nuevo Casas Grandes

Tufts History, Tisch Library, University Archives and Special Collections

University of Arizona Libraires, Special Collections

University of California, Berkeley, Bancroft Library, University Archives

University of California, Riverside, Special Collections & University Archives

University of California, San Diego, Geisel Library, Special Collections and
    Archives

University of New Mexico, Center for Southwest Research and Special Collections

University of Texas, Austin, Nettie Lee Benson Latin American Collection

University of Texas, El Paso, C.L. Sonnichsen Special Collections Department

University of Utah, J. Willard Marriott Library Special Collections

Utah State University, Merrill-Cazier Library, Special Collections and Archives

Yale University Library, Special Collections

York University, Toronto, Clara Thomas Archives and Special Collections

Published Sources:

Acosta Ramírez, Diana. "Ex Hacienda de San Diego: Patrimonio Histórico de Casas Grandes." Agave Lindo Tours, 2010.

Adler, Lorna Call, William G. Hartley and Lane Johnson. *Anson Bowman Call: Bishop of Dublan*. Lorna Call Alder, Provo, Utah, 2007.

Almada, Francisco R. *Diccionario de Historia, Geografía y Biografía Chihuahuenses*. Talleres gráficos del gobierno del estado, Chihuahua, 1927.

Almada, Francisco R. and Guillermo Porras Muñoz. *Luis Terrazas: una polémica histórica*. Ediciones del Azar A.C., Chihuahua, 1999.

Armstrong, Christopher and H.V. Nelles. "A Curious Capital Flow: Canadian Investment in Mexico 1902-1910." *The Business History Review*, vol. 58, no. 2, Summer 1984.

Azuela, Luz Fernanda. "Towards a nationwide geological survey in nineteenth Century Mexico." in *History of Science: Celebrating 50 Years of INHIGEO*, Geological Society Special Publication 442. 2017.

Baca Miranda, Roberto César. *Recopilación de datos históricos de Casas Grandes, La Antigüa Paquimé*. Artedigital, Nuevo Casas Grandes, Chih., 2007.

Baldwin, Hanson W. *Sea Fights and Shipwrecks*. Hanover House, Garden City, NY, 1955.

Ball, Eve. *In the Days of Victorio: Recollections of a Warm Springs Apache*. University of Arizona Press, Tucson, 1970.

Bartlett, John Russell. *Personal Narrative of Explorations and Incidents in Texas, New Mexico, California, Sonora, and Chihuahua*. Appleton and Company, New York, 1854.

Bautista Fregoso, Jesús. *Historia de la medicina en la región Noroeste de Chihuahua*. Editoriales Bauco, Nuevo Casas Grandes, Chih., (n.d.).

——— *50 Años, La historia médica personal*. Ediciones del Azar A.C., Chih., 2004.

Beals, Ralph L. "The Comparative Ethnology of Northern Mexico Before 1750." *Ibero-Americano,* vol. 2, University of California, 1932. Republished in 1973 by Cooper Square Publishers, NY.

Beezley, William H. *Insurgent Governor: Abraham González and the Mexican Revolution in Chihuahua.* University of Nebraska Press, Lincoln, 1973.

Betzinez, Jason. *I Fought with Geronimo.* University of Nebraska Press, Lincoln, 1959.

Blyth, Lance R. *Chiricahua and Janos: Communities of Violence in the Southwestern Borderlands, 1680-1880.* University of Nebraska Press, Lincoln, 2012.

Boyer, Christopher R. *Political Landscapes: Forests, Conservation, and Community in Mexico.* Duke University Press, Durham, 2015.

Boyer, Christopher R. and Lucricia Orensanz. "Revolución y paternalismo ecológico: Miguel Ángel de Quevedo y la política forestal en México, 1926-1940." *Historia Mexicana,* vol. 57, no. 1, July-Sept. 2007.

Braddy, Haldeen. *Cock of the Walk, the Legend of Pancho Villa.* University of New Mexico Press, Albuquerque, 1955.

——— *Pancho Villa at Columbus: the Raid of 1916.* Texas Western College Press, El Paso, 1965.

Brand, Donald. "The Chihuahua Culture Area." *New Mexico Anthropologist,* vol. 6, Issue 3, September 1943.

——— "The Distribution of Pottery Types in Northwest Mexico." *American Anthropologist,* 37, April-June 1935.

Bridgemon, Rondal R. "Mennonites and Mormons in Northern Chihuahua." *Journal of the Southwest,* vol. 54, no. 1, Spring 2012.

Bridgemon, Rondal R. and Sylvia Brenner, "San Joaquín Canyon and the 1916 Punitive Expedition." *Journal of the Southwest,* vol. 54, no. 1, Spring 2012.

Brown, Jennifer. *Ejidos and Communidades in Oaxaca, Mexico: Impact of the 1992 Reforms.* Rural Development Institute Reports on Foreign Aid and Development #120, February 2004.

Brunson, B.R. *The Texas Land And Development Company:A Panhandle Promotion, 1912-1956.* University of Texas Press, Austin and London, 1970.

Bush, Dr. I.J. "The Battle of Casas Grandes." *Sports Afield,* August, 1912.

——— *Gringo Doc.* Caxton Printers, Ltd., Caldwell, ID, 1939.

Campbell, C.E. *Mines, Cattle, and Rebellion: The History of the Corralitos Ranch.* Green Street Publications, Sunset Beach, CA, 2014.

Canales, Jaime Abundis. "Luis Terrazas: Lord and Master of Chihuahua." *Voices of Mexico,* no. 63, April-June 2003.

Carlson, Roy L. "The Polychrome Complexes." *Arizona Archaeologist,* no. 15, summer 1982.

Castillo, Máximo. "The Simple History of My Life." In *Máximo Castillo and the Mexican Revolution,* edited by Jesús Vargas Valdés, Louisiana State University Press, Baton Rouge, 2016.

Chace, Russel E. *The Mexico Northwestern Company, LTD, 1908-1914.* Working Paper #4, CERLAC, Centre for Research on Latin America and the Caribbean, York University, Toronto, 1982.

Chang, Jason Oliver. *Chino: Anti-Chinese Racism in Mexico, 1880-1940.* University of Illinois Press, Urbana, 2017.

Chávez Barrón, Héctor. *Luis Terrazas.* (primera edición), Editorial Clio, Mexico City, 2004.

Cooke, Gilmore G. "Somerville Electric Light Company 1880-1903: The Design and Evolution of a Successful Enterprise." *Society for Industrial Archaeology,* (New England Chapters), 26, no. 1, 2005.

——— *The Existential Joys of Fred Stark Pearson (1861-1915): Engineer, Entrepreneur, Envisioner.* Budget Edition, San Bernardino, CA, 2019.

Cooper, Clarence. *Sawdust and Revolutions II: The Mexican Experience of C.H. Cooper 1911-1950.* Clarence Cooper, El Paso, 2015.

Cremony, John Carey. *Life Among the Apaches.* University of Nebraska Press, Lincoln, 1983. Initially published by A. Roman Company, San Francisco, 1868.

Davis, Britton. *The Truth About Geronimo.* University of Nebraska Press, Lincoln, 1976.

Day, James M. *Mules, Mines, and Me in Mexico.* The University of Arizona Press, Tucson, 1979.

Development Company of America, Annual Report of the President, 1909.

Di Peso, Charles C. (au) and Gloria J. Fenner (ed). *Casas Grandes, a Fallen Trading Center of the Gran Chichimeca.* Volumes 1-3, Amerind Foundation, Inc., Dragoon, AZ and Northland Press, Flagstaff, AZ, 1974.

Di Peso, Charles C., John B. Rinaldo and Gloria J. Fenner, *Casas Grandes, a Fallen Trading Center of the Gran Chichimeca.* vol. 4-8, Amerind Foundation, Inc., Dragoon, AZ and Northland Press, Flagstaff, AZ, 1974.

Di Peso, Charles C. "Casas Grandes Effigy Vessels." *American Indian Art,* Autumn 1977.

Dodd, Townsend F. "The First United States Aëro Squadron: Mexican Adventures of Foulois, Carberry, Kilner and Gorrell." *U.S. Air Service Magazine,* September 1919.

Domínguez Rascón, Alonso. "Procesos agrarios en Chihuahua." *Volume 4 of Cuadernos de Investigación,* Unidad de Estudios Históricos y Sociales - Extensión Chihuahua, Instituto de Ciencias Sociales y Administración, Universidad Autónoma de Ciudad Juárez, Chihuahua, Mayo 2004.

Eisenhower, John S.D. *So Far from God: The U.S. War with Mexico 1846-1848.* Random House Inc., NY, 1989.

"Evens and Howard Brick Company." *Brick, Special Issue on St. Louis,* vol. XX, no. 5, May 1904.

Farrington, O.C. "Catalogue of the Meteorites of North America." *Memoirs of the National Academy of Science,* vol. 13, Washington D.C., 1915.

Foulois, Benjamin D. and Carroll V. Glines. *From the Wright Brothers to the Astronauts: Memoirs of Major General Benjamin D. Foulois.* McGraw-Hill Book Company, 1968.

French, William E. "Business as Usual, Mexico Northwestern Railway Managers Confront the Mexican Revolution." *Mexican Studies* 5(2), Summer 1989.

Garibaldi, Giuseppe, *A Toast to Rebellion.* Garden City Publishing Co., Garden City, NY, 1937.

Garcia, Jerry. *Looking like the Enemy: Japanese-Mexicans, The Mexican State and US Hegemony, 1897-1945.* University of Arizona Press, Tucson, 2014.

Garate, Donald T. *Juan Bautista de Anza: Basque Explorer in the New World, 1693-1740.* University of Nevada Press, Reno, 2005.

Gemoets, Mark Edward. "The Mexico-Northwest Railroad and the Maderista Phase of the Mexican Revolution, 1910-1911." Master's thesis, New Mexico State University, 2007.

Gladwin, Harold S. and Winifred Gladwin. "A Method for Designation of Cultures and Their Variations." *Medallion Papers,* XV, Gila Pueblo, Globe, AZ, 1934.

Goodwin, Grenville and Neil Goodwin. *Apache Diaries: A Father-Son Journey.* University of Nebraska Press, Lincoln, 2000.

Glick, Thomas F. "Catalonia, Factory of Spain, an Exhibition in Barcelona." *Technology and Culture,* vol. 27, no. 3, July 1986.

Griffen, William B. *Indian Assimilation in the Franciscan Area of Nueva Vizcaya.* Anthropological Papers of the University of Arizona, no. 33, University of Arizona Press, Tucson, 1979.

——— *Apaches at War and Peace: The Janos Presidio, 1750-1858.* University of Oklahoma Press, Norman, 1988.

Grant, Jay Sutherland. "Revolution and Rebellion, Mormon Colonies of Northwest Chihuahua, 1912-1917." Master's thesis, New Mexico State University, December 1991.

Guzmán, Martín. *Memoirs of Pancho Villa.* University of Texas Press, Austin, 1965.

Hammond, George P. and Agapito Rey. *Obregon's History of 16th Century Explorations in Western America.* Wetzel Publishing Co., Los Angeles, 1928.

Hansen, Elizabeth. "Madera 1965: Obsessive Simplicity, the Agrarian Dream and Che." PhD diss., University of Arizona, 2015.

Harcum, Cornelia G. "Indian Pottery from the Casas Grandes Region, Chihuahua, Mexico." *Bulletin of the Royal Ontario Museum of Archeology,* December 1923.

Hardy, B. Carmon. "The Sonora, Sinaloa and Chihuahua Railroad." *Jahrbuch für Geschichte Lateinamerikas—Anuario de Historia de America Latina,* vol. 12, Issue 1, December 1975.

Hardy, R.W.H, Lieut., R.N. *Travels in the Interior of Mexico.* Rio Grande Press, Inc., Glorieta, NM, 1977. First published by H. Colburn and R. Bentley, London, 1829.

Hart, John Mason. *Empire and Revolution: The Americans in Mexico since the Civil War.* University of California Press, Berkeley, 2001.

Haslip, Joan. *The Crown of Mexico.* Holt, Rinehart, and Winston, NY, 1972.

Hatch, E. LeRoy. *Médico: My Life as a Country Doctor in Mexico.* Jeanne J. Hatch, Mesa, AZ, 1999 and 2016.

Hatch, Nellie Spilsbury and B. Carmon Hardy. *Stalwarts South of the Border.* Ernestine Hatch, 1985.

Hatcher, Donald Charles. "Impact of the Mexican Revolution on Foreign Investment in Chihuahua and Coahuila, 1910—1920." Master's thesis, University of Montana, 1975.

Hernandez, A.C. "Yes You Can." *Southern New Mexico Historical Review,* vol. IV, no. 1, January 1997.

Hoard, L. Roy. "Memo. RE Mexico North Western Railway Company," December 31, 1928. Special Collections, El Paso Public Library.

Hogan, Michael. *Abraham Lincoln and Mexico: a History of Courage, Intrigue and Unlikely Friendships.* Egret Books, San Diego, 2016.

Hovey, Edmund Otis. "The Western Sierra Madre of the State of Chihuahua, Mexico." *Bulletin of the American Geological Society,* XXXVII, January 1905.

Hruska, Tracy V. "Agrarian Dreams, Agricultural Realities: Agricultural Land Conversion in Mexico's Chihuahuan Desert." PhD diss., University of California, 2020.

Hu-DeHart, Evelyn. "Immigrants to a Developing Society: the Chinese in Northern Mexico, 1875-1932." *Journal of Arizona History,* vol. 21, no. 3, Autumn 1980.

Hughes, Anne E. *The Beginnings of Spanish Settlement in the El Paso District.* University of California Publications in History, vol. 1, no. 3, Berkeley, 1914.

Hughes, Kiara Maureen. "The Women Potters of Mata Ortiz: Growing Empowerment Through Artistic Work." PhD diss., University of New Mexico, 2009.

Hulse, J.E. *Railroads & Revolutions: the Story of Roy Hoard.* Mangan Books, El Paso, 1986.

Jackson, Jack and William O. Foster. *Imaginary Kingdom: Texas as seen by the Rivera and Rubí Expeditions, 1727and 1767.* Texas State Historical Association, Austin, 1995.

Jacques, Leo Michael Dambourges. "The Anti-Chinese Campaigns in Sonora Mexico, 1900-1921." PhD diss., University of Arizona, 1974.

Janzen, Rebecca. *Liminal Sovereignty: Mennonites and Mormons in Mexican Culture.* State University of New York Press, Albany, 2018.

——— "Conflict and Change in the LeBaron Community in Mexico." *Journal of Mormon History*, vol. 47, no. 3, July 2021.

Johnson, William Weber. *Heroic Mexico, The Violent Emergence of a Modern Nation.* Doubleday and Co., Garden City, NY, 1968.

Juárez, Fernando Jordán. *Crónica de un País Bárbaro.* Centro Libreo La Prensa, Chihuahua, Chih., 1975.

Katz, Friedrich. *Life and Times of Pancho Villa.* University Press, Stanford, CA, 1998.

Keehr, Karen M. "Air Power in Mexico During the Punitive Expedition of 1916." *Southern New Mexico Historical Review,* vol. VII, no. 1, January 2000.

Kelley, Jane H., David A. Phillips Jr., A.C. McWilliams and Rafael Cruz Antillón. "Land Use, Looting, and Archaeology in Chihuahua, Mexico: A Speculative History." *Journal of the Southwest,* vol. 53, no. 2, Summer 2011.

Kerr, John Leeds. *Destination Topolobampo: the Kansas City, Mexico and Orient Railway.* Golden West Books, San Marino, CA, 1968.

Kidder, A.V. "The Pottery of the Casas Grandes District." in *Holmes Anniversary Volume; Anthropological Essays Presented to William Henry Holmes in Honor of his Seventieth Birthday, December 1, 1916*, edited by Frederick Webb Hodge, Washington D.C., 1916.

King, Laura and Amparo Garcia. "Mormons Found Sanctuary in Mexico in 1880s." *Borderlands*, 19, El Paso Community College, 2000.

Kinnaird, Lawrence. *The Frontiers of New Spain: Nicolás De Lafora's Description, 1766-1768.* The Quivira Society, Berkeley, 1958, Arno Press Inc., NY, 1967.

Kovach, Robert L. *Early Earthquakes of the Americas.* Cambridge University Press, Cambridge, UK, 2004.

Krauze, Enrique. *Francisco Villa: entre el ángel y el fierro.* vol. 4, Fondo de Cultura Económica, Mexico, D. F., 1987.

Krauze, Enrique (au) and Hank Heifetz (trans) *Mexico: Biography of Power, History of Modern Mexico, 1810-1996.* Harper Collins, NY, 1997.

Lange, Charles H. and Carroll L. Riley. *The Southwestern Journals of Adolph F. Bandelier 1883-1884.* University of New Mexico Press, Albuquerque, 1970.

Larson, Andrew Karl. *Erastus Snow: The Life of a Missionary and Pioneer for the Early Mormon Church.* University of Utah Press, Salt Lake City, 1971.

Lee, M. Patricia. "Analysis of the Carl Lumholtz Collection of Casas Grandes Ceramic Artifacts at the American Museum of Natural History." PhD diss., The City University of New York, 2013.

Lekson, Stephen H. *Chaco Meridian, One Thousand Years of Political Power.* Rowman and Littlefield Publishers, Lanham, MD, 2015, 2nd ed., first published 2009.

Lister, Florence C. and Robert H. Lister. *Chihuahua, Storehouse of Storms.* The University of New Mexico Press, Albuquerque, 1966.

Lloyd, Jane-Dale. "Rancheros and Rebellion: The Case of Northwestern Chihuahua, 1905-1909." in *Rural Revolt in Mexico: U.S Intervention and the Domain of Subaltern Politics* edited by Daniel Nugent, Monograph Series no. 7, Center for Mexican Studies, University of California, 1998.

——— *El distrito Galeana en los albores de la Revolución.* Secretaría de Educación, Cultura y Deporte, Gobierno del Estado de Chihuahua, 2011.

Long, Rodney. *Railways of Mexico.* Trade Promotion Series no. 16, Department of Commerce, Washington D.C., 1925.

Lumholtz, Carl. *Unknown Mexico: Explorations in the Sierra Madre and Other Regions, 1890-1898.* vol. I, Dover Publications, Inc., New York, 1982. Initially published by Scribners, NY, 1902.

Lunt, Marion, R. *Heaton Lunt of Colonia Pacheco*. CreateSpace Independent Publishing Platform, North Charleston, SC, 2013.

MacHugh, R.J. *Modern Mexico*. Dodd, Mead, and Co., NY, 1914.

Martín, Luis. *Memoirs of Pancho Villa*. University of Texas Press, Austin, 1965.

Martineau, Jess Rex and Laurie Martineau. *Colonia Chuichupa: Mormon Colony in the Sierra Madre Mountains of Mexico*. Family Heritage Publisher, Murray, UT, April 2015.

McCaa, Robert. "The Peopling of Mexico from Origins to Revolution." in *Population History of North America*, edited by Michael R. Haines and Richard. H. Steckel, Cambridge University Press, 2000.

Mecham, J. Lloyd. *Francisco de Ibarra and Nueva Vizcaya*. Greenwood Press, NY, 1968.

Meed, Douglas V. *They Never Surrendered: Bronco Apaches of the Sierra Madre, 1880-1935*. Westernlore Press, Tucson, 1993.

Méndez García, Miguel. *Ejido Casas Grandes, 1778-2013: 235 Años de Historia*. self-published, (n.d.).

Merrill, George P. and William F. Foshag. "Minerals from Earth and Sky: Part I, The Story of Meteorites." *Smithsonian Scientific Series*, 3, 1929.

"The Mexican Light and Power Co., Limited." in *The Manual of Statistics*, 1915.

Mexico North Western Railway promotional brochure. Ferris, H.C. and T.R Ryan, 1909. Obtained from The Huntington Library.

Mexico North Western Railway Company, Director's First Annual Report & Accounts 1910. Obtained from University of California, San Diego Library.

Mexico North Western Railway Company, Second Annual Report, December 31, 1911. Obtained from University of California, San Diego Library.

Mexico North Western Railway Company, Third Report of R. Home Smith, Receiver, June 22, 1921. Obtained from Yale University Library.

Mexico North Western Railway Company, Fourth Report of R. Home Smith, Receiver, November 14, 1922. Obtained from Yale University Library.

"Mexico North Western Railroad." in *The Manual of Statistics, The Stock Exchange Handbook, 1910*. The Manual of Statistics Company, NY.

"Mexico North Western Railroad." in *The Manual of Statistics, The Stock Exchange Handbook, 1913*. The Manual of Statistics Company, NY.

Meyer, Michael C., William L. Sherman and Susan M. Deeds. *The Course of Mexican History*. Oxford University Press, NY, 1999.

Miller, Roger G. *A Preliminary to War: The First Aero Squadron and the Punitive Expedition of 1916.* Air Force History and Museums Program, Washington, D.C., 2003.

Mills, Elizabeth, N. "The Mormon Colonies in Chihuahua After the 1912 Exodus." Master's thesis, University of Arizona, 1950.

Monnig, Oscar E. "How the Casas Grandes, Chihuahua, Mexico, meteorite got to Washington D.C." *Society for Research on Meteorites*, 2, Issue 5, January 1939.

Monumentos Históricos Inmuebles: Chihuahua, Catálogo Nacional. Secretaría de Educación Público, INAH, Mexico City, 1986.

Morse, Stearns. "The Yankee Spirit: Fred Stark Pearson." (Part III, unpublished manuscript), 1993, edited 2008. Tufts University, Tisch Library, Archives and Special Collections.

——— "Slots in the Streets." *The New England Quarterly,* vol. 24, no. 1, March, 1951.

Moulard, Barbara. *Within the Underworld Sky, Mimbres Ceramic Art in Context.* Twelvetrees Press, Pasadena, CA, 1984.

Mundt, Michael Norman. "Revolution and Reaction: the Mexico North Western Railway Company During the 1912 Pascual Orozco Rebellion." Master's thesis, New Mexico State University, 1991.

Naylor, Thomas H. and Charles W. Polzer. *Pedro de Rivera and the Military Regulations for New Spain 1724-1729.* University of Arizona Press, Tucson, 1988.

Ortega Urquidi, Javier. *Casas Grandes: tierra de siete culturas.* Socia Creativa, Mexico, 2008.

Paddock, Ana Livingston. *Mata Ortiz: The Art of Survival, The Survival of Art, Graciela and Héctor Gallegos.* Casa Aurora Publications, Santa Fe, NM and Juan Mata Ortiz, Chih., 2011.

Parkes, Henry Bamford. *A History of Mexico.* Houghton Mifflin Company, Boston, 1938.

Parker, Morris B. *Mules, Mines, and Me in Mexico.* University of Arizona Press, Tucson, 1979.

Paulsen, George E. 'Reaping the Whirlwind in Chihuahua: Destruction of the Minas de Corralitos, 1911-1917." *Mexican Historical Review,* vol. 58, no. 3, 1983.

Parks, Walter. *The Miracle of Mata Ortiz.* Rio Nuevo Publishers, Tucson, 2011.

Pearson, F.S. and P.O Blackwell. "The Necaxa Plant of the Mexican Light and Power Company." *Transactions from the American Society of Engineers,* vol. LVIII, June 1907.

Pershing, John J., Major General. *Punitive Expedition.* U.S. Army Military History Institute, Carlisle, PA, October 10, 1916.

Plana, Manuel. *Pancho Villa and the Mexican Revolution.* Interlink Publishing Group, Inc., Northampton, MA, 2002.

Pletcher, David M. *Rails, Mines, and Progress: Seven American Promoters in Mexico, 1867-1911.* Kennikat Press, Port Washington, NY, 1972. Also published by Cornell University Press, Ithaca, N.Y., 1958.

Plummer, W.P. "Frederick Stark Pearson, Consulting Engineer of the Metropolitan Street Railway Co." *Cassier's Magazine,* vol. XVIII, May-October 1900.

Poor's Manual of Railroads. NY, 1900.

Porras Muñoz, Guillermo. *Haciendas de Chihuahua.* Gobierno del Estado de Chihuahua, Coordinación de Comunicación Social, Chih., MX, 1993.

Powell, Fred Wilbur. *The Railroads of Mexico.* The Stratford Co., Boston, 1921.

Roberts, Lois J. "Archaeological Investigations on the San Antonio Terrace, Vandenberg Air Force Base, California, in Connection with MX Facilities Construction. Appendix II. Historical Overview of the Study Area." Stanton CA, January 1984.

Romney, Thomas Cottam. *Mormon Colonies in Mexico.* The University of Utah Press, Salt Lake City, 2005. Originally published by the Deseret Book Company, 1938.

Ryerson, Scott H. "The Potters of Porvenir: The Lesser Known Artisans of Mata Ortiz." *Kiva, The Journal of Southwestern Anthropology and History,* vol. 60, no. 1, Fall 1994.

Romero, Robert Chao. *The Chinese in Mexico, 1882-1940.* The University of Arizona Press, Tucson, 2011.

Santiago, Mark. "The Red Captain, The Life of Hugo O'Conor." *The Arizona Historical Society Museum Monograph,* no. 9, 1994.

Santleben, August. *A Texas Pioneer: Early Staging and Overland Freighting Days on the Frontiers of Texas and Mexico.* The Neale Publishing Co., New York and Washington, 1910.

Sayles, A.V. "Some Southwestern Pottery Types." *Medallion Papers,* XXI, Gila Pueblo, Globe, AZ, 1936.

Scholes, France V., Marc Simmons and José Esquibel, eds., Eleanor B. Adams, trans. *Juan Domínguez de Mendoza: Soldier and Frontiersman of the Spanish Southwest, 1627-1693.* University of New Mexico Press, Albuquerque, 2012.

Schroeder, Albert H. "Southwestern Ceramics, a Comparative Review." *The Arizona Archaeologist,* no. 15, August, 1982.

Schwatka, Frederick. *In the Land of Cave and Cliff Dwellers.* The Castle Publishing Co., New York, 1893.

Scurlock, Dan. *High Desert Land and Its Peoples: A Guidebook to the Eco-Cultural History and Archaeology of the Casas Grandes Area, Chihuahua, Mexico.* El Valle del Norte, Albuquerque, NM, 1992.

Sonnichsen, C.L. "Colonel William C. Greene and the Strike at Cananea, Sonora, 1906." *Arizona and the West,* vol. 13, no. 4, Winter 1971.

——— *Colonel Greene and the Copper Skyrocket.* University of Arizona Press, 1974.

Smith, Ralph Adam. *Borderlander: The Life of James Kirker, 1793-1852.* University of Oklahoma Press, Norman, 1999.

Spude, Robert L. "Frank Morrill Murphy, 1884-1917: Mining and Railroad Mogul and Developer of the American Southwest." in *Mining Tycoons in the Age of Empire, 1870-1945: Entrepreneurship, High Finance, Politics and Territorial Expansion,* edited by Raymond E. Dumett. Ashgate Publishing, Farnham, Surrey, UK, 2009.

Stevens, Louis. *Here Comes Pancho Villa.* Frederick A. Stokes Co., New York, NY, 1930.

Stewart, Joe D., Jane H. Kelley, A.C. MacWilliams and Paula J. Reimer. "The Viejo Period of Chihuahua Culture in Northwestern Mexico." *Latin American Antiquity,* vol. 16. no. 2, Cambridge University Press, Cambridge, June 2005.

Stover, Philip R. *Religion and Revolution in Mexico's North.* Río Vista Press, Deming, NM and Mata Ortiz, Chih., 2014.

——— *The Search for the Soul of Mexico, vol. 1, Religion and Revolution.* Río Vista Press, Deming, NM, 2018.

——— *The Search for the Soul of Mexico, vol. 2, The Anglo Quest for Naboth's Vineyard.* Río Vista Press, Deming, NM, 2018.

——— "The Exodus of 1912: a Huddle of Pros and Cons—Mormons Twice Dispossessed." *Journal of Mormon History,* vol. 44, no. 3, 2018.

Sutton, Paul Andrew. *Apache Wars.* Broadway Books, NY, 2016.

Sweeney, Edwin R. *Cochise: Chiricahua Apache Chief.* University of Oklahoma Press, Norman, 1991.

——— *Mangas Coloradas.* University of Oklahoma Press, Norman, 1998.

Tassin, Wirt. "The Casas Grandes Meteorite." *Proceedings of the U.S. National Museum,* vol. 25, no. 1277, 1902.

Taylor, Lawrence D. "The Great Adventure, Mercenaries in the Mexican Revolution, 1910-1915." *The Americas,* vol. 43, no. 1, Cambridge University Press, July 1986.

Thrapp, Dan L. *Juh: An Incredible Indian*. Texas Western Press, University of Texas, Austin, 1973.

——— *Conquest of Apacheria*. University of Oklahoma Press, Norman, 1975.

——— *Victorio and the Mimbres Apaches*. University of Oklahoma Press, Norman, 1980.

Timmons, W.H. "The El Paso Area in the Mexican Period, 1821-1848." *The Southwestern Historical Quarterly*, vol. 84, no. 1, July 1980.

Tompkins, Frank. *The Last Campaign of the U.S. Cavalry*. Originally published by the Military Service Publishing Co, Harrisburg, PA, 1934, reprinted by High-Lonesome Books, Silver City, NM, 1996.

Vázquez Lozano, Gustavo A. and Charles River, editors. *The United States-Mexico Border: The Controversial History and Legacy of the Boundary between America and Mexico*. CreateSpace Independent Publishing, North Charleston, SC, 2017.

Walter, Paul F. "Edgar Lee Hewitt, Americanist, 1865-1946." *American Anthropologist,* 49 (2) April-June 1947.

Wasserman, Mark. *Capitalists, Caciques, and Revolution*. University of North Carolina Press, Chapel Hill, 1984.

——— *Persistent Oligarchs, Elites and Politics in Chihuahua, Mexico, 1910-1940*. Duke University Press, Durham, 1993.

Weaver, Thomas. "Mapping the Policy Terrain: Political Economy, Policy, Environment and Forestry Production in Northern Mexico." *Journal of Political Ecology*, vol. 3, 1996.

Whetten, LaVon Brown. *Colonia Juárez: Commemorating 125 Years of the Mormon Colonies in Mexico*. Author House, Bloomington, IN, 2010.

Who's Who in Railroading. vol. 10, Simmons-Boardman Publishing, NY, 1940.

Wionczek, Miguel S. "The State and the Electric-Power Industry in Mexico, 1895-1965." *Business History Review*, vol. 39, no. 4, Special Latin American Issue, Winter 1965.

Worcester, Donald E. *The Beginnings of the Apache Menace of the Southwest*. University Press, Albuquerque, 1941.

Yetman, David A. *The Ópatas: In Search of a Sonoran People*. University of Arizona Press, Tucson, 2010.

Young, Desmond. *A Member for Mexico*. Cassell and Company, London, 1966.

Young, Karl E. *Ordeal in Mexico*. Deseret Book Company, Salt Lake City, 1968.

Newspapers

Boston Daily Globe, July 13, 1915, "Dr. Pearson Leaves $500,000 to Tufts." p. 8.

Deseret Weekly, Jensen, Andrew Alfred. "In Mexico." vol. 48, 1894.

Economist, Mar. 6, 1909, "Abridged Prospectus, Mexico North Western Railway Co." p. 557.

Los Angeles Times Farm and Garden Magazine, Collison, Thomas F., "Just as of Yore, Cattle Still Graze on Ancient Rancho." March 13, 1932, p. 5.

Mining and Scientific Press, Dec. 25, 1909, "Special Correspondence: Mexico." pp. 861-62.

——— "Mexico Gains Stability." Jan. 6, 1912, p. 5.

The New York Times, June 25, 1897, "New Mexican Line, Opening of the Rio Grande, Sierra Madre and Pacific." p. 3.

——— Nov. 20, 1900, "Chinese Miners For Mexico." p. 3."

——— Aug. 14, 1909, "Greene Mineral Lands Sold." p. 11.

——— Feb. 8, 1914, "Bandits Seize Americans: Castillo's Band Fire Tunnel and Train and Escape." p.1.

——— Feb. 9, 1914, "Villa Tells Wilson He'll Punish Bandit." p.1.

——— Feb. 19, 1914, "Castillo Blames Disaster on Villa." p. 1.

——— Aug. 16, 1953, "Mexico Will Take Vast Hearst Ranch, One Million Acres in Chihuahua Area to Become Small Farms." p. 29.

San Francisco Chronicle Sunday Magazine, "Mad Bandit Snuffs Out 55 Lives." Neville, Captain John T., March 15, 1914, p. 1.

Somerville Journal, "Somerville's first high tech startup." Dower, Erin, June 30, 2005, p.1.

Unpublished Citations

Bridgemon, Rondal R. "Pancho Villa and the Raid on Columbus." July 1, 2007.

——— "Madero at Hacienda de San Diego." January 2011.

——— "Maude Wright's Experience as a Captive of Pancho Villa." March 11, 2011.

——— "The Pearson and Pacheco Railroad." July 17, 2018.

Liehr, Reinhard and Mariano E. Torres Bautista. "From Free-Standing Company to Public Enterprise: Mexican Light and Power Company and the Mexican Tramways Company, 1902-1965." Presented at the XIII Conference, *Doing Business in Latin America,* Buenos Aires, 2002.

MacCallum, Spencer. Newsletter no. 6, December 1, 1981.

Phillips, Jr., David A. "The End of Casas Grandes, the Legacy of Charles C. DiPeso: Fifty Years After the Joint Casas Grandes Project," 73rd annual meeting of the Society for American Archaeology, Vancouver, Canada, March 27, 2008.

Ryerson, Scott. "Talk to Anthros." Unpublished manuscript of lecture given July 31, 1991.

Stover, Philip R. "Traición a La Boquilla." Presentation, Chihuahua State Archive, la ciudad de Chihuahua, October 16, 2021.

Internet Resource Citations

Arlington Cemetery Website, Emmet Crawford. https://ancexplorer.army.mil/publicwmv/index.html#/search-all/AP Archive. https://www.youtube.com/watch?v=CDSLb3SRzTA https://www.youtube.com/watch?v=CDSLb3SRzTA, July 10, 2015.

Boston Edison Company, Boston, Mass., Funding Universe, company histories. http://www.fundinguniverse.com/company-histories/boston-edison -company-history/

Black, Morley Larsen (au), Bruce J. Black (ed). A Short Autobiography (1875-1951). https://archive.orghttps://archive.org/details/AShortAutobiography ByMorleyLarsenBlack1875-1951/page/n1/mode/2up/

Bryant, B.H. "Letters on Regional Railroads." July, 1901, Tutt Library, Colorado College, Colorado Springs, CO. https://libraryweb.coloradocollege.edu/ library/specialcollections/CenturyChest/transcription63.html

Casas Grandes, Pueblo Mágico, Chihuahua Mexico. https://www.pueblosmexico.com.mx/casas-grandes-pueblo-magico.html.

Caslon, Bradford. *Edwin J. Marshall—304 South Westlake Ave.,* A Look Back at Vintage Los Angeles, July 22, 2012. http://www.oldhomesoflosangeles.org/2012/07/edwin-j-marshall-304-south -westlake.html

CNN Wire Staff. *Mexico's Historical Figures Exhumed.* May 31, 2010. http://www.cnn.com/2010/WORLD/americas/05/31/mexico.historical. figures.exhumed/index.html

Compton, Todd. *John Willard Young, Brigham Young and the Development of Presidential Succession in the LDS Church.* https://www.dialoguejournal.com/wp-content/uploads/sbi/articles/Dialogue _V35N04_125.pdf

Cultura INAH, *Paquimé* Centro INAH Chihuahua. http://inahchihuahua.gob .mx/sections.pl?id=43

Drew, Bernard. *Great Barrington, Great Town, Great History*. The Berkshire Eagle, September 13, 2019. https://www.berkshireeagle.com/stories/bernard-a-drew-our-berkshires-fred-s-pearson-powerful-innovator,584669

Domínguez Rascón, Alonso. "La Desintegración del Latifundio Terrazas, Historia de la Propiedad." *Chihuahua Hoy*, 2011, Universidad Autónoma de Ciudad Juárez, Libros Electrónicos. https://elibros.uacj.mx/omp/index.php/publicaciones/catalog/download/63/58/518-1?inline=1

Ejido Casas Grandes, Chihuahua, Mexico. https://sites.google.com/site/ejidocasasgrandes/acerca-del-ejido.

Galindo Hernández, Sergio. "Japanese Immigrants Who Joined the Mexican Revolution." *Discover Nikkei*, Nov. 2016. http://discovernikkei.org/en/journal/2016/11/7/revolucion-mexicana/;

Gamboa Carrera, Eduardo Pío. "La arquitectura de la Paquimé, Unidades IX y X, Los Montículos de los Héroes y Pájaro." GacetINAH (1 November 2021). https://issuu.com/pepiko/docs/gacetinah_noviembre_2021_web?fbclid=IwAR0qkDFt-gMMoegDOuirFU8RYPwyfT4i9INC6KB5c5PKBniLp36vDvduIEw

Hart, John Mason. *Foreign Proprietors and the Mexican Constitution*. Bibliotheca Jurídica Virtual Instituto de Investigaciones Jurídicas UNAM, 1993. https://archivos.juridicas.unam.mx/www/bjv/libros/7/3447/8.pdf

Hooper, Henry E. 1975, *Biography: Adolph Bandelier*. https://henryehooper.blog/witness-post-adolph-bandelier/.

Internet Archives Open Library, Alfonso Lancaster Jones. edited April 12, 2010. https://openlibrary.org/authors/OL4278177A/Alfonso_Lancaster-Jones

Krenn, Peter, Paul Kalus and Bert Hall. "Material Culture and Military History: Test-Firing Early Modern Small Arms." *Material Cultures Review*, vol. 42, Fall 1995. https://journals.lib.unb.ca/index.php/MCR/article/view/17669

McDowall, Duncan. "PEARSON, FREDERICK STARK," *Dictionary of Canadian Biography*, in EN:UNDEF: public_citation_publication, vol. 14, University of Toronto/Université Laval, 2003–2005. http://www.biographi.ca/en/bio/pearson_frederick_stark_14E.html.

Minnis, Paul. "Casas Grandes." *Expedition Magazine*, vol. 35, issue 1, 1993. http://www.penn.museum/sites/expedition/?p=4307.

Morrison, Allen. "Early Electrics." "The Tramways of Mexico City." part 2. http://www.tramz.com/mx/mc/mc20.html

Owens, Carole. "Connection: The Huckleberry King of the Berkshires." *The Berkshire Edge*, September 3, 2019. https://theberkshireedge.com/connections-51.

——— "Connection: Cottage Industry." *The Berkshire Edge,* September 10, 2019. https://theberkshireedge.com/connections-52/.

Paper Money of Chihuahua. https://papermoneyofmexico.com/

Phillips, Jr., David A., Christine Van Pool and Todd Van Pool. "Archaeology and Prehistory of Northwest Mexico, Bibliography." 2011. *https://www.unm. edu/~dap/nwm/nwm-english.html*

Phillips, Jr., David A. "Archaeology and Prehistory of Northwest Mexico: A "Rough Essay." 2011. https://www.unm.edu/~dap/nwm/introduction.html,

——— "Chaco Meridian, a Skeptical Analysis." Revision of a presentation in 2000 to the Society American Archaeology, last revised January 1, 2009. https://www.unm.edu/~dap/meridian/meridian-text.html

"Presidio San Felipe y Santiago de Janos Records 1706-1858." Benson Latin American Collection, April 1994. http://lanic.utexas.edu/project /lucasalaman/mexicanarchives/Janos.html

Quevedo Rivero, Arturo. "Rodrigo M. Quevedo Moreno, Una semblanza biográfica." *Rancho Las Voces, Revista de Arte y Cultura,* Ciudad Juárez, Chihuahua, 2004. https://rancholasvoces.blogspot.com/2005/10/rodrigo -m-quevedo-moreno.html

Railway Officials in America. The Biographical Directory of the Railway Officials of America, Edition of 1906. https://www.google.com/books/edition/The _Biographical_Directory_of_the_Railwa/c8ApAAAAYAAJ?hl=en&gbpv =1&dq=Railway+Officials+in+America,&printsec=frontcover

Russell, Yancy L. *Frederick Stark Pearson*, Handbook of Texas Online. Texas State Historical Association, June 15, 2010, modified November 10, 2017. http://www.tshaonline.org/handbook/online/articles/fpe06.

SEDATU, Boletín 316 Resuelve el Gobierno de la República conflict agrario del Ejido Casas Grandes, Chihuahua. https://www.gob.mx/sedatu/prensa /resuelve-el-gobierno-de-la-republica-conflicto-agrario-del-ejido-casas -grandes-chihuahua

Sudweeks, Leslie L. *The Miracle of the Piedras Verdes: The Story of the Founding of Colonia Juárez.* https://whipple.org/edson/piedrasverdes.html

Tippin, Brenda L. July 2013. https://www.morganhorse.com/upload/photos /904TMH_July2013_HearstMorgans.pdf

Woods, Fred E. "Finding Refuge in El Paso: the 1912 Exodus from Mexico." *Meridian Magazine* October 14, 2012. https://latterdaysaintmag.com /article-1-11596/

Acknowledgements

This book took us on a long journey made possible only by the willing help of so many friends, new and old. Some worked with us for years, following our progress, providing encouragement and help when needed. Others, we encountered just once or twice as we searched for specific bits of information.

We must first acknowledge Adalberto Pérez Meillón. This former school teacher, artist and pottery trader with so many friends in the Mata Ortiz region, guided us through our research trips, providing insight as well as contacts and key translation service.

Philip Stover and Rondal Bridgemon gave freely of their vast knowledge of the local region in numerous conversations and email exchanges. We also used their published and unpublished works extensively.

Miguel Méndez García from Nuevo Casas Grandes opened his library to us, furnished his writings, and joined us in our search for source documents. Leopoldo Horacio Chávez, official historian of the Casas Grandes Municipio, met with us several times, answered long lists of questions and joined us on research trips.

Diana Acosta Ramírez helped in so many ways over the years, graciously providing information and making contacts for us.

Sadly, our good friend, Spencer Heath MacCallum passed away before the book was finished. He constantly encouraged us, provided information, and introduced us to numerous people that further contributed to the book.

Years of conversations and note taking in Mata Ortiz generated an almost unmanageable list of people who helped. Jorge Quintana Rodríguez should be one of the first to mention as we have known him for such a long time. He provided detailed information and accompanied us on many of our research trips. Hector Gallegos and Graciela Martínez have been gracious and incredibly helpful. They provided a great deal of local information, photos, and wonderful company during our many visits to their home. Jerardo Tena Sandoval gave us insight into *matachines* history and other village lore. Hector Gallegos Jr. was a link to his parents and others whenever we needed a question answered. Manuel Rodríguez Guillén dug through the family pictures and located early day village photos, which he identified with the help of his father, Efrain Rodríguez Flores. Teodora Ortiz gave us good information about her family and the early days of the Mata Ortiz pottery movement. Julia Estrada Ortiz related her family history with the help of her granddaughter Paty Ortiz. Others from Mata Ortiz who helped include Gregorio Silveira, Lila Silveira Sandoval, Diego Valles, Fabián Hernández, Germán Galaz Levario, Mónico Corona Sr., and the late José Martínez Guillén. Juan Quezada Celado died tragically just before we completed this book. We are indebted to him for the information he gave us over three and a half decades. No one understood the landscape in and around Mata Ortiz better than Juan. The same can be said for the late Nicolás Quezada Celado, who also shared with us his unpublished memoirs. José "Pino" Molina, a close friend of both Juan and Nicolás, provided many early photos of the Pearson mill and the train system as well as detail about the operation of the railroad.

Bishop John Hatch shared his considerable knowledge of LDS history and local geography. Much of the story of the "smallest" LDS temple came from Virginia Romney.

S.A. Morse, descendant of Fred Stark Pearson, was especially gracious.

David Nelson shared all of his extensive research on the Cumbre Tunnel bypass and switchbacks.

Pat Jobin introduced us to her brother, Higinio (Gene) Luévano, who shared his memoir of a boyhood trip to Mata Ortiz before he passed away in 2017.

We spent a wonderful day at Rancho Ramos with the current owner Victor "Cacho" Barrios and his daughter Paulina. With them we walked the ground and saw remnants of occupation from the prehistoric Casas Grandes culture through the very first Spanish settlers to the present.

Information on the Chinese in the valley came from several sources, particularly from the late Agustín Chinolla and his daughter Blanca Chinolla.

Others from Casas Grandes and Nuevo Casas Grandes helped us, including Javier Pedraza, who has worked so hard on the *Pueblo Mágico* designation for Casas Grandes. Lila Orozco opened her home and all of her family pictures to us. Luis Tena answered many questions based on his long experience in Casas Grandes. Pharmacist Jesús Bautista Corral and his brother, J. Arnoldo Bautista Corral, UNAM-Tucson, gave us detailed information about their father, a physician who spent a year in Mata Ortiz, in addition to two books authored by him and allowed us access to family photographs. Jacob Jaquez in Janos cleared up important questions about that community.

We spent time with Professor Jesús Vargas Valdés in Ciudad Chihuahua, where he provided information and books and guided us through our document search at the *Registro Público de la Propiedad.* At the *Registro,* INAH representatives Sofía Pérez Martínez and Lorena Gallegos Renova assisted in our search. Professor Erik Harms, Yale University, also obtained source documents for us.

Our book would not have been possible without the assistance we received from librarians and archivists. These include: the University of California Berkeley, University of California Riverside, California State University, Fullerton, University of Arizona, Arizona State Museum, University of Texas at El Paso, El Paso Public Library, El Paso County Historical Society, University of California, San Diego, University of Texas at Austin, New York Public Library, Brigham Young University, University of Utah, Utah State University, Angelo State University, San Diego Museum of Us, San Diego Air and Space Museum, Great Barrington Historical Society and the Institute of Historical Survey Foundation.

Others who helped us in various ways with their special expertise include Jerry Boyd, Tom Bethard, Clarence Cooper, Lou Taub, Jon Goldenbaum, Dr. R.B. Brown, John Wesley Wallace, Guillermo Genaro Acosta Gutiérrez, James D. Ward, and Elias Guerrero Ramos.

Betty Parks, Kathryn Parks Wilson, and Joan O'Connor spent hours editing over the years and equally important, provided constant support.

A very special thanks is due Joyce Antorietto of the University of San Diego, who located many obscure publications for us.

To all these and countless others, thank you.

Index

G

H

I

M

Z